COMPLEXITY, SECURITY AND CIVIL SOCIETY IN EAST ASIA

Complexity, Security and Civil Society in East Asia

Foreign Policies and the Korean Peninsula

Edited by
Peter Hayes and Kiho Yi

OpenBook Publishers

http://www.openbookpublishers.com

All the external links were active on 22/05/2015 unless otherwise stated.

Digital material and resources associated with this volume are available at http://www.openbookpublishers.com/isbn/9781783741120#resources

ISBN Paperback: 978-1-78374-112-0
ISBN Hardback: 978-1-78374-113-7
ISBN Digital (PDF): 978-1-78374-114-4
ISBN Digital ebook (epub): 978-1-78374-115-1
ISBN Digital ebook (mobi): 978-1-78374-116-8
DOI: 10.11647/OBP.0059

Cover image created by Heidi Coburn, CC BY.

All paper used by Open Book Publishers is SFI (Sustainable Forestry Initiative) and PEFC (Programme for the Endorsement of Forest Certification Schemes) Certified.

Printed in the United Kingdom and United States by Lightning Source for Open Book Publishers

Contents

Contributors

Roger Cavazos served for 22 years in the United States Army at the tactical, operational and strategic levels of war in the policy and intelligence communities. The last 12 years of his career focused on U.S. policy toward China and Taiwan. He lived and worked in China and Korea and was a Minerva Initiative scholar at the Institute for Global Conflict and Cooperation at University of California at San Diego. Email: rcavazos@nautilus.org

Myungrae Cho is Professor of Urban and Regional Planning at Dankook University, South Korea. He obtained his D.Phil. from the University of Sussex, England. He is Head of Commission on Sustainable Development, City of Seoul, and Head of Commission on Cheonggyecheon Restoration, City of Seoul. He is a former member of the Presidential Commissions on Sustainable Development and on Balanced Development. He is Co-Representative of Korean Citizens' Networks for Environmental Justice and National Trust of Korea. Email: myungraecho@naver.com

Steven Denney is a doctoral student in the Department of Political Science at the University of Toronto. He is also the Managing Editor for SinoNK. com, an online collective of Koreanists and Sinologists who document events, contemporary and historical, on the Korean peninsula and in the Sino-North Korea border region. Steven speaks and reads Korean. Email: stevencdenney@gmail.com

Joan Diamond is Deputy Director and Senior Scenarist at the Nautilus Institute. She is also Executive Director of the Millennium Alliance for Humanity and the Biosphere. Prior to joining the Institute in 2001, Joan's career included executive responsibilities in business planning/ strategy, organization transformation, and all administrative functions in Fortune 500 companies, research institutes, and in the Silicon Valley telecommunications industry. Email: diamondjm@comcast.net

Christopher Green is a PhD candidate studying North Korean society and economics at Leiden University, the Netherlands. He is also the Manager of International Affairs for Daily NK, a prominent online periodical providing news about North Korea to the international community. He has been studying and writing about North Korean politics, society, philosophy, economics, and international relations for more than 10 years. Email: christopherkgreen@gmail.com

Peter Hayes is Honorary Professor, Centre for International Security Studies, Sydney University, Australia; and Director, Nautilus Institute, Berkeley, California. He works at the nexus of security, environment and energy problems. At Nautilus, he develops techniques to implement near-term solutions to interconnected global problems, and applies them in East Asia, Australia, and South Asia. Email: phayes@nautilus.org

Tetsunari Iida is Founder and Executive Director of the Institute for Sustainable Energy Policies, Japan. He has served on many government and non-government boards and committees in the field of energy and environmental policy. Tetsunari Iida is responsible for the idea of a Japanese green power scheme and was involved in developing Japan's first green power certificate and in the development of a financing scheme for Japan's first community-owned wind power project. Email: tetsu@isep.or.jp

Sanghun Lee is Associate Professor at Hanshin University where he teaches courses about environment, ecology, and urban and regional development. His research interests include the political ecology of water, energy, and risk management, especially in East Asia. Sanghun has a Ph.D. from the Department of Environmental Planning at Seoul National University (2001). Email: sanghunlee65@gmail.com

Takayuki Minato is Associate Professor at the Department of International Studies at the University of Tokyo. Prior to his career in academia, Takayuki spent ten years working in Japan, the U.S., and Thailand, including a two-year secondment from JICA (Japan International Cooperation Agency) to the Asian Institute of Technology. Email: t.spaceodyssey@gmail.com

Jungmin Seo is Professor of Political Science and International Studies at Yonsei University. He taught at the University of Hawaii at Manoa before joining Yonsei University in Korea. His research interests include Chinese and Korean politics, the politics of international migration, forms of nationalism in East Asia, and state-society relations in discursive realms. He has a Ph.D. in political science from the University of Chicago. Email: jmseo@yonsei.ac.kr

Kae Takase is a senior economist at Governance Design Laboratory, and a researcher at the Center for Low Carbon Society Strategy, the Japan Science and Technology Agency, and the University of Tokyo, specializing in energy economic model analysis, and renewable and energy conservation policies. She received her Ph.D. in environmental studies from the Graduate School of Frontier Science, University of Tokyo. She has previously worked for several major Japanese energy-related institutes. Email: kae@gdl.jp

Richard Tanter is Senior Research Associate at the Nautilus Institute, and Honorary Professor in the School of Political and Social Studies at the University of Melbourne. Email: rtanter@nautilus.org

David Von Hippel is a Senior Associate at the Nautilus Institute. His recent work with Nautilus has included extensive analyses of the patterns of fuel use and prospects for energy sector redevelopment in North Korea, and work with a group of Northeast Asian energy researchers to develop and evaluate the energy security implications of different national energy paths. He holds a Ph.D. in Energy and Resources from the University of California-Berkeley. Email: dvonhip@igc.org

Yi Wang is a professor and Director General of the Institute of Policy and Management, Chinese Academy of Sciences. Prof. Wang also serves as a Member of the Standing Committee of the National People's Congress of China and Vice Chair of the ISO Climate Change Coordinating Committee. His major publications include the annual China Sustainable Development Report (CSDR), China Study series, and *Towards a Sustainable Asia: Green Transition and Innovation*. E-mail: wangyi@casipm.ac.cn

Kiho Yi is Executive Director of the Center for Peace and Public Integrity at Hanshin University and Professor of King Jeongjo college of Liberal Arts at Hanshin University. Yi is Executive Director of the Asia Regional Initiative (ARI), a think-net in cooperation with the Nautilus Institute for Security and Sustainability. Previously, Yi worked as Secretary General of the Korea Peace Forum and served as an advisory member of the Presidential Committee of the Northeast Asia Initiative. Email: yikiho21@gmail.com

Sun-Jin Yun is a professor at the Graduate School of Environmental Studies, Seoul National University, Korea. She is a former president of the Center for Energy Alternatives, a grassroots environmental organization for energy transition, which introduced the concept of citizens' power plants in Korea. She has worked on various governmental committees on energy and environmental matters. She has a Ph.D. in environmental and energy policy from the Center for Energy and Environmental Policy, University of Delaware. Email: ecodemo@snu.ac.kr

Preface

Peter Hayes and Kiho Yi

This book was born after intensive dialogue among the staff of the Nautilus Institute for Security and Sustainability in the United States, South Korea, and Australia on the nature of complex global problems and the development of strategies to solve them in East Asia. The essence of the Nautilus approach is to shift from singular, sequential problem-solving to simultaneous, multiple problem-solving and to implement initiatives that demonstrate this shift is possible in tangible, measurable ways.

This change in approach is simple to state, but profoundly difficult to execute. Most individuals and organizations frame their identities and missions in terms of one primary issue. Doing one thing really well is the mantra of management advisors. Donors frown on projects that span issue areas and don't fit easily into predefined round or square holes. Individuals find it hard to multi-task on more than one priority at a time. It's difficult enough to comprehend the extraordinary complexity of one global problem in its real manifestation at a local, national, or regional level, let alone the interrelationships between problems that have common causes or shared solutions. There's no "global problem-solving" manual to turn to when one asks, "How do I make this shift?"

The specific genesis for the book was the convergence of the Korea Foundation's interest in emerging theories of statecraft that addressed complex diplomatic and security issues and the Nautilus Institute's interest in complex global problem-solving and the specific role played by civil society organizations and individuals in advancing this field in East Asia. For many years, the Nautilus Institute and its partners have addressed global problems such as nuclear weapons proliferation and the risk of nuclear war, energy insecurity, ecological sustainability, trade, climate change, and urban adaptation, but generally in a stove-piped manner, not dissimilar from most civil society organizations.

In 2008, the Korea Foundation provided the funding and stimulus to enable us to step back from specific applications in each of these areas so that we could examine the interconnections between these problems in terms of causality and solution, with particular emphasis on South Korea, China, and Japan, but nested in a global context. For the purposes of this research, we chose three global problems — energy insecurity, nuclear insecurity, and urban insecurity — and identified specialists in these problem areas from each country. We held two workshops aimed at identifying common understandings and conceptual differences in relation to each problem. We searched to understand the differences in the perception of solutions to each of the problems. Wherever possible, we strove to identify inter-linkages across countries in each problem and solution set and between the different problems and solutions. For example, we deliberately examined how the nexus between energy insecurity, nuclear insecurity, and urban insecurity intersect with both climate insecurity, on the one hand, and the specific challenges posed by the parlous state of North Korea, on the other.

In each of these in-depth analyses, we sought to understand the role civil society played in formulating and applying new ways to handle the complexity of these common global problems and shared solutions in East Asia. To do so, we conducted a set of case studies of the networked strategies of civil society in the region, especially those originating from South Korea, and compared these strategies and their results with those of "complex diplomacy" as developed and implemented by the South Korean government since the turn of the century. We termed these civil society efforts "civic diplomacy" to capture their civilian, value-based, and non-state characteristics, and we examined their efficacy relative to South Korea's "complex diplomacy."

The research scope of this project required the participation of nearly thirty expert participants at the two workshops (2009, 2010 in Seoul), largely from the three regional countries, but also from as far afield as Australia and the United States. To reflect the future orientation of civil society, we also convened two scenario workshops after each of the research meetings, the reports of which are summarized in the book's concluding chapter.

The result has been six years in the making. It would not have been possible without all the researchers who contributed to the 2008 and

2010 research and scenarios workshops where many of the issues were explored and debated, nor without the herculean efforts of the staff of the Asia Research Center at Hanshin University and the Nautilus Institute in the United States, South Korea, and Australia. We also thank our editors Maureen Jerrett and Arabella Imhoff. We are grateful to independent reviewers and to Alessandra Tosi at Open Book Publishers. Above all, we thank the Korea Foundation for its financial support for this research project and the resulting book.

This work is dedicated to the memory of O Jae Sik whose spirit lives on in civil society in East Asia and beyond.

1. Introduction

Peter Hayes, Kiho Yi, and Joan Diamond

This book is devoted to improving our understanding of the ability of global civil society to solve global problems. Non-state actors and civil society agencies do not act alone. Governments and their agencies, and market-based corporations must also play their parts, often more so and more importantly than civil society. Nonetheless, we argue in this book that civil society and its diplomats, in a process and strategy that we call civic diplomacy, have distinct advantages when it comes to solving global problems. Moreover, the attributes of civil society enable its actors and agencies to contribute in ways that are necessary and often unique, even if not always sufficient to solve global problems, especially when they are complex and interrelated.

Complex global problem-solving is a rapidly emerging theoretical and practical field. Unsurprisingly, there are no hegemonic or unified theoretical frameworks that encompass the available range of approaches and experience in this field. Rather, there are bursts of intense research and applied practice that, once documented, provide fragmentary insight and eclectic knowledge on how civil society organizations and individuals can undertake effective global problem-solving. Many disciplines and theories, including complexity and network theory, risk analysis, social movement theory, security analysis, international relations, political science, organization theory, information theory, urban geography, economics, etc., lend partial insight into the opaque, rigid snarls of intertwined global problems. By the same token, they also offer clues on how to untie these knots and weave together an enduring tapestry of interdependent solutions to these problems.

    http://dx.doi.org/10.11647/OBP.0059.01

We start the book by surveying these competing and complementary approaches to understanding complex global problems and solutions. The reader should be prepared for the fact that taxonomies of global problems are inconsistent, sometimes contending, and only partly overlapping. Yet these are the conceptual maps that global civil society, states, and corporations use to create order out of chaotic complexity in order to define their political and social agendas. Even the questions of what differentiates global problems from lesser problems and whether their resolution is conceivable are contested, making the field itself turbulent. Some of the global problems manifest in Northeast Asia, the region of concern to this book, are "emergent" — that is, no one anticipated them and, in some cases, not many people even see them. An example is the burgeoning urban insecurity associated with the emergence of transnational mega-urban corridors resulting from cumulative, bottom-up *in-situ* urbanization, in turn driven by globalized social and economic transformation and the dislocation of the countryside. The resultant in-fill between established cities creates a totally new urban geography that transcends state borders in Northeast Asia and will transform the task of social, economic, and cultural governance of the region. Yet cross-border interstate cooperation remains nascent and shallow as if this physical joining were somehow disconnected from governance. In contrast, cross-border city-level cooperation is vibrant and profound in some areas — as we describe in chapters 2 and 6 — and offers many clues as to how governance must change to accommodate complex realities.

Complexity itself is a concept that does not translate easily across cultures. In the West, it has a modern scientific meaning that goes beyond the simple English denotation of a phenomenon as tightly braided, interwoven, and often opaque; complexity also refers to attributes such as non-linearity, cross-level effects, and unpredictability. These characteristics of complexity demand additional efforts at control, often leading to even greater increasing social complexity through the formation of new rules and organizations to manage the response. As the Japanese sociologist Mushakoji Kinhide suggests,[1] East Asian cultures share an inclination to adapt to, rather than resist and control, complexity. Thus, he avers, Chinese culture is guided by its traditional Confucian belief in the harmonious rule of Heaven; Koreans exhibit an agile response rooted in a more shamanistic

---

1   Personal communication to Peter Hayes, 23 September 2014.

outlook that originated in a formerly nomadic lifestyle; Japanese society shows a dualistic response to complexity, partly because of its agricultural and shamanistic roots, and partly because of its modern transformation into a western technocratic social system.

These different orientations are reflected in the chapters of this book: in, for example, the distinct treatments of urban insecurity in Japan, China, and Korea, or in the collisions of lived historical time and identity in relation to future scenarios described in the final chapter. We note these authorial differences here to alert the reader to them, not to argue that one perspective or another is somehow better suited to recognizing and managing the complexity that is created by the emergence of interrelated global problems. Inevitably, these underlying cultural differences come to the surface whenever cross-border communication, coordination, and collaboration are required to define and implement shared solutions to these problems. Even defining the nature of these problems, let alone the resulting solutions, requires immediate negotiation between stakeholders in which all the pre-existing and contemporary distributions of power come into play, not just between states and companies, but also between civil society agencies and individuals seeking ways to collaborate across borders.

How complexity affects the perception of global problems as well as the most effective response is not well understood. In the field of nuclear insecurity, for example, it is possible to trace the emergence of true complexity as the number of nuclear weapons states increased from one (the United States from 1945-48) to two (the Soviet Union in 1948-51) with one to five targeted states; to six nuclear weapons states and up to about thirty-eight targeted states during the bipolar Cold War, including US and Soviet allies; and to nine nuclear-armed states since 2006 with at least forty-four states as potential targets. Reductive theoretical prisms were used to simplify the hugely complicated Cold War to the global nuclear balance of terror between the United States and the former Soviet Union. Today, however, there is no lens that can simplify the true complexity of dozens of relationships between nuclear armed states and their allies and adversaries, nor how their advanced conventional weapon systems interact with their own and others' nuclear forces in ways that could trigger nuclear war. In a complex system, a small, otherwise insignificant event may be amplified by virtue of timing and location in a complex network of relationships into system-wide failure — in this case, all-out war and nuclear war — even if all the system components at the national and organizational level work as intended, without component or technological failure or accident.

As the chapter on nuclear insecurity recounts, in this region new actors can erupt almost without warning and in a very short time. For example, the totally unanticipated explosion of social media as a form of deliberative democracy in China has introduced a completely new security factor in East Asia involving nearly half a billion people. This on-line opinion generator already drives and restrains the actions of the Chinese state on nuclear and conventional security issues in ways that are new and unpredictable. Although the Communist Party remains in control of foreign policy and often manipulates on-line opinion to buttress domestic support for its external actions, the Chinese state is increasingly driven by nationalist sentiment which may push it to act in ways that risk loss of military control in collision with other states, and uncontrolled escalation to war and nuclear war involving two or more states (and possibly non-state actors). The potency Chinese popular opinion expressed via social media is barely perceived in the realist scholarly and policy nuclear security circles of East Asia—let alone documented, studied, analyzed, and enshrined into norms, rules, procedures, and shared institutions whereby the risk of war, nuclear war, and nuclear proliferation may be managed and, over time, reduced.

In the chapter on energy security, the authors drill deeply into the terrain of complexity and the linkage between energy, climate, and urban insecurity. In both qualitative and quantitative dimensions, this chapter shows that it is possible to obtain rich local insight into these linkages, exploring them at different levels (city, national, regional) and across issues, and to identify ways in which states, energy agencies and companies, and civil society can promote global climate mitigation and adaptation and, via regional cooperation, increase economic, social, and ecological well-being at the same time. Some of these schemes could also help reduce the intensity of the threat arising from North Korea's nuclear armament and its linkage to regional agendas for cooperative problem-solving on urban or climate insecurity that are otherwise stalled by conflict created by the North Korea's actions and the response of its Great Power antagonists.

Having created a tapestry that combines very different types of analysis from divergent, sometimes antithetical starting positions, we argue that civic diplomacy, as employed by civil society agencies and individuals in combination with local governments and municipalities, presents a new and powerful way to adapt to and manage the complex interaction of global problems in this region. Of at least thirty truly global "mega-problems," such as global poverty, climate change, etc., we selected only five for close examination in this region: civil society, nuclear weapons, urban insecurity, energy, and climate change. While not underestimating the potency of uncivil society and non-state actors, we argue that civil society engaging in constructive civic diplomacy offers new and unique capacities to resolve such linked problems in this region, and often outperforms both the state and corporate sectors in specific instances. Indeed, we carefully examine the performance of official South Korean "complex networked diplomacy," which from 2006 aimed to capitalize on South Korea's location in the complex security and geopolitical relations of the region, especially in relation to how best to solve the problem of North Korea's nuclear breakout. We find that in relation to reducing the threat posed by nuclear weapons, reforestation, refugee flows, and urban and energy insecurity, civil society has proven effective in ways that the states of China, South Korea, and Japan could not hope to be via traditional diplomacy. We further conclude that there is great potential to improve the already significant contribution of civil society to solving complex global problems in East Asia, often in tandem and sometimes in opposition to states and the corporate sector, but always informed by deep and intimate knowledge of local circumstances and driven by commitment to universal values of justice, equity, ecological sustainability, peace, and security.

This book consists of three sections presented in seven chapters. In chapter 1, we provide a summary for readers seeking a quick understanding of the entire narrative. We follow this introduction with a conceptual chapter on global problems, three chapters that delve into specific global problems and their inter-linkages in Northeast Asia, and two concluding chapters on civil society and complex global problem-solving in this region.

In chapter 2, Peter Hayes and Richard Tanter disaggregate key concepts into their constituent elements to elucidate the complexity of global problems such as energy scarcity, climate change, and urban insecurity in China, South Korea, and Japan. They ask, "What is specifically 'global' about a global problem, and what underlies an issue of global concern that makes it problematic?" They show there has been only one effort — the World Economic Forum's annual Global Risk report — that provides a consistent approach to defining and identifying global problems. Yet a decade of the Forum's results suggest that, without a negotiated consensus as to what constitutes global problems, there is no basis for identifying the global problems that are sufficiently important to justify joint action in the form of shared solutions. Many of these solutions must be implemented across borders or entail international organizations to coordinate decentralized action in many states.

Next, Hayes and Tanter sketch the conceptual world of complex systems to provide a basic understanding of their nature, especially their ability to surprise us with unexpected events. They point to the emergence of a continuous city corridor stretching from Beijing to Tokyo that, by 2050, may be the world's first giga-city with a billion people. The emergence of this corridor serves as an example of a transformation that poses entirely new sustainability and security challenges transcending state boundaries and national political cultures, but that does not yet figure on national policy agendas.

Drawing on the work of eminent South Korean political scientists, Hayes and Tanter suggest that developing and mobilizing the networking capacities of civil society, organized transnationally, is one of the most productive ways to tackle the region's increasingly complex set of global problems. They review the outcomes of cooperative environmental projects undertaken by inter-city, cross-border networks between Japan and China. They suggest that linking environmental and security civil society networks to those of local governments will create a new type of resilience in the region and lend capacity to solving global problems in spite of their complexity.

In chapter 3, David von Hippel — with contributions by Kae Takase (Japan), Yi Wang (China), Myungrae Cho (Korea), Tetsunari Iida (Japan), and Sun-Jin Yun (Korea) — start to traverse the complexity of energy security in the region. The development of this chapter began before 11 March 2011, the date of the earthquake-tsunami that struck Japan and caused the Fukushima nuclear catastrophe. This event shattered conventional concepts of energy security and nuclear power and increased the complexity that already confronted policymakers on energy security at the end of the 20th century. Von Hippel and his colleagues use quantitative and qualitative analysis based on case studies in Japan, China, and South Korea to describe existing and alternative pathways for providing future energy security in each country, including the implications of these pathways for urban and ecological security. They superimpose the impact of climate change on these energy security pathways and spell out the implications of adapting to climate change. They also present key pressure points at which civil society can push for constructive changes — especially ones that reduce the North Korean threat to its neighbors. They conclude by outlining ways in which the South Korean state might not only improve energy security in the Republic of Korea (ROK), but also improve urban, climate, and nuclear security. In particular, they propose steps to promote the involvement of the Democratic People's Republic of Korea (DPRK) in regional energy infrastructure development as an inducement to engage on nuclear weapons and related issues. In so doing, the ROK would be helping to address the DPRK issue as well as its own energy, climate, and urban security needs.

Cities are inherently complex systems beset by many intractable problems. In chapter 4, Sanghun Lee and Takayuki Minato suggest that irreversible and rampant globalization has transformed every aspect of daily life and made cities even more insecure. Consequently, the security of cities remains threatened from different directions simultaneously. Developments such as the deepening inequality found in cities and the *in-situ* urbanization in the rural space between them are not planned. The result, Lee and Minato argue, is that infrastructure services for critical shelter, food, energy, and water supplies are now seriously threatened. Additionally, terrorism and inter-state war with nuclear or conventional weapons threaten city security.

By exploiting their increasing interdependence, however, cities can learn from each other and create cross-city solutions to common problems via complex, networked, and shared strategies. Lee and Minato suggest provision and good governance of "smart critical infrastructure" has become the central concern for creating secure and sustainable cities. Conversely, without provision of secure and sustainable critical infrastructure and its good governance, urbanization in an era of globalization leads to more, not less insecurity and vulnerability, thereby undermining the very essence of city formation.

They note that, while the dynamics and nature of urbanization and the delivery of security are uneven within and between countries, coastal cities in China, South Korea, and Japan face new insecurities such as climate change impacts and heat islands. The resulting thermal stress and public health risks, as well as the impact of floods, storm surge, and increasingly frequent and intense storms on cities, are common problems with global as well as local causes, and many of the solutions may be shared if adapted to local circumstances.

Networked civil society organizations working closely with city governments can precipitate a new, emergent pattern of decentralized, networked governance that supplements and supersedes, but in no way substitutes for the role of states in the region. Lee and Minato describe model cities in each country with repertoires of ecological and urban security strategies. These cities offer learning opportunities and are incubators for new strategies with implications for all cities in the region.

In chapter 5, Peter Hayes and Roger Cavazos examine the increasingly complex threat posed by nuclear weapons of mass destruction in Northeast Asia. They first sketch the evolution of the role played by nuclear weapons in international affairs and summarize the prevailing definition of the nuclear weapons problem both globally and regionally, from a conventional, policy-oriented viewpoint. They suggest the Cold War nuclear hegemony of the United States has been up-ended by the DPRK's at first slow-motion and now accelerating "nuclear breakout," leading to a renewed and likely increased threat of nuclear next-use in the region.

Hayes and Cavazos suggest the trend towards greater trade integration: mobility of labor from poor, labor-surplus countries to demographically aging, labor-short, rich countries, and the *de facto* cross-border urbanization in massive corridors, renders many of the old state-based nuclear deterrence strategies meaningless. At a certain point, likely not too far in the future and certainly by the mid-twenty-first century, targeting people and places with weapons of mass destruction will render nuclear armament not only wasteful, but absurd. The rise of non-state actors armed with nuclear weapons or materials underscores the obsolescence of relying on nuclear weapons for security.

Their conclusion in chapter 5 argues that only civil-society-based cooperative security strategies can supplant nuclear weapons and prevent related insecurity from destabilizing the region. Case studies highlight the role played by social movements in China, South Korea, and Japan in constraining or deflecting state policies on nuclear weapons (or weapons-related fuel cycle activities). They point to the rise of virtual deliberation on security issues in China using social media that involves millions of Chinese "netizens." These netizens represent a potentially constructive social force capable of changing the security landscape in the region and providing new impetus for abandoning nuclear weapons.

In chapter 6, Kiho Yi and Peter Hayes — with contributions by Joan Diamond, Steven Denney, Christopher Green, and Jungmin Seo — focus on the implications for ROK foreign policy of the actual and potential role of civil society in solving complex global problems in Northeast Asia. They highlight the emergence of independent civic diplomacy originating from civil society in South Korea, Japan, and China, rather than from the state. This diplomacy dedicates its energy to solving traditional as well as new cross-border security issues in the region. They start by tracing the rise of official South Korean complex diplomacy aimed at exploiting the ROK's middle power status and location in the international system while addressing this increasingly complex foreign policy terrain. Next, they examine the emergence of civil society networks operating across borders. They find that the characteristics of civilian actors vary from country to country, and that their capacities are also uneven when compared across China, the ROK, and Japan.

Nonetheless, at a regional level, networks of these civil society actors have formed that tackle a number of global problems as or more effectively than states, at least in particular moments and circumstances. After outlining the roles these organizations play in functional and structural (networking) terms, Yi, Hayes, and colleagues examine six case studies to derive lessons learned from four civil society networks for ROK foreign policy. Their first case study depicts the networked civil society response, often led by South Koreans, to supplant regressive Japanese history textbooks by producing the 2005 book *A History to Open the Future*. The second case study looks at how South Korean non-governmental organizations addressed deforestation and food scarcity in Northeast Asia, especially in China and North Korea. The third case study examines the critical role played by the Refugee Aid Network in the passing of South Korea's Refugee Act, the first independent refugee law passed at the national level in Asia. The fourth case study reviews the networking experience of a private initiative, Jeju Peace Forum, and its evolution from a network focused on a peace initiative to solve the North Korea problem into a multi-issue network of networks. The fifth case study traces the creation and influential intellectual role of the East Asia Institute. The sixth case study explores efforts by the most recent of these civil society initiatives — the Asan Institute for Policy Studies — to build global networks and the implications such efforts have for global community-building and cosmopolitanism.

Following this excursion into historical and empirical case studies, Yi, Hayes, and colleagues review the role of inter-city collaboration across national borders, and the implications of civil society-oriented network strategies for the ROK's state-centric, networked complex diplomacy strategy. They observe the potential for common cause between these trans-border local initiatives and issue-based civil society networks to add a new layer of social capacity to solving the problems that afflict states. They conclude the sixth chapter by proposing the adoption of civic diplomacy as a separate category to the official complex diplomacy pursued by the ROK state to implement its foreign policy. They suggest the rise of civic diplomacy working in concert with complex diplomacy, in addition to the shift to the civic state and nation, provides the extra social capacity whereby the ROK can respond best to the challenges posed by global and regional problems. In this vision there is no singular, unified civic foreign policy, but as many civic foreign policies as are needed to respond to the exigencies confronting communities and the issues evoking cross-border responses by civil society.

In the seventh and final chapter, Peter Hayes, Kiho Yi, and Joan Diamond describe how cross-cultural civil society organizations explored the true uncertainty posed by complex global problems for the future of Northeast Asia at two events held in Seoul in 2009 and 2010. In 2009, they tackled the question, "Northeast Asia 2050: Is there a role for civil society in meeting the climate change challenge?" In 2010, they responded to the focal question, "Will East Asia Mega-cities be Secure and Sustainable by 2050?"

Without giving away the storylines of the eight scenarios created at these two events and described in chapter 7, we can reveal that Hayes, Yi and Diamond suggest that, in the case of many urgent regional security and sustainability issues such as migration, energy and urban insecurity, nuclear weapons, and climate change adaptation, it is civil society organizations that cross borders to find counterparts and create the transnational networks to anticipate future crises. By doing so, these civil society organizations create a new layer of social complexity commensurate with that of the emerging problem-terrain.

Moreover, developing a common agenda with milestones for action requires all participants to incorporate their accountability into their own agendas. They note how pre-existing patterns of time inhabited by civil society actors have adjusted to the demands for new patterns of activity generated by complex global problem-solving and via actions synchronized in new ways across borders. This process of integration generates a new experience of shared time that may be termed "complex time" — constantly negotiated as civil society organizations expand and contract around common problems and implement joint problem-solving strategies. The authors suggest that the experience of communicating, coordinating, and collaborating across borders in civil society networks prefigures the creation of a new, hybrid identity for millions of individuals that transcends national identity based on statehood. For this reason, they remain optimistic about the future of civic diplomacy and argue it should often lead, not always follow, successful state-based complex diplomacy.

Returning to the overarching theme of the book — the role of civil society organizations in helping to solve interrelated, complex global problems — we believe that the strategies of civil society and their transnational networks provide at least part of the missing manual for global problem-solving. Exactly which tools and techniques are needed remains to be conceptualized and documented. The authors of this book are certain that civic diplomacy is one such tool, but there are many others — deep research methodologies, convening and facilitation techniques, communication and coordination systems that reduce transactions costs and support systems, enabling partners to co-evolve and support each other's respective strategies.

No one knows where these ideas and tools will be invented and used. The authors are convinced the methodologies will be eclectic, even inconsistent, but still necessary to provide the requisite diversity of understanding and approach. We suggest many of the tools and techniques of global problem-solving will be invented, tested, and then replicated in Northeast Asia, even as civil society organizations adopt and adapt those tools offered by comparable organizations elsewhere in the world.

2. Global Problems, Complexity, and Civil Society in East Asia

Peter Hayes and Richard Tanter

Introduction

This chapter presents an argument about the relationship between global problems, complexity, problem-solving, and East Asian civil society. In section 1, we begin by asking two fundamental questions: what is specifically "global" about a global problem, and what underlies an issue of global concern that makes it problematic? We outline three categories of global problems — those that affect the sharing of global commons, those that affect our shared humanity, and those that rely on our shared rule book for regulating human activity. We conclude there is no agreement as to which global problems are most urgent, let alone how each fits into these three categories. To demonstrate the need for a consistent approach with an explicit method and transparent values in developing a ranking of global problems, we describe the effort of the World Economic Forum to generate a map of global risks based on the perceptions of global leaders. In turn, we find this effort is limited by the privileged status of the participating experts, and we suggest that what constitutes a global problem must be negotiated across national borders and political cultures. Without convergence towards consensus on which of these issues are truly global, there is no basis for agreeing on which of these problems are common to all countries in East Asia and which are so important they justify joint action in the form of shared solutions.

In section 2, we enter the conceptual world of complex systems. We argue that international security and sustainability are dimensions of human existence that increasingly reveal the characteristics of complex systems at the start of the twenty-first century rather than the relatively simple state of affairs that pertained in the last half of the twentieth century. We suggest that one of the emergent patterns of human organization in the region — a continuous city corridor stretching from Beijing to Tokyo — presents an immense challenge to the leaders of China, South Korea, and Japan. Inherent in that development are contradictory aspects of energy insecurity, urban insecurity, and nuclear insecurity, cross cut by the challenges of climate change and the specific threat posed by an unstable, declining North Korea.

Drawing on the work of Ha Young Sun, an eminent South Korean political scientist, we suggest the basic approach to this increasingly complex set of global problems in the region is to draw on the networking capacities of civil society to organize transnationally across the region. We review the outcomes of such efforts in relation to cooperative environmental projects undertaken by inter-city, cross-border networks between Japan and China. Next, we suggest linking single-issue civil society networks to future networks of local governments will create resilience in the region and lend new capacity to framing and solving global problems in spite of their complexity.

We conclude this chapter by arguing that it is central to the role of civil society to provide a critical perspective as to what constitutes the most urgent global problems that originate in or affect the region as a whole, rather than mirroring the priority problems set by states. Otherwise, civil society networks risk being entrapped in "realpolitik" zero-sum games rather than moving to "idealpolitik" based on cooperative strategies.

What Are Global Problems?

What is a *global* problem? This might appear obvious, but in fact, it is a much more difficult question to answer than one might think at first glance. Are they just extra-large problems, otherwise similar to complex problems found at the local or regional level? If they are different, even if only in scale, what do we have to do to solve them and how does that differ from what we do now? Is there an emerging field of "global problem-solving" with its own methods and tools? Are conceptual innovations needed to undertake global problem-solving? What comprehensive approaches already exist for this purpose?

The list of questions goes on. What are the implications for policy if global problems have special characteristics, and, if so, what are these? To what extent do global problems originate in this region? How are they manifest in this region even if they don't originate here? And how does the region contribute to the solution of these problems both in the region itself and beyond?

By their very nature, global problems are complex, intractable, and interrelated. Global problems cannot be solved sequentially, one at a time. Often, our best efforts to solve global problems fail or even make them worse. Multiple, interrelated global problems demand multiple, shared global solutions; they require more complex strategies and differentiated organizational responses. Global problems often stress our decision-making processes and institutional capacities beyond their limits. Consequently, such problems may spiral out of control, sometimes catastrophically, and often they persist whatever individuals and organizations do to resolve them.

Organizations tend to focus on one problem as their core mission, pushing aside secondary, linked problems as less important. Individual humans are hard-pressed to track more than four independent variables at once.[1] Yet we live in a seamless web of interrelated global problems, each of which may feed into and shape other problems. Partly because of this tunnel vision, we do not agree on which global problems are the most important, let alone on global solutions. Consequently, humanity searches for global solutions at cross-purposes and even in conflict. The result is often "global gridlock." Meanwhile, this dissensus immobilizes the search for partial, multiple solutions that can be implemented at the local and regional level.

In fact, global problems are not just important problems, or problems that affect many people. Rather, they are those problems that affect the whole planet, and potentially all of the people who live on it. In this

---

1   "Processing loads required for the 2 x 3-way and 4-way problems differed because two 3-way problems can be processed independently, and a solution can be stored for each, whereas the two halves of a 4-way problem must be processed relative to each other, and cannot be decomposed into separate problems. Therefore, the increase in working memory load from the 2 x 3-way to the 4-way problems was not simply due to the amount of information that was stored, but was due to the number of variables that had to be related in the representations of the problems..." Halford, G.S., *et al.*, "How Many Variables Can Humans Process?," *Psychological Science*, 16(1) (2005), doi: http://dx.doi.org/10.1111/j.0956-7976.2005.00782.x

sense, all global problems are local (although the reverse is not true, see below). Climate change is an obvious example of a truly global problem. The consequences of humanly-generated changes in the atmosphere will, albeit in different ways according to region, affect everyone on the planet. In other words, the consequences are universal. Moreover, unless we profoundly change our collective behavior, climate change may well result in irreversible changes in the climatic conditions of life — a measure of the deep vulnerability of human society in the face of this problem.

There is no easy solution to the climate problem — it is truly intractable. There are many causes of climate change rooted in our economic system, our attitudes to nature, our political organization, our technological capacities and preferences, and our uses of resources. Solutions will involve all communities and every country; they must be collective, not just individual. In other words, the example of climate change suggests that global problems are complex, intractable, and make human society as a whole increasingly vulnerable. The solutions to climate change are inherently global, but in their archetypical form, the mitigation of greenhouse gases and adaptation to climate impacts will always be manifested locally and usually in ways tailored to local circumstances.

What, in contrast, is a strictly *local* problem? These are problems that are local in origin and solution and do not require global governance for resolution. Since the mid-sixties, for example, environmental organizations have existed almost everywhere. They work on local ecological problems such as habitat loss, land and forest rights, or environmental pollution.[2] Many of these groups are now networked transnationally across borders, some of them globally, to address "glocal" problems — problems that are universal but are regulated locally, not globally — in contrast to truly global problems, such as restoration and preservation of the ozone layer.[3]

Such problems for the most part are truly local, not global problems, no matter how widespread the issue. Usually, the cause is local (that is, national or smaller in scale and sub-national in terms of the governance level). Unless the problem arises from some international connection, such as foreign

---

2   Hayes, P., *The Potential for Environmental Action: Report to the UNEP* (Geneva: NGO Environment Liaison Board, 1976).

3   Lopez, G., A., *et al.*, "The Global Tide," *The Bulletin of the Atomic Scientists*, 51(4) (1995).

investment in a polluting factory (as at Bhopal) or a transnational criminal gang dumping toxic wastes (as in Somalia), the solution is primarily local. By the widely accepted principle of subsidiarity, the responsibility for solving a problem should be pushed to the lowest level possible in the institutional context where the problem demands resolution. Of course, at some point, the local problem becomes so internationalized that it becomes truly global in scope and scale—and today at least seven types of international environmental crimes exist.[4] Thus, the status of a problem is dynamic. With time, local problems may become global, both quantitatively and qualitatively and, typically, will exist on a local-global spectrum rather than at one or the other end of the scale.

Rischard's Top Twenty Taxonomy

One way to define and categorize "inherently global" problems is shown in Table 2.1. As Jean-Francois Rischard explains in *High Noon: Twenty Global Problems, Twenty Years to Solve Them*:

> Roughly a third of these have to do with how we share our planet (burning environmental issues); another third of which relate to how we share our humanity (urgent economic and social issues requiring a worldwide coalition for their effective solution); with a final third having to do with how we share our rulebook (important regulatory challenges urgently requiring a minimum critical mass of global rules to prevent free-riding and other negative consequences).[5]

We believe this taxonomy of global problems is powerful, although as we will see below, Rischard's "top twenty" list of global problems may be too narrow or inadequate. For example, not listed is a truly global and intractable global problem that originates in and affects East Asia in profound ways (see chapter 5 of this book): the risk of next-use and proliferation of weapons of mass destruction (WMD).

---

4   "They include: illegal trade in wildlife; smuggling of ozone depleting substances (ODS); illicit trade in hazardous waste; illegal, unregulated, and unreported fishing; and illegal logging and the associated trade in stolen timber," in Banks, D., *et al.*, *Environmental Crime, a Threat to Our Future* (London: Environmental Investigation Agency, 2008).

5   Rischard, J.F., *High Noon: Twenty Global Problems, Twenty Years to Solve Them* (New York: Basic Books, 2002).

Table 2.1: Taxonomy of Twenty Global Issues

Global Commons
"Sharing the Planet: Issues involving the global commons"

1. Global warming
2. Biodiversity and ecosystem losses
3. Fisheries depletion
4. Deforestation
5. Water deficits
6. Maritime safety and pollution

Global Commitments
"Sharing our Humanity: Issues whose size and urgency requires a global commitment"

7. Massive step-up in fight against poverty
8. Peacekeeping, conflict prevention, combating terrorism
9. Education for all
10. Global infectious diseases
11. Digital divide
12. Natural disaster prevention and mitigation

Global Regulatory Approach
"Sharing our Rulebook: Issues needing a global regulatory approach"

13. Reinventing taxation
14. Biotechnology rules
15. Global financial architecture
16. Illegal drugs
17. Trade, investment, competition rules
18. Intellectual property rights
19. E-commerce rules
20. International labor and migration rules

Source: J. Rischard, *High Noon: Twenty Global Problems, Twenty Years to Solve Them* (New York: Basic Books, 2002), p. 66.

The Nature of Global Problems

In addition to falling into one of these three categories, global problems exhibit a number of characteristics that make them global rather than national or local in nature. Global problems may exhibit linkage between cause and effect across societal levels from global to local. Global problems also separate cause and effect when the driving forces are highly centralized and concentrated both institutionally and spatially and, therefore, are distant or even invisible to most of humanity who nonetheless experience the effects. Other global problems are the result of highly distributed and decentralized driving forces so diffuse yet cumulatively powerful that the resulting overall impact is qualitatively transformative even though it passes unnoticed except at the local level. The global financial collapse is an example of the former; the ozone hole is an example of the latter.

Often, global problems are multi-dimensional and drive pervasive change propelled by interrelationships across superficially segmented problems or disparate issues or levels of governance. Global problems may be the result of multi-directional causes that erupt suddenly from below or without warning from above a specific level or location in the global hierarchy of place (extra-national, national, subnational, local, individual) and organization (UN Security Council, regional government unions, nation states, provincial and state governments, local governments, cities and villages, associations). Sometimes, events in one society arc around the planet to jolt another, thereby dramatically changing both their trajectories — a phenomenon that James Rosenau calls "distant proximities." [6] Acts of mass terror by non-state actors exemplify this kind of global problem. Political scientists have observed such turbulence for decades,[7] but have not contributed significantly to our understanding of the origins or outcomes of such sudden, discontinuous, and often non-linear changes in world affairs.

The impact of some global problems may not be felt for years or decades, whereas decision-making time horizons for actions that contribute to or resolve these problems are relatively short. Such enduring

---

6   Rosenau, J.N., *Turbulence in World Politics: A Theory of Change and Continuity* (Princeton: Princeton University Press, 1990).

7   Ernst Haas was an exception, with his early contribution: Haas, E.B., "Turbulent Fields and the Theory of Regional Integration," *International Organization*, 30(02) (1976), doi: http://dx.doi.org/10.1017/S0020818300018245

global problems may set severe limits on solving interrelated, medium-term global problems. Some solutions may turn out to generate further problems. These attributes and perceptions of global problems are an enormous challenge to traditional organizations, especially those that are state-based, which typically are slow to recognize problems and even slower to respond.

Disaggregating a Global Problem

Complex global problems often appear to be rigid, opaque, and immune to human agency. At the risk of losing sight of the whole, therefore, it is useful to decompose such mega-problems into constituent problems.

As a global problem, the weapons-of-mass-destruction or "WMD" issue is enormously complex. Solving it entails a great deal of regulation of human behavior. Failure to control it could result in crimes against humanity on a massive scale, to the point where it threatens human existence as well as global ecological integrity. In Rischard's framework, it is a global problem that falls into all three categories. Thus, many distinct, linked, global problems are tied together in this instance into a rigid "mega-problem."

In the case of nuclear weapons, researchers at the Carnegie Endowment for International Peace unpacked the global nuclear weapons problem into its constituent problem drivers and possible "solution strategies" (see chapter 5). They identified four key drivers — terrorism, new states, existing arsenals, and regime breakdown — each of which had four distinct sub-problems, generating no fewer than sixteen distinct possible ways in which East Asia might contribute to the global problem — including North Korea, nuclear threats, nuclear black markets, and the collapse of the Nuclear Non-Proliferation Treaty (NPT).

On the solution-strategy side of the nuclear weapons problem, they outlined six obligations (no easy exit, devalue weapons, secure materials, stop transfers, resolve conflicts, deal with the four nuclear-armed states outside of the NPT), each of which contains multiple possible strategies for a total of twenty possible ways that regional action in East Asia could contribute to the solution of the global problem.[8] Overall, the drivers and solutions present no fewer than thirty-six possible links between the global

---

8   Perkovich, G., *et al.*, *Universal Compliance, a Strategy for Nuclear Security* (Washington, DC: Carnegie Endowment for International Peace, 2007).

and regional dimensions of the nuclear weapons problem. Of these, at least fifteen of the sixteen nuclear weapons threats and at least fourteen of the solution strategies pertain to East Asia. Thus, the regional dimension of the global nuclear weapons problem is only marginally less complex (twenty-eight out of thirty-six) than the full-blown global WMD problem. Whether global or regional, the overall level of complexity in either case far exceeds human comprehension.

In this book, we will use a similar process of disaggregation into constituent, separate, but linked problems to approach and comprehend the daunting complexity of climate change, urban insecurity, energy insecurity, and weapons of mass destruction.

Contested Nature of Global Problems

If there is no definitive, authoritative list and priority ranking of global problems, how does civil society determine which global problems are most important in East Asia, and which of these are in turn amenable to solutions, in what combinations and sequencing?

One approach to setting this agenda was taken by the United Nations (UN) in 2000 when it adopted the Millennium Development Goals (MDGs). These eight anti-poverty goals were to eradicate extreme poverty and hunger; achieve universal primary education; promote gender equality and empower women; reduce child mortality; improve maternal health; combat HIV/AIDS, malaria, and other diseases; ensure environmental sustainability; and develop a global partnership for development.[9] More than a decade later, significant progress has been made to fulfill some of these goals, but we are lagging behind several of them. And while these goals are challenging, they do not capture the full range of obstacles and threats that obstruct them, let alone the full array of security and sustainability problems that are truly global in scope, many of which afflict this region.

Is it true, as the United Nations appears to assume, that overcoming global poverty entails solving all the other critical global problems that could lead humanity over a cliff of unsustainable insecurity and disorder? Although overcoming global poverty is central to fulfilling our shared

---

9   *The Millennium Development Goals* (New York: United Nations Development Programme), http://www.undp.org/content/undp/en/home/mdgoverview/mdg_goals.html

humanity, it is not clear that doing so would suffice to resolve all the problems afflicting the global commons, nor to complete the agenda of problems related to achieving equitable, just development of all humans, let alone to regulate all behaviors that could lead to global problems. Other global problems would still be universal, have global impact, and would be inescapable, for example, energy use leading to irreversible climate change that reduces food security. Nor would overcoming global poverty suffice to instigate all the behaviors needed to create global public goods (such as open, transparent government processes at every level).

At the other end of the spectrum of specificity we find that the Union of International Associations (UIA) empirically documents at least 170 *basic universal* problems (such as danger, lack of information, social injustice, war, environmental degradation).[10] These high-level problems are defined by the UIA as difficulties

> of such proportions and complexity that no single organization or discipline can claim to encompass any one of them in all its aspects. The scope and implications of such problems tends to be a matter of continuing debate. They are not sufficiently well defined to respond to well-defined solutions. The nature of an appropriate solution to such problems is also a matter of continuing debate.[11]

Another source for determining the possible priority of problems would be global civil society. Many international think-tanks offer their own laundry lists of priority global problems that form the foci of their research. The Brookings Institution, for example, offers a list of seventeen global issues, only nine of which wholly or partly overlap with Rischard's list and only three of which partly or wholly overlap with the eight MDGs.[12] Similarly,

---

10   In addition, UIA 1994 update identified a further set of 575 cross-sectoral problems (such as animal suffering, irresponsible nationalism, soil degradation), 2,162 detailed problems (such as epidemics, white-collar crime), 3,857 emanations of other problems (such as terrorism targeted against tourists, injustice of mass trials), 3,072 fuzzy exceptional problems (such as blaming victims, pacifism, unconstrained free trade), 2,153 very specific problems (such as blue baby), 214 problems under consideration for inclusion (such as feminist backlash, mudslide), for a total of 9,832 world problems. See Union of International Associations, *Encyclopedia of World Problems and Human Potential*. 3 vols (Munich: K.G. Saur, 1994). *Encyclopedia of World Problems and Human Potential* (Wikipedia), http://en.wikipedia.org/wiki/Encyclopedia_of_World_Problems_and_Human_Potential

11   *Basic Universal Problems* (Brussels: Union of International Associations), http://www.uia.be/node/328165

12   Namely, communications, corruption, crime, development assistance, economics (global finance international trade), environment (nature conservation, environment:

Rischard's list contains partial or complete overlap with the MDGs (7/8), but these constitute only a third (7/20) of his top twenty global problems. Thus, there is simply no consensus in global civil society as to what constitutes the core set of global problems.

Shifting levels, one could seek instead to identify a set of shared priority economic and security concerns from the agendas of the leading Asian-Pacific regional organizations, assuming these reflect the priorities of the participating states, and further assuming that regional and national civil society follows suit. For example, Asia Pacific Economic Cooperation (APEC), the members of which are "economies," not states, promotes free trade and economic cooperation throughout the Asia-Pacific region. Its convening and dialogic activities encompass a wide range of topics on competition policy, commercial law, trade, and investment issues (such as market access and business mobility). It also holds senior official meetings on sectoral-level economic and technical cooperation with specific attention to terrorism, gender issues, mining points of contention, and an array of ad hoc themes such as sustainable development, free trade agreements, and bio-technology.[13]

The ASEAN Regional Forum (ARF) addresses a range of regional security issues and promotes dialogue at an official level.[14] The Council for Security Cooperation in the Asia Pacific (CSCAP) convenes "Track 2" study groups[15]

---

pollution), global commons (oceans, Antarctica, atmosphere and outer space), health, human rights, labor rights, refugee protection and assistance, violence: intrastate conflict, warfare (conventional weapons, nuclear, biological, chemical weapons). See Simmons, P.J. and de Jonge Oudraat, C., *Managing Global Issues: Lessons Learned* (Washington, DC: Carnegie Endowment for International Peace, 2001).

13 See Wesley, M., *The Regional Organizations of the Asia Pacific: Exploring Institutional Change* (Basingstoke: Palgrave Macmillan, 2003).

14 ASEAN Regional Forum official activities cover confidence building measures; peacekeeping; search, rescue and disaster relief; defense; counter-terrorism; non-traditional security; maritime security; WMD proliferation; preventive diplomacy; small arms and light weapons; energy security; shipboard waste disposal; economic security; and eminent persons. See *List of Track II Activities 1994-2012* (Jakarta: ASEAN Regional Forum), http://aseanregionalforum.asean.org/library/arf-activities/list-of-arf-track-i-activities-by-inter-sessional-year.html

15 As of May 2011, CSCAP working groups were (with Asia-Pacific wide scope): Cybersecurity, Water Resources Security, Responsibility to Protect, Naval Enhancement, Safety and Security of Offshore Oil and Gas Installations, Regional Transnational Organised Crime Hubs, Countering the Proliferation of Weapons of Mass Destruction, Export Controls; and sub-regionally, Multilateral Security Governance in Northeast Asia/North Pacific. Already concluded working group topics covered: Capacity Building for Maritime Security Cooperation, Facilitating Maritime Security Cooperation in the Asia Pacific (specifically, Safety and Security in the Malacca and Singapore Straits, and a Legal experts group), Future Prospects for Multilateral

that often mirror the foci of the ARF.[16] The ASEAN Plus 3 (China, South Korea, and Japan) is an extension of the ARF process that began in 1997 and tries to develop cooperation between the member states that spans cultural, economic, functional, political, security, and social areas.[17] Likewise, CSCAP has also convened a sub-regional working group on Multilateral Security Governance in Northeast Asia and the North Pacific.

These regional concerns are listed at a high level of generality, however, and there is no more than a loose convergence of views represented in these fora. Although they show what issues national elites in the whole Asia-Pacific want to talk about, none of these regional organizations entail substantive commitments. No state in the region relies on them to preserve their vital national security and sustainability interests.

At the sub-regional level of "low politics" a set of Northeast Asian environmental inter-ministerial[18] and senior official meetings[19] have focused on critical environmental oceanic and land-based issues, but none of these dialogues have led to any concrete cooperation or collaboration.[20] At the level of high politics, the Six Party Talks addressed the specific issue of North Korea's nuclear weapons program. Again, to date the Talks have achieved nothing but acrimony, nuclear tests, and the isolation of North Korea.

Scholars have also tackled interrelated global problems in East Asia under the rubric of "human security." For example, Tsuneo Akaha examines three global insecurities arising from the extent to which the

---

Security Frameworks in Northeast Asia; Human Trafficking; Regional Peacekeeping and Peacebuilding; Enhancing the Effectiveness of the Campaign against International Terrorism with Specific Reference to the Asia Pacific Region; Preventive Diplomacy; Oceania; Energy Security; and Security Implications for Climate Change. See *Study Groups* (Kuala Lumpur: Council for Security Cooperation in the Asia Pacific), http://www.cscap.org/index.php?page=study-groups; *Concluded Working and Study Groups* (Kuala Lumpur: Council for Security Cooperation in the Asia Pacific), http://www.cscap.org/index.php?page=concluded-working-and-study-grups

16   *List of Track II Activities 1994-2012* ; ibid.; ibid.

17   See *ASEAN Plus Three Cooperation* (Jakarta: Association of Southeast Asian Nations, 2012), http://www.asean.org/asean/external-relations/asean-3/item/asean-plus-three-cooperation

18   The 13th Tripartite Environment Ministers Meeting among Korea, China and Japan since they began in 1999 was held April 29, 2011 in Korea. See *The 13th Tripartite Environment Ministers Meeting (TEMM13)* (Tripartite Environment Ministers Meeting), http://www.temm.org/sub05/view.jsp?id=20

19   The 14th Senior Officials Meeting since they began in 1993 was held on April 8-9, 2009, in Russia. See *Key Outcomes of Soms: Som-14 (8-9 April 2009; Moscow, Russian Federation)* (Incheon: North-East Asian Subregional Programme for Environmental Cooperation), http://www.neaspec.org/key-outcomes-soms

20   Jho, W. and Lee, H., "The Structure and Political Dynamics of Regulating 'Yellow Sand' in Northeast Asia," *Asian Perspective*, 33(2) (2009).

countries of the region have failed to embrace global norms regarding the rights of groups of individuals, namely humans trafficked for exploitation, migrant workers, and persons living with HIV and AIDS patients. He and other scholars conclude that a common obstacle to addressing these global problems as manifested in East Asia is the lack of common principles and regulations concerning the treatment of border-crossing mobile individuals who embody each of these pressing issues.[21] Others have tackled further human security issues in the region such as the role and status of women and the realization of human rights.[22] Yet another, more critical angle of approach investigates the existential sources of insecurity experienced by the peoples living within this region: demographic pressures, resource limitations, ecological degradation, food politics, identity challenges, health threats, and political change.[23]

Identifying Linkages

We argued above that civil society networks are particularly good at identifying links between global problems and solutions. However, doing so is not easy. As Jared Diamond points out, they are linked in complex and often unrecognized ways. He lists twelve problems that lead to "unsustainability" and notes that while these problems appear to be separate,

> [T]hey are linked: one problem exacerbates another or makes its solution more difficult. For example, population growth affects all eleven other problems; more people means more deforestation, more toxic chemicals, more demand for wild fish, etc. The energy problem is linked to other problems because use of fossil fuels for energy contributes heavily to greenhouse gases, the combating of soil fertility losses by using synthetic fertilizers requires energy to make the fertilizers, fossil fuel scarcity increases our interest in nuclear energy which poses potentially the biggest "toxic" problem of all in case of an accident, and fossil fuel scarcity also makes it more expensive to

21   Akaha, T., "Human Security in East Asia: Embracing Global Norms through Regional Cooperation in Human Trafficking, Labour Migration, and HIV/AIDS," *Journal of Human Security*, 5(2) (2009), doi: http://dx.doi.org/10.3316/JHS0502011. See also Vassilieva, A. and Akaha, T., *Crossing National Borders Human Migration Issues in Northeast Asia* (Tokyo: United Nations University Press, 2005), http://search.ebscohost.com/login.aspx?direct=true&scope=site&db=nlebk&db=nlabk&AN=148044

22   See, for example, UNESCO, "Human Security in East Asia," in *International Conference on Human Security in East Asia* (Seoul: Korean National Commission for UNESCO, 2003).

23   Renwick, N., *Northeast Asian Critical Security: Exploring Democratic Freedoms and Social Justice* (Basingstoke: Palgrave Macmillan, 2004).

solve our freshwater problems by using energy to desalinize ocean water. Depletion of fisheries and other wild food sources puts more pressure on livestock, crops, and aquaculture to replace them, thereby leading to more topsoil losses and more eutrophication from agriculture and aquaculture. Problems of deforestation, water shortage, and soil degradation in the Third World foster wars there and drive legal asylum seekers and illegal emigrants to the First World from the Third World.[24]

This interlinking of issues, or complex interdependency of problems, has implications for both the way we think about these issues — our forms of knowledge — and the way we might start to solve them. Diamond remarks:

> People often ask, "What is the single most important environmental problem facing the world today?" A flip answer would be, "The single most important problem is our misguided focus on identifying the single most important problem!" That flip answer is essentially correct, because any of the dozen problems, if unsolved, would do us grave harm, and because they all interact with each other. If we solved eleven of the problems, but not the 12th, we would still be in trouble, whichever was the problem that remained unsolved. We have to solve them all.[25]

Some international agencies have attempted to map the specific links between the global problems that they tackle. In 2004, for example, the Global Environment Facility (GEF) recognized it was missing opportunities to exploit synergies and complementarities between their different projects on biodiversity, climate change, international waters, persistent organic particulates, integrated ecosystem management, and land degradation. It was ignoring the negative impacts arising from duplicated and incomplete work because linkages were not taken into account in project design and implementation.[26] In an important study for the emerging field of global problem-solving, undertaken for the GEF by its Scientific and Technical Advisory Panel (STAP), the GEF called attention to four distinct types of linkages that were identified in its funded projects. These were:

Key Linkages (blue), for example:

- Climate change and biodiversity, land and water degradation
- Land degradation and biodiversity
- Water degradation and biodiversity

---

24   Diamond, J.M., *Collapse : How Societies Choose to Fail or Succeed* (New York: Viking, 2005).

25   Ibid., p. 498.

26   Anderson, D., et al., *A Conceptual Design Tool for Exploiting Interlinkages between the Focal Areas of the GEF*, GEF working paper (Washington, DC: Global Environment Facility, 2004).

Intermediate Linkages (light blue), for example:

- Effect of land degradation on water bodies and vice versa, disrupting the hydrological cycle and leading to declining productivity and food insecurity, accentuated poverty, and social instability

- Effect of Persistent Organic Pollutants on biodiversity due to major impact on species and ecosystems

Weak Linkages (green), for example:

- Effect of land degradation and biodiversity on climate change via changes in albedo and decreasing carbon sequestration

Multiple (3-4 way) Interactions, for example:

- Climate change and variability affect biodiversity (at genetic, species and ecosystem levels), land degradation, hydrological cycles, thus also influencing surface, ground, and international waters — possibly all at the same time[27]

Of the 119 GEF projects reviewed by the STAP, only one-fifth of the project documents revealed any recognition by GEF of the existence of these links in the underlying problems and their causal factors, and only nine tried to exploit these links in project design.[28] On the solution side, that is, the intended outcome of projects in the GEF focal areas, the STAP identified ways in which the projects could have positive or negative impacts on projects in other focal areas. In the case of establishing and managing protected areas, for example, the projects were found to have positive effects on climate change by increased carbon storage when previously overexploited habitats are restored, but negative effects on climate change if the protected areas displace human populations and/or brings tourists to the area, which can further degrade it.

The GEF recommended each project identify these links between causal factors and the positive and negative linkages in their strategies. In addition, each project was told to take specific measures to reduce vulnerability to neglecting these links. In the case of protected areas, this approach means ensuring that protected areas include buffer zones and corridors to link separated areas, for example. GEF is one of the few international agencies to explicitly address the issue of linkages between problems and solutions in their project design — although effective implementation is another question. (The UN Environment Programme has also addressed this issue

---

27   Ibid., pp. 14-19.
28   Ibid., p. 22.

by creating an "Interlinkages Unit" that attempts to strengthen interlinkages and promote synergies across multilateral environmental conventions.[29] We are not aware of a similar study of inter-linkages applicable to the work of civil society organizations and networks, although some metrics exist to determine the performance of networks independent of their contribution to the resolution of global problems). Some of the GEF's framework is usable in a civil society context — the notions of key, intermediate, and weak linkages, cross-problem impacts of solution strategies, etc. But the lack of scholarly work in this field is striking, given the scale of international civil society activity and interventions on specific problems. It appears that practitioners responding to real-world crises in intergovernmental organizations may be the most important source of knowledge in the field of global problem-solving. Although not reviewed here in detail, the Nexus Network, established in the UK in 2014, attempts to distil lessons learned about such linkages among problems — in this case water, food, energy, environment, and in some cases climate. These interlinkages were perceived by development agencies to be critically important in 2009 after the food and energy crises of 2007 and 2008.[30]

World Economic Forum Global Risk Taxonomy

In 2005, the World Economic Forum (WEF) developed a new taxonomy of global problems under the rubric of "global" risk. In its first of a series of annual reports, the WEF listed thirty-six global risks, which it classified into four categories: economic, geopolitical, societal, and environmental. From this list, the WEF focused on ten risks most likely to have a "major or extreme impact on business." These were instability in Iraq, terrorism, emerging fiscal crises, disruption in oil supplies, radical Islam, sudden decline in China's growth, pandemics and infectious diseases, climate change, weapons of mass destruction, and unrestrained migration and related tensions.[31]

---

29 Gitay, H., *et al.*, "Interlinkages: Governance for Sustainability, Section D: Human Dimensions of Environmental Change" in *Global Environmental Outlook GEO 4* (Kenya: United Nations Environment Programme, 2007).

30 See *The Nexus Network* (Brighton: The Nexus Network), http://thenexusnetwork.org/ Allouche, J., "Does the Nexus Mask a Bigger Debate? Rethinking the Food-Energy-Water Nexus and a Low Water Economy," *Knowledge, Technology and Society*, 21 March 2014, http://www.water-energy-food.org/en/news/view__1607/does-the-nexus-mask-a-bigger-debate.html?-rethinking-the-food-energy-water-nexus-and-a-low-water-economy

31 World Economic Forum in collaboration and Merrill Lynch, *Global Risks to the Business*

In 2006, the WEF reduced the list to twenty-five global risks, but added technological risks to the taxonomy. At this point, the dangers were identified by commissioned individual, scholarly, and corporate risk analysts.[32] In 2007, the WEF increased the number of "core" risks to twenty-seven, a precursor of what was called "clusters" and then "Centres of Gravity," that is, global risks that are highly interconnected with other risks of great consequence. The WEF also introduced a "risk barometer" that year to measure the probability, impact, and trend of each risk (measured in potential economic damage, growth loss as per cent of global GDP, and mortalities) and a measure of the degree of correlation between them.[33]

In the 2008 report, the WEF made the concept of global risk more granular and explicit. The WEF explained that it separated identifiable trends ("observable facts in the contemporary world"), issues of concern ("potential challenges which arise from those trends"), and risks ("specific realizations of those challenges in a format which is sufficiently specific to be open to a level of assessment in terms of relative severity and likelihood, without being so specific as to preclude them as a basis for decision-making"). In some domains, the WEF noted that the *trends-issues of concern-risks* pathway is clear. "In others, notably geopolitical risk," the WEF observed, "the pathway from trend to risk is less clear, contingency is greater and common issues can manifest in many different ways."[34] Thus, whereas for economic global risks, there were six trends, six issues of concern, and six risks, for geopolitics, there were seven trends, nine issues of concern, and twelve risks to track.

In the 2008 report, the assessments were still based on expert groups. Some of the thirty-one risks listed such as natural catastrophe were assessed using actuarial data. Others, geopolitical risks in particular, required additional, disaggregated assessment by specialists. Consequently, the WEF allowed for a wider range of possible outcomes on the latter types of global risk and correspondingly higher levels of uncertainty.[35]

In 2009, the WEF added new depth to their evolving taxonomy. This time, as the global financial crisis took grip, they listed thirty-six global risks.

Environment, 2005 (Geneva: World Economic Forum, 2005).

32   World Economic Forum, *et al.*, *Global Risks 2006* (Geneva: World Economic Forum, 2006).

33   World Economic Forum, *et al.*, *Global Risks 2007, a Global Risk Network Report* (Geneva: World Economic Forum, 2007).

34   World Economic Forum, *et al.*, *Global Risks 2008, a Global Risk Network Report* (Geneva: World Economic Forum, 2008).

35   Ibid., p. 45.

For the first time, the WEF defined global risk (see Table 2.2). To qualify, the WEF stated, a global risk must have the following attributes at a global or supra-regional level: pervasive economic impacts, high uncertainty as to its general impact, a risk of no less than $10 billion, and a multi-stakeholder approach to risk mitigation given the complex linkages with other risks.[36]

Table 2.2: WEF Definition of Global Risk

Global Scope: To be considered global, a risk should have the potential to affect (including both primary and secondary impact) at least three world regions on at least two different continents. While these risks may have regional or even local origin, their impact can potentially be felt globally.

Cross-Industry Relevance: The risk has to affect three or more industries (including both primary and secondary impact).

Uncertainty: There is uncertainty about how the risk manifests itself within 10 years combined with uncertainty about the magnitude of its impact (assessed in terms of likelihood and severity).

Economic Impact: The risk has the potential to cause economic damage of around US$ 10 billion.

Public Impact: The risk has the potential to cause major human suffering and to trigger considerable public pressure and global policy responses.

Multi-stakeholder Approach: The complexity of the risk, both in terms of its effects and its drivers as well as its inter-linkages with other risks, requires a multi-stakeholder approach for its mitigation.

Source: World Economic Forum, *et al., Global Risks 2009, a Global Risk Network Report* (Geneva: World Economic Forum, 2009), p. 32.

Unlike previous catalogues of global problems, the WEF's definition can be used to determine if a specific problem qualifies as "global" based on the qualitative and quantitative characteristics of the risk it presents. There is still a substantial overlap with older taxonomies and catalogues, however, especially with regard to the "mega-problems" or "core problems" identified by earlier studies.

The WEF also began to map the interconnections between risks, drawing on a survey initially limited to experts. By 2012, it had surveyed more than 1,000 participants in the WEF from all regions and cultures of the world

---

36   World Economic Forum, *et al., Global Risks 2009, a Global Risk Network Report* (Geneva: World Economic Forum, 2009).

for estimates of the degree of correlation and level of risk associated with a trend. Of course, this is not a representative sample in any respect. Those surveyed were mostly privileged, wealthy transnational leaders from market and public sectors (with a sprinkling from the "social" sector). But they surely constitute a relatively well-informed group alert to trends that might affect business or the exercise of power and, therefore, a priori more likely to be scanning the global risk horizon than most people on the planet.

The empirical basis of the risk assessment and linkage also allowed the WEF to break down their results on a regional basis. They found that Asian countries "are much more diverse with respect to their exposures to economic risks, but comparatively tightly clustered — however at a higher median risk level — when it comes to the geopolitical and environmental risk dimensions."[37] Moreover, most Asian economies "are heavily exposed to a hard landing in China. Asia is also subject to risks related to the price of oil, dollar fluctuations, and a retrenchment from globalization."[38]

In 2011, the WEF introduced three new elements. These were "cross-cutting global risks," "the nexus between risks," and "risks to watch." Cross-cutting risks "are especially significant given their high degrees of impact and interconnectedness [that] influence the evolution of many other global risks and inhibit our capacity to respond effectively to them" (in 2009, economic disparity and the failure of global governance were highlighted).[39] These nexuses are clusters of emerging risks (in 2009, the WEF identified three such emergent nexuses, "macroeconomic imbalances," "illegal economy," and the "water-food-energy" nexus). A separate set of "risks to watch" were also identified in 2009 through the combination of survey responses with expert opinion indicating that these risks may have "severe, unexpected or underappreciated consequences" (such as cyber-security issues ranging from cyber theft to all-out cyber warfare). [40]

The 2012 report added another characterization to its mapping of the linkages between risks. Previously, the WEF identified five "centers of gravity" in each of the categories of problems, these being "the risks of greatest systemic importance, or the most influential and consequential in relation to others" (in 2012, they were chronic fiscal imbalances, greenhouse gas emissions, global governance failure, unsustainable population growth,

---

37   Ibid., p. 8.
38   Ibid., p. 10.
39   Ibid., p. 6.
40   Ibid.

and critical systems failure).[41] The WEF then pinpointed four global risks that were most connected across these global risk "centers of gravity." (In 2012, all of these were economic in nature, namely, severe income disparity, major systemic financial failure, unforeseen negative consequences of regulation, and extreme volatility in energy and agriculture prices).[42]

Arguably, these critical connectors are the most powerful leverage point in this "ecology" of risk-generating problems. The 2013 report supplemented this with an additional set of five "X Factors" or wild cards that look beyond the fifty known problems with potentially massive impact over the next decade to survey as yet almost unknown problems, issues that have the potential to emerge rapidly and "change the game." (In 2013, the X Factors were runaway climate change, significant cognitive enhancement, rogue deployment of geo-engineering, costs of living longer, and discovery of alien life.)[43]

In 2009, the WEF had already shifted from a quantitative definition of risk to a more qualitative one: "an occurrence that causes significant negative impact for several countries and industries."[44] In 2014, the WEF used this definition to winnow down the list to thirty-one leading global threats.[45] It made this change because the quantitative valuations of risk inevitably involved many assumptions, could not account for a range of valuations for a specific risk, and could not be estimated at all for some risks such as loss of biodiversity or climate change.[46] Instead, the WEF relied primarily on surveys of perception of the leading risks in terms of possible impact and probability, with all the attendant problems of cognitive bias, etc. The 2014 report therefore identified the perceptual differences revealed by gender (women were found to be more sensitive to impact than men) and by age (the young were found to attribute higher impact to environmental and social risks such as the fiscal crisis than older respondents, for example).[47] It also showed that, in terms of probability and impact of risk, the WEF's "top ten" evolves fast —faster, in fact, than the underlying real phenomena could possibly change. This is evidence, therefore, that the WEF risk indices

---

41   World Economic Forum, *et al.*, *Global Risks 2012* (Geneva: World Economic Forum, 2012).

42   Ibid., p. 14.

43   World Economic Forum, *et al.*, *Global Risks 2013* (Geneva: World Economic Forum, 2013).

44   World Economic Forum, *Global Risks 2014, Insight Report* (Geneva: World Economic Forum).

45   Ibid., p. 55.

46   Ibid., p. 49.

47   Ibid., p. 19.

are driven by factors that rapidly affect perception (such as "global events" that generate massive media and Internet exposure). In 2014, the WEF also distinguished between risks and vulnerabilities, which they suggest are really trends that portend the emergence of a risk.

In 2014, the WEF also introduced the notion of "systemic risks." These are risks that transcend national boundaries, involve shared resources, and exhibit causality that is "indirect and time-delayed." Such systemic risks resist technical fixes and require changes to the behavior of those involved.[48] The WEF examined three such systemic risks (instability in a multipolar world, the lost generation growing up with poor prospects, and digital disintegration) and argued that unless all stakeholders are engaged in joint problem-solving, each of these risks may overwhelm humanity.[49] They noted that failing global governance may be replaced by an "intricate lattice of multiple, interconnected government agreements related to relatively simple global goals," leaving it to collaborative alliances, partnerships, and localities to figure out how to deliver solutions commensurate with the scale of the problem.[50]

We focus on the WEF framework because it is the first detailed description of global problems and solutions (in their parlance, "global risks and mitigation strategies") that describe the terrain of global problems ("risk landscape") and populates it with empirical content, expert opinion, and survey data of risk perception. Admittedly, this approach is based primarily on the perceptions of a privileged community of corporate leaders and closely-related expert communities. Another global community — for example, ecological and climate specialists, or development and human rights practitioners — might generate a different top fifty list of global risks, centers of gravity of clustered risks, critical connecting risks, risks to watch, systemic risks, and wild card risks. Indeed, this is observable already in the problems that are highlighted in the United Nations' Millennium Development Goals. Nonetheless, the WEF framework is a powerful navigation tool that can provide useful insight into interrelated global problems and shared solutions in a policy framework that can then be implemented in tangible, specific ways.

---

48   Ibid., p. 27. This section of the report drew on the conceptual work on "global systemic risk" advanced in Goldin, I. and Mariathasan, M., *The Butterfly Defect, How Globalization Creates Systemic Risks, and What to Do About It* (Princeton: Princeton University Press, 2014).

49   World Economic Forum (2014).

50   Ibid., p. 22.

In 2008, the WEF suggested that nations create country risk officers to respond both to risks that are displaced across borders and over time onto vulnerable communities (a process of so-called "squeezing" in WEF parlance) and to risks that are becoming more homogenous across countries. Examples include the universality of "lifestyle" diseases formerly limited to OECD countries or exposure to pandemics that cross borders in hours and days due to the velocity and breadth of human mobility. The WEF proposed the creation of a forum of country risk officers or agencies to overcome fragmented accountability for managing these risks, and to devise coalitions for tackling collaborative mitigation of risk squeezing and risk homogeneity.[51]

In a multi-year process beginning in 2009 and involving nearly 200 young leaders, the World Economic Forum investigated how to craft practical interventions in twenty "issues" covering ten "areas of enquiry" such as education, energy, and health, issues which could also be termed complex global problems.[52] They set out to identify positive feedback in the causal loop diagrams they visualized for each issue area. Such feedback could destabilize the entire issue area — or those linked to it — with runaway negative and positive feedback loops. Each group worked to identify interventions that would lend stability to their issue area, and in some cases, to multiple issue areas at a time. They recommended that not only the immediate effects of interventions should be considered, but also possible delayed second-order effects[53] They advised that intervention choices to induce constructive change should emerge through this mapping and testing process, stating "By exploring several levels of effects and influences, patterns emerged that indicated areas of leverage (many connections converging on one point) or root causes, which could spin a situation out of balance. By creating a broader, non-linear picture of your situation of interest, a more nuanced approach to intervention can be plotted."[54]

They then described case studies and interventions made by the young leaders such as proposed increases in transparency of governance, new uses of social media, and highly adapted and localized technological innovations. As Michael Drexler observed, all twenty loop diagrams generated by the

---

51   World Economic Forum, *et al.* (2008); World Economic Forum (2014).
52   World Economic Forum, "Young Global Leaders: Guide to Influencing Complex Systems," in *The Forum of Young Global Leaders* (Nuevo Vallarta: World Economic Forum, 2012).
53   Ibid., pp. 7-9.
54   Ibid., p. 9.

groups contained potentially destabilizing feedback loops, endowing each system with the potential to "blow up."[55] He noted how multiplier nodes often sit within each positive feedback loop, many of which are common to different complex systems and may be key to stabilizing the system once technical silos within each system are connected — for example, connecting popular mass media with specialist media in a given issue area. Drexler also noted that "meta-interventions" might work across different systems such as designing appropriate incentive schemes to overcome short versus long-term or local versus national versus global stabilizing outcomes. Finally, he concluded that as the systems are interconnected, interventions within each system will affect other systems. Thus, "An intervention to appropriately value natural resources, for example, will need at least collaboration, if not a reinforcing intervention, from financial services."[56]

It follows, Drexler asserts, that one must remove "the worst distortions first before the 'softer' measures can be given a chance to stabilize the system. One without the other will not work."[57] Given the exercise began by recognizing that what appears at first to be a cause of one issue may, in a set of interdependencies, be a symptom of another,[58] Drexler leaves open the question of how the "worst distortions" are best identified for intervention before other distortions. Despite this lacuna, the WEF's attempt to create an applied methodology to identify specific interventions — many of which have been implemented since 2009 — is an important methodological achievement in the field of global problem-solving.

In 2013, the WEF focused on how to build resilience at the national level to manage many disparate but linked risks in the form of action narratives. The WEF observed that it felt obliged to develop such narratives due to complexity: "The 50 global risks in this report are interdependent and correlated with each other. The permutations of two, three, four or more risks are too many for the human mind to comprehend. Therefore, an analysis of the network of connections has been undertaken to highlight some interesting constellations of global risks."[59] A subset of these constellations was selected, and an "action narrative" around each of these cases was developed to help leaders understand the risk, make them aware of the true complexity of the

55   Drexler, M., *Influencing Complex Systems – a Systemic Overview*, Young Global Leaders: Guide to Influencing Complex Systems (Geneva: World Economic Forum, 2012).
56   Ibid.
57   Ibid.
58   World Economic Forum (2012).
59   World Economic Forum, *et al.* (2013).

interconnected risks, and help them to envision how they might contribute to possible solutions. In 2013, three such cases were presented: "Testing Economic and Environmental Resilience" on climate change mitigation and adaptation, "Digital Wildfires in a Hyper-connected World" on virally distributed misinformation, and "The Dangers of Hubris on Human Health" on the existential threat posed by antibiotic-resistant bacteria.[60]

Dirk Helbing connects complexity with the WEF's concept of "hyper-connected" global risks that can set off cascading and concatenating risks in his 2013 essay, "Globally Networked Risks and How to Respond."[61] He argues that systemic instability is the outcome of globalization processes, increasing network densities, sparse use of resources, greater complexity, and ever-faster decision-making processes, all of which interact to create "hyper-risks." To increase resilience, Helbing suggests some general design principles for global systems. These include: fostering of diversity to ensure that at least one backup system exists in case of failure; imposition of limits on system scale to reduce the maximum damage from coupled failure; introduction of weak links within and between systems to reduce system density and, thereby, the rate of transmitted failure or "contagion"; deceleration of system processes to enable decision-makers to avoid and manage crises; devolution of sufficient authority to lower levels in command hierarchies, ensuring the top is not overwhelmed and cross-level decisions are not de-synchronized; and the design of certain critical systems to operate either partly or completely independently of other systems.[62]

Global Asia

There is, as yet, no consensus in East Asia as to which problems are paramount, let alone which shared solutions should be adopted in the search for ways to engage in solving linked global problems at the same time. Indeed, it is not surprising that there are no ready-made catalogues of the most pressing problems in the region. In many respects, East Asia is more of an anti-region than a community, with only nascent convergence towards common norms, standards, and practices, let alone institutions of consultation, coordination, and collaboration.

---

60   Ibid., p. 15.
61   Helbing, D., "Globally Networked Risks and How to Respond," *Nature*, 497 (2013), doi: http://dx.doi.org/10.1038/nature12047
62   Ibid., pp. 55-56.

To recap, we have shown that some but not all problems are truly global in their impact. Those that are fall into one of three basic categories — they relate to a global commons, to our shared values as human beings, or to the need for regulating human behavior to create global public goods. But we have also seen that the "pool" of candidate global problems that meet these criteria is very large — upwards of hundreds of such problems compete for attention — and that many of these problems are nested within or linked to other problems, creating mega-problems.

Finally, we have noted that leaders from the region of concern to this book — East Asia — are yet to present clear statements of what they consider to be global problems. They have also yet to identify what global problems manifest in, or originating from, this region might be the subject of multilateral cooperation in the search for solutions at a regional or global level.

Thus, "Global Asia," or the relationship between globalization and global issues and Asia, still needs to be defined.[63] The potential for this region to solve problems at a local, regional, and global level is immense and urgently required. As Thomas Risse-Kappen argues, the impact of transnational actors and coalitions on state policy is inversely related to the degree to which specific issue areas are regulated by international society or institutionalized, state-based relationships on the one hand, and by the capacity of these actors and coalitions to overcome the barriers set up by domestic political structures, on the other.[64] Nowhere is this clearer than in East Asia. One might also infer that the bigger the gap in institutional structure, the bigger the need and greater the role of networks of civil society. In this region, the security gap is bigger than the economic gap, and the cultural gap is greatest of all.

Before moving onto the task of specifying more precisely what is meant by complexity when discussing interrelated global problems and solution strategies in East Asia, and addressing the potential for civil society to contribute to the networked governance of these problems, we must first look more closely at the concept of "problem."

---

63 "Global Asia" is the name of an important journal published in South Korea that tackles exactly this issue. The author is on the editorial board. See *Global Asia* (Seoul: East Asia Foundation), http://www.globalasia.org/

64 Risse-Kappen, T., *Bringing Transnational Relations Back In: Non-State Actors, Domestic Structures and International Institutions* (Cambridge: Cambridge University Press, 1995).

Negotiating Definitions of Common Problems and Shared Solutions

Earlier in this chapter, we outlined different approaches to ascertaining which problems are truly global and how these problems might be framed. Now we ask: what is a problem in the first place? At the most fundamental level, we may say that humans are goal-directed animals, and goals embody values. When a goal is not achieved, values are frustrated and a problem is born.

A problem, therefore, is an obstacle to the realization of one or more human goals, either individual or collective. By implication, once this obstacle is removed, the goal may be fulfilled and the value defining the goal may be realized — provided that no other limiting conditions or obstacles are in effect. Thus, a problem measures the deficit between actual or perceived reality and what humans desire to be the case. The deficit can be viewed pragmatically or with respect to some ideal state. The former measure is generally less demanding and is often the basis of pragmatic politics in search of marginal improvements to the status quo. The latter measure is often the motivating worldview of utopians who push radical, dramatic change that ruptures the continuity of past and present. Which one is more realistic or idealistic depends on context; whether a social agent adheres to incremental rather than radical change depends more often than not on the degree to which that agent — a person or an organization — is heavily vested in the status quo.

The core values of societies are only partly overlapping. They vary by culture, language, and history. Extensive cross-cultural communication, translation, and negotiation are required to establish the common core of values that may be threatened and which therefore constitute the basis for common problems across cultures and borders. Even when this has been achieved, the same "problem" may have different meanings in different social locations due to divergent cultural values, social rank, and socialization. In some contexts, one person's problem may even be another person's solution (exploitative workplaces, for example, render some people desperately poor and others fabulously rich). In another context, the leaders of one country (say North Korea) may find salvation in nuclear weapons whereas the leaders of another (say America) may view the same capacity to be a dire threat. And the leaders of yet another country (say South Korea) may view it as less of a threat and more of an irritant

— possibly even an achievement to be admired because as Koreans they share more values with North Koreans (for instance, the distrust of great powers) than Americans.

This analysis implies that only part of the total set of views as to what constitutes a big problem is held in common. This core of shared perceptions may be called common knowledge,[65] implying that each observer of the problem is convinced that another (especially an adversary) would agree that it is a problem. It does not, however, signify a consensus as to what constitutes the problem itself — a dimension of problems that constantly ambushes attempts to solve them. We hypothesize here that the problem "tails" — the aspects of the problem that are not captured in the overlapping, common view, which we call the core of the common problem, but are only perceived separately from distinct cultural angles of interpretation — constantly disturb and undermine the effort of one party to focus on the core.

Thus, we should not be surprised to find that even the definition of problems that afflict more than one society can be highly contentious. For example, China is the source of the bulk of the acid rain in East Asia, some of which is deposited in both Koreas and Japan as the winds blow it from west to east. On the surface, this might seem like a straightforward scientific issue. But in reality, China has been hesitant to concur with trans-boundary scientific research that suggests that it is the source of much of the acid rain in these countries. In fact, the primary concern of Chinese decision-makers is not the impact of the acid rain in Korea or Japan; it is the ghastly impact of acid rain on local communities and ecosystems in the immediate vicinity of the offending sources of sulfurous emissions. Roughly the same logic operates with respect to the yellow sand storm problem.[66]

Given their true complexity, the only way to generate a common understanding across political cultures of interrelated global problems is to systematically decompose these problems into their constituent elements first at a global level, and then within each country to see where, if at all, the overlap is to be found. Inevitably, this exploration entails long and intensive dialogue and often uncovers deep assumptions and misconceptions about

---

65 Geanakoplos, J., "Common Knowledge," *The Journal of Economic Perspectives*, 6(4) (1992); Vanderschraaf, P. and Sillari, G., *Common Knowledge* (Stanford: Stanford Encyclopedia of Philosophy, 2002), http://plato.stanford.edu/entries/common-knowledge/

66 Streets, D., *Energy and Acid Rain Projections for Northeast Asia*, NAPSNet Policy Forum (Berkeley: Nautilus Institute, 1997); Jho, W. and Lee, H. (2009), p. 62.

what parties in different countries believe to be problematic or even to constitute the factual situation.

For example, it took two years of meetings, mutual learning, joint exploration of issues and concepts, and finally, an extensive process of joint writing and word-by-word editing, translation, retranslation, and revision, for Nautilus experts from the United States and their Japanese counterparts to arrive at a shared, meaningful concept of energy security. The final statement of this concept, included in a long report, reads:

> A nation state is energy secure to the degree that fuel and energy services are available to ensure: (a) survival of the nation (b) protection of national welfare, and (c) minimization of risks associated with supply and use of fuel and energy services. The six dimensions of energy security include energy supply, economic, technological, environmental, social and cultural, and military/security dimensions. Energy policies must address the domestic and international (regional and global) implications of each of these dimensions.[67]

This concept explicitly included cultural dimensions normally ignored in Western thought. Conversely, the American side identified a key attribute of energy security not previously analyzed in Japan, namely technological diversity over time[68]— an issue that caused Japan's power sector to shut down reactors starting in 2000 and again in 2002 and that was highlighted by the catastrophic Fukushima reactor failures in 2012. Notably, the resulting concept was neither American nor Japanese, but rather a hybrid concept that truly was more than the sum of the parts. Consequently, its application in either culture required extensive explanation and further work by its authors, although this has proved productive in a number of applied policy contexts, including identifying the most resilient and rapid energy security response to the Fukushima disaster.[69]

In two workshops held in Seoul in 2009 and 2010, researchers from South Korea, Japan, and China investigated energy-related and climate-related

---

67   von Hippel, D., *et al.*, "Evaluating the Energy Security Impacts of Energy Policies," in *The Routledge Handbook of Energy Security*, ed. by Sovacool, B. K. (Abingdon: Taylor & Francis, 2010).

68   Drawing on a diversity concept based on the Herfindahl index and advanced by Neff, T.L., *Improving Energy Security in Pacific Asia: Diversification and Risk Reduction for Fossil and Nuclear Fuels*, Pacific Asia Regional Energy Security (PARES) Project (Berkeley: Nautilus Institute, 1997).

69   von Hippel, D. and Takase, K., *The Path from Fukushima: Short and Medium-Term Impacts of the Reactor Damage Caused by the Japan Earthquake and Tsunami on Japan's Electricity Systems*, NAPSNet Special Report (Berkeley: Nautilus Institute, 2011).

urban insecurity to explore how these three linked global problems were manifest in East Asia. As outlined below, they discovered they had very different views as to the nature of the problem and the required solutions both within and across countries.

South Korea: Climate and Energy Linkages with Urban Insecurity

Seung Jick Yoo advanced a traditional view of energy security and its linkage to climate change in South Korea. He argued the primary source of energy insecurity in South Korea is oil import dependency, a reliance that can be directly reduced by increasing energy end-use efficiency and the supply of renewable energy, which in turn mitigates greenhouse gas reductions. The other element of official strategy is to diversify geographic supply, in particular from the Russian Far East, via a regional cooperation framework advanced by the South Korean government since 2001, albeit without much success. He argued that solving the problems of import dependency and climate change simultaneously is very difficult and best achieved by regional cooperation. At the heart of these solutions is the joint development and deployment of new technologies, especially to reduce Chinese emissions from dirty coal.[70] This approach became the core of the South Korean government's "green growth" strategy.

In contrast, Sun-Jin Yun analyzed the linkage in South Korea between energy scarcity, prices, environmental stress, and equity in terms of energy access both across households with varying incomes and between regions in South Korea (for example, the concentration of reactors and related hazards on the southern and eastern coast to primarily power Seoul).[71] She noted that South Korea essentially functions as an island because the Democratic People's Republic of Korea (DPRK) blocks the land bridge with respect to power and gas supplies from China and Russia.

She argued that technological change and regional diversification of fuel will not suffice to realize energy and climate security in urban areas. She

70 Yoo, S.J., "Issues in Climate Change and Energy Security in Northeast Asia," in *Interconnections of Global Problems in East Asia: Climate Change Adaptation and its Complexity in Perspective of Civil Society Initiative* (Paju: Nautilus Institute, 2008).

71 Yun, S.J., "Energy Security of Cities in Korea," in *Interconnections of Global Problems in East Asia, Green Economy, Urban Security And Energy Security* (Seoul: Nautilus Institute, 2010).

held that the standard energy paradigm leads to excessive energy use and overconsumption of resources, while concentrating the direct (pollution) and indirect (economic- and climate-related) impacts on the poorest and most vulnerable populations. The outcomes are energy poverty and needless suffering. The key to increasing energy equity and sustainability at the same time is not to maintain this paradigm but to provide decentralized, distributed, and renewable energy.

Lee Sang Gun approached the issue of linkage from a spatial perspective. He described the political-economic basis that allows ecological services and climate impacts to be distributed unequally across regions and income levels of South Korean society. The net result is the "apartment dominant" urban landscape of South Korean human settlements. [72] This polarization leads to a vicious circle described by Lee as "Roads and roofs of building -> impervious cover -> hydrological circulation interruption -> vulnerability increase (serious damage from heavy rainfall) at Seoul in 2010." We expand on this thesis in chapter 4.

Myungrae Cho explained that while green growth policies aim to ameliorate the negative impacts of climate and energy insecurity on urban populations in South Korea, a focus on technological solutions results in a paradoxical outcome. The benefits of green growth policies accrue mostly to the rich while the effects of environmental degradation fall disproportionately on the poor as was evident during the massive floods in Seoul in September 2010. A condition of "environmental injustice" is thereby created.[73]

In this view, green growth is blind to the distributional outcomes of policies dedicated to the development and deployment of new technology. As Sun-Jin Yun argued, the urban poor in South Korea are most vulnerable to the effects of simultaneous resource depletion (higher prices) and increased energy consumption (leaving them relatively inefficient and under-served), as well as to many of the negative environmental externalities arising from energy supply and use. They are disproportionately susceptible to the local climate change impacts arising from increased greenhouse gas emissions.

Yun suggested that interdependent changes in lifestyle, land-use, energy democracy, and community participation are central to breaking this vicious cycle. She argued that these factors are directly linked and

---

72   Lee, S., "Climate Change and Green Cities in South Korea," in *Interconnections of Global Problems in East Asia, Green Economy, Urban Security And Energy Security* (Seoul: Nautilus Institute, 2010).

73   Cho, M., "Is the Green Economy Secure in Korea? Dissecting Korea's Green Growth Strategy," in *Interconnections of Global Problems in East Asia, Green Economy, Urban Security And Energy Security* (Seoul: Nautilus Institute, 2010).

mutually reinforcing, and entail reshaping not just technology, but entire legal and institutional structures.[74] In her view, the official solution to the linked problems of energy and urban insecurity in South Korea, that is, green growth, boiled down to a stimulus, driven by the global financial crisis, that funded well-connected "construction and engineering" sectors to build nuclear reactors and huge water storage and flood control projects. These were primarily constructed to create jobs and to align voters with the ruling party. She noted the sharp turn away from an authentic solution in all aspects of the current Republic of Korea (ROK) government's policies for green growth, implying that a political change at the top was a necessary enabling condition for the full realization of the local potential for sustainability.

According to these authors, policies intended to address the linkage between climate, energy, and urban insecurity have been captured by vested interests. Put slightly differently, the "meta-problem" (the WEF would call it the critical connecting problem) that connects these clustered problems is a failure of national and regional governance. This problem in turn represents a binding constraint on what can be done to resolve each aspect of the problems of climate- and energy-related urban insecurity.

China: Multi-level Critical Connections between Energy and Urban Insecurity

China presents a very different story to South Korea. According to Wen Bo, the mechanisms of social and political feedback from environmental and victims organizations to the central government, expressing the desire to curb environmental excesses created by local governments and companies, have already reached their limit. The scale of pollution and adverse impacts arising from local development projects and resource extraction threatens to overwhelm the capacity of local governments and political authorities to manage the consequent social displacement and political disruption. Wen observed that the environmental ministry lacks human and regulatory capacity, is particularly weak in local offices, and faces inconsistent legal frameworks, contradictory policies, and overlapping institutions. In this case, the problem is not so much the appropriation of institutional capacity by vested interests in green growth garb, as in South Korea. Rather, the lack of institutional capacity generates the social stress evident in Chinese urban development.[75]

---

74   Yun, S.J. (2010).
75   Bo, W., "Urban Security in China," in *Interconnections of Global Problems in East Asia,*

Conversely, top-down, central planning and allocation of production targets and resources have had limited efficacy in reducing energy intensity or improving environmental performance, two key indicators of sustainability. Yi Wang noted that the green stimulus and recovery package China adopted to counter the global financial crisis had alleviated much poverty. But it also led to the restoration of polluting, resource-intensive traditional industries on the one hand, and by increasing demand, drove an absolute increase in energy use and emissions due to the rebound effect on the other — even though it reduced energy intensity in various sectors.[76] Ironically, China makes more photovoltaics than any other country, but exports 90 percent of them because they are too costly for local use.

Wang argued that two elements are critical to achieving a successful sustainability transition whereby energy and climate-driven insecurity in China could be tackled at the same time as rapid urbanization and development. The first is extensive administrative, managerial, and technical-scientific capacity building at the local and provincial levels of government to manage environmental issues before they become massive and disruptive. The second is a market framework that sends the right, long-term price signals to investors, the consuming public, and to private corporate management. Due to the failure of the climate negotiations, a global market framework that sends such consistent signals and creates certainty in the market is missing. Without an informed and highly capable set of local actors, including government and community organizations of many types, no bottom-up participatory or democratic approach is feasible — as was evident in the controversies in Nanjing and Guangzhou over the incineration of waste. For civil society, the most important thing is local capacity building, including scientific, administrative, managerial, and financial capacities to enable civil society to challenge the state. A related problem is the market failure created by contradictory property rights regimes in the transition from "rural village"-based land ownership to "urban" collective land ownership. This inconsistency puts local government officials seeking to increase tax revenues and party cadres under pressure to evict local residents standing in the way of development projects, often leading to corrupt land deals followed by protests and social unrest.[77]

Green Economy, Urban Security And Energy Security (Seoul: Nautilus Institute, 2010).

76 Wang, Y., "China's Approach to Green Development and Transformation of Economic Development Pattern," in *Interconnections of Global Problems in East Asia, Green Economy, Urban Security And Energy Security* (Seoul: Nautilus Institute, 2010).

77 Shin, H.B., "Development and Dissent in China's 'Urban Age,'" *openSecurity*, 25

At the level of the city, Wang noted that China has many demonstration projects and model cities. The latest project is a low carbon city led by the department of climate change. "We have invested a lot of money into these programs but have not coordinated between cities. We have a top-down approach and we do not have different regional policies. Many regions would like to set their own policies and plans, but they do not know how to realize their plans. There are a lot of conflicts between the various types of plans: low carbon, urban, etc."[78]

"In China" he explained, "mayors dominate in urban planning and each mayor has their own plans. We change our plans depending on who is in office at the time, and they don't understand how to create a modern society. This is a big challenge. We need to integrate the top-down and bottom-up approaches in urban development."[79]

Thus, in contrast to South Korea, one might say the primary problem in China is an outright institutional shortfall based on continued command-and-control planning, incomplete reform of property rights, and a deficit in local government capacity faced with these contradictory pressures. Whether this capacity can be built up without political democratization at the national level is a key issue. In China, there appear to be multiple, critical connecting problems that lead in turn to urban insecurity despite the gains in recent years to increase energy end-use efficiency and to supply renewable energy.

Japan: Social and Cultural Drivers of Energy and Urban Insecurity

Japan revealed a third picture, different from South Korea and China. In contrast to South Korea where institutional interests captured the "green solution space," and to China, where the primary problem is a lack of institutional capacity, the Japanese problem derives from rigid paradigms of growth combined with institutional gridlock. As Takayuki Minato explained, in Japan the process of innovation is driven by the feedback loop between individual consumers and producers as expressed in the

---

February 2013, https://www.opendemocracy.net/opensecurity/hyun-bang-shin/development-and-dissent-in-chinas-urban-age; O'Donnell, M.A., "Laying Siege to the Villages: Lessons from Shenzhen," *openSecurity*, 28 March 2013, https://www.opendemocracy.net/opensecurity/mary-ann-o%E2%80%99donnell/laying-siege-to-villages-lessons-from-shenzhen

78 Wang, Y. (2010).
79 Ibid.

highly regulated market system in Japan.[80] Thus, social factors that drive consumer behavior at the individual and household level in Japan, such as demographic aging, life style changes, and immigration levels, etc., are critical to system-level outcomes.

External factors such as Chinese competition for material resources and increasingly direct competition with South Korea for export markets necessitate government-driven technological innovation to reduce reliance on external resources. However, these state-led initiatives are often contradictory, slow, hazardous, and costly relative to the agile, rapid, and market-based technologies that are created to fulfill immediate social demands for goods and services and which have historically been Japan's competitive edge in global trade. Moreover, Japan's ability to implement high technology strategies that rely on imported materials such as rare earth minerals is potentially vulnerable to the loss of external suppliers (especially from China), which Minato noted is a "cross-national linkage" between energy, climate, and urban insecurity in Japan. Consequently, Japan and South Korea (which faces a similar constraint) may both need to develop new technologies that are not reliant on such minerals.

With regard to energy-driven urban insecurity, Kae Takase described the continuing difficulties faced by government and industry in making nuclear spent fuel reprocessing a viable energy strategy in Japan. She contrasted this with the adoption of a feed-in-tariff that could stimulate rapid growth in photovoltaic cell-distributed electricity production and achieve Japan's goals of reduced greenhouse gas emissions if combined with a "minimum" nuclear power pathway in Japan.[81] She suggested a shift from conventional to "comprehensive" energy security policy that would capture the full complexity of the energy security issue in Japan, and by implication, in other countries.

In Japan, where the basic minimum needs of most people are already met, a key driver of policy is how people think: that is, the basic paradigms that drive behavior at all levels. Tetsunari Iida suggested that in the energy field, the basic shift is transforming renewable energy from a fractional wedge on the "carbon flatland" to 100 percent (when combined with stringent end use efficiency) of the energy supply in a "renewable revolution."[82]

---

80   Takayuki, M., "Urban Security," in *Interconnections of Global Problems in East Asia, Green Economy, Urban Security And Energy Security* (Seoul: Nautilus Institute, 2010).
81   Takase, K., "Energy Security in Japan," in *Interconnections of Global Problems in East Asia, Green Economy, Urban Security And Energy Security* (Seoul: Nautilus Institute, 2010).
82   Iida, T., "Changing Climate Change & Energy Policy and Politics in Japan," in *Interconnections of Global Problems in East Asia, Green Economy, Urban Security And Energy Security* (Seoul: Nautilus Institute, 2010).

In his proposed "breakthrough" strategy, Iida relied primarily on local initiatives and market response to demand to drive change at the political and policy levels, but remained open not only to networking globally while acting locally, but also to cross-country, long-distance, and high-tech imports of renewable energy. Although the equity issues involved in one such project have yet to be analyzed, he referred to the "Gobitec" concept whereby solar, thermal, and other renewable sources of power generation could be undertaken in Mongolia and exported via long-distance, high-voltage, and direct-current transmission lines that would traverse China and/or Russia *en route* to the DPRK, ROK, and Japan.[83] This vision would stimulate development and local employment, create value where little currently exists in the Gobi desert, and build economic and energy interdependence between the countries of the region.

As with other regional energy networks that would traverse the DPRK (such as electric tie lines connecting the ROK and Russian Far East grids, or natural gas pipelines from Russia to the ROK), the Gobitec concept requires the resolution of the DPRK nuclear issue and the opening of the DPRK to be plausible. As a multi-billion-dollar, high-tech solution-strategy that would likely be championed by states and corporations, this top-down concept is the antithesis of the community-level strategies described by Sanghun Lee such as the bottom-up "green apartment" movement in Gwangju, South Korea, which aims to change community attitudes and consumption patterns in fundamental ways.

Many of the ideological and institutional barriers to implementing the strategies described by Takase and Iida were shattered by the March 2011 tsunami and the ensuing Fukushima catastrophe. The resulting networked strategies to realize post-Fukushima reconstruction and develop greater resilience are described in chapter 3. What is evident in Japan is that in a fully market-driven society, the linkages between climate, energy, and urban insecurity arise more from the devolved actions of very large numbers of individual, household, and corporate players and less from the policies and interventions of state-based agencies (as in South Korea or China). Ideational influences are important in all three countries, but are particularly potent in Japan, and in different ways than in China or South Korea, in part due to the different roles and institutional locations of scholars, mass media, and civil society organizations relative to state agencies and policy formation in each country.

---

83   The Gobitec Initiative led by the Hanns Seidel Foundation is described at: http://www.gobitec.org/

It is evident from the preceding section that it is not simple to determine the linkages between global problems such as energy, climate, or urban insecurity in East Asia, or even to create a common understanding of what constitutes these problems, let alone their linkages. A first step in each country to resolving shared global problems requires that the problem be decomposed into its separate drivers and constituent parts, with a focus on those elements that originate in or affect the East Asian region.

Separately, national researchers need to undertake substantial empirical research into the nature of the problem and solution in each country. Then they can attempt a joint mapping of the "complexity terrain" to see if a common core exists in the divergent views of these constituent elements of the problem and its solutions, and if this common core in turn provides a nexus that bridges the causes or the solutions between these problems across cultures. This distillation is necessary before a realistic appraisal of the potential for concerted action can even begin.

Before we commence this task (to which the bulk of this book is devoted), we must first drill deeper into the concept of complexity to ascertain whether civil society organizations and networks are able to provide unique insight into these linked problems. And, if so, we must ask what they are capable of doing to facilitate collaborative action to address these problems, within and across countries of the region.

Defining Complexity

When we say something is complex, we refer intuitively to the quality of a system's interconnectedness, the relation between parts that makes it so complicated or intricate that it is difficult to comprehend. Although there is no authoritative definition, a "complex system" has acquired a conventional modern meaning in English as one in which:

a.   The interdependent elements of a system interact in a non-linear way (meaning that quantitative and qualitative change can occur very rapidly);

b.   The elements themselves are diverse rather than similar in nature;

c.   The system is self-organizing, and the constituent agents are autonomous and can make decisions on their own behalf rather than being controlled — that is, they have "agency;"

d.   The structures that emerge at different spatial, physical, and temporal scales within the system as a result of interacting, heterogeneous agents are unpredictable, but they are also very sensitive to small changes in the initial conditions, changes that are amplified by the non-linear nature of interaction between constituent elements of the system resulting in chaotic outcomes over time, often called the "butterfly effect;" and

e. The impacts of small changes at one scale of the system may affect another scale rapidly, unpredictably, and structurally — a moment sometimes called a tipping point.[84]

These characteristics contrast with those observed in "simple systems" (see Table 2.3).

Table 2.3: Characteristics of Simple and Complex Systems

Simple Systems	Complex Systems
Few agents	Many agents
Few interactions	Many interactions
Controlled decision-making	Decentralized decision-making
Decomposable	Irreducible
Closed system	Open system
Static	Dynamic
Tend to equilibrium	Dissipative
Few feedback loops	Many feedback loops
Predictable outcomes	Surprising outcomes
Examples	**Examples**
Pendulum	Immune systems
Bicycle	Genes
Engine	Molecules in air
Boyle's Law	Ecosystems
Gravitational system	Markets

Source: N.E. Harrison, "Thinking About the World We Make," in *Complexity in World Politics: Concepts and Methods of a New Paradigm*, ed. by Harrison, N.E. (Albany: State University of New York Press, 2006), p. 3.

In ecological and human systems, such system-level transformations may be irreversible, and a system may become "stably unstable" and oscillate

---

84 See Baranger, M., *Chaos, Complexity, and Entropy. A Physics Talk for Non-Physicists* (Cambridge: New England Complex Systems Institute, 2001).

around a point of equilibrium for a long time due to multiple negative feedbacks that discourage change. Sometimes, an apparently random small event perturbs the system so much, due to multiple positive feedback loops, that it transforms the system itself. Studies of complex systems have been undertaken in many disciplines including climate science, mathematics, ecology, biology, and even in fields as far from the natural sciences as the study of organizational behavior, markets, archaeology, interstate relations, land use management, diplomatic negotiations, and security dynamics.[85]

Today, there are two basic methods for approaching complexity. One method made popular during and after the Cold War is to use models that attempt to simulate the whole system by defining state variables and the algorithms whereby these variables affect each other via defined pathways. A good example of this approach was the famous *Limits to Growth* report of the Club of Rome. These deterministic models often led to policy decisions that generated highly undesirable outcomes and a false sense of understanding and control.[86]

A second approach, which emerged in the 1980s, is to model each agent that exists in a system rather than the system itself. One then uses computer models to allow the agents to interact based on rules of environmental perception, recognition, decision-making, and learning over time.[87] Based on multiple — sometimes thousands — of model runs, recognizable patterns emerge from the interactions of large numbers of agents. These outcomes can provide insight into the determining variables, the sensitivity of outcomes to initial conditions, and the counter-intuitive outcomes that can occur in aggregate outcomes. Agent-based models are attractive in that they highlight how the heterogeneity of the agents affects their interaction with each other and their environment. Moreover, there is no presumption as to the system-level outcomes. These just happen, deriving from the defining characteristics of the agent. Intuitively and appropriately, human behavior is treated as a complex system, especially if it involves some kind of spatial or social diffusion process including large numbers of people.

---

85 See, for example, Cumming, G.S. and Norberg, J., *Complexity Theory for a Sustainable Future*, Complexity in Ecological Systems (New York: Columbia University Press, 2008).

86 See, for example, Bracken, P.J., *The Command and Control of Nuclear Forces* (New Haven: Yale University Press, 1983).

87 Berry, B.J.L., *et al.*, "Adaptive Agents, Intelligence, and Emergent Human Organization: Capturing Complexity through Agent-Based Modeling," *Proceedings of the National Academy of the Sciences*,99(Suppl 3) (2002), doi: http://dx.doi.org/10.1073/pnas.092078899

The concept of complexity can be applied to any system, natural or artificial. As defined above, global problems result from the failure of natural and artificial systems to fulfil human goals. Today, the quantity, universality, and intensity of many human problems make them global and therefore common to all humanity. The increased rate and magnitude with which complex, interrelated global problems confront us demands a correspondingly increased social differentiation and specialization to manage and resolve multiple challenges at the same time. In short, as we will see below, complex problems demand complex solutions, and complex strategies required by complex solutions entail increasingly complex organizations, which often fail in spite of their extra effort.

Complexity in Urban Security and Sustainability

Complexity theory originated partly from efforts to understand ecological systems such as interdependent predator-prey dynamics; species and food webs; the relationship of diversity, especially biodiversity, to ecosystem resilience; and social-ecological interactions and system thresholds in the context of adaptive management.[88] Since the late 1960s, the understanding that humans affect the biosphere has increased dramatically, starting with the first United Nations Conference on the Human Environment in 1972 and leading to scores of multilateral environmental accords, as well as the attempt to preserve, conserve, and restore global environmental assets and services upon which humanity depends for its very existence. Arguably, the rising costs of damages to environmental services, which in turn lead to a non-sustainable economy, have derived from increasingly complex ecological dynamics in the biosphere.[89]

Of these efforts, four "overarching" global environmental agreements have played prominent parts in East Asia sustainability agendas, both diplomatically and domestically. These are the conventions and protocols relating to ozone depletion, climate change, biodiversity, and regional

---

88 See Levin, S., "Ecosystems and the Biosphere as Complex Adaptive Systems," *Ecosystems*, 1(5) (1998), doi: http://dx.doi.org/10.1007/s100219900037; Holling, C.S., "Resilience and Stability of Ecological Systems," *Annual Review of Ecology and Systematics*, 4(1) (1973), doi: http://dx.doi.org/10.1146/annurev.es.04.110173.000245; Walker, B. and Meyeres, J., "Thresholds in Ecological and Social-Ecological Systems: A Developing Database," *Ecology and Society*, 9(3) (2004).

89 Fisk, D.J. and Kerhervé, J., "Complexity as a Cause of Unsustainability," *Ecological Complexity*, 3(4) (2006), doi: http://dx.doi.org/10.1016/j.ecocom.2007.02.007

oceans management. At regional and sub-regional levels, multilateral, government-funded dialogues and bilateral activities on acid rain, yellow sand, marine pollution, persistent organic pollutants, and biodiversity have also occurred.[90] By the first decade of the 21st century, environmental issues had become sufficiently "hot" in the region to be recognized by scholars as security concerns.[91]

These transboundary and global sustainability problems intersect with the emergent pattern of massive urban growth in this region. The developing urban corridor also poses an immense challenge for the preservation of biodiversity. As we shall see, local governments and civil society organizations have begun to tackle the issues arising from this rapidly evolving "sustainability complexity" in East Asia.

BeSeTo: An Emerging Northeast Asian Giga-City?

One of the most important patterns that emerged in the shift from a simple to a complex international system in Northeast Asia is the growth of urban corridors that now stretch across the region. This conurbation is neither planned nor controlled by any city or state. Yet it is the backbone of a tiger that cities and states will have to ride into the future. One obvious question is what new insecurities will arise from its proximity to the coastal zone, given climate change impacts?

Underlying these networked strategies, countervailing organizations and entrenched habits are uncontrolled, incremental expansion of cities and rapid connectivity (Internet and cell phones, fast trains, airplanes, etc.). This combination creates a set of linked, contiguous mega-cities, sometimes called mega-regions: organic entities that are more than the sum of their parts. This urban system includes horizontally-linked hinterlands (often called "rurbanization,"[92] a hybrid rural-urban development also called

---

90 For the early period of these regional dialogues, see Hayes, P. and Zarsky, L., "Environmental Issues and Regimes in Northeast Asia," *International Environmental Affairs*, 6(4) (1994).

91 See Schreurs, M.A. and Hyun, I., *The Environmental Dimension of Asian Security : Conflict and Cooperation over Energy, Resources, and Pollution* (Washington, DC: United States Institute of Peace Press, 2007).

92 This phrase is used partly to refer to reversal of net migration from rural to urban areas; and also widely in India to refer to the combination and infusion of traditional rural

"desakota" in poor countries,[93] referring to *in-situ* urbanization in rural areas driven by access to and demand from the globalized economy, on the one hand, and poverty-driven workforces desperate to generate income without moving to the city on the other — a process previously identified in Indonesia and now well underway in China)[94] and huge vertical, compact multi-function poleis that would serve aging populations in wealthy portions of the mega-region with super-efficient technology for healthcare, mobility, communications, schooling, and entertainment.

The emergence of this connected, contiguous, and interdependent set of mega-cities may accelerate if the DPRK opens up to trade and investment in the next decade, with huge impacts on energy and climate change risks in the region as a whole. Thus, urbanization and its underlying social, economic, and technological linkages reconnect in turn to the security and nuclear weapons issues posed by the conflict between the DPRK and the United States, on the one hand, and by unresolved inter-Korean issues on the other. The latter issues constitute a powerful mix of risks that is potent enough to register as a global risk in its own right in the WEF framework.

The BeSeTo (Beijing-Seoul-Tokyo) urban corridor concept came to international prominence in a 1996 United Nations University study by Sang-Chuel Choe.[95] In 1994, it already included 98 million urban dwellers living in 112 cities, each populated by 200,000 or more people, across 1,500 km. Today, this system has grown substantially. By 2050, it could become the world's first giga-city: an agglomeration inhabited by a billion people and crossing four countries.

---

practices with urban amenities and facilities, in a hybrid and transformational manner in the rural landscape. See Modi, N., "Introduction to Rurban and Rurbanisation," in *Panel Discussion on Rurbanisation* (Ahmedabad, 2011).

93   "The *desakota* phenomenon encompasses more than the term "peri-urban." It refers to closely interlinked rural/urban livelihoods, communication, transport and economic systems. *Desakota* systems occupy, and radiate out from a spectrum of conditions that have purely urban and purely rural as the two extreme ends. In this emerging system, large sections of the population operate a mixed household economy that straddles the urban and the rural, as well as the formal and informal sectors." Moench, M. and Gyawali, D., *Desakota: Reinterpreting the Urban-Rural Continuum* (Ecosystem Services for Poverty Alleviation, 2008).

94   Xie, Y., *et al.*, *Simulating Emergent Urban Form: Desakota in China* (London: Centre for Advanced Spatial Analysis, University College London, 2005).

95   Choe, S.C., "The Evolving Urban System in North-East Asia," in *Emerging World Cities in Pacific Asia*, ed. by Yeung, Y. and Lo, F. (Tokyo: United Nations University Press, 1996).

Although the core concept was already circulating,[96] Choe himself began to promote it as early as 1991.[97] Indeed, in 1995, Beijing, Seoul and Tokyo signed a memorandum of understanding which set the pace for inter-city cooperative relations, including all types of relations at both public and private levels. Hieyeon Keum explains that

> In 1993, the Mayor of Seoul (Lee Won-Chong) proposed that city governments take concrete steps towards inter-city cooperation at a conference in Beijing. The mayors of Beijing (Li Qiyan) and Tokyo (Suzuki) agreed to the proposal. The expression of interest by the three capital cities' mayors in Beijing was followed up in April 1994 by an international conference in Seoul to explore the scope of and approaches to cooperation. In March 1995, the three mayors met in Seoul to sign the "Memorandum on BeSeTo Cooperation." The Memorandum stated a consensus among the three capital city administrations over the necessity of further three-way cooperation as well as a working principle of trust and faith in each other. In addition, the Memorandum pledged to involve the private and non-political sectors (such as cultural, academic, and athletic exchanges) in the cooperative framework as well. More specifically, the Second Memorandum identified four sectors for cooperation and exchange among the three mega-cities: economy, urban management, science and technology, and culture and the environment. The framework envisioned a three phase development trajectory of inter-capital-city cooperation. The first stage (1995-1997) was going to be one of further exchange of ideas and agenda setting. Indeed, a series of discussions on specific cooperation and exchanges were held. The second phase (1998-2000) would involve exchanges of scholars for more discussions; development of new tourist routes; formation of joint ventures; and frequent exchanges among city officials. However, except for several cultural exchanges and administrative meetings, there has not been discussion on specific areas and issues for cooperation and exchanges. The third phase (2000-2005) was going to be a period of consolidation, leading to an institutionalization of the envisioned cooperative scheme. With the help of their respective national governments, the three capital cities were supposed to coordinate the construction of an information highway to remove the obstacles to communication. The highest stage of the BeSeTo cooperative scheme was

---

96   See Seoul Development Institute and Seoul 21st Century Research Center, *Building the BESETO Cooperation System* (Seoul Development Institute and Seoul 21st Century Research Center, 1995); Han, Y.J., *The Necessity and Role of a Cooperative System among the Northeast Asian Mega-Cities; the Future of Northeast Asian Mega-Cities* (Seoul: Seoul Development Institute, 1994); Jung, H.Y., *Seoul-toward a Regional Hub City in the Northeast Asia* (Seoul: Seoul Development Institute, 2005); Choe, S.C., *Status and Role of Seoul for the 21st Century* (Seoul: Seoul Development Institute, 1994).

97   Keum, H., "Globalization and Inter-City Cooperation in Northeast Asia," *East Asia*, 18 (2) (2000), doi: http://dx.doi.org/10.1007/s12140-000-0029-y

going to be the establishment of a permanent organization to coordinate and facilitate the cooperation in the four areas listed in the Memorandum.[98]

However, in the same year, the Seoul-led effort to stimulate collaboration between Beijing, Seoul, and Metro-Tokyo fell afoul of bureaucratic politics, and the new Mayor (elected in 1994) paid more attention to local issues with greater political payoff. Moreover, the private sector was not involved in these early dialogues.[99] Keum blames the lack of coordinated effort by the central and municipal governments to orchestrate the necessary private involvement to realize this vision.[100]

Furthermore, the extent of economic complementarity as opposed to competitiveness between the three mega-cities was unclear. Without a champion, the BeSeTo concept could not overcome other powerful obstacles, namely the deepening power rivalry within the region and nuclear proliferation, especially in North Korea.[101] Keum concludes, "At the present stage, the BeSeTo scheme remains more of a concept than a reality. In view of the political-economic complexities at the national and regional levels, the most practical step to follow is to build a BeSeTo urban information network."[102]

However, the probabilities were always stacked against a scheme based on the collaborative strategies of three capital cities, given their different economic locations in national hierarchies and global networks of trade, finance, and investment. Regional urban corridors do not emerge through top-down planning. Rather, they emerge from the uneven processes of globalization that promote rapid urbanization and de-urbanization, shifts in production location due to relative factor endowment and comparative advantage, and changes in policy environment at the local and city level. Thus, the detailed study of the Shenyang-Yanbian section of the BeSeTo corridor, by Michael Wang and Guoping Lih, found that globalization had fragmented the corridor, causing shifts from Shenyang to Yanbian in competitive conditions, domestic reform of state-owned enterprises, and changing economic conditions in relation to international markets.[103]

---

98 Ibid., pp. 109-10.
99 Ibid., p. 99.
100 Ibid., p. 111.
101 Ibid., p. 112.
102 Ibid., p. 113.
103 Wang, M. and Li, G., "The Shenyang-Dalian Mega-Urban Region in Transition," *International Development Planning Review*, 30(1) (2008), doi: http://liverpool.metapress.com/content/l03530t8627u023t/?genre=article&id=doi%3a10.3828%2fidpr.30.1.1

Overall, the authors concluded that the corridor is now characterized by "increasing divergence in the economic growth of the two urban poles of this corridor and a breakdown in rural-urban integration in the region."[104] Much of the previous rural-industrial development had been driven by contracts by big urban state-owned enterprises entered into with town- or village-level enterprises. As the former shut down, the latter followed suit.

Nonetheless, some areas around Dalian have shot ahead, and the overall result is fragmentation of the corridor in some areas and rapid integration in others. A similar story can be told with respect to the Nampo-Pyongyang, Incheon-Seoul, and other major urban corridors that collectively constitute the network of cities in the BeSeTo space.

According to Chinese analysts, a major problem with the BeSeTo concept is that Liaoning Province and even Beijing itself are in many ways lagging far behind the coastal cities stretching south. In their view, a giga-city is far more likely to emerge in the area from Beijing to the Tianjin-Binhai zone, from Shanghai to Hong Kong and beyond, than merely from Beijing to Tokyo.[105]

Interestingly, Professor Choe still suggests that the BeSeTo concept may be emerging as quickly as other regional corridors.[106] However, until the DPRK stops impeding the regional completion of dynamic networks currently blocked by its rejection of an open economy — which include road and rail transportation, telecom, pipelines, power grids, and, above all, labor mobility — the full potential vigor and likelihood that a completely interconnected BeSeTo corridor in China will emerge cannot be determined. Meanwhile, it will continue to evolve in stop-start, disconnected, and disjointed ways — exactly how most mega-urban corridors develop.

Moreover, the concept is still in motion at the policy level. In 2006, for example, three research institutes conducted a joint three-year review of the BeSeTo concept. It was led by Japan's National Institute for Research Advancement (NIRA) — the Korean and Chinese partners were the Korean Research Institute for Human Settlements and the National Development

---

104 Ibid.

105 Chen, X. and Liu, C., "The Reluctant Powerful Participant: China on, in, and out of the Pan-Yellow Sea Rim," in *2010 Presidential Committee on Regional Development International Conference* (Jeju, 2010).

106 Choe, S.C., "Incheon City-Region in Korea: Gateway to Northeast Asia — Aspiring to Be an Innovative and Learning Region," in *2nd International Conference on the Process of Innovation and Learning in Dynamic City-Region* (Bangalore: United Nations Industrial Development Organization, 2005).

and Reform Commission/ISPRE — as part of a NIRA project on "Research on a Grand Design for Northeast Asia." The project undertook:

> In concrete terms, (1) detailed examination of the construction of networks of individual transportation modes, such as conceptualization of a high-speed rail system for Northeast Asia in the near future, an expressway network including the Asia Highway, and a daily roundtrip air shuttle system linking the three cities and related major cities; (2) examination of the concept of inter-modal networks; and (3) sketching an overview of the construction of an intergovernmental platform for economic relations in Northeast Asia.[107]

In March 2007, this group published the joint *Proposal for Promotion of the Realization of the BeSeTo Corridor Vision — Toward sustained development in the Northeast Asia Region*.[108] Although they recognized the numerous impediments to the realization of this vision, including problems of energy, transport, logistics, and urban infrastructure, they argued that

> The BeSeTo corridor is a linear representation of urban agglomerations in C-J-K [sic]. It contains major centers of talents and innovation, financial and industrial capital, and manufacturing and advanced services. The corridor, if equipped with less institutional barriers and a smoothly functioning transport system, would certainly contribute to building a more or less homogenized economic space wherein agglomeration benefits can be spread to enterprises and people.[109]

"Three things," they suggested, "are essential for building the BeSeTo corridor. They are transport corridors, information highways, and inter-city networks. Without doubt, these three elements are complementary to each other and thus constitute building blocks of the BeSeTo corridor."[110] Specifically, they argued that collaborative steps can be taken to circumvent the DPRK obstacle by implementing inter-modal roll-on, roll-off train and road freight systems that load onto and off ferries between Incheon and Yantai, alongside an improved Busan-Fukuoka train-ferry system.[111] Achieving this efficiency would entail standardizing rail gauges and freight sizes, adopting a common headless-chassis for containers, and

---

107 Gangzhe, L., *Research Trends: Research on a Grand Design for Northeast Asia* (Tokyo: National Institute for Research Advancement, 2006).

108 China Institute of Spatial Planning & Regional Economy, *et al.*, *Proposal for Promotion of the Realization of the BESETO Corridor Vision-- toward Sustained Development in the Northeast Asia Region* (Tokyo: National Institute for Research Advancement, 2007).

109 Ibid., p. 24.

110 Ibid.

111 Ibid., p. 28.

harmonizing customs clearance procedures.[112] The group also suggested creating a "Northeast Asia Sky Corridor," an inter-city shuttle service that would also entail issuing a fast-visa for passengers using this service.[113]

Finally, they promoted a variety of inter-city networking and mutual learning activities. These would involve not only the three capital cities, but would expand the sub-regional inter-city networks on the rims of the Yellow Sea and the East Sea/Sea of Japan, such as the Organization for the Northeast Asia Economic Development, the Association of Northeast Asia Regional Governments, and the Conference of Major Cities in the East Sea/Sea of Japan Rim Region.[114] Along these lines, they also called for "active and positive participation" by the citizen sector. "The traditional exchange mode, which is regional government-centered with supports by local business groups and academics such as local universities and think-tanks, should be improved to the mode with participation of a broader civic sector. Getting this participation of the civic sector will widen and enhance the foundation of inter-city network."[115] Perhaps the most important single recommendation is the establishment of a virtual "BeSeTo Knowledge Corridor" whereby collaborative scholarly and policy research could be undertaken on both this concept and related issues by Chinese, Korean, and Japanese researchers.[116] This would ultimately lead to a virtual transnational civil society, especially in areas of environmental and tourism cooperation.[117]

Sceptics may see this study as yet another example of Japanese "big think," a product of a construction state in an endless search for taxpayer funds to finance massive public infrastructure markets. Indeed, behind the study lay NIRA's previous work on a "Big Loop" vision that called for a circular high-speed railway to connect major cities in Northeast Asia plus a high-speed railway system to connect the "Big Loop" to the Shinkansen bullet train networks. Also in the background was NIRA's "New Cross" vision to connect the existing main north-south transport artery in Northeast Asia with the emerging inner Mongolia-Northeast Asia, east-west traffic route, linked by sea and air to Japan.[118]

---

112 Ibid., p. 29.
113 Ibid., p. 30.
114 Ibid., p. 35.
115 Ibid., p. 36.
116 Ibid., p. 37.
117 Ibid., p. 38.
118 Mori, N., "A Grand Design for Northeast Asia," in *15th Northeast Asia Economic Forum* (Khabarovsk, 2006).

Nonetheless, nearly two decades of conceptual work, extensive inter-city investigation, the uneven but inexorable process of massive urbanization and sprawl, *in-situ* rural industrialization and urbanization, integration of transportation systems, and above all, increasing movement of people within the region, suggest that, in one form or another, a BeSeTo corridor will emerge over the next fifty years. Indeed, some analysts have already added Shanghai to "BeSeTo" to make "BESHTOSHA": the emerging mega-corridor along the east Chinese coast to the BeSeTo corridor.[119] Whatever its final form — and remote sensing data already offers evidence of the emergence of this corridor[120] — when the world's first giga-city emerges, it will present entirely new challenges of urban insecurity that, in turn, will require new forms of networked and trans-border urban governance.

Complexity and Port City Climate Adaptation

According to the United Nations Economic and Social Commission in Asia and the Pacific, the heads of ports from China, Japan, and South Korea have discussed the creation of a North-East Asian Transport Corridor. It would link East Asian ports with Europe by sea and land transport and enable the Northeast Asian countries to expand their international trade, especially Northeastern China. Major ports of call on the China-Japan route include Shanghai, Tianjin Qingdao, and Dalian in China and Tokyo, Yokohama, Nagoya, Osaka, Kobe, Moji, and Hakata in Japan. In part, these ports hope to avoid over-investment in facilities given the emerging level of need and competition for business while gaining from expanded regional flows of passengers and cargo that would be facilitated by trans-border technical standards on power supplies, rail gauges, and road safety.[121]

Almost by definition, port cities are greatly at risk from climate change, particularly from rising sea levels, increasingly frequent and intense storms and related storm surges, and degradation of physical infrastructure, such as accelerated carbonation and chloride induced corrosion of concrete and

119 Lee, S.J. and Kim, W.B., "Recent Trends of Cross-Border Cooperation and Spatial Strategies of the Northeast Asian Countries," in *Presidential Committee on Regional Development, 2010 International Conference* (Seoul, 2010).
120 Schneider, A., *et al.*, "A New Map of Global Urban Extent from MODIS Satellite Data," *Environmenal Research Letters*, 4(2009), doi:http://dx.doi.org/10.1088/1748-9326/4/4/044003
121 United Nations Economic and Social Commission for Asia and the Pacific, "Subregional Cooperation for Shipping and Port Development in North-East Asia," in *Development of Shipping and Ports in North-East Asia* (New York: United Nations, 2005).

steel, due to increased atmospheric and oceanic carbon dioxide levels.[122] These impacts will affect the operations of the already highly competitive port cities of East Asia, many of which have integrated into global shipping logistical and supply chains.[123]

As a result, smart port cities are already addressing these direct impacts on the physical infrastructure of their port facilities, as well as focusing on reducing the carbon footprint of existing operations (largely arising from container traffic and docking facilities for ships) and substituting low or zero emission vehicles and equipment for the existing greenhouse-gas-emitting stock.[124] Los Angeles is one leader in this respect, but there are many others, including some East Asian ports, that participate in the C40 network of cities cooperating to respond to climate change.[125]

Port cities contain vulnerable populations, especially those who live on the waterfront and who may gain little from the logistical operations by major production entities in the cities' manufacturing, mining, or agricultural hinterland. Worse, they may be displaced by port city expansion or heavily polluted by co-located industrial plants, especially petrochemical and energy generation facilities. Fishing communities also find their traditional homeport often dominated by major interests. Their coastal fishing operations may be further disrupted by a combination of runoff from watershed abuse and mismanagement, overfishing by industrial enterprises, and changes in fishing populations due to climate impacts on ocean temperature and circulation patterns.

In addition to these direct threats that undermine the physical and social resilience of port cities in the face of climate change, such cities are also subject to major geographic shifts of global competitive advantage in the production of globally traded and shipped fossil fuels, minerals, food, tourist cruise ships, and other bulk and high value goods that prove to be

---

122 Nicholls, R.J., *et al.*, *Ranking Port Cities with High Exposure and Vulnerability to Climate Extremes*, OECD Environment Directorate Working Paper (Organization for Economic Co-operation and Development).

123 Jacobs, W., *et al.*, "Integrating World Cities into Production Networks: The Case of Port Cities," *Global Networks*, 10(1) (2010), doi: http://dx.doi.org/10.1111/j.1471-0374.2010.00276.x. and Ducruet, C. and Notteboom, T., "The Worldwide Maritime Network of Container Shipping: Spatial Structure and Regional Dynamics," *Global Networks*, 12(3) (2012), doi: http://dx.doi.org/10.1111/j.1471-0374.2011.00355.x

124 Aerts, J., *et al.*, *Connecting Delta Cities, Coastal Cities, Flood Risk Management and Adaptation to Climate Change* (Amsterdam: VU University Press, 2009).

125 C40 Large Cities Climate Leadership Group, "The World Ports Climate Declaration and Endorsement Ceremony: Declaration," in *C40 World Ports Climate Conference* (Rotterdam: C40 World Ports, 2008).

climate-sensitive. These factors in turn have multiple non-climate change drivers that are global, sectorial, and local. As Darryn McEvoy and Jane Mullett explain with reference to Australian port cities: "Volatility in markets, for example, increasing climate change impacts on agriculture both domestically and internationally, will also need to be factored into forward planning. Port planning needs to integrate land use, freight transport and environmental issues with consideration of multi-level governance perspectives at port, local, state and national levels."[126]

Thus, climate change amplifies the existing non-climate drivers of port city economic competitiveness or decline, and thereby superimposes new risks on top of the direct threats noted above. Some agile port cities will gain from this climate-driven shift in global production and trading patterns by adopting new, climate-friendly industries; they might become import-export centers for biofuels, as well as renewable energy generation from on-site or offshore, or possibly export hubs for captured carbon. Others, wedded to carbon-intensive processing, mechanical manufacturing, and logistical systems for bulky, carbon-intensive products such as fossil fuels, may lose market share whatever their locational advantage.[127]

Some major ports and their affiliated global shipping networks have already identified this shift, one driven by indirect climate change and which may affect port cities much earlier than, for instance, slowly rising sea levels.[128] Thus, Rotterdam and affiliated global ports have created the global Rotterdam New World Alliance, redefining their primary role from industrial-era to climate-era port cities and creating integrated systems on common standards. The New World Alliance includes APL (Singapore), Mitsui OSK Lines (Japan), and Hyundai (South Korea). At a regional level, the European Union is developing new standards to promote climate-resilient best practices via ESPO, the European Sea Ports Organization. A first step is to compile a global index of clean shipping operations for carbon dioxide, nitrous oxide, and sulfur compounds emitted by ships on the ocean and in port.[129] A coalition of European port cities led by Antwerp,

---

126 McEvoy, D. and Mullett, J., *Enhancing the Resilience of Seaports to a Changing Climate: Research Synthesis and Implications for Policy and Practice* (Gold Coast: National Climate Change Adaptation Research Facility and RMIT University, 2013).

127 Stenek, V., *et al.*, *Climate Risk and Business: Ports* (Washington, DC: International Finance Corporation, 2011).

128 Rynikiewicz, C., "European Port Cities as Gateways to a Green Economy?," *Network Industries Quarterly*, 13(4) (2011).

129 *Environmental Ship Index ESI* (World Ports Climate Initiative), http://esi.wpci.nl/Public/Home.

Rotterdam, Le Havre, Bremen, and Hamburg has undertaken to create such an index.

With an eye on the horizon for the coming storm of climate change-generated shifts in energy use, cities such as Antwerp have begun to implement strategies for becoming distribution hubs for already globally-traded biofuels such as ethanol, biomass pellets, palm oil, and agricultural residues. As algal biofuels become economically viable and major producers of this new liquid fuel use existing refined oil product storage and distribution systems, port cities may turn into "energy ports." Ports may also be well-situated for the direct transport of captured carbon for injection under the seabed or to other industrial and sequestration sites — a scheme that is already in pilot stage at Rotterdam and foreshadows its future as a "carbon hub."[130]

In East Asia, this dynamic is already in play via the global shipping networks and the alliances of port city authorities and corporate terminal operators. The direct and indirect impacts of climate change on East Asian port cities such as Dalian, Nampo, Inchon, and Niigata will shape urban mega-regions along the East and Northeast Asian coastlines, with the threats and opportunities challenging each port city. Because the climate system is all-pervasive, climate change will affect every aspect of human life in the region. The adaptive responses will differ, and no-one can predict the bottom-up, networked patterns of adaptation that will make some cities resilient and leave others more vulnerable to climate-induced decline.

Fortunately, many of the measures that cities should take to withstand the accumulating impacts of climate change are similar to those needed to anticipate other catastrophic events such as tsunamis, pandemics, earthquakes, and even wars and terrorist attacks. In this regard, not only the central state (including the military) and major corporate sectors (especially the financial, insurance, and legal industries) need to prepare for climate change.[131] Local governments, city agencies, and communities represented by civil society organizations also need to act autonomously and with strategies tailored to local circumstances, not least because many

---

130 Rotterdam Climate Initiative, *Port of Rotterdam CO2 Hub: Crucial Stepping Stone Towards Sustainable Economic Growth* (Rotterdam Climate Initiative, 2012).

131 Prasad, N., *et al.*, *Climate Resilient Cities: A Primer on Reducing Vulnerabilities to Disasters,* (Washington, DC: The World Bank, 2009).

of the large, centralized institutions are likely to either implement old, brittle strategies or deliver too little change, too late, and at the wrong location.[132]

In this regard, complex networks, especially "live networks" using smart sensors and the latest social media communication devices, may enable first responders and communities to react in instantaneous swarms to catastrophic events far more efficiently than lumbering, slow, centralized agencies. In "cognitive cities," citizens equipped with smart phones become the mobile, omnipresent sensor agent for smart systems integrated across sectors.[133] As Ali Mostashari *et al.* explain, citizens "become active data generators but also active consumers of urban information." The result will be far greater accountability and efficiency in urban governance: "The transparency that a cognitive city provides will put the burden of performance on the shoulders of urban service providers, but it will also result in more efficient and effective resource allocation decisions. This is a fundamental cultural shift — thereby making urban governance far more transparent."[134]

The need to retreat in the face of climate-driven disasters, to adjust course mid-way in the midst of crisis response, and to generate a distributed, autonomous response puts the onus on networked civil society organizations and local governments to prepare for the worst while embracing climate change as the key to building multipurpose resilience in port cities.

Networked Inter-City Cooperation

Whatever its ultimate form, the sheer scale and complexity of the emerging giga-city in East Asia poses unprecedented challenges for regional security and sustainability. It will create new types of energy- and climate-related insecurity for urban areas along its corridor(s). It will require a new, cross-border form of urban governance that far surpasses the challenges of precursor "border cities" in this region.[135] Here, we address how networks

---

132 Matthias, R. and Coelho, D., "Understanding and Managing the Complexity of Urban Systems under Climate Change," *Climate Policy*, 7(4) (2007), doi: http://dx.doi.org/10.10 80/14693062.2007.9685659

133 Mostashari, A., *et al.*, "Cognitive Cities and Intelligent Urban Governance," *Network Industries Quarterly*, 13(3) (2009).

134 Ibid.

135 See studies of Russian-China border towns in Billé, F., *et al.*, *Frontier Encounters: Knowledge and Practice at the Russian, Chinese and Mongolian Border* (Cambridge: Open Book Publishers, 2012).

of cities propagate best practice in the emerging giga-city. We also explore how civil society organizations accelerate the process of inter-urban and cross-border learning and innovation on an issue-by-issue approach — and how states may facilitate (or block) this process.

How these networked processes will be affected by the emergent patterns and logic of the emerging "giga-ntic" urban corridor is as yet unexamined.[136] That the corridor will superimpose its own properties, dynamics, and cellular structure on the component mega-cities, as well as on inter-urban cooperation and transnational civil society networks, is certain.

Kiho Yi suggests that inter-city networks in Northeast Asia already contribute to a nascent transnational "solution-strategy spiral." These inter-urban networks, often connecting secondary and coastal cities, include the Niigata-Vladivostok-Wonsan triangle, the Kita-Kyushu-Pusan-Jeju triangle, and a Seoul-Dalian-Shanghai triangle. To these we might also add the Busan-Fukuoka bilateral network.[137]

Yasuo Takao provides a set of documented case studies examining transnational inter-city networked cooperation on a range of economic, infrastructure, cultural exchange, human rights, and environmental projects between Japanese cities and their counterparts in China and the Russian Far East.[138] For example, the cities of Dalian (China) and Kitakyushu (Japan) cooperated closely through 1996-2010 on the creation of a Dalian Environmental Model Zone, transferring the requisite pollution control technology and management practices.[139] Takao explains:

> The greatest potential for information dissemination lies in local government's expertise transfer to overseas counterparts. The Dalian-Kitakyushu "friendly" relationship that had been officially established in 1979 built up a high level of information exchange between the two cities.

---

136 See Douglass, M., "Toward Participatory Governance of Transborder Intercity Regions in Asia," in *Interventions in the Political Geography of Asia's Transborder Urban Networks: Working Paper Series 193*, ed. by Miller, M. A. and Bunnell, T. (Singapore: Asia Research Institute, National University of Singapore, 2012).

137 Park, S.H., "Post-Cold War Trans-Border Networks in Northeast Asia: The Busan-Fukuoka Network," in *Interventions in the Political Geography of Asia's Transborder Urban Networks: Working Paper Series 193*, ed. by Miller, M. A. and Bunnell, T. (Singapore: Asia Research Institute, National University of Singapore, 2012).

138 Takao, Y., "Transnational Coalitions in Northeast Asia: Search for a New Pathway of Japanese Local Government," *Ritsumeikan Annual Review of International Studies*, 2 (2003).

139 Ibid., p. 82.

In the field of environmental issues, as early as 1981, Kitakyushu began to transfer the know-how of local planning and management to Dalian. From 1996 to 2000, Kitakyushu City in collaboration with the KITA conducted energy efficiency improvement projects. In 1998 environmental experts, engineers and city officials presented to Dalian through the KITA a set of 18 preventive environmental proposals including pickling/heat treatment process improvement in steel works, production conversion of sulfuric acid in a chemical plant, and nitration process improvement of chlorobenzene in a dye factory. In the same year, the KITA co-organized with the UN Centre for Regional Development a training seminar in Dalian to inform outcomes of the Model Zone project.[140]

The cooperation was not merely formal or contractor-based, but involved extensive participation by local business and grassroots groups, as well as increased public awareness in both cities.[141] At both ends, local government officials were able to compel their national governments to support the project, putting political pressure on the Japanese aid agency to provide the requisite resources, eventually amounting to over $300 million of investment in the Model Zone.[142] Importantly, city officials from Kitakyushu were able to deal directly with Chinese central government officials without having to pass via Tokyo. This transnational network enabled the project to proceed quickly and with state blessing, but unencumbered by the normal bureaucracy. As Takao concludes, "In so doing, they [the city level leaders] brought together otherwise unconnected domestic actors in a manner that produced a transnational interest that had not existed before."[143]

Takao shows how the Niigata Prefecture played a similar role in establishing and hosting a regional acid rain training center in the city of Niigata:

In 1998 the Acid Deposition and Oxidant Research Center (ADORC) was established in Niigata. The ADORC started its activity as a branch of the nonprofit organization Japan Environmental Sanitation Center, which was located in Kawasaki. Since 1993, expert meetings on air pollution and acid deposition have been held by several East Asian countries, and in 1998 Niigata was designated as the interim network center for dissemination of monitoring data and other information to the participants.[144]

---

140 Ibid., p. 85.
141 Ibid., p. 87.
142 Ibid., pp. 98-99.
143 Ibid., p. 104.
144 Ibid., p. 84.

Having delved into the complex connections linking energy and urban insecurity and deriving from the bottom-up nature of urbanization in East Asia, we now turn to the relationship between complexity and geopolitical security issues in the region. In the course of doing so, we will discuss networked solution strategies that have been implemented by civil society networks to increase security and sustainability in East Asia.

Complexity and Security

Orthodox, *realpolitik* accounts of international security assume the unitary nature of the key actors (states), the nature of the game that they play (balance of power), the anarchic nature of the international system, and the key determinant of outcomes in the competition for power and influence (military capacity). In the Cold War period, a relatively simple bipolar model of the international system dominated, at least in the West: the nuclear balance-of-terror stabilized the system through fear of mutual annihilation by the American and Soviet blocs.

In reality, these are theories that overlap considerably. From a theoretical perspective, the concept of security propagated by all of them suggests that the state system is closed, determinate, and rests ultimately on the attempt to exert top-down control over unruly social and political phenomena. Fear is the fundamental basis of security in this realist world, dominated by the means of coercion and destruction, and the main way to understand the relative power of states or the structure of the region is to examine both these means and the elite's perceptions of threats.[145] The primary goal of the national security state is to maintain order. At the international level, the goal of great powers in a nuclear-armed world is to preserve the status quo, often termed "stability." Thus, one of the main security challenges in the region, the North Korean nuclear weapons program, is viewed as a threat to the existing balance of power. It threatens not only to rupture the regional order, a "punctuated equilibrium" in what was previously viewed to be a homeostatic system, but to herald the dawn of a new global nuclear era in which nuclear-armed rogue states and non-state actors disturb strategic stability.[146]

---

145 See, for example, Hassig, K.O., *Northeast Asian Strategic Security Environment Study* (Alexandria: Institute for Defense Analyses, 2001).
146 Wilson, P., "Does 'Strategic Stability' Have a Future in Northeast Asia?" in *Strategic Stability in a Turbulent World: SAIC Report of 5th Nuclear Stability Roundtable to Defense*

The constraints on independent behavior within this rigid, bipolar system became less effective with the reconstruction and rise of Japan and Europe. Consequently, new and less mechanistic theories emerged that reflected the shift in the underlying political-economy of American global hegemony. *Liberal institutionalism* proposed that states are able to cooperate even in a system without an overarching authority by concentrating on the norms, rules, and organizations that regulate and manage international affairs.[147] A variant, *Gramscian hegemonic theory*, suggests that less powerful states not only defer to great powers, but also consent to their subordination; they should therefore share the ideology of common political, economic, and security interests that legitimates the leadership of an external great power. And finally, *state formation theory* argues that nuclear weapons are one of the ways in which state elites not only project threat against external adversaries, but also employ it to reinforce domestic control.[148]

Since the mid-nineties, a "complexity paradigm" has begun to challenge these traditional theories of the international system. In this view, there is no world or regional system of states, but only the macro-outcome aggregate results of the systematic interaction of large numbers of constituent agencies within and between states. The results of this interaction at any point in time are highly unpredictable. A further consequence of this view is that there is no homeostatic "balance-of-power" between states; rather, the power flux is always dynamic and never the same.[149] As James Rosenau explains:

> Even the most complex system can maintain long equilibrium before undergoing new adaptive transformations, or what complexity theorists call "phase transitions." Put differently, their progression through time can pass through periods of stasis or extremely slow, infinitesimal changes before lurching into a phase transition, thereby tracing a temporal path referred to as "punctuated equilibrium."[150]

Threat Reduction Agency Advanced Systems Concepts Office (McLean: Science Applications International Corporation Strategies Group, 2003).

147   Mann, S.R., "Chaos Theory and Strategic Thought," *Parameters* (1992).

148   Tanter, R. and Hayes, P., "Beyond the Nuclear Umbrella: Re-Thinking the Theory and Practice of Nuclear Extended Deterrence in East Asia and the Pacific," *Pacific Focus*, 26 (1) (2011), doi: http://dx.doi.org/10.1111/j.1976-5118.2011.01053.x

149   Harrison, N.E., "Thinking About the World We Make," in *Complexity in World Politics : Concepts and Methods of a New Paradigm*, ed. by Harrison, N. E. (Albany: State University of New York Press, 2006).

150   Rosenau, J.N., "Many Damn Things Simultaneously: Complexity Theory and World Affairs," in *Complexity, Global Politics, and National Security*, ed. by Alberts, D. S. and Czerwinski, T. J. (Honolulu: University Press of the Pacific, 2002).

As a defining case in point for our purposes, the rigid boundaries and spheres of American and Soviet Cold War influence fractured, splintered, and flew apart in 1991, and then re-aggregated in ways that were inconceivable a mere decade before. In the two decades since 1990, new states were founded at the net rate of 1.6 per year,[151] and international non-governmental organizations and transnationally active corporations were created at an astonishing rate. Today, there are some 27,000 internationally active non-governmental organizations,[152] 63,000+ multinational corporations,[153] and about 3,000 cities with over 100,000 people, plus another ~19,000 human settlements with populations between 5,000 and 100,000. Overall, therefore, there are roughly 110,000 leaders with global reach. (Good data are hard to come by, but according to C. van Marrewijk *et al.*, there were about 2,957 cities with 100,000 or more people on Earth in the early 1990s.[154] J. Vernon Henderson and H.G. Wang estimate that there were 2,684 cities with populations of at least 100,000 or more people in 2000.[155] Yet another accounting states that there are currently about 21,905 urban areas each populated by more than 5,000 people, of which about 18,948 contain between 5,000 and 100,000 people).[156]

The leadership of many of these non-state entities conduct their own international activities across state borders. Clearly, a theory that concentrates on the dynamics of only 190 interacting states does not capture the full complexity of the international system today. One of the tenets of complexity theory is that as the number of agents and the degree of their freedom in a system increase, so the outcomes become increasingly difficult to predict. This happens because the agents in a complex system have agency — they must make decisions based on available information,

---

151 Net because some states flew apart (Yugoslavia into five states) and others unified (Germany, Yemen).

152 For INGOs, see Union of International Associations, *Yearbook of International Organizations 2012-2013: Geographical Index: A Country Directory of Secretariats and Memberships* (Boston: Brill, 2012).

153 For multinational corporations, see Gabel, M. and Bruner, H., *Global Inc: An Atlas of the Multinational Corporation* (New York: New York Press, 2003).

154 C. van Marrewijk, *et al., International Economics* (Oxford: Oxford University Press, 2006) (data tables at: http://www2.econ.uu.nl/users/marrewijk/international/zipf.htm).

155 Henderson, J.V. and Wang, H.G., "Urbanization and City Growth: The Role of Institutions," *Regional Science and Urban Economics*, 37(3) (2007), doi: http://dx.doi.org/10.1016/j.regsciurbeco.2006.11.008

156 *Data Sets, Global Rural-Urban Mapping Project* (New York: SocioEconomic and Applications Data Center, Colombia University), http://sedac.ciesin.columbia.edu/data/collection/grump-v1/sets/browse

and these decisions are undetermined in advance because of the stochastic way that different types of agents interact over time.

Thus, in the post-Cold War period, when rigid division between two essentially closed, relatively simple systems of states collapsed into an open flux across borders, new and powerful players entered the field of cross-border relations within the East Asian region. Indeed, some agents — corporations, unions, civil society organizations such as development agencies or religious movements, diasporas, and sometimes even individuals — may cross over and act simultaneously in more than one open, complex system at a time (a state, a market, and a church, for example). Some may cross state borders and operate simultaneously in multiple state systems or in international commons under the jurisdiction of no state (like pirates on the ocean). Others may be transnational actors working at the same time at different levels and locations through networks and influential webs such as the virtual diasporas supporting irredentist movements,[157] thus creating a kind of quantum politics. Neil Harrison calls such actors "meta-agents"[158] because they are both agents at a lower, domestic scale of the larger international complex system and acted upon at the same time by other states in the international system, itself a dynamic complex system that is not controlled centrally and constitutes an open-ended, evolving structure.[159]

By this perspective, a state — a very large emergent system in its own right — adapts to other states, or constantly *co-evolves* with them to regenerate the international system of states. In this view, global or regional level interstate relations are not stable *per se* — an attribute that is often referred to as a positive value, the maintenance of which, by virtue of lending predictability to the outcomes of inter-state transactions, should guide the exercise of great power. Rather, the relationships between states are continuously reinvented and the "balance" between contending forces is always dynamic, a "fleeting embodiment" of the underlying deep organization of the domestic and international systems, never returning to the same equilibrium point.[160]

---

157 *The Internet and International Systems: Information Technology and American Foreign Policy Decision-Making Workshop* (Berkeley: Nautilus Institute, 1999), http://oldsite.nautilus.org/gps/info-policy/workshop/papers/
158 Harrison, N.E. (2006), p. 8.
159 Ibid., p. 27.
160 Ibid.

Complex Adaptive Systems and Networked Governance

The agents that constitute a complex state system — that is, individuals, civil society organizations, state bureaucracies, etc. — are all purposeful and able to learn and adjust their behavior in response to other agents and environmental factors. They may be able to change their behavior very quickly to adapt to external stress, and thereby lend resilience to the whole system — at least for a while. In doing so, they will often innovate and create new types of social agents, or differentiate those that exist to specialize in particular types of adjustment — as occurred, for example, when nuclear weapons were deployed, forcing whole new types of military organization and thinking to affect the traditional posture of military forces. Each of these kinds of innovation represents an increase in social complexity, or as Joseph Trainter puts it:

> [Complexity] is a fundamental problem-solving tool. In its early phases, complexity can generate positive feedback and increasing returns. Confronted with challenges, we often respond by strategies such as developing more complex technologies, adding more elements to an institution (specialists, bureaucratic levels, controls, etc.), increasing organization or regulation of transactions, or gathering and processing more information. Each such action represents increasing complexity. Their effectiveness comes in part because changes in these dimensions can be enacted rapidly. While humans may be complexity-averse when we personally bear the cost, our problem-solving institutions can be powerful complexity generators. All that is needed for growth of complexity is a problem that requires it. Since problems always arise, complexity seems to grow inexorably. Since complexity is an adaptive problem-solving strategy that has costs, it can be viewed as an economic function. Societies invest in complexity.[161]

Unsurprisingly, complexity theory has been applied not only to the international system as a whole, as outlined above, but also to the realm of military security in the aftermath of the Cold War. Just as realist theories of the international system were mechanical in nature, so theories of war and military strategy in the industrial era were "Newtonian": that is, they posited that war was linear in nature, that its effects could be observed and predicted, and that military organization and warfighting itself were

---

161 Tainter, J.A., "Problem Solving: Complexity, History, Sustainability," *Population and Environment*, 22(1) (2000), doi: http://dx.doi.org/10.1023/A:1006632214612

subject to effective centralized command and control from above. Today, war is viewed dynamically. As John Schmitt states:

> War is fundamentally a far-from equilibrium, open, distributed, nonlinear dynamical system highly sensitive to initial conditions and characterized by entropy production/dissipation and complex, continuous feedback. Rather than thinking of war as a structure at equilibrium, we should think of it as a standing wave pattern of continuously fluxing matter, energy, and information.[162]

Like other social domains, Northeast Asia's militaries have faced a general shift from simple to complex environments, from simple to complex warfare. Instead of defined battlegrounds with distinct frontiers and dedicated forces, the military in each country faces diverse types of adversaries. (The exception is the Korean Demilitarized Zone, frozen in the 1950s on the northern side). Many possible adversaries for each military operate without central direction. They do not present fixed targets. Yaneer Bar-Yam argues that the military is particularly susceptible to the general law that an organization's repertoire of possible actions must be at least as complex as the challenge confronting it. As Bar-Yam argues, "In a high complexity environment, high complexity forces are more capable than low complexity ones. Thus, an effective analysis of warfighting capability must include both scale and complexity of the forces and the environment where the conflict occurs."[163]

The scale at which the military applies force becomes a critical issue because its practices must match the level of complexity of the countervailing military. "A force that is organized, trained and otherwise prepared to apply large scale force," he writes, "is not well suited to high complexity conflicts."

> Similarly, a force that is designed for high complexity conflicts is not well suited to large scale conflicts. More generally, the complexity of a force's capabilities at each scale of a possible encounter is a key property that describes the abilities of that force. This, then, is the central basis for

---

162 Schmitt, J.F., "Command and (out of) Control: The Military Implications of Complexity Theory," in *Complexity, Global Politics, and National Security*, ed. by Alberts, D. S. and Czerwinski, T. J. (Honolulu: University Press of the Pacific, 2002); Rosenau, J.N. (2002), p. 37.

163 Bar-Yam, Y., *Complexity of Military Conflict: Multiscale Complex Systems Analysis of Littoral Warfare* (Cambridge: New England Complex Systems Institute, 2003).

evaluating the effectiveness of force design in the face of a specific complex military mission or conflict.[164]

As Trainter noted above, the argument that the complexity of organizations and problems must match to find solutions is a general proposition about the relationship between problem-solving organizations and the issues they tackle. As the number of complex global problems increases, so the level of social complexity must increase to solve these problems. This imperative creates a need for new forms of organization to fill the "complexity deficit," as we shall see below.

Perhaps the most intractable and profound security problem in the region is the divided Korean Peninsula. The North Korean nuclear threat is the only geopolitical global risk originating in East Asia that can be found among the WEF's top fifty global risks — in which the criterion is that a risk could impose a cost of more than $10 billion dollars. Therefore, we will examine the evolution of the Korean Peninsula from a simple to complex security environment.

Korea's Complex Regional Security Environment

The security environment of a small nation like Korea is especially complex, due in part to its division into North and South Korea, but also to the nature of great power relations. Five decades after the end of the Korean War, and two decades after the end of the Cold War, Korea remains trapped in a set of mutually reinforcing security dilemmas. These are partly driven by geopolitical circumstances in which great powers continue to exercise influence over the two Koreas. These external powers aim to realize their own interests in Korea by exercising diplomatic and military power in response to the DPRK's nuclear breakout, on the one hand, and by attempting to pursue their divergent interests with respect to the future of the Peninsula regarding territorial disputes, resource management, military deployments, and crisis management, etc., on the other.

In this manner, classic geopolitical concerns such as the nuclear non-proliferation regime, the maintenance of the reputation of United States as nuclear and global hegemon, Sino-Japanese hostility, Sino-US distrust and the Taiwan Straits issue, and the desire of Russia to participate in regional security and development schemes are all super-imposed on and shape the

---

164 Ibid., p. 4.

fundamental insecurity of Korea. This insecurity includes its division by war and the long standoff between its two halves. These external drivers over-determine inter-Korean relations and make it almost impossible to align the internal and external variables that influence progress or regress in those relations. When domestic Korean political and economic variables are added to the conflict equation, especially the isolated nature of the DPRK regime and the volatility of the ROK's democratic polity, it is almost certain that one or more of the critical external variables will be out of alignment at the brief moments when the two Koreas are able to accommodate each other. This makes periods of inter-Korean rapprochement short and virtually ensures their brutal, often abrupt termination and reversion to chronic conflict.

Thus, one could compare regional security problems to a classic six-sided Rubik's Cube with an additional layer of complexity arising from the domestic variables. As is well-known, the solution to the Rubik's Cube requires that each of the six faces — just as there are six states in East Asia — show only one color: each of these faces has nine cells, totaling fifty-four independent externally-oriented variables. The combination of cells by permutation is enormous, and solving the Cube takes practice, skill, and knowledge of solution algorithms that exceed the ability of most people.

As Changrok Soh has observed, since the Cold War ended, non-state actors have transformed what was a strict hierarchy of hegemonic state control into a "horizontal self-autonomous system" organized into networks composed of states and non-state actors. These diverse actors interact in transnational networks and contribute a new type of "networked governance" to the traditional, state-dominated system. This hybrid organizational innovation has been critical, for example, in developing a human rights regime in East Asia, and in creating a multilayered strategy to promote human security in the region.[165]

Such networks have inaugurated a loose web of multilateral dialogues and concerted activities in the East Asia region that supplement rather than supplant the dominance of existing states.[166] Ha Young Sun has described this phase of international relations in East Asia as the "wolf spider"

---

165 Soh, C., "Enhancing Human Security in North Korea through Development of a Human Rights Regime in Asia," *Korea Review of International Studies*, 10(1) (2006).

166 Yeo, A., *Bilateralism, Multilateralism, and Institutional Change in Northeast Asia's Regional Security Architecture*, EAI Fellows Program Working Paper Series (Seoul: East Asia Institute, 2011).

stage, in which great powers still hunt for prey, but also form complex, multi-sectoral networks of diplomatic, economic, cultural, and ecological interdependence built on a foundation of information and knowledge.[167] Although it is small, South Korea is ahead of the pack in developing a networked strategy as a global actor, and may even lead China, still preoccupied with consolidating its economic development. North Korea lags far behind in this view, and to co-evolve with the other states without collapsing, to survive at all, it must introduce networked strategies.[168] Moreover, it must integrate with South Korea at the same time or fall apart. Along the way, leaders in each country must become cosmopolitan and adopt multiple identities as national and regional citizens.[169] Koreans face the extra challenge of adopting a triple identity as citizens of a divided nation, citizens of separate Korean states, and citizens of the East Asian region.[170]

Thus, in Ha's view, South Korea should develop its thickest, stickiest webs with the United States and Japan, but over time, he suggests its web of relationships with China will be equally important. From this perspective, it is particularly important that South Korea do everything possible to ensure that China and the United States do not tear apart their web of increasing interdependence; South Korea can play the role of network mediator (sometimes called a border-spanning role in network theory), using its information power and knowledge to weave together the American and Chinese webs.

South Korea should also find ways to work around the "structural holes" that exist in the Japanese and American webs with respect to North Korea — a state almost bereft of networks in the sense used here.[171] South Korea, he avers, can use its network power to overcome its relative scarcity of resources in terms of size and military power, but not, he implies, if it continues to be distracted by petty competition with North Korea rather than forging joint strategies.[172] In short, as he suggests, "The complex time of the twenty-first century calls for complex networks."[173]

---

167 Ha, Y.S., *Path to an Advanced North Korea by 2032: Building a Complex Networked State*, EAI Asia Security Initiative Working Paper (Seoul: East Asia Institute, 2011).
168 Ibid., p. 13.
169 Ibid.
170 Ibid., p. 14.
171 See Mansourov, A., *Bytes and Bullets: Information Technology Revolution and National Security on the Korean Peninsula* (Honolulu: Asia Pacific Center for Security Studies, 2005).
172 Ha, Y.S. (2011).
173 Ibid.

Ha Young-sun's concept is controversial in South Korea, not the least because the Lee Myung-bak government funded his South Korean-Japan project in 2009, to develop a joint concept of Korean-Japanese future relationships, as part of Lee's "Global Korea" strategy.[174] In support of this strategy, it proposes to maximize the soft power and public diplomacy of a middle-sized power by creating networks that promote national goals.[175] Others from the Ha study-group of complex diplomacy have suggested that South Korea implement a networked middle-power strategy to cope with the pressure placed on it by the US-China power transition in the region. Instead of having to choose between the United States and China, as Lee Sook-Jong states, South Korea should

> pursue middle power diplomacy on global issues based on its Unites States support while staying away from some regional security issues that would invite US-China rivalry, such as the Taiwan issues and the South China Sea maritime disputes.[176]

The September 2011 opening of the China-Japan-Korea Trilateral Cooperation Secretariat in Seoul was the epitome to date of the pursuit of this complex networked statecraft at a regional level, while the convening of the 2010 Seoul G20 summit exemplified it at a global level.[177]

Ha and colleagues have not fully embraced the role of civil society in their concept of the "complex networked state," a polity in which civil society would not necessarily align with the goals of the nation state, but instead develop a cosmopolitan agenda that may counter rather than facilitate advances by the state. In part, Ha's state-focused concept reflects the relatively weak civil society sector in China, Japan, the two Koreas, and Russia. Nonetheless, civil society is in play in different and powerful ways within each society and across borders, even in North Korea. Civil society has already demonstrated its capacity to affect state agendas and to

174 "Korea-Japan Joint Research Project for New Era," *KBS World Radio*, 27 January 2009, http://world.kbs.co.kr/english/archive/program/news_zoom.htm?no=4709&current_page=44

175 Sohn, Y., "Searching for a New Identity: Public Diplomacy Challenges of South Korea as a Middle Power" in *Opening New Horizons for Public Diplomacy and Culture in the 21st Century, 2012 Korean Association of International Studies-Korea Foundation International Conference* (Seoul: Korea Foundation, 2012); Sohn, Y., "Middle Powers' Like South Korea Can't Do without Soft Power and Network Power," *Global Asia*, 7(3) (2012).

176 Lee, S.J., *South Korea as New Middle Power Seeking Complex Diplomacy*, EAI Asia Security Initiative Working Paper (Seoul: East Asia Institute, 2012).

177 The history of the Secretariat: *Politics* (Seoul: Trilateral Cooperation Secretariat), http://www.tcs-asia.org/dnb/board/list.php?board_name=3_1_1_politics

assert its own priorities in the region in different issue areas. We examine complex diplomacy in greater depth in chapter 6. We turn now to the role that networked civil society has already played in responding to global ecological problems in Northeast Asia, implementing its own foreign policies or "civic diplomacy" across national borders.

Civil Society's Networked Search for Cooperative Solutions

In networked governance strategies, civil society actors have already contributed significantly to weaving the kinds of web espoused by Ha. They are particularly adept at creating networks that identify where global problems intersect, where solutions may jointly address more than one problem at a time, and where different linked problems might be tackled simultaneously to solve a common problem. In principle, civil society networks are also particularly suited for sensitive security tasks such as engaging North Korea, having the agility to forge relationships and deliver joint benefits quickly, without regard for the old "decision rules" adhered to by slow-moving, conservative bureaucracies.

Here we use networks to refer to structured patterns of communication and coordination originating with social actors who are not part of the state. As the degree to which the state encompasses social, economic, cultural, and even religious life varies in each society, so too does the relative autonomy and organizational capacity of civil society organizations originating in these spheres. Civil society organizations may reside primarily in the market or in the social sphere in all its diversity. The networks they spawn may incorporate actors from multiple sectors, including the state, provided the impetus is generated and maintained by civil society organizations. Their influence arises by virtue of their structural position. This is due either to their degree of connectedness, which enables them to increase the speed and quality of information flow across networks, thereby making the world smaller, or to their ability to fill structural "holes" between other networks by spanning borders or boundaries, thereby creating networks of networks enabling other organizations to communicate in ways otherwise thought impossible. The Nautilus Institute's NAPSNet information service, with readers in every country in the region and, often, contributors from the "community of readers," is the former case in point.[178] "Track 2" dialogues such as the Northeast Asia Cooperation Dialogue are the classic instance of the latter.[179]

Civil society actors are defined here not just with respect to the degree to which they are civilian, but also to the point to which they are committed to universally accepted values. John Keane argues that to the extent that civil society organizations realize the latter, they are truly part of "global civil society."[180] Because many societies contest these values, what one society views as civilizing may be viewed negatively in another (gender-based rights, for example). Some "dark" non-state networks engage in activities that are arguably barbaric, such as human trafficking, drug or arms trading, or the propagation of international terrorism.

Thus, not all non-state networks are civil society networks as defined here, and some of these dark networks may contribute to the global problems that afflict the region.[181] In this book, we have not sought out to illustrate this point, or to make a net assessment of the contribution of civil society and its diplomacy as described in subsequent chapters. There are plenty of failures to point to in which an uncivil society campaigned for socially and culturally regressive goals (historical revisionism and Japan's textbooks are described in chapter 6); and there are also many instances in which single-issue civil society groups caused more chaos by mis-specifying their goals, seeking to bring about an ill-conceived or poorly understood solution, or failing to implement it in a competent, sensitive manner. In this book, we try to understand how civil society and its agencies may succeed, not fail, and we recognize that much research remains to be done in relation to the activities of uncivil society and its agents, as well as the performance metrics and record of civil society in this region.

---

178 See Hayes, P., *et al.*, "The Impact of the Northeast Asian Peace and Security Network in US-DPRK Conflict Resolution," in *Internet and International Systems: Information Technology and American Foreign Policy Decision-making Workshop* (Berkeley: Nautilus Institute, 1999).

179 See *The Northeast Asia Cooperation Dialogue* (La Jolla: University of California Institute on Global Conflict and Cooperation), https://igcc.ucsd.edu/research-and-programs/programs/regional-issues/northeast-asia/northeast-asia-cooperation-dialogue.html

180 Keane, J., *Global Civil Society?*, Contemporary Political Theory (Cambridge: Cambridge University Press, 2003).

181 Such as DPRK drug smuggling across the border to China. See Meng, L., "Study on Problem of Trans-Border Drugs Crimes on Sino-DPRK Border," *The Journal of Chinese People's Armed Police Force Academy*, 1 (2009).

To succeed, the leading agents in a networked complex adaptive system must have internal decision rules, the ability to learn from interaction with other agents and their environment, and thus the flexibility to adjust their decision rules and strategies. Most critical of all, civil society networks build enduring relationships that make trust possible, especially in conflict zones. Each of these engagements will change attitudes, build relationships, and make it possible to conceive of a world in which communication leads to cooperation and, in turn, to collaboration between warring parties. As Raul Lejano put it (in relation to establishing peace parks in conflict zones such as the Korean Demilitarized Zone), the process of creating such networks may lead to relationships "between actors, between groups of actors, between subsets of each group, etc. That is, we do not simply model cooperation as occurring between states, but between individuals, organizations, epistemic communities, and others. This follows from the fact that relationships are multiplex, unbounded, and dynamic."[182]

By *multiplexity*, Lejano means the "multiple contexts of a relationship whereby roles, exchanges, or affiliations overlap in a social relationship." In addition to their structural attributes, networks are powerful because their social agents, especially individuals, live many lives at once, and each of these public and private lives intersects with other social networks, often not related directly to the primary concern of the issue-based network. Yet information will travel over any connected network, not just one that is designed around an issue. This is why taxi drivers, hairdressers, and other agents whose location leads them to connect with many people at the boundaries of their multiple identities are such good sources of rumor or hard information.

A good example of a regional multi-sectoral network is the Northeast Asian Forest Forum (NEAFF). Launched by South Korean foresters in 1998 and initiated by businessperson Moon Kook-Hyun, participants include forestry and paper companies, environmental organizations, forester associations, scholars, and individuals in China, Mongolia, and South Korea. It aims to "restore degraded forest lands, to combat desertification and deforestation, and to promote environmentally sound and sustainable management of forest ecosystems in the region."[183] NEAFF worked in the DPRK to reforest 1.6 million hectares of land deforested for fuel wood and

---

182 Lejano, R.P., "Theorizing Peace Parks: Two Models of Collective Action," *Journal of Peace Research*, 43(5) (2006), doi: http://dx.doi.org/10.1177/0022343306066565

183 *Keep Northeast Asia Green* (Seoul: Northeast Asia Forest Forum), http://www.neaff.org/

timber by establishing and upgrading forest nurseries. It also planted trees and fixed sand dunes in China's Inner Mongolia and the Gobi Desert of Mongolia.

A closely related civil society initiative was Forests for Peace (FFP), an inter-Korean reforestation project that aimed to restore degraded forestland and food production in North Korea. Begun in April 1999, FFP worked on a bilateral basis with the DPRK Asia Pacific Peace Committee and shipped pine tree seeds, spray machines, branching shears, plastic sheeting, and fertilizer on 22 May 1999 to the DPRK via the Inchon-Nampo sea route. Following that initial shipment, five more consignments containing various supplies and forestry equipment were dispatched by the end of 2000.[184]

In the 1990s, a network of civil society organizations in Northeast Asia actively worked to address regional acid rain and yellow sand issues as well as to reduce greenhouse gas emissions. In 1995, the Atmospheric Action Network in East Asia (AANEA) launched with members from South Korea, Japan, China, Hong Kong, Taiwan, Mongolia, and Russia. AANEA's funding came from Japan and the secretariat was based in Seoul.[185] It aimed to reduce acid rain emissions, monitor the impact of acid rain by promoting citizen air quality measurement techniques, and address co-related greenhouse gas emissions.[186] However, the group faded away after achieving few concrete reductions in emissions. It suspended operations not long after 2000.[187] Another regional network, EnviroAsia, is sustained by a coalition of Japanese environmental groups. The project shares information about the environment between groups in South Korea, China, and Japan.[188]

Esook Yoon argues that the failure of state-based environmental dialogues and meetings to reduce trans-boundary air pollution in East Asia opens a political space that may be filled by non-state civil society

---

184 Moon, K.H. and Park, D.K., "The Role and Activities of NGOs in Reforestation in the Northeast Asian Region," *Forest Ecology and Management*, 201(1) (2004), doi: http://dx.doi.org/10.1016/j.foreco.2004.06.013

185 Jho, W. and Lee, H. (2009), p. 55.

186 Yoon, E., *et al.*, "The State and Nongovernmental Organizations in Northeast Asia's Environmental Security," in *The Environmental Dimension of Asian Security: Conflict and Cooperation over Energy, Resources, and Pollution*, ed. by Schreurs, M. A. and Hyon, I.-T. (Washington, DC: United States Institute of Peace Press, 2007).

187 Jho, W. and Lee, H. (2009), p. 55.

188 For background in English, see *East Asia Environmental Information Center* (Tokyo: Asia 3R Citizen's Network), http://www.asia3r.net/en/link/eden-j.html. See also the sharing platform in three languages (Chinese, Japanese, and Korean) *Enviro Asia* (East Asia Environmental Information Centre), http://www.enviroasia.info/

networks. In spite of the severe and already-noted constraints on the ability of civil society organizations to affect state policy in East Asian countries, Yoon suggests:

> Such informal social networks may facilitate official governmental level negotiation by opening dialogue on politically sensitive or ignored issues. NGOs also can play a role enhancing public awareness about the environment through information circulation, campaigns, and education programs. Grassroots actors may not be able to alter the fundamental distribution of power that explains the official and bureaucratic character of environmental politics in NEA today. Still, through the mobilization of social concern, civil society may achieve the goal of placing the environment higher on the NEA political agenda and slowly crack open a space for greater citizen participation in regional politics.[189]

In this state-centered political culture, civil society networks may still play a critically important ideational role by convening and supporting the emergence of epistemic communities in each culture that share an understanding of sustainability problems. As Jho and Lee argue, the yellow sand issue was first raised at an expert forum in 1988, and in 1992 an information cooperation network called the Northeast Asian Conference on Environmental Cooperation (NEAC) was formed by experts, civil society organizations, scholars, and research institutes. NEAC held fourteen regional meetings from 1992-2006.[190] This group revealed facts about yellow sand and desertification that were previously unidentified and provided a rationale for a formal governmental investigation.[191]

Nonetheless, these early efforts by pioneering civil society environmental networks armed only with scientific information produced relatively few results. On yellow sand for example (whereby huge volumes of airborne dust laced with toxic materials are transported from inner Mongolia and the Mongolian desert across Korea and Japan, reaching all the way to North America), these networks succeeded in publicizing the issue and possible solutions. Yet they were unable to persuade governments to fund a proposed Northeast Asia Environment Cooperation Core Fund.[192]

---

189 Yoon, E., "The Growth of Environmental Cooperation in Northeast Asia: The Potential Roles of Civil Society," *The Good Society*, 12(1) (2003), doi: http://dx.doi.org/10.1353/gso.2003.0032

190 See *Northeast Asian Conference on Environmental Cooperation* (Tokyo: Environmental Cooperation Office, Japan Ministry of Environment, 2005), https://www.env.go.jp/earth/coop/coop/neac_e.html

191 Jho, W. and Lee, H. (2009), p. 59.

192 Ibid.

This shortfall suggested to Yasuo Takao that environmental and other single-issue networks needed to make common cause with cities and local governments engaged in their own transnational, networked activities as described above. Cities can provide the resources and a degree of accountability to civil society organizations that increase their autonomy for the central state. He argues that local governments are located strategically between transnationally linked local civil society organizations and central state governments.[193] Exactly how this coordination would be achieved is not clear. Regional single-issue networks focused on air pollution, climate change, gender, etc., tend to emanate from the primary mega-city of each country, whereas many of the cross-border urban networks described by Takao are activated in second-tier cities, in part to compete with the primary capital city. We do not have a good picture of how these single-issue networks work between South Korea and China or how they interact with nascent Chinese non-governmental organizations.[194]

In contrast, other civil society groups have managed to affect government policy. For example, at the center of the warzone — the Korean Demilitarized Zone — that forms the greatest barrier of all to the interlocking urban corridor stretching from Beijing to Tokyo, the DMZ Forum has set out to create a park. The goal of creating the park is to preserve biodiversity, restore Korean ecology and contribute to peacemaking, historical reconciliation, and cultural preservation by linking the Sorak, Keumkang, and Cheolwon regions north and south of the DMZ.[195]

This proposed peace park is at the center of the very same bio-geographical region where the BeSeTo giga-city is emerging, along with a multi-sectoral network of geographers, botanists, and ecologists from government and private sector conservation organizations in each country of Northeast Asia. In meetings convened by the United Nations Economic and Social Commission for Asia and the Pacific (ESCAP) in Bangkok, a regional inter-governmental organization proposed a set of trans-border biodiversity corridors through Mongolia, China, Russia, and North Korea. They want to ensure sufficient habitat remains for keystone and "flagship" species,[196] the successful conservation of which would ensure that a host

193 Takao, Y. (2003), pp. 78-79.
194 Xie, L., *China's Environmental Activism in the Age of Globalization* (London: City University London, Department of International Politics, 2009).
195 See the DMZ Forum's website for details: http://www.dmzforum.org/
196 See United Nations Economic and Social Commission for Asia and the Pacific, *Saving the Flagship Species of North-East Asia : Nature Conservation Strategy of NEASPEC* (New York:

of other species survive the emergence of the giga-city and its networked infrastructure, such as pipelines, roads, railways, and power lines.

In turn, a biodiversity corridor that would link the northern habitat preservation zones with the DMZ Peace Park, and stretch southward to Jeju and on to Japan, has also been proposed by this author.[197] As a result of the Forum's work, key government officials in the United States and South Korean militaries have indicated they support a DMZ Peace Park and biodiversity conservation, although they have not yet managed to elicit a response from the North Korean side.

Civil society networks have addressed other "hot" topics. These include the proposed Taiwan-North Korea nuclear waste deal[198] and the marine oil pollution clean-up networks in which civil society organizations played an effective role either in stopping governments outright (as in the case of the nuclear waste deal) or in mobilizing massive, bottom-up civilian efforts to achieve what governments could not (as when confronted by the massive 1997 oil spill off the western coast of Japan).[199]

Conclusion

This chapter presented an argument about the relationship between global problems, complexity, problem-solving, and East Asian civil society. In section 1, we asked what is "global" about a global problem and what makes it "problematic" in the first place. We reviewed categories of global problems — those that affect the sharing of global commons, those that affect our shared humanity, and those that rely on our shared rule book

---

United Nations); *Meeting on Nature Conservation in Transboundary Areas in North East Asia Expert Group* (Incheon: North-East Asian Subregional Programme for Environmental Cooperation); Futrell, W.C., "Shallow Roots: Transnational Environmental Civil Society in Northeast Asia" in *American Sociological Association's 103rd Annual Convention* (Boston: American Sociological Association, 2008); Futrell, W.C., "Environmental Networks and Flows in Northeast Asia: NGOs and Institutes Working on Sandstorms and Migratory Birds" in *ISA's 49th Annual Convention, Bridging Multiple Divides* (San Francisco: International Studies Association, 2008).

197 See Hayes, P., "Sustainable Security in the Korean Peninsula: Envisioning a Northeast Asian Biodiversity Corridor," *The Korean Journal of International Studies*, 8(10) (2010).

198 See *TED Case Studies: Taiwan Nuclear Waste Exports (NKORNUKE)* (Washington, DC: American University), http://www1.american.edu/ted/nkornuke.htm

199 For the spill, see *Tanker NAKHODKA Oil Spill in the Sea of Japan* (Fukui: Environmental Research Centre, Fukui Prefectural Institute of Public Health and Environmental Science), http://www.erc.pref.fukui.jp/news/Eoil.html. For the citizen clean-up, see *TED Case Studies: Japan Oil Spill* (Washington, DC: American University), http://www1.american.edu/ted/japanoil.htm

for regulating human activity. We described the World Economic Forum's map of high-impact, most-probable global risks. And we suggested that only by cross-border and cross-cultural dialogue and negotiation could we determine the priority and strategy for solving global problems via coordination and collaboration at a regional level in the form of jointly implemented, shared solutions.

In section 2, we confronted complexity head-on. We suggested that the world is becoming not merely more complicated, but more complex in the sense that all realms of human existence are increasingly unpredictable, opaque and uncertain. We added that the possible emergence of the world's first giga-city — a continuous city corridor stretching from Beijing to Tokyo — would make worse the already contradictory aspects of energy insecurity, urban insecurity, and nuclear insecurity, cross-cut by the challenges of climate change and the specific threat posed by an unstable, declining North Korea.

Drawing on the work of Korean political scientists, we suggested that complex issues require a complex, networked response, organized transnationally across the region by states or by civil society. We examined cooperative environmental projects undertaken by inter-city, cross-border networks linking Japan, South Korea, and China, and suggested that integrating the single-issue environmental and security civil society networks in future networks of local governments will create a new type of resilience in the region and generate new capacity for framing and solving global problems in spite of their complexity.

We concluded this chapter by arguing that it is central to the role of civil society networks that they provide a critical perspective as to what constitutes the most urgent global problems that originate in or affect the region as a whole, rather than mirroring the priority problems set by states. Otherwise, civil society networks risk being entrapped in *realpolitik* zero-sum games, rather than moving towards *idealpolitik* based on cooperative strategies. To this end, we will present detailed case studies of energy, urban, and nuclear insecurity in the next three chapters of this book. In each case, the nature of the core problem, the "center of gravity" of urban insecurity, climate change, energy insecurity, or nuclear insecurity, differs. As a starting point in mapping the complexity landscape, each chapter considers the extent to which the authors can identify common causes and shared solutions in the problem area and country of primary concern, across problems, and across borders.

This mapping is similar to any exploration of uncharted terrain. What is important is to identify multiple pathways between problems and solutions, to identify the high ground that can serve as navigation points in the future, and to find ways around barriers without having to climb over the highest peaks. In reality, there is little terrain left on Earth that has not been lived in before. The same is true of conceptual territory and of the corpus of specialized insight into specific problems. Thus, the question is not to uncover but to identify the paths not taken, while learning from those with intimate knowledge of the local ground.

3. Energy Security and the Role of Green Economies in East Asia

David von Hippel

Contributing authors: Yi Wang, Kae Takase, Tetsunari Iida, Myungrae Cho, and Sun-Jin Yun

Introduction

Energy Security in a Post-Fukushima World

On March 11, 2011, a massive earthquake and subsequent tsunami devastated a substantial area of Japan on the Pacific coast of Honshu, north of Tokyo, with tragic consequences for the citizens of Japan and unfolding impacts in the country and elsewhere. Among the many facilities affected by this natural disaster was the Fukushima I nuclear power plant. Over the weeks and months following the earthquake (continuing, in fact, to the time of this writing), several reactors and spent nuclear fuel storage areas at the Fukushima I plant underwent slow-motion destruction. The result was fuel decomposition and the release of more radioactivity to air and water than in any nuclear power accident, save the 1986 explosion at the Chernobyl reactor in Ukraine. Damage to Fukushima I was initiated by the impacts of the earthquake and tsunami on the plant itself and on the local area — knocking out grid power to the plant, for example.[1] The continued degradation of the plant, however,

---

1   For background on the Fukushima I disaster and its immediate aftermath, see, for example, Hayes, P., *et al.*, *After the Deluge: Short and Medium-Term Impacts of the Reactor Damage Caused by the Japan Earthquake and Tsunami* (Berkeley: Nautilus Institute, 2011).

    http://dx.doi.org/10.11647/OBP.0059.03

has been sustained by a cascading series of events. Some of these events resulted from unavoidable choices made during in the frantic triage of the reactor crisis. Others were arguably set in motion by decisions made years ago by those who determined the shape of Japan's path to energy security.

The lessons of Fukushima continue to unfold, and are perhaps only just beginning to be appreciated. These lessons are having and will have significant impacts on the way that public policy is developed and carried out in Japan,[2] in the Northeast Asia Region,[3] and beyond.[4] Among these impacts is the recognition that new paradigms are needed to deal with expanding complexity in the relationships between the issues and actors involved in energy sector-related decisions. The old paradigms of traditional supply-focused "energy security" are insufficient for the task. Trends toward regional energy-sector, economic, and in some cases social integration, the expanding role of civil society and local government in affecting key energy decisions, and the tightening connections between climate change considerations, economic development (including development of "green economies"), and addressing North Korean nuclear weapons and related issues, are only a few of the complex threads that affect, and are affected by, energy sector decisions.

Even before Fukushima, energy security issues had increased in complexity at the end of the 20th century and in the early years of the 21st century. Drivers of this increase included a greater number of energy importers and exporters, and different relationships between traditional suppliers and buyers (most notably, between Europe, Russia, and the other former Soviet Union states, but also between China and its sources of fuel). The change was also shaped by China becoming a large net oil and even coal importer and the Republic of Korea (ROK) becoming a supplier of nuclear power technology. Furthermore, a combination of price rises, wars, technological and physical bottlenecks tended to

---

2   See, for example, World Nuclear News, "Japan to Reconsider Energy Policy," *World Nuclear News*, 11 May 2011, http://www.world-nuclear-news.org/NP-Japan_to_reconsider_energy_policy-1105114.html von Hippel, D. and Takase, K. (2011).

3   See, for example, Hayes, P., "Fukushima's Implications for Korea's Nuclear Dilemmas," *East Asia Forum*, 14 May 2011, http://www.eastasiaforum.org/2011/05/14/fukushima-s-implications-for-korea-s-nuclear-dilemmas/

4   "Germany to Reconsider Nuclear Policy: Merkel Sets Three-Month 'Moratorium' on Extension of Lifespans," *Spiegel*, 14 March 2011, http://www.spiegel.de/international/world/germany-to-reconsider-nuclear-policy-merkel-sets-three-month-moratorium-on-extension-of-lifespans-a-750916.html

increase complexity; that is, they resulted in a marked increase in the number of connections between those nations and other organizations affected by energy issues, in the types of relationship existing between organizations, in the groups that are connected, and in the kinds of links made between energy security-related issues. New types of connection included, for example, energy security considerations related to climate change, in which countries were much more modestly engaged pre-1990.

Standard Definition of Energy Security

Many of the existing definitions of energy security begin, and usually end, with a focus on maintaining energy supplies — particularly supplies of oil.[5] Cornerstones of this supply-based focus include reducing vulnerability to foreign threats or pressure, preventing a supply crisis from occurring (which would arise either from restrictions in physical supply or an abrupt and significant increase in energy prices), and minimizing the economic and military impact of a supply crisis once it has occurred. As noted above, however, national and international energy policies are currently facing many new challenges and, as such, need to have their effectiveness judged by additional criteria.

Why has oil been the primary focus of energy security policy? First, oil is still the dominant fuel (~33 percent) in the global primary energy supply (as of 2012).[6] (Primary energy use refers to inputs to energy transforming sectors such as power generation or oil refining before it becomes useful energy for society). Second, the Middle East, where the largest oil reserves exist, is still one of the most unstable areas in the world. Third, and related to this last observation, oil supply and prices are often influenced by the political decisions of oil suppliers and buyers. Fourth, world economic conditions, as the last several years have shown, are still vulnerable to oil price volatility, since there are certain key sectors that are heavily dependent on oil (such as transportation, petrochemicals, agriculture, and others) with limited short-term alternatives for substitution. Fifth, the key words here are "volatility" and "instability." Although globalization has improved the transparency of the oil market, prices remain to some extent at the mercy of speculators, fluctuations in currency values (which

---

5   See, for example, Clawson, P., "Energy Security in a Time of Plenty," *Strategic Forum*, 130 (1997).

6   British Petroleum, *BP Statistical Review of World Energy* (British Petroleum, 2013).

are subject to manipulation by oil suppliers), and, of course, the forces of market supply and demand.[7] This instability has been dramatically demonstrated recently, with oil prices roughly doubling between mid-2007 and mid-2008, followed by a 75 percent decline in price by early 2009 and a return to early-2008 price levels (of ~$100 per barrel) by early 2011, continuing at more or less that level through 2013.[8]

Few works have made a serious attempt to clarify the concept of energy security. One effort was that of the Working Group on Asian Energy and Security at the Massachusetts Institute of Technology (MIT)'s Center for International Studies. The MIT Working Group defined three distinct goals of energy security:

1. Reducing vulnerability to foreign threats or pressure,

2. Preventing a supply crisis from occurring, and

3. Minimizing the economic and military impact of a supply crisis once it has occurred.[9]

These goals implicitly assume that an "oil supply crisis" is the central focus of energy security policy. In essence, the two tenets of conventional energy security policy are (1) reducing threats to oil supply and (2) operating in a mode of crisis management. These tenets have traditionally constituted the primary shared view among key energy policy-makers in the East and West.

Though the major energy consuming/importing countries share the above characterization of conventional energy security thinking, there are critical divisions in policy. Two important factors influencing energy policy

---

7   Harris, J. (2008), *Written Testimony of Jeffrey Harris, Chief Economist, Before the Committee on Energy and Natural Resources United States Senate*, April 3, 2008, http://www.cftc.gov/stellent/groups/public/@newsroom/documents/speechandtestimony/opaharris040308.pdf

8   For example, Chavez-Dreyfuss, G., "FOREX-Dollar Falls as Oil Prices Rise on Iran News," *Reuters*, 9 July 2008, http://www.reuters.com/article/2008/07/09/markets-forex-idUSN0943813620080709 Kebede, R., "Oil Hits Record above $147," *Reuters*, 11 July 2008, http://www.reuters.com/article/2008/07/11/us-markets-oil-idUST14048520080711. *Petroleum and Other Liquids: Europe Brent Spot Price Fob* (Washington, DC: Energy Information Administration, United States Department of Energy, 2013), http://www.eia.gov/dnav/pet/hist/LeafHandler.ashx?n=PET&s=RBRTE&f=D

9   Samuels, R., "The MIT Japan Program Science, Technology and Management Report," in *Securing Asian Energy Investments: Geopolitics and Implications for Business Strategy* (Massachusetts Institute of Technology, 1997).

differences between countries are natural and geopolitical conditions. One country might have abundant natural resources and another may not. Some consuming countries are located close to energy-producing countries; others are far away and require transportation of fuel over long distances. Those conditional differences can lead to variances in energy security perceptions.

In sum, there are three major attributes that define differences in energy security thinking between countries: (1) the degree to which a country is energy resource-rich or energy resource-poor, (2) the degree to which market forces are allowed to operate as compared to the use of government intervention to set prices, and (3) the degree to which long-term versus short-term planning is employed.[10] Despite these differences, however, energy policies in both resource-poor and resource-rich countries are arguably converging. Both recognize the need to construct a new paradigm in energy policy, driven by common considerations such as climate change and informed and affected by events in the increasingly networked global community.

Energy Security Issues in Northeast Asia

Over the last two decades, economic growth in Northeast Asia — a region of more than 1.5 billion people comprising Japan, the Republic of Korea, the Democratic Peoples' Republic of Korea (DPRK), Mongolia, China, Hong Kong (Special Administrative Region of China), and Chinese Taipei (Taiwan), plus the Far Eastern Federal District (*okrug*) of the Russian Federation — has rapidly increased regional needs for energy services. In China and the Republic of Korea in particular, growth in the need for energy services, and for the fuels used to supply that need, has brought with it a raft of environmental problems, including rapidly mounting greenhouse gas emissions and increased emissions of other air pollutants, the latter significantly impacting local and regional air quality. The countries of the region already constitute the largest import market for liquefied natural gas (LNG) and are a major (and growing) oil import

---

10   For a more comprehensive discussion of these attributes see von Hippel, D., *et al.*, "Energy Security and Sustainability in Northeast Asia," *Energy Policy*, 39(11) (2011), doi: http://dx.doi.org/10.1016/j.enpol.2009.07.001

market as well. Northeast Asia accounts for a progressively larger share of world primary energy use; even as energy use in the rest of the world has increased, Northeast Asia's share rose from 18.6 percent in 1999 to 25.2 percent in 2007.[11]

Though the region as a whole possesses resources that could contribute substantially toward its future energy needs, many major energy resources, including natural gas, oil, coal, hydroelectric power in the Russian Far East, and gas and hydro in Western China, are far from population centers. The spread of interest in shale gas production, including imports of US shale gas to the ROK and China, and production of gas from Chinese shales, was of keen interest in 2012-2013, but prospects for both of these potentially significant initiatives remain unclear at best. Major infrastructure investments will be required to bring these resources to market, and additional economic, political, technical, and environmental considerations also apply. This is particularly true when these resources cross one or several borders, and most particularly when one or more of the borders (as with pipelines or power lines from Russia to the Republic of Korea) are shared by the DPRK. Furthermore, the Six-Party Talks on denuclearization of the DPRK — and whatever forum for discussion succeeds the Six-Party Talks once the parties return to the table — link international assistance in rebuilding the DPRK's economy and energy sector to the nuclear weapons issue. Nuclear power is heavily used in the region, but issues related to the nuclear fuel cycle (uranium enrichment, nuclear waste/materials management, and prevention of proliferation of nuclear weapons and related technologies, for example) remained substantially unresolved before Fukushima and are even more uncertain today. Increasing infrastructural, political, economic, and civil society connections between many of the cities of the region, including those located on the geographical arc from Beijing to Tokyo via Seoul, mean that problems related to urban development and security are increasingly shared between nations. As a result, regional energy cooperation, approaches to the DPRK nuclear weapons dilemma,

---

11   von Hippel, D. and Hayes, P., "Future Northeast Asian Regional Energy Sector Cooperation Proposals and the DPRK Energy Sector: Opportunities and Constraints," *ERINA Report*, 82(2008). Hayes, P. and von Hippel, D., "Growth in Energy Needs in Northeast Asia: Projections, Consequences, and Opportunities," in *2008 Northeast Asia Energy Outlook Seminar, Korea Economic Institute Policy Forum* (Washington, DC: Korean Economic Institute, 2008).Korea Economic Institute Policy Forum (Washington, DC: Korean Economic Institute, 2008

nuclear fuel cycle issues, urban security, military security, and perhaps even partial solutions to global and regional environmental problems are intertwined in the region. All of these issues have significant implications for the energy security of the region and beyond.

Addressing Energy Security in a Complex World

Given the many entwined issues affecting and affected by energy policies in Northeast Asia and beyond, a broader definition of energy security is needed to address the problems (and opportunities) facing the region both today and in the coming years, particularly as the deeply interconnected issues of urban security/insecurity, the development of green economies, climate change, and problems associated with North Korea must be considered in any policies that seek to increase energy security in the countries of the region. All of these issues strongly affect the ROK; therefore, the formulation of effective ROK energy, environmental, and economic development policies requires the application of a broader energy security definition. The development of government policies that are "robust" across multiple dimensions of these problems, including (but not limited to) the implementation of aggressive programs of energy efficiency, renewable energy, and distributed generation — taking advantage of nascent and growing civil society and commercial networks that promote such changes — will be among the key methods for improving energy security, defined in the broad sense in Northeast Asia.

Chapter Road Map

Section 2 of this chapter begins with a discussion of the general issues associated with energy security in Northeast Asia, noting recent, current, and likely future patterns of energy use that form the background of energy security dilemmas in the region. Elements of a broader concept of energy security are presented — including traditional energy security elements such as supply and price security, but also extending to intimately-related energy security challenges in multiple dimensions — along with suggested methods to evaluate the energy security implications of different future "paths" for providing energy services. Section 3 describes key linkages between energy security and urban security/insecurity, suggesting that the calculus of energy security may be extended to evaluate urban insecurity issues in order to identify solutions that address both types of insecurity at the same time. Section 4 discusses the linkages between the green economy — the movement toward adopting economic patterns that help to reduce human-caused pollutant emissions and environmental impacts while also addressing human development needs — globally and in the region, and examines approaches to improving the overlap between energy security and green economy considerations as they affect both climate change and DPRK issues (that is, regional and global security issues caused by the combination of the DPRK's nuclear weapons program and its humanitarian and economic problems). We review case studies of green economy policies in Japan, China, and the ROK. Section 5 details key connections between climate change (including climate change mitigation and adaptation efforts, as well as the impacts of a changing climate) and energy security, and between DPRK issues and energy security. Section 6 provides an illustrative application of the energy security analysis of alternative policies, including considerations of urban insecurity and the green economy. We emphasize impacts related to climate change and the DPRK. We conclude with a summary of lessons learned regarding policies that appear to provide important benefits in improving energy security in the region while simultaneously addressing other goals. We also offer insights on key "pressure points" for civil society to move such policies along. Section 7 emphasizes the potential role of ROK foreign policy, if influenced by the voices of civil society, in improving the energy security of the region while simultaneously ameliorating urban insecurity, securing the benefits of the green economy, and making progress on climate change and DPRK issues.

Energy Security in Northeast Asia

Northeast Asia's Energy Sector: Recent Past, Current Status, and Future Trends

Energy supply and demand in Northeast Asia drive the large and vibrant (as well as the not-so-large and/or not-so-vibrant) economies of the region. The energy sector of Northeast Asia is a central factor in the creation and growth of environmental problems, such as local air pollution and climate change, and of local, regional, and international problems ranging from competition over energy resources to the DPRK nuclear weapons issue.

How these problems are dealt with in the future will arise from how the nations of the region and beyond pursue their energy policies. An appreciation of where the Northeast Asia energy system has come from in recent decades, where it stands now, and where, based on "business as usual" projections, it may be in the future, is key to identifying those policies that the ROK and the other nations of the region (and beyond) might adopt in addressing these issues.[12]

Energy Demand and Demand Growth in Northeast Asia

The countries of Northeast Asia — mainly Japan, the ROK, and Taiwan, but increasingly China as well — already constitute the world's largest market (63 percent of 2012 global exports) for LNG[13] and one of the largest for crude oil and petroleum products (nearly 20 percent of global demand). Table 3.1 shows the distribution of primary energy use by fuel in the countries of Northeast Asia. The region also uses more than half (57 percent, up from about 33 percent in 1999) of global coal production, with 75 percent of regional coal use occurring in China. In 2012, the countries of Northeast Asia consumed over 21 percent of the world's petroleum, 12.4 percent of its nuclear energy (a significant decline from previous years, caused by the shut-down of many Japanese reactors for post-Fukushima safety checks), 26.1 percent of hydroelectric generation, and 10 percent of natural gas, the latter up from 5.5 percent in 1999.

Table 3.2 provides 2012 (for the most part) estimates of population in each of the countries (or, in the case of the Russian Far East and Hong Kong, sub-country regions) of Northeast Asia and shows the use of primary energy per capita by country. By way of comparison, the DPRK consumed approximately 0.8 tonnes of oil equivalent (TOE) of primary commercial fuels per capita in 1996 and China about 0.6 TOE/capita in 1999, while South Korea used 3.9 TOE per capita and Japan 4.0 TOE per capita in 1999. Since that time, as shown in Table 3.2, energy use per capita has decreased slightly in Japan, increased significantly in the ROK, and more than tripled in China, while decreasing in the DPRK.

---

12   Some of the text and figures in this section are adapted and updated from von Hippel, D., *et al.*, "Overview of the Northeast Asia Energy Situation," *Energy Policy*, 39(11) (2011), doi: http://dx.doi.org/10.1016/j.enpol.2009.07.004

13   British Petroleum (2013).

Table 3.1: Primary Energy Use in Northeast Asia and the World, 2012 (except as noted)

Primary Energy Use in Northeast Asia and the World, 2012*
(Unit: PJ)

Country/Area	Natural Oil	Gas	Coal	Nuclear Energy	Hydro-electric	Renew-ables	Total	Fraction of NE Asia	Fraction of World
China	20,250	5,420	78,432	923	8,155	1,336	114,516	74.70%	21.90%
Chinese Taipei	1,765	614	1,720	383	51	48	4,581	3.00%	0.90%
DPRK (North Korea)	38	-	342	-	43	213	423	0.30%	0.10%
Hong Kong (China SAR)	751	106	318	-	-	0	1,175	0.80%	0.20%
Japan	9,135	4,399	5,207	170	767	342	20,021	13.10%	3.80%
Mongolia	33	-	98	-	-	4	136	0.10%	0.00%
ROK (South Korea)	4,554	1,885	3,427	1,424	29	33	11,352	7.40%	2.20%
Russian Far East	442	120	483	2	47	-	1,131	0.70%	0.20%
Total Northeast Asia	36,969	12,544	90,027	2,902	9,093	1,976	153,334	100.00%	29.40%
NE Asia Fraction of World	21.40%	10.00%	57.60%	12.40%	26.10%	19.90%	29.40%		
Total Rest of World	135,968	112,518	66,144	20,561	25,705	7,964	369,038		70.60%
TOTAL WORLD	172,937	125,062	156,171	23,463	34,798	9,940	522,371		100.00%

Sources: Gulidov, R., et al., "Update on the RFE Energy Sector and on the RFE LEAP Modeling Effort," in Asian Energy Security Project Meeting Energy Futures and Energy Cooperation in the Northeast Asia Region (Beijing; Nautilus Institute, 2007); Victor Kalashnikov, Ruslan Gulidov, and Alexander Ognev, "Energy Sector of the Russian Far East: Current Status and Scenarios for the Future," Energy Policy, 39(11) (2011), doi: 10.1016/j.enpol.2009.09.035

Table 3.2: Population and Energy use Per Capita in Northeast Asia, 2012

Country/Area	Population (million)*	Primary TOE/cap*	Primary GJ/cap*
China	1,376.90	1.99	83.2
Chinese Taipei	23.3	4.69	196.4
DPRK (North Korea)	24.5	0.41	17.3
Hong Kong (China SAR)	7.2	3.92	164.3
Japan	127.1	3.76	157.5
Mongolia	2.7	1.19	50
ROK (South Korea)	49	5.54	231.8
Russian Far East	6.6	4.1	171.5
Total Northeast Asia	1,617	48.24	2019.7

Note: Estimates are for 2012 except in the cases of the DPRK (2010), RFE (2005), and Mongolia (2009/2010).

Sources: Population figures used for these calculations are from United Nations Population Projections, Medium Variant (2012), http://esa.un.org/unpd/wpp/unpp/panel_population. htm, except for those of Chinese Taipei (Taiwan), which are from "Population Projections for R.O.C. (Taiwan): 2012-2060," and the RFE, which is based on data from P.A. Minakir, "Russia and the Russian Far East in Economies of the APR and NEA," in Minakir, P.A., *Economic Cooperation between the Russian Far East and Asia-Pacific Countries* (2007).

Despite the explosive recent growth, energy use in Northeast Asia — particularly in China, DPRK, and Mongolia — would seem to have substantial room to grow more before it reaches the levels currently maintained by Japan, the ROK, and other developed nations. Transport services, which the Chinese and North Koreans currently use relatively lightly and very lightly respectively, is one of the key areas of growth (as any recent visitor to a major Chinese city will affirm), and in all probability transport energy use will increase significantly. Residential energy use can also be expected to rise in these countries. Projected continued increases in energy use (see below) underscore the need for policies that consider the multiple connections between energy supply and demand and other issues in the region.

Figure 3.1 summarizes primary energy use in the countries of Northeast Asia (plus the Far Eastern District of Russia) over the period from 1990 through 2006. During those 16 years, the total energy use by the region increased by a factor of two, led by a tripling of energy use in China and an increase of about 150 percent in the ROK and Taiwan. This happened despite primary energy use in Japan, the second largest energy user in the region, growing hardly at all from 2000 through 2007 (after having grown by about 20 percent during the previous decade). During the period from 1990 through 2007, Northeast Asia's share of global primary energy demand grew by half, from about 17 percent to over 25 percent. Note that the totals shown in Figure 3.1 do not (with the exception of the DPRK) include use of biomass fuels, which provide a significant (though decreasing) portion of residential energy use in China and in Mongolia, as well as in the DPRK.

Figure 3.1: Primary Energy Use in Northeast Asia by Country, 1990-2012

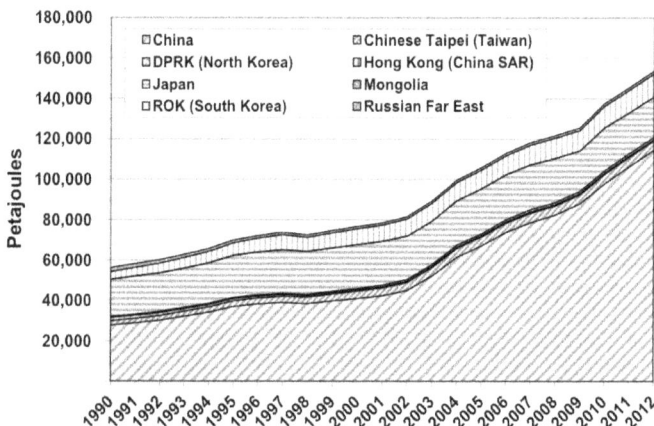

Sources: Data for all countries except the DPRK, Mongolia and the RFE are from British Petroleum Co., "BP Statistical Review of World Energy"; DPRK data are based on David F. von Hippel and Peter Hayes, "An Updated Summary of Energy Supply and Demand in the Democratic People's Republic of Korea (DPRK)," EGS Working Paper 2014-02, April 2014, http://nautilus.org/wp-content/uploads/2011/12/Russia-Energy-Changes.ppt; Mongolia data are from USDOE/EIA, 2013, "Mongolia Overview/Data" http://www.eia.gov/countries/country-data.cfm?fips=MG#tpe; and RFE data are compiled from Victor Kalashnikov, "Electric Power Industry of The Russian Far East: Status and Prerequisites for Cooperation in North-East Asia," Draft Report Prepared for the Working Group Meeting on *Comparisons of the Electricity Industry in China, North Korea and the Russian Far East*, East-West Center, Honolulu, Hawaii, 28-29 July 1997; Victor Kalashnikov, Alexander Ognev, and Ruslan Gulidov, "Updates on the RFE Energy Sector and the RFE LEAP model, and Inputs to and Results of RFE Future Energy Paths," presentation prepared for the *Asian Energy Security Workshop*, May 13-16, 2005, Beijing, China; and Ruslan Gulidov and Alexander Ognev, "The Power Sector in the Russian Far East: Recent Status and Plans," prepared for the 2007 Asian Energy Security Project Meeting *Energy Futures and Energy Cooperation in the Northeast Asia Region*, Tsinghua University, Beijing, China, October 31–November 2, 2007, http://nautilus.org/wp-content/uploads/2011/12/Russia-Energy-Changes.ppt. 2011 and 2012 data for the DPRK and RFE, 2011 and 2012 data for Mongolia, and 2007-onwards data for the RFE are extrapolations from previous years' data.

The trends in primary energy use by fuel in Northeast Asia are shown in Figure 3.2. Coal use has dominated the absolute growth in energy use over 1990 through 2012, with China accounting for the bulk of that increase.

Figure 3.2: Primary Energy Use in Northeast Asia by Fuel, 1990-2012

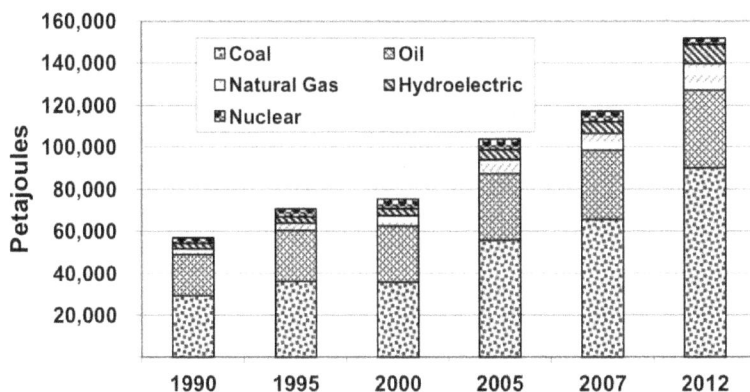

Sources: Data for all countries except the DPRK, Mongolia and the RFE are from British Petroleum Co., "BP Statistical Review of World Energy" (2013); DPRK data are based on David F. von Hippel and Peter Hayes, "An Updated Summary of Energy Supply and Demand in the Democratic People's Republic of Korea (DPRK)," EGS Working Paper 2014/02, April 2014, http://www.egskorea.org/common/download.asp?downfile=2014-2_workingpaper_NK_Energy_Hippel_Hayes0.pdf&path=board; Mongolia data are from USDOE/EIA, "Mongolia Overview/Data" (2013), http://www.eia.gov/countries/country-data.cfm?fips=MG#tpe; and RFE data are compiled from Victor Kalashnikov, "Electric Power Industry of The Russian Far East: Status and Prerequisites for Cooperation in North-East Asia," Draft Report Prepared for the Working Group Meeting on *Comparisons of the Electricity Industry in China, North Korea and the Russian Far East*, East-West Center, Honolulu, Hawaii, 28-29 July 1997; Victor Kalashnikov, Alexander Ognev, and Ruslan Gulidov, "Updates on the RFE Energy Sector and the RFE LEAP model, and Inputs to and Results of RFE Future Energy Paths," presentation prepared for the *Asian Energy Security Workshop*, May 13-16, 2005, Beijing, China; and Ruslan Gulidov and Alexander Ognev, "The Power Sector in the Russian Far East: Recent Status and Plans," prepared for the 2007 Asian Energy Security Project Meeting *Energy Futures and Energy Cooperation in the Northeast Asia Region*, Tsinghua University, Beijing, China, October 31-November 2, 2007, http://nautilus.org/wp-content/uploads/2011/12/Russia-Energy-Changes.ppt. 2011 and 2012 data for the DPRK and RFE, 2011 and 2012 data for Mongolia, and 2007-onwards data for the RFE are extrapolations from previous years' data.

Coal, natural gas, and hydroelectric power use have expanded the most in relative terms, with average growth rates of between 8 and 9 percent annually between 2000 and 2012. Coal and hydroelectricity use grew by an average of just under 5 percent annually between 1990 and 2007, but by 2.7 and 4.1

percent annually, respectively, from 2007 through 2012. In part, the slower growth was a function of the global recession of 2008-2010 and of China's effort to diversify away from coal use. Nuclear power use expanded by an average rate of 3.7 percent annually between 1990 and 2007, but at a much slower pace — 1.2 percent annually — between 2000 and 2007, as the nuclear power fleets in Japan and the ROK have filled many of the few remaining reactor sites. Since 2007, nuclear power use in the region actually contracted by an average of 4.4 percent annually, largely as a result of the shutdown for safety evaluations of the Japanese reactor fleet and, to a lesser extent, the reactor fleets of other nations. Oil use has grown by about 3 percent annually between 2000 and 2012, with large increases in use in China offset by a trend away from oil use in the non-transport sectors in Japan and the ROK.

Figure 3.3: Electricity Generation in Northeast Asia, 1990-2012

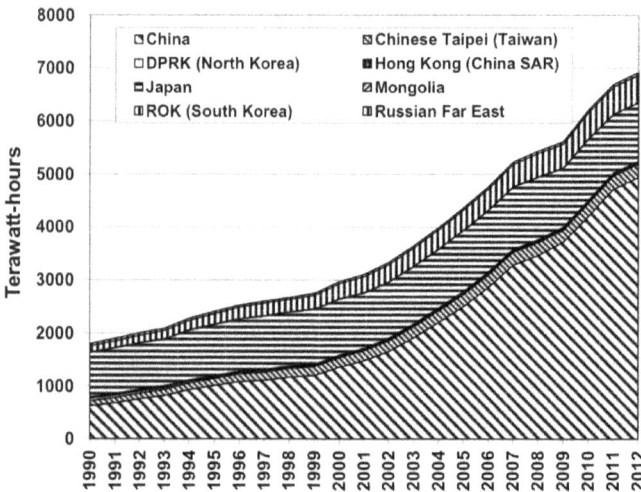

Sources: DPRK is from Peter Hayes and David von Hippel, "Foundations of Energy Security for the DPRK: 1990-2009 Energy Balances, Engagement Options, and Future Paths for Energy and Economic Redevelopment," *NAPSNet Special Report* (Nautilus Institute, 2012). Mongolia data is from USDOE/EIA, "Mongolia Overview/Data" (2013), http://www.eia.gov/beta/international/country.cfm?iso=MNG; and RFE data is from Ruslan Gulidov and Alexander Ognev, "The Power Sector in the Russian Far East: Recent Status and Plans," prepared for the 2007 Asian Energy Security Project Meeting *Energy Futures and Energy Cooperation in the Northeast Asia Region*, Tsinghua University, Beijing, China, October 31-November 2, 2007, http://nautilus.org/wp-content/uploads/2011/12/Russia-Energy-Changes.ppt. Generation figures shown are for gross generation (that is, including in-plant electricity use), except for Mongolia and the RFE. All other data is from British Petroleum Co., "BP Statistical Review of World Energy" (2013).

Even more striking than the growth in primary energy use — and indeed one of its main drivers — has been the increase in electricity generation (and consumption) in the region. As shown in Figure 3.3, total electricity generation in the region nearly quadrupled between 1990 and 2012, with generation in China increasing by a factor of nearly eight, generation in Taiwan increasing by a factor of nearly three, and generation in the ROK increasing by a factor of 4.4. Even though electricity production in Japan, which in 1990 had the highest generation in the region, grew by only 31 percent (an average of 1.2 percent annually), the fraction of global generation accounted for by the Northeast Asia region grew from just over 15 percent in 1990 to nearly 31 percent in 2012. Electricity generation in the rest of the world grew at an average rate of 2 percent annually during the period.

Although population growth has been a driver of energy use in the region, it has not been the key driver. The total number of people in the region surpassed 1.5 billion in the year 2000, but overall population in the region increased by only 12.7 percent between 1990 and 2006, an average of less than 1 percent (0.75 percent) annually. The rate of population growth has further decreased, to an average of 0.57 percent/year from 2007 through 2012. Most of the region's countries either have populations that are already declining — Japan, Russia and the Russian Far East, and (possibly) the DPRK — or that are expected to start declining in the next decade or so.[14]

Economic growth, on the other hand, has certainly been a key driver of expanding energy use in Northeast Asia. Figure 3.4 presents trends in gross domestic product from 1990 through 2010 for the countries of the region, expressed in Purchasing Power Parity (PPP) terms. Real GDP in China increased by a factor of 6.6, and GDP in Taiwan and the ROK more than doubled (increasing 2.5- and 2.7-fold, respectively) during the 20 years covered by the graph, while the Japanese economy grew by less than one quarter overall.

---

14 See, for example, United Nations, Department of Economic and Social Affairs, Population Division, *World Population Prospects: The 2012 Revision, DVD Edition* (United Nations, Department of Economic and Social Affairs, Population Division, 2013).

Figure 3.4: Northeast Asia GDP by Country, 1990-2010

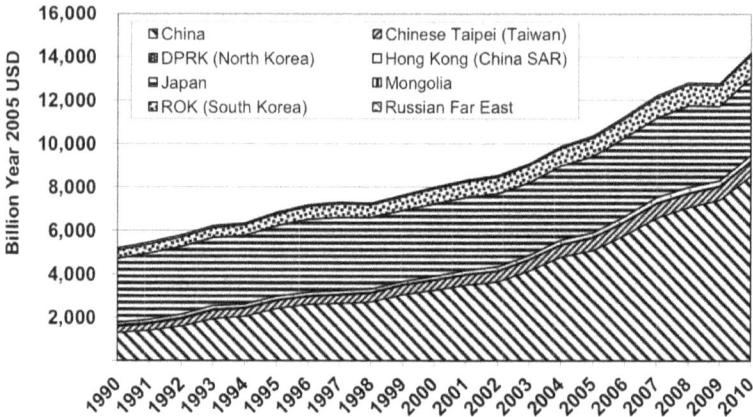

Sources: Data were derived from Primary Energy Use data from British Petroleum Co., "BP Statistical Review of World Energy and Primary Energy Use per unit PPP" (2013); GDP data from USDOE/EIA, "International Energy Statistics – Energy Intensity Using Purchasing Power Parities, 1990-2011" (2013), http://www.eia.gov/cfapps/ipdbproject/iedindex3.cfm?tid=92&pid=47&aid=2&cid=regions&syid=1990&eyid=2011&unit=BTUPUSDP. Note that though DPRK data were derived as above from USDOE/EIA data, they should be considered highly approximate. Data for the Russian Far East through 2006 have been estimated very roughly from data in P.A. Minakir, "Russia and the Russian Far East in Economies of the APR and NEA," in Minakir, P.A., *Economic Cooperation between the Russian Far East and Asia-Pacific Countries* (2007). After 2006, the RFE GDP was assumed to grow at approximately the rate of growth of GDP in the Russian Federation as a whole.

The efficiency with which an economy uses energy as an input in its overall economic output is reflected in its energy use per unit of GDP. Figure 3.5 charts primary energy use in the countries of Northeast Asia per unit of economic output in units of kilojoules (kJ) per year-2005 US dollar of PPP-adjusted Gross Domestic Product. For the more established economies (Taiwan, Hong Kong, Japan, and the ROK) primary energy use per unit of GDP varied somewhat year to year, but changed very little over the period from 1990 through 2006. In contrast, in the economies in transition — Mongolia, the DPRK, and the RFE — energy use per unit of GDP fell markedly. This decrease was due to a number of factors, including structural adjustment (a reduction in activity in a number of high-energy-input industries) and an improvements in efficiency as some Soviet-era infrastructure was replaced or decommissioned (mostly in the RFE and Mongolia). In China, primary energy use per capita fell from 1990 through about 2000, likely due to a combination of replacing older industrial equipment with more efficient newer equipment, phasing out smaller, older infrastructure (such as smaller, less-efficient coal-fired power plants), and an economy gradually shifting toward less energy-intensive industries. After 2000, trends in consumption caused primary energy use per unit GDP in China to rise somewhat — for example, more road vehicles and per capita transportation use, homes with greater floor space (and energy requirements) per resident, and construction of more commercial building space per person.

Figure 3.5: Primary Energy Use per Unit GDP in the Countries of Northeast Asia, 1990-2010

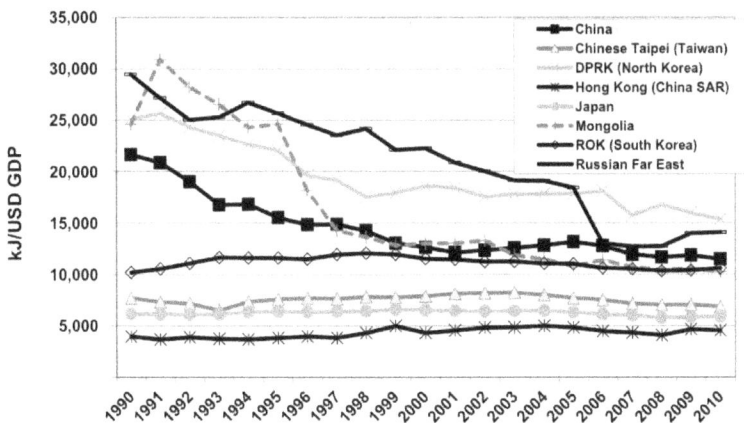

Sources: Data from USDOE/EIA, "International Energy Statistics – Energy Intensity Using Purchasing Power Parities, 1990-2011" (2013), http://www.eia.gov/cfapps/ipdbproject/iedindex3.cfm?tid=92&pid=47&aid=2&cid=regions&syid=1990&eyid=2011&unit=BTUPU SDP, except for RFE, where primary energy use per unit GDP was derived from the sources noted for Figures 3 and 4.

Projections of Energy Use in Northeast Asia

Figures 3.6 and 3.7 present projections of primary energy use by country and by fuel for the countries of Northeast Asia. These projections were largely derived from initial or draft "reference" or "BAU" (Business-as-Usual) case projections, most of which have been developed or conveyed by country working groups in the Nautilus Institute's collaborative Asian Energy Security project. The exception is the projections for China, which were derived and extrapolated from energy use trends shown in Zhou *et al.* (2008).[15]

---

15 Zhou, N., *et al.*, *Energy Use in China: Sectoral Trends and Future Outlook* (Berkeley: Lawrence Berkeley National Laboratory, 2008).

This composite is just one of many possible energy sector "futures" for the region, and it is based on assumptions regarding changing trends in energy use that are affected by national, regional, and global economics, as well as by evolving national policies. With this limitation in mind, the projections shown suggest that energy use in Northeast Asia will nearly double between 2010 and 2030, with approximately 90 percent of that growth coming from China. On a fuel-by-fuel basis, demand for oil and for hydroelectric energy are projected to double in the 20 years between 2010 and 2030, while coal use increases by more than 50 percent, gas use nearly triples, and nuclear power and hydro use roughly double. In terms of absolute increases, oil shows the second largest growth — driven by expansion of transport energy demand, especially in China — with coal just ahead.

Figure 3.6: Projected Reference-Case Primary Energy Use in Northeast Asia by Country

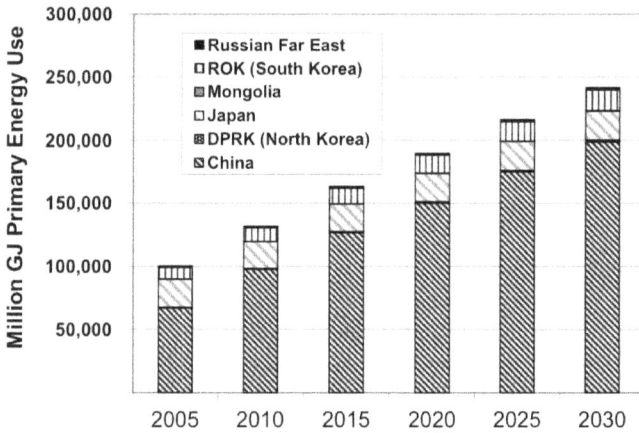

Source: These projections were largely derived from initial, draft "reference" or "BAU" (Business-as-Usual) case projections, most of which have been developed or conveyed by country working groups in the Nautilus Institute's collaborative Asian Energy Security project, except for projections for China, which were derived and extrapolated from energy use trends derived from Nan Zhou, Michael A. McNeil, David Fridley, Jiang Lin, Lynn Price, Stephane de la Rue du Can, Jayant Sathaye, and Mark Levine, *Energy Use in China: Sectoral Trends and Future Outlook*, Report # LBNL-61904, Lawrence Berkeley National Laboratory, 2008.

Placed in perspective, for example, the additional 31 EJ (Exajoules, equal to 1000 Petajoules) of annual oil demand for the region projected here corresponds to about three quarters of a one billion tonnes, or roughly

5.5 billion barrels, not much less than the 7.4 billion barrels produced in 2010 by Saudi Arabia and Russia — the world's two largest oil producers — combined. Given estimates by some researchers that show the world's output of petroleum peaking soon (see, for example, Zittel and Schindler, 2007),[16] if not already, this projected increase in oil demand in just one region is clearly cause for concern.

Figure 3.7: Projected Reference-Case Primary Energy Use in Northeast Asia by Fuel

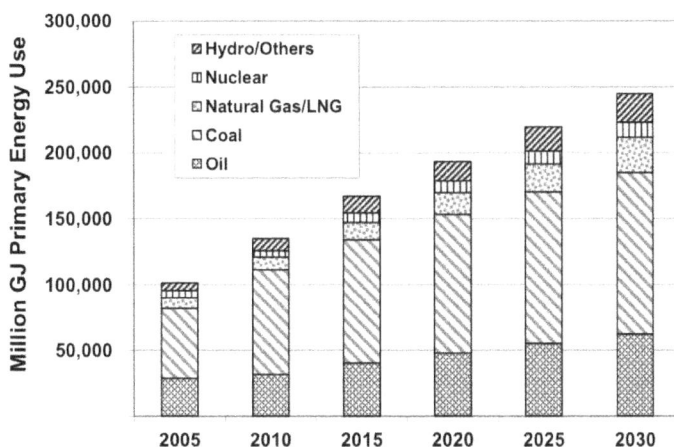

Source: These projections were largely derived from initial, draft "reference" or "BAU" (Business-as-Usual) case projections, most of which have been developed or conveyed by country working groups in the Nautilus Institute's collaborative Asian Energy Security project, except for projections for China, which were derived and extrapolated from energy use trends derived from Nan Zhou, *et al., Energy Use in China. Sectoral Trends and Future Outlook*.

In addition to implications for global energy supplies, the growth in energy needs projected above has significant implications for global greenhouse gas emissions, Table 3.3 provides a summary of historical estimates and projections for emissions in the countries of Northeast Asia and a view of the increasing importance of emissions of carbon dioxide (CO_2) from the region relative to the rest of the world. Northeast Asia's share of world CO_2 emissions increased from 17.9 percent in 1990 to over 32.6 percent by 2010, and, based on a variety of estimates, it will account for 40 percent of global emissions by 2030.

---

16   Zittel, W. and Schindler, J., *Crude Oil, the Supply Outlook* (Energy Watch Group, 2007).

Table 3.3: Historical and Projected Emissions of Carbon Dioxide in Northeast Asia

Carbon Dioxide Emissions (Unit: million tonnes of carbon dioxide)								
Country/Area	1990	1995	2000	2005	2010	2015	2020	2030
China	2,178	2,723	3,272	5,464	7,997	10,022	11,532	14,028
Chinese Taipai	118	182	256	289	287	318	353	435
DPRK (North Korea)	131	80	34	39	33	48	79	90
Hong Kong (China SAR)	40	47	56	80	92	[Included in China total]		
Japan	1,047	1,116	1,201	1,241	1,180	1,243	1,220	1,215
Mongolia	10	9	6	6	8	10	13	21
ROK (South Korea)	242	381	439	494	581	600	627	666
Russian Far-East	80	71	71	80	92	98	105	135
Total Northeast Asia	3,845	4,610	5,335	7,693	10,269	12,340	13,930	16,590
Total Rest of World	17,678	17,400	18,815	20,569	21,233	21,477	22,516	24,874
TOTAL WORLD	21,523	22,010	24,150	28,262	31,502	33,817	36,446	41,464

Sources: Historical data from USDOE EIA, "International Energy Statistics – Total Carbon Dioxide Emissions from the Consumption of Energy, 1990-2011" (2013), http://www.eia. gov/cfapps/ipdbproject/iedindex3.cfm?tid=90&pid=44&aid=8&cid=regions&syid=1990& eyid=2011&unit=MMTCD, except DPRK from David F. von Hippel and Peter Hayes, "An Updated Summary of Energy Supply and Demand in the Democratic People's Republic of Korea (DPRK)," EGS Working Paper 2014-02, April 2014, http://www.egskorea.org/common/ download.asp?downfile=NK_Energy_2014-2_final_Hippel_Hayes.pdf&path=board;   and RFE, rough estimates from Ruslan Gulidov, Victor Kalashnikov and Alexander Ognev, "Update on the RFE Energy Sector and on the RFE LEAP Modeling Effort," prepared for the 2007 Asian Energy Security Project Meeting *Energy Futures and Energy Cooperation in the Northeast Asia Region*, Tsinghua University, Beijing, China, October 31-November 2, 2007, https://www.google.com.au/url?sa=t&rct=j&q=&esrc=s&source=web&cd=1&ved=0CB8QFj AA&url=http%3A%2F%2Fnautilus.org%2Fwp-content%2Fuploads%2F2011%2F12%2F01.- RFE.pptx&ei=c6EkVMLdIYvioATF64KQCA&usg=AFQjCNEPDMEV0Pdg5FttVejt2FYcaQwq Ug&bvm=bv.76247554,d.cGU&cad=rja; and Victor Kalashnikov, "Electric Power Industry of The Russian Far East: Status and Prerequisites for Cooperation in North-East Asia," Draft Report Prepared for the Working Group Meeting on *Comparisons of the Electricity Industry in China, North Korea and the Russian Far East*, East-West Center, Honolulu, Hawaii, 28-29 July 1997. Projections data from USDOE EIA, *International Energy Outlook 2013*, Table A10, World carbon dioxide emissions by region, Reference case (2013), http://www.eia.gov/oiaf/ aeo/tablebrowser/#release=IEO2013&subject=0-IEO2013&table=10-IEO2013&region=0- 0&cases=Reference-d041117, for China, Japan, ROK, and Total World.

Energy Supplies in Northeast Asia: Resources, Energy Imports and Exports

To supply the energy needed to meet current and projected demand, the Northeast Asia region as a whole already has a considerable endowment of energy resources, including both fossil fuels and renewable energy resources. Most, however, of the remaining untapped fossil fuel reserves and hydroelectric potential in the region are far from population centers and often in difficult-to-access areas — they are mostly found in the Russian Far East. As a result, there has been rapid growth in the region's net energy imports, including oil, gas, and coal.

Japan and the ROK have limited coal reserves — an estimated 350 and 126 million tonnes, respectively[17] — and have ceased (or all but ceased) domestic production. Neither country has significant reserves of gas or oil, though exploration, particularly in offshore areas, continues. Available hydroelectric resources in both countries are largely already in use, though both countries have wind energy resources in some areas. China has a reported 115 billion tonnes of coal reserves — about a 45-year supply at current production levels, along with 2.1 billion tonnes of oil (just an 11-year supply at 2007 production levels), and about 1.9 trillion cubic meters of natural gas — about a 27-year supply. China's exploitable hydroelectric resources are the largest in the world, at about 400 GW (gigawatts, or million kilowatts), of which roughly one-third have been tapped. The bulk of China's gas and hydroelectric resources are located in the western part of the country and require the construction of transmission pipelines and power lines to reach the major cities in eastern China. China has significant wind resources, largely in remote areas in the northwest and northeast, including Inner Mongolia, although offshore wind resources in areas of eastern China are also significant. The DPRK has abundant coal deposits, with estimates ranging from "reserves" of 600 million tonnes to "resources" of up to 15 billion tonnes. The DPRK has some remaining untapped hydroelectric potential, though mostly at smaller sites, and no significant oil or gas production, though some resource finds have been reported.[18]

---

17   British Petroleum, *BP Statistical Review of World Energy June 2011* (British Petroleum, 2011).

18   Hayes, P. and von Hippel, D., *Foundations of Energy Security for the DPRK: 1990-2009 Energy Balances, Engagement Options, and Future Paths for Energy and Economic Redevelopment*, NAPSNet Special Report (Berkeley: Nautilus Institute, 2012).

The Russian Far East's energy endowment includes a reported 10.8 billion tonnes of oil, 24.3 trillion cubic meters of natural gas, and 1.2 trillion tonnes of coal, as well as hydroelectric potential on the order of 200 GW and 20 billion cubic meters of wood stocks that can be harvested at a rate of about 66 million cubic meters annually.[19] These vast resources are located in remote and often forbidding terrain, requiring major investments to bring them to market.[20] As such, even if developed rapidly, these resources will only provide a fraction of the regional energy requirements projected in the coming years.

China was a net oil exporter until 1993, but its imports net of exports has since grown to over 260 million tonnes of crude oil and oil products by 2010, second only to the United States.[21] Japan had net imports of about 210 million tonnes of crude oil and oil products in 2010, the ROK had net imports of 775 million barrels (just over 100 million tonnes) in 2009,[22] and Taiwan had net imports of 54 billion liters of oil equivalent (about 60 million tonnes).[23] Japan, the ROK, and Taiwan were also top importers of liquefied natural gas (LNG), at about 93, 44, and 15 billion cubic meters, respectively, during 2010. Though Japan and the ROK once produced most of their own coal, both now produce only 1 percent of what they consume, importing coal with energy value of 123 and 75 million tonnes of oil equivalent (Mtoe), respectively, in 2010. Taiwan imported 40 Mtoe of coal in 2010. China both imports and exports coal, but its trade flows of coal are dwarfed by its vast domestic production (over 3.2 billion tonnes, or 1800 Mtoe). The near-total dependence on energy imports by Japan, the ROK, and Taiwan has been perceived as a significant energy-supply security liability. It is one reason that all three countries, and especially Japan and the ROK, have invested so heavily in nuclear power and worked to ensure that their own energy companies (especially oil companies) secure (own and develop) fuel supplies in other nations, in addition to taking other steps to improve their energy security. As China's energy needs continue to outpace its own

19 Minakir, P.A., "Russia and the Russian Far East in Economies of the APR and NEA," in *Economic Cooperation between the Russian Far East and Asia-Pacific Countries* (Khabarovsk: RIOTIP, 2007).

20 von Hippel, D., *et al.*, "Northeast Asia Regional Energy Infrastructure Proposals," *Energy Policy*, 39(11) (2011), doi: http://dx.doi.org/10.1016/j.enpol.2009.08.011

21 British Petroleum (2013).

22 *Korea Energy Statistics Information System* (Seoul: Korea Energy Economics Institute, 2011), http://www.kesis.net/flexapp/KesisFlexApp.jsp?menuId=Q0109&reportId=& chk=Y#app=5dd0&7a56-selectedIndex=2 The ROK is a major oil refiner, and actually exports more oil products than it imports.

23 Taiwan Bureau of Energy, *Energy Balance Sheet of Taiwan, 2010* (Taiwan: Taiwan Ministry of Economic Affairs, 2011).

production of many fuels, it has also sought to secure energy supplies abroad and take steps domestically to improve its energy supply security.

Introduction of an Inclusive Concept of Energy Security

Need for a Broader Definition of Energy Security

Although improving energy-supply security, or addressing energy-supply insecurity, has been a traditional focus of energy policy, today the variety of challenges related to energy provision and use argue for a much broader consideration of what energy security really means. The challenges facing national and regional energy policy in today's interconnected world, and in the increasingly interconnected Northeast Asia region, include such multi-faceted problems as mitigating and adapting to global climate change; addressing the security threat of North Korean nuclear weapons, with its strong ties to energy, economic, and social issues; and adjusting to the increasing role of civil society in energy sector decisions. All these challenges go beyond what can be handled by a narrow energy-supply/ energy-cost perspective.

The energy sector is not the only source of the anthropogenic greenhouse gas emissions that are causing the earth's climate to change, based on the conclusions of the Intergovernmental Panel on Climate Change[24] and the vast majority of scientists working on the topic. The energy sector is, however, the largest contributor to global climate change, particularly in Northeast Asia, where emissions from coal combustion dominate. The reduction of greenhouse gas emissions — that is, mitigation of climate change by reducing the emissions that drive it — is already a major element of the stated policies of most of the countries of Northeast Asia. Given the strong connection between greenhouse gas emissions and the energy sector, climate change considerations play an increasing role in energy policy and thus need to be considered a part of the energy security calculus. Furthermore, as some degree of climate change is inevitable (indeed, has already occurred), no matter what steps to mitigate the problem are undertaken, some degree of adaptation to climate change will be required. A number of certain or likely adaptation strategies are directly or indirectly related to the energy sector. A far-from-exhaustive list of examples here

---

24   Pachauri, R. and Reisinger, A., *Climate Change 2007: Synthesis Report. Contribution of Working Groups I, II and III to the Fourth Assessment Report of the Intergovernmental Panel on Climate* (Geneva: Intergovernmental Panel on Climate Change, 2007).

would include the reinforcement of seawalls and other structures against rising seas and storm surges to protect coastal power plants and port facilities used for fuel imports and exports, the reinforcement of electricity transmission and distribution networks against the impacts of severe storms, and the provision of additional peak power-supply capabilities to meet the needs for summer air conditioning as average temperatures rise. Thus, climate change adaptation also needs to be considered when evaluating the energy security impacts of different policies.

Although climate change affects and involves all nations, the countries of Northeast Asia are the most affected, or potentially affected, by the DPRK nuclear weapons dilemma. The problem of how to secure the DPRK's nuclear weapons, nuclear materials, and nuclear know-how is arguably not a direct energy issue, but it is intimately linked to the energy insecurity (the lack of energy security) in North Korea. The DPRK began using its nuclear program — which was at first, ostensibly, geared toward creating a civilian nuclear power program — as a threat and a bargaining chip after 1990 when the dissolution of the Soviet Union deprived the DPRK of a considerable fraction of outside support for its energy sector. Since then, several international negotiations with the DPRK have focused on members of the international community providing different types of energy aid to the DPRK, including most prominently the "Agreed Framework" of 1994 and the "Six-Party Talks" in the mid-2000s.[25] Energy aid was to be provided in exchange for steps toward winding down the North Korean nuclear weapons program and securing the DPRK's nuclear materials. As the lack of sufficient energy supplies plays a role in preventing the DPRK from redeveloping its economy and providing its population with adequate food, heat, and other services, the energy security/insecurity of the DPRK is tightly connected with economic, security, social, humanitarian, and political issues. These issues not only affect the DPRK but spill over to its neighbors, with impacts on border security, refugee concerns, and, for the ROK, military security (witness the sinking of the ROK naval ship *Cheonan* and the shelling of the island Yeonpyeong in 2010).[26] In addition, some regional policies that might help to improve regional energy security, such as infrastructure to share the vast energy resources of the Russian Far East with China, the ROK, and Japan, are in part at the geographical mercy of the DPRK, which lies on the route for pipelines and power lines between

---

25   Liang, X., *The Six-Party Talks at a Glance* (Washington, DC: Arms Control Association, 2012), http://www.armscontrol.org/factsheets/6partytalks

26   See, for example, McDonald, M., "Crisis Status' in South Korea after North Shells Island," *New York Times*, 23 November 2010, http://www.nytimes.com/2010/11/24/world/asia/24korea.html?pagewanted=all&_r=0

the Russian Far East and Seoul. For Northeast Asia, the North Korean nuclear weapons issue is inextricably linked with energy security issues.

Another pervasive trend in Northeast Asia and in other regions has been the increased voice of civil society in key policy decisions. This voice, which differs in strength, to be sure, in different nations, affects and is affected by energy policy discussions and outcomes. In the ROK and Japan, for example, the concerns of local residents and their civic representatives, as well as local and national non-governmental organizations, are significant factors in deciding where nuclear energy facilities may and, more significantly, may not be sited. The Fukushima incident, by raising the profile of the potential impacts of nuclear energy on local communities, seems to be further increasing the response of civil society on the nuclear power issue. Similarly, civic groups of various kinds have had an increasing role in affecting decisions on other types of major energy infrastructure, as well as on overall energy and environmental policy. As a consequence, the impact of civil society on policies affecting the energy sector, and vice versa, needs to be a considered part of any comprehensive concept of energy security.

Elements of the Concept of Broader Energy Security

National energy policies in the new century face challenges on multiple fronts.[27] The substance of these challenges needs to be incorporated into a new concept of energy security and used when evaluating policies designed to improve energy security/address energy insecurity. Energy security policies in various countries are now showing trends of convergence rather than divergence, in part due to the increasing speed with which news and ideas are shared among peoples in our increasingly complex and interconnected world. This convergence does not eliminate regional and national differences. Yet it is an encouraging sign that may minimize the potential conflict stemming from differences in energy security concepts as reflected in the energy security policies adopted by different countries.

The following is a quick review of the major challenges that need to be included in an energy security concept sufficiently comprehensive as to

---

27 Some of the materials provided below have been adapted from previous publications by the authors, including von Hippel, D., *et al.*, "Energy Security (East Asia)," in *Berkshire Encyclopedia of Sustainability: China, India, and East and Southeast Asia: Assessing Sustainability* (Great Barrington: Berkshire Publishing Group, 2012). Suzuki, T., *et al.*, *A Framework for Energy Security Analysis and Application to a Case Study of Japan*, Synthesis Report for the Pacific Asia Regional Energy Security (PARES) Project, Phase 1 (Berkeley: Nautilus Institute, 1998).

be broadly applicable to the complex impacts of energy-sector and related policies.

Economic

Though the economic impacts of policies addressing energy security have typically been a part of the standard energy security calculus, at least in a limited way through considerations such as stockpiling fuel supplies to avoid or reduce shocks to the economy arising from sudden increases in the costs of imported energy, a more comprehensive approach to energy security requires looking beyond the impacts of price shocks. A nation's choice to pursue different energy strategies may have a significant effect on the future of its economy. For example, a decision to aggressively pursue energy efficiency or renewable energy may have a significantly positive influence on the domestic development of those industries. Similarly, a conscious decision to move away from a coal-powered economy will cause economic dislocation for workers in the coal mining industry. The complex and dynamic nature of economies often makes it difficult to determine with any certainty the economic impacts of a policy designed to improve energy security, but consideration of the impacts of energy policies on key economic sectors, including both the direct and interactive effects of the policies, is a necessary part of a comprehensive energy security analysis.

Environment

Perhaps the most serious challenge to traditional (supply-security-oriented) energy policy thinking is the need to protect the environment. If environmental problems are to be solved, energy policies will have to be reformulated. International environmental problems present the greatest impetus for change. Two international environmental problems inherently linked with energy consumption, particularly fossil fuel consumption, are acid rain and global climate change.[28] Trans-boundary air pollution (acid rain) has been an international issue in Europe and North America and is a developing issue in East Asia. It even has trans-Pacific elements.[29]

---

28   Asuka, J., *A Brief Memo on Environmental Security Regimes in the Asian Region*, PARES project (Berkeley: Nautilus Institute, 1997). Yamaji, K., *Long-Term Techno-Management for Mitigating Global Warming*, PARES project (Berkeley: Nautilus Institute, 1997).
29   Wilkening, K.E., *et al.*, "Trans-Pacific Air Pollution," *Science*, 290(5489) (2000), doi: http://dx.doi.org/10.1126/science.290.5489.65

As noted above, global climate change poses an even broader and more complex challenge to energy policy than trans-boundary air pollution. Although there are relatively straightforward technical solutions to reduce the emissions of acid rain precursors — including flue-gas desulfurization devices — greenhouse gas emissions cannot be so easily abated by "end-of-pipe" methods.[30] A comprehensive approach toward greenhouse gas emissions is necessary. The climate change issue also brings in a much longer time perspective than businesses and governments are used to dealing with, in terms of planning both for climate change mitigation and, increasingly, for adaptation to the inevitable (or likely) impacts of ongoing changes in climate. Other environmental issues, such as radioactive waste management, require long-term perspectives. In sum, environmental issues must be incorporated into the energy security concept.[31]

Technology

Risks associated with the development and deployment of advanced technologies challenge current energy policy assessments. Conventional thinking understates such risks and tends to see them as short-term rather than long-term. Risks include nuclear accidents such as those at Three Mile Island in the United States (1979), Chernobyl in the former Soviet Union (1986), and, of course, Fukushima in Japan (2011); natural disasters with impacts on energy infrastructure such as Hurricane Katrina's impacts on oil and gas production in the Gulf of Mexico, the impact of the July, 2007 earthquake near Niigata, Japan on the seven-unit Kashiwazaki-Kariwa nuclear plant; and the combination of nuclear technology and natural disaster risks that have surged into the world's general consciousness with the Fukushima disaster. Other examples of manifestations of technological risk include the failure of research and development efforts to perform as expected (such as the synthetic fuel, fast-breeder reactor, and solar thermal programs in the United States during the 1970s and 1980s).

Technological risks can be transnational. The accident at Chernobyl is a good example of an incident with decidedly cross-boundary direct

---

30 Research on carbon capture and storage (CCS), a means of capturing carbon dioxide from fossil fuel combustion for permanent disposal, continues, and some results have been promising, but costs, and in some cases, efficiency penalties associated with CCS are projected to be significant, and concerns remain regarding the reliability of permanent disposal options for the captured carbon.

31 Khatib, H., *et al.*, "Energy Security," in *World Energy Assessment*, ed. by United Nations Development Programme (New York: United Nations Development Programme, 2000).

implications, and the Fukushima incident, though its radiological impacts on other nations is unclear, has had a reverberating impact on the public's opinion of the nuclear industry worldwide.[32] Also, markets for advanced technologies are becoming global. As a result, technological risks can be exported. Nuclear technology, for example, is being exported to a number of developing countries, most notably China and India, but also Vietnam and potentially Indonesia, Thailand, Pakistan, and Malaysia,[33] in addition to Middle Eastern nations such as the United Arab Emirates.[34] As the world rapidly moves toward a technology-intensive energy society, a new energy security concept must address the various domestic and international risks associated with advanced technologies.

Demand-side management

Another challenge to energy policy thinking is the need to address energy demand. Conventional energy policy seeks to assure supply while assuming that demand is given. This notion has been changing since the mid-1980s, when the concept of demand-side management (DSM) was first incorporated into energy planning. Now, management of energy demand is almost on an equal footing with management of supply — new technologies such as distributed generation and "smart grids" blur the distinction between demand and supply — and it is recognized as a key tool in the achievement of climate change mitigation and other environmental goals. DSM does not, however, eliminate uncertainties that are inherent in energy policy planning. Unexpected demand surges and drops occur depending on, for instance, changes in weather patterns and economic conditions.

There are risks associated with energy demand just as with supply. Conventional energy policy thinking has tended to underestimate demand-side risks. Risks stem from, for example, demand surges (periods of peak demand in response to extreme conditions resulting from global climate change). These are a serious concern for utility management, but

---

32　See, for example, Kurokawa, K., *et al.*, *The Official Report of the Fukushima Nuclear Accident Independent Investigation Commission: Executive Summary* (Tokyo: The National Diet of Japan, 2012).

33　IAEA Staff Reporter, "Asia Leads Way in Nuclear Power Development," *International Atomic Energy Agency*, 30 October 2007, http://www.iaea.org/newscenter/news/2007/asialeads.html

34　World Nuclear Association, "Nuclear Power in the United Arab Emirates," February 2010, http://www.world-nuclear.org/info/Country-Profiles/Countries-T-Z/United-Arab-Emirates/

managing peak demand is not easy, particularly given uncertainties in consumer behavior. Long recessions are another major concern for energy industry managers, since recession means large supply-capacity surpluses. Uncertainty (risk) on the demand side of the total energy picture is therefore a key component of a new concept of energy security.

Social-cultural factors

Not In My Backyard (NIMBY) and environmental justice concerns are becoming global phenomena, making it increasingly difficult, time-consuming, and costly to site "nuisance facilities" such as large power plants, waste treatment and disposal facilities, oil refineries, or liquefied natural gas terminals. Although the public recognizes the need for such facilities, many communities prefer not to have the plants in their neighborhood. Opposition to plant siting has elevated the importance of local politics in energy policy planning. Who has the right to decide where to locate the facilities? Who has the right to refuse? Can any rational policymaking process satisfy all stakeholders? These questions pose not only a challenge to energy security policy, but also to democratic institutions themselves. NIMBY epitomizes the social and cultural risks that need to be recognized in policymaking agendas and which present a challenge to current energy policy thinking. As noted above, the increasing role of civil society in energy sector decisions is a part of this challenge.

There are "enviro-economic" concerns as well. It is often the case that the party who bears the risk should get economic compensation. But how much compensation is reasonable, and who should be qualified to receive such compensation? These issues are often difficult to decide.

Public confidence represents another social factor influencing energy policy. Once lost, public confidence becomes hard to recover. "Public confidence" should be distinguished from "public acceptance," which is commonly used in traditional energy policy thinking. Promoting public acceptance is often the object of public relations campaigns. Promoting public confidence involves more than public relations. Examples of efforts to increase public confidence in energy decisions include, for example, efforts by the U.S. Department of Energy (DOE) to increase information disclosure and by the Japanese government to make the nuclear policymaking process more transparent through holding roundtable discussions. Accounting for social-cultural factors and increasing public confidence in energy choices are therefore central components of a new concept of energy security.

International relations and military risks

New dimensions in international relations and military risks challenge traditional energy policy-making. The end of the Cold War brought in its wake a new level of uncertainty in international politics. Although the risk of a world war is drastically reduced, the threat of regional clashes has increased, as ongoing conflicts in the Middle East, the Balkans, North Africa, and the former Soviet states of the Caucasus demonstrate. The international politics of plutonium fuel-cycle development, with its associated risks of nuclear terrorism and proliferation, remains an area where energy security and military security issues meet, with the North Korean nuclear dilemma, as noted above, a special case of this set of problems. The brave new world of post-Cold War international relations must be accounted for in a new concept of energy security.

A Comprehensive Definition of Energy Security

The above key components — environment, economics, technology, demand-side management, social and cultural factors, and post-Cold War international relations — are central additions to the traditional supply-side point of view in the following comprehensive energy security concept.

> A nation-state is energy secure to the degree that fuel and energy services are available to ensure (a) survival of the nation, (b) protection of national welfare, and (c) minimization of risks associated with supply and use of fuel and energy services. The six dimensions of energy security include energy-supply, economic, technological, environmental, social and cultural, and military/security dimensions. Energy policies must address the domestic and international (regional and global) implications of each of these dimensions.[35]

What distinguishes this energy security definition is its emphasis on the imperative to consider extra-territorial implications of the provision of energy and energy services while also recognizing the complexity of implementing national energy security policies and measuring national energy security. This emphasis is particularly apt in a region like Northeast Asia, where the energy security and other policies of neighboring nations significantly interact. The definition is also designed to include emerging concepts of environmental security, which include the effects of the state of

---

35   von Hippel, D., *et al.* (2010).

the environment on human security and military security and the effects of security institutions on the environment and on prospects for international environmental cooperation.[36]

Methods for Evaluating the Broader Energy Security Impacts of Different Energy Paths or Scenarios

Given the broader definition of energy security provided above, the application of a suite of analytical tools and methods, and a framework within which to apply them, are called for in order to systematically compare the various attributes of different energy security policies or policy scenarios.

Such a framework should help to identify the relative costs and benefits of different "energy futures" — essentially, future scenarios driven by suites of energy and other social policies. Below we describe some of the policy issues associated with the dimensions of energy policy presented earlier and offer a broadly defined framework for evaluating energy security.

A Conceptual Framework for Energy Policy

We provide a listing of each dimension of energy security as defined below in Table 3.4, along with a sampling of the policy issues associated with which each dimension of energy security. The two right-hand columns of Table 3.4 provide examples, many drawn from the energy security approaches described above, that might be used to address the types of both "routine" and "radical" risk and uncertainty faced in the planning, construction, and operation of energy systems. While Table 3.4 provides a broad, though by no means complete, list of policy issues, the categories shown are not necessarily independent. Certain energy technologies will be influenced by climate change (hydroelectric power and inland nuclear power plants, for example, may be affected by changes in water availability) and/or by requirements for climate change adaptation. And there are many other examples of interdependence that need full consideration of the energy security impacts of candidate energy policies.

---

36 Matthew, R.A., *Environmental Security: Demystifying the Concept, Clarifying the Stakes*, Environmental Change and Security Program Report (Washington, DC: Environmental Change and Security Program, Wilson Centre, 1995).

Table 3.4: Energy Security Conceptual Framework

Dimension/ Criterion of Risk and Uncertainty Associated with Energy Security	Energy Security Policy Issues	Energy Security Strategies/Measures	
		Reduction and Management of Routine Risk	Identification and Management of Radical Uncertainty
1. Energy Supply	□ Domestic/Imported □ Absolute scarcity □ Technology/Fuel Intensive? □ Incremental, market-friendly, fast, cheap, sustainable?	□ Substitute technology for energy □ Efficiency first	□ Technological breakthroughs □ Exploration and new reserves
2. Economic	□ Cost-benefit analysis □ Risk-benefit analysis □ Social opportunity cost of supply disruption □ Local manufacturing of equipment □ Labor □ Financing aspects □ No regrets	□ Compare costs/ benefits of insurance strategies to reduce loss-of-supply disruption □ Investment to create supplier-consumer inter-dependence □ Insurance by fuel (U, oil, gas, coal) stockpiling, global (IEA) or regional quotas (energy charters)	□ Export energy intensive industries □ Focus on information intensive industries □ Export energy or energy technology
3. Technological	• R&D Failure • Technological monoculture vs. Diversification • New materials dependency in technological substitution strategies	• Invest in renewables • Mixed Oxide Fuels recycling • Plutonium /Fast Breeder Reactors • Uranium from seawater • Spent fuel management issues	• Ultimate Nuclear Waste Storage
4. Environmental	• Local externalities • Regional externalities both atmospheric and maritime • Global externalities • Requirements for adaptation to climate change □ Precautionary Principle	• Risk-benefit analysis and local pollution control • Treaties • Mitigation planning • Adaptation planning □ Technology transfer	□ Thresholds and radical shifts of state such as sea level rise and polar ice melt rate

Table 3.4, cont.

5. Social-Cultural	• Consensus/conflict in domestic or foreign policy making coalitions • Institutional capacities • Siting and downwind distributional impacts • Populist revulsion or rejection of technocratic strategies • Perceptions and historical lessons • Role of civil society in energy decisions	• Transparency • Participation • Accountability • Side payments and compensation • Education • Training • Engagement with civil society organizations	
6. Military-Security	• International management of Plutonium • Proliferation potential • Terrorism and energy facilities • Sea lanes and energy shipping • Geopolitics of oil/gas supplies • North Korean nuclear weapons issues	• Non-proliferation Treaty/Safeguards regimes • Security alliances • Naval power projection • Transparency and confidence building • DPRK Energy assistance and denuclearization agreements	• Disposition and disposal of excess nuclear warhead fissile materials • Military options for resolving energy-related conflicts, securing infrastructure

Source. Modified from David von Hippel, Tatsujiro Suzuki, James H. Williams, Timothy Savage, and Peter Hayes, "Energy Security and Sustainability in Northeast Asia," *Energy Policy*, 39 (2011), pp. 6719-30, http://dx.doi.org/10.1016/j.enpol.2009.07.001

Testing the Energy Security Impacts of Different Energy Scenarios

Given the broad definition of energy security provided above, how should a framework be organized for evaluating the energy security impacts of different policy approaches? Some of the challenges in setting up such a framework include deciding on a manageable but useful level of detail, incorporation of uncertainty, risk considerations, comparison of tangible and intangible costs/benefits, comparison of impacts across different spatial levels and time-scales, and balancing analytical comprehensiveness and transparency. To meet these challenges, we devised a framework based on a variety of tools, including the elaboration and evaluation of alternative energy/environmental "paths" or "scenarios" for a nation and/or region (for example, with the Long-range Energy Alternatives Planning System (LEAP)[37] software tool used in the Asian Energy Security Project), diversity indices, and multiple-attribute (trade-off) analyses, as described below. Central to the application of the framework is the search for "robust" solutions — a set of policies that meet multiple energy security and other objectives at the same time.

The framework for the analysis of energy security includes the following steps:

1. Define the objective and subjective measures of energy (and environmental) security for evaluation. Within the overall categories presented in Table 3.5, these measures could vary significantly between different analyses.

2. Collect data and develop candidate energy paths/scenarios that yield roughly consistent energy services, but use sufficiently different assumptions to illuminate the explored policy approaches.

3. Test the relative performance of paths/scenarios for each energy security measure included in the analysis.

4. Incorporate elements of risk.

5. Compare path and scenario results.

6. Eliminate paths that lead to clearly suboptimal or unacceptable results, and iterate the analysis as necessary to reach clear conclusions.

---

37   *LEAP: Long-Range Energy Alternatives Planning System* (United States: Stockholm Environment Institute), http://www.energycommunity.org/#sthash.g5LLFKXm.dpbs

Some of the possible dimensions of energy security, and potential measures and attributes of those dimensions, are summarized below in Table 3.5. The right-hand column includes a listing of possible interpretations — that is, a listing of the direction in which a given measure would typically indicate greater energy security. It should be noted that many of these dimensions and measures can and do interact — and that a solution to one problem may exacerbate another. Formal or informal application of analytical methods such as "systems thinking" can assist the execution of steps 4 and 5, above. These methods allow the interaction of the different elements of complex processes to be seen more clearly than if pairs of systems interactions are viewed independently.[38]

There is often a temptation in step 5 of the energy security analysis procedure to place the attributes of energy security into a common metric: for example, an index of relative energy security calculated through a ranking and weighting system. We recommend avoiding this temptation. Such systems almost invariably involve procedures that amplify small differences between paths/scenarios, play down large differences, and give an illusion of objectivity to weighting choices that are by their nature quite subjective. Instead, as described below, we recommend laying out the energy security attributes of each path/scenario side by side in a matrix, or table, allowing reviewers, stakeholders, and decision makers to see the differences and similarities between different energy futures for themselves, and to apply their own perspectives and knowledge, in consultation with each other, to determine what is most important in making energy policy choices. Also, not explicitly included in steps 5 or 6 are mathematical tools for optimizing energy security results over a set of paths or scenarios. Optimization can be attractive as it appears to identify one "best" path for moving forward. Optimization models can in some cases offer useful insights, provided the underlying assumptions and algorithms in the analysis are well-understood by the users of the results. Like weighting and ranking, however, optimization involves subjective choices made to appear to be objective, especially when applied across a range of different energy security attributes, and as such it should be employed only with caution and with a thorough understanding of its limitations in a given application.

---

38   See, for example, Aronson, D., *Overview of Systems Thinking* (1998), http://www.thinking.net/Systems_Thinking/OverviewSTarticle.pdf

Table 3.5: Dimensions and Measures/Attributes of Energy Security

Dimension of Energy Security	Measures/Attributes	Interpretation
Energy Supply	Total Primary Energy	Higher = indicator of other impacts
	Fraction of Primary Energy as Imports	Lower = preferred
	Diversification Index (by fuel type, primary energy)	Lower index value (indicating greater diversity) preferred based on index formula as derived by Neff (1998)
	Diversification Index (by supplier, key fuel types)	Lower index value preferred (see above)
	Stocks as a fraction of imports (key fuels)	Higher = greater resilience to supply interruption
Economic	Total Energy System Internal Costs	Lower = preferred
	Total Fuel Costs	Lower = preferred
	Import Fuel Costs	Lower = preferred
	Economic Impact of Fuel Price Increase (as fraction of GNP)	Lower = preferred
Technological	Diversification Indices for key industries (such as power generation) by technology type	Lower = preferred
	Diversity of R&D Spending	Qualitative—higher preferred
	Reliance on Proven Technologies	Qualitative—higher preferred
	Technological Adaptability	Qualitative—higher preferred
Environmental	GHG emissions (tonnes CO_2, CH_4)	Lower = preferred
	Acid gas emissions (tonnes SOx, NOx)	Lower = preferred
	Local Air Pollutants (tonnes particulates, hydrocarbons, others)	Lower = preferred
	Other air and water pollutants (including marine oil pollution)	Lower = preferred
	Solid Wastes (tonnes bottom ash, fly ash, scrubber sludge)	Lower = preferred (or at worst neutral, with safe re-use)
	Nuclear waste (tonnes or Curies, by type)	Lower = preferred, but qualitative component for waste isolation scheme
	Ecosystem and Aesthetic Impacts	Largely Qualitative—lower preferred
	Exposure to Environmental Risk	Qualitative—lower preferred
Social and Cultural	Exposure to Risk of Social or Cultural Conflict over energy systems	Qualitative—lower preferred
Military/ Security	Exposure to Military/Security Risks	Qualitative—lower preferred
	Relative level of spending on energy-related security arrangements	Lower = preferred

Source: Modified from David von Hippel, *et al.*, "Energy Security and Sustainability in Northeast Asia," http://dx.doi.org/10.1016/j.enpol.2009.07.001

Other Tools and Methods for Energy Security Analysis

One set of analyses critical to the comprehensive evaluation of energy security, but not directly performed by LEAP[39] or similar tools, is the evaluation of the energy security impacts of risk for different energy paths. The incorporation of the elements of risk in energy security analysis can involve a more qualitative but systematic consideration of different potential futures in order to "arrive at policy decisions which remain valid under a large set of plausible scenarios";[40] sensitivity analysis — which studies variations in one or more plans (or paths) when key uncertain parameters are varied; probabilistic analysis — in which "probabilities are assigned to different values of uncertain variables, and outcomes are obtained through probabilistic simulations";[41] "stochastic optimization" — in which a probability distribution for each uncertain variable is assigned during an optimization exercise, incorporating uncertainty in the discount rate used in an economic analysis; and "search for a robust solution," which Hossein Razavi describes as using "the technique of trade-off analysis to eliminate uncertainties that do not matter and to concentrate on the ranges of uncertainty which are most relevant to corresponding objective attributes."[42]

Although any or all of these six techniques could be applied within the energy security analysis framework suggested here, probably the most broadly applicable and transparent of the techniques above are scenario analysis, sensitivity analysis, and "search for a robust solution." In the Pacific Asia Regional Energy Security (PARES) analysis of the energy security implications of two different medium-term energy paths for Japan, for example, we used a combination of paths analyses and sensitivity analyses to test the response of the different energy paths to extreme changes in key variables.

Diversification indices

In a paper prepared for the PARES project, Thomas Neff borrows from economics, financial analysis, and other disciplines to create a set of tools, based on diversity indices, which can help to provide a metric for the energy security implications of different energy supply strategies.[43]

39 *LEAP: Long-Range Energy Alternatives Planning System*
40 Razavi, H., *Economic, Security and Environmental Aspects of Energy Supply: A Conceptual Framework for Strategic Analysis of Fossil Fuels* (Berkeley: Nautilus Institute, 1997).
41 Ibid.
42 Ibid., p. 6.
43 Neff, T.L. (1997).

Neff starts with a simple diversification index, the Herfindahl index, written in mathematical terms as:

$$H = \sum_i x_i^2$$

where x_i is the fraction of total supply from source "i." This index can measure, for example, the diversity of the types of fuels used in an economy (where x_i would then be the fraction of primary energy or final demand by fuel type). Alternatively, within a single type of fuel (such as oil), the index can be applied to the pattern of imports of a particular country by supplier nation. The index has a maximum value of 1 (when there is only one supplier or fuel type) and goes down with increasing diversity of number of suppliers or fuel types, so that a lower value of the index indicates more diverse, and perhaps more robust, supply conditions.

Deliberation of risk in specific fuel import patterns can be worked into the index, Neff argues, through consideration of the variance in the behavior of each supplier and by application of correlation coefficients that describe how variance in the behavior of pairs of suppliers (for example, the oil exporters Saudi Arabia and Indonesia) are or might be related. The correlation might be positive for countries that tend to raise and lower their exports together, or negative as when supplier A increases production to compensate for decreased production by supplier B.

Neff also addresses the topic of market, or systematic, risk: that is, the risk associated with the whole market changing at once — whether the market is for stocks, oil, or uranium. Applying parameters that describe the degree to which individual suppliers are likely to change their output when the market as a whole shifts (the contribution of the variance of an individual supplier to overall market variance) allows the calculation of the variance of a given energy supply pattern. Hence, the calculation of such as "portfolio variance" provides a measure of the relative risk inherent in any given fuel supplier pattern versus any other.

Multiple attribute analysis and matrices

Deciding upon a single set of energy policies (or a few top options) from a wide range of choices is a complex process, necessarily incorporating both qualitative and quantitative aspects, and should be approached systematically for credible results. There are different methods with many gradations for deciding which set of policies or which energy path is the most desirable. These range from simply listing each attribute of each policy set or path in a large matrix and methodically eliminating candidate paths, noting why each is eliminated, to more quantitative approaches involving "multiple attribute analysis."

In one type of application of multiple attribute analysis, each criterion (attribute) used to evaluate energy policies or paths is assigned a numerical value. For objective criteria, the values of the attributes are used directly (present value costs are an example), while subjective criteria can be assigned a value based on a scale of 1 to 10. Once each attribute has a value, a weight is assigned. These weights should reflect a consensus as to which attributes are most important in planning. Multiplying the values of the attribute by the weights assigned, and then summing up the attributes, yields "scores" for each individual policy set or path that can be compared. Although this process may seem like an attractive way to organize and make more objective a complicated decision/evaluation process, great care must be taken to apply the analysis so that (1) all subjective decisions — for example, the decisions that go into defining the system of weights used — are carefully and fully documented, and (2) the system avoids magnifying small differences (or minimizing large differences) between policy or path alternatives.

Whatever tool or technique is used to decide between policy sets or paths, it is ultimately the policymakers and their constituencies who will decide which policies are to be implemented or which energy path is worth pursuing. As a consequence, one of the most important rules of applying multiple attribute analysis is to present the analytical process in a transparent manner so that others can review the assumptions and decisions made along the way.

The most straightforward approach to comparing paths is to simply line up the attribute values for each path side by side and review the differences, focusing on those that are truly significant. For example, if the difference in the net present value (NPV) cost of plan A is one billion dollars greater than that of plan B, this disparity may seem at first glance like a lot of money, but it must be examined relative to the overall cost of the energy system or to the cost of the economy as a whole. To an energy system that accrues, say, one trillion (10^{12}) dollars in capital, operating and maintenance, and fuel costs over twenty years, a difference between plans of one billion (10^9) dollars is not only trivial, it is dwarfed by uncertainties in even the most certain elements of the analysis. The key, then, is to search for differences in the plans' attributes by including truly meaningful qualitative and quantitative values.

One straightforward way to visualize the similarities and differences between paths, both quantitative and qualitative, is the use of a comparison matrix or matrices. These tables show the different attributes and measures of each path (cost, environmental emissions, military security, and others) as rows, while the results for each scenario/path form a column in the table.[44] In theory, the matrix format allows for the comparison of a large number of different attributes for a large number of different paths. In practice, the more that the attributes can be reduced to a significant few, and the more that the paths can be reduced to those showing clear differences relative to each other, the more the comparison matrix will be useful and easy to comprehend. The matrix format is also compatible with the use of other tools and methods for evaluating aspects of energy security, including, but by no means limited to, the sampling of tools and methods presented above.

One advantage of the matrix method of paths comparison is that it allows input on both quantitative and qualitative attributes and measures of energy security. In some cases, comparing attributes quantitatively across paths is theoretically possible (for example, employment impacts or spending on security arrangements), but it is not feasible from a practical perspective, at least for the study at hand. In other cases, quantitative measures may simply not exist (as in the case of exposure to social and cultural risk). In these types of cases, the only option for measuring the relative attributes of different paths may be qualitative analysis. There is no one correct way to accomplish a qualitative analysis, but such an analysis should address the issue from different points of view (for example, cultural impacts on different segments of society), clearly define operating assumptions, and show a thinking-through of the relationship between cause (differences between energy paths) and effect (differences in attribute outcome).

---

44   An example of a comparison of two energy paths for Japan (done for the PARES project in the late 1990s) laid out in a "matrix" format is available in von Hippel, D., *et al.* (2010). In this comparison, a "BAU" path roughly echoed Japanese government plans at the time, while the "Alternative" path featured an emphasis on aggressive application of energy efficiency and renewable energy in end-use demand and electricity (and heat) supply. For readers interested in more detailed descriptions of updated versions of these paths for Japan, see Nakata, M., *et al.*, *Carbon Dioxide Emissions Reduction Potential in Japan's Power Sector — Estimating Carbon Emissions Avoided by a Fuel-Switch Scenario* (World Wildlife Fund Japan, 2003). Takase, K. and Suzuki, T., "The Japanese Energy Sector: Current Situation, and Future Paths," *Energy Policy*, 39(11) (2011), doi: http://dx.doi.org/10.1016/j.enpol.2010.01.036

Qualitative analysis is by definition subjective, but it is a necessary part of the overall analysis of different energy paths, which otherwise runs the risk of confusing the attributes that are *countable* with the issues that *count*.

Energy Security and Urban Security Issues

Definition of Urban Security

Like energy security, urban security and its converse, urban insecurity, consist of a complex combination of many overlapping and interlinked factors. All of the factors that help to define human security in general —including access to adequate food, clean water, shelter, health care, transportation and other energy services, employment, meaningful and pleasant human interaction, educational opportunities, and reasonable safety from the risks of natural and man-made disasters, crime, oppression by others, and other stresses — are magnified in urban environments by the simple concentration of people. As Sanghun Lee notes, two-thirds of the world's population live in cities, and cities produce three-quarters of the world's greenhouse gas emissions. [45] At the same time, half of the world's urban residents live in substandard housing (or worse). Poverty exacerbates urban insecurity.

Not all urban security problems relate directly to energy security/insecurity, but many do, either directly or indirectly. When urban security and energy security problems interact, many urban security issues tend to exhibit a concentrated microcosm of energy security issues that affect nations as a whole, while other issues are almost unique to urban areas. Special urban insecurity challenges include urban poverty, the fragility of aging infrastructure, water supply problems, and the interaction of a variety of issues with climate change vulnerabilities such as sea level rise or extreme weather events.

Overlaps Between Urban Security/Insecurity and Energy Security

Below we outline key areas where urban security considerations overlap with energy security considerations and vice versa. We note the key

---

45   Lee, S., "Latent Layers beneath the Relationship between Urban Insecurity and Climate Change: Case of South Korea" in *Interconnection Among Global Problems in Northeast Asia* (Paju: Nautilus Institute, 2009).

pressure points that can be affected by policies in areas of overlap. The list is by no means exhaustive. Our purpose here is to identify some of these key overlaps as a prelude to describing how the energy security analysis methods summarized earlier in this chapter might be applied to related urban security issues as well.

Energy security-related policy choices, whether made by public entities or effectively left to private markets/decision makers, have special impacts on cities because cities are the planet's major consumers of energy services; they consume these services in a concentrated manner that requires focused energy supplies. Viewed another way, choices made to increase or reduce urban security by adjusting the way that cities are organized and provide goods, services, and employment for their residents often have ramifications for the energy sector, and thus for energy security. There are a number of examples of choices for energy and urban policy-making in which urban security and energy security intersect and interact. To illustrate some of these connections, we focus on two policy areas with coupled energy and urban security aspects — electricity supply and demand and transportation system policies — then explore them with respect to five indicative areas of energy security/urban security interactions: implications for climate change and local/regional pollution, distribution and implications of risk of accidents or attacks at critical facilities, implications of energy choices for economic development, implications of new modes for urban organization, and implications of the growing role of civil society in cities.

Electricity Supply and Demand

Choices related to the provision of electricity services, whether at the national or urban level, can have a profound effect on urban security. These choices include the positioning of power generation and electricity transmission facilities, the sufficiency of electricity supplies, the fuels/energy sources used to power generation, the degree to which energy efficiency is emphasized, and the degree to which distributed generation is undertaken. These choices offer many energy and urban security tradeoffs.

Situating power plants inside cities, depending on the generation of fuel and the technology used, may subject lower-income and other populations to local air pollution and related health issues. At one time, the siting of power plants inside cities was fairly typical in many nations, with the practice most recently demonstrated in the Northeast Asian context by parts of China and the DPRK. Power plants were co-located with cities for labor reasons as well as for easy access to heat for buildings and industrial facilities. Siting power plants outside cities may (or may not, depending on power plant design, location, and the prevailing atmospheric conditions) reduce local air pollution concerns; however, it requires an extensive transmission infrastructure to bring power into a city. This approach may have its own health and safety outcomes. The choice of power generation technologies and fuels can have a profound impact on emissions of local and regional air pollutants, as well as on greenhouse gases. Relative to coal-fired power, natural gas-fired power plants can emit half the greenhouse gas emissions per unit of electricity provided, reduce sulfur oxide and particulate emissions, and eliminate production (and required disposal) of coal ash, but they generally produce power at a higher cost. Nuclear power and renewable energy produce few or zero air pollutant emissions, but involve varying tradeoffs relative to fossil-fueled plants, as noted below.

Choices related to the spatial organization and type of power supply imply different risks for cities. These risks may arise from accidents — through human error or natural disasters — but also include the possibility of attacks on key facilities. Major fossil fuel storage facilities, such as coal terminals and liquefied natural gas storage tanks, are often located at ports surrounded by cities. These waterfront facilities are potentially vulnerable to tidal surges during severe storms, which may occur with greater frequency as global climate change continues. They are also potentially vulnerable to attack, either by other nations (a potential DPRK attack on ROK fossil fuel facilities has to be a consideration for urban planners) or by subnational groups such as terrorists. The placement of these facilities within major population centers amplifies the implications of a successful attack both for human life and the economy. Similarly, and underscored by the Fukushima reactor disaster, the placement of nuclear power and nuclear fuel cycle facilities within cities means that successful attacks on those facilities could expose large populations to radiation risks. The impact of locating nuclear facilities within cities on facility security is less clear. Placing facilities in cities may mean that more "eyes" are on the facility at any given time, but, on the other hand, with many more people moving around the facility's area due to its location, an attacker may have more of an opportunity to blend in with the crowd. In the case of nuclear facilities, there are at least two reasons why even locating them outside cities does not necessarily reduce risk to nearby populations. First, a radiation plume from a severe accident will go where the wind takes it, and though location of nuclear facilities in a generally downwind direction from population centers may help to reduce the risk of exposure to radioactive aerosols, it cannot eliminate it completely. Second, a nuclear facility located outside an urban area today may find itself part of a highly-populated suburb before its lifetime of 40 years or more is complete, as has happened many times in the United States. At that point, plans to evacuate local populations in the event of a nuclear emergency may become unusable due to the increase in traffic congestion.

Having sufficient and affordable supplies of power throughout the day and year is crucial to the economy of a city and to the well-being of its residents. Power outages can grind the local economy to a standstill and create opportunities for criminals to prey on homes and businesses while power is off-line. It can also affect the delivery of basic services such as food, water, sanitation, public lighting, and health care. Citizens and businesses in cities under-served by power supplies are forced, if they can afford it, to invest in on-site power supplies that are expensive, difficult to keep fueled, and which contribute to local pollution. Lagos, Nigeria was (as of 2011) an example of a city hamstrung by poor power supplies and other infrastructure issues despite its vibrant economy.[46] Apart from power interruptions, electricity that is unduly expensive can make an economy less competitive than it if its electricity supplies were cheaper. For example, high energy prices can affect whether certain industries decide to leave a city and can thus influence employment opportunities in urban areas.

A city's aggressive emphasis on improving energy efficiency can help to improve the reliability of electricity systems by contributing to local employment and reducing system loads, pollutant emissions, the amount of new supply infrastructure required, and "urban heat island" impacts (though decreasing the amount of heat the city generates). Likewise, a commitment to developing distributed generation, especially when powered by renewable energy, can improve the reliability of electricity supplies in a city and create local employment, among other benefits and depending on how it is implemented.

The degree to which urban areas around the world are developed in a planned and orderly fashion varies from intensive controls on urban growth to practically no controls on growth at all. Many cities have begun to embrace new modes of urban organization with careful land use planning for "livability." Clustered residential and commercial services with easy access to parks and other recreation reduce the need for transportation and

---

46   Abuja, *et al.*, "A Man and a Morass," *The Economist*, 26 May 2011, http://www.economist.com/node/18741606

lower traffic congestion. Clustered growth can also significantly impact the use of energy. For example, planned residential/commercial clusters can share distributed generation facilities, including renewable energy facilities, as well as heat and power systems to provide electricity, heating, and cooling to nearby buildings. In addition, planned developments may give designers more control over the energy performance of the buildings in the development, for example, by designing and arranging building units for optimal cooling by prevailing breezes in the summer, and for heat retention and passive solar heating in the winter.[47] Enhancing the "livability" of cities can, therefore, enhance both urban security and energy security.

The rising influence of civil society on energy sector choices, including those involving electricity generation facilities, is particularly strong in urban areas. The concentration of people both potentially affected by and with a strong interest in affecting energy sector decisions can catalyze further civil actions on topics ranging from the review of power plant siting and power supply choices, to the siting of transmission and distribution facilities, to decisions on land use and urban development, which, as noted above, can have their own impacts on energy use. One could argue that the increasing power of civil society to influence decisions that have in the past been made by public and private-sector actors with much less public input, coupled with some of the concerns above (pollution and risk reduction, urban development/redevelopment concerns), may favor the development of electricity sources that are often more limited in scale and in impact, including distributed generation, energy efficiency, and renewable energy sources. These choices will, in turn, affect both urban and energy security.

Transportation Policy Choices

Transportation policy choices in urban areas affect urban security and energy security. Cities that provide wide access to convenient, low-cost public transportation will likely require less energy input (with its attendant energy security benefits, including reduced fuel imports). They will also produce lower air pollution (with its attendant health and safety impacts), particularly if they limit the use of private vehicles, than cities that rely on private autos for most transport. Depending on how public transportation

---

47 See, for example, Chuanjiang, J. and Ruixue, Z., "Shandong's 'Solar Valley' Basks in Success," *China Daily*, 11 August 2010, http://www.chinadaily.com.cn/cndy/2010-08/11/content_11134110.htm

is implemented, such cities can also be made safer and more pleasant for residents by providing opportunities for more non-motorized transport.

Many of the transportation policy choices that a city makes have significant impact on local pollution emissions. Policy options, including developing subway, light rail, and bus rapid transit systems, can bring people into the urban core efficiently without requiring private vehicles. Some cities have restricted the use of private vehicles in the urban core, and others have implemented vehicle fleets (such as taxis) using cleaner-burning fuels, such as liquefied petroleum gas (LPG) or compressed natural gas (typically for larger vehicles such as buses). All of these measures are designed to enhance livability and improve efficiency for urban residents and workers, but they also reduce air pollutant emissions and related health impacts, thus providing additional urban and energy security benefits. To the extent that transport policies are effective in moving people or goods more efficiently and with lower energy intensity, a decrease in greenhouse gas emissions is also likely. Some fuel-switching measures for road vehicles (gasoline or diesel to LPG, CNG, or fossil-fueled electricity) can also reduce greenhouse gas emissions, but typically not as much as by shifting modes. Other transportation policies with potential impacts on both urban and energy security include the development of electric vehicle charging stations, possibly in combination with distributed generation (including renewable generation) and the introduction of "smart grid" concepts to use electric vehicle batteries as electricity storage devices for the distribution grid,[48] both of which can affect urban and energy security.

Some of the transportation policy choices that arguably enhance urban security from the points of view of livability and congestion/pollution reduction, however, may also reduce urban security by concentrating travelers in transport hubs (main subway or rail stations, for example) and thus increasing the potential damage and disruption from attacks or accidents at those hubs. Of course, other facilities associated with private-vehicle-oriented transport systems, including major intersections often beset by gridlock, fuel storage facilities, and key freeway interchanges or river bridges, may also be vulnerable to major disruptions due to terrorist attacks or accidents. Evaluating the net effect on urban and energy security of transportation policy tradeoffs requires an assessment of the vulnerability of multiple transport infrastructure development scenarios.

---

48   See, for example, Slack, G., "Electric Vehicles for Energy Storage to Stabilize Utility Grid," 11 April 2012, http://citris-uc.org/electric-vehicles-for-energy-storage-to-stabilize-utility-grid/

Transportation policy choices in cities, like urban electricity sector choices, will have implications for economic development. The map of new mass-transit facilities and, alternatively, the map of new road networks can and do guide the development of housing and commercial zones. Spatial choices strongly influence where workers can live while still being able to hold jobs in the urban core.

Beyond its economic impact, transportation planning is a key element of urban land use planning in general, and thus has a significant impact on the viability, for example, of the types of clustered residential and commercial developments described briefly above. Without access to mass transit facilities, clustered development would either have to depend on private vehicles to allow residents to get to their jobs, with attendant impacts on local parking and pollution, or be more or less self-contained in terms of employment for residents (with the exception of telecommuters).

Civil society in urban areas can and does impact on transportation policy. This influence can drive policies in different directions. Urban areas with clogged freeways may see a groundswell of public support either for transportation alternatives to freeways or for the construction of additional freeways, with very different impacts on urban and energy security. Civil society groups can help to identify development projects that appear to have given inadequate consideration to transportation needs, and thus force changes in plans to enhance urban security. The input of civil society groups favoring clustered development patterns can force city and private planners to take quality-of-life considerations seriously. The presence or absence of a vibrant civil society response to (or drive for) urban renewal has in many cases shaped, or failed to shape, the redevelopment of urban districts in neighborhoods. As such, the response of civil society to transportation policy issues helps to influence urban security and, in many cases, has implications for energy security as well.

Evaluating Urban Security Issues Within an Energy Security Calculus

The sampling of relationships between energy security and urban security policy choices in the issues described above underscores the complexity of these choices and the need to evaluate them using a framework that considers energy and urban security issues together. One approach is to identify how candidate policies with energy security impacts touch upon urban security and how urban security policies affect energy security. The next step would be to identify measures of those interactions/impacts and evaluate different policy scenarios (energy policies, urban policies, or a combination of the two) qualitatively and quantitatively as appropriate to the different measures. Then, one would provide a side-by-side comparison of the impacts of different scenarios in a way similar to that outlined above for the six categories of energy security attributes. Below we offer a sampling of how this approach might work.

Extension of Energy Security Analysis to Intersecting Urban Security Issues

In Table 3.6, we provide a brief adaptation of Table 3.5 that, for each of the dimensions of energy security, suggests a set of measures and attributes, and offers interpretations of those measures and attributes that could be relevant to the evaluation of the combined energy/urban security impacts of different policy choices. The measures and attributes in Table 3.6 could be considered in addition to or instead of the attributes in Table 3.5, depending on the scope and goal of the security analysis. Note that this is just a sampling of the possible measures and attributes that could be considered and is by no means an exhaustive list.

Table 3.6: Urban Security Measures/Attributes with Energy Security Implications

Dimension of Energy Security	Measures/Attributes	Interpretation
Energy Supply	Urban energy self-sufficiency/use of local resources	Higher = generally preferred
	Diversification Index for electricity (by electricity plant, plant type, or incoming transmission line)	Lower index value (indicating greater diversity) preferred
	Intensity of urban energy use (as measured by energy use per person or per unit GDP)	Lower = preferred
	Urban area stocks of key imported fuels as a fraction of imports (key fuels)	Higher = greater resilience to supply interruption
Economic	Total urban energy system internal costs	Lower = preferred
	Total urban energy system capital costs for required upgrades	Lower = preferred

Table 3.6, cont.

Economic	Impact of energy sector investments/ policy choices on local employment and income	Higher = preferred
Technological	Contribution of energy policies to development of local expertise in new technologies	Qualitative—Higher preferred
	Reliance on proven technologies	Qualitative—Higher preferred
	Technological adaptability (including in response to climate-change-driven events)	Qualitative—Higher preferred
Environmental	GHG emissions (tonnes CO_2, CH_4) caused by activities in the urban area (even if not emitted there)	Lower = preferred
	Urban area acid gas emissions (tonnes SOx, NOx)	Lower = preferred
	Impacts on or risks to local/urban water supplies	Lower = preferred
	Urban area local air pollutants (tonnes particulates, hydrocarbons, others)	Lower = preferred
	Local ecosystem, aesthetic, and "livability" impacts	Largely Qualitative—Lower preferred
	Exposure to environmental risk, including climate change-driven risk	Qualitative—Lower preferred
Social and Cultural	Exposure to risk of social or cultural conflict over development of energy or related systems in the urban area	Qualitative—Lower preferred
	Potential for civil society to help shape policies to yield improved urban security	Qualitative—Higher preferred
	Degree to which energy sector choices contribute to urban security (through improved employment, quality of life, poverty alleviation, access to key services, for example)	Qualitative—Higher preferred
Military/Security	Exposure to security risks related to attack on key energy or other urban infrastructure facilities	Qualitative—Lower preferred
	Relative level of urban spending on security arrangements	Lower = preferred

Source: Adapted from Table 5 by the authors for application to urban security issues.

Interaction of Energy Security and Urban Security Policies: Examples

As noted above, policies designed to improve urban security/reduce urban insecurity and policies designed to improve (typically national) energy security/reduce energy insecurity can interact in numerous ways. Below we provide two hypothetical examples of overlapping policies, and we explore their possible impacts with respect to some of the measures and attributes described in Table 3.6. We should emphasize that both of these scenarios are intended to be purely illustrative of the potential for complex policy interactions, and thus are not intended to represent policy recommendations. To facilitate the illustration, both scenarios are assumed to apply to a coastal urban area of 10 million people located somewhere in Northeast Asia. In both cases, the scenarios are evaluated relative to a "business as usual" baseline in which the urban area undertakes limited targeted development/redevelopment, continues to be dependent on a mix of private and public transport, continues to obtain virtually all of its energy, food, and other resources from outside the urban area, and relies principally on fossil fuels to provide energy services.

Urban Security Improvement Scenario

In the Urban Security Improvement (USI) scenario, policies focus on improving the quality of life in urban areas by promoting a combination of urban development and redevelopment that emphasizes clustered residential and commercial developments so that people may live in neighborhoods and districts with everyday services readily available nearby and significant open space provided in the form of parks, playgrounds, community gardens, and nature preserves. A comprehensive, effective, and affordable mass transit system is developed to move people between neighborhoods/districts to a compact urban core and to industrial and other areas where workplaces are located. Some or all of the neighborhood areas emphasize the availability of affordable housing for low-income residents. Throughout the urban area, there is a commitment to deploying local resources for food and energy and to using energy and other resources as efficiently as possible. The possible performance of the Urban Security Improvement scenario with respect to the energy/urban security dimensions and measures/attributes in Table 3.6 is discussed below.

- Energy Supply: Relative to the baseline scenario, the USI scenario offers higher urban energy self-sufficiency, likely higher diversity (a lower value of the diversity index) in terms of electricity supply sources, and a lower intensity of energy per person and (probably) per unit of GDP. The impact of the scenario on stocks of imported fuels is unclear, though the types of development patterns suggested by the USI scenario may suggest less emphasis on fuel storage.

- Economic: The USI scenario's total energy costs relative to a baseline scenario will depend largely on the capital costs of the distributed technologies, renewable and otherwise, and the prices of any fossil fuel use avoided. The total energy cost of the USI scenario could therefore be either higher or lower than the baseline scenario. It is likely that the capital cost of the USI scenario, which depends on more advanced and smaller-capacity technologies, would be higher overall than in a baseline case. Given the local energy/resources development emphasis of the USI scenario, as well as its emphasis on efficiency, recycling, and other labor-intensive activities (in addition to imported fuel use reduction), it seems likely that local employment and income generation will be stimulated more by the activities implied by the USI scenario.

- Technological: The USI case offers greater learning potential for the development and application of new technologies, but as a consequence relies less on proven technologies. The loss of the latter may be compensated for by increased adaptability through the use of distributed energy systems of different types, which are less likely to be simultaneously at risk from technological failure or from failure caused by catastrophic storms or floods, for example. They may also prove more flexible in adapting to a changing climate.

- Environmental: The USI case is likely to reduce net GHG emissions relative to the baseline case through a combination of greater efficiency in energy use, more aggressive use of renewable and low-carbon fuels, and some sequestration of carbon in biomass in urban open spaces. The USI case is likely to reduce emissions of some pollutants relative to the baseline case, such as sulfur oxides, but to the extent that distributed generation using gas or other fuels is a major feature of the case, it may increase local emissions of some pollutants. Impacts on water use and quality are likely to be positive in the USI case due to the availability of open space for groundwater recharge and water efficiency/recycling efforts. We expect local ecosystem, aesthetic, and "liveability" impacts to be positive and exposure to environmental risk lower overall than in the baseline case.

- Social and Cultural: With its emphasis on small projects and the preservation and creation of neighborhoods, as well as on collaboration between stakeholders in project design, the USI scenario probably offers less risk of social conflict and a greater role for civil society than the baseline scenario. By emphasizing the development of residential/commercial clusters, the USI scenario likely improves the local economy, resulting in reduced poverty, lower crime rates, and thus increased urban security.

- Military/Security: The USI scenario focuses in part on distributed generation and the use of local energy resources, which would tend to reduce the consequences of an attack on any one facility, and may or may not reduce the overall costs of securing critical facilities. With its emphasis on mass transport, however, the USI scenario probably offers targets for attack (busy train and subway stations, for example, or other transit hubs) that represent greater risk of damage and disruption than the more distributed transportation sector targets in a baseline scenario.

Energy Supply Security Improvement Scenario

A second illustrative alternative to the baseline scenario is one with many components that are similar to the overall energy policies pursued by a number of Northeast Asian nations, including Japan and the ROK, until at least the last decade or so. Here, the nation looks to develop nuclear power as an alternative to fossil-fueled electricity generation, and consequently builds up large stockpiles of fossil fuels, most notably crude oil and oil products, to reduce the potential disruption caused by constraints in imported fuel supplies or by rapid increases in world fuel prices. These nuclear and fuel storage facilities are assumed to be on the periphery of the urban area. Some of the possible implications of the Energy Supply Security Improvement (ESSI) scenario with regard to the measures/attributes in Table 3.6 are as follows:

- Energy Supply: Relative to the baseline scenario, the ESSI scenario offers higher urban energy self-sufficiency through expanded use of nuclear power. It may or may not yield higher diversity in terms of electricity supply sources. The ESSI scenario would be expected to have little or no impact on intensity of energy use. By definition, the scenario would increase stocks of imported fuels.

- Economic: The ESSI scenario's total energy costs relative to a baseline scenario will likely be higher due to the cost of nuclear power and its related infrastructure. The scenario's capital costs would also be higher. Although the ESSI may provide some short-term economic benefits relative to the baseline scenario, during the construction of nuclear and fuel storage facilities it seems likely that the lasting positive impact on local employment and income generation would be modest at best, since the negative economic impacts of likely higher prices for electricity offset the impacts of any additional long-term jobs arising from the nuclear and fuel storage facilities.

- Technological: The ESSI case implies little learning potential for the development and application of new technologies, assuming that the nuclear power plant is of a standard type previously built in the country where it will operate and that it relies on proven technologies. The large new facilities that are part of the ESSI case are more likely to be at risk from technological failure or from failure caused by catastrophic storms or floods (or earthquakes); they are also likely to prove more flexible in adapting to a changing climate.

- Environmental: The ESSI case is likely to reduce net GHG emissions relative to the baseline case through the use of nuclear power (displacing some fossil-fueled generation included in the baseline case). Depending on the type and location of the generation displaced, moreover, it is likely to reduce nearby emissions of local and regional air pollution. Impacts on water use and quality may be slightly negative in the ESSI case due to routine leakage from expanded oil storage and handling facilities, with the potential for catastrophic oil releases and subsequent impacts in the event of a major accident or natural disaster. Local ecosystem, aesthetic, and "liveability" impacts of the ESSI case would be expected to be related to whether the new nuclear and oil storage facilities are located on previously "virgin" lands (in which case the impacts are likely to be negative) or in existing industrial areas (in which case impacts are likely to be minor).

- Social and Cultural: Recent history suggests that many proposals for large, new energy facilities are at risk of social and cultural conflict, particularly proposals for nuclear facilities (in the post-Fukushima era). Civil society groups could be expected to oppose, or at least to demand thorough and critical examination of, proposals for the types of energy facilities included in the ESSI scenario. The scenario is likely to have minimal impacts on the local economy, poverty, crime rates, and other social and cultural urban security issues.

- Military/Security: The ESSI scenario, with its focus on large projects, would tend to increase the consequences of an attack on any one facility and would probably increase the overall costs of securing critical facilities.

The examples above offer brief illustrations of how to evaluate the complex interactions, across many different attributes, of the relative energy and urban security benefits of a given policy direction. Different criteria for comparison can be employed, and an infinite number of different scenarios can be considered. As in the energy security framework described earlier in this chapter, many of the results of the analysis will be difficult to compare quantitatively across attributes, so it will be up to the analyst, and the stakeholders supported by the analyst, to develop their own subjective weighting of the different attributes to reach a decision as to which scenario is most attractive. In general, the goal is to search for policies that are "robust" — that is, contribute positively — across a range of energy and urban security evaluation criteria.

Energy Security and Green Economics

Energy security, particularly as we have broadly defined it earlier in this chapter, has considerable overlap with "green economics." Green economy advocates and policy thinkers see the development of a green economy as a way of achieving multiple objectives related to improving energy (and, often, urban) security. In this section of the chapter, we review the concept of the "green economy." We then provide three case studies relating how policymakers and others in China, Japan, and the ROK have interpreted green economy concepts and how they have begun to implement policy.

"Green Economies" and Related Concepts: Origin and Drivers of Green Economy Movements

Recent years have seen many nations, as well as sub-national jurisdictions such as provinces, states, and cities, identifying the development of or shifting to a "green economy" as a key policy goal. The United Nations Environment Programme (UNEP) defines a "green economy" as follows: "A Green Economy is one that results in improved human well-being and social equity, while significantly reducing environmental and ecological scarcities. In its simplest expression, a green economy can be thought of as one which is low carbon, resource efficient, and socially inclusive."[49] This

---

49   See, for example, *About GEI: What Is the "Green Economy?"* (United Nations Environment Programme), http://www.unep.org/greeneconomy/AboutGEI/WhatisGEI/tabid/29784/Default.aspx UNEP has just made available a major report on the green economy

general and overarching definition leaves plenty of room for interpretation. Indeed, many authors and nations have interpreted the concept differently.

The concept of a green economy generally denotes a way of producing goods and services so as to make a reduced or, ideally, minimal impact on the environment while still building a robust and sustainable economy. Much-improved energy and resource use in the production and consumption of goods and services is a major part of the green economy. Examples of technologies and processes typically considered part of a green economy include the development and widespread deployment of "zero-net-energy" buildings,[50] an emphasis on the development of renewable energy sources, the shifting of production of locally-consumed items (including food) toward local suppliers to reduce transport costs (and support the local economy), waste management with reduced environmental impacts and the reduction of waste generation overall, and improvements in recycling of materials and in planning for reduced life-cycle impacts of the goods and services that people use.

Beyond these examples, the green economy also entails much-improved stewardship over the world's agricultural lands, fisheries, oceans, fresh water, forest resources, and atmosphere, with goals of long-term preservation and, where needed, remediation and revitalization, as well as sustainable resource use. Green economy concepts are applicable throughout the economy, including in the building, manufacturing, and transport sector (as noted above). They also apply to tourism and city planning, as illustrated by the "Urban Security Improvement" example evaluated earlier in this chapter.

The implementation of green economy concepts requires the consideration, management, and coordination of a wide variety of complex

---

topic, United Nations Development Programme, *Towards a Green Economy: Pathways to Sustainable Development and Poverty Eradication* (United Nations Development Programme, 2011).

50 Zero-net-energy buildings are typically defined as buildings that require no net fossil fuel use to operate. That is, they use a combination of very efficient use of energy plus some on-site energy conversion (in the form, for example, of solar photovoltaic panels, biomass energy use, combined heat and power systems, and active and/or passive solar space and/or water heating technologies) such that their net import of fossil-derived energy is zero. In his written response to questions from two US Senators, Edward Mazria of the building energy efficiency advocacy group Architecture2030 cites a similar definition of zero-net energy buildings derived from the United States' 2007 Energy Independence and Security Act. "Senate Committee Calls on Edward Mazria to Testify on Building Energy Efficiency," in *United States Senate Committee on Energy and Natural Resources* (Washington, DC: United States Senate Committee on Energy and Natural Resources, 2007).

interdependencies in numerous dimensions and at many different scales.
Examples of these interdependencies are endless, but include:

- Nations attempting "green" management of their natural resources
  are dependent on both nearby countries and far-flung nations to
  do their part (and to do so consistently over years, decades, and
  centuries) in managing shared and contiguous resources.

- Industries seeking to produce "green" products and services are
  dependent on the development of markets for those products
  and, if needed, the development and enforcement of regulations
  to guide the markets as well as the development of suppliers and
  service providers that will allow and promote "green" operations.

- Households, groups, firms, and governments seeking to implement
  green economy principles are dependent on accurate and persuasive
  information about green economy development, much of which
  has been and will be developed by civil society organizations.

- Substantial progress on green economy development will depend
  on the availability of investment capital, which will in turn entail a
  shift in how investors evaluate investment opportunities to more
  fully reflect criteria such as environmental sustainability.

These interdependencies have a negative side. It makes it hard in many
cases for individual households, businesses, or governments to affect
substantial change by acting on their own. On the positive side, however,
the coordination and information-sharing between groups transitioning
to green economies means the spread of green economy concepts, once
begun, could be quite rapid.

The introduction to a recent UNEP report on the green economy
suggested the green economy concept "moved into the mainstream of policy
discourse" in 2008. The UNEP report goes on to state, "This recent interest in
a green economy has been intensified by widespread disillusionment with
our prevailing economic paradigm, emanating from the many concurrent
and recent crises – particularly the recession of 2008-2009. At the same
time, increasing evidence is pointing to an alternative paradigm, in which
increased wealth does not lead to growing environmental risks, ecological
scarcities and social disparities."[51]

Despite the recent rush by many in government and industry to embrace
(at least in theory) green economy concepts, the theoretical foundations of

---

51   United Nations Development Programme (2011).

the green economy were laid long ago by luminaries including Margaret Mead, Buckminster Fuller, Dennis and Donella Meadows, Amory Lovins, and many others, as well as global movements toward sustainability and environmental preservation, of which the 1992 UN Conference on Environment and Development was a major milestone.[52] The implementation of green energy concepts on various scales has been going on for decades, manifest in organic and local farming movements, environmental education efforts, local materials recycling programs, and numerous others, many of which are the products of civil society actions and efforts by determined and committed individuals. The question remains whether these many, mostly small-scale efforts can be successfully knitted together by governments and other actors into a cohesive, global green economy movement that makes real and continuous progress toward sustainable development goals, or whether the green economy concept will be eased out of the policy mainstream by the next global crisis or, alternatively, by the next global economic upturn. The role of civil society, and of local governments, in keeping the pressure on national and global organizations to continue pursuing green economy goals will likely be pivotal.

The case studies of green economy policies in China, Japan, and the ROK provided below are based on presentations prepared for the conference, *Interconnected Global Problems in Northeast Asia: Energy Security, Green Economy, and Urban Security*, which was held in Seoul, ROK, in October, 2010. Each demonstrates different interpretations of the green economy concept in the three nations, and each suggests different ramifications for the implications of green growth policies for their energy security.

Case Study of Green Economy Policies: China

With by far the largest population, the fastest economic growth, and, in recent years, the largest economy in Northeast Asia, China faces special challenges in transitioning to a green economy. Below we present a brief overview of the background to China's energy and economic situation, a summary of recent legislation related to green economic development and of progress toward a green economy in recent years, and a discussion of

---

52   See, for example, *Green Economy and Sustainable Development* (New York: United Nations Conference on Sustainable Development, Rio +20).

China's policies and challenges for moving forward with the development of a green economy in the near-term and more distant future.[53]

Background: Recent Trends in China's Energy and Economic Situation

Since 2000, China's economic and energy sector has been characterized by another round of rapid growth, building on the gains of the 1990s and before. The high economic growth rate — about 10 percent annually, on average — has many positive effects, but it has also created new problems. Although the economic rise of China has markedly raised the standard of living for a huge proportion of China's residents and made China the world's second-largest economy, it has also led to significant environmental problems and obliged China to become a large net importer of energy, among other impacts. At present, China finds itself in what might be termed the "middle stage." Although the services and light industrial sectors of the Chinese economy are growing, the heavy and chemical industries remain responsible for about 70 percent of China's industrial output, and these industries are extremely resource, energy, and pollutant discharge-intensive. Rapid urbanization has been a key element of China's growth, with the fraction of China's population accounted for by urban dwellers rising by over 1 percent annually in recent years. With urbanization and overall economic growth has come a transition in household consumption patterns. As average per capita GDP has risen to over US $1000, many more Chinese households can afford major appliances, cars, and larger homes. These new acquisitions have helped to drive rapidly expanding energy use. Since about late 2002, the overall stress on resources and energy use, and the attendant, serious environmental pollution caused by resource and energy use, has been increasingly recognized as a major problem that needs to be addressed.

Figure 3.8 shows the trends in overall energy consumption in China. Between 2000 and 2008, overall energy use more than doubled, increasing at an average rate of 8.9 percent annually, though the growth rate of energy consumption has decreased substantially from the early years of the decade. Figure 3.9 shows the trend in coal production in China. Between 2001 and 2008, coal production increased by an average of about 200 million tonnes each year.

---

53   This description of China's green growth challenges and initiatives is based on Wang, Y. (2010).

Figure 3.8: Overall Energy Consumption and Growth Rates in China,
2001-2008 (units: 10,000 tonnes coal equivalent)

Source: Wang, Y., "China's Approach to Green Development and Transformation of Economic Development Plan," Presentation for the workshop *Interconnected Global Problems in Northeast Asia*, Seoul, Korea, October 20, 2010.

Figure 3.9: Coal Production in China, 2001-2008
(units: million tonnes coal)

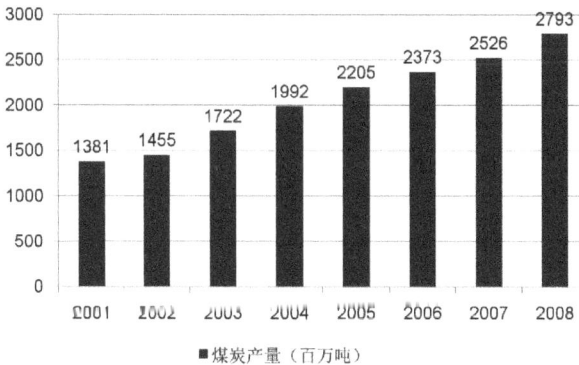

Source: Wang, Y., "China's Approach to Green Development and Transformation of Economic Development Plan," Presentation for the workshop *Interconnected Global Problems in Northeast Asia*, Seoul, Korea, October 20, 2010.

As a result of urbanization and an increased overall standard of living, among other factors, China's electricity needs have increased even faster than average energy use. As Figure 3.10 shows, China's installed generation capacity increased by a factor of more than 2.5 between 2000 and 2008, with more than 100 GW of capacity (the equivalent of about 1.5 ROK electrical systems) added in China in recent years.

**Figure 3.10: Electricity Generation Capacity in China, 1978-2008
(units: gigawatts)**

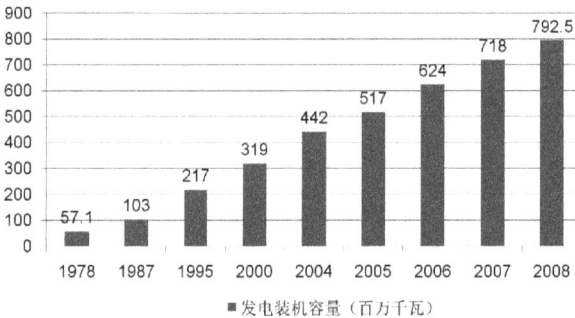

发电装机容量（百万千瓦）

Source: Wang, Y., "China's Approach to Green Development and Transformation of Economic Development Plan," Presentation for the workshop *Interconnected Global Problems in Northeast Asia*, Seoul, Korea, October 20, 2010.

Figure 3.11: Fraction of Chinese Energy Supply by Fuel Type, 1978-2007

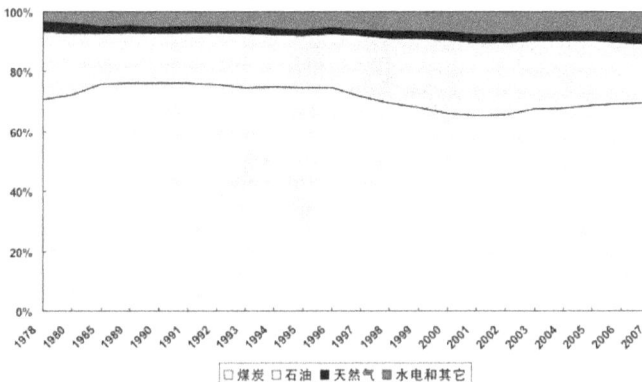

□ 煤炭 □ 石油 ■ 天然气 ▨ 水电和其它

Source: Wang, Y., "China's Approach to Green Development and Transformation of Economic Development Plan," Presentation for the workshop *Interconnected Global Problems in Northeast Asia*, Seoul, Korea, October 20, 2010.

The huge growth in overall energy use, coal use, and electricity generation, however, has had barely any impact on the structure of fuel supply in China. Coal remains the dominant energy resource, as shown in Figure 3.11.

China's Sustainability Challenges and Related Recent Legislation

China faces a number of key sustainability challenges on which action in the next five to ten years will be crucial. China became a net oil importer in 1993[54] and has since become a major importer of both crude oil and natural gas, mostly as LNG. The lack of sufficient domestic resources to fuel its economy has made energy supply security a major concern. At the same time serious environmental pollution, much but not all of which has been related to energy consumption and production, has emerged as a key issue for China's future. Though China's economic growth has rebounded faster than in most of the rest of the world, the impacts and lessons of the global financial crisis on China continue to be felt and learned. Improving energy security, making a transition to a sustainable economy, and addressing global climate change are emerging as significant issues. But the continued importance of other development issues, including poverty alleviation, providing sufficient employment, developing a system of social insurance, and alleviating economic and social disparities in the different regions of China, poses a number of dilemmas and conflicts in developing policies to achieve multiple goals. Resolving these dilemmas and conflicts in the coming years will determine whether China continues on a path that looks unsustainable in many ways, or transitions to a new model of sustainable development.

China has begun to develop laws and regulations intended to guide the country toward a more sustainable "green" economy. Some of the ideas that have come into the Chinese consciousness in the past decade, and have been instrumental in initiating government action, are as follows. All of these ideas bolster the theme of making a transition toward market-based, regulation-oriented, and sustainable development.

- 2002: A new industrialization pathway
- 2003: Scientific outlook on development: balanced development; people-centered, comprehensive, coordinated, and sustainable development
- 2004: Resource-Efficient and Environment-Friendly Society (REEFS) and Circular Economy (CE)

---

54   British Petroleum (2013).

- 2005: Harmonious society including relationship between man and nature, with China becoming an innovation-oriented country
- 2009: Green economy and low carbon development
- 2010: Transformation of economic development pattern

Based on the ideas above, a number of laws have been developed over the past decade that define China's current legislative framework for sustainability. They include:

- Environmental Impact Assessment Law (2002)
- Cleaner Production Promoting Law (2003)
- Renewable Energy Law (2006)
- State Council Circular on REEFS (2006)
- Industrial regulations, codes, standards
- Energy Conservation Law (amended, 2007)
- Plan of Renewable Energy Development in Mid- and Long-Term (2007, under revision)
- Circular Economy Promotion Law (2008)
- Regulations on E-Waste Management (2009)
- Renewable Energy Law (amended, 2009)
- Energy Law (under review by the National People's Congress as of 2010)

In the last five years, China has undertaken a number of actions to provide guidance in combating climate change. China set mandatory targets of energy efficiency during the period 2006-2010, targeting an increase in efficiency of about 20 percent nationwide, designed to yield about 1.5 billion tonnes of carbon dioxide equivalent emissions reduction (CO_2e). A National Climate Change Assessment Report was released in December 2006, and an update was produced in 2010. The National Climate Change Program was released in June 2007, along with a volume on China's Science and Technology Actions on Climate Change. In October 2008, a white paper entitled *China's Policies and Actions on Climate Change* was released. The National Leading Group on Climate Change, chaired by Premier Wen Jiabo, was established along with the Department of Climate Change under the NDRC (National Development and Reform Commission) in 2008. A new NPC (National People's Congress) Resolution on Climate Change was signed on August

27, 2009, and the National Energy Commission was established in 2010 as a super-coordinating body on energy-related policies in China.

Achievements and Problems During the 11th Five-Year Plan

The ideas, laws/regulations, and actions described above have laid the framework for the green economy achievements under China's 11th Five-Year Plan, spanning the period from 2006 through 2010. Below we describe a summary of the Plan's major goals, achievements, and problems encountered.

The 11th Five-Year Plan aimed to use comprehensive measures, together with a continued growth model modified by transfer and structural adjustment, and an orientation toward innovation, to accomplish several main goals in improving energy efficiency and reducing pollutant emissions. The mandatory targets the plan set for 2006-2010 included reducing energy consumption per unit of GDP by 20 percent, reducing the discharge of key pollutants such as sulfur dioxide (SO_2) and Chemical Oxygen Demand (COD) — a measure of the pollutant load of organic material discharged to water — by 10 percent, reducing water use per unit of industrial value-added by 30 percent, and reforestation to increase the forest coverage rate by 1.8 percent annually.

The mandatory 20 percent reduction in energy intensity below 2005 levels by 2010 received clear policy support from government. Energy intensity reduction targets averaging about 20 percent, but varying in different regions of China (see Figure 3.12), were assigned to provinces, as well as to the "Top-1000 Enterprises" (the 1000 largest, mostly industrial enterprises nationally) and to the economic sectors, with reductions to be obtained under central government supervision. Energy efficiency improvements (as opposed to shifts in industrial structure) were intended to make the largest contributions to support the target, with industrial restructuring, such as closing small and inefficient plants where possible, also playing a role.

The longer-term target for the policy was to make a cumulative reduction below BAU emissions totaling 5.6 Gt (Billion tonnes) CO_2e from 2007 to 2020. It is estimated that from 2005 through 2009 a 15.61 percent cut in energy intensity was achieved, along with 13.14 percent and 9.66 percent reductions in SO2 and COD emissions, respectively. Other supporting policies promulgated during the 11th Five-Year plan included a renewable energy policy that featured, as of 2009, connection and "must-buy" provisions related to utility additions of renewable capacity to their grids, including a provision for planned Mandatory Renewable Portfolio standards for utilities and the extension of grids to accommodate renewable supply sources (especially wind power). Special feed-in tariffs for renewables and a Special Fund to support research and development, demonstration projects, and renewable energy industry development and commercialization were also implemented. Other policies for the 11th Five-Year plan included fuel efficiency standards for cars and vehicles, excise tax restructuring to promote the purchase of vehicles with smaller engines, and ambitious water conservation/water quality and waste management targets.

Figure 3.12: Distribution of Energy Intensity Reduction Targets in China by Province

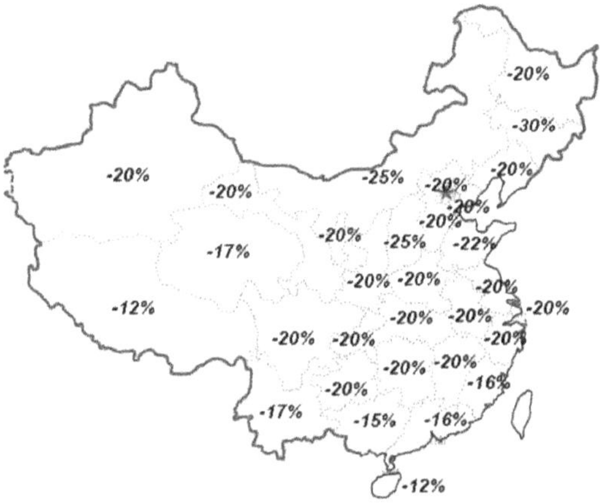

Source: Wang, Y., "China's Approach to Green Development and Transformation of Economic Development Plan," Presentation for the workshop *Interconnected Global Problems in Northeast Asia*, Seoul, Korea, October 20, 2010.

China used various approaches to improve energy efficiency during the 11th Five-Year Plan. These approaches included controlling the growth rates of the economy and of energy use; adjusting existing stocks of fuels and energy-using equipment; optimizing the industrial structure for improved energy intensity, implementing an objective-based responsibility system among enterprise managers to implement energy efficiency (EE) improvements; implementing a "Ten Key EE Programs" initiative and a Top 1000 Enterprises energy conservation action plan (with its own target of reducing energy use by 100 Mtce in five years); improving the collection and management of energy statistics and meteorological data; improving EE in governmental agencies ("lead by example"); and providing public information, education, and training on energy efficiency throughout China.

In response to the global economic downturn, the Chinese government used a combination of economic stimulus measures designed, in part, to promote a "green recovery" in China. These measures included direct investment in environmental areas totaling 5 percent of a total 4 trillion Yuan 2008-2010 stimulus package, with another 10 percent of the funds in the stimulus package devoted to energy efficiency investments. An additional 10 percent was devoted to "green direct investment," while an additional 38 percent of the package was indirectly designed to benefit the green economy. Other stimulus measures with "green" impacts included investments in the development of new strategic industries, including EE and environmental industries; investment of over 7 billion Yuan in research and development targeted at energy efficiency improvement, pollution reduction, and addressing climate change; and large scale construction of new technologies and infrastructure, such as renewable energy and high speed rail transport. Despite the focus on green economy investments, the impact of the economic stimulus program on China has not been entirely straightforward. For example, the stimulus program had the side-effect of helping to somewhat restore activity in traditional, energy-intensive industries. In addition, a "rebound effect" was noted, whereby the reduction in energy use through energy efficiency resulted, in the short term, in helping to expand domestic energy demand, as consumers applying EE measures found themselves spending less on energy and availing themselves of some of those savings to increase their use of energy services (for example, by purchasing and employing more energy-using devices).

The transportation sector has been another focus for green economy policies in China during the 11th Five-Year Plan. The overarching policies in the sector have stressed fuel economy improvement, electric vehicle development, and the promotion of public transport. A clean vehicle demonstration project includes conventional vehicle improvement as well as the development of battery electric, hybrid, and fuel cell vehicles, in part through expansion of China's "10 cities and 1000 vehicles" program to twenty cities. Through the "10 cities and 1000 vehicles," launched in December 2007, the Ministry of Transportation has placed 1,000 or more "new energy" vehicles and their fueling/charging infrastructure in each of ten cities to catalyze the deployment of new energy vehicles.[55] These efforts have been supplemented by policies to boost the promotion of plug-in vehicles in China, starting in June 2010 with a pilot program in five cities offering subsidies of 50,000 Yuan for plug-in hybrid cars and 60,000 Yuan for all-electric (battery-powered) cars. Other transportation sector measures in the last five years have included bus rapid transit demonstration and full-scale construction projects in over twenty cities, aggressive expansion of high speed rail with 6552 km in service as of late 2010 and over 18,000 km planned for service by 2020, as well as local activities to promote the use of green vehicles.

Over the past decade and more, the pace at which the skylines of China's cities have been changing is truly breathtaking. All of this building sector activity is both a challenge and an opportunity, since the most cost-effective way to improve the energy efficiency of buildings, which may be in service for thirty years or more, is to make sure that high energy efficiency is a key consideration when buildings are initially constructed. Figure 3.13 shows the scope of this challenge. The floor area of buildings in China is projected to more than double in the two decades between 2010 and 2030, with most of that growth in the residential sector. Growth in residential housing floor area occurs despite population growth rates that are falling toward zero and an aging population, with key factors being rapid urbanization and rising incomes, meaning that households can afford larger homes. To improve the energy efficiency of new buildings, the Chinese government has implemented programs including National Design Standards for Green Buildings, a Green Building Development Strategy, Green Building Technology Guidelines, Best Design for Demonstration Buildings, as well as programs to develop advanced building materials and windows to integrate renewable energy products and improve the efficiency of central heating and cooling systems.

---

55   See, for example, Gao, G., "1,000 New-Energy Cars to Have Trial Run in 10 Cities," *Gasgoo.com*, 24 October 2008, http://autonews.gasgoo.com/china-news/1-000-new-energy-cars-to-have-trial-run-in-10-citi-081024.shtml

Figure 3.13: Estimated floor area of buildings from 2010 to 2030

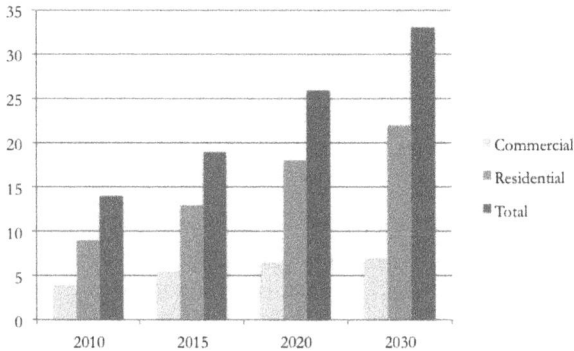

Source: Wang, Y., "China's Approach to Green Development and Transformation of Economic Development Plan," Presentation for the workshop *Interconnected Global Problems in Northeast Asia*, Seoul, Korea, October 20, 2010.

China is the worldwide leader in renewable investment, the world's largest exporter of solar cells and the world's largest solar water heating market. China's renewable electricity targets by 2020, as expressed in 2009, include:

- 80 GW small hydro (increased from 55GW in 2009)
- 200 GW wind (up from 25.8 GW in 2009, with considerable capacity in Inner Mongolia — as shown in Figure 3.14)
- 30 GW biomass
- 20 GW solar PV
- 300 million m² of solar water heaters
- 24 billion m³ of annual biogas production capacity

Renewable electricity deployment is supported by the development of energy storage technologies and increased efforts to strengthen the power grid and implement "Smart Grid" technologies, including an emphasis on developing and deploying distributed energy systems. As of the late 2000s, the on-grid prices of coal-fired power fitted with sulfur dioxide removal systems (0.47 Yuan/kWh) were within the range of costs for different types of renewable power systems. Wind and biomass power, in some applications, were nearly competitive with coal-fired power in China as of 2010, with wind at 0.5 to 0.65 Yuan/kWh and biomass at 0.4 to 1.0 Yuan/kWh. The rapid increase in wind power generation capacity has been a major achievement of the 11th

Five-Year Plan. China's wind power increased at an annual growth rate of over 100 percent during 2004-2009. Supported by the Renewable Energy Law and related policies and regulations, China's installed wind power capacity ranked number two globally by 2009 and, at 25.8 GW, was over five times the initial capacity projected for 2009 when the 11th Five-Year Plan was completed in 2010. As of late 2010, wind power capacity is projected to be 200 GW in China by 2020, whereas the target set in 2007 called for only 30 GW. There are 80 companies in China producing wind power systems, and 70 percent of the parts for the key 1.5 MW wind power unit are made in China.

During the 11th Five-Year Plan, China has also become the world's leading country for solar photovoltaic (PV) cell and panel production. In 2009, China produced solar cells with a total capacity of 4 GW, of which most were exported; the total installed capacity in China in 2009 was 300 MW. Major photovoltaic and polysilicon industry clusters are located in the eastern and central provinces of China as shown in Figure 3.14. Ongoing policies, including subsidies for Solar Building Integrated Photovoltaic systems (BIPV) and a national Solar Roofs plan, are designed to build Chinese demand for PVs; meanwhile, growth in PV exports are continuing. China is also the world's leading producer of solar water heaters, accounting for 65 percent of the world's total. In 2009, China's annual production capacity for solar water heaters stood at 30 million m^2 of water heating panel area, with a cumulative output through 2009 of 145 million m^2.

Figure 3.14: Location of Photovoltaic Industry Centers in China

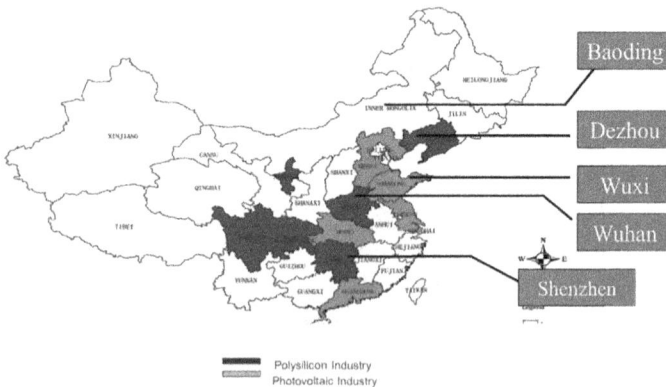

Source: Wang, Y., "China's Approach to Green Development and Transformation of Economic Development Plan," Presentation for the workshop *Interconnected Global Problems in Northeast Asia*, Seoul, Korea, October 20, 2010.

Biomass has historically been a staple fuel in China, particularly in rural areas, although its use has lessened substantially in recent years as commercial fuels have been introduced (primarily coal and oil products). Recent efforts have focused on diversifying sources of biomass as well as on developing new technology paths and products. Over the last thirty years, China has been researching and deploying digester systems to convert manures and other organic wastes to a methane rich "biogas" for household and other uses. As of 2009, biogas production in China stood at 14 billion m^3 annually, supplying fuel for 80 million people in mostly rural areas. Some deployment of biomass-fired power systems has also taken place with installed capacity of 3.24 MW achieved by 2009. Biomass-derived fuels for vehicles are in the initial stages of production in China, with annual fuel ethanol production of 1.65 million tonnes and bio-diesel production of over 0.5 million tonnes in 2009, but biofuels production in China, as elsewhere, raises concerns of food security to the extent that crops destined for biofuels compete for farmland and other agricultural inputs with food crops.

The accomplishments and goals of China's 11th Five-Year Plan also included progress on "clean coal" technologies and nuclear power. The combustion of coal in Integrated Gasification Combined Cycle (IGCC) units offers opportunities for "polygeneration," that is, the co-production of electricity, coke, chemical products, and heat from coal, in different combinations as needed, combined with carbon capture and sequestration (CCS) to reduce the greenhouse gas emissions from coal production. The generation of valuable co-products helps to make the systems more economic. The IGCC system also allows the removal of pollutants, such as sulfur oxides and particulate matter, and promises higher thermal efficiency for power production. The goal of IGCC and polygeneration development is to make the technology cheap and available for use throughout China. A related technology under development in China is the production of liquid fuels from coal via "Coal to Liquids" (CTL) systems. These systems produce liquid fuels from coal via indirect liquefaction and can be coupled with CCS systems. Like IGCC systems, they allow the removal of key air pollutants.

Nuclear power use in China has been growing faster than in any other nation. In 2009, nuclear capacity totaled 9 GW and spread over eleven operating reactor units, and while this total represented about 1 percent of the total installed generation capacity in China at the time, with an additional thirty reactors permitted (about 33 GW) and twenty units under construction, the share of nuclear power will rise. The goals of the 11th Five-Year Plan included nuclear generation capacity of 40 GW in 2015 and over 70 GW in 2020; the latter goal translates to more than 150 million tonnes of reduced

CO_2 annual emissions relative to coal-fired generation. Nuclear technology priorities for China include the development of a "third generation" pressurized water reactor, such as the "AP1000" and "CAP1400," and the development of safe and effective systems for nuclear spent fuel disposal. Longer term projects include research on high-temperature gas-cooled reactors, low-temperature heat-supply reactors, fast breeder reactors, and the use of accelerator-driven systems (ADS). These transform some of the radioactive materials in nuclear wastes to elements and isotopes that are easier to dispose of. Other projects include the development of thorium-fueled reactors, as well as participation in fusion power research projects such as the ITER (originally, International Thermonuclear Experimental Reactor) effort, which is building a fusion reactor prototype in the south of France.[56]

The green economy elements detailed above — energy efficiency, vehicle efficiency, clean vehicle development, mass transit, renewable energy, clean coal technologies, and nuclear power—are among the key components of China's "Energy Technology Roadmap to 2050," published in 2009 toward the end of the 11th Five-Year Plan.[57]

China's Approach to Sustainable Energy Development in the 12th Five-Year Plan and Beyond

China's general approach to continuing the process of sustainable energy development through the next (12th) Five-Year Plan and beyond 2020 is to transform economic development patterns by building a resource-efficient and environment-friendly society. As part of this process, China aims to maintain the development of new strategic industries such as EE, clean energy, new energy vehicles, environmental services, and others. It aims to set in place a special plan of energy savings and environmental protection at the State Council level including a roadmap, priorities, an action plan, and demonstration projects designed to facilitate movement toward a green economy.

The process of governmental restructuring in 2013, taking a "mega department" approach, is expected to facilitate the operation of the green economy through integration and implementation of coordinating mechanisms related to the energy sector. Green economy transformations

---

56   See, for example, *The Way to New Energy* (St. Paul-lez-Durance: ITER Organization), http://www.iter.org/

57   Chen, Y., *Energy Science and Technology in China: A Roadmap to 2050.* ed. by Chinese Academy of Sciences (Berlin: Springer, 2010).

will also be supported by policy reviews and mandatory target-setting encompassing targets for energy and carbon intensity, control over energy consumption, economic incentives including energy product price reforms and green taxation, and capacity building, including in the collection of energy statistics and the monitoring/enforcement of compliance with energy-related regulations. "Green innovation" will be supported to lower the cost of green economy products and services, with measures involving subsidies for low-carbon technology development in areas such as small renewable energy systems, biochar production,[58] and other technologies.

The 12th Five-Year Plan continues the approach of the 11th Plan by instituting a mandatory energy intensity reduction of about 18 percent for China as a whole (varying from 16 to 20 percent in different provinces). New targets for carbon intensity reductions (carbon emissions per unit of GDP) were announced on November 26, 2009, targeting a 40 to 45 percent cut by 2020 compared with 2005 levels.

The emphasis on the development of new and clean energy sources will continue, with a goal of increasing non-fossil energy from its 7.5 percent share of overall energy use (excluding traditional biomass use) in 2005 to 15 percent in 2020, with nuclear power constituting at least 5 percent of total power generation in 2020. China will continue to pursue clean coal technologies with advanced technologies such as super-critical and ultra-super-critical coal-fired generation, IGCC, polygeneration, and CCS supported as demonstration projects.

Clean vehicle research and development will also continue with alternative fuel vehicles, hybrid cars, electric cars, and fuel cell vehicles. The 12th Five-Year Plan will also include further efforts to enhance the carbon sinks in China's ecosystems, including a target of increasing forest cover from the 18 percent it was in 1999-2003 to around 23 percent in 2020, representing about 40 million ha of reforested land.

The 12th Five-Year Plan also includes capacity building for and carrying out of climate change adaptation planning, as well as more mandatory targets for reduction of atmosphere pollutants such as nitrogen oxides (NOx) and water pollutants such as nitrogen, phosphorous, and others.

Reaching the green economy targets of the 12th Five-Year Plan will call for a number of different approaches. Energy efficiency is the preferred starting point, yielding the least-expensive reductions in energy use and emissions.

---

58   "Biochar" is a charcoal made from the pyrolysis (combustion with limited oxygen) of biomass and intended for use a soil amendment to both improve the fertility of soils and to provide long-term sequestration of carbon.

But given China's dependence on coal, the development of clean coal use is crucial (including, as appropriate, with CCS). If overall energy consumption amounts to 4.6 billion tce in 2020 as projected and the non-fossil energy contribution to primary energy reaches the target of constituting 15 percent of non-fossil energy, hydro power will need to rise to an estimated 8 to 9 percent of total primary energy supply by 2020, wind power capacity will need to be 200 GW, solar capacity 20 GW, and biomass-fired 30 GW to total 4 percent of total primary energy use. Nuclear power will need to be 70 GW, producing 1 percent of primary energy needs. Other sources of energy will together need to provide 2 percent of primary energy needs, including solar water and space heating (800 million square meters by 2020), bio-diesel (2 million tonnes/year), and bio-ethanol (10 million tonnes/year).

In reaching these targets, technology development will certainly play an important role, but an even more serious effort is required to overcome non-technical barriers to moving to a green economy in China. Comprehensive solutions are needed to reform and develop the legal, administrative, and economic instruments that will provide the proper climate for the green economy. Policies for green and low carbon technology innovation and development need to be matched with policies for cooperation on these issues. Technology demands assessment at the level of reporting, monitoring, and verification by the technology, classification, and demand sector to properly focus green economy efforts.

Collaboration among newly industrialized and developing countries will play a role in developing and disseminating green economy concepts and products, as will joint research, development, and distribution at the bilateral and multilateral levels. Sharing of best practice in technologies, policies, and other green economy needs will also help catalyze China's (and the world's) progress toward a green economy, and the establishment and operation of a multi-lateral Green Transition Fund, together with its implementing mechanisms, would help to fund and guide green economy efforts.

For China to succeed in its green economy transition, a systematic and integrated approach will be required that includes elements of technology development and deployment, policy improvements, preparation of a clear plan/roadmap for the transition, and the practicing of green economy concepts including demonstrations, industry development, and market development.

Case Study of Green Economy Policies: Japan

The challenges that Japan faces in transitioning to a green economy are substantially different to those faced by China but, in many ways, no less daunting. Japan is one of the wealthiest countries in the world. With the world's third largest economy, its technological capabilities are of the first order. The population is highly educated. Japan also has a tradition of saving and frugality, as well as a spiritual connection with the natural world. Japan's economy, however, has shown modest growth at best for over a decade, and a declining and aging population is an impediment to future sustained growth. Although Japan's energy use and greenhouse gas emissions have changed relatively little since 2000, with CO_2 emissions even decreasing in recent years, this decline has been largely the result of the recent economic stagnation rather than of government policies. Energy supply security has, for many decades, been a major focus of Japan's policy because it has very limited fossil fuel resources of its own. This focus remains, though a number of policies have been developed that nominally steer Japan towards a greener economy. Their implementation, as described below, has generally been slow.[59]

Recent Trends in Japan's Energy Sector and Economy[60]

As of 2009, Japan had the world's third-largest economy (among individual nations) in terms of GDP (purchasing power parity-adjusted), after the United States and China. It ranked third in electricity consumption, third in oil consumption, and fifth in natural gas consumption.[61] Lacking major deposits of fossil fuel resources, however, Japan is reliant on energy imports and was, as of 2004, the second largest importer of fuels after the United States and the third largest importer of oil (after the United States and China). Japan's modest coal resources are still mined at a very low level, but domestic coal production in recent years has been heavily subsidized and uneconomic relative to coal imports from Australia, South Africa, the United States, and China. Domestic coal production has disappeared from public statistics.

Japan has a few operating oil and gas wells and some reserves of both oil and gas, but less than 2 percent of its oil and gas needs are produced domestically.[62] Japan has an estimated 34 GW of hydroelectric resources, of which about 65 percent have already been tapped.[63] As a result, Japan's

---

59 This description of Japan's green growth challenges and initiatives is based on Takase, K. (2010). Iida, T. (2010).

60 Takase, K. and Suzuki, T. (2011).

61 Central Intelligence Agency, *The World Factbook* (Washington DC: Central Intelligence Agency, 2011), https://www.cia.gov/library/publications/the-world-factbook/index.html

62 Ministry of Economics, Trade, and Industry, *Energy Balance of Japan for Fiscal Year 2009* (Tokyo: Japan Ministry of Economics, Trade, and Industry, 2011).

63 Asia Pacific Energy Research Centre, *Electric Power Grid Interconnections in the APEC Region* (Tokyo: Japan Institute of Energy Economics, 2004).

economy is highly dependent on imports — particularly imported coal, oil, LNG (liquefied natural gas), and uranium for its nuclear power industry. Over 80 percent of Japan's oil imports come from the Persian Gulf (as of 2011), while about two thirds of its natural gas imports — as LNG — come from Southeast Asia and the Pacific (Indonesia, Malaysia, Brunei, and Australia), as of 2010, with additional LNG sourced from the Middle East and from Russia, among other locations.[64]

Figure 3.15: Ratio of Imported Energy to Total Primary Energy Use in Japan, 1965-2011 (Values shown are ratios as of 2011)

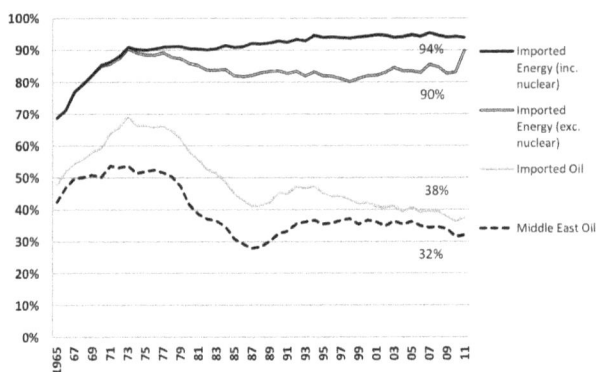

Source: Derived by Kae Takase from data in *EDMC Handbook of Energy & Economic Statistics in Japan 2012.*

Despite some diversification since 1980 — mainly stemming from an increased use of nuclear power and natural gas — Figure 3.15 shows how Japan's very high import dependency continues. It is not surprising, therefore, that concerns over energy supply security have historically dominated energy policy debates in Japan.

Japan has one of the lowest rates of energy use per unit of GDP among the industrialized nations of the world. This status reflects, among other factors, an emphasis since the "energy crises" in the 1970s on energy efficiency in manufacturing and other sectors, as well as the displacement, over the last few decades, of much of Japan's heavy industrial base to other countries as high value-added industries such as electronics and services

---

64   United States Department of Energy, *Country Analysis Briefs — Japan* (Washington, DC: United States Department of Energy, 2011). *Countries* (Washington, DC: Energy Information Administration, United States Department of Energy), http://www.eia. gov/countries/

have come to dominate Japan's economy. Figure 3.16 shows the division of final energy demand by consuming sector in Japan in 2011. Figure 3.17 compares trends in energy demand by sector over the period 1990-2011, showing industrial demand has remained nearly static, while commercial sector demand, for example, has increased by over 40 percent.

Figure 3.16: Final Demand by Sector in Japan, 2011

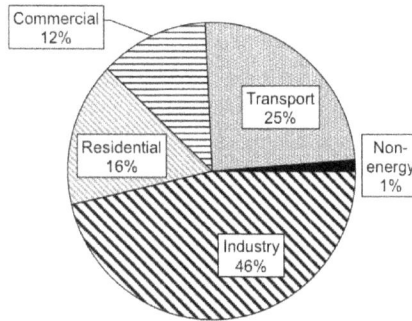

Source: Derived by Kae Takase from data in *EDMC Handbook of Energy & Economic Statistics in Japan 2012*.

Figure 3.17: Index of Final Demand by Sector in Japan, 1990 to 2008 (1990 = 100)

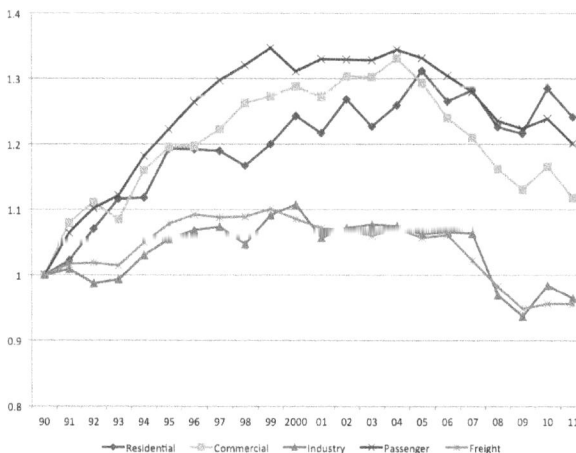

Source: Derived by Kae Takase from data in *EDMC Handbook of Energy & Economic Statistics in Japan 2012*.

Japan's population — about 127.8 million as of 2011 — has reached its peak and is starting to decline.[65] After a period of slow or no growth — average annual GDP growth was about 1.2 percent from 1990 through 2005 — Japan's economic picture had begun to improve somewhat in the years prior to the global economic crisis and the March 2011 earthquake and its aftermath. Japan's energy use and carbon dioxide emissions have also continued to grow, but more slowly than the economy (see Figure 3.18).[66]

Figure 3.18: Energy and Economic Trends in Japan, 1965-2012 (Index at left relative to 1965 values, scale at right represents change in energy use per unit change in GDP)

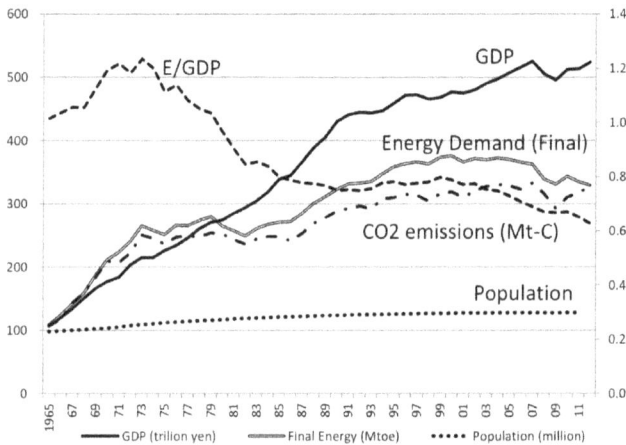

Source: Derived by Kae Takase from data in *EDMC Handbook of Energy & Economic Statistics in Japan 2012*. Kae Takase, "The Japanese Energy Sector, Energy Policies, and the Japan LEAP Modeling Effort," presentation prepared for the Nautilus Institute project *Spent Fuel and Reduction of Radiological Risk After Fukushima* (2013), http://nautilus.org/wp-content/uploads/2013/08/Takase_201305.pdf.

Japan's CO_2 emissions trends can be decomposed into three contributing factors. The so-called "Kaya equation" expresses the annual change ("Δ") in CO_2 emissions as the product of the change in energy use per unit of

---

65   See, for example, National Institute for Population and Social Security Research, *Social Security in Japan* (Tokyo: National Institute for Population and Social Security Research, 2011).

66   Energy Data and Modeling Center, *Handbook of Energy & Economic Statistics in Japan '08*, Japan Energy Conservation Center (Tokyo: Institute of Energy Economics, 2009).

GDP ("$\Delta E/GDP$"), the change in CO_2 emission per unit of energy use ("$\Delta CO_2/E$"), and the change in GDP ("ΔGDP") over a given time period.[67] Figure 3.19 shows the contributing factors to Japan's trends in energy use emissions from 1965 through 2011 in ten-year increments (except for 2010 through 2011). In general, the energy intensity of GDP ("E/GDP") is falling, reflecting a combination of true energy efficiency increases and reduced energy intensity due to the continued restructuring of Japan's economy away from heavy industries.

Japan's CO_2 emissions, as shown in Figure 3.20, rose only modestly from 1990 through 2007, in part due to a reduction in CO_2 intensity of energy use (CO_2/E) — mostly reflecting a trend toward expanded use of natural gas and nuclear energy. CO_2 emissions from 2005 through 2009 fell due to a combination of decreased energy intensity and CO_2 intensity, along with negative trends in GDP, particularly as a result of the global recession of 2008-2009.

Figure 3.19: Contributing Factors to Trends in Energy Use in Japan, 1965-2011 (Units: percent average annual change)

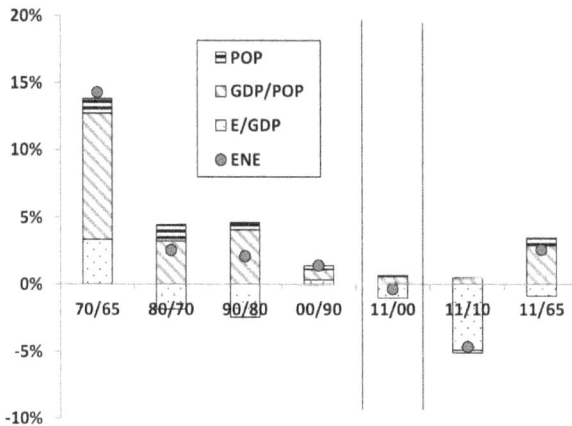

Source: Kae Takase, "The Japanese Energy Sector, Energy Policies, and the Japan LEAP Modeling Effort," presentation prepared for the Nautilus Institute project *Spent Fuel and Reduction of Radiological Risk After Fukushima* (2013), http://nautilus.org/wp-content/uploads/2013/08/Takase_201305.pdf.

---

67 For a discussion of the "Kaya identity" see, for example, Nakicenovic, N. and Swart, R., *Emissions Scenarios* (Geneva: Intergovernmental Panel on Climate Change).

Figure 3.20: Energy Use (1010 kcal) and CO_2 Emissions (Mt CO_2) in Japan, 1990-2012

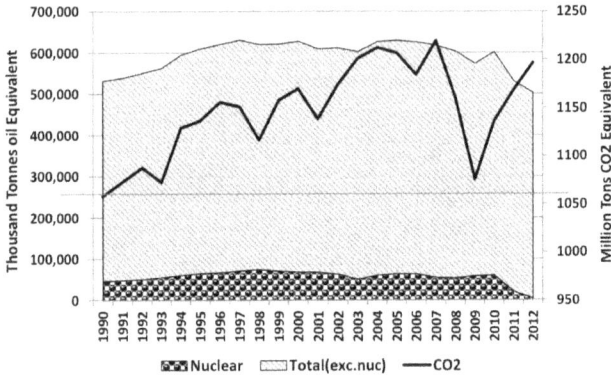

Source: 1965-2011 data derived by Kae Takase from *EDMC Handbook of Energy & Economic Statistics in Japan 2012*. Data for 2012 estimated by Governance Design Laboratory from various sources.

Greenhouse Gas (GHG) Reduction Policies in Japan

The historical trends in the evolution in Japan's energy sector, economy, and emissions form the backdrop for Japan's energy security and green economy-related policies in recent years. As of a few years ago, the prospects for meeting Japan's 2012 greenhouse gas emissions reduction commitments under the Kyoto Protocol to the United Nations Framework Convention on Climate Change looked relatively bleak, as achieving the target (before accounting for carbon sink credits from such sources as growing forests and Kyoto Mechanism credits) would have required a 12.7 percent reduction from 2007 emissions.[68] The impact of the global economic downturn, however, made Japan's task in meeting its short-term Kyoto Protocol obligations much easier. As shown in Figure 3.21, Japan achieved a 0.6 percent reduction compared to base-year emissions levels in the period between 2008 and 2012 and, with additional help in the shape of Kyoto Mechanism credits, the target of 6 percent reduction from 1990 level was achieved.

---

68   Ministry of the Environment, *FY 2007 Greenhouse Gas Emissions in Japan (Provisional Data)* (Tokyo: Japan Ministry of Environment, 2008)

As it turned out, Japan's GHG emissions did stay below the 2012 target, though offsetting drivers — economic dislocation as a result of the remnants of the global recession, a driver compounded by the impacts of the Sendai earthquake and tsunami, but countered in part by greater consumption of fossil fuels used for electricity generation to compensate for nuclear plants shut down after the Fukushima catastrophe — make this drop in emissions less than straightforward to explain.

Figure 3.21: Greenhouse Gas Emissions in Japan in Comparison with Kyoto Protocol Commitments (Units: Million tonnes CO$_2$ equivalent)

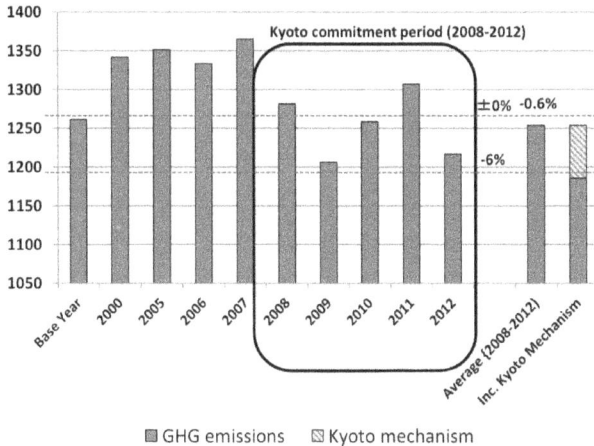

Source: Ministry of Economy, Trade and Industry (METI), "Past Emission Reduction Targets and Achievement, and policy measures" (2013), http://www.meti.go.jp/committee/summary/0004000/pdf/035_02_01.pdf.

Reaching Japan's medium and long-term targets for emissions reduction, however, is another matter. Table 3.7 shows the transitions over time in Japan's greenhouse gas emissions reduction targets. Japan most recently committed to a 25 percent reduction from 1990 emission levels by 2020 under the Copenhagen code, as shown in Figure 3.22 (with an extrapolation to 2050). But after the governing political party in Japan changed from the Democratic Party of Japan (DPJ) to the Liberal Democratic Party (LDP) in late 2012, the target underwent a "zero-based review" according to the "Japan Revitalization Strategy" set forth by the new cabinet.[69] (A zero-based review is one conducted without consideration for funding, staffing, or organizational constraints.)

Table 3.7: Historical Transitions in Japanese Greenhouse Gas Emissions Reduction Targets

	Plan	Prime Minister (Party)	Target
1997.12	Kyoto Protocol	Ryutaro Hashimoto (LDP)	Reduce 6% compared to the 1990 levels in the period of 2008-2012 (Japan)
2007.5	Cool Earth 50	Shinzo Abe (LDP)	Reduce 50% of World emissions
2008.6	Fukuda Vision	Yasuo Fukuda (LDP)	Reduce 60-80% (Japan)
2009.6	Aso Target	Taro Aso	Reduce 15% compared to 2005 levels by 2020 (8% compared to 1990 levels) (Japan)
2009.9	Speech by Hatoyama	Yukio Hatoyama	Reduce 25% compared to 1990 levels by 2020
2012.9	Innovative Strategy for Energy and the Environment	Yoshihiko Noda	Reduce 5-9% compared to 1990 level by 2020 (if GDP grows, reduction will be 2-5%)

Source: Mainichi Newspaper, "Discussion of CO_2 reduction target disrupted," 26 August 2013.

Japan's overall policies for improving energy supply security traditionally focused on three principles: improving self-sufficiency in energy use, diversifying sources of energy (including energy types and geographical sources), and reducing GHG emissions as described in "The Energy Basic Plan" approved by the cabinet in 2010. The Basic Energy Plan of 2010 set a very ambitious target calling for a high rate of energy efficiency improvement, especially in the household sector, and a high rate of development of zero-emission sources of electricity (namely nuclear power

---

69   Prime Minister of Japan and his Cabinet, *Japan Revitalization Strategy-Japan Is Back* (Tokyo: Government of Japan, 2013).

and renewable electricity). After the earthquake, the cabinet considered the possibility of a zero-nuclear power future for Japan and, after much discussion, published a document entitled "Innovative Strategy for Energy and the Environment" in September 2012. This document, however, was not approved by the cabinet due to strong opposition to the concept of a zero-nuclear future.

Figure 3.22: Historical Greenhouse Gas Emissions in Japan, and Required Trends to Reach Medium and Long-term Targets (Units: Million tonnes CO_2 equivalent)

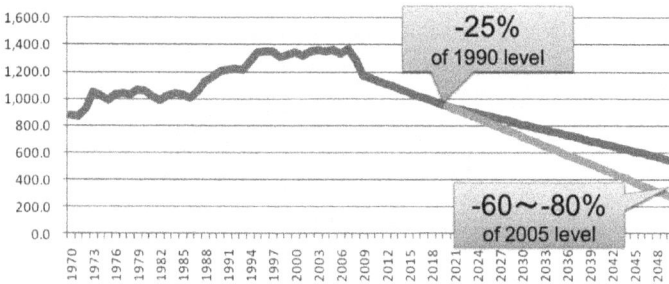

Source: Historical statistics from data in *EDMC Handbook of Energy & Economic Statistics in Japan 2012*. Future extrapolations derived by Kae Takase based on stated Japanese climate policies.

After the LDP regained power in December 2012, Prime Minister Abe announced the CO_2 emission target for 2020, as well as the Energy Basic Plan and any other energy related plans, should be "zero-based" reviewed and revised. In Prime Minister Abe's economic recovery plan, the "Japan Revitalization Strategy," which was approved by the cabinet in June 2013, it is clearly stated that every target or plan related to CO_2 emissions and energy are to be reviewed and revised.

In the meantime, Feed-in Tariffs (FIT) for renewable electricity sources in Japan have been fully implemented, and the tariff for the first year (beginning in July 2012) and second year of the FIT program have been high enough to encourage many companies to start renewable generation businesses. Table 3.8 provides a summary of the FIT schedule.

Table 3.8: Tariff Levels for Renewable Energy Sales to the Japanese Grid

Energy source	Type	Coverage of Purchase	Price (Yen per kWh)		Purchase period (years)
			2012 FY	2013 FY	
PV	Up to 10kw	Surplus	42	38	10
			(34 w/FC)	(31 W/fc)	
	10kW and above	All	42	37.8	20
Wind	Up to 20kW	All	57.75	57.75	20
	20 kW and above	All	23.1	23.1	20
Small hydro	Up to 200 kW	All	35.7	35.7	20
	200-100 kW	All	30.45		20
	Above 1000 kW	All	25.2		20
Geothermal	Up to 15,000 kW	All	42	42	15
	15,000 kW and above	All	27.3	27.3	20
Biomass	Methane fermentation gasification	All	40.95	40.95	20
	Unused wood combustion (1)	All	33.6	33.6	20
	Wood combustion (2)	All	25.2	25.2	20
	Waste (non-wood) combustion (3)	All	17.85	17.85	20
	Recycled wood combustion (4)	All	13.65	13.65	20

Note: "FC" denotes tariff when a PV system is coupled with a home fuel cell system fueled with oil or gas, with the combined output (net of home use) sold to the grid. 1) Using "unused" timber from forest thinning or regeneration cutting. 2) Using wood other than "unused" or "recycled"(waste wood from lumber sawing or imported woods), and palm chaff, rice husk sourced biomass. 3) Burning biomass such as domestic waste, sewage sludge, food waste, refuse-derived fuel (RDF), refuse paper and plastic fuel (RPF), or black liquor from the wood pulp industry. 4) Burning biomass such as construction and demolition waste.

Source: Ministry of Economy, Trade and Industry (METI), "Portal site for renewable policy of Japan" (2013).

As a result, renewable generating capacity has been rapidly growing in Japan since 2012, and the sum of capacity approved for FIT by May 2013 was exceeded by total accumulated capacity in March 2013. Most of the approved (in other words, future) capacity consists of non-residential photovoltaics (PV), which refers to megawatt-class and medium-class PV power plants on the roofs of buildings, and similar large PV systems. The dominance of PV power among FIT-qualifying systems stems from the short lead time for installing PV; wind and geothermal power projects will also be commissioned in the coming years.

Figure 3.23: Recent and Planned Short-term Additions to Renewable Energy Capacity in Japan (Units: Megawatts)

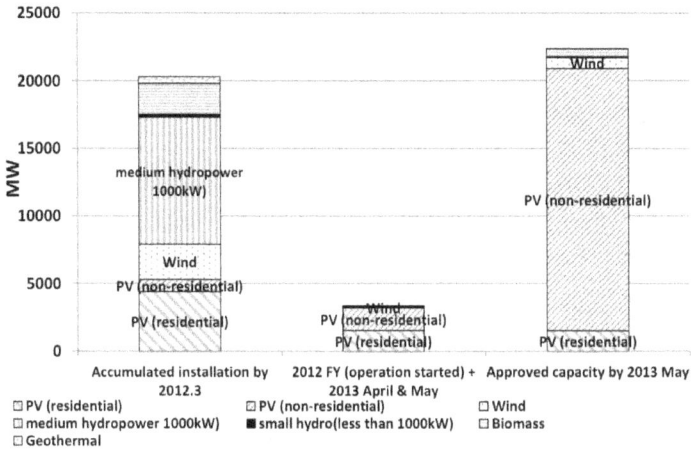

Source: Ministry of Economy, Trade and Industry (METI), "Status of Renewable Energy Generation Facilities" (2013), http://www.meti.go.jp/press/2013/08/20130820005/201308200 05-2.pdf

As of 2010, Japan's nuclear reactor fleet included fifty-four plants with a total capacity of 49 GW and an additional two plants under construction. Twelve more units are planned. Recent trends in reactor usage in Japan, however, have not been encouraging, with the annual capacity factor of nuclear power (the equivalent fraction of the year that reactors were running at full capacity) falling from over 80 percent in the late 1990s to about 60 percent in recent years. As shown in Figure 3.24, nuclear output in Japan had fallen from its peak of the late 1990s even before the 2011 Fukushima accident. Note that the 2007 decline in nuclear output shown in Figure 3.25 is the result of the July 2007 earthquake near Niigata, which caused the temporary shut-down (followed by continuing outages for safety checks) of the 7-unit Kashiwazaki-Kariwa nuclear power station. A combination of events, including accidents at nuclear power plants and revelations about nuclear mismanagement, were already causing public confidence in nuclear power to wane even prior to the disaster at the Fukushima I plant, which resulted in the drop to zero output shown on the right side of Figure 3.25.[70] The small rise from zero shown for 2012 in Figure 3.25 represents the restart of the Ohi #3 and #4 units in July-August 2012. As the Fukushima I accident has played out over the months, the Japanese government's commitment to nuclear power has looked progressively weaker, to the point where, in July 2011, Prime Minister Kan called for a phase-out of nuclear power.[71] These events, coupled with ongoing delays, cost overruns, and technical problems at the Rokkasho reprocessing plant, which was to have been the model for nuclear fuel recycling and waste management in Japan, combine to make the future contribution of nuclear power to Japan's GHG emissions reduction goals increasingly uncertain.

Figure 3.24: Historical Trends of Nuclear Power Monthly Output in Japan, 1986 through 2012 (10[10] kcal)

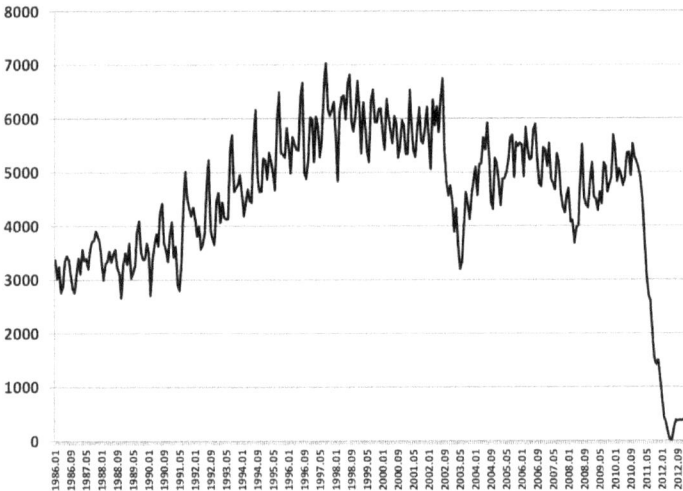

Source: Ministry of Economy, Trade and Industry (METI), "Monthly Report on Electric Power Statistics" (2013).

---

70   von Hippel, D. and Takase, K. (2011). Hayes, P., *et al.* (2011).
71   See, for example, Tokyo Times staff writer, "Kan: Nuclear Energy to Take a Back Seat," *Tokyo Times*, 11 May 2011, http://www.tokyotimes.com/2011/Kan-Nuclear-energy-to-take-a-back-seat/ Harlan, C., "Japanese Prime Minister Naoto Kan Calls for Phase-out of Nuclear Power," *Washington Post*, 13 July 2011, http://www.washingtonpost.com/world/japans-prime-minister-calls-for-phase-out-of-nuclear-power/2011/07/13/gIQAXxUJCI_story.html

Prospects for Meeting GHG Reduction and Green Economy Targets in Japan

Despite the modest progress on renewable energy to date, and the currently bleak outlook for the nuclear power industry in Japan, concerted green economy policies focusing on renewables and energy efficiency offer the potential for Japan to realize its environmental and energy security goals. Figure 3.25 shows the results of quantitative energy paths analysis by Kae Takase, co-author of this chapter, indicating that very significant reductions in Japan's GHG emissions are possible even in a scenario in which Japan's nuclear capacity declines by 60 percent (to about 20 GW) by 2030, so long as an aggressive program of energy efficiency and renewable energy deployment is undertaken (the "National Alternative with Minimum Nuclear" or "NA+Nuc. Min." See case in Figure 3.23).[72] The high-renewables, high-efficiency scenario with a "Maximum Nuclear" deployment (about 68 GW by 2030) would reduce emissions still further, but the relative contribution of the additional nuclear capacity in the Maximum Nuclear case, relative to the Minimum Nuclear, contributes only about 15 percent to the overall 2030 GHG reductions.

It is also more than conceivable that if the significant additional costs of the Maximum Nuclear deployment were directed toward energy efficiency and renewable energy, the reduction in emissions could be even greater than in the "NA+Nuc. Max" case. What is more, as shown in Figure 3.26, the rates of change of the factors in GHG emissions reduction implied by the various scenarios are not inconsistent with recent experience in Japan. Even assuming relatively robust (for Japan) economic growth, the change in energy use per unit of GDP, reflecting ongoing shifts in Japan's industrial structure and energy efficiency, will decrease at a lower rate than in 2002-2007. And while the change in CO_2 emissions per unit of energy use, reflecting "de-carbonization" of energy supplies, would decrease at the highest level ever in the "NA+Nuc. Max" scenario through 2020, the rate of change is not unfathomable given Japan's experience over the years.

---

72   Takase, K. and Suzuki, T. (2011).

Figure 3.25: Scenarios of GHG Emissions Reduction in Japan
(Units: million tonnes of CO_2)

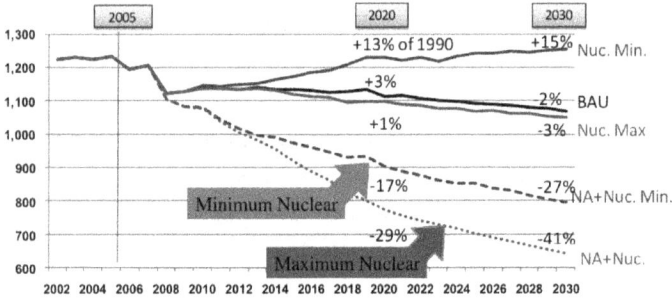

Source: Prepared by Kae Takase (2013/2014) based on LEAP (Long-range Energy Alternatives Planning) modeling results as undertaken for the Nautilus Institute project *Spent Fuel and Reduction of Radiological Risk After Fukushima.*

Figure 3.26: Factors Analysis for GHG Emissions Reduction Scenarios
(Units: annual change in factors)

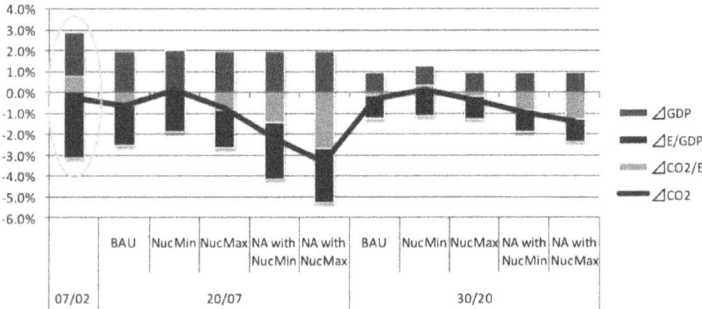

Source: Prepared by Kae Takase (2013/2014) based on LEAP (Long-range Energy Alternatives Planning) modeling results as undertaken for the Nautilus Institute project *Spent Fuel and Reduction of Radiological Risk After Fukushima.*

Recent years have seen some encouraging developments in Japan with respect to policy and social trends that relate to GHG reduction efforts and green economy development. An "Eco-points" program has been developed that awards points for the purchase of high-efficiency electric home appliances and equipment (for example, refrigerators, TVs, air conditioners, insulation, and high-performance windows). Points can be exchanged for green products or travel vouchers, gift certificates, and other items. It is estimated that the program has already resulted in a reduction of national CO_2 emissions of 0.1 percent at a net cost (that is, factoring in fuel cost savings) of 2000 yen per tonne of emissions reduction over the lifetime of the high-efficiency devices installed. Programs providing subsidies for "eco-cars" (hybrid and high-efficiency cars) and efficient boilers have also been provided. The combination of these programs, in addition to green economy publicity and other factors, has resulted in social change in Japan. It is becoming "fashionable" to buy hybrid cars, to live in a house with PV on the rooftop, to exchange old air conditioners for efficient units, and to receive eco-points.

Economic modeling of different ways of reaching Japan's GHG emissions reduction goals underscores the utility of "green economy" investments. Matsuhashi and his co-authors modeled a 15 percent reduction in Japan's GHG emissions by 2020, excluding credits for carbon sinks and other Kyoto protocol mechanisms.[73] Their results suggest that an emphasis on improving energy efficiency —such as for vehicles, homes, and appliances — and lowering costs for efficient devices and for photovoltaic power systems yield much higher household utility (that is, reduces household expenditures) across all income classes relative to approaches that rely mostly on fuel-switching (toward gas and nuclear power) and carbon taxes, but not on energy efficiency.

Although the implementation of strong policies related to green economy development has been relatively slow in Japan, a number of groups both within and outside of the Japanese government have given significant thought to a green economy transition for Japan. A Roadmap Committee on GHG emissions reduction, convened by the Central Environmental Council of Ministry of the Environment, has developed a set of Low-Carbon Society (LCS) scenarios and policies to promote an LCS in Japan.[74] This comprehensive effort (of which only selected results are discussed here) studied environmental options geared toward achieving a

---

[73] Matsuhashia, R., *et al.*, "Sustainable Development under Ambitious Medium Term Target of Reducing Greenhouse Gases," *Procedia Environmental Sciences*, 2(2010), doi: http://dx.doi.org/10.1016/j.proenv.2010.10.135.

[74] See, for example, Fujino, J., "Japan and Asian Low-Carbon Society Scenarios and Actions" in *East Asia Low Carbon Green Growth Roadmap Informal Brainstorming Meeting* (Bangkok, 2010).

Low-Carbon Society in Japan, including "Techno-Socio Innovation" studies of elements such as changes in urban structure (including green buildings, self-sustained cities, decentralized services), information technology, social development (eco-awareness, effective communication, and dematerialization), and transportation system evolution (next generation vehicles, efficient transportation system, and advanced logistics). Scenarios built out of these elements were developed and evaluated using economic and technical models to determine their sufficiency for reaching GHG reduction goals. The scenarios also proposed directions for long-term global warming policies. Junichi Fujino notes that the LCS effort identified a dozen changes that are consistent with a green economy that would make it possible for Japan to achieve 70 percent CO_2 emissions reductions by 2050, namely:

1. Comfortable and green built environment
2. Anytime, anywhere appropriate appliances
3. Promoting seasonal local food
4. Sustainable building materials
5. Environmentally-enlightened business and industry
6. Swift and smooth logistics
7. Pedestrian-friendly city design
8. Low-carbon electricity
9. Local renewable resources for local demand
10. Next generation fuels
11. Labelling to encourage smart and rational choices
12. Low-carbon society Leadership.[75]

Significant reductions in Japanese GHG emissions will require a necessarily complex, integrated combination of elements incorporating many of the aspects of the broad energy security definition articulated earlier in this chapter (energy supply, technology, environment, economics, and social/policy considerations).[76]

---

75   Fujino, J., "Backcasting and a Dozen Actions for 70% CO2 Emissions Reductions by 2050 in Japan," in *Low Carbon Society Symposium* (Tokyo, 2009).
76   Fujino, J. (2010).

Requirements for Successful Green Economy/Renewable Energy Development in Japan

Japan's traditional focus on energy supply security, with its emphasis primarily on diversifying oil and gas imports and on nuclear power, is being tested by the requirements of greenhouse gas emissions reduction and a host of other economic, political, and social factors. Japan's modest efforts at promoting renewable energy development and its solid commitment (at least until very recently) to nuclear power both run contrary to recent international trends. As shown in Figure 3.27, Japan's renewables and nuclear energy policies are not consistent with trends in the rest of the world, which show an accelerating deployment of renewable power systems and a very limited net new nuclear capacity, contrary to the claims of several organizations that nuclear power is undergoing a "renaissance." The major exception to this pattern, as noted earlier in this chapter, is China, which is adding both nuclear and renewable capacity at a rapid rate. The European Union added significant gas-fired, wind, and PV capacity from 2000 through 2008, while decommissioned coal-fired and nuclear capacity exceeded new capacity additions.

Recent experience in a number of cases shows cost estimates for nuclear power and solar photovoltaic power heading in opposite directions. A nuclear plant under construction in Finland seems to be perpetually forty-five months from completion, and its estimated costs have risen by a factor of three, with "busbar"[77] costs of power from the reactor (including interest) estimated at 0.12 euros per kWh, or about 17 US cents/kWh. According to at least one group, and based on historical and projected costs in the United States, the relative busbar costs of solar PV power and nuclear power, on average, "crossed over" in 2010, such that costs for electricity from solar PV systems are now less than those for nuclear power plants.[78] Annual global investment in new renewable energy capacity rose 500 percent from

---

77 "Busbar" costs are the costs of power generation, including fuel, capital costs, and operations and maintenance costs, measured at the point where power from a generator enters the transmission and distribution grid. Busbar costs are typically used to compare the full costs and benefits of power sources, though in fact distributed generation options, such as rooftop solar PVs and other on-site power sources, have an additional advantage over central power stations because less transmission and distribution capacity is required to move power form on-site systems to consumer, and less transmission and distribution losses are incurred.

78 Blackburn, J.O. and Cunningham, S., *Solar and Nuclear Costs — the Historic Crossover* (Durham: NC WARN: Waste Awareness & Reduction Network, 2010).

2004 to $150 billion in 2009. Around the world, national and regional plans are emphasizing renewable power and the development of transmission systems, including international transmission connections to accommodate the sharing of renewable capacity. Plans and proposals, including the European Wind Energy Association's Offshore Network Development Master Plan and the "Gobitec" scheme to move wind power from the Gobi desert of Mongolia and China to population centers in China, Korea, and even Japan, are examples of such international transmission connections that seek to share the risk and benefit for a future international "energy community."[79]

Figure 3.27: Global Trends in Annual Additions to Wind, Solar, and Nuclear Power Capacity (GW)

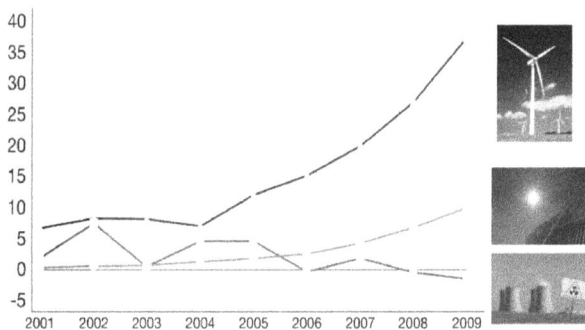

Source: Iida, T., "Changing Climate Change & Energy Policy and Politics in Japan," Presentation for Nautilus Institute Workshop *Interconnections of Global Problems in Northeast Asia*, Seoul, Korea October 18, 2010.

In 2010, the two major political parties in Japan had different policies on renewable energy and GHG emissions targets. The Democrats called for medium-term GHG reductions of 25 percent relative to 1990, while the LDP called for 8 percent reductions from 1990. The Democrats sought a fairly substantial rise in the fraction of electricity generated from renewable

---

79 See for example, Seliger, B. and Kim, G.E., "Tackling Climate Change, Increasing Energy Security, Engaging North Korea and Moving Forward Northeast Asian Integration – "Green Growth" in Korea and the Gobitec Project," *Gobited Outline Paper*, 1-03 10112009 (2010).

fuels (from 9 percent — including existing hydro — to 24 percent in 2020), while LDP policy only proposed to increase non-hydro renewables by 1.6 percent in 2014, a move that was already legislated! The Democrats wanted to extend Feed-in Tariffs to all renewables, abandon the renewable portfolio standard, and introduce cap and trade legislation by 2012. The LDP would apply Feed-in Tariffs only to rooftop PVs, retain the renewable portfolio standard, and have no plans for cap and trade legislation. As of late 2010, however, following the historic change in Japan's government, with voters re-installing the Liberal Democratic Party and unseating the long-serving LDP, policies on GHG reduction and renewable energy in Japan became highly uncertain over the following years. .

A large part of the reason why Japan's GHG and renewable energy policies remain ineffective relative to other nations that have embraced FIT and renewable portfolio standard policies (Germany is a prime example)[80] is that much of Japan's decision making on these issues happens at the ministerial level. The Ministry of Economy, Trade, and Industry (METI) has jurisdiction over the energy sector, while the Ministry of Environment (MoE) has jurisdiction over climate change. The two ministries tend to have different attitudes about policies promoting renewable energy. METI, along with the Japanese electric utility monopolies, tends to have negative or reluctant attitudes about renewable energy policies, while MoE, siding with non-governmental organizations and the bulk of the general public, takes a more positive attitude. The leadership of Japan's industrial firms gravitates towards a middle position on the issue.

More generally, the structure of policymaking as it has traditionally been practiced in Japan does not lend itself to effective policymaking on GHG, renewable energy, or green economy issues. As shown in Figure 3.28, there tends to be a disconnect in Japan between policymaking on the macro scale (national policies), with detailed promulgation of and enforcement of regulations, and other policies within Japanese ministries ("meso sub-politics" in Figure 3.27). Then there is a further disconnect between the ministries and micro-scale results and goals (individual projects, for example). In addition, the press, non-governmental organizations, and

---

80   Starting from the introduction of feed-in-tariffs in 2000, Germany's total solar PV installations reached over 9000 MW by 2009, compared with less than 3000 MW in Japan. Meanwhile, Japan's former dominance in PV manufacturing (47 percent of the market in 2005) has fallen dramatically to 12 percent in 2009, as new manufacturers have entered the market causing global output to grow by more than 50 percent per year, while Japan's PV output has grown at about 10 percent annually.

members of civil society, tends to be less engaged at each level of the knowledge economy than is desirable in a society where the free flow of information and opinion between levels of government and the various actors in society combine to achieve a policy goal.

Figure 3.28: The Political Structure of and Information Flow in Energy and Climate Issues

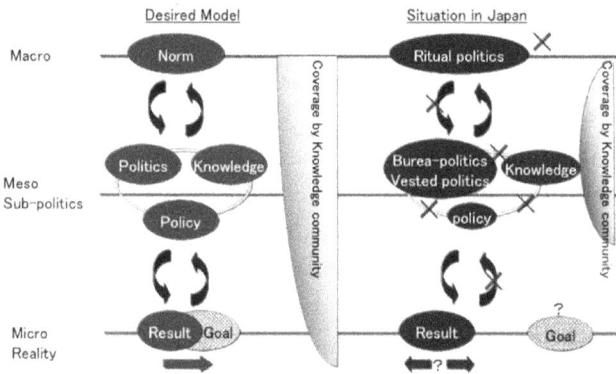

Source: Iida, T., "Changing Climate Change & Energy Policy and Politics in Japan," Presentation for Nautilus Institute Workshop *Interconnections of Global Problems in Northeast Asia*, Seoul, Korea, October 18, 2010.

Despite the traditionally top-down or ministry-driven structure of energy and climate politics in Japan, there is a significant history of key environmental policies actually being led at the local/municipal level. The development of Japan's national legislation on air and water pollution in the 1960s and 70s was initiated by Tokyo municipal ordinances from the late 1940s onward. Similarly, municipal initiatives in Tokyo on GHG reporting, energy efficiency labeling, and solar energy use preceded national action by several years. Japan's successful development of a green economy, and of the renewable energy systems that will help to power it, depends on making use of imaginative vision at all levels of government and civil society, seizing political windows of opportunity afforded by unforeseen events (such as the Fukushima accident), and then using innovative policies and financing techniques to create markets for green products and services. These same resources are likely to be required to address problems of urban insecurity in Japan; indeed, many of the approaches necessary for green economy development will also improve urban security, as well as directly addressing problems of climate change mitigation (through GHG emissions reduction) and adaptation (through moving to distributed energy systems). In addition, the regional and international networks developed in moving toward a green economy in Japan are likely to assist in addressing Japan's relationship with the DPRK by offering multiple opportunities for engagement on issues that are both highly useful to the DPRK and politically non-threatening to either nation.

Case Study of Green Economy Policies: Republic of Korea

The ROK's economy has been one of the economic marvels of the last few decades, growing rapidly and steadily, with few downturns. By 2010, the ROK had the world's 12th largest GDP and was ranked 10th among nations in electricity consumption and production, 10th in gas imports, 9th in oil consumption, and 4th in oil imports.[81] The ROK has become an international force in several industries, including steel, automobiles, and electronics, and it has seen a vast increase in the living standards of its people, as well as in urbanization. Like Japan, much of the ROK's energy needs are supplied by imports, and like Japan, the ROK has embraced nuclear power as a key source of electricity. Unlike Japan, however, for the ROK the DPRK serves as a much more significant factor, albeit a quite uncertain one, in its development of energy systems and drive toward energy security.

The last decade has seen some transitions in the ROK energy sector, including a move toward partial restructuring of its electricity, expanded investment in oil and gas producer nations, and a drive toward exports of nuclear technologies. The last few years, as of 2011, have also seen the development, and the very early phases of implementation, of green economy principles in the ROK and of policies related to the reduction of greenhouse gas emissions.

In the section that follows we provide background on the energy sector and energy security policies in the ROK, describe the genesis and current status of green economy and GHG emissions reduction policies and projections, review the strengths and weakness of existing green economy policies, and suggest how green economy and energy security policies in the ROK might interact with issues such as urban security, climate change, and improvement of the DPRK situation.[82]

---

81   Central Intelligence Agency (2011).
82   This description of the ROK's green growth challenges and initiatives is based on Sun-

Overview of the ROK's Energy and Economic Situation

At of the end of the Korean War, the ROK's economy and infrastructure, to the extent that it had survived the ravages of conflict, was largely agricultural, with most energy provided by biomass (wood and crop wastes) and from the ROK's modest reserves of anthracite coal. The country's rapid industrialization, particularly in the last thirty years, has been fueled by imported energy to the extent that, as of now, only a small percentage of energy is supplied from domestic sources, and much of that comes from the combustion of municipal and other wastes. Already by 2006, domestic coal constituted only about 2 percent of total ROK coal use, and much less than one per cent of total energy use. Figure 3.29 shows the trends in ROK GDP, primary energy use (that is, including inputs to processes such as electricity generation and oil refining), and final energy use (use of energy by consumers).

Both GDP and primary energy use have increased since 1981, with strong growth throughout the period with the exception of the Asian Financial Crisis of 1997 to 1998 and the global recession of 2008-2009. GDP grew approximately seven-fold from 1981-2013, while primary energy use grew by a factor of 6. As implied in Figure 3.29 and shown more clearly in Figure 3.30, the trend in intensity of energy use (that is, the use of energy per unit of ROK GDP) has shown two distinct trends, increasing (more energy use per unit of GDP) until about 1997 and then slowly decreasing through 2013, a fall due to a combination of greater efficiency of energy use and a slow shift to less energy-intensive industries. Although, as shown in Figure 3.30, the growth in energy consumption exceeded growth in GDP in every year from 1990 through 1997, from 1999 to 2009 growth in GDP surpassed growth in energy consumption in every year except 2003. Since the recession of 2008-9 this pattern has changed again, with primary energy consumption growing somewhat faster than GDP. Electricity consumption has consistently grown faster than primary energy consumption, as ROK consumers' end-uses of electricity have increased faster than those for other fuels.

Jin, Y. (2010). Cho, M. (2010). Elements of this discussion of green energy policies in the Republic of Korea provided in this section are also presented in Yun, S.J., *et al.*, "The Current Status of Green Growth in Korea: Energy and Urban Security," *The Asia-Pacific Journal*, 9(44) (2011).

Figure 3.29: GDP, Primary Energy Use, and Final Energy Use in the ROK, 1981-2013

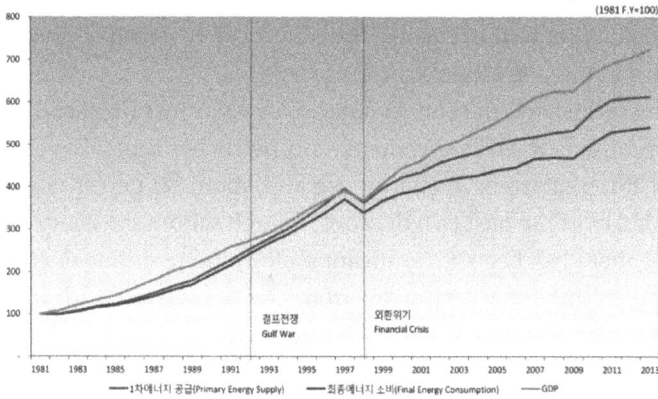

Source: Derived by Sun-Jin Yun from Korea Energy Economics Institute (KEEI), 2010, *Yearbook of Energy Statistics*.

Figure 3.30: Trends in Economic and Energy Sector Activity and Intensities in the ROK, 1990-2012

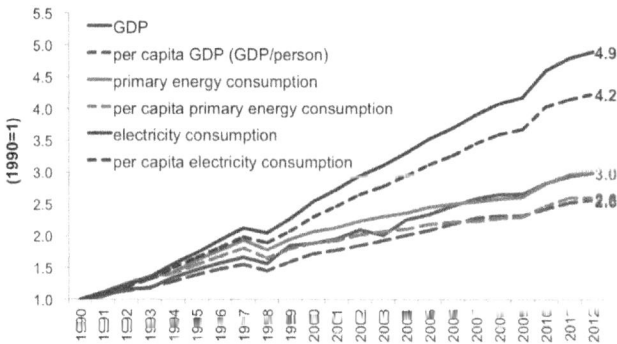

Source: Derived by Sun-Jin Yun from Korea Energy Economics Institute (KEEI), 2010, *Yearbook of Energy Statistics*.

One of the most notable changes in the last two decades in the ROK energy sector has been the increase in the use of natural gas, with a corresponding decrease in the use of oil. Industry still consumes the majority of final energy use in the ROK, with nearly half of industrial energy use coming from feedstock materials, mainly the oil product "naptha," which is used as an input in the petrochemicals industry.

Among industries, the energy-intensive subsectors (iron and steel, non-metallic products including cement, and petrochemicals) have accounted for about three quarters of energy use and about 30 percent of industrial value added over the past two decades, though within the energy-intensive industries there has been a significant shift in the fractions of energy used toward petrochemicals and away from the other two traditional heavy industries, even as the fractions of value added by heavy industries have remained roughly constant.

The largest change since 1990 has been the vast increase in the fraction of industrial value added in the ROK economy that has come from the fabricated metal subsector, including vehicle production, though the fraction of energy consumed in that subsector has risen only modestly. The fraction of industrial energy used and value added produced by the paper and publishing, textile and apparel, food and tobacco industries has declined over time, and though the fraction of energy used in "other" industries, including, for example, the electronics industry, has increased substantially since 1990, its share of value added has declined.

Limited domestic energy resources, a growing manufacturing base in industries highly relevant to nuclear power development, and the desire to develop expertise in nuclear technologies, among other considerations, led the ROK to emphasize nuclear power as an energy supply security measure. Twenty nuclear reactors are now under operation, with ongoing expansion expected to result in twenty-eight operating reactors by 2016. Nuclear generation accounted for 35 percent of generation in 2007, and plans call for an additional twenty-two reactors to be constructed by 2022. By 2007, the ROK's nuclear capacity and generation ranked sixth among the world's nations, its fraction of generation produced by nuclear power ranked fourth, and the ROK was first by a wide marge among nations in nuclear capacity per unit of land area.[83] The ROK has also been actively

---

83   *Key World Energy Statistics* (Paris: International Energy Agency, 2009), http://large.

promoting nuclear technology exports, including a recent deal to build reactors in the United Arab Emirates.[84]

The Development of the ROK's Climate and Green Economy Policies

A combination of factors has focused ROK attention on climate and green economy policies in recent years. Over the last century, climate records show that Korea's temperature has increased by 1.5°C, a rate double the global average (0.7°C), and the temperature in Seoul has increased by 2.5°C.[85] At the same time, the ROK's high energy consumption and near-complete import dependence are strong inducements to reduce exposure to energy supply security risks by developing domestic resources. The ROK also ranks ninth among the world's nations in CO_2 emissions, sixth in overall greenhouse gas emission, and first in the rate at which its GHG emissions grew between 1990 and 2004, nearly doubling (increasing by 90.1 percent) over that span. As of 2006, energy use constituted by far the largest fraction of the ROK's GHG emissions, at over 84 percent, with industrial sector non-energy emissions, including emissions of chlorofluorocarbons from refrigeration systems and other sources; sulfur hexafluoride, perfluorocarbons, and other compounds used as solvents and cleaning agents in the electronics and other industries; and CO_2 from cement production constituting the next largest source of emissions at somewhat less than 10 percent.[86] Of energy-related sources of GHG emissions, energy transformation (dominated by electricity generation) was the largest, at over 35 percent, with industry accounting for 30 percent.

The ROK's first major set of climate change-related policies was set out in the 1999 draft of the "1st Comprehensive Counter Plan for the Framework Convention on Climate Change (1999-2001) Act on Countermeasures

---

stanford.edu/courses/2009/ph204/landau1/docs/key_stats_2009.pdf. Schneider, M., *et al.*, *Nuclear Power in a Post-Fukushima World: 25 Years after Chernobyl Accident* (Washington, DC: Worldwatch Institute, 2011).

84 Yonhap News Agency staff writer, "The Consortium of Korea Electric Power Corporation Won a Nuclear Power Contract of 40 Billion Dollars," *Yonhap News*, 27 December 2009.

85 Kwon, W.T., "Changes in Land Use Resulting from Abnormal Climate and Natural Disaster," *Kugto*, 353 (2007). Some of the increase in temperatures measured in Seoul are doubtless due to the increase in the urban "heat island" effect as the city has grown.

86 *Handbook of Energy and Climate Change* (Yongin City: Korea Energy Management Corporation, 2010).

Against Global Warming." From 1999 through 2007, the ROK's policy responses relating to climate change tended to be modest in scope, calling for emissions reduction from "business as usual" levels that were not particularly aggressive and which were protective of what was seen as the required increases in energy use to drive a growing economy. In the Basic National Plan for Energy as of 2007, growth in energy use slows from the levels of the last decade, but overall energy use continues to climb, even assuming a program of demand-side management (DSM) is implemented.

In 2008, however, and as indicated in Table 3.9, a major change occurred in the ROK's climate policies, which shifted from what can be termed a "defensive" position to one that is relatively proactive in addressing climate issues. Though the Lee Myung-bak administration began its tenure with an emphasis on high economic growth, supported by massive civil engineering development, its second year (2008) saw a sudden turn toward the principles of green growth. This policy change was underscored by presidential announcements, at the G20 meetings in Japan and Italy in 2008 and 2009, of the ROK's plans for aggressive mid-term GHG emissions reduction targets, followed by the release in August 2009 of three scenarios for the ROK's reduction targets as produced by the Presidential Committee on Green Growth.

Both domestic and international considerations played into the Lee administration's change in approach. In his speech on the 60th anniversary of national independence, President Lee emphasized green growth as a "new national development paradigm" that would allow future generations to secure a reasonable standard of living, in contrast to the focus in the previous sixty years on economic growth and export targets, with reductions in GHG emissions now a key indicator of "low-carbon green growth." At the same time, the administration sought to upgrade the ROK's international image by positioning it as an "early mover" in the green economy transition, thus improving the ROK's "brand value," and also as a trusted and respected mediator between developing and developed nations, building on the ROK's status as a (relatively) newly industrialized nation with strong economic links to both the developed and developing world.[87]

---

87   It is possible that this change in the ROK's position was influenced in part by the status of Ban Ki-moon as the Secretary General of the United Nations. Ban began his term as UN Secretary General in January, 2007.

Table 3.9: Evolution of the ROK's Climate Policies, 1999-2008

Plans	Sector/ project	Detail	Note
The 1st comprehensive counter plan (1999)	4/36	1. Decreasing GHG emissions (27)	
		2. Applying the flexible mechanism (1)	* Korea's first national plan on climate change
		3. Decreasing PFC, HFC, SF6 emissions (1)	* A three year plan
		4. Creating infrastructure for reducing GHG emissions (7)	
The 2nd comprehensive counter plan (2002)	5/84	1. Building negotiation capacity (6)	* Establishing basic framework
		2. Exploiting technologies for GHG emissions reduction (20)	
		3. Enhancing GHG reduction measures (40)	
		4. Kyoto mechanism and building statistical database	
		5. Scaling up citizens' participation and cooperation	
The 3rd comprehensive counter plan (2005)	3/91	1. Establishing a foundation for the implementation of agreements (30)	* Adding adaptation measures
		2. Reducing sectoral GHG emissions (45)	
		3. Building infrastructure for adapting to CC (16)	
The 4th comprehensive counter plan (2007)	5/19	1. GHG emissions reduction (6)	* Presidential transition period
		2. Climate change adaptation (3)	* A five year plan
		3. Research and development (4)	
		4. Building infrastructure (4)	
		5. International cooperation (2)	
The comprehensive plan on combating climate change	4/176	1. Developing climate industry as a new economic driving force (48)	* 'Low carbon, green growth' vision
		2. Improving the quality of life and the environment (106)	* A five year plan
		3. Contributing to the global efforts to combat CC (12)	
		4. Key policy tools (10)	

Note: The authors would like to gratefully acknowledge the assistance of Nyun-Bae Park, Research Professor, Sejong University, ROK, in assembling this Table.

The nominal goals of the ROK's recent climate and development policies are to pursue the development of a "new economy coupled with ecology," in effect creating a virtuous circle between economy and ecology, leading to a green economy that can be a new growth engine for the ROK. Despite the development of an array of related policies, however, it is too early to discern significant actual green economy progress in the ROK resulting from green growth strategies promulgated during 2009 and 2010. Figure 3.31 summarizes a mid-term "target" scenario for the year 2020, based on GHG emissions reductions announced by the Ministry of Environment in 2014. The target scenario represents a considerable departure from the pattern of emissions growth to date and from the BAU (business as usual) case, since the BAU case includes a continued reduction in emissions per unit of economic output that is overwhelmed by the impacts of increasing affluence on per-capita emissions in the ROK, even as the ROK population begins to decline. The target scenario shown in Figure 3.31, with 2020 emissions 30 percent lower than the BAU case and a few percent lower than in 2005, calls for reductions in emissions in all sectors of the ROK economy, with reductions of 25 to 34 percent in the transportation, building (including residential and commercial), transformation (for example, power production), and public sectors, and somewhat lower reductions in other sectors, including industry. This 2014 target scenario follows the pattern of an earlier set of emissions reduction scenarios adopted by the ROK government in November 2009[88] and submitted to the UN in January of 2010.

Figure 3.31: Mid-term GHG Reduction Target and Road Map in the ROK

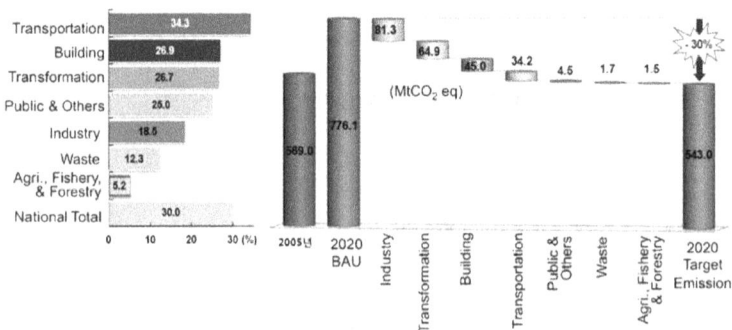

Source: Ministry of Environment, "GHG reduction road map was prepared" (2014) (press release).

---

88   See, for example, Presidential Committee on Green Growth, *Greenhouse Gas Reduction Target* (Green Growth Korea, 2011).

Following President Lee's speech on the 60th anniversary of the National Foundation Day (August 15, 2008), all government ministries were almost immediately engaged in producing a plethora of policy programs to institutionalize green growth strategy, with competition between ministries not uncommon. In just over five months between August 2008 and January 2009, the following policy programs below (and others) had been put forward, all of which focus on developing new energy and industrial technologies and generating new jobs in the field of the green economy:

- The National Energy Basic Plan and Industrial Development Strategy for Green Energy
- The Basic Plan for Comprehensive Action against Climate Change
- The Long-term Master Plan for National Research and Development on Climate Change
- The "Green New Deal"
- Comprehensive Measures for R&D on Green Technologies
- The Vision and Development Strategy for New Growth Power

The three institutional pillars for green growth in the ROK to date have been the establishment of the Presidential Commission on Green Growth in January 2009, the launching of the National Strategy and Five-Year Plan for Green Growth in July of 2009, and legislation of the Basic Act on Low-Carbon Green Growth in December 2009, which went into effect on April 14, 2010. A "Five-Year Green Growth Plan" envisioned the elevation of the ROK to the 7th-leading "Green Power Country" as of 2020, and to the 5th by 2050, based on three strategies and ten policy directions:

- Strategy 1: climate change adaptation and energy independence, including effective reduction of GHG emissions, reduction of petroleum use, increasing energy independence, and strengthening of the ROK's adaptation capability against climate change impacts.
- Strategy 2: creation of "new growth power" through green technology development and its utilization to promote green industries, deepen the ROK's industrial structure, and build the base of the green economy.
- Strategy 3: quality-of-life improvement and upgrading of national status through the construction of green space and green transportation systems, green reform of the patterns of everyday life, and embodiment of the global model nation of green growth.

These strategies are supported by a number of sector-specific goals and targets, including those in Table 3.10 below for the building, transportation, industrial, and energy transformation sectors; the latter, notably, includes and extends the ROK's goals for expansion of nuclear power.

Table 3.10: ROK GHG Emission Mitigation Policies

Building sector	Transportation sector
31% reduction by '20 compared with BAU	33~37% reduction from BAU by '20
Strengthening energy performance standards: 50% reduction in heat and cooling from '12, passive house level from '17, mandatory zero energy from '25	Designating green transportation zone; green vehicle first; discount point from mass transit
Energy consumption cap from '10	Expansion of rail road in the share of total SOC ('Shipper-owned container') traffic 29% in '09 to 50% in '20)
Energy management in energy intensive building from '11	Over 65% share of mass transit
Certificate of energy consumption from' 12 in case of purchasing and rent	
Industrial sector	**Transformation sector**
Energy target setting program from '10 (for energy intensive industries with more than 0.5 MTOE)	Expansion of nuclear (41% of installation by '30, 59% of generation)
	Introduction of RPS in '12
	Building smart grid

Source: Presidential Committee on Green Growth (PCGG), "Presidential Committee on Green Growth suggests national GHG emission reduction targets," 11/04/2009 press release.

To implement these strategies, the ROK was to spend 107 trillion won (0.107 trillion US dollars) on green growth projects between 2009 and 2014, equivalent to 2 percent of GDP, with an annual growth rate of 10.2 percent.

Strengths and Weaknesses of Current Green Economy Policies in the ROK

Although the green energy policies developed during the last few years in the ROK are a notable departure, at least nominally, from earlier policies, it is not clear that the ROK's policy shift represents a heartfelt conversion to the green economy concepts as defined earlier in this section. Rather, ROK green economy policies to date have tended to focus on the establishment of techno-bureaucratic and hardware-oriented institutions for green growth, and they have resulted in the over-politicization of green growth without building much of a constituency and concern for green growth among the general public. Instead of improvements in the ROK's environment, the last few years have arguably seen a deterioration of the environmental performance of the national economy. The 2010 Environmental Performance Index released by the World Economic Forum rated the ROK 94th of 163 countries, a drop of forty-three places since 2008 and the lowest ranking among OECD member nations.[89]

It can be argued that the idea of "green growth" as it is currently being implemented in ROK policy is a largely a product of conceptual and ideological degradation of previous meanings of the term. The "two ecos" (economy and ecology) have been at the heart of environmental policy in the ROK since the Kim Dae-Jung government (1998-2003). Moreover, sustainable development, a higher-level conception of green growth, was instituted as a national priority policy during the Kim Dae-Jung and the Noh Moon-Hyun governments (2003-2008). The current advocates of green growth in the ROK misinterpret sustainable development as a Western-centered and ecology-biased concept, and thus not suitable for the ROK. There has thus been a process of excluding and discriminating against traditional "green" views, beginning with the degradation of the original Presidential Commission on Sustainable Development (PCSD) into a ministerial commission under the control of Minster of Environment, with its policy review position taken over by the current Presidential Commission on Green Growth (PCGG).

Although the PCSD was typical of a governance body representing a wide range of different stakeholders, the PCGG is composed almost entirely of pro-governmental techno-bureaucratic experts representing largely the interests of the business community and excluding traditional green advocates from civil society. This has resulted, essentially, in the representation in green-growth policymaking of just one perspective, that of advocates for market-driven green growth. When the second term of the PCGG commenced in July 2010 and took up the theme of market-driven green growth in its 8th general meeting, suggestions from the industrial and business communities were the primary topics debated, with business and allied interests complaining loudly that green growth policies included in the proposals offered "only green, no growth," a reversal of the "only

---

89   See, for example, Yale Center for Environmental Law & Policy, *et al.*, *Environmental Performance Index 2010, South Korea* (New Haven: Yale University, 2010).

growth, no green" complaints of the environmental community at an earlier stage of the policy debate.

As a result of this shift in how the concept of green growth is put into practice in the ROK, the prospects for true reform of the ROK's environmental performance based on current policies are limited by the paradox of the ROK's policies of green growth and the green economy. Essentially, these policies presently emphasize the economy first and "green" second. The current green growth strategy comprises two key approaches: (1) "low-carbonization," meaning reduction of greenhouse gas emissions and other environmental pollution to accomplish "defensive green growth" and (2) "green industrialization," meaning the generation of new growth, power, and jobs for "offensive green growth." These priorities are reflected in the chapter structure of the "Basic Act on Low-Carbon Green Growth," which reads:

1. Promotion of Green Economy and Industry
2. Measures for Climate Change and Energy
3. Construction of Sustainable Territory and Environment

Operationally, in green growth policy implementation, priority has been placed on "the promotion of green economy and industry," while policies to address climate change, energy security, sustainable land use, and other environmental causes are implemented only to the extent that they support the priority agenda. This reveals the standpoint of the current Korean government: "the economy (growth) is first, green is second." Such growth, even if considered "green," is unlikely to result in significant environmental clean-up due to the following chain of logic. First, the linkage between low-carbon development and green industrialization is "green technology." Green technologies, in turn, are eco-efficient technologies that offer a relative reduction in the amount of environmental pollution per unit of economic (resource and energy) input, but do not necessarily imply that the absolute amount of environmental pollution produced by the economy will be lower than "business as usual" or some other policy scenario. This further implies that the more green growth based on the principle of eco-efficiency is successfully pursued, the more environmental pollution it generates. As a result, the green economy generated by the ROK's current green growth policies is likely to end up being neither sustainable nor secure.

The ROK's "green growth" energy policy may be efficient, but by more standard global definitions of the concept, it is rather un-green. Although the ROK's 2020 target for greenhouse gas reduction is 30 percent of the 2020 BAU emissions estimate, on closer examination the largest portion of green energy included in policies to achieve the target comes from nuclear power, a type of efficient but un-green energy. It is planned that nuclear power use will increase from 36 percent of total 2007 power generation to 59 percent in 2030, while absorbing the largest share of the budget for green technology development (35.9 percent in 2009). This planned nuclear development, however, is not without opposition in the ROK. Within a few years, the ROK's existing sites for nuclear power plants will have all of the reactor units they can reasonably accommodate, and new plant sites will be required. As of 2009, although more than 80 percent of ROK residents acknowledged the need for nuclear power, a growing number (over 60 percent) were concerned about nuclear safety, and just over a quarter of survey respondents found the prospect of new nuclear plants in their own communities acceptable.[90] It is likely, in the aftermath of the Fukushima accident, that a similar survey would find less positive public perceptions of nuclear power in the ROK.

Meanwhile, renewable energy, more typically considered to be a form of green energy, will continue to occupy a minor proportion of the total energy consumption during the forthcoming fifty years or so, rising from about 2.7 percent in 2009 to 6 percent in 2020, and only then to a more substantial 30 percent in 2050. Concern for energy independence as manifested in the ROK's green power policies is not so acute: the ROK's rate of energy independence (the fraction of energy supplies from domestic sources) excluding nuclear power in 2007 was 3.4 percent, but rose to 16 percent if nuclear power is considered a domestic resource (though the ROK imports nuclear fuel and licenses some nuclear technologies from other nations).

There is no clear target for energy independence based on green energy. As the ROK's export-oriented economic growth system operates almost entirely through imports of cheap energy from overseas, the proposed goal of energy independence through the application of current policies appears merely rhetorical in anything but the very long run, and only then with the most aggressive of fuel substitution policies. This likely

---

90   Korea Nuclear Energy Promotion Agency, *Survey Results of People's Nuclear Awareness in 2010* (Seoul: Korea Nuclear Energy Promotion Agency, 2010).

lack of progress on energy supply security implies that without changing Korea's economic growth regime, which is sustained by the lowest energy efficiency (measured as income per unit of energy use) among OECD countries, in part because of the concentration of heavy industries in the ROK, substantially improving energy supply security seems infeasible in the ROK under current green growth policies.

A substantial fraction of the ROK's green growth program is an outgrowth of a bias toward large civil engineering projects as drivers of development. As such, the green growth program features arguably "high-carbon" construction of so-called "green cities." In this focus, the green growth strategy stems from the civil engineering growth that the current ROK administration, with its renewed (relative to previous administration) emphasis on civil engineering projects, is inclined to pursue emphatically. The Green New Deal program, part of the green growth strategy package, clearly shows this propensity. 64 percent of the total program budget (some 50 trillion won, or nearly half of the total green growth budget) is to be allocated to projects associated with civil engineering work, including the restructuring of four major rivers, generating 910,000 construction jobs out of the total 950,000 jobs estimated to be created under the Green New Deal.

Though the ROK is a highly urbanized society, there is as yet no national target to reduce the total energy consumed and greenhouse gas produced in urban areas, though globally cities consume 75 percent of total final energy and produce 80 percent of total GHG emissions. In the ROK, most of the policy efforts planned for the greening of cities tend to be skewed toward constructing new green cities, which are projected to use 30 percent less energy than existing cities consume, rather than improving the energy efficiency of existing built areas. It is unclear from existing plans whether the considerable GHG emissions used in constructing new cities have been factored into the overall carbon budget for the project, or whether GHG emissions savings will somehow be achieved by retiring existing built areas as new cities are built. As a case in point, the pilot project to build a low-carbon city now underway in the district of Keongpyo in Kangneung (Gangneung)[91] is largely a demonstration of new promising

---

91   For a description of this project, see, for example, Kim, K.G., *Urban Development Model for the Low-Carbon Green City: The Case of Gangneung* (London: University College London), http://www.weitz-center.org/uploads/1/7/0/8/1708801/urban_development_model_kwi_gon_kim.pdf.

green technology and industry, and it is understood by local residents to be primarily a new regional development project.

Typical of the ROK's focus on civil engineering in its green growth program is the government's plan to supply 1 million "green homes" as a flagship project for the green economy. The green home project is designed to generate new housing technologies and industries in the ROK. The approach used in this project is typical of a top-down government-initiated policy program in that it expands the supply of more environmentally efficient housing by addressing the "hardware" of the housing stock, but with little effort to involve consumers in greening the patterns of their everyday life. By contrast, in Ireland, a program also called "Green Homes" has a vastly different focus.[92] Ireland's program has been initiated by community-based organizations and focuses on greening family life as well as community life (for example, through a "green school" component).

The ROK's green growth strategy, if pursued as currently planned, has a significant probability of running afoul of Jevon's Paradox, which states that as the efficiency with which a resource is used increases, the use of the resource tends to increase as well, absent measures (such as higher taxes) to prevent it, as consumers find they can afford more of the resource. As a result, it is likely that the more South Korea's green growth is pursued, the more energy its economy will consume and the more greenhouse gases it will produce because the green economy policies rely on the intriguing principle of eco-efficiency. Thus, more investment in eco-efficient hardware such as passive housing, green industries, and green cities will be likely to end up causing more total energy to be consumed and producing more total greenhouse gas than is presently produced.

Conclusion: Green Economy Policies in the ROK

The ROK's green growth strategy, as currently formulated, includes some impressive targets and demonstration projects, but at its heart emphasizes economic growth and national industrial competitiveness rather than the true "greening" of the South Korean economy. As such, the ROK's current "green" policies are in effect mostly policies for further benefiting existing ROK industries, including the nuclear and construction industries. As a

---

92   See, for example, *What Is Green Home?* (Dublin: An Taisce and the Ireland Environmental Protection Agency, 2011), http://www.greenhome.ie/

result, energy and urban security in South Korea's feeble green economy can be secured only insofar as South Korea's current growth policy regime is either abandoned or recast/reborn as a genuine environmental welfare regime. To do so, more autonomy, and likely more resources, should be granted to the civil society organizations that are best placed to initiate the greening of the everyday lives of South Koreans in cities and towns at the grassroots level.

Such a shift calls for analysis of the additional inputs nascent local policies will need to succeed, and for a re-alignment of the development goals of the green economy with the goals of sustainable development. Such a re-alignment would, among other aims, seek to change patterns of energy consumption in existing cities, pursuing a green economy that makes better use of local resources and reduces the separation, which is considerable in the ROK, between where energy (especially electricity) is produced and where it is consumed by adopting much more distributed (including renewable) generation.

Tools to accomplish such a re-alignment would include energy pricing schemes that favor local electricity generation (such as attractive Feed-in Tariffs for distributed generation) and promote energy efficiency (such as rates that increase as a household or business consumes more). Efforts should be made to site power plants closer to consumers so as to more directly relate the impacts of electricity generation and transmission to those who use the power (and reduce the impacts on those who do not). Again, support for distributed generation and "smart grid" development can help.

In addition, green economy strategies in the ROK should seek to improve the affordability of energy services to low-income residents[93] and to take advantage of the fact that after energy consumption reaches a certain level, long since exceeded in the ROK, human welfare, as measured by the Human Development Index, rises very little with increasing energy use,[94] meaning that an emphasis on improving the efficiency with which

---

93   The lowest-income residents of the ROK, the "energy poor," spend a much higher proportion of their income on energy than higher-income residents, and tend to use lower-quality fuels. Korean Ministry of Economy and Knowledge, *Reports of Energy Census* (Seoul: Korean Ministry of Economy and Knowledge, 2008).

94   Ebenhack, B.W. and Martinez, D.M., "Understanding of the Role of Energy Consumption in Human Development through the Use of Saturation Phenomena," *Energy Policy*, 36 (2008), doi: http://dx.doi.org/10.1016/j.enpol.2007.12.016; Anderson, D., *et al.*, *World Energy Assessment* (New York: United Nations Development Programme, 2004). Gaye, A., *Access to Energy and Human Devel* (New York: United Nations Development Programme, 2008).

energy is used but not necessarily expanding the use of energy services, on average, by Koreans, should be a central goal.

Existing ROK green growth policies tend to use the type of top-down policy strategies that are traditional in South Korea. Achieving true sustainable energy and economic development, founded on the three goals of economic, environmental, and social sustainability, will require a different approach, one that blends considerations of efficiency and energy supply security with low-carbon and low-pollution systems, as well as a commitment to equity and democratic participation. Energy sector approaches such as energy efficiency improvement, renewable energy adoption, use of decentralized energy systems, and enhanced participation of residents in energy decisions and the running of energy systems can be combined with other approaches, such as changes in land use to promote more balanced and low-impact use of the ROK's land, enhanced production and use of local food, and lifestyle transformation.

As a part of a sustainable development approach, expanded local energy use may offer several advantages, including:

- More energy democracy, providing local residents with opportunities (and responsibilities) to participate in production and consumption decisions;

- A transition to soft-path energy, moving from centralized supply-oriented systems to more decentralized, demand management-oriented systems, with an expansion of the use of renewable energy;

- Improving energy security through efficiency improvement and renewable energy development, thus responding to peak oil and energy resource depletion problems;

- Improving energy justice in that local communities would be more responsible for both the costs and benefits of energy production; and

- Revitalizing the local economy, in that money required for energy production and consumption would circulate within a community to a greater extent, rather than leaving the community (and often the country).

These approaches to the achievement of a green economy address issues of energy security, urban security, and climate change. These green economy/sustainable development approaches can also, if developed and implemented appropriately, help to improve the ROK's relationship with the DPRK, and thus make progress on resolving the DPRK nuclear weapons situation.

First, by addressing sustainable energy and economic development issues on the local level, but implemented with national coordination, processes in the ROK can serve as models for use in the DPRK, and the local emphasis may provide good opportunities for engagement with DPRK counterparts on non-political and grassroots levels that are likely to be less threatening to the DPRK than engagement on large, centralized projects. Second, if the ROK is seen to be moving away from nuclear power to less centralized alternatives, the DPRK may feel less pressure to move forward on nuclear energy and nuclear weapons development. Third, as the ROK develops expertise in local power, it will be in a position to share that expertise with the DPRK, including, for example, in joint ventures on energy production and other technologies appropriate for use in both countries and contributing to the local economies in both nations.

Conversely, the threat of a DPRK attack arguably affects, at least in some ways, how the ROK government develops and implements its policies, in that when threatened, any organization tends to concentrate decision-making power and limit access to information. On a less theoretical level, the threat of a DPRK attack may, for example, argue against the placement of key energy infrastructure in areas near the Demilitarized Zone (DMZ) where they would be more vulnerable to attack or sabotage. If progress is made in addressing the DPRK nuclear weapons issue, thereby reducing tensions between the two Koreas, it may help to stimulate the ROK government to promote a less-centralized, more local approach to a green economy transition, one more in keeping with the more usual concepts of sustainable development.

Conclusion: Green Economy Efforts in Northeast Asia — Key Similarities, Differences, and Ways Forward

Green economy policies in China, Japan, and the ROK show some similarities, but also significant differences. Below we briefly summarize what we see as the consistent and diverging elements in the policies reviewed, identify the needs for moving green economy policies forward, and identify policies that seem to be generally "robust" region-wide — that is, applicable to a wide variety of policy goals in multiple settings.

Consistent Elements in the Genesis and Shape of Green Economy Policies in the Region

Green economy policies in China, Japan, and the ROK have all grown out of the recognition that current patterns of environmental degradation due to the use of energy and other resources are not sustainable, and that changes are needed. In each case, though to varying degrees, the goal of being perceived as a global leader/early adopter in the green economy movement also played a role in promoting interest in green economies among policymakers, as did the promise of the economic benefits of being a leader in the production of green technologies. Most elements of the green economy plans in the three countries are similar — improvements in residential and industrial energy efficiency, land stewardship, mass transit systems, vehicle efficiency, and building energy performance all feature in the green economy plans in each nation, as does a greater effort at deploying renewable energy systems and nuclear power (with the exception of very recent announcements in Japan). Official plans in none of the three countries, to date, have much emphasized the role of local governments and civil society in achieving a green economy, which is at least in part because all three countries have a strong tradition of top-down government.

Differing Elements in the Genesis and Shape of Green Economy Policies in the Region

Despite these similar green economy elements, the three countries are starting from different points in terms of development, resources, and social situations, and thus the policies developed to date differ. China, with a lower (but rapidly rising) state of economic development than the other two nations and with greater indigenous energy resources, but also ten and twenty times the populations of Japan and the ROK, is promising (and, in some cases, already delivering) a more aggressive effort on energy efficiency and certainly on renewable energy than the other two. Japan's green economy plans have tended to be less ambitious than the others, in part due to the poor state of the economy in recent years, as well as to the utility-dominated structure of Japan's energy sector policymaking.

The ROK has, since 2008, shown a sudden shift toward the development of green economy policies, but to date, most of these policies appear to have benefitted established industries more than the environment or energy users in South Korea.

The three countries also seem to place differing levels of importance on the use of energy pricing and energy taxes to move markets toward greener consumption, with China showing more willingness to use price signals (albeit starting from lower price regimes for energy and energy-using devices), and Japan and the ROK being rather less willing to do so. In addition, the three countries are at different levels when it comes to the influence of civil society and local government on key energy sector decisions (among others). Civil society and local government groups in Japan likely have more influence, at present, over major decisions than similar groups in the ROK, with the civil society movement in China currently less developed than in the other nations.

A final, specific difference between nations is in their likely response to the Fukushima nuclear plant accident in Japan. With a stronger tradition of civil society and as the nation directly affected by the Fukushima disaster, the influence of the disaster on Japan's policies, and most notably its nuclear policies, is likely to be more profound than in South Korea or China,[95] though it seems likely that the incident will affect nuclear power in those countries as well, as it has elsewhere.

Consistent Needs in the Region for Bringing the Goals of Green Economy Policies to Fruition

Throughout the region, achieving the goals of green economy policies will now require a number of inputs. First, it will require sustained and detailed planning, as green economies tend to be more complex in terms of interaction between sectors, between regulators and producers, and between central and local actors than more standard industrial economies.

---

95   Japan's Prime Minister Kan announced in mid-2011 that Japan would gradually phase out its reliance on nuclear power, likely in large part as a result of the reconsideration of nuclear policies forced by the Fukushima accident. See, for example, Sekiguchi, T. and Nishiyama, G., "Japan's Kan Seeks Exit from Nuclear Power," *The Wall Street Journal*, 14 July 2011, http://online.wsj.com/article/SB1000142405270230491110457644 3542422110936.html Whether this change in Japan's nuclear policies will survive intact in the current government (Abe) administration is unclear, and perhaps unlikely, see for example, Torres, I., "Abe's Government Will Reconsider Previous Nuclear Power Phase out Policy," *Japan Daily Press*, 28 December 2012, http://japandailypress.com/ abes-government-will-reconsider-previous-nuclear-power-phase-out-policy-2820569 However it seems undeniable that the Fukushima accident and its aftermath have permanently altered the way Japan thinks about nuclear power.

Second, the needs for capacity development to bring about green economies is vast everywhere. In China, by our rough estimate, hundreds of thousands of trained building inspectors will be needed to enforce China's building efficiency laws; how that cohort of inspectors will be trained to effectively monitor China's building sector at the local level is at present unclear. Third, a patient, consistent approach will be needed on the part of governments to retooling existing economies toward green principles. An important element here is that these efforts need to be consistent not just within individual administrations, but spanning administrations, as the transitions necessary to address long-term issues such as climate change will require ongoing efforts for decades and generations. Fourth, implementing green economies will require a continuous program of public education reaching to and involving the grassroots level, in addition to a program of educating leaders in politics and industry to convince them of the imperative for action. Finally, and probably most difficult, the implementation of an effective green economy transition depends on a gradual devolution of decision-making authority and activity in a number of sectors from the central level to the local level, as local production of energy, food, and other goods, and local efforts at conservation, education, and pollution reduction, must underpin green economy efforts. At the same time, communications between the central and local levels must be dramatically increased, as achieving an effective green economy requires combining many actions at the local level to effect changes at the national level. Local actions must also coordinate with ongoing national-level goals and systems, be they overall GHG emissions reduction targets, national electrical grids, or, perhaps eventually, carbon capture and sequestration facilities.

Differing Needs in the Region for Bringing the Goals of Green Economy Policies to Fruition

Although the list of common needs for bringing green economy concepts into effective practice is long, there are also some needs that are more specific to the individual countries of the region. China, for example, has arguably much further to go in terms of adopting effective air and water pollution control measures to support a green economy. The ROK may need to undergo a significant change in the way that it does business, including its emphasis on heavy industries and top-down economic management in the private and public sectors, in order to effectively implement a green economy. Japan will likely need to reorganize the institutional structure of its energy sector to provide both institutions and individuals with the proper incentives to build and operate green energy systems, as well as to promote energy sector cooperation among the regions of Japan (in building a truly national gas transmission grid, for example)[96] and in sharing resources with other nations in the region.

Overall Findings and the Value of Civil Society/Local Government Networks

The process of building toward green economies in ways that also put nations, regions, and the globe on a path toward true sustainable development, together with the numerous policies, programs, and changes in economies and society that this transition requires, can generally be "robust" throughout the region in delivering green economy benefits to many groups. In addition, this process may, depending on its implementation, serve as a vehicle to ease international tensions related to economic development and resource acquisition by requiring and fostering engagement networks at multiple levels (see below). Many of the policies intended for building green economies are also, either incidentally or by design, effective in improving energy security, addressing climate change, and, in some cases, positively affecting the DPRK situation, as described in the country case studies above.

In Northeast Asia and, indeed, globally, there are currently a wealth of fast-growing networks in which local jurisdictions are banding together to share experiences and jointly work toward green economy goals. A sampling of these organizations is provided in Table 3.9, and the connections between them and other actors, many of them civil society and local government organizations that are "networking globally, but acting locally," are growing fast.[97]

Successful development of a green economy, and of the renewable energy systems that will help to power it, depends on imaginative vision at all levels, seizing political windows of opportunity afforded by unforeseen events (such as the Fukushima accident) and then using innovative policies and financing techniques to create markets for green products and services. The process of development is and will continue to be an evolutionary one, as Japan and other nations make the transition from the 20th-century

---

96 See, for example, Soligo, R., "Facilitating Development of the Natural Gas Market in Japan: Pipelines Gas and Law," in *New Enerty Technologies in the Natural Gas Sectors: A Policy Framework for Japan* (Institute for Public Policy, Rice University, 2001).

97 See, for example, Martinot, E., *et al.*, *Global Status Report on Local Renewable Energy Policies* (REN21, *et al.*, 2009).

standard of an energy system dominated by centralized, mostly fossil- and nuclear-fueled technologies decided upon through top-down decision-making in an industrial economy to a 21st-century paradigm featuring distributed renewable energy, energy efficiency, and information technologies developed in response to market and social forces within a knowledge-based economy and through a process of local innovation and global networking.

Figure 3.32 provides a schematic of the type of "triple decoupling" needed to achieve a transition to a green economy. The three types of decoupling are separating environmental impacts from energy use and economic activity, the provision of energy services from economic activity, and the welfare of human beings from both the amount of energy services consumed and economic growth as conventionally defined, relying instead on improvements in the quality of economic activities to boost welfare. This last economic decoupling has also been described as "shifting from debt-financed consumption (which is unsustainable) as the primary economic driver of our economies, to sustainability oriented investments in innovation as the primary economic driver of our economies."[98]

Figure 3.32: Triple Decoupling for a Green Economy

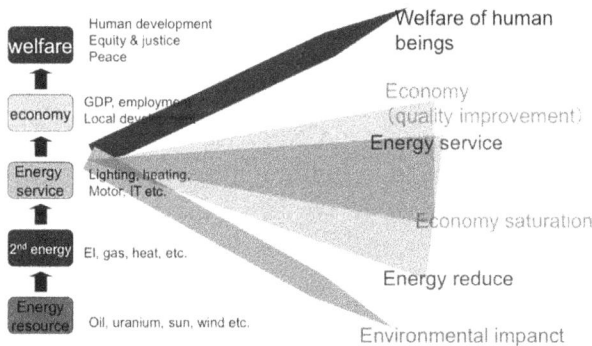

Source: Iida, T., 2010, "Changing Climate Change & Energy Policy and Politics in Japan," presented at *Interconnected Global Problems in Northeast Asia: Energy Security, Green Economy, and Urban Security*, Seoul, Korea, October, 2010.

98 Swilling, M., *Decoupling Natural Resource Use and Environmental Impacts from Economic Growth* (United Nations Environment Programme, 2011). Fischer-Kowalski, M., *et al.*, *Decoupling Natural Resource Use and Environmental Impacts from Economic Growth* (Nairobi: United Nations Environment Programme, 2011).

Accomplishing this decoupling will require consideration and integration of a complex set of factors in each nation, and across the region. These factors include (but are not limited to) technology and energy infrastructure, existing and new laws, government and other institutions, national and sub-national budgets, evolutions in lifestyles (including as populations in the region age), making good use of social capital and experience (both within and across nations), and making room for the participation in decision processes of stakeholders representing many points of view.

Another key to bringing about green economies in the region will be the sharing of information, experience, and resources of all types across nations, through both the civil society and local government networks described above and through economic links between nations. These types of connections in Northeast Asia will be facilitated by, and will themselves facilitate, a solution to the DPRK nuclear weapons issue. The process of building connections between nations will not be easy, and will require considerable coordinated patience and political will among all parties over the span of a generation or more, but it will certainly be worth the effort.

Implications of Climate Change and North Korean Issues for Energy Security in Northeast Asia

Introduction

As is evident from the discussion on green economy policies above, the quest for progress on climate change mitigation — in the form of reduction of greenhouse gas emissions — is a key driver of recent energy security and green economy policies. Climate change also influences energy security because different plans for addressing energy security result in different levels of risk to energy facilities (and those served by them) from the impacts of climate change; thus, different climate adaptation strategies have different implications for different approaches to energy security. Given the importance of cities in any energy security assessment, urban security is also affected by climate change itself, as well as by efforts to mitigate and adapt to climate change.

Another issue that has potential impacts on energy security in the region — though unlike climate change, this one is (mostly) specific to Northeast

Asia — is the regional security challenge posed by the North Korean nuclear weapons program, by its tenuous economy, and, more broadly, by relations between the DPRK and its neighbors. The status of the DPRK in relation to its neighbors affects a number of potential energy infrastructure choices in the ROK, and also significantly affects the prospects for regional energy cooperation. In addition, the ways in which other countries, in particular the ROK, choose to develop their own green economies may either open up opportunities to engage with the DPRK or reduce the possibilities for meaningful engagement.

Below we briefly outline how climate change and North Korean security might drive influence the results of policies designed to address energy security, urban security, and the development of green economies.

Influence of Climate Change on Energy Security Policies

Other chapters in this book, and earlier sections of this chapter, have touched upon the many interactions of the climate change issue with energy security policies, ranging from climate change mitigation as a driver of energy security policy to adaptation to climate change-related risks as a requirement of energy security, with challenges posed by the direct impacts of climate change on energy systems and energy users somewhere in between. Most of these interactions also have ramifications for urban security and green economy policies. A full and detailed listing of the interactions of climate change and energy security is well beyond the scope of this volume; a small sampling of these issues is provided below.

Climate Change Challenges in Northeast Asia

Some (but hardly all) of the energy security-related climate change challenges that are facing Northeast Asia include the following (and as alluded to in more detail in the country case studies earlier in this chapter):

Key Mitigation Challenges

- Reducing greenhouse gas emissions starting from a point of heavy fossil fuel dependence, while at the same time allowing for economic growth.
- Greatly increasing the efficiency of energy use.

- Developing alternative, non-fossil energy sources in nations where energy resources are limited without significant negative impacts on economies.

- Retooling existing energy sector institutions (both private and public) to facilitate the accomplishment of emissions mitigation, including capacity-building and public education on a vast scale.

Key Direct Challenges

- Protecting coastal energy (and other) infrastructure from storm/ tidal surges and sea level rise.

- Protecting energy systems from the impacts of more severe weather brought on by climate change.

- Adjusting to the impact of higher temperatures on energy systems (such as the impact of water temperature increases and changes in fresh water availability on thermal power plant performance/ availability and the impact of higher air temperatures on transmission line performance).

- Providing energy services for displaced populations.

Key Adaptation Challenges

- Compensating for climate impacts on human needs through greater use of energy services, with specific requirements ranging from greater use of air conditioning, to additional water pumping, to additional water treatment required due to factors such as saline intrusion into aquifers or climate-induced changes in soils in key watersheds.[99]

- Adapting energy systems to compensate for the greater risk to those systems due to a more variable climate (ranging from hardening/ raising seawalls for coastal energy facilities, to strengthening or burying transmission lines, to diversifying energy sources so that damage to one source yields less economic disruption).

- Selecting and planting biofuels crops in a way that factors in changing climates.

- Development of necessary technologies for adaptation in a timely manner, and funding that development.

---

99   As just one specific example, see Park, J.H., *et al.*, "Potential Effects of Climate Change and Variability on Watershed Biogeochemical Processes and Water Quality in Northeast Asia," *Environment International*, 36(2) (2010), doi: http://dx.doi.org/10.1016/j. envint.2009.10.008

Climate Change Mitigation as a Driver of Energy Security Policies

Given these challenges (and many more), climate change mitigation has already become a key driver of energy security policies as demonstrated by the country studies provided above. Nations are now obliged to report impacts on greenhouse gas emissions as a key feature of their future energy sector plans, and climate mitigation performance is a central tenet of the green economy movement, though the balance between "green" and "economy" varies considerably depending on whose interpretation one looks at. Measures of climate change mitigation appear explicitly in the multi-attribute energy security calculus provided earlier in this chapter. In general, climate change mitigation requirements drive energy security policies in the direction of improving the efficiency of energy use and increasing the diversity and absolute capacity of non-carbon-based (or low-carbon) energy systems. The international impacts of national climate change mitigation policies must also be considered, however, and one nation's progress on GHG emissions reduction may either improve the global climate — for example, by expanding markets and expertise in energy efficiency and renewable energy systems — or be effectively climate-neutral or negative — such as when countries close their own energy-intensive industries, and thus effectively supply their own demand for the products of those industries by using the output of other nations.

Impacts of Climate Change Adaptation on Energy Security Policies

Anthropogenic greenhouse gas emissions stretch back to prehistoric deforestation, but since the beginnings of significant use of fossil fuels during the Industrial Revolution, they have increased the degree to which the earth's atmosphere retains solar heat to the extent that a significant increase in average global temperature is inevitable in the coming half-century and beyond, no matter what mitigation measure are taken. In fact, measurable global warming has already occurred. The inevitability of some level of climate change does not mean that mitigation efforts are not worthwhile, but it does mean that policies, programs, and actions to adapt to a changing climate will be necessary. Climate change adaptation policies can affect energy security policies in many ways. A very small selection of these possible impacts follows:

- Location of energy facilities: Climate change adaptation considerations will affect the location of some energy facilities. In the most basic instance, it will be necessary to site many coastal power plants or fuel transport terminals at higher elevations to protect them from sea level rise and storm surges. However, adaptation may mean that some power plants cannot be sited on rivers if the impacts of changing climate make inadequate the flow of cooling water at certain times of the year.

- Modifications to energy supply infrastructure: Adaptation to climate change will require a host of modifications to energy infrastructure, ranging from the construction of higher seawalls and levees to protect facilities near oceans, rivers, and lakes; to hydroelectric reservoirs to accommodate higher peak flows; to hardening transmission networks, wind turbines, and offshore oil and gas rigs against severe weather; to increasing peaking power capacity to accommodate power demand during periods of extreme heat. Other examples of required changes are increased capacity to provide power, clean water, and other necessities in an emergency (including, for example, emergency distributed generation), providing energy supplies for refugees from climate events, and even planning and implementing energy systems for new cities that must be created as existing low-lying urban areas are inundated by rising seas.

- Modifications to energy demand infrastructure: Examples of demand-side modifications to adapt to changing climate conditions include constructing buildings that require less water and energy to operate, re-sizing the capacity of systems such as air conditioning to meet expected demand, and, in extreme cases, moving to where climate may be more favorable.

- Modifications to planning: Climate change adaptation will affect energy security in many ways through its impact on planning requirements. Adapting to climate change will require changes in the ways that societies at virtually every level plan for the future. Urban and land use planning, for example, will have to strengthen its consideration on the interaction and integration of energy supply, demand, and climate considerations, as well as of how systems such as water, energy supply, and agriculture might need to be altered. Planning horizons will need to extend further into the future than is typical now, and there may need to be an increase in the regulation of the energy sector to ensure that planning is sufficiently long-range, coordinated, and integrated to serve society's needs for adapting to a changing climate.[100]

Impact of North Korean Issues on Energy Security Policies

The presence of a nuclear-armed, often-belligerent, yet in many ways desperately energy-insecure DPRK in the middle of Northeast Asia affects energy security, and energy sector options that might be used to address energy security, throughout the region. Some of the ways in which DPRK issues affect energy security were alluded to above in the context of ROK energy policy. In general, North Korean security issues affect energy security in Northeast Asia, now and possibly in the future, in the following ways:

- Considerations related to defenses against potential DPRK attack: In designing and siting its energy systems — including nuclear power and other fuel-cycle facilities, as well as major conventional energy systems such as thermal power plants, refineries, and LNG terminals — the ROK, and to a lesser extent, Japan, needs to be cognizant of the vulnerability of energy systems to a direct or covert attack by the DPRK. This requirement limits and affects some energy system choices and has broad implications for many energy security criteria.

- Influence of a nuclear DPRK on nuclear fuel cycle choices by others: The fact that the DPRK has nuclear weapons and nuclear weapons capability, and has furthermore been developing missile technologies, cannot help but alter the way that the ROK and Japan think about nuclear deterrence. This topic is dealt with in much more detail in other chapters in this book, but in general, it seems highly likely that nuclear energy fuel-cycle decisions by Japan and the ROK are colored by DPRK nuclear weapons issues. For the ROK and Japan, developing or retaining nuclear energy fuel cycle processes that build or maintain the ability to, in a crisis, construct their own nuclear weapons to counter a DPRK threat, has to be a consideration, however tacit or denied, in their own energy security thinking.

- The DPRK as a "player" (or not) in regional mega-projects: There have long been proposals and even plans to move some of the vast

---

100 See, for example, Ebinger, J. and Vergara, W., *Climate Impacts on Energy Systems: Key Issues for Energy Sector Adaptation* (Washington, DC: The World Bank, 2011).

energy resources — gas, coal, hydroelectricity, and oil — of the lightly-settled Russian Far East to the major demand centers of the ROK, China, and even Japan. Though some of these proposals have begun to come to fruition in recent years, progress in developing these large resource-sharing projects (power transmission lines, pipelines, transport facilities, and jointly-owned refineries, for example), particularly given the potential benefits for all participants in such trade, has been slow.[101] It seems very likely that if the DPRK enjoyed more "normal" relations with its neighbors (and the rest of the international community), these projects would have moved much more rapidly. So long as the DPRK nuclear stalemate continues, progress on these mega-projects for regional resource-sharing with the Russian Far East, and the energy security benefits (and costs) they represent, is not likely to accelerate.

- DPRK energy sector assistance considerations: When and if a breakthrough occurs in negotiations on the DPRK's nuclear weapons program, one of the key demands that the DPRK will make in return for freezing and eventually eliminating its nuclear weapons program will be energy sector assistance. This assistance will obviously affect the DPRK's energy security, but it will also likely impact the energy security of its neighbors in many ways. For example, the ROK may choose to help the DPRK complete the nuclear reactors at Simpo and purchase the power from those reactors, with impacts potentially both good and bad on its electricity supply security. As a very different example, the ROK and other nations might be obliged to increase their own commitment to and expertise in renewable energy and energy efficiency in order to provide energy assistance to the DPRK in those areas.[102]

- Clean Development Mechanism considerations: Again, when and if a breakthrough in negotiations with the DPRK occurs, the ROK and other nations will likely see opportunities to earn carbon credits through investment in a wide range of potential emissions-reduction projects in the DPRK. These will in turn likely have an impact on the energy security of other Northeast Asian nations by affecting investment in their own energy sectors in ways that could either be positive (through furnishing good examples of GHG reductions, and by cutting national GHG reduction costs) or

---

101 See, for example, von Hippel, D., *et al.* (2011). Also papers by a number of authors prepared for Nautilus Institute workshops, *Power Grid Interconnection in Northeast Asia* (Seoul: Nautilus Institute), http://nautilus.org/projects/by-name/asian-energy-security/workshop-on-power-grid-interconnection-in-northeast-asia/

102 See, for example, von Hippel, D. and Hayes, P., "DPRK Energy Sector Development Priorities: Options and Preferences," *Energy Policy*, 39(11) (2011), doi: http://dx.doi.org/10.1016/j.enpol.2009.11.068. Hayes, P. and von Hippel, D. (2012).

negative (by diverting potential investment funds from domestic to DPRK projects).

- DPRK "collapse" considerations: In the unlikely (in our view,) events of a collapse of the DPRK regime or a negotiated political (or *de facto* economic) reunification of Korea, the international community, with the ROK at the forefront, will likely bear much of the costs for redeveloping the DPRK energy sector and addressing DPRK energy insecurity. This will by definition increase energy security in the DPRK, but it is also likely, at least in the short run, to strain attempts at increasing energy security elsewhere by diverting investment funds and the attention of planners, for example. A special, short-term (possibly longer) case for the DPRK's immediate neighbors would be the need to provide energy services for a large number of border-crossing refugees in the event of a DPRK regime collapse.

- Green economy preparations: Consideration of the DPRK as a market for and/or potential supplier of green economy goods and services may affect green economy preparations in the countries of the region.

Assessing the Energy Security Impacts of Climate Change and DPRK Issues

Initiatives to address climate change and the DPRK nuclear weapons impasse (along with the related problems of energy/economy/development) can have significant impacts on energy security in the countries of Northeast Asia. Identifying and, where possible, estimating the extent of those impacts in a consistent and transparent manner is a necessary element in an even-handed and thorough comparison of energy policy alternatives. In the section that follows, we suggest an extension of the energy security analysis structure presented in the second section of this chapter to accommodate these (and potentially other) cross-cutting issues.

Energy Security in a Complex World

Interaction of Energy Security and Related Issues

Once the traditional, narrow focus on energy security as the means to obtaining sufficient fuel at a reasonable price is abandoned, a broader and far richer interaction of energy security policy choices with other issues is evident. The framework for energy security analysis summarized earlier in this chapter, and in writings by the authors and our collaborators dating back to 1998, emphasizes the multi-disciplinary aspects of energy security, with six energy security dimensions — energy supply, economic, technological, environmental, social/political, and military security — used to organize the evaluation of the energy security impacts of alternative policies.

In this chapter, many (though hardly all) of the interactions of energy security issues with other cross-cutting concepts and issues have been identified. Energy security and urban security are closely tied because providing energy services to urban populations typically consumes the bulk of national energy needs, and because many aspects of urban security depend on how and when energy services are provided. The "green economy" movement, though implemented in very different ways and at very different levels of effort in different nations, is in large measure an attempt to address the six dimensions of energy security in a comprehensive manner. Climate change mitigation and adaptation are policy goals that are intimately related to the dimensions of energy security, with desired outcomes primarily related to the environmental dimension, but with impacts on all of the other dimensions of energy security. Responding to the North Korean nuclear weapons program and to the DPRK's related "energy insecurities" is a policy issue unique to Northeast Asia, though a number of countries around the world are intimately involved. Policy solutions (or lack of solutions) to DPRK nuclear weapons-related issues can and do also affect the energy security of the nations of the region in multiple ways, from altering the siting of energy facilities, to limiting international resource sharing options, to influencing domestic energy system choices. Identifying and evaluating the interaction of policies to address these cross-cutting issues with the dimensions of energy security, and the impacts of energy security policies on these issues, is a crucial step in the policy evaluation process. Failure to consider cross-cutting impacts may lead to over- or under-appreciation of the costs and benefits of specific policies, unintended consequences from policy applications, and missed opportunities for applying policies that are "robust" across multiple energy security dimensions and with respect to multiple issues. As a result, a complete analysis needs to be able to look at the implications of policies for these multiple, related issues together, rather than separately.

Working Multiple Considerations into the Energy Security Calculus

In an ideal world, analysts would be able to quantify all relevant parameters of a policy choice, weight those parameters in a manner that everyone could agree on, and thereby come up with a single index of energy security for any given policy plan.[103] Unfortunately, this energy policy analyst's dream is just that. Some of the most important dimensions of energy security stubbornly, and probably indefinitely, defy quantification, while some of the measures for those that can be quantified have shortcomings and/or special interpretations that must be fully understood.[104] Parameter weightings may seem objective when applied, but even the best weighting formulations include (and often obscure) substantial subjective judgment. Even when the weightings are arrived at through open, inclusive, transparent processes that involve a wide range of stakeholders, which is possible and appropriate, comparison of the resulting weightings across categories may result in conclusions that defy common sense, thereby jeopardizing the validity of the analysis.

The alternative to attempting a single index of energy security is to use the approach outlined earlier in this chapter, in which the different energy policies, plans, paths, or scenarios are scored, qualitatively and quantitatively, for their performance among the multiple dimensions of energy security in a "matrix" approach. The resulting matrix allows side-by-side comparison of options, with policymakers and stakeholders free to explicitly weight the different dimensions in the identification of a preferred strategy. This method does not avoid the application of subjective judgment — as such judgment is largely unavoidable in these

---

103 For further discussion of some of the difficulties involved in establishing composite metrics for energy security, see von Hippel, D., *et al.* (2010).

104 A common measure of the energy efficiency of an economy, energy use per unit of GDP (or its inverse, GDP per unit of energy used) is an example here, as it depends on multiple factors, including how efficiently energy is used to accomplish specific tasks, which fuels are used (as some can be used at higher efficiencies than others), and to what extent changes in the index are the result of shifts in the economy to less energy-intensive industries, which can be accomplished either by reducing the materials-intensity of the domestic economy or by moving the production of energy-intensive goods and services to other nations — two approaches with very different impacts on global energy and environmental problems.

complex decisions — but it does render such judgments much more explicit and transparent, facilitating understanding among parties on major policy decisions.

The matrix approach to energy security policy analysis can be adapted to include consideration of cross-cutting issues such as urban security, green economy development, climate change mitigation and adaptation, and DPRK nuclear weapons/energy insecurity issues. One way to accomplish this is to add measures and attributes under the different energy security dimensions (as identified in Table 3.5, above, for example) that reflect the performance of different policies with regard to the cross-cutting issues. Each cross-cutting issue may require one or more indicative measures and attributes in each of several energy dimensions. For example, possible energy security measures and attributes specifically related to urban security might include (but, again, are certainly not limited to):

- Diversity of energy supply sources for a particular city (Supply dimension).
- Capital and overall costs of a city's energy supplies and the impacts of energy sector outlays on the urban economy (Economic dimension).
- The impact of an energy policy on the technological diversity of energy supply and demand systems in an urban area (Technological dimension).
- GHG emissions produced in providing a city's energy needs, non-GHG air pollutants and water pollutants emitted within the urban boundaries, and the effect of an energy policy on the urban area's climate change adaptation needs and processes (Environmental dimension).
- The degree to which an energy policy lends itself to input by civil society and local government in the urban area (Social/Political dimension).
- The degree to which an energy policy increases or decreases the risk to an urban population of a major accident or state/non-state attack on energy facilities in the urban area (Military security dimension).

To explore the impact of cross-cutting issues on the energy security implications of different energy (or related) policies, an individual energy security matrix could be prepared for each cross-cutting issue of interest. A perhaps better, though possibly more cumbersome, approach is to attempt to develop key measures and attributes relating to each cross-cutting issue, and to evaluate the performance of several energy policies/plans with respect to all of those measure and attributes at the same time. Shading or coloring can be used to more clearly identify which attributes affect which cross-cutting issues. It is only by seeing the performance of the policies with regard to multiple issues that the links between issues, and the cross-issue impacts of policies, can be properly appreciated.

Lessons Learned: National and Regional Energy Policies that Address Multiple Issues

Discussions in this chapter on the complex linkages between energy security, urban security, the development of green economies, climate change, and the DPRK nuclear weapons/energy insecurity considerations have pointed to a number of energy policies that appear to be "robust" — that is, useful and productive to implement under a variety of conditions — with respect to these many different, but intimately linked, issues. Some of these policies with likely positive impacts on many different issues are offered below, along with a discussion of how civil society and local government actors could help bring them to fruition.

- Energy (and water use) efficiency improvement policies: Improving the efficiency with which electricity and other fuels are used has benefits across the spectrum of energy security dimensions and with regard to all of the cost-cutting issues. Efficiency improvements reduce urban insecurity by making supplies of energy and water go further, and by effectively increasing reserve capacity in times of stress. Using less energy reduces GHG emissions and is by definition a key feature of a green economy. Building and demonstrating expertise in energy and water efficiency offers Northeast Asian (and other) nations a key opportunity to peacefully engage the DPRK on a topic that is of use to and largely non-controversial for North Koreans. Local governments are key players in implementing energy efficiency efforts, due to the basic "bottom-up" requirements of most efficiency programs. Civil society groups contribute expertise to energy and water efficiency efforts, and help to catalyze and keep watch on both local efficiency programs (for example, programs offered by local or regional utilities) and national energy efficiency efforts, such as the promotion of energy efficiency standards for appliances, equipment, vehicles, and buildings.

- Land-use/urban planning to retain/remake green space and provide easy access to essential services: Related to energy efficiency improvements are planning and implementing changes in land use and land use development in such a way as to simultaneously reduce the need for energy and transport services and improve quality of life by building integrated living, work, and commercial spaces that serve as communities. Again, these activities are central to most concepts of the green economy, assist with climate change mitigation and potentially adaptation, and address a number of urban insecurity concerns. Here, the involvement of civil society and local government are central and crucial to making sure that land-use decisions make long-term sense and are consistent with the needs of residents and other stakeholders.

• Development of renewable energy resources: Much-expanded development and use of renewable energy systems is required if GHG emissions reduction is to become a reality. Renewable energy systems need not necessarily use domestic resources, but to the extent that they do, they can be used to address energy supply security concerns, help build local economies, and reduce non-GHG pollution from fossil fuel use, among other attributes. Local governments and civil society in Northeast Asia can and do play active roles in promoting renewable energy use, including technology development, and in assuring that renewable energy systems offer a positive social impact.

• Development of distributed energy systems: Coupled with but not the same as renewable energy policies, the development of high-efficiency distributed energy systems, harnessing local production of electricity for use both on-site and on a shared grid, often in combination with heat for use locally, makes sense from the perspective of energy security (across multiple dimensions) and also provides urban security benefits, climate change mitigation/adaptation benefits, and helps with issues related to the DPRK (ranging from being another good topic for DPRK engagement to making the consequences of a DPRK attack on a single-energy facility less devastating). Renewable or fossil-fueled (for example, combined heat and power) energy systems can be integrated with buildings and industrial facilities, or can be shared in neighborhoods. Here, as with renewable energy systems, civil society and local government need to be active in promoting distributed energy systems through advocacy, expertise, and the development of local programs and regulations that support them. But they will also need to put pressure on central governments to fine-tune national policies in order to provide favorable treatment for distributed energy systems. Such treatment would include, for example, laws, regulations, and utility policies that stimulate the purchase of distributed renewable energy (such as grid interconnection rules and Feed-in Tariffs). Civil society and local government also need to encourage the development of "smart grid" systems that can help in encouraging energy efficiency, adapting in the event of climate events, and smoothly integrating distributed generation, electricity storage, and electric vehicles (as well as electricity storage using electric vehicles) into grid planning and into the grid itself.

- Planning for nuclear waste management: Although not a major topic of this chapter, making plans, and especially plans shared across nations, for the safe and effective management of nuclear fuel cycle materials and wastes is key to future energy security in multiple dimensions. Nuclear waste management affects the prospects for nuclear power (and new nuclear technologies), thereby affecting any GHG emissions mitigation impact that the deployment of nuclear power might have. Waste management also affects the cost of nuclear power, though not hugely. Whether the nuclear reactor fleet grows substantially in the coming decades or never grows at all, the volume of nuclear wastes currently extant and that will be produced by the current generation of reactors requires secure management. Options for nuclear materials management vary widely in terms of their impact on the environment and society, and here civil society can play a crucial role in making sure that the many issues related to waste management are clear to both decision-makers and to the public. Moreover, local governments have and will have a considerable influence on the types and locations of waste management facilities.

Implementing any or all of the above strategies, however, requires one element in short supply nearly everywhere — the human capacity to thoughtfully design, discuss, evaluate and carry out these types of policies within government, industry, and civil society. With typically highly-developed educational systems, the countries of the region have the necessary foundations to build such capacity, but the involvement of civil society and other groups will be crucial in making sure that sufficient financial and human resources are direct into programs to adequately prepare green economy leaders and workers for the future.

Developing and Applying Methods of Analysis of Energy and Related Policies

In this chapter we have outlined methods for evaluating the impact of energy and related policies on energy security, in its multiple dimensions, as well as on intimately related cross-cutting issues. Further methodological development is needed in order to more fully integrate the evaluation of the impacts of policies on cross-cutting issues and, especially, to develop better ways of highlighting and summarizing the results of policy comparisons for easy access by relevant decision-makers, as well as by the civil society groups and others that would use the results of comparisons to guide policy development. A major challenge is how to make such summaries approachable and useful, while still retaining the richness and salience of the multi-dimensional analysis. A second general area of "next steps" is to develop more detailed energy policy paths, similar to those reviewed above for the ROK, in each country of the region, evaluate their energy security results using the "matrix" analytical structure and other tools, and use the combination of this analytical framework and national energy paths to evaluate how coordinated energy policies in Northeast Asia might contribute to improved regional energy security.

Opportunities for ROK Foreign Policy to Drive Energy Security in Northeast Asia

Although it is not the country with the largest land area, population, or economy in the region, the ROK occupies a crucial and central place not just in the geography of Northeast Asia, but in its policy future as well. Below we summarize how the ROK influences energy security policy in the region in general, identify some specific ROK policies that affect regional energy security and related issues, and describe how ROK policies might be adjusted to provide for improvements in energy security and in the other cross-cutting issues discussed in this chapter, both domestically and region-wide.

The ROK's Influence on Regional Energy Security

The Korean peninsula in general, and the ROK in particular, is geographically located in a central hub among Northeast Asian nations, connected by land to the lightly populated but resource-rich expanse of the Russian Far East via populous, rapidly developing China, and separated by only a few hundred kilometers of sea from highly-industrialized Japan. As a result of this geographical position, most proposals for regional energy and transport hubs go through the ROK.[105]

---

105 See, for example, Paik, H., "Northeast Asian Energy Corridor Initiative for Regional Collaboration," *Journal of East Asian Economic Integration* 16(4) (2012).

As a major fuels importer, the ROK's choices of how it obtains fuel supplies affect potential fuel suppliers, including Russia (with whom the ROK has for years been in consultations regarding potential power-line and pipeline projects, as well as road and rail projects), but they also have implications for other major energy importers, including Japan and China, who might either share or compete for Russian Far East resources exported via major international energy (and transport) infrastructure projects. The ROK's decisions to pursue LNG and refinery projects affect the international markets for LNG and crude oil, and thus also influence transport and production projects in those sectors worldwide. ROK commercial interests seek, with government backing, to develop and secure oil and gas supplies on several continents, where they compete with Northeast Asian and other "players" for economic and political influence in resource-rich nations.

As the home to companies that are major manufacturers and exporters of a large number of energy demand devices and equipment — ranging from household appliances to vehicles to machinery — the ROK's own efficiency standards, and those that apply to goods for export, affect energy demand throughout the world. As a major user of nuclear power, as well as a producer and, as of 2015, planned exporter of nuclear technologies,[106] the ROK affects the use of nuclear power in other nations. In addition, and as noted in more detail in other chapters of this book, the ROK's positions on nuclear fuel cycle activities in general, and particularly on the reprocessing of nuclear wastes by extracting plutonium for further use in reactors (the ROK nuclear sector's favored, though not yet developed, technology for reprocessing is a variant known as "pyroprocessing"),[107] affects (and is affected by) the positions on nuclear fuel cycle technologies taken by neighboring countries, especially the DPRK and Japan. And, as a major electronics manufacturer, the ROK is in a position to be a leading force for the development and implementation of low-cost solar photovoltaic power systems.

---

106 See, for example, *Nuclear Power in South Korea* (London: World Nuclear Association, 2013), http://www.world-nuclear.org/info/Country-Profiles/Countries-O-S/South-Korea/#. UgPXcW33M5s

107 "Pyroprocessing" is a variant of reprocessing in which "the plutonium separated from spent fuel by pyroprocessing remains mixed with other elements." See, for example, Horner, D., *Pyroprocessing Is Reprocessing: U.S. Official*, Arms Control Today (Arms Control Association, 2011). See also Kim, D. and McGoldrick, F., *Decision Time: US-South Korea Peaceful Nuclear Cooperation*, Academic Paper Series (Washington, DC: Korea Economic Institute, 2013).

The ROK is at once a nation with aspirations to lead the world in the development of green technologies and in transitioning to a green economy, and a nation with significant political, financial, and mercantile connections with industrialized and developing nations around the world. It is thus poised to provide an example — for good or for bad — to other countries on how to affect a transition to a green economy.

As one of the two main players in the sixty-year-plus saga that is the partition of the Korean peninsula, the ROK has a major influence on when, if, and how conflicts with the DPRK are to be resolved, and, once resolution is underway, the path by which the DPRK's evolution (or not) to a modern economy and "normal" nation, up to and including reunification with the ROK, will take place.

Finally, but as just as importantly, as a nation where civil society and local governments are just beginning to exert their influence in the national energy policy arena, the ROK is in a position, through networks with similar groups across the region and the globe, to be a catalyst for changes in the way that the ROK and its neighbors respond to energy security and related challenges.

Potential ROK Policies to Enhance Regional Energy Security

The ROK's policy choices, and how it pursues them in the coming decade, have significant potential to shape energy security — broadly construed to include not only the six dimensions described above, but elements of urban security, green economy, climate change mitigation/adaptation, and DPRK issues as well — both domestically and in the Northeast Asia region for years to come. A complete listing of the policies that the ROK might pursue, and their impacts, is beyond the scope of this chapter, but a sampling of such policies follows, briefly describing their potential impact and keyed to the ROK's influences on regional energy security.

- The ROK's policies of seeking to diversify energy sources by purchasing oil, gas, electricity, and perhaps coal from the Russian Far East have helped to move along discussions of regional energy networks, but more could be done to support such infrastructure projects. For example, the ROK could continue to work with governments in the region and commercial interests to move closer to resolving some of the key financial, technical, and environmental issues that have to some extent slowed the development of regional energy supply infrastructure. Key among these is resolution of the North Korean nuclear and energy insecurity problem. The ROK could use the prospect of the DPRK's involvement in (and profiting from) regional energy infrastructure development as an inducement to engage on nuclear weapons and related issues. In so doing, the ROK would be helping to address the DPRK issue as well as its own energy security needs. The ROK could also condition its involvement in regional energy sharing schemes on making sure that such schemes result in a net reduction of greenhouse gas emissions region-wide.

- In order to enhance energy efficiency as much as possible both at home and abroad, and thereby build demand-side and manufacturing infrastructure for both a domestic and export-oriented green economy, the ROK should adopt stringent energy efficiency standards for the energy- and water-using devices made in the ROK, including both standards as to the efficiency of devices sold for use in the ROK and standards of devices destined for export. By adopting the most stringent practical efficiency standards, the ROK will contribute to energy and GHG savings at home and abroad, and will also serve help to raise standards for energy efficiency worldwide.

- Relatedly, and to help move green economy activities forward, the ROK should rapidly adopt local and national regulations, standards, and guidelines to recycle all types of materials, and to incorporate recyclability into manufactured goods, as much as possible. This will reduce the energy and materials intensiveness of the ROK economy, and indicate to the world that the ROK is serious about its green economy efforts.

- In the nuclear sector, the ROK should undertake a serious and even-handed exploration of the benefits of different fuel cycle options, but do so in a way that also considers the probable implications of its policies on the nuclear policies of Japan and, in particular, the DPRK. Moreover, the ROK should open its nuclear policy discussions to a much wider group of stakeholders, including those from civil society and local government. Specifically, the ROK should carefully examine the costs (including social and political costs) and benefits of any kind of reprocessing activity, and seriously consider officially abandoning reprocessing, which would likely be a helpful step in getting the DPRK to agree to give up its nuclear weapons program. And the ROK should also carefully examine different alternatives for storage and eventual disposal of nuclear wastes and spent fuel, again in close consultation with local governments and other stakeholders. Finally, as a nuclear technology exporter, the ROK should explore and adopt export regulations designed to strictly meet non-proliferation standards, and work with other nuclear suppliers to make sure that client countries adhere to the IAEA Additional Protocol and other stringent nuclear oversight mechanisms.

- The ROK should encourage domestic manufacturing of advanced renewable energy and distributed generation devices through, for example, a combination of national competitions for renewable energy innovation, Feed-in Tariffs for renewable power that are consistent with the most aggressive among developed nations, utility incentives for customers to adopt renewable power, renewable portfolio standards for distribution utilities, and much more aggressive national targets for renewable energy development. Local governments, encouraged by civil society, could develop their own renewable energy ordinances and incentives, as well as equipping local government buildings and other installations with renewable energy systems (and energy efficiency measures) in "lead by example" programs.

- The ROK should review its green economy initiative to focus on bottom-up measures to build the green economy rather than top-down impositions, including de-emphasizing mega-projects such as new "green cities" and nuclear power. This will mean working closely with local governments and civil society organizations at the local level to design custom green-economy solutions that work for specific communities, as well as working with industry on green economy-related research and development.

- The ROK should rethink its approach to engagement with the DPRK, which as of 2015 largely consisted of non-engagement. The ROK has much to gain, both for its near-term and long-term energy security future, if engagement with the DPRK bears fruit. Possible benefits to the ROK include access to the DPRK's mineral and energy reserves, the potential to move forward with mutually-beneficial regional energy sharing options, the possibility of sharing energy facilities (potentially including nuclear power sites and LNG terminals) with the DPRK, access to the DPRK's markets and labor force, the potential to receive Clean Development Mechanism credits for GHG-reducing measures in the DPRK, and, most importantly, the opportunity to help rebuild the DPRK's entire energy system and other infrastructure in advance of eventual Korean reunification.

Key Lessons for ROK Domestic and Foreign Policies

The suggested policies that the ROK might pursue to improve domestic and regional energy security have several basic common threads. With respect to its activities and policies abroad, the ROK should develop strict guidelines for how it interacts with other nations so as to strongly support green economy, sustainability, and non-proliferation goals everywhere through its products, services, international aid, and other interactions. In order to develop and maintain international leadership in these areas, the ROK government should adhere to these guidelines in all of its activities abroad, embody them in its activities at home, and demand adherence to the guidelines by ROK companies. Civil society should be involved in helping the government develop its green economy/sustainability support guidelines and, once the guidelines are implemented, should maintain oversight of ROK activities globally to make sure that they are adhered to. Local governments could help support these guidelines by fostering relationships (for example "sister city" ties) with local governments in other nations geared toward modeling and promoting green economy principles.

With respect to the special case of interactions with the DPRK, the ROK should look for and embrace engagement opportunities wherever and whenever it is prudent to do so; focusing on green economy engagement in particular is likely to be more acceptable in the ROK and easier for the DPRK to say "yes" to. Civil society groups can support such engagement through pressuring the government to engage, and by carrying out their own capacity-building and aid projects with the DPRK, to the extent that such cooperation is possible.

With respect to domestic energy security policies, many of the energy sector and related policies that are the most robust in terms of both the broad energy security dimensions and their impacts on cross-cutting issues are policies that, for the most part, need to be implemented at the grassroots level. This means that local governments will have a key role in developing, implementing, and supporting these activities, but national government actors will need to support the bottom-up efforts with consistent, patient policies and enforcement, and with funding. Companies will need to develop products and services to support the local green economy effort. And civil society will need to assist efforts at all levels, press for more aggressive action where appropriate, and demand transparency in the development and implementation of green economy and related energy policies.

The complexity of the energy security dilemmas facing the ROK, the region, and the world mean that many different government and non-government actors will have stakes in energy security decisions. It is crucial that these actors have the opportunity to talk with one another to share information and ideas, but the Korean government (as with many other governments) has traditionally been structured so as to discourage discourse between key analysts and decision-makers in different ministries, except for those at the very top. The access to government officials by those outside the government has also been uneven, with some groups — notably business-related — enjoying much better access than others. Setting up and operating inter-ministerial task forces with both responsibility and authority to address issues that cross ministerial boundaries may help to alleviate this problem, but a general society-wide move toward inclusive decision-making is desirable, though the transition is unlikely to be rapid. Civil society is in the best position to try and catalyze such a transition by calling for transparency and accountability on issues of importance.

Key Lessons for ROK and Northeast Asian Energy Policies

Energy security has traditionally been viewed as simply or largely a matter of securing sufficient and consistent supplies of fuel at a reasonable cost. Energy security policies, however, have consequences in so many different dimensions that this narrow definition is woefully insufficient for the evaluation of possible future actions. Consideration of at least six dimensions of energy security policies — energy supply, economics, technology, environment, social/political, and military security — is needed in order to begin to understand the full level of candidate policies' impacts. Moreover, energy security concepts overlap considerably with Northeast Asian issues such as urban security, development of green economies, climate change mitigation and adaptation, and addressing the coupled issues of DPRK nuclear weapons and energy insecurity. When energy and related policies are developed in a way that fails to adequately consider the complex, cross-cutting nature of these issues, the resulting policies are liable to face major problems in implementation and result in significant unintended consequences, many of them undesirable. Adopting a more comprehensive analytical framework for energy policies is hardly a guarantee against policy failure, as the future is nothing if not capricious, but it does provide expanded opportunities to spot and address problems before they develop, and, perhaps most importantly, it provides a comprehensive way to transparently explore issues and simultaneously offer opportunities for stakeholders from a variety of different backgrounds, disciplines, and interests to contribute to policy analysis and development. The involvement of a broader coalition of stakeholders, notably including civil society and local government, as well as elected officials, government ministries, and commercial interests can help assure that energy policies, if chosen by broad consensus based on a review by many parties across multiple attributes, will be easier to implement, and more likely to perform as intended, than policies developed and considered more narrowly.

Energy policies that focus on energy efficiency, renewable and distributed energy development, consideration of local community development, and related, largely bottom-up types of measures are typically likely to make the most progress on moving the ROK and its regional neighbors toward green economy goals and solutions to other problems. Bottom-up approaches in the ROK, as in most if its neighboring states, have not, however, been the traditional means of policy development — rather the opposite. This fundamental disconnect of top and ministry policymakers with those that need to be involved in on-the-ground program/project design and implementation must be addressed if significant progress is to be made on developing energy-secure green economies in the region while simultaneously addressing climate, DPRK security, and other issues as well.

4. Urban Security and Complexity in Northeast Asia

Sanghun Lee and Takayuki Minato

Contributing author: Peter Hayes

Introduction

Irreversible and rampant globalization has transformed every aspect of the economic, social, cultural, legal, political, military, and environmental spheres of daily life. "In this respect," writes David Held,

> [G]lobalization is akin to a process of 'structuration' in so far as it is a product of both the individual actions of, and the cumulative interactions between, countless agencies and institutions across the globe… But it is also a highly stratified structure since globalization is profoundly uneven… Globalization is best understood as a multifaceted or differentiated social phenomenon. It cannot be conceived as a singular condition but instead refers to patterns of growing global interconnectedness within all the key domains of social activity… Under conditions of globalization, 'local,' 'national' or even 'continental' political, social and economic space is re-formed such that it is no longer necessarily coterminous with established legal and territorial boundaries.[1]

Due to globalization, we face not only local and national problems, but also manifold global problems like climate change, biodiversity and

---

1   Held, D., *Global Transformations: Politics, Economics and Culture* (Redwood City: Stanford University Press, 1999).

© 2015 Sanghun Lee and Takayuki Minato , CC BY 4.0 http://dx.doi.org/10.11647/OBP.0059.04

ecosystem loss, fisheries depletion, deforestation, water deficits, maritime safety and pollution, global financial crises, illegal drugs and trafficking, the digital divide, terrorism, the international migration of laborers, the inappropriate regulation of international investment, the lack of reliable and safe biotechnology, and so forth.[2]

The most significant characteristic of a global problem is that it is very complex. Cities have become complex systems by virtue of their intersection with multiple global problems. In complex systems, there are more agents, more interactions, more decentralized decision-making, more feedback loops, and more unpredictable outcomes than in a simple system.[3] Beset by global problems, the security of cities is threatened from many different directions at the same time. As a result, cities face new vulnerabilities and uncertainties as globalization proceeds apace. Conversely, by exploiting their increasing interdependence, cities can learn from each other and contribute to creating cross-city solutions to these common problems via complex, networked, and shared strategies.

The spatial inflection of globalization is vast and drives rapid urbanization across the globe. According to the UN Department of Economic and Social Affairs (UN DESA) *World Urbanization Prospects* report in 2010,[4] almost two thirds of humanity already live or soon will live in urban areas. "Between 2009 and 2050," states the report, "the world population is expected to increase by 2.3 billion, passing from 6.8 billion to 9.1 billion. At the same time, the population living in urban areas is projected to gain 2.9 billion, passing from 3.4 billion in 2009 to 6.3 billion in 2050."[5]

Even more striking is the rise of "mega-cities" (those with more than 8 million) and "hyper-cities" (those with over 20 million inhabitants).[6] During the period from 1950-1975, only three cities (Tokyo, New York, and Mexico City) had more than 10 million inhabitants. From 2009-2025, however, twenty-nine cities are expected to have more than 10 million inhabitants. Tokyo, for example, will have 37 million inhabitants in 2025.[7]

---

2   Rischard, J.F. (2002).

3   Harrison, N.E., *Complexity in World Politics: Concepts and Methods of a New Paradigm* (New York: State University of New York Press, 2006).

4   United Nations, Department of Economic and Social Affairs, Population Division, *World Urbanization Prospects, the 2009 Revision* (New York: United Nations, 2010).

5   Ibid., p. 1.

6   Davis, M., *Planet of Slums* (London: Vigo, 2006).

7   United Nations, Department of Economic and Social Affairs, Population Division (2010).

The burgeoning of megacities has two distinct characteristics. First, this unprecedented urbanization increases inequality within and between cities with different sizes and economic functions. Although most of the population will still live in smaller cities in an urbanized world in 2015, "there is little or no planning to accommodate these people or provide them with services" due to the dominant demand of the megacities.[8] That is, megacities will gain the benefits of globalized investment, trade, and financing while the costs arising from the growth of urban populations will remain concentrated in small and medium-sized cities.[9] And with the dominance of neoliberal capitalism, the daily life of ordinary people will be affected profoundly by the continued existence of inequality of income and wealth between the relatively wealthy and the vastly poor. This dichotomy results in social conflict between and within cities.

Second, globalization also changes the relationship between cities and rural areas. Traditionally, we have conceptualized cities and the countryside at opposite ends of one spectrum. However, with the extension of megacities into rural areas, especially in China and Indonesia, cities and countryside have fused. As Michael Davis puts it, "In many cases, rural people no longer have to migrate to the city; it migrates to them."[10] Such rural-urban hybrid settlements are called "*desakotas*" (city villages). In this case, rural areas are urbanizing "not through rural depopulation to the cities with their subsequent outward growth, but through a process of spontaneous change in which a majority of the rural population are transforming their lifestyles and activities into urban pursuits *in situ*."[11]

Deepening disparity or inequality of cities and the rise of *desakota* settlements are emergent phenomena that reflect the bottom-up transformation of human settlement and land use by globalization. In the wake of this transformation, the provision of appropriate services to the increased population is under serious threat. In particular, the provision of infrastructure to provide important services like water, food, energy, and transport is critically important for urban security in each city. Because the provision and management of infrastructure entails the investment of capital, implementation of new technology, management of social conflict,

---

8   Davis, M. (2006), p. 7.
9   Ibid.
10   Ibid., p. 9.
11   Xie, Y., *et al.* (2005).

and solving of environmental problems, infrastructure becomes highly politicized.[12] Superimposed on this political economy are other challenges such as climate change, resource constraints, violence and conflicts, economic depression, non-state terrorism, and so forth. Sustainable provision and good governance of "smart critical infrastructure" has become, therefore, the central concern for creating secure and sustainable cities. Conversely, without provision of proper critical infrastructure and its good governance, urbanization in an era of globalization leads to more, not less, insecurity and vulnerability, thereby undermining the provision of human security in various forms — the very essence of city formation. Thus, Martin Coward juxtaposes urbanization and security as reciprocal dynamics. He suggested that the security agenda is urbanized and that urbanity is securitized. He calls this antithesis the "urbanization of security."[13] Security in this sense has many dimensions. Some dimensions are contradictory and many are intricately connected to external, often global forces unamenable to local control.

The "urbanization of security" and "politicization of urban infrastructure" leaves urban infrastructure managers with multiple dilemmas. Key questions to answer include the following:

- Who is responsible for sustaining and reproducing the critical infrastructures of cities facing multiple threats like climate change, resources constraints, violence, terrorism, and other insecurities?

- How are they held responsible?

- Is critical urban infrastructure resilient to those threats?

- Which urban form is more resilient to those threats? Closed, separated cities or networked, open, agglomerated cities?

In this chapter, we examine how globalization affects cities in Northeast Asia. We begin by noting the different historical origins of urban form and land use, which in turn affect a city's relative vulnerability to a variety of global threats. We note how the evolution of land use and urban form varies greatly due to local, historical, and contemporary factors, but we also observe how the evolution of urban corridors and *in-situ* urbanization

12   Hodson, M. and Marvin, S., "'Urban Ecological Security': A New Urban Paradigm?," *International Journal of Urban and Regional Research*, 33 (1) (2009), doi: http://dx.doi.org/10.1111/j.1468-2427.2009.00832.x

13   Coward, M., "Network-Centric Violence, Critical Infrastructure and the Urbanization of Security," *Security Dialogue*, 40(4-5) (2009), doi: http://dx.doi.org/10.1177/0967010609342879.

of "rural" settlements in a globalized economy may surpass the capacities of traditional urban authorities and stimulate new forms of networked, cross-border governance. Next, we investigate how cities in the region adapt to energy insecurities. We note how local urban form and density are major drivers of multiple dimensions of energy insecurity that arise from exogenous factors associated with the potential failure of global energy markets and the vulnerability of cities to energy-driven climate impacts—especially thermal stress and heat islands in major cities.

In the next section, we identify the already visible impacts of global climate change on cities in Northeast Asia, including its amplification of the already noted effects of land use on energy insecurity, as well as those of floods, storm surges, and the increasing frequency and intensity of storms on cities.

In the final section, we observe that traditional forms of international cooperation executed by central governments are slow, bureaucratic, and often result in little change. We argue that city-city linkages are far more likely to create solutions commensurate with these rapidly evolving, linked problems. Moreover, we suggest that such a networked approach will create extra-city, networked forms of resilience, thereby preparing cities to respond to the shared shocks that may arise as climate change reaches various tipping points or to bottom-up, game-changing dynamics such as non-state threats to urban security. This inter-city approach, supplemented by agile civil society networks able to span borders and fill structural holes between different cities, and between cities and central authorities, increases social complexity to match the increasing complexity of the problems that beset cities.

In this respect, we suggest that civil society organizations working closely with city governments are seeds dropped into an already super-saturated solution. Although they are small, they lead to the rapid precipitation of crystals and to a new, emergent pattern of decentralized, networked governance that supplements and supersedes, but in no way substitutes for, the role of states in the region.

Multiple Threats to Cities in Northeast Asia

We will now apply these arguments and questions to cities in Northeast Asia. Northeast Asian countries have some common features. Except for Japan, they all experienced post-colonial, nation-state-led urbanization.

In Seoul, Tokyo, and Shanghai, cities relied on a "growth-only-oriented" urban policy. Central states designated specific cities to pursue this growth strategy. Additionally, for some cities in South Korea and Japan, North Korea poses a concrete military and economic threat due to its ability to deliver an artillery or rocket attack, implicating these cities in an inter-Korean war. Thus, cities in this area also live in a potential warzone that poses additional risks in common.

However, Northeast Asian cities also differ from each other in many ways. Some are on socialist paths of urbanization; others are completely capitalist in nature. The cities have different locations in the global network of cities, and they are positioned differently in the topology of global cities. In fact, it is easy to get lost in the diverse characteristics of cities in each country. In each country, there is a hierarchy of urban scale. In addressing the challenges posed by globalization, we must specify what type of cities we are dealing with: small- and medium-scale cities, large cities, metropolises, megalopolises, urban corridors, and so on. Here, we focus on world cities like Tokyo, Beijing, and Seoul. Smaller cities can be included for discussion, however, provided we recognize how the specificity of the issue varies as a function of scale. As we shall see, smaller cities are often more agile and more creative than mega-cities in adopting new strategies to respond to the pressures of globalization and globalized threats. In Table 4.1, we present a taxonomy of the multiple threats faced by world cities in Northeast Asia in four dimensions: political, social, environmental, and economic.

Table 4.1: Multiple threats to Cities in Northeast Asia

Political aspect	Social aspect	Environmental aspect	Economic aspect
DPRK threat of attack	Demographic instability	Natural /artificial disaster	Unsustainable supply chain
Dependency upon central government	Migration/ immigration (households)	Climate change related disaster	Japanese recession
City-rural relations	Limited professional opportunities	Food dependency on imports	Market investment trend
Non-state terrorism	Asymmetry of population structure	Water from long distance	Construction-biased economy
Territorial disputes	Aging city	Concentration of risky facilities	Shortage of jobs

Urbanization of Northeast Asian Cities

In this chapter, we will not attend to all of these dimensions —many more could have been included in Table 4.1. Rather, we will begin with an overview of the urban form and land use of major cities in South Korea, Japan, and China. We will identify some of the drivers that explain their different vulnerabilities to global threats and their strategies in response to these threats.

Urbanization of Seoul

The urbanization of South Korea can be characterized as "compressed urbanization," meaning that all the steps and cycles of modernization, the transformation of social life, occurred in a short time.[14] The urbanization was relatively smooth and successful, although there social conflicts arose as a result of redevelopment and providing houses. As the locational inertia of traditional cities has affected the urbanization process, most large cities in South Korea were built on the sites of older big cities.[15] In particular, Seoul, the capital of the Chosun dynasty (1492-1910), accumulated advantages such as physical infrastructure, economic and social/cultural capital, educational opportunities, human resources, social services, networking, and so forth. Therefore, concentration on the Seoul Metropolitan Area (hereafter SMA) is the single most noticeable feature of urbanization in South Korea. The capital region population increased from 21 percent of the national population in 1960 to 48 percent in 2005. In 1960, there were only two million-sized cities in South Korea, but by 2003, there were eight. Overall, the urbanization rate increased from 37 percent in 1960 to 90 percent in 2000. Today, therefore, most South Koreans live in urban areas. We list the socio-spatial characteristics of the South Korean urbanization process in Table 4.2.

The government used many policies during the 1990s to cope with the problems of population concentration in SMA, such as land shortages for housing and the skyrocketing price of housing for the middle class. The regulation of the floor area ratio, for example, was reduced by up to 400 percent, enabling the construction of high-rise buildings and five

---

14   Cho, M., "Trends and Prospects of Urbanization in Korea: Reflections on Korean Cities" (Korean Language), *Economy and Society*, 30(29) (2003).

15   Ibid., p. 27.

new satellite cities near Seoul. The "joint redevelopment method" for the provision of high-rise apartments was adopted, and the restructuring or remodeling of dilapidated houses and the building of multi-owner or multi-family houses was promoted.

Table 4.2: Urbanization and Socialization of South Korea

Period	Mid 50s-early 60s	Mid 60s-mid 70s	Late 70s-late 80s	Early 90s-present
Steps of urbanization	Leaping stage	Growing stage	Accelerating stage	Maturing stage
Mode of urbanization	Selective urbanization	Concentrating urbanization	Regional urbanization	Dispersed and metropolitan urbanization
Pattern of social change	• High mobility • Leaving rural community • State-led economic development • Military dictatorship	• Settling in urban area • Urban slums and apartments • Informal sectors and conglomeration • Export and heavy industry oriented industrialization • Authoritative regime	• Expansion of urban employment • Expansion of urban culture • Urban middle class • Domination of conglomeration • New industrialization • Democratization	• Urban generation • Intensive consumption • Liberalization • Economic crisis • Knowledge/venture capital • Segregation of employment and class relation • Vitalization of civic politics

Source: Adapted from Cho, M., "Trends and Prospects of Urbanization in Korea: Reflections on Korean Cities" (Korean language), *Economy and Society*, 30(29) 2003.

Of these, the "joint redevelopment method" for the provision of housing was uniquely South Korean. In projects designated for "joint redevelopment," owners of land or houses within the designated area for redevelopment could establish a "house redevelopment union" and pursue redevelopment by financial support from private construction companies. In most cases, high-rise apartments replaced dilapidated houses, and the number of houses exceeded that of union members. Then they sold the surplus house stocks (including their own new houses) on the open housing market, earning windfall profits in the rapidly growing South Korean real estate market at that time. The only role of public agencies was to set the spatial boundary for redevelopment. In fact, joint redevelopment was sort of a win-win game for stakeholders — but not for tenants. Typically, the tenants of dilapidated houses were evicted violently without proper compensation before enactment of the "law of protection of housing tenants" in 2001.

Private construction companies that exploited public sector support, which provided legal and institutional means to privatize a public asset, led this process of urbanization. Thus, the urbanization process was commercialized and houses were only provided that could be sold privately for profit. In this system, the public sector did not provide housing for low-income populations who could not compete in the private real estate market. Thus the human right to shelter, a meaningful housing-welfare system, and the basic dignity of the poor were neglected. During this period of South Korean urbanization, only money mattered, not people. As a result, high-rise apartments dominate the urban landscape of South Korea.

This development pathway was heavily biased by commercial interests and deepened the vulnerability of cities. Land used for agriculture had low market returns and was transformed into commercial land for housing, paved roads, and industry. According to the 2009 survey, total agricultural land amounted to 1.8 million hectares[16] — a 1.3 percent drop from 2008. As a result, rice paddy fields fell by 3.4 percent (36 thousand hectares) over the same period. As rice is a domestically produced staple crop for Koreans (unlike other food crops), the food security of cities is thus being steadily reduced from year to year.

To serve the residence of apartment dominant cities, roads were constructed. In 2008, the roads of South Korea totalled 104,236 km, of which 79 percent paved. In the case of metropolitan cities, 99 percent of roads were paved.[17] The increase in paved roads was expected to improve the speed of traffic, but it turned out to have the opposite result: heavy traffic jams followed the surge in private cars. Also, paved roads decreased the number of permeable surfaces and open spaces. In particular, developed hillsides do not hold water well. Urban development relying solely on drainage systems cannot solve the problem of draining away heavy rainfall, nor the problem of landslides. Consequently, Seoul is vulnerable to flooding. On

---

16   Statistics Korea, *Survey on Agricultural Land* (Daejeon: Statistics Korea, 2009).
17   Ministry of Land, Transportation and Maritime Affairs, *Report on Status of Roads* (Seoul: Korean Ministry of Land, Transportation and Maritime Affairs, 2009).

July 27, 2011, for example, an unimaginable disaster occurred in downtown Seoul after unexpected heavy rain.

In addition to these escalating vulnerabilities that stemmed from the redevelopment strategy, citizens were obliged to depend heavily on fossil fuels. According to Gupta, South Korea is the second most vulnerable among twenty-six net oil importing countries in 2004.[18] Gupta's oil vulnerability index shows a country's relative sensitivity to the international oil market, with a higher index implying higher vulnerability. The index is based on various indicators like the ratio of value of oil imports to gross domestic product (GDP), oil consumption per unit of GDP, GDP per capita and oil share in total energy supply, the ratio of domestic reserves to oil consumption, exposure to geopolitical oil market concentration risks as measured by net oil import dependence, diversification of supply sources, political risk in oil-supplying countries, and market liquidity.[19]

Urbanization of Tokyo

Tokyo presents a different story to Seoul. As the capital of the Tokugawa Shogunate, established in 1603, Tokyo was named *wad Edo*. Edo became Japan's political center with a population surge in the early 18th century. It quickly developed into a metropolis of more than a million people. In 1868, after the collapse of the Shogunate, the city came under the control of the Meiji government and was renamed Tokyo. In the Taisho period, the influx of people to Tokyo went further and the population reached approximately 3.5 million by the beginning of the 20th century. Most of the city was destroyed, however, by the Great Kanto Earthquake in 1923. Toward the end of World War II, moreover, Tokyo was again destroyed by massive air raids. Most areas were totally ruined.

The urbanization of Tokyo underwent massive societal change after World War II, as shown in Figure 4.1. In 1897, Japan already had a highly-skilled labor force employed by the Yawata Iron & Steel Works. In the second half of the 20th century, essential public technologies such as the Shinkansen railway network (1959) and the Kasumigaseki skyscraper (1968) symbolized the development of cities through robust economic growth. Post-war reconstruction was virtually complete by the Tokyo Olympics in

---

18   Gupta, E., "Oil Vulnerability Index of Oil-Importing Countries," *Energy Policy*, 36(3) (2008), doi: http://dx.doi.org/10.1016/j.enpol.2007.11.011.

19   Ibid.

1964, and the city is now the paramount political and economic center of Japan, with a population of more than 10 million. Tokyo is still advancing, and, for a giant city, its public places are unusually safe and clean.

Figure 4.1: Post-WWII Transition in Japanese Society

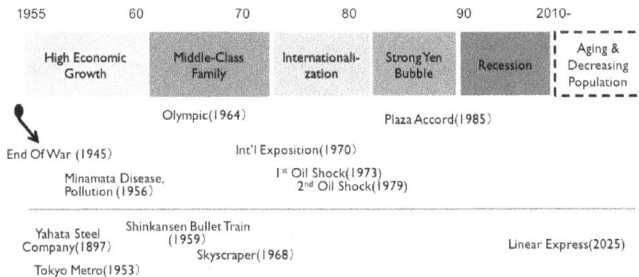

1955	60	70	80	90	2010-
High Economic Growth	Middle-Class Family	Internationali-zation	Strong Yen Bubble	Recession	Aging & Decreasing Population

Olympic(1964)   Plaza Accord(1985)

End Of War (1945)

Int'l Exposition(1970)

Minamata Disease, Pollution (1956)

1ˢᵗ Oil Shock(1973)
2ⁿᵈ Oil Shock(1979)

Yahata Steel Company(1897)   Shinkansen Bullet Train (1959)

Skyscraper(1968)   Linear Express(2025)

Tokyo Metro(1953)

Source: Minato, T., "Urban Security," presentation prepared for the Nautilus Institute workshop *Interconnected Global Problems in Northeast Asia*, Seoul, Korea, October 20, 2010.

Although Tokyo has led Japanese economic development, there are still unresolved issues. The areas of unused land around Tokyo Bay (nearly 900 ha) have been left vacant after factories were relocated, and many of these sites are contaminated and cannot be used easily. Redevelopment of these sites is also constrained by lack of accessible infrastructure and by contending stakeholders who block a public consensus for action.

In Japan, economic and political resources such as population and capital are over-concentrated in Tokyo. The transportation system, for example, followed a steady expansion to satisfy increasing demand. While some efficiency was achieved, there is a deadly commuter rush on workdays, in addition to pollution, garbage, and the omnipresent danger of the capital city being destroyed by earthquake and floods, or even terrorism and war. As a result, there is a need to take action on the over-concentration in Tokyo.

A blueprint of Tokyo in the future will be determined by socio-economic factors and by technological progress that may influence the basic structure of cities. Japan's aging population is an especially powerful driver of change. Aging leads to an increase in social welfare budgets and, at the same time, to falling personal savings. A decrease in the birthrate will lead to a smaller workforce, in turn dampening economic growth. Conversely, technological change is also a powerful driver and induces changes in lifestyle. Table 4.3 shows a projected image of urban life in Japan should economic development gradually deteriorate due to key causes such as the aging population.

Table 4.3: Boundary Image of Futuristic Cities in Japan

	Compact	Pastoral
Description	Homogeneous 'parasite' families moving in cities	Heterogeneous landscape (food, resorts, etc.)
Key drivers	Economic growth	Innovative technologies
Business	Ventures by elderly, women	Telecommuting work
	Conglomerate	P to P business
Transportation	Public and vertical	Personal and horizontal
	Automated commuter, walking	Hybrid-car, rapid train network
Welfare	Multifunctional services in one residence, intensive care	Self medical care, robots
		Remote education
Energy	Centralized, Building & Home Energy Management Systems	Distributed, de-commercialized, self-generation
	Micro, mobile electricity	
Security/safety	Centralized	Individual monitoring, tracing, alarm system
	Gated city	Open City

Source: Minato, T., "Urban Security," presentation prepared for the Nautilus Institute workshop *Interconnected Global Problems in Northeast Asia*, Seoul, Korea, October 20, 2010.

In Table 4.3, we refer to "compact" and "pastoral" models of future cities in Japan. By compact, we mean the maintenance of a smaller scale in every aspect of urban existence. The model of compacted urbanization also makes it easier to work close to home and vice versa. In compact cities, this integration of living spaces and workplaces will rest in the uniform control of information for the protection of safety and security as well as on a stock of new technologies to optimize production/usage of energy and food. In

Tokyo, for example, facilities such as shops and restaurants, called "Eki-naka," already exist inside railway stations and are developed in ways that meet the needs of communities. Some compacted towns such as Roppongi Hills have already been established in the midst of the Tokyo metropolis.

Compacted urbanization will have a significant impact on the sociology of housing and work. Aged parents, for example, may move to the city to live with their children, thereby creating a "reverse-parasite" living environment. In such urban habitats both women and the elderly may play important roles in business. Businesses that attract people with special skills and interests may also congregate in specialized, compact cities. The transportation range of people will also shrink, habitation styles will become vertical (that is, more residential skyscrapers), and energy efficiency will be achieved through highly automated, sensor-based Building and Energy Management Systems (BEMS) and Home Energy Management Systems (HEMS). In the realm of safety and security against crime and international terrorism, society will deploy a new suite of technologies, such as intelligent city gates and universal surveillance systems.

Pastoral cities lie at the opposite end of the spectrum of possible urban futures. Here, pastoral refers not to farms, but rather to the decentralized, combined urban-rural settlement or "rurbanization" that occurs when technological developments enable people to actualize their diverse values, and economic growth suffices to allow them to express their personal needs and desires in locational and lifestyle decisions. Such lifestyles may lead to communities that aspire to create democratic, autonomous societies in which human values and perceptions limit government control, and a set of diverse values are bonded into a networked, decentralized society.

In such societies, individual preferences would be respected and, therefore, diversification of lifestyles would occur. Furthermore, peer-to-peer businesses, working at home, and remote learning/remote medicine may become more viable through open network technologies. An increase in population distribution using high-speed transportation and eco-cars would require the deployment of energy-efficient technologies. Electronic authentication in online services, ciphering processes in mail circulation, embedded microchips in the medical treatment of the elderly, and practical use of traceability are all examples of technologies that realize pastoral societies. In addition, the social costs of food, medicine, or energy may increase in a decentralized society, which would then make it essential to implement innovative technologies such as nanotechnology and IC tags using radio frequency identification (RFID) technology to keep track of items to optimize the increase in social costs. Should compact or pastoral cities become widespread, society may shift from a growth-oriented economy to one based on steady-state energy and resource flows with minimum or zero pollution. As both types of ideal society require populations to devote increasing time to achieving energy efficiency and material flows, technology will be critical to making the transition from a mega-city such as Tokyo to a secure, sustainable city in the future.

In a decentralized social structure, decision-making processes in civil society-type social entities will become more important than they are today. For example, the realization of an "informed society" requires technological literacy so that people can discuss and select the most useful advanced technology as well as facilitate the introduction and diffusion of technology in concert with experts. For example, young people today exchange through social networks private, personal information that their parents could have never have imagined sharing in their youth, but this is not yet a virtual society in which the connection between people is very strong. On the other hand, the values and perspectives of people regarding information security are diverse. Information is free, and people are becoming increasingly indifferent about releasing previously private information. This involves risks and dangers for a society in which the private-public divide may become vague and chaotic and the "community" a group of anomic, unspecified, mostly unknown individuals except for their online identity.

In compact and pastoral cities, it seems likely that people will use energy ever more efficiently, and that cities will become even more integrated than they are today. This future portends much regulation, surveillance, and even heavy-handed urban security systems unless a strategy of extraordinary de-concentration occurs to increase local resilience in a network of coupled, diverse, urban systems. If enough people demand a decentralized lifestyle, whether in pastoral or compact cities, the provision of innovative technologies will be essential to monitor and track individuals in remote areas and have sensor-based services deliver to them wherever they may be — without reducing their autonomy from the state by virtue of the continuous surveillance inherent in many of these technologies.

Urbanization of China

Given its socialist history, post-revolutionary urbanization in China followed a very different trajectory to that of post-war capitalist societies like South Korea and Japan. In capitalist cities, the main impetuses of urban development are economic factors like capital investment, property ownership, and market structure. In China, however, political factors like the strategic considerations of central government, control over the migration of people from rural to urban areas, and the designation of specialized cities have played a significant role in the process of urbanization, at least before the economic reforms of 1978. After those reforms, the Chinese economy engaged with the global economy and marketized in a capitalist manner, albeit with Chinese characteristics. Thus, as in the capitalist cities of Seoul or Tokyo, Chinese urban development was greatly affected by the political and economic drivers of globalization in the last three decades.

The urbanization of China can be divided into two phases. The first phase lasted from the establishment of People's Republic of China in 1949 until 1977. The second phase dates from the economic reforms in 1978 to today. The rural-urban relationship has played an important role in the process of Chinese urban development. After 1949, the Chinese Communist Party (CCP) pursued a rural rather than urban-based strategy of rapid industrialization to support the basic needs of people. As George Lin states, "To achieve rapid industrialization, a large agricultural population was retained in the countryside for the production of food and other materials to support a small and privileged industrial workforce in the cities."[20] This strategy relied on the ideology of socialist egalitarianism to mobilize the population to implement this uniquely Chinese urban development path. China tried to eliminate the "big three differences" between industry and agriculture, the city and the countryside, mental labor and physical labor. Thus, as manifested in the "downward transfer" (*xia fang*) campaign (1957-1958), almost 2.3 million of urban cadres (university professors, intellectuals, white collar workers, factory hands and so forth) were sent to the countryside to receive re-education from the peasantry.[21] Concurrently, the central government strictly controlled the migration of people from rural to urban areas. Moreover, political considerations of national security led to an emphasis on increasing the prosperity of inland cities rather than

---

20 Lin, G.C.S., "The Growth and Structural Change of Chinese Cities: A Contextual and Geographic Analysis," *Cities*, 19(5) (2002), doi: http://dx.doi.org/10.1016/S0264-2751(02)00039-2

21 Ibid., p. 303.

eastern coastal cities that were vulnerable to external attack. Despite rapid industrialization, there were different stages of urban development: slow urbanization (1949-61), de-urbanization (1962-65), and under-urbanization (1966-77).[22] Notwithstanding the many problems associated with the Maoist ideology and the Cultural Revolution, Chinese cities overcame their previously crowded and poorly-serviced status and by the end of this first phase in 1977, as Youqin Huang puts it, "they were virtually free of many of the urban problems that were widespread and seemed unavoidable in other developing nations, such as high crime and unemployment rates, and acute inequality."[23]

After the economic reforms of 1978 and the adoption of an open door policy, the pattern and driving factors of urbanization changed dramatically. With the transition from a socialist planning and control system to a market-regulation regime, the fate of Chinese cities was redrawn. State control over city designation and the operation of market forces was relaxed, as was the role of ideology. The authorities began to recognize cities as growth generating machines. The central government set up the first four "Special Economic Zones" (SEZ) in 1979 and designated fourteen coastal cities as "open" in 1984.

As a result of the new geographically-biased open door policy, SEZs and open coastal cities enjoyed more economic, social, political, and cultural benefits from globalization than inland cities, many of which remained closed to external markets. For example, most foreign investment was concentrated in SEZs and coastal cities.[24] They became the center of capital investment. According to George Lin,

> Because of their inherent advantages of agglomeration economies, these larger urban settlements received more than 60% of all fixed assets capital invested in cities in the 1990s. Moreover, the share of fixed assets capital invested in the extra-large cities was raised from 46.5% in 1990 to 52.5% in 1998..., suggesting that the extra large cities have clearly been chosen by the Chinese government as the center of fixed assets capital investment.[25]

22   Ibid., p. 305.
23   Huang, Y., "Urban Development in Contemporary China," in *China's Geography: Globalization and the Dynamics of Political Economic and Social Change*, ed. by Gregory Veeck, Clifton Pannell, Christopher J. Smith, and Youqin Huang (Boulder: Roman & Littlefield Publishers 2006).
24   Fan, C.C., "Foreign Trade and Regional Development in China," *Geographical Analysis*, 24(3) (1992), doi: http://dx.doi.org/10.1111/j.1538-4632.1992.tb00264.x
25   Lin, G.C.S. (2002), p. 311.

This trend continues today. Unsurprisingly, the inland cities of China lag behind the coastal cities in terms of population and economic growth. Experts on Chinese urbanization predict the population of urban areas will reach 1.0-1.1 billion and the urbanization level will skyrocket to 75 percent by 2050. In addition, "there are likely to be 50 ultra-large cities with a population of more than 2 million, some 150 big cities, 500 medium sized cities, and 1,500 small cities."[26]

The vast social and economic disparity between cities and within cities, however, now prevents China from becoming a prosperous society. According to the World Bank, 91 percent of the poor are from rural areas and 50 percent of them are from western provinces. Moreover, "the urban underclass is concentrated in second-tier cities. The four largest mega provincial cities (Beijing, Shanghai, Chongqing and Tianjin) have the lowest urban disadvantaged rate of around 1 percent. More than 80 percent of the urban underclass live in prefectural or lower-level cities."[27] This disparity is likely to deepen under current conditions of globalized growth in the aftermath of the global financial crisis.

Urban Insecurity in Northeast Asia

In Asia, many major cities are located in coastal zones. This means that they may face similar types and levels of impact from climate change, earthquakes, and tsunamis, as well as from other global threats to all open cities, such as pandemics and food insecurity. Here, we highlight the risks arising from the ultimate global threat: rapid climate change driven by anthropogenic causes.

Many major coastal cities may face existential threats within the next twenty years due to the increased frequency and intensity of storms and surges as well as to relative and absolute sea-level rise associated with climate change.[28] According to the Japanese Ministry of the Environment,[29] 93 percent of the seashore will disappear in Japan if the sea level rises by 1

---

26 Yeh, A.G.O. and Xu, J., "China's Post-Reform Urbanization: Trends and Policies," in *IIED-UNFPA Research on Population and Urbanization Issues* (London, 2009).

27 Lall, S. and Wang, H.G., "China Urbanization Review: Balancing Urban Transformation and Spatial Inclusion. An Eye on East Asia and Pacific" (The World Bank, 2011).

28 Gray, D., "Keeping Its Head above Water," *Associated Press*, 27 October 2007, http://v1.theglobeandmail.com/servlet/Page/document/hubsv3/Travel/travelPages?activities=floods; Margolis, J., "Sinking Bangkok," *PRI's The World*, 2007

29 Ministry of the Environment, 地球温暖化の日本への影響 (Tokyo: Japan Ministry of the Environment, 2001).

meter, and the expansion of levees from 2.8 to 3.5 meters would be necessary to protect the inland. Another simulation shows the inundated area would increase by approximately 50 percent in Tokyo and Osaka Bays if the mean sea level were to rise by 60 centimeters.[30] According to the Japanese Ministry of Land, Infrastructure, Transport, and Tourism,[31] the inundated area would reach a maximum 25,000 ha under the worst scenario. The situation is the same as in other mega-cities located near the sea.

In big cities like Tokyo, climate-induced sea-level rise intersects with the threat of tsunamis. In the 2011 earthquake in eastern Japan, for example, the number of dead and injured exceeded 20,000, and many people went missing. In some areas, massive fires broke out after the tsunami, and whole cities were burned if they had not already been washed away or irradiated by the Fukushima reactor catastrophe. The damage included more than 1.2 million destroyed and damaged buildings, and more than 400,000 people were evacuated.[32] Power and water systems were devastated, cutting off millions of households. The tsunami was 40 meters high in some places and resulted in catastrophic damage to the coastal areas of Tohoku facing the Pacific Ocean.

In addition to the tsunami damage in 2011, various lifeline networks were also shredded by liquefaction, ground subsidence, and dam failure. Five stations in the Tohoku Shinkansen were affected, and the Sendai airport runways were submerged. In many industries, factory operations stopped and the international supply chain was interrupted. These events caused procurement problems outside Japan in the automobile industry, among others. According government estimates, property and livelihood damage may reach up to 25 trillion yen, excluding the Fukushima nuclear power plant accident.[33]

Since South Korea is a peninsula, its coastal cities are also vulnerable to sea level rise from climate change as well as watershed saturation and flash flooding. An estimate of the number of people and places that

---

30   Ministry of Land, Infrastructure, Transport and Tourism, *Climate Change Adaptation Strategies to Cope with Water-Related Disasters Due to Global Warming (Policy Report)* (Tokyo: Japan Ministry of Land, Infrastructure, Transport, and Tourism, 2008).

31   Ibid.

32   Vervaeck, A. and Daniell, J., "Japan – 366 Days after the Quake... 19000 Lives Lost, 1.2 Million Buildings Damaged, $574 Billion," *Earthquake-Report*, 12 March 2012, http://earthquake-report.com/2012/03/10/japan-366-days-after-the-quake-19000-lives-lost-1-2-million-buildings-damaged-574-billion/

33   Nakamichi, T. and Ito, T., "Tokyo Estimates Disaster Costs of Almost $200 Billion," *Wall Street Journal*, 24 March 2011, http://online.wsj.com/news/articles/SB10001424052748704050204576217852022676740

may be affected by sea level rise in South Korea is projected in Table 4.4. Major ports in South Korea have already registered a measureable sea level rise.

Table 4.4: Population and Area affected by Observes Sea Level Rise at Korean Ports (cm/y)

Population and area affected by sea level rise			
Sea level rise	Potential population affected	Potential area affected	Reference
0.5m	278,745	856.13 Km^2	1.4 x the size of Seoul
1m	312,855	984.30 Km^2	1.6 x the size of Seoul
Observed Sea Level Rise at Korean Ports (cm/y)			
Port			Level
Sokcho			0.2
Mukho			0.06
Ulreungdo			0.2
Busan			0.2
Yeosu			0.2
Jeju			0.5
Seogwypo			0.6
Mokpo			0.08
Gunsan			0.1

Source: Korea Economic Institute, *Economic Analysis on Climate Change in South Korea* (2009), p. 166.

In many ways, China is even more vulnerable to climate change than cities in South Korea or Japan due to inherent risks associated with its climatic zones, susceptibility to severe natural disasters, huge population, vulnerable ecosystems, coal-dominated energy mix, and relatively low level of per capita income, etc.[34] The impacts of climate change on its coastal cities deserve particular attention. According to the National Development and Reform Commission, "Firstly, the sea level along the Chinese coast will continue to rise. Secondly, the frequency

---

34 National Development and Reform Commission, *China's National Climate Change Programme* (Beijing: China's National Development and Reform Commission, 2007).

of typhoon and storm surge will increase, aggravating the hazards induced by coastal erosion. Thirdly, some typical marine ecosystems, including coastal wetlands, mangroves, and coral reefs will be further damaged."[35]

In Japan, four major typhoons have struck Tokyo since World War II: Typhoon Kathleen (1947), Typhoon Kitty (1949), Typhoon Kanogawa (1958), and Typhoon Eleven (1993). Recently, there has been frequent torrential rain in urban areas and serious urban flooding. In addition to the traditional water damage, cities experienced a new form of fatality due to people being trapped and drowned by rapid, widespread basement flooding in 1999. Because of this trend, the Tokyo Metropolitan Government has continued to develop flood control facilities.

In the case of South Korea, casualties from natural disasters have decreased between 2001 and 2011, but in monetary terms the damage has increased, as Table 4.5 shows.

Table 4.5: Impact of Natural Disasters in South Korea, 2001-2011

Year	2001	2011
Dead and missing	42	24
Refugees	338	-
Flooded houses	0	14,855
Cost of damage (1,000KRW)		
Total	24,883,087	31,319,101
Building	3,402,000	9,286,200
Vessels	0	-
Farming land	117,529	23,931
Public facilities	21,219,205	21,928,860
Other	144,353	80,110

Source: Seoul Statistics, http://stat.seoul.go.kr/jsp3/

In 2010, super-Typhoon Gonpas hit South Korea. On September 21, a month's worth of rain fell on Seoul in three hours. The Cheong-Gye-Cheon stream and public space, a famous achievement of the ex-mayor

---

35   Ibid., p. 18.

of Seoul and later president of South Korea, Lee Myung-bak, was flooded along with Gwang-Hwa-Moon Square, a symbolic site, and much of southern Seoul.[36] Today, South Korea can expect to be hit by two to three typhoons a year,[37] and the intensity of these storms may increase with further climate change.

China, too, is vulnerable to climate change. In 2010, almost 210 million people in China were affected by flood and drought. Overall, more than 3,000 people died, and the economic damage totaled around 3,745 million Yuan. The floods damaged 3,751 reservoirs (of which 57 were large and middle-sized reservoirs, while 3,694 were small-sized reservoirs) and 81,824 dykes extending over 19,146 km, with associated economic losses of about 692 million Yuan.[38] Climate-induced out-migration in China may increase the number of unregistered, "floating" urban migrants, many of who will be homeless. One careful examination of this prospect found that natural disasters of the type associated with climate change not only increase the total number of migrants to cities, but also expand the number of low-skilled workers in the cities and swell the ranks of the urban poor in China.[39] Thus, climate change would amplify the already anticipated doubling of China's urban population by 2030. The increased share of this population constituted by the labor force — due to internal migration of younger workers, leaving rural areas with older and under-skilled workers — will likely constrain the transition to a service economy.[40] Unsurprisingly, China's cities are highly exposed to climate impacts. Of its estimated urban population of 0.4 billion people, about 130 million live in coastal cities.[41] One study found that six of the top twenty most at-risk cities in the world are in China (see Table 4.6).

---

36 Kim, J.E., *et al.*, "Disaster Management of Local Government: Comparison between the UK and South Korea" in *Korea Association of Public Administration 2012 Summer Conference* (Korea Association of Public Administration, 2012).

37 City Safety Agency of Seoul, *Report of Disasters in Seoul 2010* (Seoul: City Safety Agency of Seoul, 2011).

38 Ministry of Water Resources, *Bulletin of Flood and Drought Disasters in China* (Beijing: China Ministry of Water Resources, 2010).

39 Deng, Q., "Natural Disasters, Migration and Urban Insecurity in China" in *Interconnection Among Global Problems in Northeast Asia Workshop* (Paju: Nautilus Institute, 2009).

40 Cao, G.Y., *et al.*, "Urban Growth in China: Past, Prospect, and Its Impacts," *Population and Environment*, 33(2-3) (2012), doi: http://dx.doi.org/10.1007/s11111-011-0140-6

41 Prasad, N., *et al.*, *Climate Resilient Cities: A Primer on Reducing Vulnerabilities to Disasters* (Washington, DC: The World Bank, 2009).

Table 4.6: City Vulnerability to Climate Impacts, China

Qingdao	Highest proportional increase in population at risk from climate change extremes, estimated 2070 population at risk: 1.9 million; assets: $601.6 billion.
Ningbo	Highest proportional increase in assets at risk from climate change extremes, estimated 2070 population at risk: 3.3 million; assets: $1.1 trillion.
Hong Kong	With 450 miles of coastline and 19 sq. mi of water in its territory, an estimated 687,000 people and $1.2 trillion in assets by 2070 are at risk.
Tianjin	Exposed to dangers from severe flooding, putting at risk an estimated 3.8 million people and $1.2 trillion in assets by 2070.
Shanghai	Heavy storms in 1997 flooded over 170 roads and cost Shanghai millions in economic losses. The city established flood security measures in the last decade. Estimated 2070 population at risk: 5.5 million; assets: $1.8 trillion.
Guangzhou	Over $500 million in damages due to recent "meteorologically unusual," heavily damaging storms exposed this wealthy city's vulnerability to climate extremes. Estimated 2070 population at risk: 10.3 million; assets: $3.4 trillion.

Source: R. J. Nicholls, S. Hanson, C. Herweijer, N. Patmore, S. Hallegatte, J. Corfee-Morlot, J. Château, R. Muir-Wood, "Ranking Port Cities with High Exposure and Vulnerability to Climate Extremes: Exposure Estimates," OECD Environment Working Paper No. 1, OECD (2008), http://www.aia.org/aiaucmp/groups/aia/documents/pdf/aias076737.pdf

The fact that so many Chinese cities are at "high risk" may affect international investment in manufacturing, especially water-intensive industries, which already face water stress in China.[42] This incidence of climate disaster in vulnerable regions of China is a challenge to local, city, and provincial governments. In 2007, following central government direction, local governments established "leading groups" with the responsibility of developing mitigation and adaptation plans to build resilience capacity, not because of climate concerns per se, but because of the close linkage of climate action with energy efficiency, a key indicator of economic competitiveness.[43]

---

42 *Climate Change and Environmental Risk Atlas 2013* (Bath: Verisk Maplecroft, 2013), http://maplecroft.com/about/news/ccvi_2013.html

43 Ye Qi, *et al.*, "Translating a Global Issue into Local Priority: China's Local Government Response to Climate Change," *The Journal of Environment & Development*, 17(4) (2008), doi: http://dx.doi.org/10.1177/1070496508326123.

Urban and Climate-Induced Heat Stress

Another urban problem associated with extreme weather conditions and climate change is the heat island: a phenomenon whereby average and peak temperatures in urban areas are higher than in non-urbanized areas due to energy use, changes in albedo, etc. According to the Japan Meteorological Agency, the annual average temperature in Tokyo rose 3 degrees Centigrade over the last century, which is 1 degree higher than in medium-size cities. The proportion of days spent in temperatures rising above 35 degrees Centigrade and nights not falling below 25 degrees Centigrade has also increased since 1970. Recently, the heat island has been correlated with heat stroke and even death, particularly among small children and the elderly. In July 2011, approximately 1,500 people affected by heat were transported to medical facilities.[44] Consequently, the Tokyo metropolitan government office issued new guidelines to implement green infrastructure and so reduce the heat island.[45]

With rapid urbanization, Seoul also exhibits a heat island. From 1971 to 2007, the frequency of daily maximum temperatures above 30 degrees Centigrade increased in Seoul. In 1994, for example, there were 56 days above 30 degrees, while in 1997 there were 61.[46]

Like Tokyo and Seoul, Chinese cities endure thermal stress in heat islands. An early review of three decades of paired rural and urban climate stations showed the average heat island effect was 0.23 degrees Centigrade over the period 1953-1973, and that the heat island effect had increased by about 0.1 degrees Centigrade. Trends in the heat island effect could be correlated with the level of urbanization and industrial activity before 1966 and after 1977, that is, with the rise and fall of the Cultural Revolution in China.[47]

A more recent study of Shanghai showed summer mortality rates in and around Shanghai have increased. Scientists directly attribute these deaths to exposure to extreme thermal conditions due to the heat island effect.

---

44 Ryall, J., "Japan Struggles to Cope with Heatwave, with 26 Dead of Heatstroke," *The Telegraph*, 18 July 2011, http://www.telegraph.co.uk/news/worldnews/asia/japan/8645326/Japan-struggles-to-cope-with-heatwave-with-26-dead-of-heatstroke.html

45 Guidelines for Heat Island Control Measures (Tokyo: Tokyo Metropolitan Government, 2005).

46 Korea Environment Institute, *Research on Policies for Mitigating Heat Island Phenomenon to Adapt to Climate Change in Urban Area* (Seoul: Korea Environment Institute, 2009).

47 Wang, W.-C., *et al.*, "Urban Heat Islands in China," *Geophysical Research Letters*, 17 (13) (1990), doi: http://dx.doi.org/10.1029/GL017i013p02377.

Jianguo Tan and his colleagues found the average mid-summer maximum temperature in the urban center is rising at about 0.07 degrees Centigrade per year, with the maximum extreme temperature rising by 0.09 degrees Centigrade per year. The number of hot days (above 35 degrees Centigrade) is also increasing in Shanghai by 0.6 days per year (0.3-0.4 days per year in suburban areas with no increase in ex-urban areas).[48] The heat island effect in Shanghai is most intense during the daytime and reached an average 0.9 degrees Centigrade differential temperature between urban center and exurban areas, with the range amounting to a 0.5-2 difference in degrees during the midday period.[49]

The heat island effect has caused a measurable increase in deaths in Shanghai's central region, especially during the 1998 and 2003 heat waves. In 1998, for example, excess mortality among city dwellers was 27.3/100,000 residents versus 7/100,000 in exurban areas.[50] Researchers concluded that this heating effect was mostly local in nature, and not the result of a larger, regional warming pattern. Their investigation did not examine concurrent determinants of mortality such as air pollution (itself caused in part by heat), cloud cover, humidity, or social variables that affect mortality under conditions of heat stress. Nonetheless, there seems little doubt that cities in China that lack effective offsetting green strategies to reduce the heat island effect increase the vulnerability of their residents to thermal stress, sometimes to the point of death.[51] This conclusion applies not only to eastern coastal cities in the tropics or sub-tropics but also to northeastern cities such as Harbin, which researchers have shown to be similarly vulnerable to such climate effects as the heat island.[52]

Energy and Urban Security

Japan is one of the biggest energy consumers in the world. Since 1973, it has tried to diversify its energy supplies among hydroelectric, natural gas, coal, petroleum, and nuclear sources. The major driver of this diversification

---

48   Tan, J., *et al.*, "The Urban Heat Island and Its Impact on Heat Waves and Human Health in Shanghai," *International Journal of Biometeorology*, 54 (1) (2010), doi: http://dx.doi.org/10.1007/s00484-009-0256-x

49   Ibid., p. 77.

50   Ibid., p. 80.

51   Ibid., p. 78.

52   Zhang, L., *et al.*, "Analyzing and Forecasting Climate Change in Harbin City, Northeast China," *Chinese Geographical Science*, 21 (1) (2011), doi: http://dx.doi.org/10.1007/s11769-011-0441-9

was two oil supply cutoff shocks in the 1970s. Overall, Japanese energy self-sufficiency today is about 20 percent, falling to 4 percent if nuclear power is excluded (Japan relies on imported uranium). The country's secondary energy production is heavily reliant on imports. Natural gas is the major source of energy, supplying nearly 50 percent of primary energy. Before the Fukushima-driven nuclear shutdowns, nuclear accounted for about 25 percent. Japan's energy efficiency is very high, about twice that of the United States and eight times higher than in China and India.

Tokyo is a major energy-consuming entity in its own right. Electricity in the Kanto area (Tokyo and the surrounding seven prefectures) is supplied mostly by thermal and nuclear power plants. The Tokyo Electric Power Company (TEPCO) has a virtual monopoly within its service region. Before the March 2011 Fukushima catastrophe, total power generation capacity was about 9 gigawatts from hydroelectric plants, 38 gigawatts from thermal (oil and coal) power plants, and 17 gigawatts from nuclear power plants. The capacity of the renewable electricity supply was roughly 0.01 gigawatts.

Electricity supply is characterized by daily fluctuations in demand and by seasonal peaks. In Japan, this peak usually occurs in summer due to air conditioning loads. To meet this demand profile, the utility allocates base-load demand to nuclear generators, most of the rest to thermal power, and matches peak demand from stored hydropower. Until 2011, nuclear power played a critical role in energy policy. After the Fukushima nuclear disaster, however, the regional power grid suffered irreversible damage. TEPCO relied on nuclear power plants for about 20 percent of its power. The impacts of the loss of nuclear supply were severe in the Tokyo metropolitan area. After the accident, renewable energies such as photovoltaic cells received more attention. Renewables are insufficient to meet the gap, however, and are expensive to boot. Therefore, the transition from nuclear to renewables may not be easy in the short run, and largely voluntary energy conservation has filled the gap in Tokyo.

Japan grew rapidly after 1950 and energy consumption grew with the economy. In the 1970s, Japan's economy was hit by the oil shocks. Economic growth also slowed. Since the 1980s, energy demand has increased due to lifestyle changes based on comfort, convenience, and increased automobile ownership. Today, energy use by the commercial and transport sectors have doubled relative to four decades ago, while industrial energy use has remained the same.

Air conditioning, refrigeration, lighting, and TVs account for more than 60 percent of household energy use, the growth of which has been driven by increased floor space, office automation equipment, and larger appliances. In the transportation sector, the shift to individual passenger automobiles caused most of the increased energy consumption. Energy consumption in this sector dependents on oil more than in the industrial sector. Undoubtedly, alternative energy conversion technologies must be a critical driver of future energy use.[53] To improve energy efficiency and reduce greenhouse gas emissions, the Ministry of Economy, Trade and Industry has produced the Technology Strategy Map of critical technologies.[54] Those include natural gas thermal power, coal thermal power, carbon capture and sequestration, innovative solar power, advanced nuclear power, and superconductivity in the energy sector; fuel cell automobiles, plug-in hybrid cars, and biomass fuel in the transportation sector; material processing technologies and innovative steel in the manufacturing industry sector; energy conservation in houses and buildings, lighting, decentralized fuel cells, heat pumps, information devices/systems, energy management systems in homes and commercial and industrial buildings of all kinds; and electricity storage, power electronics, and hydrogen production/storage as common technologies.

Like Tokyo, Seoul is also a major energy consumer. The service sector dominates electricity use in Seoul (60 percent) followed by residential use (28 percent), industrial (10 percent), and public use (8 percent).[55] Unlike in China, where industry still dominates urban energy, Seoul's industrial energy use remains small. And whereas many Chinese households today are powered by coal — even in Beijing — 90 percent of households in Seoul use natural gas. Overall, Seoul energy use is fuelled mostly by oil (37 percent), liquid natural gas (33 percent), and electricity (26 percent), as shown in Table 4.7. Although Seoul accounts for nearly a quarter of the population of South Korea, it uses only about 8 percent of the total energy consumed (in 2010), mostly because industrial energy use is so small in Seoul relative to other cities based around heavy and energy-intensive industry, as shown in Table 4.8.

53   *Research Organization for Information Science & Technology* (Tokyo: Research Organization for Information Science & Technology), http://www.rist.or.jp/ehome.html
54   Ministry of Economy, Trade and Industry, *Innovative Energy Technology Plan* (Tokyo: Japan Ministry of Economy, Trade and Industry, 2007).
55   Ministry of Knowledge and Economy and Korea Energy Economics Institute, *Yearbook of Energy Statistics* (Tokyo: Japan Ministry of Knowledge and Economy and Korea Energy Economics Institute, 2011).

Table 4.7: Seoul, Final Energy Consumption By Source Unit: 1,000toe

Total Seoul	Coal	Petroleum	Town gas	Electricity	Heat	Renew-ables
15,717	117	5,800	5,127	4,067	510	97
100%	0.70%	37%	32.60%	25.90%	3.20%	0.60%
Total national						
193,832	27,968	100,381	21,081	37,338	1,718	5,346
100%	14%	52%	11%	19%	1%	3%
Seoul as fraction of total national						
8.10%	0.40%	5.80%	24.30%	10.90%	29.70%	1.80%

Source: Ministry of Knowledge Economy, Korean Energy Economics Institute, *Yearbook of Regional Statistics* (Seul, 2011).

Table 4.8: Seoul, Final Energy Consumption By Sector Unit: 1,000toe

Total Seoul	Industry	Transportation	Residential/commercial	Public
15,717	1.023	4,846	9,153	696
100%	7%	31%	58%	4%
Total national				
193,832	115,155	36,938	37,256	4,483
100%	59%	19%	19%	2%
Seoul as fraction of total national				
8%	1%	13%	25%	16%

Source: Ministry of Knowledge Economy, Korean Energy Economics Institute, *Yearbook of Regional Statistics* (Seul, 2011).

As in South Korea and Japan, cities in China play a major role in national energy use. Wenji Zhou and his colleagues have described how residential households, transportation, and the building materials industry propel most of China's urban energy use [56] The main determinants of these drivers are (a) shifts in industrial structure that change the energy intensity of key inputs into urban construction, such as cement, glass, aluminum, and steel; (b) net effects of increasing income on household energy use via the

---

56   Zhou, W., *et al.*, "Energy Consumption Patterns in the Process of China's Urbanization," *Population and Environment*, 33(2-3) (2012), doi: http://dx.doi.org/10.1007/s11111-011-0133-5

acquisition of more end-use equipment, as opposed to increasing the unit efficiency of such equipment over time, as well as the substitution of cleaner, more efficient fuels such as natural gas for dirty coal in household cooking and heating; and (c) shifts in transport and mobility, especially from public transport to cars, and from inefficient older vehicles to more efficient newer vehicles that offset efficiency-driven reductions with increased absolute usage provided by the more efficient vehicles.[57] These three drivers — household equipment, transport mode, and building materials — account for about 20 percent of overall urban energy use in China. Within that 20 percent, residential use is declining relative to transport and building energy use. The other 80 percent comes from urban industrial energy use.[58]

The International Energy Agency notes that urban energy use in China is controlled more by the central government and national policies than it is by cities or provincial policies. Nonetheless, Chinese cities still influence local energy usage because they often own much of the public infrastructure and energy utilities. Overall, the Agency estimates that China's cities account for about 75 percent of total primary energy demand (2006), forecast to increase to 83 percent by 2030. "On average," the Agency states, "each urban citizen in China consumes 2.6 Mtoe (million tonnes of oil), compared with 1.4 Mtoe nationally, reflecting higher urban incomes." About 87 percent of this usage is still fuelled by coal although natural gas has been substituted for much coal in the mega-cities.[59]

Cities in China are charged with implementing energy and emissions reductions. Investment competition between cities drives them to address strong local concerns about air pollution and reliable energy supplies. To this end, cities focus on increasing natural gas and limiting coal use in residential and commercial sectors, building knowledge-based industry, increasing energy efficiency, and improving mass transit.[60]

In addition to increasing energy efficiency, China has promulgated the concept of a "circular economy" based on a zero-emissions recycling and efficient resource-use system, formally bringing it into law in 2009.[61] In this concept, the waste of high-grade heat is treated as a resource in a

---

57   Ibid., p. 202.
58   Ibid.
59   International Energy Agency, *World Energy Outlook 2008* (Paris: International Energy Agency, 2008). http://www.worldenergyoutlook.org/media/weowebsite/2008-1994/weo2008.pdf
60   Ibid., p. 193.
61   Zhou, W., *et al.* (2012), p. 217.

cascade of co-located end-users. Coupled industrial waste heat flows allow wastes from one factory (carbon dioxide, for example) to be used in the production of industrial chemicals in another factory. This model will take enormous effort to adopt throughout China, not just in the mega-cities. The "coal cities" of northeastern China, for example, were built around coal mining and manifest very poor integration of urban form and function. The energy transition implied by a circular economy and by increasing material and energy efficiency highlights the economic vulnerability and lack of resilience of such cities to economic losses and climate impacts at the same time.[62]

Finally, energy use in Chinese cities is very uneven. On average, the relative urban energy use per capita in China is small. But in the really big cities like Beijing, Shanghai, and Tianjin, it is huge and exceeds that of Tokyo, London, or New York. Shobhakar Dhakal, an energy researcher based at the Global Carbon Project who investigated China's urban energy use with the International Energy Agency, recommends that China's mega-cities look to the Tokyo model for excellent public transportation and mixed land uses.[63]

Complex, Networked Urban Security

In an era of globalization and complex global problems, no city is an island. No city can solve its problems alone. Cities must cooperate to prosper and subordinate globalization to local goals rather than allow their infrastructure to be fragmented and identity to be dissolved by new interdependencies. Above all, cities need to collaborate to create and share solutions to complex global problems, some of which must be implemented jointly.

The traditional approach of inter-governmental cooperation to urban development is to promote *project-based cooperation*.[64] Each project, such as

62 Bo, L. and Lianjun, T., "Vulnerability and Sustainable Development Mode of Coal Cities in Northeast China," *Chinese Geographical Science*, 18(2) (2008), doi: http://dx.doi.org/10.1007/s11769-008-0119-0

63 Gaffney, O., "Tracking China's Urban Emissions," *Global Change Magazine*, 1 December 2009, http://www.igbp.net/news/opinion/opinion/trackingchinasurbanemissions.5.1b8ae20512db692f2a680003075.html

64 This section is based on Minato, T. and Sutheerawatthana, P., "Exploring Possible Cooperation for Climate Change Adaptation: How Civil Society Could Work with Government Strategies," in *Interconnections of Global Problems in East Asia: Climate Change Adaptation and its Complexity from the Perspective of Civil Society* (Paju: Nautilus Institute, 2009).

the construction of a water treatment plant, is treated and implemented separately, in part conforming to local needs and stakeholders and in part driven by the intentions of the project sponsors. This is typically how assistance agencies, such as the Japan International Cooperation Agency and Korea International Cooperation Agency, have operated. Sometimes, however, resources allocated to projects are hotly disputed, especially where there is a divergence between the goals set by central government agencies and the aspirations of locals who wish to exercise authority over the project or at least participate in its design and implementation. This has often occurred, for example, in "slum" renovation projects. Another approach, *the sectoral approach*, was recently promoted in the region in relation to greenhouse gas mitigation technologies. In this case, a coalition of global industrial corporations was promoted to develop and deploy technologies that could be used to tackle sector-specific problems. With this method, advanced technologies will be transferred or developed and owned jointly. The proprietary nature of corporate intellectual property embodied in such technologies, however, often reduces the incentives for technology sharing.

A *city-based approach* founded on alliances between cities demonstrates the possibility of powerful synergies in contrast to the traditional and corporate-coalition approaches to building capacity for urban security in the region. It may facilitate the dissemination of useful knowledge, enable technology transfer, facilitate sharing of resources, support capacity building, and permit new types of co-financing, etc. Because cities can act relatively independently from national-level policy, it can circumvent many political obstacles that otherwise block international cooperation. For example, the Clinton Climate Initiative applies a business-oriented approach by seeking economic opportunity in the urban response to climate change while nurturing the sharing of best-practice between forty of the world's largest cities.

Kitakyushu-Dalian cooperation exemplifies a city-based coalition approach. As one of Japan's four major industrial areas suffering from severe pollution caused by heavy and chemical industry, Kitakyushu was able to transform itself from a city with "a smoke-filled sky and the sea of death" to an "environmental city" with cutting edge technologies. Starting in the 1970s, it began to share this experience with other cities. In 1996, it initiated formal cooperation with Dalian, China. The local government played a significant role in obtaining funding from not only the central government, but also affiliated agencies such as the Japan International Cooperation Agency (JICA). It also organized the participation of private firms by addressing plausible technology transfers for the Dalian Environmental Model Zone Project. The project successfully created a master plan for environmental improvement, and Dalian became the first city in China to receive the "Global 500" awarded by the United Nations Environment Programme in 2001.[65]

The attempts made by Kitakyushu demonstrate that the city-based approach could help reinforce both intergovernmental environmental cooperation and market mechanisms relying on a production network of firms. Other than Dalian, Kitakyushu has cooperated to solve environmental problems with other cities in the East Asia region such as Incheon, Busan and Tianjing, Ho Chi Min, Cebu, and Surabaya.

The number of sister cities sharing environmental best practices has proliferated. Particularly in China, the State Environmental Protection Administration (SEPA) has encouraged local authorities to implement their own environmental policies through cooperation with cities in other countries.[66]

Scale in Social and Technological Solutions

Cities are under intense pressure to lessen the effects of natural disasters, especially those driven by climate change. In addition to institutional resilience, new technologies can reduce vulnerability to climate change impacts. One example is the Metropolitan Area Outer Underground Discharge Channel, a massive "underground river" in Tokyo. This artificial river, built 40 meters under the ground with a diameter of more than 10 meters, runs 30 kilometers under the Seven Ring Road from the Channel uptown into Tokyo Bay. The system prevents the overflow of four major waterways in Tokyo. When the swollen river exceeds capacity, the flood system functions as a reservoir, eventually draining the water into the sea.[67]

---

65 Council of Local Authorities for International Relations, *Local Authorities International Cooperation Network* (Council of Local Authorities for International Relations, 2003); Kitakyushu Office for International Environmental Cooperation, *Eco, Thereby Enhancing Global Partnership* (Kitakyushu: City of Kitakyushu, 2007)

66 Shin, S., "East Asian Environmental Co-Operation: Central Pessimism, Local Optimism," *Pacific Affairs*, 80 (1) (2007), doi: http://dx.doi.org/10.5509/20078019.

67 *The Metropolitan Area Underground Discharge Channel* (Tokyo: Japan Ministry of Land, Infrastructure, Transport and Tourism), http://www.ktr.mlit.go.jp/edogawa/gaikaku/

At the macro-scale, smart grids could make city-level energy much more secure. A smart grid uses information technology to radically change the way electricity is delivered. Smart grids monitor the flow of electricity to and from generators and consumers, use transmission lines to reduce power loss and accommodate intermittent and renewable power generators, enhance multi-layered network resilience, and facilitate demand-side management.[68]

In 2009, about $69 billion was spent globally on smart grids, of which about $21 billion was allocated to "Unified Smart Grid" implementation in the United States. Europe is developing a "SuperSmart" grid. Australia committed to a "Smart City, Smart Grid" in 2009,[69] and China has announced plans to create its own hybrid "Strengthened Smart Grid" by 2020.[70] Dozens of technological innovations in hardware and software are needed to achieve this shift from a unidirectional, centralized grid system to one that is omni-directional, decentralized, polycentric, and locally controlled.

In general, smart grid technology can be grouped into five key areas – integrated communications, sensing and measurement, advanced components, advanced control, and improved interfaces and decision support.[71] But most technologies enabling the smart grid are off-the-shelf. As envisioned, smart grids will develop incrementally and will not be transformational. In China, the initial emphasis on very high-voltage transmission lines — and the decision to delay the integration of renewable energy generation to a later stage — reinforces the traditional electric utility culture dominated by engineering values.

---

68 National Energy Technology Laboratory, *A Vision for the Modern Grid* (Pittsburgh: United States Department of Energy, Office of Electricity Delivery and Energy Reliability, 2007).

69 CTBR staff writer, "Australia's Rudd Government Invites Industry Bids to Transform Its Energy Grid through Smart Grid, Smart City Initiative," *Clean Technology Business Review*, 29 October 2009, http://www.cleantechnology-business-review.com/news/ australias_rudd_government_invites_industry_bids_to_transform_its_energy_grid_ through_smart_grid_smart_city_initiative_091029

70 Li, J., "From Strong to Smart: The Chinese Smart Grid and Its Relation with the Globe," *Asian Energy Platform News*, 2009, http://www.aepfm.org/ufiles/pdf/Smart%20Grid%20 -%20AEPN%20Sept.pdf

71 National Energy Technology Laboratory, *A Compendium of Smart Grid Technologies* (Pittsburgh: United States Department of Energy, Office of Electricity Delivery and Energy Reliability, 2009).

To become transformative, the smart grid needs to be combined with new technologies for urban redesign, transportation systems, and different modes of power generation, distribution, and end use — all of which are driven by sustainability imperatives. Of these, the vision of electric and hybrid cars serving as generators when not re-charging or in use presents a possible combination that makes the smart grid and hyper-car, taken together in a fusion, truly transformative.[72]

For this to occur, hyper-cars need to move from concept to sales in large numbers, and smart grids will need to accommodate millions of new, small auto-generators feeding electrons back into the grid. The hyper-car entails shifting from fossil fuels or a centralized power supply stored in batteries to industrially-produced bio-fuels, as well as genetically enhanced plants with high-efficiency photosynthetic conversion of sunlight to biomass. Another concept is to convert underground coal or natural gas *in situ* into hydrogen, storing the carbon dioxide underground and using the hydrogen in fuel cell-powered hyper-vehicles.

Such a shift from centralized generation, whether of fossil fuels or renewable sources such as wind, to millions of small-scale generators that are also consuming machines would turn the smart grid upside-down and reap huge gains in energy efficiency, avoid billions of tonnes of greenhouse gas emissions, increase network resilience in the face of climate impacts on the power system, and yield massive economic savings.

To work, the system would need high bandwidth wireless monitoring and decision-support systems that could maintain tens of millions of parked auto-generators. It would also require the development of automatic power dispatch algorithms that reflect the interaction of driving patterns with power generation capacity. The fusion of the smart grid with hydrogen and bio-fueled hyper-cars is a possible transformative technology that could become the platform for a sustainable civilization. No less radical a technological shift will be needed to secure largely coal-powered cities in China in the face of dwindling oil supplies and accelerating climate impacts.

Of course, no one can predict exactly how such a transformative technological fusion will emerge. But let us assume something along these lines happens in the coming generations. What else is on the sustainability

---

72 Lovins, A., "Hypercars, Hydrogen, and Distributed Utilities: Disruptive Technologies and Gas-Industry Strategy," in *Operations & Marketing Conferences, American Gas Association* (Denver: Rocky Mountain Institute, 2000).

horizon that might complement the IT-enabled smart grid combined with the hyper-car?

At the other end of the scale, the East Japan Railway Company has reportedly installed an experimental "floor electricity generator" using the energy of the pressure and vibration of pedestrians at the Marunouchi North Ticket Gate in Tokyo station.[73] Such "micro-energy" may also be applicable in many public buildings as well as in private housing for keyless entry systems, battery-free remote control, and other monitoring systems such as automobile locks and ignition. Some hope that this type of electricity generation could provide auxiliary power during disaster emergencies.

In addition to physical strategies or "hard adaptation," cities must also undertake "soft adaptation." Cities increasingly face "infrastructure congestion" or bottlenecks such as traffic jams. Japan, for example, loses more than 12 trillion yen per year due to traffic jams.[74] "Smart infrastructure" is a concept that applies not only to grids, as explained above, but also to transportation (to traffic light controls, for example), water, buildings, etc.[75] Using the full network capabilities of infrastructure, not just its stand-alone function, is critical to achieving urban sustainability as well as security. The two goals are served by creating adaptive networks to achieve efficiencies through substitution across infrastructure or by adding resilience, as in the case of cross-infrastructure cascading or concatenating failures. Seoul has begun to "smarten" its infrastructure and is moving quickly from phase 1 (application to specific services in a sector such as public transport system), to the phase 2 (vertical integration across services within a sector such as inter-modal transport information), and then onto phase 3 (horizontal integration across sectors).[76]

---

73   Japan for Sustainability, "Walking on New Power-Generating Floor Creates Electricity," 22 March 2007, http://www.japanfs.org/en/pages/026618.html [accessed 22 July 2013]; Arai, M., "New Energy Systems in Railroads" in *Confederation of Asia-Pacific Chambers of Commerce and Industry* (East Japan Railway Company, 2009).

74   Nissan Motor Company, "Urban Mobility: Breaking the Chain of Urban Traffic Congestion," *Nissan Technology Magazine*, 19 July 2010, http://www.nissan-global.com/ EN/TECHNOLOGY/MAGAZINE/report1.html

75   Lee, S.H., *et al.*, "Ubiquitous and Smart System Approaches to Infrastructure Planning: Learnings from Korea, Japan and Hong Kong," in *Sustainable Urban and Regional Infrastructure Development: Technologies, Applications and Management*, ed. by Yigitcanlar, T. (Hershey: IGI Global, Information Science Reference, 2010).

76   Hwang, J.S. and Choe, Y.H., *Smart Cities Seoul: A Case Study*, ITU-T Technology Watch Report (International Telecommunications Union, 2013).

Operational Strategies to Make Cities Secure

In Japan, governments have responded to threats to urban security such as climate change on an ad hoc, top-down basis, organization by organization. Central government tends to create catalogues of policies to be implemented in vertically-separated stovepipes by national ministries and agencies.

In contrast, cities tend to weave together their programs around local circumstances in a much more effective manner. In 2009, for example, the Tokyo Metropolitan Government initiated its "Tokyo in 10 Years" strategies. More than forty strategies were adopted to fulfill eight goals and objectives, including the development of a green city, infrastructure stock management, low-carbon society, disaster prevention, a new model for aged society, a creative city, the promotion of sport activities, and challenging society. As part of this plan, Tokyo also considered adaptive measures. Use of advanced technologies, personnel training, and promoting collaboration and solidarity among Asian cities were designated as important.

The March 2011 earthquake, tsunami, and Fukushima catastrophe revealed the underlying importance of local and urban resilience, and the fragility and brittleness of national and oligopolistic corporate responses. The national government proved slow and ineffective in its response while TEPCO, the main corporate organization responsible for the Fukushima plant, demonstrated not only its corruption, but also its incompetence in that it utterly failed to respond effectively.[77] This response deficit was filled mainly by the bottom-up actions of civil society,[78] including massive voluntary energy conservation,[79] combined with emergency capacities fielded autonomously by first-responder organizations and supplemented by the military.

Perhaps the most significant long term impact of the disaster will be the direct challenge to the oligopolistic structure of the electric power industry in Japan. Led by cell phone entrepreneur Masayoshi Son, who laid out a

77   Onishi, N. and Belson, K., "Culture of Complicity Tied to Stricken Nuclear Plant," *New York Times*, 26 April 2011, http://www.nytimes.com/2011/04/27/world/asia/27collusion.html?_r=1&hp=&pagewanted=print

78   Ferris, E. and Solís, M., "Earthquake, Tsunami, Meltdown – the Triple Disaster's Impact on Japan, Impact on the World," *Up Front*, 11 March 2013, http://www.brookings.edu/blogs/up-front/posts/2013/03/11-japan-earthquake-ferris-solis

79   Inajima, T. and Okada, Y., "Japan to Have Surplus Power in Summer without Additional Nuclear," *Bloomberg*, 9 April 2013, http://www.bloomberg.com/news/2013-04-09/japan-to-have-surplus-power-in-summer-without-additional-nuclear.html

networked vision of renewable energy for a "solar belt" on the eastern coast of Japan that would render nuclear power unnecessary and obsolete, and in alliance with municipal governments across the country, a political struggle over nuclear power and electricity sector regulation has raged in Japan since the Fukushima event.[80] A number of tsunami-devastated towns are planning to resurrect themselves as altogether off-grid towns.[81]

After the disaster of 11 March 2011, consciousness of the danger of nuclear power plants increased greatly in the region. In spite of the Korean government's continuing commitment to constructing twenty-three more nuclear reactors by 2030 and to exporting eighty nuclear power plants abroad, civil society in South Korea has expressed alarm about this expansion. Small but significant operating errors and reactor accidents have occurred in dilapidated nuclear power plants in South Korea and almost three out of four plants are located near heavily populated urban areas. The Korean Green party was established on October 30, 2011, with non-nuclear power as its motto.

Perhaps the most significant example of the civil society reaction to the Fukushima catastrophe came from the local government. The new mayor of Seoul, Park Won Soon, a famous and leading NGO activist and lawyer, declared that by 2014 Seoul would eliminate the equivalent of one nuclear power plant through energy demand management and an energy saving movement.[82] The basic plan was for the 10 million citizens of Seoul to reduce their electricity consumption by 10 percent per year, rendering a nuclear power plant unnecessary. To achieve this goal, various policy tools were employed. These included the establishment of fuel-cell power plants, expansion of photovoltaic panels on the roofs of buildings (290MW), eco-mileage, a specialized school for climate change, energy retrofitting projects for buildings, total maximum energy consumption limits for buildings, changing low-efficient lighting bulbs into high-efficient LED bulbs, and

---

80 Masayoshi, S., *Creating a Solar Belt in East Japan: The Energy Future*, NAPSNet Policy Forum (Berkeley: Nautilus Institute, 2011); Kingston, J., *Ousting Kan Naoto: The Politics of Nuclear Crisis and Renewable Energy in Japan*, NAPSNet Policy Forum (Berkeley: Nautilus Institute, 2011); De Wit, A., *Japan's Nuclear Village Wages War on Renewable Energy and the Feed-in Tariff*, NAPSNet Policy Forum (Berkeley: Nautilus Institute, 2011).

81 Herman, S., "Japan Urged to Invite Foreign Expertise When Re-Building Tsunami Communities," *City Mayors Development*, 4 March 2012, http://www.citymayors.com/development/japan-post-tsunami.html

82 RTCC staff writer, "Mayor of Seoul Aims to 'Cancel out' a Nuclear Power Plant with Climate Action," *Responding to Climate Change*, 25 October 2012, http://www.rtcc.org/mayor-of-seoul-aims-to-cancel-out-a-nuclear-power-plant-with-climate-action/

so forth. Since Seoul consumes the electricity generated by seven nuclear power plants, this campaign had a significant impact on energy policy and also on the consciousness of ordinary people. As a result of this campaign, Seoul has set the goal of increasing its urban self-reliance in electricity generation from 3 percent in 2011 to 8 percent in 2014, and 20 percent in 2020.

This policy goal confronts many obstacles like low electricity tariffs, the indifference of many people to the danger of nuclear power plants, the pro-nuclear power plant policy of the central government, long-lasting economic depression, unfavorable circumstances for the anti-nuclear power movement, and so on. The campaign requires social consensus and strong support from civil society for its success.

Another post-Fukushima urban security project is the city farming project of Seoul, which began in the summer of 2012. Seoul's mayor outlined the "Ten commandments of city farming" on June 2, 2012. It gives residents guidelines on how to grow food in Seoul including advice on, for example, the provision of spare plots for city farming, education on city farming, community building through city farming, eco-friendly city farming, networking with professional farmers, establishing legal support for city farming, and so forth. Seoul established a 1-hectare model city farm on Nodle Island in the middle of the Han River. The Nodle farming plot consists of a citizen plot, a community plot, a paddy field, an indigenous seeds plot, and community facilities such as picnic tables, small pavilions, and chairs. The project offers environmental education programs like "farm school," "kids' farm class," and "paddy field school." The environmental education facilities use eco-toilets to recycle feces into fertilizer.

In China, the Sino-Singapore Tianjin Eco-City (SSTEC) project deserves scrutiny as an example of a city coping successfully with urban insecurity. SSTEC is located 45 kilometers east from the Tianjin city center and covers about 30 square kilometers of formerly contaminated land. The goal is to recover this area and create a sustainable city by 2020. The Tianjin eco-city is envisioned as a harmonious and sustainable community that would meet the needs of an urbanizing China. The term harmony is meant to include harmony among humans, harmony between social and economic activity, and harmony between humans and the environment. SSTEC will be a modern township where 350,000 residents can live, work, and play.

The vision of SSTEC is for an environmentally-friendly and resource-conservation city in China.[83]

SSTEC is an audacious Chinese experiment to explore alternative models for city development. The site lacks water due to low precipitation in Tianjin. There is also almost no arable land in the city. In the Tianjin eco-city, salt water will be desalinized into freshwater. Waste is to be managed in a comprehensive manner including reduction, reuse, and recycling. In other words, China is now trying to define and test a completely new model for city development in the face of an insufficient supply of water, food, and other environmental services.[84]

---

83   Lang, G. and Miao, B., "Food Security for China's Cities," *International Planning Studies*, 13 (1) (2013), doi: http://dx.doi.org/10.1080/13563475.2013.750940.
84   Ibid., p. 9.

5. Complexity and Weapons of Mass Destruction in Northeast Asia

Peter Hayes and Roger Cavazos

This chapter examines the increasingly complex problem of the threat posed by nuclear weapons of mass destruction (WMD) in Northeast Asia. The first section sketches the recent evolution of the role played by nuclear weapons in international affairs and provides a summary of the nuclear weapons problem both globally and regionally from a conventional, policy-oriented viewpoint. It argues that US nuclear hegemony was constructed to contain the contradictions at the core of its nuclear-based state security strategy.

The second section argues that bottom-up incremental changes due to nuclear weapons proliferation led to tipping points whereby the system of US nuclear hegemony was transformed. The threat of nuclear war metamorphosed and metastasized from a Cold War-era "manageable" threat in Northeast Asia to a rapidly changing, turbulent, and uncontrolled "nuclear breakout" by the DPRK and potentially by non-state actors. In the third section, we note that this phase-shift in the nature of the nuclear weapons problem has led to a renewed and likely increased threat of nuclear next-use in the region. In the fourth section, we examine state-based strategies for solving the nuclear weapons problem, commonly framed as "arms control" or "disarmament" measures. We note that because these approaches do not attend to the underlying drivers of the bottom-up proliferation and increased risk of nuclear next-use, nor to the cross-cutting issues that exacerbate these dynamics, these conventional measures may stabilize, but not eliminate the twin nuclear threats associated with declining

US nuclear hegemony, namely horizontal proliferation and increasing risk of nuclear war. Rather, as the chapter concludes, only civil society-based cooperative security strategies can supplant nuclear weapons and related insecurity from destabilizing the region.

Introduction

Since the end of the Cold War, the world in which nuclear weapons exist has changed dramatically. The basic elements of the global system into which nuclear weapons are interwoven include the following: (a) great powers with enormous superiority over most states due to their conventional and nuclear forces, that is, of the United States (and its allies), of Russia, and of China; (b) states locked into conflicts that are stabilized by defense-dominated deterrence and have no recourse to nuclear weapons, such as Taiwan and formerly North Korea; (c) states engaged in traditional nuclear and conventional high-risk standoffs based on deterrence by retaliatory threat with constant danger of preemption, such as Israel, India and Pakistan; and (d) states with no adversaries in sight and which are not driven to acquire defensive or offensive deterrent capabilities either directly or indirectly extended by others, such as New Zealand and Mexico.[1]

Consequently, nuclear weapons are now woven into international affairs in a more complicated and multi-dimensional fashion than during the Cold War. Four tributaries feed into this river of turbulent change, namely:

Trend 1: The triangular nuclear standoff between the United States and its nuclear allies in Asia and Europe, the former Soviet Union, and China has shifted to one of general deterrence rather than one aimed at sustaining immediate deterrence against the threat of pre-emptive attack. At the global level, nuclear weapons have receded into the "background" of great power politics and serve as hedging insurance against regression to confrontational postures by any one of these great powers against the others, whether because of domestic or external causes. This move away from imminent global nuclear war led to significant reductions in American and Russian-deployed nuclear forces and the abandonment of Soviet nuclear weapons and material by those nations (except for Russia) who inherited them. Today, the global strategic triangle is constituted of relatively symmetric and stable deterrence between the United States and Russia; latent deterrence between

---

1   Morgan, P.M., *Deterrence Now* (Cambridge: Cambridge University Press, 2003).

Russia and China; and asymmetric, relatively unstable deterrence between the United States and China.[2]

Trend 2: Regional conflicts and local security dilemmas have driven small and regional powers to proliferate nuclear weapons in recent years — most obviously between India and Pakistan, but also in Korea and potentially, in the future, Iran, offsetting Israel's undeclared but widely acknowledged nuclear force. These arsenals are primarily targeted against neighbors who are geographically proximate rather than across continents, or against great powers that have forward-deployed forces or project power into these conflict zones. These nuclear forces are small in number and arguably serve immediate deterrent roles due to locally "hot" conflicts that could bring these smaller nuclear powers into head-on collisions.[3] Consequently, nine states now wield nuclear weapons of varying levels of technological maturity — the United States, Russia, China, Britain, France, Israel, India, Pakistan, North Korea, and soon, possibly, Iran.

Trend 3: Transnational and networked terrorists and sub-national actors such as religious cults actively seek nuclear weapons capacities ranging from "dirty" radiological weapons to nuclear weapons that may leak out of state stockpiles kept by the great nuclear powers or be acquired from a small nuclear state. If these non-state actors achieve nuclear status, they are likely to use these weapons for coercive threats rather than for deterrence — or they may simply detonate them as part of their insurgent strategy against local targets (detested political elites, for example), regional targets (Israel, for instance), or global targets (the United States or its allies, Russia, and China).[4]

Trend 4: The revolution in military affairs has made it easier for the great nuclear powers to extend deterrence without relying on nuclear weapons of mass destruction. Forward-deployed conventional forces are still slow and bulky — but over the next two decades, they will become stealthier, smarter, faster, smaller, and, therefore, much harder to target by local conventional or nuclear weapons. Three effects of this fourth trend are already observable and will accelerate:

---

2   Arbatov, A. and Dvorkin, V., *The Great Strategic Triangle*, The Carnegie Papers (Moscow: Carnegie Moscow Center, Carnegie Endowment for International Peace, 2013).

3   Ochmanek, D. and Schwartz, L., *The Challenge of Nuclear-Armed Regional Adversaries* (Santa Monica: RAND Corporation, 2008).

4   Allison, G., "Confronting the Specter of Nuclear Terrorism," *ANNALS of the American Academy of Political and Social Science*, 607 (Special issue) (2006), doi: http://dx.doi.org/10.1177/0002716206290912

1. Great nuclear powers, especially the United States, are likely to intervene against threatening states, especially those that seek nuclear weapons and/or lend support to non-state actors – witness Iraq;

2. Small and regional nuclear powers will accelerate their development and acquisition of medium and long-range delivery systems to directly threaten the homelands of the great nuclear powers and thereby deter them from entering local frays;[5] and

3. Great nuclear powers, especially the United States, will invest heavily in defense-dominant strategies and technologies to counter crude, minimalist nuclear threats from third-rate nuclear powers attempting to counter local conventional dominance. Wholly new weapon systems based on converging information technology-computation, nanotechnology, and nano-biotechnology will accelerate this trend and endow the United States and other technologically powerful states with ways to partly or completely neutralize such long distance threats both to homeland security and to extended deterrence based on forward interventions.[6]

Considered separately, none of these trends would necessarily lead to nuclear next-use. Ordinarily, great powers will keep their distance. Local and regional nuclear-armed states will either avoid hot wars or run them as limited wars under the deterring influence of their crude nuclear weapons. All nuclear powers may keep fissile material and weapons stockpiles secure enough to avoid leakage via any route to non-state actors. Great power intervention may topple nuclear proliferating states and replace them with non-nuclear states. Small nuclear states may be unable to acquire long-range delivery systems or, if they do, be deterred from rattling their own nuclear weapons by the overwhelming offensive nuclear and conventional forces of the great nuclear powers and their local allies and friends.

Nevertheless, the complexity and unpredictability associated with the interaction of these different players at different levels is more likely than not to overwhelm controls and rational decision-making. The Cold War was managed as a nuclear balance of terror because the security elites in Washington and Moscow developed and, over time, observed some rules to the game. Nuclear weapons became the ties that bound the two adversaries in an intimate, lethal embrace. Even then, they ran close to the brink of nuclear disaster on more than one occasion. In short, these four trends converge

---

5   Gormley, D.M., *Missile Contagion: Cruise Missile Proliferation and the Threat to International Security* (Santa Barbara: Praeger Security International, 2008).

6   Anton, P.S., *et al.*, *The Global Technology Revolution*, Monograph Reports (Santa Monica: RAND Corporation, 2001); National Intelligence Council, *Disruptive Civil Technologies: Six Technologies with Potential Impacts on US Interests out to 2025* (Washington, DC: National Intelligence Council, 2008).

to increase the probability that nuclear weapons will be used in war in the coming two decades.

In a four-way standoff where two local nuclear adversaries, each with backing from an external nuclear great power, may come to blows over a contested area (Kashmir, for example) with ties to global terrorism and great power interests (the Taliban and Al Qaeda, say), and in which transnational terrorists could then acquire nuclear weapons through persistent attempts to penetrate poorly secured nuclear stockpiles (in Russia, for example) and use them against one of the local nuclear powers or its backers (India, United States, or its allies), each player must become increasingly concerned about pre-emption and escalation risks to their own existence. The apocalyptic prospect contained in the core ideas of *mutually assured destruction* based on *existential deterrence* does little or nothing to avoid nuclear next-use in such complex and chaotic conflicts — especially *ambiguous* next-use that seeks to gain political and military advantage in the midst of fast-moving conflicts and the source of which cannot be demonstrated or is simply unknown (by ambiguous, we mean no-one claims responsibility or is easily identified as the source of the attack).

Put another way, great powers may not keep their distance if and when global stakes embroil them in regional conflicts such as that between the two Koreas. Local nuclear powers such as North Korea may collapse under pressure and lose control of their nuclear weapons in the midst of civil war and external intervention in the Peninsula. Nuclear weapons may be used pre-emptively by one faction or another in such a war to fend off further intervention or the South Korean occupation of the North. In the event of a nuclear attack on Seoul, Tokyo, Beijing, or Guam, we may never know who pulled the trigger. All this tension takes place in the midst of other transecting global issues that affect how states respond to insecurity. As the US Department of Defense put it with reference to the difficulty of US statecraft, "A series of powerful cross-cutting trends, made more complex by the ongoing economic crisis, threatens to complicate international relations… The rising demand for resources, rapid urbanization of littoral regions, the effects of climate change, the emergence of new strains of disease, and profound cultural and demographic tensions in several regions are just some of the trends whose complex interplay may spark or exacerbate future conflicts."[7]

---

7   United States Department of Defense, *Quadrennial Defense Review* (Washington, DC: United States Department of Defense, 2010).

Defining the Nuclear Weapons Problem

The threat of weapons of mass destruction in Northeast Asia in the post-Cold War world is complex and multifaceted. In the conventional perspective (top-down and state-driven),[8] the global threat of nuclear weapons may be disaggregated into four distinct but related problems (namely, terrorism, new nuclear armed or nuclear weapon states (NWS), existing arsenals, and regime breakdown), thereby generating roughly sixteen separate interrelated problems, as outlined in Table 5.1. On the solution-strategy side of the nuclear weapons issue, there are six obligations (no easy exit, devalue weapons, secure materials, stop transfers, resolve conflicts, deal with the now four nuclear-armed states outside of the Non-Proliferation Treaty), each of which contains multiple possible strategies for a total of twenty possible ways that regional action in East Asia could contribute to a solution of the global problem. Overall, the drivers and solutions present no less than thirty-six possible links between the global and regional dimensions of the nuclear weapons problem.

Table 5.1: Disaggregation of the Nuclear Weapons Global Problem

A. THREAT ASSESSMENT			
Terrorism	**New Nuclear Weapons States**	**Existing Arsenals**	**Regime Breakdown**
1. Terrorist acquisition	5. Nuclear Korea	9. 1000s of weapons on hair-trigger	13. Dual use nuclear plants
2. Fissile material in Russia, Pakistan, North Korea	6. Nuclear Iran	10. New weapons, new tests	14. Nuclear armed states outside Treaty on the Non-proliferation of Nuclear Weapons (NPT) problem*
3. Highly enriched uranium in 40 nations	7. Nuclear war in South Asia	11. New threats of use	15. End of negotiated reductions
4. Nuclear black market	8. War in Taiwan Straits	12. Nuclear Example	16. Collapse of NPT

8   Perkovich, G., *et al.* (2007).

Table 5.1, cont.

B. SIX OBLIGATIONS (SOLUTION-STRATEGIES)					
No Easy Exit from NPT	Devalue Weapons	Secure Materials	Stop Transfers	Resolve Conflicts	Three* Nuclear Armed States Outside NPT
1. No new fuel plants	7. *No new weapons, reaffirm test moratorium, ratify test ban*	11. *Group to prevent nuclear terrorism, secure fissile material*	13. *Implement UNSC 1540 to secure, restrict, criminalize non-state proliferation*	18. Special obliga-tions of nuclear states	19. *Recognize 3 states will not disarm absent regional peace and global elimination but they must assume obligations*
2. *Guaranteed fuel*	8. *De-alert weapons*	12. Global cleanout to identify, secure, remove nuclear materials within four years	14. *Make Additional Protocol mandatory*	*Focus on underlying causes*	20. *Yes, nuclear safety, no, new reactors*
3. *End fissile material production*	9. One-way reductions		15. *Export transparency*		
4. *Punish withdrawals*	10. Plan to disarm		16. *Voluntary actions*		
5. *Nuclear repossession*			17. *Ground Proliferation Security Initiative in law*	A unified approach	
6. *No compliance, no trade*				Starts at the top	

* This table was drafted before the DPRK became the 4th nuclear-armed state outside the NPT.

Note: Items in italics are judged to be relevant to East Asia.

Source: George Perkovich, Jessica T. Mathews, Joseph Cirincione, Rose Gottemoeller, and Jon B. Wolfsthal, *Universal Compliance: A Strategy for Nuclear Security*, Carnegie Endowment for International Peace (2007), http://www.carnegieendowment.org/files/univ_comp_rpt07_final1.pdf

On the solution side of the nuclear weapons equation, states must fulfil at least twenty disparate obligations to resolve the sixteen nuclear threats. These obligations are broken into six solution-strategies, namely, ensuring that there is no easy exit from the NPT; that nuclear weapons are devalued; that fissile materials are secured; that transfers of weapons and requisite technology, knowledge, and materiel are controlled; that conflicts are resolved; and that the special problem of extra-NPT nuclear-armed states is addressed in a way that strengthens rather than weakens the NPT system. Overall, therefore, the conventional paradigm has a complexity measure of thirty-six distinct problems and solutions, all of which are related to each other, and each of which is related in turn to other problems and solutions at various levels of the international system.

One can compare in a highly subjective manner how the global nuclear weapons problem is manifested in the Northeast Asian region by designating which elements are regional in origin or application. Of these, thirteen of the sixteen problem elements clearly originate in the region (such as the proliferation of nuclear weapons by North Korea) or are expressed in the region (such as the threats of nuclear use by the United States against the DPRK).

On the solution side of the nuclear weapons problem, roughly fifteen are solution-strategies that must either originate from states in the region (such as increasing security over nuclear materials and facilities post-Fukushima) or be applied to the region based on a global framework or the emulation of a regional or national strategy elsewhere in the world (for example, the creation of an inter-Korean fuel cycle organization like that between Argentina and Brazil).

Overall, therefore, about twenty-nine of the thirty-six facets of the global nuclear problem as viewed conventionally are to be found at play in Northeast Asia. Thus, the regional dimension of the global nuclear weapons problem is only marginally less complex (twenty-nine out of thirty-six) than the full-blown global nuclear weapons problem. Whether global or regional, the level of complexity in either case exceeds human comprehension.

Although the global nuclear weapons problem is not the same as the nuclear weapons problem in Northeast Asia, all four types of problem and all of the six obligations-solutions are at work in the region. This high degree of global-regional correspondence suggests that the underlying problems in this region may not diverge radically from those elsewhere in the world.

The solutions adopted, while they must be tailored to regional realities, must also be consistent with global solution-strategies. This complexity contrasts with the formerly simple system of nuclear capacity, which commenced with a short-lived US nuclear monopoly from 1945-1949 and continued for the next four decades as a tight bipolar structure led by the United States (with its nuclear allies Britain, France, and, silently, Israel).

From Uni-polar Nuclear Power to a Bi-polar Balance of Terror

The nuclear bombs dropped on Hiroshima and Nagasaki in 1945 marked the zenith of American power in the 20th century. In the next half-decade, the former Soviet Union tried to catch up and as the Cold War began, the United States viewed nuclear weapons as extraordinarily powerful weapons of war, not of deterrence and peace.

The Korean War was the first major conflict in which nuclear weapons played a political-symbolic as well as a military role. Not only did US presidents attempt to compel Chinese leaders to abandon their intervention in the Korean War and to negotiate an end to hostilities on terms advantageous to the United States, but also the shadow of nuclear threat was cast over Korea itself and affected the conduct of the war by the military. For example, in the Korean War, US navy ships were distributed rather than left concentrated in Korean ports and vulnerable to nuclear attack. However, Korea was primarily a protracted conventional conflict based on attrition, maneuver, and air superiority. Nuclear weapons barely affected political or military outcomes although the War did serve as a laboratory for American strategic practitioners to explore how the nuclear threat worked in psychological terms against Chinese and North Korean personnel. Thus, the Korean War prefigured the role of nuclear weapons, but it did not yet reflect the operation of the nuclear threat in a pronounced manner.

In the aftermath of the Korean War (and in response to the demobilization of US forces), the United States substituted nuclear weapons for conventional forces and positioned itself to retaliate massively against the former Soviet Union and China. This was also the moment in which the United States laid down the strategic architecture that combined the ideology of nuclear deterrence with the institutional framework of integrated forces and joint organizations to support combined nuclear and conventional forces, based on unique American nuclear weapons capabilities — including the full spectrum of warheads, delivery systems, bases, command-and-control, and communications-and-intelligence systems needed to fight a nuclear war.

Starting in the mid-1950s in Japan and in 1958 in Korea, US nuclear weapons were forward-deployed to land bases as well as carried aboard US naval forces. By now, the former Soviet Union had tested and deployed its own nuclear weapons, and US strategic thinkers were starting to develop rationales for nuclear forces that recognized their uniquely destructive nature — so much so that they were repulsed from forward-deployment in post-war occupied Japan by a popular movement that led to the removal of land-based weapons from Japan itself in 1960 (but left unrestrained the transit by air and sea of US nuclear weapons in a secret understanding that came to light only in 2010, although it was known to exist for many decades beforehand).

Although China had not yet developed, tested, or deployed its own nuclear weapons, US nuclear forces routinely targeted the former Soviet Union and China as one bloc in the US nuclear war plans maintained at the headquarters of the regional Commander-in-Chief in Hawaii. By now, the United States had created a set of bilateral alliances across the Pacific, and the Cold War was fully underway. The two blocs came closest to direct military confrontation in the 1958 Taiwan Straits Crisis, in which the United States positioned nuclear forces in Taiwan to deter any expansion of the Chinese efforts to occupy Nationalist-controlled islands, thereby risking the use of nuclear weapons against China should Beijing have decided to escalate. This was the first instance in which American strategists began to comprehend fully the risks being run by over-reliance on nuclear weapons to substitute for conventional force.

The escalating Vietnam War was the next theater in which nuclear weapons played a role. Again, due to the primarily counterinsurgent nature of the war, and overwhelming American control of the air war, the United States could not find a way to bring the enormous firepower of nuclear weapons to bear on the ground — although the option was studied carefully in the Pentagon.[9] However, it is possible that the Southeast Asia Treaty Organization (established by the United States with its local allies to prosecute the Vietnam War) played a role in deterring Chinese direct intervention in the war due to the image it projected of being ready and

---

9   Hayes, P. and Tannenwald, N., "Nixing Nukes in Vietnam," *Bulletin of the Atomic Scientists*, 59(3) (2003).

able to fight nuclear war — an option regularly exercised by US forces operating in the region with allied navies.

Tri-polar Nuclear Deterrence

Although the United States (plus Britain and France) and the former Soviet Union fielded the vast majority of nuclear weapons at home, on ships, or on land (the former Soviet Union did not deploy nuclear weapons on allied territory, only on its ships in the Indian and Pacific Oceans), China joined the nuclear club in 1964, launched its first missile in 1966, and tested its first fusion bomb in 1967. With subsequent bomber and long-range missile deployments in the early 1970s, the bipolar balance of terror became a triangle of nuclear threat. This included a 1968 artillery shootout between the former Soviet Union and China at a time when the United States targeted both with nuclear weapons, but tilted towards China as Nixon made his famous move to meet with Mao in 1972, a central aspect of his global redesign of world power.

The trend of integrating nuclear and conventional forces as complements for war-fighting rather than as substitutes for deterrence accelerated in the 1970s to the point where US military emphasized to their own troops and to allies that no distinction could be made between the two types of forces — they were dual use. The ferocity of the Cold War in the 1980s led to an escalation of risk-taking in the region in two cases, both of which came perilously close to direct combat between the United States and the other two nuclear states in the region.

The first was a series of incidents in Korea that stretched back to the late 1960s, during which North Korea conducted provocative covert conventional attacks on South Korean territory or abroad (in Rangoon, for example, when it attempted to assassinate the majority of the ROK Cabinet). This series of attacks culminated in the August 1976 confrontation over a poplar tree in the Demilitarized Zone during which forces on both sides mobilized for full-scale war. On August 18, 1976, the US military decided to remove a poplar tree in the Joint Security Area in the Demilitarized Zone that was blocking the northward view.[10] As a team of US and ROK soldiers began to cut the tree, they were attacked by North Korean soldiers. In the

---

10   For an account of this crisis, see Hayes, P., *Pacific Powderkeg: American Nuclear Dilemmas in Korea* (Lanham: Lexington Books, 1991).

melee, two Americans were killed, bludgeoned by axe handles. On August 21, US and South Korean forces mounted Operation Paul Bunyan, backed by mobilized forces across the entire Peninsula, including the movement forward of tactical nuclear weapons.[11] The then-US Commander in Korea, General Richard Stillwell, had pre-delegated authority to use artillery to bombard a barracks north of the DMZ should the DPRK respond to the task force. In fact, not long after the tree was cut down, the North Koreans fired on a US helicopter flying over the DMZ and hit it — a *casus belli* if Stillwell had chosen to act on it. Luckily, he did not. For the next month, the United States sent flights of B52 bombers up the Korean Peninsula, veering off at the last moment. Henry Kissinger noted at the time that this huge show of force was to "overawe" the North Koreans.[12] "I have never seen the North Koreans so scared," Kissinger commented on August 26, 1976.[13]

The second case was the prospect of a naval-nuclear shootout between American and Soviet naval-nuclear forces in the North Pacific or one of the coastal seas close to the former Soviet Union. The peak of this risk may have been after the former Soviet Union's air defenses shot down the South Korean airliner KAL 007 in 1983, leading to naval collisions in the area where debris splashed into the ocean. Elsewhere, Soviet submarines engaged in a cat-and-mouse game with American adversaries. The risk was more that the forces themselves would go awry and inadvertently start a nuclear war rather than that some strategic interest would bring American forces to blows with Soviet forces, leading to nuclear war.

At the same time, American allies including Australia, Taiwan, South Korea, and even Japan began to explore directly and indirectly the acquisition of independent nuclear forces due to their fear that the American extension of nuclear and conventional deterrence was of deteriorating credibility and utility after US forces had been driven out of Vietnam in abject defeat. Of these efforts, South Korea did most at the time when

---

11 Singlaub, J.K. and McConnell, M., *Hazardous Duty: An American Soldier in the Twentieth Century* (Mandaluyong City: Summit Books, 1991).

12 United States Department of State, *Minutes of Washington Special Actions Group Meeting, Washington, August 19, 1976, 8:12-9:15 A.M*, Foreign Relations of the United States, 1969-1976, Volume E–12, Documents on East and Southeast Asia, 1973-1976, Document 285 (Washington, DC: United States Office of the Historian, 1976).

13 United States Department of State, *Minutes of Washington Special Actions Group Meeting, Washington, August 25, 1976, 10:30 A.M.*, Foreign Relations of the United States, 1969-1976, Volume E–12, Documents on East and Southeast Asia, 1973-1976, Document 286 (Washington, DC: United States Office of the Historian, 1976).

unilateral conventional and nuclear withdrawal was imminent. But they did not go far down the proliferation pathway due to American pressure in each of the four decades since, even during periods when they toyed with the idea of developing and deploying their own nuclear or chemical weapons. Japanese explorations concluded that proliferation was a bad idea because it was unlikely to create a strong deterrent force in a short time, and that it would come at a high political, economic, and military cost. Taiwan capitulated quickly to pressure from the United States that exposed its dependency on US military aid and direct support against the threat of mainland attack. Thus, this period demonstrated the resilience of American nuclear hegemony, but also revealed the powerful stress that was starting to affect the political-ideological basis of allied consent to American nuclear leadership in the region.

Nonetheless, until the late 1980s, American nuclear hegemony ruled supreme. The popular overthrow of the South Korean military dictatorship in 1987 was in part due to the subordination of local military forces to American nuclear forces aimed at the Soviet Union, and this bottom-up rebellion directly collided with the deployments that undergirded nuclear hegemony. Another key factor in declining hegemony was the region-wide Nuclear Free and Independent Pacific Movement that coordinated anti-nuclear warship and basing protests, which led to the abdication from the nuclear alliance of New Zealand — the mouse that roared when it banned nuclear ship visits by its putative American ally.

In an adroit move to defuse this opposition and respond to the dissolution of the former Soviet Union, then-President George H. W. Bush ordered the removal of all theater and tactical nuclear weapons in the region from bases and surface warships — a task completed in 1992. This adjustment recognized the limits of American hegemonic power to attend to the most urgent security tasks in the region, including the rapidly emerging threat of a North Korean nuclear weapons program. It also reflected the judgment that American and allied conventional forces were able to fulfill almost all the war-fighting missions formerly attributed to crude nuclear weapons, a judgment justified by the increase in range, precision, and lethality demonstrated during the Gulf War with Iraq in 1990-91. Moreover, conservative strategists were disenchanted with the passive notion of deterrence based on mutually assured destruction. They were anxious to test and deploy missile defenses to increase the ability of the United States to achieve its own security with or without allied support, and without regard to the intentions and capacities of other nuclear-armed adversaries — at this stage, Russia and China.

Things Fly Apart

After popular opposition pushed nuclear weapons out of public view in Japan in 1960, states became almost completely predominant in deciding how nuclear weapons affected security in the region. Anti-nuclear sentiment pushed nuclear weapons out of Okinawa in 1972, and the democratic uprising in South Korea in 1987 laid the foundations for the removal of nuclear weapons in 1991. With offshore nuclear submarines, home-based long-range missiles, and long-range bombers, the United States and the former Soviet Union deployed enormous numbers of nuclear weapons to strike fear into the minds of adversary leaders and the hearts of their populations. China deployed nuclear weapons to keep the two superpowers from coercing it. Two small powers — Taiwan and South Korea — attempted to get out from under the American thumb by developing their own nuclear forces, but were stopped almost immediately by the United States.

When the Cold War ended abruptly and the former Soviet Union dissolved, the region flew apart and fractured in many different directions. The relatively simple bipolar and even the more complicated tri-polar balance of state-based nuclear forces became far more complex — not just in the quantitative sense that the number of states began to increase, making it difficult to live, in Albert Wohlstetter's memorable phrase, in a "nuclear-armed crowd." But also in the qualitative sense that many different types of states and social entities, including non-state actors, became influential agents of change. The dynamics were embedded in a global set of processes and networks that linked the local, regional, and global aspects of the nuclear weapons problem and solution in a way that quickly surpassed the management capacity of the United States as nuclear hegemon.

Unsurprisingly, North Korea emerged as the most serious contender in the region for state-based nuclear proliferation when, in early 1992, the International Atomic Energy Agency (IAEA) declared the North's declaration did not include plutonium known to have been reprocessed at Yongbyon. The DPRK's nuclear aspirations had been apparent for many years. Alarm bells began to ring over its nuclear program in the early 1980s, leading the United States to enlist the former Soviet Union to induce the DPRK to join the NPT and to allow IAEA safeguards to come into force over its declared nuclear facilities. North Korea's breakout not only tore a hole in the fabric of the NPT, it threatened the foundations of US nuclear hegemony: its legitimating deterrence ideology, institutional integration with allies, and uniquely powerful nuclear forces. It also introduced a new element, in that it primarily used its nuclear threat for compellence purposes, whereas the other nuclear weapons states had reserved their nuclear threat for deterrence (except for the United States on a few, failing occasions). Nonetheless, North Korea was still a state playing a nuclear deterrence-compellence game that other states had played for decades in one way or another; while its trajectory was an unnerving departure from past state practice, it was a latecomer that reinforced the role of nuclear weapons in international relations between states and thereby reaffirmed the status quo.

In contrast to North Korea's entirely predictable nuclear proliferation, a relatively serious attempt by a non-state actor to develop nuclear weapons in the region was completely unanticipated. This development originated in Japan in the form of a murderous, apocalyptic religious cult, the *Aum Shinrikyo*. At one point, they had assets of more than a billion dollars and scientists in laboratories developing chemical and biological weapons, some of which they tested in Australia on sheep in 1991. They had attempted to buy a nuclear weapon in Russia before attacking a subway system in Matsumoto City with sarin nerve gas in 1994, followed by a second attack on the Tokyo subway system in 1995.

Aum Sinrikyo prefigured the rise of mega-terrorism that culminated in the September 11, 2001 attack on New York City by Islamic fundamentalists operating in networked cells. Thus, in the few years between the collapse of the former Soviet Union and the rise of *Aum Shinrikyo*, the nuclear weapons problem shifted radically from being merely complicated to becoming one of enormous complexity.

Complexity-based Definition of the Nuclear Weapons Problem

In contrast to the conventional paradigm of the nuclear weapons problem delineated above, here we will attempt to define the true complexity that characterizes the nuclear weapons problem in Northeast Asia in the 21st century. To do this, we will examine the nuclear weapons problem anew using the attributes of simple systems versus complex systems, as outlined in chapter 2. In sum, a complex system has many agents, many interactions between these agents, decentralized decision-making by these agents, is irreducible, is open to flows across borders with other systems, is dynamic, tends towards entropy, has many positive and negative feedback loops, and generates surprising outcomes.

As we noted above, humanity survived half a decade of uni-polar American nuclear power; a decade and a half of a perilously simple, bipolar US-Soviet balance-of-terror system; and three and a half decades of a tri-polar US-China-former Soviet Union nuclear triangle. Even then, the strategic calculations entailed by a nuclear "truel" were mind-boggling.

As Paul Bracken explains, "truels" — or three-way standoffs — are inherently more unstable than duels due to the inability of each party to know if the third is holding fire in the hope of the other two eliminating each other. He notes that in a three-way "'truel', in which each of three competitors is in direct opposition against the other two…The players have to decide (l) whether to shoot at all, and (2) if so, which countries to shoot at, with how many missiles, at what targets, and in what order." Moreover, "solutions to the problem require more stringent assumptions about communication, trust, and commitment than with two players, where only weak assumptions are needed to achieve crisis stability. The number of possible scenarios is enormous compared to the two-person duel." Part of the problem with the emerging global triangle at the end of the Cold War was precisely that no one knew if China recognized or played by the same rules.[14] This led to some weird policy options. At one point, for example, the United States considered conducting a nuclear strike on Soviet forces in Asia, weakening them so that China could occupy central and Far Eastern Soviet territory.[15]

Now, we face a future in which no fewer than nine nuclear-armed states co-exist. Still, a relatively manageable level of complicated, multi-polar nuclear threat involving 21 possible relationships (or 42 one-way links) is shown in Figure 5.1 — but this is embedded in a fluid set of alignments and

---

14   Bracken, P., *The Structure of the Second Nuclear Age*, E-Notes (Philadelphia: Foreign Policy Research Institute, 2003).

15   Braddock, J.V., *et al.*, *Targeting the Soviet Army Along the Sino-Soviet Border* (The BDM Corporation, released under US Freedom of Information Act request to Nautilus Institute, 1978).

coalitions over novel issues and problems such as huge tsunamis, global pandemics, regional conflicts, economic crisis, and uncontrollable climate change. when North Korea is added the mix, its nuclear breakout further complicates relationship management, so that now 28 relationships or 56 links must be constantly monitored.

Figure 5.1: Phase Transition from Complicated to Complex Nuclear Weapons Problems

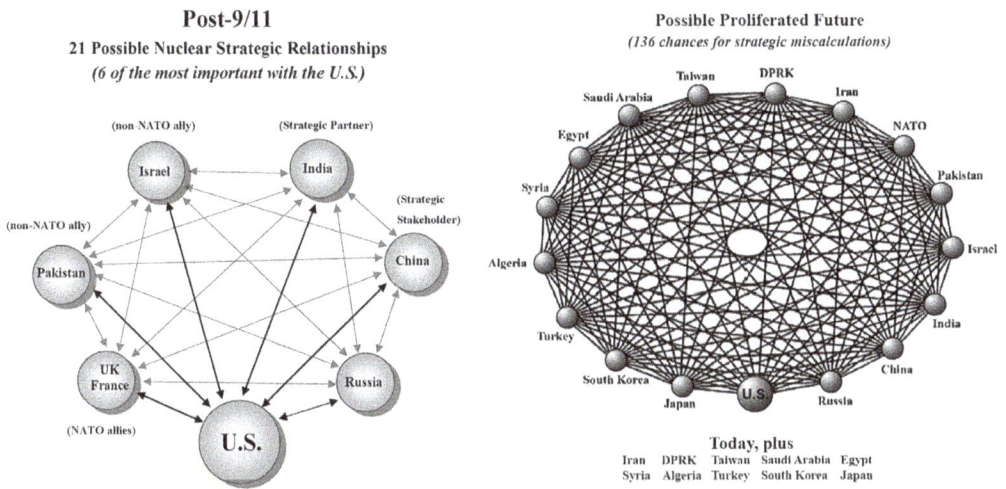

Post-9/11
21 Possible Nuclear Strategic Relationships
(6 of the most important with the U.S.)

Possible Proliferated Future
(136 chances for strategic miscalculations)

Source: Henry Sokolski, "Nuclear Abolition and the Next Arms Race," in *In the Eyes of the Experts: Analysis and Comments on America's Strategic Posture, Selected Contributions by the Experts of the Congressional Commission on the Strategic Posture of the United States,* ed. by Taylor Bolz (United States Institute of Peace Press, Washington DC), pp. 207-08, http://www.usip.org/files/In%20the%20Eyes%20of%20the%20Experts%20full.pdf

This complexity looks ready to increase exponentially in less than a decade should the existing nuclear states be joined by an additional eleven nuclear-armed states in Northeast Asia, the Middle East, and North Africa: the state of affairs will move from 21 to 136 relationships and from 42 to no fewer than 272 one-way links.

In the first nuclear era (1945-1990), the state-based nuclear threat system exhibited a strong degree of central control by the United States with respect to the nuclear decisions of its allies. Even those countries that were nominally independent, such as France, eventually aligned with NATO — and the system was able to directly block and redirect a number of proliferating states.

Thus, in the conventional paradigm, two of the most critical characteristics of the second, post-1990 nuclear era are, firstly, that a number of states — most importantly, North Korea — have proliferated in direct opposition to the great powers, including those represented on the UN Security Council; and secondly, the Kahn non-state network has emerged and proved capable of evading Western intelligence for decades while trading in material, technology, and knowledge essential for the development, deployment and use of nuclear weapons — thereby demonstrating that non-state actors are nuclear weapons-capable.

The combination of exponentially increasing inter-state nuclear threat relationships that must be managed with adversarial states such as North Korea and Iran breaking out of the Cold War control system reconstitutes the nature of the nuclear weapons problem, both globally and regionally. However, the qualitative transformation of the international system arises not merely from the addition of more nuclear-armed states per se, but from other powerful trends. These include the following: accelerating functional integration, especially economic, within the region and especially between China and the other major economies in Northeast Asia; the simultaneous convergence and diffusion of information and of nano- and bio-technology that may result in new types of weapons of mass destruction alongside nuclear, chemical, and biological weapons; generational change in the established nuclear weapons and nuclear-armed states, meaning that historical lessons may be lost and have to be relearned at great risk; and the increasing probability that a non-state actor will obtain access to nuclear weapons and either take a state hostage or use a nuclear weapon against a state. The latter risk is closely related to the rise of global crime networks on the one hand, and global terrorist networks on the other. They converge in locales with weak or no governance, and the general globalization of trade and mobility of people results in the increased porosity of society to bottom-up, networked nuclear weapons strategies.

These modern attributes of the nuclear weapons problem in a new, more diverse, and turbulent context make it a truly complex problem and no longer amenable to central control. There are now many autonomous state-based decision-making centers, each capable of starting a nuclear war and each susceptible to errors of information, misinterpretation, misjudgment, biased interpretation, and degradation of decision making at times of stress. Interacting with these states across levels and borders are numerous non-state entities, at once political-ideological in the orthodox sense of insurgencies aimed at overthrowing and supplanting specific governments, but also motivated by a range of core goals including religious, cultural, and other values that are not amenable to deterrence. Not least of these problems is the fact that many non-state actors "have no fixed address" and may welcome rather than fear capture or death, being thereby largely immune to deterrence in the standard military frame of reference.[16]

Increased Risk of Nuclear Next-Use

In the Cold War, the main risk of nuclear war in the region emanated from a global nuclear war that would begin in Europe (or the Middle East) and escalate to the Asia-Pacific region; in a naval-nuclear Soviet-American shootout in the North Pacific that would escalate to a regional or global nuclear war; or in a war in Korea that would escalate to nuclear war on the doorstep of China and the Soviet Union — either of which might have become involved.

Today, the risk of nuclear next-use is far more diffuse and unpredictable. There seems to be no reason to anticipate a global nuclear war between the United States and Russia, let alone a war pitting either of these nuclear weapons states against China. A nuclear war between North Korea and the United States and its allies is conceivable and could escalate to involve China. A naval-nuclear shootout in the Taiwan Straits between the United States and China is also conceivable given the stakes, the structure of the situation, and the forces involved. The situation could become even more complex should all states in the region become nuclear-armed, as was suggested at one point during the Cold War as a possible and (some argued) even desirable state of affairs.

Nuclear terrorism in the form of an attack on a spent fuel pond, reprocessing center, or nuclear reactor, or through the acquisition and threat of deployment and/or use of a nuclear weapon, especially a nuclear

---

16 Kroenig, M. and Pavel, B., "How to Deter Terrorism," *The Washington Quarterly*, 35(2) (2012), doi: http://dx.doi.org/10.1080/0163660X.2012.665339

weapon, is conceivable. A nuclear terrorist attack would likely be against a port city (but any city could be held hostage or attacked). Such an attack might not be attributed to a specific aggressor, or its point of origination might be ambiguous, leaving everyone guessing as to what comes next. This section examines this spectrum of possible nuclear next-use situations, and concludes that after declining in the aftermath of the end of the Cold war, the cumulative risk of another nuclear attack is again on the rise.

Nuclear Next-Use in Korea

To anyone conversant with the Korean Peninsula, the simplistic realist notion that states strive constantly for stability and dominance at the same time, thereby generating instability, sounds all too familiar.

Viewed from the perspective of complexity theory, states as the international system's highest level or meta-agents are indeed independent, as are many of their constituent elements; even in North Korea, some players have a degree of autonomy. No one controls how events unfold in and around Korea because there are too many driving forces involved at the same time for the system to behave predictably. The interstate system in Northeast Asia is composed of states of very different sizes, political cultures, and power capacities, creating asymmetric relationships that are themselves difficult to understand.

In this complex terrain, market and civil society non-state actors are active both domestically and transnationally and can, without warning, ignite change or induce states to shift their strategic direction by a few degrees. In situations as super-charged with restrained force as the Korean Demilitarized Zone, simple incidents involving the actions of only a few people can bring the conflict system close to a shooting war in only a few seconds. In May 2010, for example, hungry North Korean soldiers desperate to find food entered the Demilitarized Zone to go fishing, leading to a shootout with South Korean soldiers.[17] In 2011, marines on a small ROK-controlled island fired upon a South Korean commercial airliner thinking it was a North Korean jet attacking the South. In North Korea itself, the slow,

---

17   "Fish Hunting of the North Korean Soldiers," *Korea DMZ*, 2001, http://www.korea-dmz.com/en/s/sa/ssa_01_en.asp For a fishing-shootout in May 2010, see CBS/Associated Press, "Shots Fired as North Koreans Cross DMZ," *CBS News*, 11 February 2009, http://www.cbsnews.com/stories/2006/10/07/world/main2072358.shtml

incremental, but inexorable degradation of the electricity transmission and distribution substations has gone so far that a long cold period could shut down many substations forever — no matter what is done by North Korean technicians to improvise solutions. Such an event could lead to a massive humanitarian crisis in the midst of winter to which South Korea and its partners have no solution — indeed, they are not even aware of the existence of this crack rising to the surface of North Korean "stability." These are examples of small changes at one scale of the system which can affect another scale of a problem rapidly, unpredictably, and structurally — a moment sometimes called a "tipping point."

Exactly how would a nuclear war unfold in Korea? No one knows. But we do know the US Strategic Command (STRATCOM) maintains a database of possible nuclear targets in North Korea that includes wide-area attacks on ground forces massing to attack South Korea, key command and control sites that would be attacked to "decapitate" North Korea's leadership, and many other military and logistical sites all over North Korea. Warheads could be delivered to these targets by strategic bombers flying all the way from the United States and back, by land-based intercontinental missiles, or by submarine-launched missiles from the Pacific Ocean. STRATCOM would send Nuclear Employment Augmentation Teams or teams of nuclear-targeting specialists to US Forces Korea to advise the local commanders on nuclear targets. The locals would likely find many of these options useless due to lack of local knowledge and would end up improvising selection of targets and target coordinates for nuclear weapons against North Korean sites or mobile units in the midst of a war, under immense stress.[18] For its part, the DPRK has a small number of warheads, probably fewer than ten, and in our assessment, these would be used near the DMZ in either a pre-emptive or retaliatory attack to create craters in the corridors through which US-ROK ground forces might otherwise attempt to pass. Our best guess is that for all the hubbub over its long range missile tests (four out of five failed) and nuclear tests (one out of three failed), the DPRK has no reliable way to deliver its warheads outside its own territory.[19]

---

18 Cockle, J., "The Army's Role," *NBC Report*, 1998, http://www.hsdl. org/?view&doc=11715&coll=limited

19 Hayes, P. and Bruce, S., "Translating North Korea's Nuclear Threats into Constrained Operational Reality," in *North Korean Nuclear Operationality: Regional Security and Nonproliferation*, ed. by Moore, G. (Baltimore: John Hopkins University Press, 2013), pp. 15-31.

There are still a number of pathways by which a war in Korea could escalate to nuclear war. Bruce Bennett at RAND has imagined a number of such cases.[20] One is that for whatever reason, likely inadvertently, a major artillery exchange occurs north of Seoul along the DMZ. This escalates into an attack on northern Seoul by the DPRK in an attempt to stun the ROK into halting a push to move the DMZ northwards to reduce Seoul's vulnerability to future artillery and rocket attacks. Bennett suggests the move would induce the DPRK to switch to chemical weapons to reverse the tide. Such an attack, depending on targeting, wind, and the agent used, could lead to immense civilian casualties, which could then lead to pressure on the United States to reply with nuclear weapons to deter further escalation by the DPRK or to eliminate its chemical weapons capacities. Such a spiral is all too easy to envision and, historically in other conflicts, has proved very hard to halt once under way.

Factors that might deflect or shape American nuclear attacks in a renewed war with Korea (other than wind and weather, which could lead to an unacceptable radiological threat to US and ROK forces as well as to civilian populations whether north or south of the DMZ) include the "balance of blame" as to who started the war, the question of whether China enters the war, and what other regional and global contingencies would already pre-occupy American leaders or interact with a war in Korea. The latter could include tension and/or war in the Taiwan Straits, a Middle Eastern crisis involving Iran, instability in China itself, and the speed and type of South Korean response to North Korean provocation (which could become extremely bloody should it entail rapid occupation of North Korea to suppress a civil war after the collapse of the North Korean regime). In such a context, deterrence is unlikely to be a straightforward exercise in communication of threat, as conceived during the Cold War. Instead, the situation would be more like an arena full of bucking broncos, with each rider cracking whips to try to control the other riders and scare their horses, creating chaos and mayhem.

20   Bennett, B.W., "North Korea's WMD Capability and the Regional Military Balance: A US Perspective," *Korean Journal of Security Affairs*, 14(2) (2009). Bennett, B.W., *Uncertainties in the North Korean Nuclear Threat*, Document Briefing (Santa Monica: RAND Corporation, 2010).

Nuclear Next-Use between Nuclear Weapons States in East Asia

Nuclear war in Korea would be bad enough, but it would likely remain confined to North Korea. Of even greater consequence would be a confrontation between China and the United States over Taiwan, should Taipei declare independence from the mainland. If such a thing occurred, then China has declared that it would have no option but to attack and occupy Taiwan. Moreover, some Chinese security officials have let slip that its no-first-use declaration (with regard to the use of nuclear weapons) applies only to external conflicts — and because it regards Taiwan as an integral part of China, no-first-use does not apply to it. One may conclude that China would not use nuclear weapons against Taiwanese forces attempting to stop a cross-straits, air-sea attack by China. But it is far from clear whether China would feel restrained against first-use of nuclear weapons against US aircraft carrier groups that would otherwise operate beyond striking range of most of China's air and naval forces — thereby bringing China's nuclear-tipped intermediate range missiles into the equation. Also ambiguous is whether nuclear missiles might be fired at US forward bases on American and allied territory in the region if they were used to support a conventional naval and aerial defense of Taiwan against Chinese attack, thereby linking the fate of the allies to America's extended deterrence of attacks on Taiwan, both conventional and nuclear. Because China has the assured capacity to fire nuclear weapons at these allies, whereas North Korea does not, the Taiwan Straits issue is far more significant in terms of the risk of nuclear attack on Japan than is North Korea. For South Korea, however, the North Korean military and nuclear threat to the South is far greater than that arising from China via a conflict with the United States over Taiwan — not least because US forces in South Korea have little direct bearing on the United States' ability to prosecute such a war (and therefore, China would have little military reason to waste warheads on South Korea).

Currently, it is clear that from a military viewpoint the United States has absolute and relative superiority, including "escalation dominance," which in almost every respect would block a Chinese attack on Taiwan — even without Taiwanese forces playing a role.[21] But the balance of military

---

21   Shaplak, D., *et al.*, *A Question of Balance Political Context and Military Aspects of the China-Taiwan Dispute* (Santa Monica: RAND Corporation, 2009).

forces is not the only determinant of the robustness of deterrence. The balance-of-will, based on relative interest in the independence of Taiwan, is clearly tilted in China's favor, whereas the interest of the United States lies primarily in its reputation as a reliable ally able to stand up to rising Chinese power in the region. Of course, Taiwan is not an ally of the United States, but the impact on other allies such as South Korea or Japan of allowing China to militarily occupy Taiwan and reverse its secession from China would be to shatter the credibility of the United States as a security patron. It could also set in motion proliferation dynamics among US allies and motivate North Korea to use conventional force to put pressure on South Korea to evict US forces.

Due to the centrality of Taiwan's decision on whether to slowly reunify with China or declare independence, the United States plays a role in this conflict zone as a "pivotal" deterrent. On the one hand, it reassures China that it will restrain such a move by Taiwan's leaders, which requires that it demonstrate the military capacity able to defend credibly against Chinese attack, with all the attendant risks of escalation, including nuclear escalation. On the other, the United States deploys forces in the region to deter China from attacking, thereby reassuring Taiwan and underlining the point that a declaration of independence would be a needless provocation that risks degrading US protection against China.

Unfortunately, it is not as if these two scenarios — war and nuclear war in Korea, and war and nuclear war in the Taiwan Straits, China, and the wider region—exist in separate worlds. In the real world, the decisions of Taiwanese and North Korean leaders will be made in the midst of crises with an eye to how the other's possible conflict affects their respective great power's adversaries and abilities to respond. A war in Korea would so entangle China and the United States that the Taiwanese might think that they could declare independence in the belief that China would be unable to fight on two fronts at once, thereby achieving a *fait accompli*.

Conversely, in a war over Taiwan, North Korea could decide to move decisively while a window of opportunity remains open; meanwhile, the ability of the United States to reinforce its troops in Korea would be constrained by mobilization to support Taiwan.

Moreover, even in times of routine insecurity, North Korea and Taiwan have potential joint interests that could come into play. In 1997, Taiwan's power company contracted with North Korea to store nuclear waste.[22] Taiwan had previously attempted to build its own bomb in the 1980s and has an advanced nuclear fuel cycle capacity to support its nuclear power program. Taiwan is also a "black hole" in terms of non-state-based trading in dual-use and nuclear-specific commodities needed for a nuclear weapons program, and it has been the transshipment point for a number of such transactions between Japanese firms and North Korea. If these two international outcasts found themselves isolated and highly insecure — especially in the case of Taiwan — it is possible that North Korea could assist Taiwan to gain its own nuclear weapons capability in return for hard currency, technology, and even informal alignment with regard to how to play hard ball with China and the United States in a concerted manner. As Dingli Shen put it, "Even if China would not ask for it, a nuclear North Korea's ability to pin down US forces in a Taiwan Strait contingency deters America's consideration of possible military intervention."[23]

Thus, the Taiwan factor overlays all other considerations for China and the United States, and it also affects the calculus of US allies and North Korea in all their bilateral relationships. Nuclear risk in Korea is linked directly and indirectly to nuclear risk in Taiwan. Although both can be resolved separately, the two ongoing regional conflicts must be managed jointly — and adroitly — by the United States and its allies, and by China, if war and nuclear war are to be avoided. Moreover, the reverse is also true. If the Taiwanese situation is resolved peacefully and reunification is achieved without the use of military force, then North Korea's geo-strategic significance for China would be greatly diminished, and the conflict in Korea would likely become much easier to resolve as well.

Nuclear Next-Use in a Nuclear-Armed East Asia?

In 1982, John On-Fat Wong wrote a bleak dissertation at the University of Wisconsin positing that every state in Northeast Asia had gone nuclear,

---

22 Kato, C., *TED Case Studies: Taiwan Nuclear Waste Exports (NKORNUKE)* (Washington, DC: American University, 1977), http://www1.american.edu/ted/nkornuke.htm

23 Shen, D., "North Korea's Strategic Significance to China," *WSI China Security*, 2(3) (2006).

leaping from three nuclear weapons states (United States, Russia, and China) to seven (the additional countries being North and South Korea, Japan, and Taiwan).[24] In this imagined world, superpower conflict continued, local conflicts drove local proliferation, leaderships changed explosively, and regimes disintegrated.

Wong examined four geopolitical scenarios (1990) for Northeast Asia (he included Taiwan). These were: general détente, limited bilateral détente, a new cold war, and a general cold war. Next, he listed strategic targets for nuclear weapons in each country, basically cities and industrial areas, and then determined the firing point from which a nuclear weapon attacking each of these targets would be launched. From this, given blast effects and other means of degradation such as warhead fratricide, he derived the warhead yields and delivery systems required to achieve varying levels of desired annihilation. These targets were "countervalue" in nature rather than "counterforce" in Wong's approach. He wanted to determine what a generalized nuclear-veto system of multilateral nuclear deterrence would look like if McNamara's notion of Mutual Assured Destruction were applied to each target country in the search for stable deterrence. Then, he set out to rejig the nuclear postures required to conform to the local requirements for strategic deterrence given the size of each state and its insecurities as defined in each of the four scenarios.[25]

Wong's regional nuclear nightmare vision is worth revisiting today because we now have four nuclear-armed states and only two non-nuclear states in the region, and the trend is moving toward his imagined world of full proliferation.

Wong began by determining that lesser versions of mutual assured destruction were feasible between small and middle powers armed with nuclear weapons. Even without secure assured retaliatory forces on the American model of a three-service strategic triad, these powers could still wreak "assured heavy damage" on each other (though not the 70 or 80 percent damage demanded by McNamara's best and brightest as sufficiently "deterring" during the Cold War). Of course, the great powers armed with thousands of warheads could still exterminate the medium powers, so the

---

24   On-Fat Wong, J., *Security Requirements in Northeast Asia* (Madison, University of Wisconsin, 1982).

25   Ibid., pp. 12-14.

reliability of the medium power arsenals to deter great power pre-emptive attack is inherently low. The inevitable lack of a secure retaliatory capacity on the part of small states suggests that a generalized nuclear veto-system based on universal proliferation in Northeast Asia would be prone to pre-emptive strike in the search of some states for damage limitation.[26]

Wong noted that small nuclear powers — like North Korea — are more of a nuisance than a threat to the status quo of the nuclear threat system between the great powers. The existence of a number of middle power, nuclear-armed states such as Japan or South Korea could affect the force ratios between the great power, nuclear-armed states. Moreover, the small nuclear power is vulnerable to pre-emption at any time, whereas the middle power is much less so, although it could not hope to conduct a pre-emptive strike against a great power nuclear state and hope to survive, at least not for very long.

Wong pointed out that the relationship between two small nuclear-armed states — if both Koreas gained nuclear weapons, for example — would be one of mutual vulnerability, as neither would have a secure nuclear retaliatory force and both would have relatively concentrated and easily targeted industry and populations.[27] In a region composed of great, middle, and small powers like Northeast Asia, only the great powers can wreak mutually *assured destruction* on each other (in fact, only Russia and the United States could do that then or today to each other). The great powers could also inflict assured destruction on middle and small powers, and middle powers in turn could inflict assured destruction on small powers.

Moving along the other direction in scale, small powers and middle powers could assuredly *heavily damage* each other, but not the great powers. And all the powers could massively *retaliate* against each other (for example, by destroying one or two cities, equivalent to "ripping off an arm" as the Gaullists used to say of the French nuclear *force de frappe*) against any power, small, middle, or large. Summarized in Table 5.2, these distinctions capture some of the effects that Wong anticipated could arise from universal nuclear proliferation in the region.[28]

---

26 Ibid., pp. 65-66.
27 Ibid., p. 69.
28 Ibid., p. 78.

Table 5.2: Probable Doctrinal Preferences

Deterrer	Deterree		
	Superpower	Medium Power	Small Power
Superpower	AD	AD	AD
Medium Power	AR	ARD	AD
Small Power	AR	AR	MD/PD

AD Assured Destruction AHD Assured Heavy Destruction
AR Assured Retaliation MD/PD Mutual (or Probable) Destruction

Source: John On-Fat Wong, *Security Requirements in Northeast Asia* (PhD dissertation, University of Wisconsin, 1982), p. 77.

It is worth quoting Wong at length to highlight the implications for "stability" in conflicts between middle and small powers if nuclear hawks in each country of the region have their way:

> Given the vulnerability of the small power and its nuclear forces, enemy destruction is more "probable" than "assured." This condition of pre-emptive instability suggests that among the small powers, "mutual vulnerability" or "mutual probable destruction" is a much more appropriate description of their strategic relationship than "mutual assured destruction." Once they have acquired some quantity of nuclear weapons, the condition of "mutual vulnerability" has been created. It is possible to imagine asymmetry of doctrines among small nuclear powers (e.g. one pursuing assured destruction while the other superiority). However, the differences in their nuclear arsenals will not alter their vulnerability. This is not surprising since (1) regardless of their doctrinal preference, there are real limits to their nuclear arsenals, and (2) the effectiveness of pre-emption by conventional means is enhanced by relatively small and dense target structures and geographical proximity.[29]

The significance of this situation is immediate in Korea today. As Wong explained:

> [T]he paucity of means usually forces the small power to adopt a relatively rigid strategic posture and force structure vis-à-vis the large power. This rigidity of posture has a paradoxical effect on the credibility of the small power nuclear deterrent and the stability of the nuclear deterrence system. In a sense, the enhancement of the small power deterrent contributes to the greater overall stability of the deterrence system. However, due to the severe limitations on its capabilities, the real choice of the smaller power in time

---

29   Ibid., pp. 79-80.

of crisis is between strategic surrender and suicidal war. There is a built-in instability in this type of situation. Overall crisis stability has been eroded, in fact, by the possession of nuclear weapons by small powers.[30]

Wong calculated that for one country (in this case, South Korea) to achieve a second strike capability against the other six countries in his most insecure scenario for 1990 (a revived Cold War), it would have taken 820 one-megaton warheads capable of being fired against 600 cities with over 300 million people — an enormous and incredible arsenal for a small power like South Korea.[31]

More realistically, he noted, to bomb North Korea into the stone age would have taken "only" seventy-five 200-kiloton weapons, buttressed by ten more one-megaton warheads aimed at China, Russia, and Japan (which was assumed in his scenarios to also have become a nuclear weapons state) to deter them from entering a war with the North.[32]

We dwell on Wong's extremist heuristic to highlight the threat that past, present (North Korean), and any further proliferation poses to national and human security in Northeast Asia. The risk of nuclear next-use in such a world would increase dramatically and likely in non-linear ways, giving rise to what Wong called "probable assured destruction" — although he reserved this term for the likely fate of small nuclear-armed states in his scenarios.

We have referred in previous sections to how American, Korean, and Chinese nuclear weapons could lead to nuclear next-use. Here, we should note that Russia also maintains nuclear forces and some may still be deployed in the Russian Far East, remaining salient to Chinese and American strategic forces and to Russia's relationships with the three small powers in the region, that is, North and South Korea and Japan. Russia's Far Eastern provinces are militarily weak and isolated from European Russia. Russia has re-emphasized the role of tactical and theater nuclear weapons in its nuclear doctrine, relying on the concept of early-use to stun conventional attack.[33] Facing rapid Chinese military modernization, Russia may reassert the enduring nature of its nuclear forces in this region, thereby contributing — yet again — to the vulnerability of its neighbors in the region, especially of Japan and South Korea.

---

30   Ibid., pp. 80-81.
31   Ibid., pp. 358-59.
32   Ibid., pp. 315-19.
33   Kipp, J., *Asian Drivers of Russia's Nuclear Force Posture* (Arlington: Nonproliferation Policy Education Center, 2010).

Nuclear Next-Use and Nuclear Terrorism

The proliferation, acquisition, deployment, and use of weapons of mass destruction, especially nuclear weapons, are no longer the sole province of states. Globally-networked insurgencies and ideologically-motivated terrorist organizations, have begun to converge[34] with global criminal organizations that traffic in people[35] and contraband,[36] and in many countries are allied to powerful political figures, sometimes providing private militia to them.[37] Conditions of global trade, finance, and investment make borders increasingly porous to these flows and portend the risk that non-state actors will become nuclear-armed. This is a different but related concern to the role that non-state actors such as A.Q. Khan and his network may play, legal or otherwise, in state-based proliferation. The issue of greatest concern is that non-state actors — individuals, companies, cities, or non-states (secessionist movements, theocracies) — may seek and obtain WMD capabilities.

As is well documented, ideological and criminal networks originate in as well as cross through all the countries of East Asia.[38] North Korea has been highlighted as a potential source of dual-use or of nuclear weapons-specific knowledge, material, skills, or hardware due to its combination of supply (of nuclear commodities) with its established proclivity to conduct drug, arms, and other contraband smuggling.[39] Taiwan is another "black hole" where such transactions have occurred,[40] however, and the existence of nuclear fuel cycles in all countries of the region creates a nuclear security control problem that is universal.[41]

---

34   Shelley, L.I., "Trafficking in Nuclear Materials: Criminals and Terrorists," *Global Crime*, 7(3-4) (2006), doi: http://dx.doi.org/10.1080/17440570601073335

35   di Nicola, A., "Trafficking in Human Beings and Smuggling of Migrants," in *The Handbook of Transnational Crime and Justice*, ed. by Reichel, P. L. (New York: Sage Publications, 2005).

36   Kafchinski, J., *Global Counterfeit Trade* (George Mason University, 2009).

37   Kaplan, D.E. and Dubro, A., *Yakuza: Japan's Criminal Underworld* (Oakland: University of California Press, 2003).

38   Ward, R. and Mabrey, D., "Organized Crime in Asia," in *The Handbook of Transnational Crime and Justice*, ed. by Reichel, P. L. (New York: Sage Publications, 2005).

39   Lijun, M., "Study on Problem of Trans-Border Drugs Crimes on Sino-DPRK Border," *Journal of Chinese People's Armed Police Force Academy* (2009).

40   Kassenova, T., *A 'Black Hole' in the Global Nonproliferation Regime: The Case of Taiwan*, NAPSNet Policy Forum (Berkeley: Nautilus Institute, 2011).

41   Bunn, M., *et al.*, *Controlling Nuclear Warheads and Materials: A Report Card and Action Plan*, Project on Managing the Atom (Cambridge: Belfer Center for Science and International Affairs and Nuclear Threat Initiative, 2003).

Post-Fukushima Spent Fuel Vulnerability

In addition to the rise of non-state smuggling, threats, and acquisition of nuclear weapons, the Fukushima nuclear disaster highlights the vulnerability of nuclear facilities to non-state attack, as well as to the diversion of nuclear materials by non-state actors. Fatal design flaws in boiling water reactors (BWR) in Japan and elsewhere became evident. They included:

- Locating spent fuel ponds and reactors at a coastal site subject to massive tsunamis without establishing sufficient defenses to avoid the plant being overwhelmed and destroyed;

- Placing the spent fuel ponds at the top of reactor containment buildings to minimize the core-pond transfer distance and the handling cost and errors (thereby making access to the ponds very difficult in a crisis involving radiological release from the reactor cores);

- Using active, powered cooling systems for spent fuel ponds that have common failure modes with the reactors, thereby leading to loss-of-coolant-induced melting of spent fuel in the ponds and reactors, resulting in the generation of hydrogen and the subsequent explosions that devastated the Fukushima containment buildings;

- The ad hoc use of fire trucks and sea water to provide coolant to spent fuel ponds and reactors that ultimately exacerbated the cooling problem via salt deposition on fuel rods and salt build-up in the ponds and reactor cores;

- Packing increasing amounts of fuel onto racks in spent fuel ponds due to "constipation" (lack of immediate capacity caused by technical and political delays) in the off-site spent-fuel processing and waste storage and disposal systems in Japan. The resulting crowding and heat generation from tightly packed ponds made it even harder to cool the spent fuel rods;

- Using insufficiently strong structures and support for the spent fuel ponds themselves. As a result of less-than-robust design, the spent fuel pools may have cracked due during earthquake and tsunami-related stresses, leading to leakage of radioactive water into the containment building.

Some of these lessons apply to all kinds of reactors; some are BWR-specific. A complete accounting of the failure pathways and design problems at Fukushima will not be available for years. The Fukushima reactor disaster has not yet fully played out, as the reactors and spent fuel ponds remain far from stabilized. Site stabilization and recovery, including dismantlement of the broken spent fuel ponds and reactor cores, will likely take ten to thirty years.[42]

Meanwhile, a huge quantity of radiation has been released in gaseous, particulate, and liquid forms, and a 40 km exclusion radius has been established around the reactor site.[43] No one knows how badly contaminated the land is and therefore when, if ever, the residents of this area who survived the tsunami and earthquake will be allowed to return and rebuild their shattered lives.

There will be many lessons for Northeast Asia to take from Fukushima. One of the most important is how brittle the spent fuel ponds proved to be to the loss of coolant, especially as a result of co-location with reactors, and that the loss of coolant and subsequent release of radiation could lead to wholesale evacuations of cities and towns on a very large scale. In this sense, Fukushima was a "wet run" at what could happen not only after a technological failure or malfunction, but as a result of a malevolent attack on a nuclear facility by a state or non-state actor, or as a result of terrorist diversion of spent fuel and its subsequent use to threaten or attack concentrated populations or military targets.[44]

In such an attack, one might also expect — as occurred at Fukushima — a set of unpredictable consequences and concatenating effects caused by the initial accident. For example, wildly contradictory statements made by authorities about radiation levels at the site and in the exclusion zone amplified the risks perceived by residents and government agencies. Furthermore, forced electricity outages in the form of rolling blackouts were implemented to conserve power. These outages in turn led to accidents, medical malfunctions, and other problems, but were abandoned relatively quickly, in part due to reduced economic activity and electricity use in the wake of the earthquake, but also because consumers conserved in a self-organized manner to reduce peak electricity demand by an estimated 3 gigawatts almost immediately after the accident. Additional evidence of these concatenating impacts included ripple effects on the global economy

---

42 Tokyo Electric Power Company, *Roadmap Towards Restoration from the Accident at Fukushima Daiichi Nuclear Power Station* (Tokyo: Tokyo Electric Power Company, 2011). Yasu, M. and Shiraki, M., "Hitachi, Ge Submit Proposal to Dismantle Crippled Fukushima Nuclear Plant," *Bloomberg*, 13 April 2011, http://www.bloomberg.com/news/2011-04-13/hitachi-ge-file-proposal-to-scrap-fukushima-dai-ichi-plant.html
43 Hayes, P., *et al.* (2011).
44 Robichaud, C., "The Consequence of a Dirty Bomb Attack," *The Hill*, 12 April 2011, http://thehill.com/blogs/congress-blog/homeland-security/155493-the-consequence-of-a-dirty-bomb-attack

due both to the tsunami and earthquake damage and to the implementation of the radiation exclusion zone which shut down critical component plants for a variety of global industries, particularly the automotive and electronic.

Finally, the culturally- and historically-determined fear of radiation due to the Hiroshima and Nagasaki experience, which affected the Japanese response to the Fukushima accident, and the recent history of scandal and cover-ups in the nuclear sector, particularly at the Tokyo Electric Power Company, the operator of the Fukushima reactor-complex, shook the public's trust that the accident would be resolved. In all these ways, Fukushima demonstrates and provides insight into the range of possible impacts of a successful attack on radiological targets such as spent fuel ponds.

Concern about nuclear facilities as radiological targets began with discussions of targeting these sites during the Cold War to "enhance" the effects of nuclear strikes. An early debate occurred over the risk of nuclear terrorism in light of Theodore Taylor's work on the topic.[45] The first public systematic treatment of the issues associated with targeting nuclear facilities by terrorists (by Bennett Ramberg) included the targeting of spent fuel ponds and other ancillary facilities that support reactors, but concentrated on the risk of attacks by states on reactors and the consequent radiological risks.[46]

In the United States, non-governmental researchers, especially scientists, have been at the forefront of research on the risks posed by poorly-protected and badly-designed spent fuel ponds in reactor containment buildings, putting pressure on the Nuclear Regulatory Commission to respond with limited but significant success to date.[47] These experts raised the risk that non-state actors could attack spent fuel ponds and casks at reactor sites. They estimate quantitatively and qualitatively the truly immense, catastrophic possible releases that could result from successful attacks.[48] In some cases, a simple repositioning of casks could reduce the risk and

45 Willrich, M. and Taylor, T., *Nuclear Theft: Risks and Safeguards: A Report to the Energy Policy Project of the Ford Foundation* (Pensacola: Ballinger, 1974). Taylor was profiled in McPhee, J., *The Curve of Binding Energy* (New York: Ballantine, 1974).

46 Ramberg, B., *Nuclear Power Plants as Weapons for the Enemy: An Unrecognized Military Peril* (Berkeley: University of California Press, 1984).

47 Beyea, J., *et al.*, "Damages from a Major Release of 137 Cs into the Atmosphere of the United States," *Science and Global Security*, 12 (2004), http://dx.doi.org/10.1080/08929880490464775. Alvarez, R., *et al.*, "Reducing the Hazards from Stored Spent Power-Reactor Fuel in the United States," *Science and Global Security*, 11 (2003), http://dx.doi.org/10.1080/08929880309006

48 Thompson, G., *Robust Storage of Spent Nuclear Fuel: A Neglected Issue of Homeland Security* (Institute for Resource and Security Studies and Citizens Awareness Network, 2003).

impacts of attacks substantially. Some redesign of storage casks could also greatly reduce the risks that a successful non-state actor could breach such spent fuel containers.

Importantly, the Massachusetts Institute of Technology (MIT) *Future of the Nuclear Fuel Cycle* study, for which an update was released in March 2011, strongly recommended that spent fuel be stored in a central repository, noting that "requirements for on-site spent fuel management may increase and design basis threats may be elevated" because of the Fukushima disaster.[49] Due to the expanded risk of radiological contamination from attacks on dry casks or spent fuel ponds located outside the reactor building but co-located with reactors, it appears necessary to consider separating dry cask storage, at least surface storage, from reactor sites. This relocation would ensure failure in either reactor or storage technology due to accident, malfunction, or malevolence does not lead to disablement by contamination of the adjacent facility.

Such spatial rearrangement of spent fuel storage on-site at various types of power reactors, and from reactors to centralized sites, entails costs, but it could also increase vulnerability to possible state and non-state diversion and/or attack on such storage. Ironically, so long as the spent fuel ponds were contained inside the reactor containment building, they were somewhat secured by the facility security systems from armed attacks by non-state actors, although various modes of non-state attack such as crashing aircraft into reactor buildings on the 9/11 model still posed a conceivable threat to these enclosed ponds. The fact that guards were discovered asleep at one American reactor suggests security issues are not always taken seriously.[50]

Once removed from the reactor building, various cost and design choices need to be made with regard to spent fuel storage and disposition. Each of these choices entails different levels of risk of diversion or successful attack by state and non-state groups. One such choice pertains to the cost and longevity of spent fuel storage technologies. Options include deciding between pools and dry casks, and between dry casks suitable for high-level waste almost straight out of the reactor versus dry casks used only after five or ten years of decay and cooling off, which are therefore less expensive — but also more vulnerable to attack. Other choices include:

49   Kazimi, M., *et al.*, "Postscript," in *The Future of the Nuclear Fuel Cycle* (Cambridge: Massachusetts Institute of Technology, 2011).

50   Mufson, S., "Executive Resigns in Storm over Sleeping Guards," *Washington Post*, 10 January 2008, http://www.washingtonpost.com/wp-dyn/content/article/2008/01/09/AR2008010903 368_pf.html Holt, M. and Andrews, A., *Nuclear Power Plant Security and Vulnerabilities*, Report for Congress (Washington, DC: Congressional Research Service, 2008).

- The use of ancillary barriers to reduce the possibility of successful attack on and/or diversion of dry casks in storage on reactor sites;

- The use of surface versus underground storage facilities at reactor sites to reduce the possibility and consequences of land or aerial attack on dry casks;

- The use of various combinations of dry cask storage on reactor sites versus rapid removal of spent fuel to a centralized repository, located either on the surface or underground, that uses either pools or dry cask storage; and

- The selection of choices outlined above in relation to retrievable forms of storage for eventual spent fuel reprocessing versus those designed for medium or longer term irretrievable disposal, such as deep borehole disposal.

These and other design considerations affect the possibility that a devastating radiological attack by a state or a non-state actor could occur by exploiting the measures taken, post-Fukushima, to reduce the reciprocal risk of reactors and spent fuel storage systems, as well as the radiological outcome of a successful attack. The steps taken to reduce reciprocal risk may also affect the probability of successful diversion of spent fuel for use in a dirty bomb or in actual nuclear weapons at another location. Evaluation of alternative disposition of spent fuel must also take the risk of diversion into account to the extent it can be shown to exist at the margins.

States in the region have been dilatory in the extreme in addressing this risk. The Seoul Nuclear Security Summit in March 2012 called for coordination to make this connection between nuclear fuel cycle management, safety, and security, noting, "We affirm that nuclear security and nuclear safety measures should be designed, implemented and managed in nuclear facilities in a coherent and synergistic manner… Noting that the security of nuclear and other radioactive materials also includes spent nuclear fuel and radioactive waste, we encourage States to consider establishing appropriate plans for the management of these materials."[51] Although it called for action to address risks related to the management of spent fuel and wastes, the Summit focused on control of fissile material, did not have a panel on nuclear safety and security, and failed to offer any concrete recommendations for how nuclear facilities should be designed or secured so as to reduce the risk of accident or attack and the attendant

---

51 Nuclear Security Summit leaders, "Seoul Communiqué at 2012 Nuclear Security Summit," *Council on Foreign Relations*, 27 March 2012, http://www.cfr.org/proliferation/seoul-communiqu-2012-nuclear-security-summit/p27735

radiological consequences of such events. Thus, it appears to have been left to civil society organizations in Northeast Asia to tackle this question directly.[52]

Even if states succeed in establishing near-perfect control over nuclear facilities and material, controlling the movements of nuclear-capable scientists and technicians is even more difficult. Proliferation activity by non-state actors that does not end up as nuclear weapons activity does not matter in the real world. To move from merely hypothetical to WMD-reality, proliferating states or non-state entities with WMD-nuclear aspirations must obtain scarce expertise in nuclear weapons.

There are no public figures for how many WMD knowledge-endowed and technically capable individuals exist in nuclear weapons and non-nuclear weapon states (NNWS), either globally or in the East Asia region. Often, large global numbers are cited based on American or Russian experience (125,000 personnel is often mentioned for the former Soviet nuclear weapons complex). But in one study of South Africa, the total nuclear weapons workforce was estimated to be quite small, about 400 personnel over the duration of the program (1970-1993).[53] By 1989, the total staffing was about 270, of which about half —or 135 —were estimated to be directly involved. However, other former participants in this program assert that only about ten of these people were truly WMD-nuclear capable and posed a true proliferation risk before the program was terminated in 1989. One, at least, is reportedly under house arrest and the others are reportedly under surveillance in South Africa. Based on his survey of this workforce, Andre Buys notes that "Of the former NEWP personnel that were retrenched the majority (71%) of were "very dissatisfied," and of the sample (about 40% of the total late period workforce), about 16% had worked overseas; at least one was location unknown." A study in Russia found a similar level of high dissatisfaction with jobs in its nuclear and missile cities and a proclivity to migrate to better conditions, irrespective of the proliferation risks of potential destination countries.[54]

In the case of the DPRK, of the 5-10,000 workers in the nuclear-industrial and military complex related to nuclear weapons, a similarly small number of truly nuclear-capable individuals, perhaps up to 200, reportedly exist.

---

52   *Security of Spent Nuclear Fuel* (Berkeley: Nautilus Institute), http://nautilus.org/projects/by-name/security-of-spent-nuclear-fuel/#axzz2STq2M8Ed

53   Buys, A., *Proliferation Risk Assessment of Former Nuclear Explosives/Weapons Program Personnel: The South African Case Study*, NAPSNet Special Report (Berkeley: Nautilus Institute, 2011).

54   Tikhonov, V., *Russia's Nuclear and Missile Complex: The Human Factor in Proliferation* (Washington, DC: Carnegie Endowment For International Peace, 2001).

Larger numbers likely exist in China's nuclear weapons complex. States with latent nuclear weapons capabilities — South Korea, Japan, and Taiwan — also have many scientists and technicians who could work on nuclear weapons and related delivery systems.

Another consideration is the difficulty of deterring acquisition, deployment, threatened use, and actual use of nuclear weapons by non-state actors, especially if they are not connected to any particular place or state. One taxonomy of non-state actors includes what Brad Roberts calls jihadi movement-networks:

> foot soldiers; the terrorist professionals who provide training and other logistical guidance and support; the leaders of al Qaeda; groups affiliated by ideology and aspiration (so-called franchisees); operational enablers (financiers etc.); moral legitimizers; state sponsors; and passive state enablers (generally weak states that are unable or unwilling to prevent terrorists from exploiting their territory or other assets).[55]

To this list, Daniel Whiteneck adds the "larger societal sponsors (networks of financiers, supporters, scientists, smugglers) of nuclear terrorism,"[56] and then expands this taxonomy to include more moderate, less ambitious, or more risk-adverse terrorist groups, or groups competing for the same constituencies. These groups might be influential within terrorist networked movements with a propensity to adopt nuclear weapons strategies. They are, therefore, potential subjects of strategies aimed at inducing them to exercise a restraining influence over the more nuclear weapons-oriented networked movements.

From the global, regional, and local perspectives, other types of non-state actors must be differentiated. These include "homegrown" loners or groups in "target" countries; ideologically motivated insurgencies, separatist movements, free-floating and self-generating terrorist cells and cults; alienated or corrupt officials or disaffected or unemployed scientists; unaffiliated, non-ideological and for-profit and -hire opportunist suppliers (corporate, criminal, diasporic); corrupt, incompetent, or alienated officials (border agents, intelligence agents in states of primary origin of nuclear weapons, having facilities and dual use capabilities that can be diverted, or in states of potential nuclear weapons transit, deployment, and actual

---

55   Roberts, B., *Deterrence and WMD Terrorism: Calibrating its Potential Contributions to Risk Reduction* (Alexandria: Institute of Defense Analysis, 2007).

56   Whiteneck, D., "Deterring Terrorists: Thoughts on a Framework," *The Washington Quarterly*, 28(3) (2005), doi: http://dx.doi.org/10.1162/0163660054026452

targeted delivery-detonation); and leaders and operatives of state sponsors of controlled, arms-length or disavowable non-state networked movements.

The impossibility of controlling a large number of diverse, self-organizing agents, especially individuals and ideologically motivated networks with top-down control strategies orchestrated by states, suggests fundamental issues of vulnerability may drive urban forms and building designs that provide greater resilience against possibly inevitable nuclear threats and even attacks by non-state actors in the coming decades. The trend in major cities is exactly the opposite, towards even bigger primary and secondary cities with gigantic urban corridors emerging between these mega-cities. But, as noted in chapter 2, there is also an opposite trend of *in-situ* and networked urbanization known as "rurbanization" in India and *desakota* in China and elsewhere in Asia, which may prove less vulnerable.

After the risks of nuclear next-use between states in a universally nuclear-armed East Asia, especially attacks aimed at populations, the risk of nuclear next-use by non-state actors may be the second most important source of risk — not the least because it could vastly complicate inter-state conflicts during times of high tension or even in the midst of war.

Grappling with the Complexity of Nuclear Weapons in East Asia

This section examines three types of strategies to reduce and eliminate these types of nuclear next-use risk. These are state and market-based solutions, regional networked solutions, and civil society-based solutions.

The primary state-based means to contain nuclear weapons proliferation are a combination of international treaties and conventions that establish the basic framework of nuclear and non-nuclear weapons states under the NPT and the closely related system of safeguards run by the International Atomic Energy Agency and related regional safeguards systems. These are supplemented by ad hoc UN Security Council resolutions that mandate national sanctions against proliferating states, their officials, and corporate and non-state entities involved in their proliferation activities. This system of direct regulation by nations is supplemented by the Proliferation Security Initiative, an ad hoc coalition of states organized by the United States and intended to interdict illegal shipments of nuclear weapons-related hardware or material.

These global regimes are supplemented in many regions by nuclear weapons-free zones (but not in East or Northeast Asia), by specific bilateral or national declarations such as the 1992 Denuclearization Declaration of North and South Korea, and the 1968 Three Non-Nuclear Principles of Japan. More recently, another ad hoc mechanism was instigated by the George W. Bush Administration, the "Six Party Talks" devoted to denuclearizing North Korea. However, no regional security mechanism exists in the region, and prospects are dim for a state-based institution emerging in the near future.[57]

In the case of past proliferation activity, primarily on the part of its own allies, namely South Korea and Taiwan, the United States exerted considerable leverage by threatening to reduce military aid while offering financial support for expanded nuclear power programs. However, the solutions adopted in both instances — no reprocessing or enrichment allowed — contrasts strongly with the treatment accorded to Japan by the United States, which agreed in 1979 to allow the latter to build enrichment and reprocessing plants after blocking the same in South Korea in 1975. This consequently gave rise to a discriminatory and inherently unstable system of state-based restraints on nuclear fuel cycle activities in the two American allies that persists to this day.

With regard to adversarial proliferation by North Korea, the United States first enlisted the former Soviet Union to induce North Korea to join the NPT and to accept safeguards. After North Korea was discovered out of compliance with its safeguard's declaration, they attempted from 1992-2004 to bilaterally compel and to some extent induce North Korea to reverse direction and to denuclearize.[58] As is well known, these efforts, most importantly in the form of the Korean Peninsula Energy Development Organization, failed, and the Bush Administration treated North Korea with malign neglect and then malign engagement, leading rapidly to North Korean nuclear testing in 2006 and again in 2009, and the subsequent collapse of the Six Party Talks.

57 Snyder, S., "Envisioning a Northeast Security Framework: The Korean Peninsula," in *Towards a Northeast Asian Security Community: Implications for Korea's Growth and Economic Development*, ed. by Seliger, B. and Pascha, W. (New York: Springer, 2011), pp. 27-38.

58 Morgan, P.M., "Deterrence and System Management: The Case of North Korea," *Conflict Management and Peace Science*, 23(2) (2006), doi: http://dx.doi.org/10.1080/07388940600665768

Another possible approach that rests heavily on states cooperating for common security is the creation of a regional nuclear weapons-free zone (NWFZ). To date, restrictions on nuclear deployments have been established in Japan and the two Koreas (now abandoned in the North), and the United States withdrew all its forward-deployed tactical and theater nuclear weapons from the region in 1992.

Four different zonal concepts have been examined since the end of the Cold War, all at the behest of security intellectuals and social movement activists. The first by a study group led by John Endicott tested the idea of a limited nuclear weapons-free zone. It would cover part of the territory of the nuclear weapons states (NWS) in the region (that is, China, Russia and the United States) and therefore some of their intermediate-range nuclear forces, as well as the territory of the three then non-nuclear states (NNWS) in the region, the two Koreas and Japan.[59] Aside from the obvious asymmetries that made negotiating such a treaty difficult, as well as likely problems with monitoring and verification of the status of nuclear forces in the nuclear weapons states, the eruption of the North Korean nuclear weapons tests in 2006 and the subsequent strategic bifurcation of Northeast Asia into states aligned with China versus those aligned with the United States (with Russia on the sidelines) made the concept obsolete.

The second concept was developed in Japan, specifically by the peace researcher Hiromichi Umebayashi and by Peace Depot, a civil society activist and research organization, which was influential in political circles in Japan, especially with the former Foreign Minister Katsuya Okada in 2010.[60] They based their approach on the notion of three non-nuclear weapons states — the two Koreas and Japan — receiving a guarantee from the nuclear weapons states of non-use of nuclear weapons against the non-nuclear states. However, this concept has also been shunted aside by the DPRK's nuclear breakout.[61]

The third concept was advanced by Morton Halperin in 2000. It is similar to the Umebayashi concept, but proposes to include Taiwan, either by incorporating it into the treaty as a non-state (not done in any other nuclear weapons-free zone to date) or through a side agreement between China and Taiwan. Essential to Halperin's concept is the simultaneous adoption

59 Endicott, J.E., "Limited Nuclear-Weapon-Free Zones: The Time Has Come," *Korean Journal of Defense Analysis*, 20 (1) (2008), doi: http://dx.doi.org/10.1080/10163270802006305.
60 Hiromichi, U., "Toward a Northeast Asia Nuclear Weapon-Free Zone," *Japan Focus* (2005).
61 Hayes, P., "The Status Quo Isn't Working: A Nuke-Free Zone Is Needed Now," *Global Asia* (2010).

by the United States of a no-first use policy with regard to nuclear attack on the one hand, and the notion that Taiwan also be covered by the zone on the other — a legal and political question that unless addressed could lead to China refusing to participate in the zone.[62]

The fourth concept proposes that Japan and South Korea should not wait for North Korea to disarm and fully denuclearize. Instead they should proceed apace to create a bilateral nuclear weapons-free zone, thereby either leaving the DPRK isolated but with the door open for its later entry or inviting it to join from the outset as a non-compliant party — much as occurred with Brazil and Argentina when the Latin American Treaty of Tlatalelco was signed on the basis of differentiated entry.[63] Separately, the NWS would calibrate their no-use against NNWS party to the Zone treaty to the extent to which they are denuclearized, that is, as a function of the DPRK's incremental disarmament.

The crux of this idea is to create an institutional mechanism that "captures" the DPRK's breakout and creates a stabilizing framework to avoid further nuclear risk-taking behavior in areas of high tension, such as Korea in 2010. The Six Party Talks were to have created such a security mechanism in Northeast Asia but failed. Instead, a six party treaty would take its place as the enduring institutional security mechanism in the region. It is premised on the hypothesis that the DPRK really wants a legally binding treaty commitment of non-use of nuclear weapons against it. And, even the negative security assurance offered in the latest American Nuclear Posture Review (2010), should the DPRK disarm, would not cut the mustard because it is only an executive-branch and not a sovereign commitment, let alone a commitment in effect backed by the other nuclear weapon states that would be party to a NWFZ treaty.[64]

Finally, one partly market-based strategy for reducing nuclear insecurity has also been proposed, variously called PACATOM and ASIAATOM. The notion is to create regionally integrated nuclear fuel cycles, either at the front-end through an enrichment consortium that would offer increased security of supply in all participating countries, in return for which enrichment would not be undertaken anew in any non-nuclear country, or

---

62 Halperin, M., *The Nuclear Dimension of the U.S.-Japan Alliance*, NASPNet Special Report (Berkeley: Nautilus Institute, 1999).

63 Redick, J., *A Differentiated Entry into Force Procedure — Precedents and Legacies: Tlatelolco's Contribution to the Next Century* (Agency for the Prohibition of Nuclear Weapons in Latin America and the Caribbean, 1997).

64 Hayes, P. and Hamel-Green, M., "Paths to Peace on the Peninsula: The Case for a Japan-Korea Nuclear Weapon Free Zone," *Security Challenges*, 7(2) (2011).

at the back-end through cooperative management of spent fuel and nuclear waste disposal. To date, none of these market-based schemes have moved from concept to implementation, partly due to asymmetries of corporate capacity and interest, concern to maintain proprietary technology and market shares, and cost. Some form of regional cooperation seems inevitable, however, if only to ensure long-term secure and sustainable separation of nuclear wastes from the biosphere — an imperative underscored by the radiological exposures imposed by the Fukushima disaster. Of particular salience is the potential for "deep borehole" direct disposal of nuclear wastes in Northeast Asia.[65]

The Role of Civil Society in Networked Governance over Nuclear Weapons Threats

Contrary to conventional wisdom, at least among security analysts focused on Northeast Asia, David Shambaugh has argued:

> The core actor in this area is not the nation-state, but a plethora of non-state actors and processes — many of which are difficult to measure with any precision — that operate at the societal level. These multiple threads bind societies together in complex and interdependent ways. Indeed, they point up another significant way in which the Asian region is changing: its traditional geographic subcomponents — Northeast Asia, Southeast Asia, South Asia, Central Asia, and Oceania — are no longer useful intellectual constructs for dividing or distinguishing the macro processes occurring throughout the region.[66]

Moreover, as he points out, this interdependence is accelerating, and in itself deters conflict and creates resources that can be used to maintain peace and stability in each conflict zone. In Northeast Asia, these non-state actors and processes are still relatively weak, even nascent. Transnational civil society networks in this region, constituted largely by cosmopolitan, multilingual, and highly mobile younger elites, do not themselves create

---

65 Kang, J., *An Initial Exploration of the Potential for Deep Borehole Disposal of Nuclear Wastes in South Korea*, NAPSNet Special Report (Berkeley: Nautilus Institute, 2010). von Hippel, D. and Hayes, P., *Deep Borehole Disposal of Nuclear Spent Fuel and High Level Waste as a Focus of Regional East Asia Nuclear Fuel Cycle Cooperation*, NAPSNet Special Report (Berkeley: Nautilus Institute, 2010). Zhou, Y., *An Initial Exploration of the Potential for Deep Borehole Disposal of Nuclear Wastes in China*, NAPSNet Special Report (Berkeley: Nautilus Institute, 2012).

66 Shambaugh, D.L., "China Engages Asia: Reshaping the Regional Order," *International Security*, 29(3) (2004).

a security community — an urgent priority even from a purely military perspective.[67]

Nonetheless, these networks already play multiple roles in resolving security issues in the region, including in relation to the threat of nuclear next-use. Many organizations and individuals have played important roles in convening Track 1.5 and Track 2 dialogues with North Korea, for example. Others have gone where states cannot go and implemented actual development projects inside the DPRK to plant the seeds of future cooperation and improved mutual understanding between the antagonists in the Korean conflict.

Civil society organizations and intellectuals outside of the state and market have also developed important security agendas to be addressed by states — such as the nuclear weapons-free zone concept outlined in the previous section — but also in terms of building the local foundations of cooperative security at the community level. Thus, local governments have coordinated development projects across borders, even across the Korean Demilitarized Zone, and have begun to promote networked sharing of sustainable and secure communities regardless of national borders.

Civil society organizations have a long tradition in this region of promoting human rights, opposing military dictatorships, evicting nuclear weapons forward-deployed by great powers, and pushing for nuclear weapons-free zones. This critical tradition is likely to continue in the future on a more transnational and instantaneous basis due to modern connectivity. This enables civil society networks to swarm around rapidly emerging security problems, even in the midst of war or near-war, as happened in South Korea after the *Cheonan* incident in March 2010, when the South Korean government found itself unable to act decisively in part due to the international mobilization of critics of its anti-North Korean stance on the sinking of the ship.

Social Media and Security Issues in China

Almost unnoticed by the world of analysts focused on state-based security issues, a new factor has erupted onto the strategic landscape in Northeast Asia — the rise of the Chinese "netizen" with access to Chinese social

---

67   Blair, D.C. and Hanley, J.T., "From Wheels to Webs: Reconstructing Asia-Pacific Security Arrangements," *The Washington Quarterly*, 24(1) (2001), doi: http://dx.doi.org/10.1162/016366001561393

media. This new voice — or scores of millions of voices — adds a new layer of complexity to regional security issues that affects not only the Chinese leadership, but also the calculus of external players, whether they are states or non-state actors of various kinds.

Among China's security and foreign elites, different policy currents may diverge over core domestic issues of political reform versus democracy. But when it comes to shared notions such as China's rightful place in the world, the nature of external threats, and the appropriate geostrategic response — including nuclear and conventional force structures — these elites converge on the status quo. The policy currents that shape China's national security and foreign policy orientations are relatively insulated from direct pressure from a range of societal entities in Chinese society. External information flows to and from officials are channeled via bureaucracies and are, to some extent, controlled. Well-known gatekeepers meet and extract various rents from external visitors at these points of entry and control, whether they are official Track 1.0, semi-official Track 1.5, or non-official, non-state Track 2 foreign entities and individuals coming to China to engage. The currency of rent may be financial in the business world, but in the security and foreign policy domain, it is often kept in cumulative *guan-xi* accounts through which Chinese officials extend assistance to outsiders and expect reciprocity in the future — the basis of the intensely personal, networked and fluid forms of power that are the core of modern Chinese politics.[68]

Both the inner and outer circles of this national security and foreign policy-making elite are highly Internet-connected. Even here, however, Chinese security analysts must tread carefully to ensure that what they write abroad does not transgress what they can say at home. They must self-censor or be edited by domestic publishers in any media. Nonetheless, these elite analysts clearly read what is published by their international counterparts, many of whom have invested much effort in mapping China's institutional terrain and listing the key personnel and entry points for information flows in these relatively well-understood organizations.[69]

Today, however, China's rapidly emerging civil society is already a significant factor affecting China's security policy. Many foreign policy and security issues, including nuclear weapons-related security issues, are

---

68 Brown,K.,"China:WhatWeThinkWeKnowIsWrong,"*OpenDemocracy*,15May2013,http:// www.opendemocracy.net/kerry-brown/china-what-we-think-we-know-is-wrong

69 *Chinese Nuclear Arms Control and Disarmament: Principal Players and Policy-Making Processes* (Monterey: Center for Nonproliferation Studies, James Martin Center for Nonproliferation Studies, 2009), http://cns.miis.edu/opapers/op15/chart_11x17_china.pdf

spilling into or arising from within China itself. Many of these issues lead to a massive social response. They bear directly on domestic agendas that determine the stability of the rule of the Chinese Communist Party, or the relative power of local, provincial, and central governments, especially on economic, social equity, and ecological issues. As with all ruling parties, maintaining power and stability are at the top of the hierarchy of institutional imperatives. Undoubtedly, the bulk of popular use of the Internet and social media concerns relatively apolitical and low-level issues that do not bear directly on the high politics of national security and foreign policy. Official censors and self-censoring by Chinese security analysts ensure that will remain the case for the foreseeable future.

Nonetheless, there is much "space" for open discussion of domestic and international issues. Empirical studies by Yang have documented that China's social media focuses on distinct themes: popular nationalism, rights defense, corruption, and manipulation of how the "netizens" (people active in online communities) of China use virtual media to collectively comment on or criticize official policies and actions. Here, the scale shifts from some thousands of officials who make security and military policy, and with whom one might purport to relate via face-to-face visits or systematic distribution and promotion of Internet services, to a wholly different order of mass communication, unprecedented in human history, involving millions of contributors and consumers of on-line media conversing almost instantaneously and often without warning.

Before we examine such on-line civil society, first we must note the extraordinary speed and breadth of individual connectivity to the Chinese Internet. At the end of 2012, China had about 560 million Internet users.[70] By 2015, this figure will double breathtakingly to about 1.1 billion users of Internet-connected digital devices, or about 87 percent of the projected population. The biggest expansion will be that of digital devices used in social media.

The use of email, micro-blogs, and social media over smart phones and tablets operates at a velocity and scale in China that is qualitatively and quantitatively new. Social media in China is a vast electronic landscape, but it revolves around two Weibo platforms. These are Tencent and Sina, each of which has about 500 million subscribers, although it is unclear how much the memberships overlap.

---

70 *China Internet Statistics Whitepaper* (Singapore: China Internet Watch, 2013), http://www.chinainternetwatch.com/whitepaper/china-internet-statistics/

Also, the typical Chinese netizen is not simply absorbed in private or domestic concerns. A significant level of virtual and often virulently critical commentary now exists on "core" foreign policy and security issues, much of it highly critical of the central government and its policies. In Table 5.3, we present a selection of social media "storms" that relate to foreign policy and security issues, including China-DPRK relations and Japan's military white paper.

Undoubtedly, some of the nationalist and even xenophobic positions articulated in China's popular social media are encouraged by officials and official agencies to buttress the central government's position in dealing with external adversaries such as the United States, Japan, and even the DPRK. This is evident in the case of their response to Japan's white paper in 2013. Typically, however, although some bloggers (often officials in private capacity) support government policy, the vast majority of China's netizens are critical or even condemnatory of government policy when the case calls for outrage (as in the case of the DPRK arrest of a Chinese fishing vessel).

Table 5.3: Selected Social Media Commentary On Security Issues, 2012-2013

January 2012, Rumors of DPRK Coup: Chinese netizens mostly dismissed as "implausible" rumors of a DPRK coup d'état.

February 2012, Rumors of North Korea Assassination Attempt: PRC netizens discussed a rumor that DPRK leader Kim Jong-un was assassinated in his house in Pyongyang.

April 2012, PRC-DPRK Account Gains Following: Pro-North Korea "Today Korea" account opened on *Sina Weibo* and attracted over 100,000 followers in only a few days.

September 2012, Anti-Japan Protests Become Hot Topic: Anti-Japan protests related to Sino-Japanese territorial disputes over the Senkakus (Diaoyu Islands in China) discussed on Chinese social media.

April 2013, PRC Netizens Report Military Mobilization on DPRK Border; Oil Aid Unaffected: Despite foreign media reports that China suspended crude oil exports to the North in February, *Sina Weibo* user "Chaoji Da Benying" said that the operation of the oil pipeline from Dandong to North Korea appeared to be undisrupted (1 April). "RyanEquilibrium" claimed to see DPRK "officials" at an oil measurement station in Dandong, which the user said was visited every month (1 April). • User "mickeymouse" said in a posting on local forum Dandong Fengyun Wang that Dandong Customs officials turned a blind eye to oil products carried by trucks "travelling to North Korea daily" (24 March).

Table 5.3, cont.

May 17-24 2013, DPRK Seize Chinese Fishing Boat: PRC netizens commented on May 5 seizure by DPRK of a Chinese fishing boat and its crew. Most condemned the DPRK for the abduction, calling the country "ungrateful." • Noting that it is not the first such seizure, Hu Xijin, editor-in-chief of Huanqiu Shibao (*Global Times*) called the captors "a bunch of scoundrels" and suspected that the DPRK had its own people in Dandong. (*Sina Weibo*, 20 May). • Retired Major General Luo Yuan, vice president and secretary general of the China Council for the Promotion of Strategic Culture, expressed anger over the incident, saying the DPRK had "gone too far" (*Sina Weibo*, 20 May). • Responding to the release of the fishing boat and its crew, PRC diplomat nicknamed "Vegetarian Cat 2011" opined that there were "no winners" and that both sides were "losers" (*Sina Weibo*, 20 May).

When DPRK special envoy Choe Ryong Hae arrived on 22 May, soon after the release, most rejected the visit, calling the DPRK "shameless" and "ungrateful." QQ Weibo user "Wang Yong Liang" called the DPRK "shameless," criticizing Choe for "having the nerve to come and ask for money" and urged China to stop giving aid (*QQ Weibo*, 23 May). *Sina Weibo* user "Zheng Yu 2011" asserted that China should "stand firm" and show its "determination to denuclearize the DPRK." (*Sina Weibo*, 23 May). Calling the DPRK an "ungrateful wolf," user "TimeU, Qing Tu Yin Xu" maintained that the DPRK is "useless" to China and that Choe only visited China to "seek protection and food" (*Sina Weibo*, 23 May).

June 2013, PRC Netizens Discuss Japan's Defense White Paper: PRC microblogs *Sina Weibo* and *QQ Weibo* posted 11,938 and 7,800 comments on Japan's defense white paper, which accused China of attempting "to change the status quo by force based on its own assertion." Bloggers on *Jiefangjun Bao's* official weibo criticized Japan for "playing up the China threat" and "creating tensions and conflicts" (*QQ Weibo*, 10 July). Most condemned Japan for its ambitions and said its "ultimate goal" is to "break away" from the United States. *Sina Weibo* user "Bu Jian Zheng," for example, maintained that Japan is only "using" the United States and that it is "biding its time to stab the United States in the back" (*Sina Weibo*, 10 July). *Sina Weibo* user "Qiao Xin Ting Xue" urged China to "speed up" its process of bolstering the military (*Sina Weibo*, 10 July).

July 2013, PRC Microbloggers on Li Yuanchao's Presence at DPRK's Armistice Day Events: While some microbloggers such as *Sina Weibo* user "Di Daren" (*Sina Weibo*, 29 July) argued that in view of Japan's threat, China must ally with the DPRK, others such as *Sina Weibo* user "nta" criticized Chinese Vice President Li Yuanchao's 25-28 July visit to the DPRK to mark the 60th Korean War Armistice anniversary for "aiding a tyrant to do evil" and "assisting the Kim dynasty to prolong its dictatorship" (*Sina Weibo*, 27 July). Another *QQ Weibo* user called "Blue" wrote, "Wallowing in the mire with the DPRK! Why do we have to commemorate the most terrible war that should not have happened?" (*QQ Weibo*, 27 July)

Sometimes, the virtual commentary directly punctures the legitimacy of existing central government foreign policy. It also resonates widely within segments of the e-literate elites, shaking the ideological foundations of policy lines and, in some instances, threatening to sweep away or at least severely erode whole policy lines. China's alliance with and support for the DPRK is a case in point. In Table 5.4, Chinese social media commentary on the DPRK's extraordinary nuclear threats against the United States and South Korea in the March-April 2013 period were unreservedly critical not only of the DPRK ("a dog that bites the ones who feed it") and the United States (which deserves to be "attacked by other countries"), but also of China itself (the crisis is "entirely of China's own making" and the result of China's "conniving behavior" toward the DPRK).

Thus, high-level officials, especially younger leaders who are strongly connected to the Internet and to social media, are alert to early signs of "Internet events" like these that activate Chinese super-bloggers (those with more than a million followers) and stimulate social media to swarm all over an issue. (Internet events are "public events with the participation of netizens, which are entities or persons that are actively involved in online communities expressing their opinions or giving comments."[71]) The presence of their own avatars and virtual names is an important status symbol of modernity and leadership to many of the younger officials who participate in social media. Due to the pervasive nature of connectivity, this virtual presence includes officials in provincial governments with international borders and those in major trading cities exposed to flows to and from the external world of people, trade, and finance — not just those at the center of power in Beijing.

Exactly how social media plays out in the power dynamics of foreign policy and geo-strategic decision-makers is opaque. On a cultural level, Chinese officials in the academic and policy advisory inner circles often float a trial balloon by mentioning a concept or proposal and saying they heard it from a foreign source if the idea is deemed too controversial or if it is unclear how the idea might be received. The risk posed by raising new ideas can be diluted even further by qualifying the post to the effect that the blogger is only relaying an idea attributable to another party, especially from overseas.

---

71   Tan, Z., *et al.*, "Agent-Based Modeling of Netizen Groups in Chinese Internet Events," *Society for Modeling & Simulation International Magazine*, 3(2) (2011).

Conversely, even at the very center — the Party's International Affairs Division — younger officials have been observed proudly reporting their aggressive, even emotional stances on various high profile issues gripping social media, their private voices publicly venting views that are clearly at odds with official policy. These statements are often made in the presence of older and traditional charismatic leaders from an earlier era who carry unquestionable organizational and political authority. Undoubtedly this dissonance has many dimensions. At times, the younger official's avatar may be using an international post as permission to discuss an issue in China and set agendas. An official's private avatar may be voicing a trial balloon in policy terms, testing the waters or pushing an alternative policy on highly visible social networks viewed by the personal networks of younger officials connected to him by cohort, mentor, origin, or family. In some cases, these positions even may be encouraged by a silent opponent in order to push an official across a line of permissible versus non-permissible contention with official policy in an attempt to trap the official as part of a line struggle within or across agencies and between policy currents. At some point, the party leadership will deem officials who become serious players on social media to be potential threats to their organizational power in the form of personality cults and populist demagoguery — a possible reason for Bo Xilai's downfall. Unsurprisingly, therefore, while the Chinese Communist Party and media entities such as *Xinhua* and *People's Daily* have social media accounts in China, senior leaders do not.

The massive reach of super-bloggers in China should not be underestimated. In July 2013, for example, ten Chinese super-bloggers were invited to tour and blog in South Korea — trips that undoubtedly required central government approval.[72] Two of these ten have a combined social media following of 23 million Chinese. If only half read their posts, then 11.5 million active followers were exposed to their posts from South Korea. Assuming just two percent of active followers re-tweeted these messages, then the 230,000 re-tweets may have reached a further 1.1 million readers (assuming 500 followers for each of these re-tweeters)! Therefore, just two of the ten super-bloggers likely reached 13 million plus followers in China, demonstrating the huge potential for communication.

---

72 Yonhap News Agency staff writer, "Chinese 'Power Microbloggers' to Visit S. Korea This Week," *Yonhap News Agency*, 1 July 2013, http://www.globalpost.com/dispatch/news/yonhap-news-agency/130701/chinese-power-microbloggers-visit-s-korea-week

Table 5.4: Netizens Respond To DPRK Nuclear Threats, April-March 2013

April 4-11, 2013, PRC netizens were observed to comment on the DPRK's recent warning of a "merciless, sacred, retaliatory war" against its neighbors and the United States…

As of 11 April on the popular PRC microblogs *Sino Weibo* and *QQ Weibo*, approximately 2,389,173 and 1,347,200 postings were observed respectively to discuss the DPRK's threat to wage what DPRK KCNA termed a "merciless, sacred, retaliatory war" on its neighboring countries and the United States.

Lu Shiwei, a senior researcher of the Institute of Modern International Relations at Tsinghua (Qinghua) University, contended that "the US sanctions, pressures, and isolation against the DPRK for the past few decades" are "one of the root causes of the conflict on the Korean Peninsula" (*Sina Weibo*, 10 April).

Yue Gang, renowned military commentator and former colonel of the PLA General Staff Department, opined the United States had "gone too far" and that "its losses will outweigh its gains" if it decides to make war "with a country that possesses nuclear weapons." Conjecturing that the United States and the ROK will make certain compromises with the DPRK, Yue maintained that the DPRK will become the "big winner" if no war is launched in the end (*Sina Weibo*, 9 April).

Military expert Zhao Chu asserted that the reason the DPRK had managed to stay "safe" since the Cold War was not due to its nuclear weapon capabilities. Rather, it was because of (1) the complicated situation on the Korean Peninsula, (2) the ROK's inability to reunite with the DPRK, and (3) former US President George W. Bush's focus on fighting terrorism (*Sina Weibo*, 8 April).

Many PRC netizens remarked that China was responsible for the current crisis on the Korean Peninsula.

QQ Weibo user "Du Qiu" said that China had "raised a dog that bites the ones who feed it," adding that the DPRK will "destroy" China's "stability" and the "good progress of the country's reform and opening up" (*QQ Weibo*, 10 April).

QQ Weibo user "Zhai Cheng Feng" condemned China for double standards, as it "did not say a word" when the United States and the ROK were conducting military drills near the DPRK, but then attacked the DPRK for launching a nuclear test (*QQ Weibo*, 10 April).

Sina Weibo user "Cool Is My Trademark" argued that the current Korean Peninsula crisis "has much to do with China's conniving behavior" toward the DPRK. Another user, "ItsRyaning," maintained that the crisis is "entirely of China's own making" (*Sina Weibo*, 10 April).

Other PRC netizens, however, blamed the United States for the current situation.

QQ Weibo user "Stroll in Rainy Night" said that while it was "necessary" for the DPRK to "put up a front," it was "impossible" that the DPRK would conduct a missile launch unprovoked. He then urged people to "stop chastising only the DPRK," which behaves the way it does because it has been "pushed into a corner by the United States" (*QQ Weibo*, 10 April).

Table 5.4, cont.

Sina Weibo user "Mini Young Melon" asked why everyone points their finger at the DPRK but not at the "culprits" – the United States, Japan, and the ROK (*Sina Weibo*, 10 April).

Calling the United States a "nation that does not know how to respect other countries," *Sina Weibo* user "Tian Xiang Shan Bu Yong Xue Xi" blamed the United States for the crisis and said it deserves to be "attacked by other countries" (*Sina Weibo*, 10 April).

Similar reach can be prompted by external posts circulated inside China. *North Korea On the Cusp of Digital Transformation*,[73] a report on the large-scale adoption and use of cell phones in North Korea and published by the Nautilus Institute on November 1, 2011, went viral on social media in China. On one site,[74] the following conversation (summarized after translation) occurs:

A young lady posts a brief excerpt of Nautilus's *North Korea On the Cusp of Digital Transformation*. She, her friends, and others chat about it. The first comment is "I had no idea there were so many cell phones in North Korea." Her friends jump in and start wondering how people can afford cell phones when they can't eat (a clear indicator that some average Chinese citizens understand North Korea is experiencing a famine). One remarks that a structure is determined by its foundation. And another disparages "Fat Kim / Fat Gold" (in Chinese, the character for "Kim" is "gold").

Exactly what exposure triggered this netizen interest is unknown. The essay was re-posted by the (official) China Arms Control and Disarmament Association on their website inside China's firewall on November 4, 2011,[75] but social and digital news media did not latch onto it until November 21. Social media interest may have been triggered by international media coverage that mentioned the report on November 21 (a Reuter's bulletin,[76] for example). Perhaps it was domestic digital news coverage that morning (at 163.com, for instance).[77] Whether the news media reporters followed the

---

73 Mansourov, A., *North Korea on the Cusp of Digital Transformation*, NAPSNet Special Report (Berkeley: Nautilus Institute, 2011), http://nautilus.org/wp-content/uploads/2011/12/DPRK_Digital_Transformation.pdf

74 The exchange is found in Chinese at http://tieba.baidu.com/p/1292015149

75 Mansourov, A., *North Korea on the Cusp of Digital Transformation*..

76 Jiawei, Z., "Korean Mobile Phone Users to Reach One Million Four Years after Mobile Phone Ban Lifted (in Chinese)," *Reuters*, 21 November 2011, http://cn.reuters.com/article/CNAnalysesNews/idCNCHINA-5247520111121?pageNumber=2&virtualBrandChannel=0

77 China Daily staff writer, "British Media Says North Korean 3G Mobile Phone

path of social media swarming around the topic or social media were set off by the news media is unclear but also unimportant.

What is evident is that an external report triggered social and news media storms that fed off each other, resulting in massive coverage of a topic highly salient to sensitive external relationships between China and the Koreas, and China and the United States. Consequently, "Internet events" on social media have profound bottom-up and sideways potential to pressure central government officials and agencies to change policy, realign provincial or local government policy, scapegoat a specific individual, company, or agency, etc., in order to preserve the legitimacy and power of the central government or its provincial agents. For example, in the blame game that ensued after the horrific July 2011 crash of a high-speed train in Wenzhou city in Zhejiang Province, Beijing officials used the Internet to put the onus on lax local government and the line agencies responsible for the accident, keeping the focus away from the center.[78]

One can only conjecture exactly how these information vectors based on virtual, bottom-up citizen mobilization intersect with the personal, intimate politics of networked patronage and mutual obligation at the center. One answer is to argue that such influence can only be inferred indirectly from observed effects, always subject to the problem of counter-factuality (what else might have changed or been influential, which can never be known in full). Another answer is to use either formal or informal agent-based modeling to simulate the true complexity of this interplay and then interpret the patterns that result from the specification of the agents and their decision rules.

For example, using agent-based modeling, Tan, Li and Mao simulated two public Internet events in China in 2010: the Synutra baby milk powder scandal and the conflict between Qihoo and Tencent software companies over privacy protection software.[79] In both cases, Internet events erupted and resulted in hundreds of reports, scores of thousands of comments, and, ultimately, government intervention to resolve both situations.

The model specified five entities: main party, opposite party, netizen group, media, and government. The main party refers to the people or the

Users to Reach One Million," *China Daily*, 21 November 2011, http://news.163. com/11/1121/11/7JCM79DL00014JB5.html

78   Xu, X., *Internet Facilitated Civic Engagement in China's Context: A Case Study of the Internet Event of Wenzhou High-Speed Train Accident* (Columbia University, 2011).

79   Tan, Z., *et al.* (2011). Tan et al refer to Tecent, but the proper name (from the website http://t.qq.com/) in English is Tencent, which is used here instead.

group who initiate a hot event. The opposite party is the group which has interests regarding the event that conflict with the main party. Their actions usually trigger the Internet event. The netizen group is the netizens who are associated with the Internet event via online participation. Media refers to traditional mass media. Government is assumed to be an intermediary in some respects in this model, rather than the primary target of netizen ire.

Each of these five parties has one or more "belief states" (for example, that of government is concern and its own credibility) affected by interaction during the Internet event. Each also has a set of possible actions. Government actions, for example, are to get involved, judge the winner, appease, award, punish, and not to respond. Each of these has an associated estimate intensity and target. Interactions between the entities are governed by rules that specify how the actions of one entity influence the others. Thus, when conflicts increase between the main and opposite party, media and netizen concern also increases. Actions by other parties such as netizen criticism also increase the concerns of all parties. Often, negative actions (in the case of netizens, these include to praise, donate, digitally broadcast or suppress, and criticize) have more influence than positive actions, which is reflected in the models.[80]

Tan, Li, and Mao used a standard agent-based modeling tool (Repast) to represent these entities, states, and interactions and compared their interaction over time with actual social media data mined from postings. In the case of the Synutra, the skepticism and anger of the netizens clearly contributed to the media attention and eventual government intervention after official inaction and cover-up.[81] The simulated pattern of interaction over time closely, but not always, matches that of the actual data — as in the modeling of the Qihoo and Tecent conflict. Of particular interest is the way that social media and mass media coincide in putting the main party in the Internet event, and thereby the government, in a negative limelight that forced official response.

In a foreign policy or national security context — especially one involving high levels of secrecy such as nuclear weapons policy, deployments, threats, delivery systems, or outcomes of use — a relatively simple five agent model such as that above may be difficult to specify, but not impossible. In some cases, the object of ire may be a local embassy of a target main group (for

---

80   Ibid., pp. 40-42.
81   Ibid., pp. 42-43.

example, as occurred with protests against Japan in China in recent years). At present, we are not aware of any agent-based modeling of the interaction of social media with elite perceptions, views, and policy-making in China.

Nonetheless, we are always free to infer how social media influences officialdom and vice versa, starting with the fundamentals and taking into account the contextual and structural parallels between domestic Internet events and official policy with foreign policy and national security concerns. As noted earlier, contending Chinese policy currents that transect China's pyramid of power (composed of the party, military, and line agencies) confront a set of "master narratives" about domestic and international issues that frame modern China. In terms of the legitimacy of power at the center, these policy currents propose different approaches to the primary issues of the distribution of wealth and power, equity and social justice, political reform and democracy, ecological integrity, and the fate of the oppressed minorities. When such issues explode into Internet events, they provide an opportunity for central authorities to monitor local developments, to direct ire against local agencies, or to promote local solutions to concrete local social problems. Bottom-up reporting of local events, combined with expression of local resentment, are amplified by social media into Internet events and enable the center to be responsive to social grievances in a long tradition of petitioning for redress against local abuses of power and authority. The Internet and social media become a means whereby Chinese citizens can participate in deliberations within China's rigid political system, thus avoiding the structural changes required to create a democratic, pluralist system.

In some of the key concepts that legitimate Communist Party rule, such as restoring China's rightful place in the world,[82] national security and foreign policy concerns loom large. In the case of North Korea, for example, the explosion of social media commentary on DPRK issues and its sensitivity to the latest rumors, as well as field reporting along the border, included at various times strongly stated views concerning China' diminished prestige, its (lack of) ability to impose its will on its small but nuclear-armed ally, and its passive role relative to the United States in coercing the DPRK to capitulate on nuclear and other issues. This time, the social media commentaries coincided with a policy line struggle that continued for months in Beijing as to whether to demote the DPRK from a

---

82   Monitor 360, *Master Narratives Country Report: China* (Open Source Center, 2012).

full alliance to a marginal and possibly negative relationship in the context of regional and global geo-strategic considerations.[83]

In this instance, social media not only criticized core tenets of Chinese policy towards the DPRK, including its emphasis on slow reform before regime change. It also focused directly on previously taboo topics for public discussion, such as the nuclear weapons issue arising from the DPRK's campaign of nuclear threats against the United States and its allies, and even, some admitted, against China itself. We summarize the breadth and depth of this discussion in Table 5.4. Similar sentiments and debates to those expressed in social media were observed within the foreign policy and security elite at the center. In some cases, officials used the stereotype of ugly North Koreans to whip up nationalist sentiment (as in the fishing boat incident). But in general, Chinese virtual opinion and much of the central officialdom have shifted their emotional and political loyalties away from an alliance born in the blood of 900,000 Chinese casualties in the Korean War towards eventual cutting adrift the North Korean ingrates. There are also generational fault lines: those who were directly involved in the Korean War as Chinese People's Volunteers fighting in Korea have been out of power for almost a decade, while the e-literate elites are present at most levels of government and account for almost all provincial and municipal level leaders. The China-DPRK alliance holds, but remains strictly based on brutal self-interest without regard to emotional and ideological ties forged during the Korean War.

The points at which social media form flash floods that feed into tributaries that, in turn, merge into slower moving policy currents down-river are chaotic and indeterminate. Sometimes social media will be driven by central government policies, statements, and actions and accelerate a bottom-up or sideways push effect. In other instances, social media will amplify pressure building in a policy current to the point that it can burst through resistance and lead to change instigated at the highest level, often by the replacement of senior officials. The ultimate flood, a burgeoning social movement demanding democratic pluralism, faces a massive dam — the Party. But all sorts of billabongs, holding reservoirs, spillways, and other devices exist to forestall the day when virtual deliberative discourse would contribute to sweeping away the dam represented by the Party's monopoly on political power.

---

83 Jun, J., "Dealing with a Sore Lip: Parsing China's "Recalculation" of North Korea Policy," 29 March 2013, http://38north.org/2013/03/jjun032913

Overall, the always shifting edge of the chaotic interplay between personalized, networked politics at the center and massive social media mobilization increases the volatility and turbulence of policy making processes, not least because social media accelerates the propagation of errors and thereby increases uncertainty. Top-level officials and political figures are driven by this dynamic to seek ever-broader social and political bases in order to share risk and diversify their sources of legitimacy — and to demonstrate the breadth of their support.

Observable trends in social media may affect how this interaction takes place. Already, Chinese social media have begun to establish "rumor refutation" groups, such as *weibo piyao* in 2010. Others have created "self-purification" networks dedicated to exposing fake or false information, in part to offset the amplification by social media of erroneous field reporting or rumor propagation associated with Internet events.[84] This self-corrective feature of social media combined with more reflective, less event-driven posts may herald the emergence of a mature civil society in China able to address national security and foreign policy issues in ways that are more amenable to uptake and to policy reformation at the center.

Social media in China allows nascent civil society to have a voice, albeit only a limited voice, in the expression of values and views that are incorporated into China's foreign policy and security policies. Although constrained, social media may play an important supplementary role to the state and to market entities in terms of situational awareness, self-surveillance, and direct regulation of behavior in time-critical situations that arise from non-state populations in the first place — such as criminal networks moving drugs, trafficking in humans, or smuggling nuclear weapons-related knowledge or items. Many of the leaders of Chinese social media, including elite security analysts and officials, already network with external parties and receive constant infusions of information and analysis in spite of the Great Firewall.[85] How these new players affect China's foreign policy and security calculus is a critical variable in future security challenges confronting its neighbors and competitors. In this regard, civil society networks which communicate directly and effectively with social media in China may be far more influential in shaping China's policies

---

84   Xu, X. (2011).
85   In China, online adults fall into the following categories (individuals can be in more than one): creators (40%), critics (44%), collectors (34%), joiners (23%), spectators (71%), and in-actives (25%). See *China Social Media Usage* (Shanghai: Resonance).

than governments, especially on security conflicts in which governments are at loggerheads.[86]

Conclusion

In this respect, therefore, we have already entered a post-hegemonic era in which the foundations of US nuclear hegemony are already so corroded, and its failure to contain North Korean proliferation so obvious,[87] that American reassurances increasingly have little meaning to ordinary citizens in allied countries such as South Korea or Japan, or may even evoke opposition to continued alliance. The many cross-border integrative processes that follow from the globalization of culture, economy, and technology — especially massive urbanization — make state-based nuclear deterrence strategies obsolete and absurd. By mid-century, the absurdity of targeting people and places with weapons of mass destruction may become so evident that the fixation of state leaders on gaining nuclear weapons will be viewed as a strange detour in an already archaic past: a time when humans put the very biosphere on which they rely for daily survival at risk of nuclear conflagration, all in the search for deterrence of aggressive intentions that, for the most part, may have never existed in an immediate sense.

For most of the nuclear weapons era, the policies and postures of states have been immune to social movements and civil society. There were significant exceptions, for example, when nuclear weapons were forced out of Japan in 1960 by anti-government protestors, out of Okinawa in 1971 due to popular revulsion to nuclear weapons in Japan, off US surface warships by protestors from the Nuclear Free and Independent Pacific Movement, out of the Philippines and New Zealand due to the rise to power of anti-nuclear advocates in the 1980s, and out of South Korea in 1991 after the overthrow of the military dictatorship in 1987 by the democratic movement.

Soviet nuclear forces were almost completely unaffected in this entire period by civil society, a situation which remains largely unchanged since the end of the Cold War. Chinese and North Korean nuclear weapons

---

86   Melissen, J., "Concluding Reflections on Soft Power and Public Diplomacy in East Asia," in *Public Diplomacy and Soft Power in East Asia*, ed. by J., M. and Lee, S. J. (New York: Palgrave MacMillan, 2011).

87   Hayes, P., *The Stalker State: North Korean Proliferation and the End of American Nuclear Hegemony*, NAPSNet Policy Forum (Berkeley: Nautilus Institute, 2006).

programs were also state-based, although they were more implicated in nuclear nationalism than in the other two nuclear weapons states in the region and were therefore more "populist" in ideological terms.

In the era of globalization and transparency, such exclusively state-based nuclear weapons programs are increasingly not viable. Networks of civil society groups dedicated to realizing peace, green agendas, non-nuclear futures, democracy, and human rights will increasingly demand accountability from nuclear weapons establishments and national leaders. Secrecy is always relative, and even the most reclusive, closed states now find themselves ambushed by non-state organizations wielding state-of-the-art surveillance techniques such as satellite imagery, crowd-sourced field reports, and open source intelligence analysis. These networks also produce visions of nuclear disarmament that they propagate via networks across borders, establish deep roots at the local government and city level (as in the 800-strong Mayors for Peace in East Asia), and promulgate new norms and shared practices on nuclear security issues, such as the operation of nuclear fuel cycle facilities. In this manner, civil society organizations have demonstrated great potential to span borders and fill structural holes in Northeast Asia, thereby expanding social capacity to respond to the increasing complexity of the nuclear weapons challenge in this region.

6. The Implications of Civic Diplomacy for ROK Foreign Policy

Kiho Yi and Peter Hayes

Contributing authors: Joan Diamond, Steven Denney, Christopher Green, and Jungmin Seo

Introduction

This chapter focuses on the Republic of Korea and the implications for its foreign policy of the actual and potential role of civil society in solving complex global problems in Northeast Asia. It looks at the impact on ROK foreign policy of the emergence of independent civic diplomacy originating from civil society rather than the state. We commence this chapter by examining the characteristics of international affairs and inter-state relations in Northeast Asia since the end of the Cold War — basically, the shift from twentieth-century, backwards-looking foreign policy focused on military power and nation-state building to a twenty-first century, forwards-looking foreign policy aimed at building a regional community. This transition left many "traditional" security issues outstanding, such as the living history of past colonial and imperial adventures in some states, the multigenerational imprint of wars, and territorial disputes. New, often cross-border issues have arisen, however, many of which originate in the region but are global in nature: they are urgent and beyond the ability of any single nation-state to address.

    http://dx.doi.org/10.11647/OBP.0059.06

Concurrently, new types of actors, including powerful individuals, civil society organizations, and local governments, have emerged in potent ways that both constrain and enable the foreign policy of each country in the region to address these traditional and new issues — sometimes in synchrony with diplomacy and other standard instruments of state-based foreign policy, but sometimes marching to their own tune. In the second section, therefore, we review the rise of the ROK's "complex diplomacy," which aims at exploiting its "middle power" status and location in the international system, while also addressing this increasingly complex foreign policy terrain.

In the next section, we examine the emergence of civil society networks operating across borders. The characteristics of these types of civilian actors vary from country to country, and their capacities are also uneven when compared across China, the ROK, and Japan. Nonetheless, at a regional level, networks of these non-governmental, non-profit actors have formed and tackled a number of global problems as effectively or more so than states, at least at particular moments and circumstances. After outlining the roles that such organizations may play in functional and structural (networking) terms, we examine six case studies to derive lessons learned from these civil society networks for ROK foreign policy.

In the fifth section, we examine the role of local governments in initiating cross-border cooperation, either by sharing solutions to common problems or managing a cross-border region. We note the potential for common cause between these "trans-border" local initiatives and issue-based civil society networks to add a new layer of social capacity to solving problems that afflict states.

We conclude the chapter by proposing the adoption of "civic diplomacy" as a separate category to the official "complex" diplomacy pursued by the ROK state to implement its foreign policy, arguably since 2000, but explicitly so since 2008. We note the further implication that the "civic state" — that is, a state that aims to provide expertise, remove obstacles, and act as an arbiter, regulator, and orchestrator while enabling civil society, regulating the market, and nesting in rather than dominating networked, autonomous communities — might find civil society and local governments to be more effective in addressing pressing problems of foreign policy than the relatively blunt, brittle, and distant tools of traditional diplomacy — military power — and the efficient but often amoral instrument of market power.

New Global Challenges for the 21st Century

The 21st century began with two major shocks that forced people to rethink the traditional concept of security. These were the September 11, 2001 (9/11) attack on the World Trade Center and the March 11, 2011 (3/11) earthquake, tsunami, and Fukushima catastrophe in Japan. The former redefined the foreign policy of all states and forced them to elevate non-state actors to the same or even a higher level of threat than other states. The 9/11 attacks challenged the very basis of the claim by some in the United States that the global state power system was unipolar,[1] creating a new layer of complexity in international security.

The 3/11 catastrophe challenged the underlying legitimacy of the state and of market institutions due to their failure to anticipate, let alone overcome the impact of the natural disasters and the collapse of the engineered safety systems of the four reactors at Fukushima.[2] Like home-grown terrorism, this incident underscored the fact that the greatest source of risk may be domestic rather than foreign, non-state instead of state-based, and linked to other problems such as energy insecurity or climate change rather than existing in isolation. The further implication — that even problems that arise domestically within the territory of one nation-state cannot be solved or managed by only one state,[3] and that even in coalitions, states alone cannot solve such complex, interrelated, and global problems — is also profoundly disruptive of the standard practice of foreign policy, which relies almost completely on state apparatuses. Many of these problems pose new ethical issues, are focused on human rather than state-based security,[4] and require new forms of trust and cooperation to emerge as the basis for transnational coordination and international cooperation, placing a new morality at the core of foreign policy rather than military power.

---

1   Krauthammer, C., "The Unipolar Moment," *Foreign Affairs*, 70(1) (1990); Hayes, P. (2006).
2   Rauhala, E., "How Japan Became a Leader in Disaster Preparation," *Time*, 11 March 2011, http://content.time.com/time/world/article/0,8599,2058390,00.html
3   Kissinger, H., *Diplomacy* (New York: Simon & Schuster, 1994).
4   In 1994, UNDP defined the new dimensions of human security with emphasizing "interdependence, early prevention than later intervention, and people-centered." According to their report, people-centered human security is concerned "with how people live and breathe in a society, how freely they exercise their many choices, how much access they have to market and social opportunities and whether they live in conflict or in peace." United Nations Development Programme, *Human Development Report: New Dimensions of Human Security* (New York: United Nations Development Programme, 1994).

Complexity and Northeast Asian Diplomacy

In Northeast Asia, 21st-century complex security issues are superimposed on 20th-century traditional security issues. These old issues include history books in Japan, Japanese politicians visiting the Yasukuni Shrine, sexual slavery during World War II, and territorial disputes such as the conflict surrounding the Senkaku/Diaoyu, Dokdo/Takeshima, and Kuril islands. Territorial disputes in particular have shown that they could lead to small-scale military conflict between the parties involved.[5] They have become a tool for politicians in Japan, both Koreas, Russia, and China to gain popular support and strengthen virulent nationalism.[6]

The Korean Peninsula is one of the last vestiges of the Cold War. It is integral to the post-Cold War international system, which places the United States at the "unipolar" center of an international hierarchy of states based on the size of their economy (the G2, G7, G20 system, for example), their military (NATO), or their regional affiliations (the EU, ASEAN, MERCOSUR, etc.). In such a system, North Korea's land-based trilateral alliance stood against South Korea's maritime-based trilateral alliance, reproducing the bifurcation of Northeast Asia in the 21st century that arose from Cold War global bipolarity. In this context, the DPRK issue is partly global in that it presents unconventional challenges (such as the risk of non-state nuclear terrorism), partly regional (in that it reinforces and at the same time disrupts the post-Cold War state system), and partly local (in that it continues the ideological and physical division of Korea with the attendant social, economic, and ecological cost to the Korean people).

Additionally, Northeast Asia is characterized by asymmetry between the power capacities and interests of each state that makes it difficult to create regional institutions based on power sharing and collaboration. The issues of hegemony and neo-imperialism further strain relations among states. In economic terms, Japan was the dominant economic power until 2010, when China overtook the nation in terms of GDP.[7] China has an overwhelming geopolitical advantage in terms of population, sheer physical size, and

---

5   The Economist, "Could Asia Really Go to War over These?," *The Economist*, 22 September 2012, http://www.economist.com/node/21563316

6   Nair, D., "Regionalism in the Asia Pacific/East Asia: A Frustrated Regionalism?," *Contemporary Southeast Asia*, 31(1) (2008).

7   *GDP (Current US$)* (Washington, DC: The World Bank), http://data.worldbank. org/indicator/NY.GDP.MKTP.CD?order=wbapi_data_value_2011+wbapi_data_ value+wbapi_data_value-last&sort=desc

geography — but the presence of the United States holds this advantage in check. The United States is still the world's largest economy (roughly double that of China) and its relative military power is overwhelming.[8]

The most important security issue framed in these terms is the transition by which the United States and its allies adjust to the rise of China to economic and military co-equal status over the coming generation and to the many related issues posed by this transformation — such as the huge increase in acid rain from China falling on Korea and Japan. In a similar vein, the leaders of each country are greatly concerned about China's desire to be a state with revisionist aspirations to reconstruct the status quo of inter-state relations and possibly become the new regional hegemon. The June 2013 Obama-Xi presidential summit did little to allay concerns that the two great powers had not figured out how to create the new "great power relationship" sought by China.[9]

In addition to these 20th-century issues, Northeast Asia has uniquely 21st-century challenges in terms of development and democratization. Openness and transparency of decision-making by states are generally assumed to be integral to democracy in the West, but are not necessarily part of the definition of democracy in Northeast Asia, let alone of foreign policy. Indeed, the latter is typically viewed as a domain of secrecy and quiet conversations outside of public view. The deepening of democracy in the ROK and Japan, the challenges facing democracy in the Russian Far East, the possibility that China will democratize in the future,[10] and the prospect of post-totalitarian, "pluralist" authoritarian government in the DPRK all obstruct the evolution of a common vision for the future at any level, let alone the emergence of a regional community and common Northeast Asian identity.

For all these reasons — the historical legacies, a divided Korea, US-China economic interdependence and competition for trade with regional states, and the impact of globalization, democratization, and the information revolution in each country, the Cold War balance of power co-exists with

---

8   Swaine, M.D., *et al.*, *China's Military and the U.S.-Japan Alliance in 2030: A Strategic Net Assessment* (Washington, DC: Carnegie Endowment for International Peace, 2013).

9   Calmes, J. and Myers, S.L., "U.S. And China Move Closer on North Korea, but Not on Cyberespionage," *New York Times*, 8 June 2013, http://www.nytimes.com/2013/06/09/world/asia/obama-and-xi-try-building-a-new-model-for-china-us-ties.html?pagewanted=1&_r=0&ref=world

10   Liu, Y. and Chen, D., "Why China Will Democratize," *The Washington Quarterly*, 35(1) (2011), doi: http://dx.doi.org/10.1080/0163660X.2012.641918

a new, as yet-nascent regional system. This new system-in-formation does not create clearly defined blocs or spheres of influence as existed during the Cold War. Nevertheless, it does pose a far more complicated set of foreign policy options for small and middle powers to shape policy options, not least because China and the United States have to compete with these states and new non-state actors to maintain their status and power.[11]

Modern ROK Foreign Policy Phases and the Rising Complexity of Foreign Policy

The ROK's foreign policy emerged during the hot war of Korea as subordinate to a great power and as a partner in the Cold War that ensued, ensuring the continued division of Korea and the implication of the ROK in the regional dimension of the evolving US-Soviet rivalry. Although the ROK under military rule was never the compliant junior partner often portrayed by pundits at the time, it was not until military rule ended with civilian uprising in 1987 that South Korea began to develop a truly independent foreign policy, with military policy lagging behind due to the integration of the US-ROK military in the Combined Forces Command.

At the end of the Cold War that ensued shortly after the eviction of the military from the Blue House, the ROK developed an independent *nordpolitik* that quickly established a set of fundamental principles for inter-Korean relations.[12] The ROK also took advantage of the brief breakthrough in relations with the DPRK in 1991-92 to negotiate a series of inter-Korean agreements, especially the Basic Agreement and the 1992 Denuclearization Declaration, which became the cornerstone of the ROK's foreign policy in the next two decades.

By this time, it was clear the ROK's competition to match the DPRK's diplomatic presence around the world was no longer of significance and that, in almost all respects, the ROK had won the game for recognition and reputation everywhere that mattered — including in China and Russia, the DPRK's erstwhile allies. Gaining cross-recognition from both in 1991, the ROK was free to pursue much broader foreign policy goals.

---

11   Ranger, S. and Kim, Y.G., *The Balance of Power in a "Complex" Northeast Asia* (Seoul: East Asia Institute, 2012).

12   Lim, D.W., *Peacemaker: Twenty Years of Inter-Korean Relations and the North Korean Nuclear Issue* (Stanford: Shorenstein Asia-Pacific Research Center, 2012). Levin, N.D. and Han, Y., *Sunshine in Korea: The South Korean Debate over Policies toward North Korea* (Santa Monica: Rand Corporation, 2002).

Once the ROK "graduated" from the UN list of "developing countries," abandoned diplomatic competition with the DPRK around the world, and became a UN member state in 1991, it joined the OECD and became a full-fledged diplomatic player on the global stage. The acme of this achievement was the selection in 2007 of former foreign minister Ban Ki Moon to be Secretary General of the United Nations, followed in 2010 with hosting the G20 annual meeting.

Promotion of trade, investment, and financing relations remained an important driver of ROK foreign policy. The ROK began to view itself as an important contributor to peace, security, and prosperity by virtue of its funding and supply of experts who became international civil servants in UN functional and specialized agencies, its own aid program[13] which included an active role in the Organization for Economic Co-operation and Development (OECD) Development Assistance Committee (2009), its role in fielding peacekeeping forces, and even its "soft power" cultural exports.

For much of the 1990s, however, South Korean diplomacy remained consumed by the cycles of cooperation and confrontation with the DPRK over its nuclear weapons proliferation threats and actions and the need to align closely with the United States while maintaining Korean interests in any prospective settlement engineered by its patron ally. The ROK's nuclear diplomacy in response to the DPRK's nuclear proliferation activity attempted primarily to ensure its interests were not subordinated in negotiations between the United States and the DPRK over the latter's nuclear weapons program. An unenviable position for a small state to find itself in, one that led to vacillating hot-cold stances, often in opposition to the policies of its patron state. Relatedly, the ROK sought to enhance its reputation as a non-nuclear state by polishing a squeaky-clean non-proliferation record, but found itself embarrassed by enrichment experiments during the 1990s that transgressed its commitments with the International Atomic Energy Agency (IAEA).

Only when Kim Dae-Jung was elected in 1998 did the ROK shift its foreign policy in a strategic manner — most importantly, by steering enormous investment by South Korean firms into China's economy. This move ensured that the ROK would always be heard in Beijing on how to respond to the DPRK's latest challenge to the legitimacy and policies of

---

13   Chun, H.M., *et al.*, "South Korea as an Emerging Donor: Challenges and Changes on Its Entering OECD/DAC," *Journal of International Development*, 22(6) (2010), doi: http://dx.doi.org/10.1002/jid.1723

the South, while also offsetting the ROK's economic dependency on Japan. Kim Dae-Jung also negotiated the establishment of the Kaesong Industrial Park with the DPRK — the most important arms control measure in Korean history that opened up a cross-DMZ conduit for trade and investment in the DPRK, while breaking the DPRK army's monopoly control of the DMZ itself. The June 2000 summit between Kim Dae-Jung and then-DPRK leader Kim Jong-il set in motion a decade of attempts to engage the DPRK on ROK terms.

At this time, security and foreign policy intellectuals — many of them professors who spent time as ministers in successive administrations — began to examine the ROK's options to move out from under actual or perceived subservience to the United States' interests. The Roh Moo-hyun administration declared that the ROK would position itself to be the "hub" (later bridge) of Northeast Asia serving to connect the powers of the region.[14] The hub concept referred to the notion that the ROK could hasten the integration of Northeast Asia by facilitating exchange and cooperation across borders, and drawing on its economic and cultural power to promote such processes. Faced with American resistance to his pro-engagement posture towards the DPRK, Roh shifted to promotion of ROK free trade agreements and global investment.

Roh's successor, Lee Myung-bak, began to promote an explicit "middle power" diplomacy after 2008 and positioned the ROK to host a series of global events including the G20 and Seoul Nuclear Security Summit meetings. Such convening on global issues was the main achievement of "complex diplomacy" under the Lee administration.[15] The Lee Administration also developed core strategies aligned with global policy agendas in the areas of climate change and sustainability ("green growth") and peacekeeping, while maintaining a hard line against engaging the DPRK. To the extent that this posture employed a strategic logic against ideological drivers aimed at isolating and squeezing the DPRK, it aimed to keep the ROK from becoming embroiled in regional conflicts that could put strain on its relations between the United States and China. It also reflected the increasing complexity of regional and global problems that exceeded the ability of great powers to manage and demanded new and unconventional policies to deal with cross-border and often highly uncertain prospects for solving these problems.

---

14   Lee, S.J., *et al.*, *The Vision of the Korean Peninsula and Territorial Networking Strategies* (Korea Research Institute for Human Settlements, 2009).

15   Lee, S.J. (2012).

To assert its good citizen credentials on these global issues, ROK diplomacy deployed various "soft power" tools to promote the ROK's interests, including the creation of networks, hosting of regional meetings, and "public diplomacy" which aimed to promote the ROK "brand" with overseas audiences. At the same time, the ROK reinforced its alliance with the United States, especially in the aftermath of the 2010 clashes with the DPRK military arising from the sinking of the ROK warship *Cheonan* in March and the exchange of artillery fire in November.

The rise of China, the stalling of Japan's recovery after Fukushima, and the US "rebalancing" of its military forces back to the Asia-Pacific region after the Iran and Afghanistan wars all reaffirmed the value of the ROK to the United States, especially in taking a hard line against the DPRK's nuclear and missile armament and testing. This alignment tightened in 2013 after President Park Guen-Hye's inauguration after her election the previous December. In response to the DPRK's rocket and nuclear tests, the United States conducted simulated nuclear strike bombings in March, and the DPRK issued a series of threats to use nuclear weapons against Seoul and American cities should war break out.

The ROK's room to use middle power brokerage was constrained by the increasing bifurcation of the region around American and Chinese spheres of influence, in spite of clear tensions between China and the DPRK. Thus, the ROK struck a "Strategic Cooperative Partnership" with China at the May 2008 Korea-China summit,[16] a partnership reconfirmed and expanded at the June 2013 Park-Xi summit in Beijing. After 2008, the ROK's attempts to create regional and global networks either convened by the ROK, or including the ROK as a key node, were critical to its ability to "stay in the great power game" as a creative middle power, while steering clear of direct embroilment in regional security issues swirling around the Korean Peninsula, especially as Sino-Japanese relations began to decline rapidly in 2010. The ROK offer to host the Trilateral Cooperation Secretariat in Seoul (which opened in September 2011) is indicative of its aspirations to play a regional middle power role — but little has come of this initiative in terms of modifying the postures of the two "heavyweight" wrestlers in the Japan-Korea-China triangle.[17]

---

16   Snyder, S., "China-Korea Relations: Establishing a 'Strategic Cooperative Partnership,'" *Comparative Connections* (2008). Bodeen, C., "Skorean President in Beijing for Summit with Xi," *Associated Press*, 27 June 2013, http://bigstory.ap.org/article/skorean-president-beijing-summit-xi

17   *Trilateral Cooperation Secretariat Website* (Seoul: Trilateral Cooperation Secretariat), http://www.tcs-asia.org/dnb/main/index.php

This focus on how to maximize the exercise of "middle power" has preoccupied many Korean diplomacy and foreign policy intellectuals since 2009. Their work has concentrated on how the networking theory concepts of positional power and filling structural holes in the network of states and their respective agencies apply to the ROK.

The critical roles that arise due to these networking, rather than power capacity, attributes of the ROK as a middle power include what mediating "broker" roles the ROK could play.[18] Scholars seek to determine whether the structure of regional relationships contain actors largely isolated in "structural holes"; do "weak links" exist with them that can be activated to connect interested third parties who otherwise would remain disconnected from the structural-hole agents?[19] By establishing this connectivity, Songbae Kim notes that the ROK can simply facilitate the mutual flow of information. That is, the ROK can establish communication between the third party and the agent located in a structural hole, or it can add information value — meaning that it can provide a form of translation services that enable the two parties to be "interoperable." That is, the ROK can establish sufficient common codification of meaning for them to coordinate with respect to each other, or, at a higher level of relationship, to facilitate collaboration or the production of a joint value by virtue of recognition and exploitation of compatibility between the two parties.[20] Thus, Kim suggests that, in theory, a networking state can either broker *information* as a connector (enable information to flow) or as a transformer (provide compatibility needed to exchange information). Conversely, he suggests, it can broker *meaning* as a messenger (add meaning needed for information to flow) or as a translator (provide meaning needed for compatibility to be recognized).[21]

Arguably, diplomats use such techniques constantly in the search for common knowledge with adversaries inhabiting a different political culture and isolated from direct reach by virtue of their structural geopolitical location or conflicts. What is new is that small and middle powers may find ways around congealed institutional and geopolitical barriers to facilitate contact with officials of adversary states and to lay the groundwork for

---

18 Kim, S., "Roles of Middle Power in East Asia: A Korean Perspective," in *International Conference on the Role of Middle Power in the 21st Century International Relations* (Seoul: Korean Association of International Studies, 2013). (This publication has since been published as Sangbae Kim, "Roles of Middle Power in East Asia: A Korean Perspective," in *Working Papers: MacArthur Asia Security Initiative* (East Asia Institute, 2014)).

19 Ibid., p. 7.

20 Ibid., p. 8.

21 Ibid., p. 9.

trust-building based on formal and informal networks of communication. The inter-penetration of cultural industries in the region, the high levels of globalization and related technological and economic inter-dependence, and the instantaneous nature of electronic media and networks all devolve capacities to initiate network-wide effects on the image and reputation of a state such as the ROK, and to exert ideational influence on many constituencies simultaneously.

Such "public diplomacy" is a competitive game, but the ROK has been skillful in playing it in Northeast Asia, especially in China, using Twitter, Facebook, and YouTube and even inviting Chinese super-bloggers to visit the ROK.[22] Nonetheless, it is easy to overstate the gains from such state-sponsored attempts to improve reputation and create a networked "attraction" for tourism and trade. Chinese bloggers tend to be critical not only of the DPRK, but also of the ROK for what is often viewed to be its one-sided, partisan interference in China's foreign policy while slavishly supporting the policies and forward-deployment of the United States, the main great power competitor.[23]

Having access to vastly greater resources than civil society organizations, state-based networking initiatives can operate at a far greater scale, bringing together large numbers of influential persons from many different sectors and countries at the same time. The result is the creation of a web of connected persons who form a "resilience" resource at times of stress, one that can crystallize around common positions by virtue of prior contact and shared information and meaning. Such networks must be constructed by a networking middle power[24] through constantly convening meetings and exchanges to weave networks making South Korea increasingly central to how others frame issues critical to the ROK — as occurred in the cases of Jeju Forum and the Asan Institute, outlined below.

Songbae Kim suggests that for a networked state, the network strategy is akin to creating a beehive with many collaboratively constructed cells, rather than a web designed to capture insects for the spider to devour (the great power's diplomatic strategy). Thus, he states, "middle powers seek to

---

22 Yonhap News Agency staff writer, 2013. *What Is PD?* (Los Angeles: Center on Public Diplomacy, University of Southern California), http://uscpublicdiplomacy.org/page/what-pd

23 Gries, P., "Disillusionment and Dismay: How Chinese Netizens Think and Feel About the Two Koreas," *Journal of East Asian Studies*, 12(1) (2012), http://journals.rienner.com/doi/abs/10.5555/1598-2408-12.1.31

24 Kim, S. (2013).

exercise the collective power through cooperative alliances. These alliances are meant for all neighbors to enhance their influence over regional and world politics by collecting and integrating their fragmented capabilities."[25] Likewise, civil society organizations create networks based on shared, differentiated, and rotating divisions of labor to offset each other's strengths and weaknesses and to create a regional capacity that is more than the sum of the parts of each national constitutive element of the network.

However, unlike state-based networks, civil society networks are far less susceptible to politically driven closure by the broker and/or by the agent in a black hole at times of increasing tensions, that is, at exactly the time when they are most needed. In short, they are resilient networks from the viewpoint of sustained communication, cooperation, and collaboration. Finally, rather than promoting a unified or singular state-originated view, transnational civil society networks create new, shared, often hybrid images of the future and common knowledge that transcend the national and generate a truly cosmopolitan identity for participants in the network. Universal values of shared humanity guide these images rather than the national interests of a specific state.

Moreover, the level at which the ROK state deploys networked middle power strategies and the goals it pursues are different to those of civil society networks that either drive urgent specific-issue campaigns to motivate and mobilize constituencies or seek to realize long-term, value-based common futures. Thus, official ROK networked strategies have aimed at positioning the ROK to broker information related to the DPRK as a structural hole, while framing the DPRK issue for third parties at the same time. Songbae Kim suggests the ROK could also attempt to bridge territorial conflicts between China and Japan, or even to help the United States and China moderate their relationship, although he admits that the latter goal may exceed the ROK's networking capacity.[26] In this aspect of the exercise of networked state power, what matters is the ROK's ability to promote norms and value-based diplomatic strategies that moderate the raw exercise of power based on military or economic assets. Constructivists in academic political science have long argued that this approach boils down to creating "habits of dialogue." These habits lead to routinized interactions, patterns of dependable cooperation in low politics spheres (for example, pollution control or coast guard coordination), or collaboration to create value where none existed before (for example, airline routing agreements to reduce

25   Ibid., p. 16.
26   Ibid., pp. 15-16.

fuel costs, or standardized railway and port container technology). These efforts cannot displace big powers, but they can induce them into enduring institutional frameworks that may moderate their unilateral actions and increase the influence of small and middle powers in negotiated outcomes.[27]

Since 2000, ROK civil society has also effectively connected disparate players to address urgent nuclear, social, and ecological security issues in the DPRK. Unlike ROK official attempts to broker or interpret the DPRK as a policy issue for states, autonomous civil society actors were able to circumvent or overcome barriers to communication and cooperation with DPRK counterparts without imposing a particular interpretation of the nature of the adversary (the DPRK). To some extent at least, civil society's networking strategy succeeded (as is evident in the case studies in the next section). Conversely, to the degree to which civil society organizations insisted on the prior imposition of meaning (for example, imposing political recognition conditionality on such communication with the DPRK by ROK autonomous entities such as UNESCO-ROK, as occurred in the case of proposing dialogue on the DMZ Peace Park),[28] it failed.

Moreover, the networking roles of civil society organizations diverge considerably from the networking goals of official ROK foreign policy agencies. In addition to the specific convening and maintenance roles, regional civil society networks require careful integration of asymmetric civil society agents in each country, as we explain in the next section of this chapter.

States do not attempt to create sustained trans-boundary issues or trans-local networks in this manner. To some extent, however, the ROK has encouraged local governments and cities to construct enduring networked collaborations based on complementary economic capacities — as in the case of the Busan-Fukuoka cross-border cooperation described below.

And, as was suggested in chapter 2, the "multiplexity" of social networks whereby participating agents can draw on more than one type of associational commonality at a time over a given link with another agent endows civil society networks with a vastly superior reach. Civil society networks are inherently and instantly reconstituted, and are far more flexible and responsive than simple networks supporting large

---

27 Ibid., pp. 16-17.
28 Lee, S.H., "A New Paradigm for Trust-Building on the Korean Peninsula: Turning Korea's DMZ into a UNESCO World Heritage Site," *The Asia-Pacific Journal*, 35(2) (2010). Jeon, S.W., *et al.*, "Policies on Conservation of the DMZ District Ecosystem," *Environmental Policy Bulletin*, 5(1) (2007).

organizations such as states that share only a few common interests or attributes. In this regard, civil society networks are like swarming immune systems whereas state-based complex networked strategies are more rigid, skeletal structures.

The Limits of ROK State-Centered, Complex Diplomacy

Even within diplomatic circles, not everyone is convinced the ROK should pursue a "middle power" complex networked strategy and attempt to "box above its weight." Some diplomats argue that the foreign policies of states should not be defined by the relative hierarchy of power. Instead, it should be based on their ability to solve shared global problems according to their capacity — an approach used in the 1992 climate change treaty negotiations known as "common but differentiated responsibility," something that may be combined with subsidiarity (the European principle of devolving implementation to the lowest competent level of social organization).

Along the same lines, rather than relying on military alliances, middle powers such as the ROK should join and promote multilateral institutions with global scope, recognizing that the main measure of great power for realists — military force — is largely irrelevant to the solution of most global problems. Finally, rather than conceptualizing and propagating strategies for others to follow, the ROK should figure out the best way for it to contribute to the resolution of global problems, and lead by doing.[29]

However, the difference between official "complex networked middle power diplomacy," as it has been termed, and the strategy of civic diplomacy is not merely one of relative efficacy of focusing on global versus regional concerns, or of a more or less independent diplomacy. Nor does it rest on whether the ROK's Ministry of Foreign Affairs and Trade (MOFAT) "complex diplomacy" includes non-state actors and civil society (it does). The core distinction between a state-based networking and a civil society-based networking strategy is more fundamental, and it presents ROK foreign policy with a far greater challenge than is recognized in its current concept of "complex diplomacy."

At stake is the underlying moral basis or legitimacy of the ROK's foreign policy. Historically, ROK foreign policy has put national interest (or often a truncated form of national interest in the shape of narrow corporate

---

29   Fujita, E.S., "Middle Power Diplomatic Strategy of Brazil and Policy Recommendations for South Korea's Middle Power," in *The Third Roundtable Discussion for Middle Power Diplomacy* (Seoul: East Asia Institute, 2013).

interests) first rather than the realization of human or ecological security. This approach cannot resolve genuinely interconnected and complex global problems. Such problems demand that states implement shared solutions based on cooperation — which is not easy to achieve when national interests clash. Thus, when it comes to global problems, it is crucial to be guided by core values and to apply moral legitimacy to foreign policy rather seek to benefit short-term, often-narrow interests — as Joseph Nye argued in relation to the attractiveness of soft power versus military and economic power.[30] Often, it is bottom-up non-state actors, especially local governments and civil society, who insist that this moral element guide foreign policy. Combining their impulse with the traditional "hard power" basis of realpolitik and adding the "smart power" of complex diplomacy may constitute and be termed "new public diplomacy." The different elements of public diplomacy are often in tension with each other, but may be far more potent than traditional diplomacy when aligned (See Table 6.1).

Table 6.1: Traditional, Complex, and Civic Diplomacy

	Traditional Diplomacy	Complex Public Diplomacy	Civic Diplomacy
Actor	State	State + Non-State Actors	State + Non-State Actors including Local Governments
			(Network State/Civic State)
Goals	Strength and Wealth	State-Based Strength, Wealth, Collective Security System	People's Security and Ecological Security
		(limited issue linkage)	(Climate Change, Pandemics, etc.)
Strategy	Competitiveness, Balance of Power	Competitiveness, Balance of Power	Mutual Respect and Cooperation
		+ Cooperation, Mutual Living	
Tool	Hard Power	Smart Power (Hard+Soft) and Network Power (NGOs, Media)	Networked Smart Power (Hard+Soft) and People's Power

---

30   Nye, J., *Soft Power: The Means to Success in World Politics* (New York, United States: PublicAffairs, 2004).

In traditional usage, public diplomacy refers to the management of "external" public perceptions of a nation as orchestrated by a state.[31] In the 21st century, the obvious role of non-state actors of all kinds in influencing perceptions of significant constituencies and social movements that could affect, challenge, or even overthrow states implies the need by states to mobilize such non-state actors in an integrated national "public diplomacy" strategy. This led to the establishment, for example, of the US State Department's Undersecretary for Public Diplomacy and Public Affairs in 1999. This office defines its mission as "informing and influencing foreign publics by expanding and strengthening the relationship between the people and Government of the United States and citizens of the rest of the world."[32] This "new public diplomacy" relies heavily on non-state actors, but it retains state and national security as the primary goal of public diplomacy.

The diplomatic strategies and foreign affairs concerns of non-state actors may overlap, but may also diverge substantially from those of specific states. By definition, transnational civil society organizations cannot be subordinate to the public diplomacy foreign affairs strategies of a single state and do not participate in "public diplomacy" (although constituent national nodes might). It is therefore necessary to select a term that encompasses the independent foreign policy orientations and diplomatic activities of non-state actors working across borders, whether they engage states, market entities, or other civil society organizations. We chose "civic diplomacy" to reflect the civilian status of non-state actors; their commitment to "civility," or universal norms and values in the UN Charter and international law (to distinguish them from un-civil non-state actors such as transnational organized crime or transnational terrorist networks); and the implied commitment to a locale, city, or community that is the ethical call of citizenship.

The ROK government's complex public diplomacy attempts to mobilize (and sometimes reign in) domestic non-state actors, but mostly these non-state actors are organizations linked to the state such as the Korean Trade-Investment Promotion Agency (KOTRA). They also include large

---

31   *What Is PD?*

32   *Under Secretary for Public Diplomacy and Public Affairs* (Washington, DC: United States Department of State), http://www.state.gov/r/

corporations intimately tied to the national government by a web of personal and commercial transactions. They seldom include city governments or local governments in their list of non-state actors. In short, complex diplomacy is a truncated version of the full potential of networked civic diplomacy that exploits the full capacities for cross-border activities of civil society and local governments in the ROK. Indeed, civic diplomacy puts city and local governments at the forefront of foreign policy along with civil society organizations, including transnational religious organizations, in place of governments and corporations.

The rest of this chapter examines the structure and roles whereby networked civil society organizations contribute to the solution of complex, interrelated global problems, and the challenges that this approach presents to ROK foreign policy. The history of regional civil society organizations stretches back to at least the 1970s in Japan, the ROK, and China. It accelerated in the 1990s due to the emergence of ROK civil society after the end of the military dictatorship in 1987 and the end of the Cold War, which opened many possibilities for trans-border communication and cooperation in the region. These early efforts by ROK civil society organizations contributed to regional human rights networks, to the removal of nuclear weapons on forward-deployed American warships and bases in the ROK and Japan, and to various anti-colonial and anti-pollution struggles in the region, especially in the island states of the Pacific.

Moreover, we will argue that ROK civil society systematically developed regional and global networking strategies in the late 1990s, partly in response to the DPRK nuclear challenge and partly due to the rise of the ROK economy to global status. At the same time, as global and regional problems accelerated and became far more challenging at the end of the Cold War, so the same globalization processes that fractured and displaced local communities and sometimes whole nations demanded networked responses that only civil society organizations could supply — not states or corporations. Thus, it is noteworthy that the long-lasting networks we will examine below were not initiated by the ROK state as part of its foreign policy. Instead, the networks had roots outside of the state, often well before the rise of official complex diplomacy, and, because of this disparate origin, they frequently have the stamina to operate across borders for decades whereas diplomatic strategies may fade after a few years.

Regional and Local Civil Society Networks and Complexity

Just as the ability of states to undertake middle-power "networked" strategies is rooted in regional history and context, so are the strategies arising from civil society in Northeast Asia. In Japan, civil society is most advanced in its key characteristics of autonomy, social capacity, and ability to supply critical services either uniquely or more efficiently than the state or the market sector. On foreign policy and security issues, the institutions of the central state are largely insulated from direct participation by most Japanese civil society organizations, although a set of elite private institutions serve as think tanks, sounding boards, holding shelves, and gatekeepers to the external world. In many respects, the most critical aids offered by Japanese civil society to collaborative problem-solving by regional civil society networks are financial and technical resources to sustain long-term efforts in partnership with sister organizations in China, Japan, the ROK, Russia, Mongolia, and even the DPRK.

In the ROK, civil society organizations are still nascent and recovering from decades of military dictatorship. Consequently, their membership is weak, endowing them with relatively small resources compared to their Japanese counterparts. They also tend to revert to large-scale, mass mobilization based on oppositional stances rather than undertake routine, policy-oriented work in alignment with state agencies or corporations. The structural bipolarity arising from South Korea's electoral system (winner takes all), the strong presidential office, and the lack of checks and balances in the state and judicial systems make it difficult for civil society to develop strong representational and policy roles.[33] As the leadership of civil society organizations and of governments both often originate from universities, individual intellectuals often keep lines of communication open between the state and civil society organizations through school and military graduation cohort networks which bypass formal institutional hierarchies.

In China, civil society organizations are either mass-based or local associations sanctioned by the Chinese Communist Party, central state ministries, or proto-nongovernmental associations with limited autonomy from the central authoritarian state.

---

33   Choi, J.J., "The Democratic State Engulfing Civil Society: The Ironies of Korean Democracy," *Korean Studies*, 34 (2010).

From these asymmetric, uneven capabilities in each country, civil society organizations in Northeast Asia have cobbled together many issue-based networks. Rizal Sukma and James Gannon have documented how civil society organizations in the region have responded to five urgent regional security threats: piracy, disaster relief, human trafficking, health, and climate change.[34] These mature networks stand in contrast to the weak early capacities of emerging civil society in the region at the end of the Cold War.[35] Each participating organization has strengths it can lend to offset the weaknesses of others in the course of creating vibrant transnational networks, as shown in Table 6.2.

Table 6.2: Civil Society Strengths and Weaknesses in Northeast Asia

	Strength	Weakness	Contribution to Transnational Civil Society
Japan	Local revitalization, autonomy, resources	Access to media and policy makers	Trans-local cooperation, partnerships with local governments
ROK	Social movement mobilization, personal connections with officials	Policy engagement of state agencies	Issue campaigns
China	Intellectual contribution, ability to work with government agencies, policy makers	Distance from local proto-NGOs	Green models of sustainability
			Limited ability to circumvent central government controls by concert with local agencies in ROK or Japan

---

34 Sukma, R. and Gannon, J., *A Growing Force: Civil Society's Role in Asian Regional Security*, ed. by Sukma, R. and Gannon, J. (Tokyo: Japan Center for International Exchange, 2013).

35 Yamamoto, T., ed., *Emerging Civil Society in the Asia Pacific Community: Nongovernmental Underpinnings of the Emerging Asia Pacific Community* (Tokyo: Japan Center for International Exchange, 2006).

In chapter 2, we argued that civil society networks offer distinct *networking* capacities that overlap but are not the same as those available to states such as the ROK. Civil society-based organizations use networks for many reasons, including to:

- Create sustained relationships with counterparts trapped or hidden inside structural holes, who are otherwise incommunicado due to isolation or partisan alignments, and build bridges between those living in a structural hole and third parties with whom no other connectivity exists (for example, between the United States and the DPRK).

- Activate "weak links" in times of crisis to reduce tension or to communicate key information or common knowledge that enables decision-makers to avoid inadvertent escalation or to find ways to resolve the crisis. This ability rests on relationships with counterparts in structural holes; but these relationships must be based on trust to work and, in turn, require time and investment to establish, nurture, deepen, and activate them when needed. That is, although weak or even inactive for long periods, these links are long-term and are not available in crisis if they are not already well established.

- Exploit the "small world's effect" whereby information is communicated instantly and precisely due to direct connectivity instead of passing via many nodes or layers of culture and organization, degrading the information and slowing its transmission.

- Supply "missing link" information that is otherwise unknown to enable decision-makers to correctly interpret the situation prevailing in a "structural hole" in a timely manner on a critical and urgent issue related to crisis avoidance or management, or to enable dialogue to occur at times of crisis or high tension.

- Inspire distributed participants across borders with a common vision, understanding, or shared image of the future, which serves as a guide to concerted but distributed action. The networks thereby create an epistemic community based on common understanding and shared discourse, including cross-generational and cross-cultural lessons and norms to guide future orientations on key issues dividing nations and peoples.

- Mobilize large numbers of individuals and propagate an interpretation of current events by social media, mass media, and direct communication using virtual means with key players in many organizations by simultaneously swarming in very large numbers either on the ground or virtually (for example, social media events in China).[36]

- Identify multiple pathways or solution strategies that can be implemented separately or jointly to ensure that fallbacks exist when tension increases or failure occurs in one strategy — that is, to realize complex, multiple solutions at the same time, as opposed to the operation of singular, sequential, problem-solving strategies.

- Convene key players to address specific problems without a central command authority, to implement joint strategies relying on distributed coordination capacities, and to deliver solutions in the absence of states — especially in disaster relief and humanitarian crises.

- Anticipate possible discontinuities and radical failures of institutions or state agencies and develop adaptive strategies that increase resilience in the face of uncertainty, especially by creating multiple pathways to solve the problems that are in play simultaneously.

Although they are often referred to as the "third" sector — defined in part by what they are not, non-governmental and not-for-profit, as much as by what they are, individual and community associations based on universal values of peace, security, and sustainability — genuinely autonomous civil society organizations do not exist in isolation but are intimately interwoven and commingled with state state-based agencies and with market-sector entities, primarily corporations. In addition to exhibiting the network attributes outlined above, civil society organizations fulfill societal roles in which they have proven to be efficient and often far more equitable in their delivery of services than states or corporations. Viewed functionally, networked civil society organizations can realize the following:

- Address simultaneously many peace, security, and sustainability issues in detail and on a highly disaggregated basis, thereby creating a new diversity of social responses that supplements and sometimes supplants the relatively limited repertoire of big state and market based organizations, adding resilience to the societal response to complexity.

- Provide early warning of local developments — disasters, conflicts, and less challenging surprises such as cross-border crimes, epidemic

---

36 Hayes, P. and Cavazos, R., *Internet Events, Social Media and National Security in China*, NAPSNet Special Reports (Berkeley: Nautilus Institute, 2013).

breakouts, etc., where the first signals of a cascading or avalanching event are obscured by the noise of routine events.

- Hold governments and corporations accountable for routine and crisis performance by demanding transparency, by monitoring and reporting implementation, and by "flaming and shaming" rule-breakers by swarming on the Internet (or mobilizing supporters at the street level).

- Mobilize resources contributed by private citizens on a massive scale, sometimes exceeding that of governments in response to disasters such as earthquakes and tsunamis.

- Develop and advocate for constructive policies to be adopted by governments, state agencies (such as climate change policies or policing policies related to human trafficking) and for corporations (such as codes of conduct and certification schemes).

- Deepen public understanding and support for value-based policies via publicity, outreach, and education programs.

- Facilitate mutual learning and rapid diffusion of innovation across borders and sectors, in part by encouraging "open source" non-profit and self-organizing replication of solutions and methods by partner civil society organizations.

- Provide technical assistance and expertise to implement direct (for example, humanitarian assistance to refugees or survivors of wars or natural disasters) or contracted (government food assistance) aid programs, or to build local capacity by training and providing funds and equipment (for local development or environmental projects).

- Participate directly in governmental delegations to international conferences and meetings, or advise corporations directly in the revision of their strategy and standards.

- Innovate in terms of lifestyles, technology, and hybrid identities that enliven communities and build bridges across borders of all kinds.

In the next section, we describe this combination of networked structures and functions in six ROK-initiated cross-border networks.

ROK Transnational Civil Society Networks

The explosive growth in global and local civil societies, and the emergence of a new global consciousness since the end of the Cold War, precipitated the creation of transnational networks and nascent cosmopolitan communities centered on civil society. The antecedents of this conjunction stretch back to the early 20th century, as documented by the Union of International Associations. Although states have continued to accrete power and influence, they have also become dependent upon civil-society and non-government-driven network strategies to succeed in solving cross-border problems, especially complex global problems.

Although a "latecomer" to civil society in Northeast Asia and the Pacific due to rentier-landlord and then military-dominated governments that from 1953-87 were antithetical to endogenous civil society, and before that, to war and colonial rule, the ROK has demonstrated it can originate leading regional transnational civil society networks that are oriented towards addressing global problems. Here, based on interviews and recently published studies, we present six case studies on South Korean civil society's latest efforts to confront global issues through transnational networks.[37] We conclude by reviewing the implications that civil society-oriented network initiatives have for the official "complex diplomacy" state-centric network strategy described earlier in this chapter.

New Discourse, New Policies: South Korea in the Era of Globalization

Few Asian-Pacific countries have leaders who are more supportive of a "global" agenda than the ROK.[38] South Koreans in all sectors welcome the prospect of further globalization. In spite — or perhaps partly because of — the regressive nature of the DPRK, as well as the desire to position itself as a convening state high in the ranks of developed countries, the ROK has been exceptionally willing to bear the financial burden of hosting events of transnational importance like the Summer and Winter Olympics, the FIFA World Cup, and the G20 Summit. Furthermore, South Korea's burgeoning civil society and non-governmental sector have begun to play an increasingly vital role in constructing transnational networks and utilizing them for solving global problems that manifest in, or originate

---

37 This section is based on an unpublished report for the Nautilus Institute by Jungmin Seo, Steven Denney, and Christopher Green, prepared in 2013. The fourth case, the Jeju Forum, was written by Peter Hayes with assistance from Hyung-taek Hong of the East Asia Foundation.

38 For one recent example, see Yonhap News Agency staff writer, "S. Korea to Conduct Worldwide Survey on National Image," *Yonhap News Agency*, 28 July 2013, http://english.yonhapnews.co.kr/news/2013/07/28/0200000000AEN20130728000900315.html

from, the wider Asia region. However, this development did not happen overnight.

The ROK's modern history is marked by several critical junctures and transition periods. Among them, the decade following the end of the Cold War is of great importance, especially when it comes to understanding the contemporary political and social landscape. The end of the bipolar world order fundamentally changed the way all countries perceived themselves vis-à-vis others. Because the ROK was on the ideological frontline during the Cold War, the impact of its end was great although the Peninsula remained divided. During the Cold War and South Korea's developmental period, security concerns dominated public discourse and policy. Talk of global issues advocacy, such as human rights, was seen as seditious and harmful to development, ergo the national interest, and was discouraged by the authoritarian government in Seoul.[39] However, with the fall of the Berlin Wall, the overthrow of the military regime in 1987, the democratic transition in the late 1980s, and the rise of progressive administrations in the late 1990s, an enormous shift began as to the dominant focus of ROK public affairs. Although military and geopolitical security remained important, the social and political discourse was largely "de-securitized."[40] The shift is illustrated in the way perceptions of the DPRK changed during the Kim Dae-jung and Roh Moo-hyun administrations (1998-2008). The DPRK became, for the most part, just another country.[41]

At the same time, the ROK state also began to re-position South Korea's economy within the new global capitalist system and post-Cold War Northeast Asia. With roots in the liberalization policies of President

39   Chaihark, H., "Human Rights in Korea," in *Human Rights in Asia: A Comparative Legal Study of Twelve Asian Jurisdictions, France and the USA*, ed. by Peerenboom, R., *et al.* (Abingdon: Taylor & Francis, 2006), pp. 265-97.

40   De-securitization of discourse is an ongoing process and is by no means complete. This point is made, among other sources, in Schattle, H. and McCann, J., "The Pursuit of State Status and the Shift toward International Norms: South Korea's Evolution as a Host Country for Refugees," *Journal of Refugee Studies* (2013), doi: http://dx.doi.org/10.1093/jrs/fet003. The shift in discourse is also reflected in the way people and the government understand "security threats." See Denney, S., "The Public Sphere in South Korea: Kim Young-Hwan on the National Security Act," *Sino-NK*, 26 September 2012, http://sinonk.com/2012/09/26/the-public-sphere-in-south-korea-kim-young-hwan-on-the-national-security-act/

41   The normalization of North Korea in the eyes of the people and policymakers alike is a point made throughout Moon Chung-in's book on the positive effects of the Sunshine Policy on North-South relations. Moon, C.I., *The Sunshine Policy: In Defense of Engagement as a Path to Peace in Korea* (Seoul: Yonsei University Press, 2012).

Kim Young-sam (commonly referred to as *saegyehwa*), South Korea began to diversify its international trading relationships and to rebrand itself regionally. Following what some have called its middle power strategy,[42] South Korea concluded Free Trade Agreements (FTAs) with the European Union and the United States and entered into FTA negotiations with other major trading partners such as Australia and China. In addition to its network-based trading strategy, South Korea also initiated the "New Asia Initiative" (NAI) in 2008, a regional policy aimed at more substantive engagement with the countries of Northeast Asia, especially those of ASEAN.

The NAI, announced during a presidential visit to Southeast Asia in early 2009, best reflects the government's efforts to rebrand and reposition the country. The initiative claims three major objectives: (1) increasing ODA contribution to Asian countries; (2) enhancing regional trade ties through the expansion of Korea's FTA networks and other means; and (3) fostering stronger inter-regional ties to address global issues more effectively, such as global warming and disaster management.[43] As noted earlier in this chapter, via regional strategies such as the NAI, the ROK attempted to posit itself as the region's "honest broker," or "bridge," between the major and minor powers as well as the developed and developing countries.

This state-centric model of complex diplomacy and middle power strategy was effective in expanding the scope of the public sphere and was prescient in its attempt to set in motion a networking strategy that positioned the ROK to design innovative solutions to regional problems in the first decade of the new millennium. However, this state-based networking model of middle power proved insufficient when it came to implementation. Although the state has been eager to portray itself as concerned with global issues such as climate change, such concerns in the ROK have been primarily a reaction to bottom-up pressure from an emerging civil society.[44] As will be illustrated in the case studies that follow,

---

42   For a discussion of South Korea's Middle Power status and strategy, see Mo, J., *Middle Powers and G20 Governance* (Basingstoke: Palgrave Macmillan, 2013).

43   Hwang, B.Y., "Korea: A Model for Southeast Asia?," *The Diplomat*, 17 April 2012, http://thediplomat.com/2012/04/korea-a-model-for-southeast-asia/. Ministry of Foreign Affairs and Trade, *Introduction to New Asia Initiative* (Seoul: Korean Ministry of Foreign Affairs and Trade, 2009).

44   See Chung, S.-Y., "Climate Change and Security in East Asia: Mapping Civil Society Organizations' Contributions," in *A Growing Force: Civil Society's Role in Asian Regional Security*, ed. by Sukma, R. and Gannon, J. (Tokyo: Japan Center for International Exchange, 2013).

by working through transnational networks, South Korean civil society has been more effective in stimulating long-term, transformational change at a regional level than through state-based strategies. Whether these networks will endure or be replaced by new ones remains an open question, however. Civil society in the ROK is still young and relatively underdeveloped, and many of its regional and cross-border initiatives continue to rely on the ingenuity and drive of individuals. As we shall see, it remains uncertain whether civil society-led movements can survive the loss of their driving thinkers, their "lone wolves."

The rest of this section examines six case studies to show how ROK non-governmental organizations (NGOs) and other institutions are both working through and actively creating transnational networks for the purpose of solving global problems. The first case study depicts the networked civil society response, led by South Koreans, to respond to and supplant regressive Japanese history textbooks by producing the 2005 book *A History to Open the Future*. The second case study looks at how South Korean non-governmental organizations addressed deforestation and food scarcity in Northeast Asia, especially in China and North Korea. The third case study examines the critical role played by the "Refugee Aid Network" in the passing of South Korea's Refugee Act, the first independent national refugee law in Asia. The fourth case study reviews the networking experience of a private initiative, the Jeju Peace Forum, and its evolution from a network focused on a peace initiative to solve the North Korea problem into a multi-issue network of networks. The fifth case study traces the creation and influential intellectual role of the East Asia Institute. The sixth case study explores efforts by the most recent of these civil society initiatives — the Asan Institute for Policy Studies — to build global networks and the implications such efforts have for global community building and cosmopolitanism.

Following this excursion across historical terrain, we conclude with a summary of the key findings from the case studies on Korean civil society networks, the role of inter-city collaboration across national borders, and the implications of civil society-oriented network strategies for the ROK's state-centric, networked complex diplomacy strategy.

Case Study 1: A History to Open the Future

In the previous section, we noted that civil society organizations are adept at activating otherwise inactive or weak links in social networks. When weak links are activated or strengthened, civil society can go beyond the creation of common knowledge. It can inspire a common vision and understanding of the future based on a shared discourse drawn from mutual learning that spans many generations. By using networks skillfully, civil society is able to mobilize large numbers of people to promote strategies or solutions to urgent problems. No clearer example of this capacity — and its relative advantage compared to slow, ineffective, and politicized state agencies — may be found in Northeast Asia than the work of the Japanese-Chinese-Korean Committee for Common History Teaching Materials of the Three Countries. This Committee produced the landmark history textbook, *A History to Open the Future*, written in Japanese, Korean, and Chinese and published in May 2005.[45]

The significance of this contribution emanating from civil society can be understood in light of the immense weight of history in Northeast Asia. This legacy includes many centuries of Chinese hegemony, two centuries of Western imperialism, Western and Japanese colonial occupation, and more than a decade of regional and world war, related sexual slavery, and concentration camps. It also includes the immolation of whole cities by fire bombing, the annihilation of cities by nuclear bombing, atrocities committed by the militaries of all states in the region upon their own people as well as subjugated populations, full-scale civil wars, externally imposed national divisions, political and military dictatorships, political assassinations, and the use of terror and surveillance to control populations. Capping this legacy was four decades of Cold War and the threat of nuclear annihilation.

Much of this history occurred in living memory. The scale, frequency, and international nature of these horrific events increased with the accelerating expansion of the territorial scope and integrative political, economic, and military capacities of imperial and non-imperial nation-states in Northeast Asia. Thus, historical dimensions of national and personal identity are increasingly intertwined with the twin themes of cruelty and irony, the victimization of and by the other (especially the outsider). Today, historical memory contributes to the complexity of international affairs in the region at every level. It is one of the most critical dimensions of regional affairs,

---

45 Japanese-Chinese-Korean Committee for Common History Teaching Materials of the Three Countries, *History to Open the Future* is published as follows. In Korean, "한중일 3국공동역사편찬위원회," Hanibook, May 26, 2005, at: http://www.hanibook.co.kr/ In Chinese, "东亚三国的近现代史(修订版)," Social Sciences Academic Press, Beijing, June 19, 2005, at: http://www.ssapchina.com/ In Japanese, "東アジア3国の近現代史," Kôbunken, Tokyo, 2005, at: http://www.koubunken.co.jp

affecting as it does subjective and national identity in ways that make Northeast Asia more of an anti-region than a nascent regional security community. Every aspect of this violent history is contested, often from multiple angles. Even the meaning of the bombing of Hiroshima and Nagasaki in August 1945 is fractured. For many Japanese, these bombings were such a radical rupture with the past that they represented a new crime against humanity that must never be repeated, whatever prior atrocities led to the attacks.[46] For many Americans, the conventional narrative is that the bombings caused Japan to surrender, thereby ending the Pacific war. For many Koreans — thousands of whom perished in the two explosions due to their impressments into Japan's war effort — it was a deserved punishment for decades of cruel oppression of Korean independence movements.[47] For millions of Chinese, it was a welcome event that signified the end of Japanese imperialism, but it also portended a new external threat once the country was unified under Communist Party rule in 1949.[48]

Because history shapes national identity and individual attitudes, states invest in official histories and, in many instances, oversee and approve the production of school textbooks through which official narratives and core values are inculcated into each generation of students.[49] This long tradition of official and dynastic history in China, Korea, and Japan has its modern equivalent in European and North American states. However, in many regions of acute conflict, states have managed to produce jointly shared histories, including textbooks that have nurtured political and cultural reconciliation between many former warring states and their peoples. Textbook revision is the subject of considerable intellectual and pedagogical effort in many post-conflict contexts.[50]

46   Morris-Suzuki, T., *The Past within Us: Media, Memory, History* (Brooklyn: Verso, 2005).

47   Hayes, P., "Wonpok," in *Pacific Powderkeg, American Nuclear Dilemmas in Korea* (Lanham: Lexington Press, 1991).

48   Harrison, H., "Popular Responses to the Atomic Bomb in China 1945-1955," *Past & Present*, 218 (Supplement 8) (2013), doi: http://dx.doi.org/10.1093/pastj/gts036

49   Wang, Q.E., "Remember the Past; Reconciling for the Future: A Critical Analysis of the China-Japan Joint History Research Project (2006-2010)," *The Chinese Historical Review*, 17 (2) (2010), doi: http://dx.doi.org/10.1179/tcr.2010.17.2.219

50   Pingel, F., *UNESCO Guidebook on Textbook Research and Textbook Revision* (UNESCO, 2010), http://unesdoc.unesco.org/images/0011/001171/117188E.pdf. Cole, E.A. and Barsalou, J., *Unite or Divide?: The Challenges of Teaching History in Societies Emerging from Violent Conflict*, Special Report (Washington, DC: United States Institute of Peace, 2006). Kim, S., "International History Textbook Work from a Global Perspective: The Joint Franco-German History Textbook and Its Implications for Northeast Asia," *Journal of Northeast Asian History*, 6 (2) (2009). Schneider, C., "The Japanese History Textbook Controversy in East Asian Perspective," *The ANNALS of the American Academy of Political*

In Northeast Asia, official sponsorship of history textbooks has generated hostility and mistrust because they are viewed as a litmus test of the extent to which former aggressor states recognize that past colonial and imperial policies and actions, such as conducting wars, occupying neighboring states, and condoning atrocities, were wrong and must never be repeated. Thus, official and private attempts in Japan to whitewash its military atrocities in Korea, China, and Southeast Asia are monitored closely and evoke powerful responses at the state and societal levels. In turn, these scars on the collective historical memory exacerbate strongly nationalist responses that overwhelm efforts to create a shared basis for aligning states and societies to communicate, cooperate, and collaborate to solve common problems. As Chung-in Moon and Seung-won Suh state, "Simply because most countries in a given region are usually afflicted with the fractured pain of the past, identity and collective memory are crucial variables in forging shared values and common goals vital to the formation of a 'community of security.' It is virtually inconceivable for nations to engage in cooperative practices without first healing the pain and then recognizing and respecting the identity of others."[51]

The Japanese Society for History Textbook Reform produced a revisionist history that denied the sexual slavery of comfort women and the occurrence of the Nanjing Massacre. When the Japanese Ministry of Education approved it for use in Japanese schools in 2001, it triggered a strong reaction from the region. Of the many countervailing efforts, those arising from civil society are particularly significant in that they broke new ground, both intellectually and politically, in the production of shared history in the region.

The origins of this effort stem from a 1992 declaration signed by South Korean, Chinese, and Japanese universities in Yokohama calling for a joint review of history textbooks. This eventually led to the creation of the "Asian Educational History Network" in 2001 that began, in 2002, to collaborate with the "Korean Civilian Movement for Correction of Japanese Textbooks," in turn leading to the formation of the "Joint Japanese-Korean Organization of Historical Research." In March 2002, the Asian Network and the Joint Organization in addition four other Chinese, Japanese, and South Korean organizations convened the "Forum for historical awareness and peace in

and Social Science, 617(1) (2008), doi: http://dx.doi.org/10.1177/0002716208314359
51   Suh, S.-W. and Moon, C.I., "Burdens of the Past: Overcoming History, the Politics of Identity and Nationalism in Asia," *Global Asia*, 2(1) (2007).

East Asia" in Nanjing and initiated the trilateral textbook project.[52] Japanese participants proposed the joint production of a multinational history and, supported by scholars from South Korea and China, established committees immediately leading to a meeting in Seoul in August 2002. The trilateral history writing committee had 53 members (17 from China, 13 from Japan, and 23 from South Korea — mostly professors or scholars from national research institutes, although teachers participated from South Korea and Japan).[53] All acted in a private capacity, and no official support was received for the eleven meetings that took place to revise the text three times before it was published in 2005 (on May 26 in South Korea, May 27 in Japan, and June 9 in China).[54]

Instead of tracing separated national trajectories, *A History to Open the Future* was organized around the interactions of the three countries, arguing the "three countries possess profound geographical and historical ties that cannot be severed."[55] It is written in six chapters, each of which focuses on these interactions, starting with the opening of ports, the arrival of Western intrusion, and the response of each country to this integration into the global system of domination and exploitation.[56] The book covers the entire period of the Japanese occupation of Korea and China, the Pacific War, the Korean War and national division, and the Cold War up to recent diplomatic and treaty recognition of interstate relationships between South Korea, Japan, and China. It not only transcends typical one-sided victor-victim narratives, it also adopts a reflective narrative that suggests structural causes of tragic conflicts. To avoid an over-emphasis on structure, it highlights the suffering of ordinary people in all three countries throughout these historical events. An epilogue outlines seven issues judged critical for building peace and a shared future in the region: compensation to victims of aggression, the

---

52   Babicz, L., "South Korea, Japan, and China: In Search of a Shared Historical Awareness," in *6th Biennial Conference of the Korean Studies Association of Australasia* (Sydney: University of Sydney, 2009).

53   This section draws on Wang, Z., "Old Wounds, New Narratives: Joint History Textbook Writing and Peacebuilding in East Asia," *History and Memory*, 21(1) (2009).

54   "Truth Can Never Be Distorted, the History Compiled by Three East Asian Countries, an Interview with Zhu Chengshan," *Xinhua News Agency*, 5 July 2007, http://www.js.xinhuanet.com/xin_wen_zhong_xin/2005-07/05/content_4569047.htm

55   Japanese-Chinese-Korean Committee for Common History Teaching Materials of the Three Countries, *A History That Opens the Future — Unauthorised English Language Translation* (Washington, DC: Memory and Reconciliation in the Asia-Pacific, George Washington University), http://www.gwu.edu/~memory/issues/textbooks/jointeastasia.html

56   Ibid.

comfort women, history textbooks, the Yasukuni Shrine, youth exchange, peace and citizen movements, and reconciliation and peace-building in Northeast Asia.

The preface notes: "While there were numerous occasions during the three-year preparation when our views differed, we were able to reach a common historical understanding through dialogue and discussion, and we succeeded in publishing this book simultaneously in three countries." The most difficult issues were the number of Chinese killed by the Japanese military in the Nanjing Massacre in 1937-38, sexual violence and comfort women, and Japan's use of poison gas in China.[57] Thus, rather than suppress divergent views, the writing team attempted to find sufficient common ground based on comparative and jointly authored multinational research of a type pioneered in Europe since World War II.[58] This approach was almost unknown in Northeast Asia, where national and bilateral official history projects mostly reinforced existing views and led to more recrimination rather than mutual learning and reconciliation. Nonetheless, the authors left some contentious issues alone. For instance, who started the Korean War, and what was the role of the Chinese Communist Party in the war against Japanese imperial forces? Much remains unaddressed on trilateral relations among the three countries, not to mention the introduction of North Korean, Southeast Asian, and other views on the history of Northeast Asia.[59]

Of course, such an immense non-governmental scholarly effort over three years did not emerge in isolation. First, starting in the mid-1990s, conservative Japanese scholars attacked the portrayal of "comfort women" in Japanese textbooks as biased and undocumented.[60] The first public declaration by a Korean comfort woman occurred in 1991, and the political campaign for Japan to compensate comfort women from many countries, but especially from China and South Korea, expanded thereafter. In 1996, the Japanese Society for History Textbook Reform announced it planned to publish its *New History Textbook* for junior high schools in 2002, attacking

---

57 Wang, Z. (2009), p. 112.
58 Pingel, F., "Old and New Models of Textbook Revision and Their Impact on the East Asian History Debate," *Journal of Northeast Asian History*, 7 (2) (2010).
59 Yi, K., *et al.*, *Development Model for the Increased Cooperation for Northeast Asian Social Culture Exchange: A Network Based on Peace, History and Knowledge (in Korean)* (Seoul: National Research Council for Economics, Humanities and Social Sciences, 2006).
60 Nozaki, Y. and Selden, M., "Japanese Textbook Controversies, Nationalism, and Historical Memory: Intra- and Inter-National Conflicts," *The Asia-Pacific Journal*, 24-5-09 (2009).

existing textbooks for their portrayal of comfort women and the Nanjing Massacre. The stimulus for this attack was the increasing profile of comfort women following Kim Hak-Soon's public testimony in 1991. Diverse civil society groups had made sporadic but very active campaigns to demand an apology from the Japanese government and compensation for the victims, starting with the Asian Solidarity Conference on Japanese Military Sexual Slavery Issues[61] held in Seoul in 1992.[62] Thus, civil society, rather than states, repositioned the comfort women issue as a question of living history in the present, not one of a closed past, and it demanded accountability for these official crimes.

Second, South Korean and Japanese national leaders recognized only top-level direction could reconstitute the relationship between the two former enemy states, the antagonism of which worked against the grain of ever increasing economic and cultural integration. In May 1995, the then-Prime Minister of Japan, Murayama Tomiichi, apologized personally for the colonization and invasion of Korea.[63] This act became an opportunity for joint historical research between South Korea and Japan with Professor Choi Sang-ryong (Korea University) and Professor Masao Okonogi (Keio University) as the Korean and Japanese representatives, respectively. The co-research on topics of history, politics, economics, culture, and North Korea was carried out between 1996 and 1998 with support from the Japan-Korea Cultural Exchange Fund and the Korea-Japan Cultural Foundation. The findings were published in fifteen volumes between 2001 and 2010 both in Korea and Japan.[64]

---

61 The Asian Solidarity Conference was held in Seoul in 1992 led by Professor Yun Chung-ok, Ewha Women's University, from the Korean Council for the Women Drafted for Military Sexual Slavery by Japan. Participants of the 1st Asian Solidarity Conference, "The Joint Resolution of the First Asian Solidarity Conference on Military Sexual Slavery by Japan" (1992).

62 The timeline of the movement against sexual slavery is given the Korea Chongshindae's Institute (in Korean) at: http://www.truetruth.org/know/know_04.htm

63 When Prime Minister Abe's denial of the Kono talks and the definition of invasion according to Prime Minister Murayama were questioned, Murayama confronted Abe's statement by saying that "invasion" could be defined as when Japan enters another country by military force when issues such as the comfort women become problems of historical concealment. Jeong, N.-K., "Former Japanese Prime Minister Criticizes Abe's Remarks," *The Hankyoreh*, 21 May 2013, http://www.hani.co.kr/arti/english_edition/e_international/588357.html

64 The 15 volume results of this comparative scholarly research was published by Ayeon Press in Korean and Japanese as the Japan-Korea Joint Study Series and are found in Korean at: http://asiaticresearch.org/front/board/list.do?board_master_seq=4162

This high-level engagement with history continued in 1998 when President Kim Dae-Jung and Prime Minister Obuchi Keizo announced the "New 21st Century Korea-Japan Partnership."[65] This statement supported and encouraged the necessity of the joint historical research. After Fusosha Publishing released their new conservative Japanese history textbook in 2001, the Korean and Japanese heads of state agreed to support joint research on both countries' history in October that year. The official Japan-South Korea Joint History Research Project was established in March 2002 and held forty-five subcommittee meetings and six joint meetings in Tokyo and Seoul over three years. However, the outcome of this official process was limited mostly to reaffirming divergent historical perspectives on critical historical issues dividing the two countries.[66] Ultimately, the government-led research could not overcome virulent nationalism to produce a shared history that could serve as a basis for a common approach to the future.

One metric of success is that the denialist *New History Textbook* almost completely failed to achieve its goal of ten percent usage in Japanese schools. In contrast, although not actually a textbook, *A History to Open the Future* sold well in all three countries, with over quarter of a million sales by 2006. The book was not only read widely, but it also stimulated a campaign starting in August 2004 in which local civic activists in South Korea and Japan developed sister-city campaigns to put pressure on Japanese education officials to refuse the *New History Textbook*. This campaign began in 2005 when Japanese civic groups visited South Korean sister cities. They focused on Japanese cities that had close ties to twelve South Korean cities including Seoul, Anyang, Jeonju, Jeongeup, and Daegu. Twenty South Korean civic groups and fourteen Japanese groups participated.[67] According to Yang

---

65   Restoration of ROK-Japanese diplomatic relations occurred in 1965 but was limited to political, diplomatic and economic levels. The movement of citizens and cultural exchange started in 1998 with the talks between President Kim and Prime Minister Obuchi. This declaration, which had 11 articles and 5 additional points, served as a turning point for future Korean-Japanese relations.

66   Dyun, D.K., "S. Korea, Japan Inch Closer to Shared Perception of History," *Yonhap News Agency*, 23 March 2010, http://english.yonhapnews.co.kr/national/2010/03/23/24/0301000000AEN20100323004800315F.HTML

67   For a description of the solidarity movement between cities of Korea and Japan for the campaign against the selection of Japanese new history book see Asia Peace and History Education Network, "Look at the History of That Obligation for Future Generations!," *Asia Peace and History Education Network Blog*, 11 May 2001, http://yespeace.tistory.com/2

In Suginami-ku in Japan, civil groups also made statements against the decision of the board of Education in Suginami-ku's to adopt the New History Textbook, which are found (in Japanese) at: http://www.ne.jp/asahi/kyokasho/net21/seimei050812.htm

Mi-Gang, who was one of the leaders of the campaign, in some sister cities such as Seocho-Gu (Seoul, South Korea) and Suginami-Ku (Tokyo, Japan), Anyang and Saitama, Korean Assemblymen or city councilors visited Japan to plead personally against its adoption, and Korean and Japanese civic groups also visited the Board of Education to press against its selection.[68] As a result, the Fusosha textbook's selection rate only achieved a 0.4 percent uptake by schools in Japan. Thus, civil society mobilization resulted in a successful countervailing and shared history on the one hand and blocked Japan's most vehement denialist history on the other — a major achievement for transnational civil society networks in Northeast Asia at the time.

Of course, the history battles continue unresolved. But *A History to Open the Future* established a standard that will endure of an open-ended history, of a multinational historical text that is amenable to reflection and revision based on mutual research and dialogue, and can serve as the foundation for common memory — in turn, the basis for the formation of community.[69] In this regard, the rapidly evolving civil society networks that activated the issue campaigns and produced a shared history served a visionary role that transcended the constrained ability of governments to come to terms with divided memories. Ultimately, visionary leadership and official recognition at the level of states[70] will be needed to overcome the vicious effects of denialist attempts to revise history textbooks — sometimes termed "weapons of mass instruction" — while respecting that fissures and silence run through all knowledge and that histories can never fully capture the past, only its residual meaning in the present.[71]

Case Study 2: Forestry and Agriculture

Trans-boundary environmental issues are among the most pressing problems afflicting Northeast Asia. They are also among the most difficult to address due to their transnational nature. The sovereign state system in Northeast Asia (and elsewhere) is not conducive to resolving complex transnational issues of this sort. At the same time, environmental problems

---

68 Yang, M., *Talks of History in Civil Society for the Reconciliation of East Asia, Transcending Boundaries of Historical Perspectives in East Asia* (Seoul: Asia Peace and History Education Network, 2008).

69 Wang, Q.E. (2010), p. 219.

70 Pingel, F. (2010), p. 23.

71 Morris-Suzuki, T. (2005).

do not recognize state borders. The most powerful nation-state cannot resolve even one of the many global and regional environmental problems afflicting the region, let alone all of them at the same time.

China, Japan, the Korean peninsula, Mongolia, and the Russian Far East form a single ecological "unit."[72] Within that unit, any activity undertaken by one actor affects the whole region as a matter of course. No single actor can unilaterally make the region ecologically sustainable. Trans-boundary environmental issues are many in number and include:

- The Russian Far East is a zone of high biodiversity that links with habitats in Korea, China, and Mongolia, but it is also the transit point for a vast trade in endangered species, as well as a lumber extractive industry that threatens the biodiversity that sustains the region. Denuded land on the margins of China's deserts throws vast amounts of sand into the westerly wind each year, swathing the two Koreas and parts of Japan in a thin blanket of noxious dust each spring. This yellow sand has grown in scale since the late 1990s, and scientists agree that it is getting more serious.[73]

- China's rapidly growing use of fossil-fuelled vehicles and fertilizer is increasing the already high levels of acid rain that cross borders and is deposited on the two Koreas and Japan (as well as on much of Northeast China) with deleterious impacts on forests, ecology, and even urban structures.

- The shared maritime coastal region of the Sea of Japan/East Sea of Korea and the Yellow Sea/West Sea of Korea remain afflicted by climate-induced surface sea temperature rises and a change from more to less valuable species, as well as threatened by oil spills and past radioactive waste dumping.

- In the middle of this region of environmentally deleterious yet compellingly dynamic economic activity is North Korea. The nation-state perpetually threatens to tip itself and the broader region into instability through its failure to guarantee the minimum food security of its population. This lack of food security stems from poor agricultural decisions over decades, acidified soil, moribund machinery, shortages of fertilizer, fuel, and spare parts,[74] and its inability to trade exported goods and services for food imports.

72 Park, D.K., interview with Denney, S. (July 22, 2013).
73 "Yellow Dust Be Gone-Thanks to Youth Groups," *Nature's Crusaders*, 7 November 2009, http://naturescrusaders.wordpress.com/2009/11/07/yellow-dust-be-gone-thanks-to-youth-groups/
74 "Interview with Denney, S." (July 2013, 2013). Further information: Bates, M., "Growth Prospects and the Potential for Progress in the DPRK's Agricultural Sector: Infrastructure and Incentives," *Sino-NK*, 23 June 2013, http://sinonk.com/2013/06/23/

To break these vicious downward spirals, the region badly needs integrated and transnational solutions. Yet doing so necessitates first overcoming political tensions that exist between the states in the region.

Fitting Farming and Forestry into the Bigger Picture

In the words of Tom Morrison, an agronomist with decades of experience dealing with agricultural issues in North Korea, the need for building trust between peoples "is where trees and agriculture fit into the bigger picture."[75] Farms and forests are "truly transnational" and intrinsically apolitical; moreover, sustainable yields make good economic sense. Those who exploit forests can extract short-term gains, but only by foregoing far greater benefits over time. Key figures in South Korea who have driven environmental conservation activities in Northeast Asia for the last two decades understood this basic tradeoff earlier than many others and had the motivation, ideas, and financing to do something about it.[76]

In 1989, the South Korean democratization process yielded freedom of foreign travel for all South Korean citizens via the *yeohaeng jayuhwa jochi* (Travel Liberalization Measure). This laid the foundations for nascent South Korean civil society to enter the broader region. However, it was not until financial disaster enveloped the South Korean economy in 1997 that the focus shifted to a second phase of forestry resource management in South Korea (the first being the community reforestation or Saemul movement in South Korea during Park Chung Hee's military rule). Forestry was chosen during this period of economic contraction, driven by the goal of economic recovery after the financial crisis. The government asked civil society groups to help initiate this movement. Forests for Life (FFL) was launched in March 1998 as part of this job creation strategy. The money was from the state, the action was civilian, and the link between the two was the Korea Forest Service. The objective was to spread out the closely planted trees in South Korea's ill-managed forests to expand overall forest coverage threefold and raise the value of the resource, thereby combining social, economic, and ecological objectives.[77]

growth-prospects-and-the-potential-for-progress-in-the-dprks-agricultural-sector-infrastructure-and-incentives/
75   "Interview with Denney, S." (July 2013, 2013); ibid.
76   Park, D.K., "Interview with Denney, S." (July 22, 2013).
77   Ibid.

FFL embodied the vision of Moon Kook-hyun, then-CEO of Yuhan-Kimberley.[78] Under his 13-year leadership, Yuhan-Kimberley initiated the "Keep Korea Green" movement in the 1980s, creating one of the first corporate social-environmental responsibility campaigns in the ROK. Moon went on to pursue the creation of domestic, forestry-based civil society networks. He sought out expertise to bring his goals to fruition, teaming up with Professor Lee Don-koo of Seoul National University and Dr. Park Dong Kyun, then employed by a private forestry company. By combining the financial resources of South Korean commerce with civic drive and the administrative resources of state, FFL drove not only the adoption of forestry as an important element in domestic policy, but it also envisioned a transnational network encompassing the entire region.[79]

Inaugurated on November 24, 1998, the Northeast Asian Forest Forum (NEAFF) was one of the earliest fruits of this vision, one that systematically tapped into the potential of the new domestic forestry movement for moving to a transnational format. NEAFF became a vehicle for connecting forestry networks in Mongolia (MOFF) and China (CFF), led by partner entities from the Institute of Geoecology of Mongolia and Beijing Forestry University respectively. International forestry networks in Northeast Asia would not have come into being so rapidly had it not been for this South Korean leadership. Partner organizations flourished, in particular MOFF (Mongolia Forest Forum), directed by Russian-speaking forestry scientist Dr. Jamsram Tsogbaatar. With South Korean civil society leaders serving as network conveners and activating weak links in these nascent networks when needed, a transnational network emerged that coordinated distributed activities and led to new forms of collaboration at a regional level.

South Korean leadership and funding expedited the creation of the network and incentivized its initial growth. According to Dr. Park Dong Kyun,[80] 70 percent of the operating cost of NEAFF came from Yuhan-Kimberley, some from government sources, and much of the remainder from "Korean firms with an interest in forests," including steel giant

---

78 "6년만에 기업인으로 돌아온 문국현 '한솔섬유 히든챔피언 만들겠다," *Hankyoreh*, 4 July 2013, http://www.hani.co.kr/arti/economy/economy_general/594451.html

79 Park, D.K., "Interview with Denney, S." (July 22, 2013). In a follow-up exchange, Dr. Park reaffirmed this dream, explaining, "It started with Forests For Life, then for North Korea there was Forests For Peace, and for China and Mongolia NEAFF was established."

80 Ibid.

POSCO, Korean Air, and Hyundai Motors. Without Mr. Moon and Drs. Lee and Tsogbaatar, not to mention Dr. Park himself, the network would not have been intellectually possible. Equally, without South Korean social and financial capital, the network would not have emerged, at least not as effectively.

Another outgrowth of this passionate transnational community, Forests for Peace (FFP), reflects the same origins and dependency on a South Korean convening node. However, in attempting to facilitate reforestation in the DPRK, FFP confronted the political and military realities of the division of Korea. The DPRK was always leery of dealing with a ROK-based civil society organization such as FFP. The emergence of an actively hostile inter-Korean relationship following the election of President Lee Myung-bak in late 2007 and a number of North Korean acts of violence, at Mt. Geumgang in 2008 and in the West Sea during 2010, made it impossible to continue FFP's small-scale reforestation projects in the DPRK. This is a tragedy because, as Park and Moon wrote in 2004, the DPRK urgently needs a forestry and agricultural revolution, and thus "it is desirable to establish an international cooperation network for the reforestation of [North Korean] forest. The NGO movement in Korea is still in its infancy and therefore must be nurtured with broader public participation."[81]

The inability to inspire a revolution in North Korean environmental best practice is just one way that South Korea's potential as a civil society leader and global honest broker is coming under threat. China is also emerging as the new dominant player in civil society movements in the modern age, a role borne of overwhelming financial strength.[82] According to Dr. Park, "South Korea is interested in Northeast Asia for its environmental impact on Korea, Japan is interested in Southeast Asia for its logging potential, but China is interested in everywhere."

The story of this network is not yet complete. The DPRK's reforestation officials have been aware of the deficits of its reforestation efforts since the early 1990s, facing as it does a shortage of raw materials, fertilizer, seed stock, and intense acid rain from China, which especially in winter afflicts seedlings planted on shaded slopes. In 1999, the DPRK embarked

---

81   Following up on his 2004 comments, Dr. Park noted during a follow-up exchange on July 29, 2013, "I believe that NGOs are not in their infancy now, rather they are in a stagnant period, and more active movement is needed."

82   Many of the movements led by Chinese entities are also close to the state, and do not reach the internationally accepted definition of a civil society organization.

on a participatory agro-forestry pilot project, sending expert study tours to Thailand (2003), China (annually from 2004-2010), and Nepal (2010).[83] The pilot project was funded by Swiss aid agencies and involved a partnership of the Academy of Forestry Sciences, State Academy of Science, Land Use Planning Institute, Central Forestry Designing and Technical Institute, Wonsan University of Agriculture, and Kim Il Sung University. The Kungmin Institute of Botany and the Chinese Academy of Science also sponsored the training of DPRK forestry scientists in the project from 2009-11. Other players include the World Agroforestry Centre in Bogor, Indonesia and the Consultative Group on International Agricultural Research.

To what extent FFP (and other small-scale reforestation projects in the DPRK) helped to prepare the DPRK Ministry of Land and Environmental Protection to explore the potential for agro-forestry — and vice versa — is unknown. The pilot project involving eighty-seven plots in north Hwanghae province began in 2004 and was first evaluated only in 2011. However, the chances are that these two cross-border bridges reaching at the same time into the "structural hole" of North Korean reforestation institutions jointly facilitated the flow of information, funds and materials that assisted local authorities to test new approaches to the reforestation of the DPRK's denuded mountain slopes. This case, however, illustrates a general point about the role of civil society networks. Creating multiple channels that enable solutions to complex problems in a structural hole such as the DPRK may create a synergistic effect inside the hole, and also provide resilience in case one channel becomes blocked.

Case Study 3: Refugees

More than half of all international refugees worldwide originate in just five countries: Afghanistan, Somalia, Iraq, the Syrian Arab Republic, and Sudan. As a result, the burden of supporting a high percentage of them falls predominantly on countries that are geographically adjacent to these sources. Most Afghan refugees are in neighboring Pakistan or Iran, for example, while most Somali refugees are in Kenya to the south or Ethiopia to the west. However, refugees fleeing a handful of particularly vicious or protracted conflict situations are only part of the story.

---

83   Xu, J., *et al.*, "Participatory Agroforestry Development for Restoring Degraded Sloping Land in DPR Korea," *Agroforestry Systems* (2012), doi: http://dx.doi.org/10.1007/s10457-012-9501-0

In a 2012 report on global trends, the United Nations High Commissioner for Refugees (UNHCR) pointed to no fewer than 7.6 million people newly displaced by conflict or persecution in just one year and the creation of more than a million new refugees.[84] Many acknowledge the year 2012 as exceptional in the context of new refugees and internally displaced persons, but the high figures only add fresh urgency to the issue of 45 million refugees or displaced persons worldwide. Moreover, UNHCR data reveals the existence of more than 35 million people deemed worthy of concern, implying immense potential for global instability due to refugees and IDP flows. South Korea does not appear to be an important actor in this particular arena. The country is currently home to a statistically insignificant proportion of the existing refugee total (487 according to the UNHCR report cited above) and has just 1,548 outstanding asylum-seeker cases (in stark contrast, Germany has more than 85,000, and France almost 50,000).

Nevertheless, the government in Seoul is acutely aware of the latent potential for instability that is inherent in this global issue. UNHCR statistics understate South Korean involvement in refugee issues because they do not take into account the constant trickle of refugees fleeing from North Korea. UNHCR treats North Korean refugees as non-statistics because they automatically receive South Korean citizenship — whether or not they reach the ROK (due to Chinese policies, statistics on these flows of people from China do not distinguish between economic migrants and refugees from the DPRK). Refugees arriving from the DPRK are also eligible for substantive resettlement funding and other state assistance such as housing. Thus, North Koreans arriving in South Korea are privileged compared with refugees elsewhere.

Moreover, North Korean citizens who wish to resettle in South Korea have to transit through at least one, and usually three, countries en route, turning the problem into a much larger one that crosses several national borders. Most North Koreans attempt to reach Thailand, which has both a positive relationship with the ROK government and a well-established system for processing incoming North Korean refugees and sending them onward to Seoul. Other countries in the region are relatively more ambivalent toward the new arrivals, as evidenced by the 2013 case of a

84   United Nations High Commissioner for Refugees, "New UNHCR Report Says Global Forced Displacement at 18-Year High," 19 June 2013, http://www.unhcr.org/51c071816.html

group of nine young North Koreans deported back to the DPRK through China by the government of the Laos People's Democratic Republic.[85] In these transitions, refugees from the DPRK live in a twilight zone of uncertainty. All these issues present the outward-looking ROK state with a major foreign policy challenge in coping with these refugee flows. At the same time, South Korean civil society is also actively crossing borders to address the severe human rights problems experienced by refugees from the DPRK.

Bottom-up Change: South Korean Civil Society and the Refugee Act

In its last plenary session of 2011, South Korea's National Assembly passed the "Law on the Status and Treatment of Refugees" (Refugee Act hereafter). It was the first national refugee and asylum seeker law passed in Northeast Asia.[86] As such, it indicates the extent to which South Korea has positioned itself to deal with refugee flows in the region. The passage of the Refugee Act was the cumulative effect of several interacting forces: the pressure towards convergence from international institutions and norms; the South Korean government's commitment to a "global" agenda; and, most significantly, bottom-up pressure from Korean civil society working in tandem with domestic legal organizations and international institutions through domestic and regional networks. The law does not relate to DPRK defectors or their UNHCR status (North Koreans are covered under the entirely separate Act on the Protection and Settlement Support of Residents Escaping from North Korea).

In the latter half of the 20th century, as South Korea's export-oriented industrialization and favorable trading relations began paying huge dividends, South Korea found itself quickly approaching the threshold that divides newly industrialized countries from fully developed countries. As a country more concerned with its global image than others, international norms and the roles associated with developed countries have, arguably, a greater impact on South Korea's domestic and foreign policies than in other countries. In September 1991, Korea became a United Nations member state

85 Reuters Staff Writer, "U.N. Fears Nine North Korean Defectors Sent Home by China," *Reuters*, 31 May 2013, http://www.reuters.com/article/2013/05/31/us-mhh-korea-north-rights-idUSBRE94U0GM20130531

86 Kim, C., "A Step Forward to Refugee Protection? South Korea's New Refugee Act," *Oxford Monitor of Forced Migration*, 2(1) (2012).

and shortly thereafter joined the 1951 UNHCR Refugee Convention, which defines refugees and their rights. In 1996, South Korea ascended the ranks of the world's most developed countries when it joined the Organization for Economic Co-operation and Development. In its quest for international recognition as an "advanced" country,[87] South Korea began to portray itself as a country concerned with humanitarian assistance to refugees. In 2000, South Korea became a member of the UNHCR Executive Committee of the High Commissioner's Programme, an international body comprised of member states with an "interest in, and devotion to, the solution of the refugee problem."[88]

South Korea's economic ascent and its successful efforts to improve its position within international and regional networks represent the backdrop against which the Refugee Law was passed. A state-centric, top-down perspective shows a global Korea whose elites are concerned with addressing this important transnational issue. Such a view, however, would be misleading and obscures the instrumental role played by civil society organizations and other non-governmental institutions in bringing about this policy shift. Although government and political elites may be sensitive to the ROK's reputation, they are not nearly as concerned with ground-level implementation as civil society organizations. Indeed, politicians and officials are often constrained by broader political and strategic concerns. In their research on Korea's progress as a host country for refugees, Hanns Schattle and Jennifer McCann find that change occurred bottom-up. "The main thrust of national-level policy change," they wrote, "has come from South Korea's vibrant civil society." Indeed, after signing of the Refugee Convention, "the government did nothing to advance its position on refugees at home."[89]

South Korea's rhetoric-policy disconnect is similar to Japan's contribution-policy divide, known alternatively as "checkbook diplomacy." In 2011, Japan contributed more than $200 million to the UNHCR, yet its refugee policies were (and remain) woefully regressive

---

87   The word used in Korean for "advanced country" (*seongjinkuk*; 선진국) is better understood as an aspiration for Koreans: a source of motivation rather than something that can be achieved.

88   Hankyoreh, "S. Korea Becomes First Former Aid Recipient to Join OECD Development Assistance Committee," *The Hankyoreh*, 26 November 2009, http://english.hani.co.kr/arti/english_edition/e_editorial/389918.html

89   Schattle, H. and McCann, J. (2013), p. 10.

by international standards.[90] In South Korea, the small number of asylum seekers that are granted refugee status highlights the divide between real implementation and official policy. Since granting the first refugee status in 2001 to an Eritrean, the process of application for refugee status has been prohibitively cumbersome, slow, and inefficient.[91] Thus, rather than the ROK government's commitment, it was, according to Schattle and McCann, the "mounting pressure by lawyers and activists who have taken an interest in advocating for refugees as well as other segments of the country's growing migrant population by drawing on international human rights law" that pushed the ROK to accept refugees.[92] It is precisely where the ROK's realpolitik conception of national interest meets with international laws and norms and bottom-up pressure from South Korean civil organizations that the potential lies for South Korea to emerge as a leading actor in a complex transnational network.

Two South Korean networks address the issue of refugees: one mainly domestic and oriented towards national-level priorities, and the other regional in scope. The "Refugee Aid Network," a loose association of refugee support and public interest legal advisory groups, represents the domestic network. This network was responsible for writing and submitting the original Refugee Act legislation to the National Assembly. Sometimes referred to as the "Refugee NGO Network," this association of non-governmental activists and human rights lawyers began meeting informally once a month in 2006. Built on the early efforts of Lee Ho-taeg, founder of *Refugee pNan*, and his close associates Choi Won-geun, one of the founders of the refugee advocacy group NANCEN, and Kim Hee-jin, former director of Amnesty International (Seoul office), most of the civil and legal organizations involved early on were associated with refugee advocacy through personal contacts. The group would eventually come to include Hwang Pill-kyu, a public interest lawyer in Gong-gam who was largely responsible for writing the refugee bill, and Kim Jong-chul, another public interest lawyer who founded Advocates for Public Interest Law (APIL).[93]

90 United Nations High Commissioner for Refugees, *Asylum Levels and Trends in Industrialized Countries – 2012* (Geneva: United Nations High Commissioner for Refugees, 2013).

91 Um, J.W., "Refugees Still Not Cared for with New Law on the Way," *The Hankyoreh*, 20 June 2013, http://www.hani.co.kr/arti/english_edition/e_international/592578.html

92 Schattle, H. and McCann, J. (2013), p. 3.

93 Lee, H.T., interview with Denney, S. (July 17, 2013).

In the formation of an "informal networked community," personal relationships and associations outside institutional frameworks are often more important in South Korea than in other countries. However, by the end of 2007, the loose association of activists and lawyers had become a recognized, semi-formal network that eventually included both conservative and progressive civil society groups, in addition to the National Human Rights Commission of Korea, the Ministry of Justice, and Assemblyman Hwang Woo-yeo (the Refugee Act's sponsor in the National Assembly). In other words, a civil-society network strategy had succeed in institutionalizing the Refugee Aid Network — a notable feat for a civil society better known for its militant street-mentality and highly contentious relationship with the government. Although most of the network is constituted by domestic organizations, the various civil and legal organizations in the Refugee Aid Network work closely with Amnesty International, UNHCR, and the National Human Rights Commission of Korea. In fact, when the drafting of the new law began in 2009, the UNHCR, at the request of civil and legal groups in South Korea, provided advice and detailed comments on ways the bill could be improved.[94]

The second network is the Asia Pacific Refugee Rights Network (APRRN), headquartered in Bangkok. Founded in 2008 at the first Asia Pacific Consultation on Refugee Rights (APCRR) in Kuala Lumpur, the APRRN is a regional forum through which 116 civil society groups from 21 different Asian Pacific countries (including the UK and the US) meet to exchange ideas and information and partake in mutual capacity building and joint advocacy efforts. In addition to conferences and meetings, APRRN members are given the opportunity to receive specific legal and medical training and apply for logistical and travel support.[95] Korea has eight member organizations in APRRN, six of which are currently, or were at some point in the past, also members of the Refugee Aid Network. Through the APRRN network, civil organizations can network with other regional member organizations — or with civil society groups from the same country. In fact, the APRRN network helped strengthen the Korea-centered Refugee Aid Network.

---

94   United Nations High Commissioner for Refugees, *UNHCR's Comments on the Republic of Korea 2009 Draft Bill on Refugee Status Determination and Treatment of Refugees and Others* (Geneva: United Nations High Commissioner for Refugees, 2009).

95   *Asia Pacific Refugee Rights Network* (Bangkok: Asia Pacific Refugee Rights Network), http://www.aprrn.info/1/

According to Lee Ho-Taeg, regional and thematic working groups within the APRRN were central to its organizational networking. He credits the East Asia Working Group — a regional working group comprised of civil society organizations from South Korea, Japan, Thailand, and Hong Kong — with "giving Korea a sense of responsibility." Although the East Asia regional working group did not directly support the Refugee Aid Network's drafting and submission of the Refugee Act, they indirectly aided their efforts by "setting expectations for the Korea network and thus holding us [the Refugee Aid Network] to account."[96] Before the passage of the Refugee Act, one such regional working group meeting took place in September 2010 on the campus of Yonsei University in Seoul, South Korea. With support from the Toyota Foundation, members of the East Asia Working Group, the director of legal studies at Yonsei University, the Representative of UNHCR Korea, and other core members of the Refugee Aid Network met to report on the status of refugee protection in East Asia and the role played by civil society in promoting the rights of refugees. Further efforts at network building have occurred since then. In August of 2012, the APRRN hosted the "Fourth Asia Pacific Consultation on Refugee Rights." With a scope going behind the regional working group level, this conference brought together specialists from all over Asia.[97]

According to Lee, it was these sorts of meetings that strengthened the Refugee Aid Network's resolve and made it clear to the South Korean members that, given their structural and network position, they would be the ones taking the lead within the regional network.[98] Outside of South Korea, the exact composition and layout of the refugee network is far less clear. What is evident is that through the APRRN network, particularly the regional working group, bridges are being built and, through working group meetings, structural holes in the legal fabric of global refugee support are being overcome. Although it is difficult to pinpoint the location and time when weak ties between two networks help facilitate the connection between hitherto-unconnected members, it is certain that key contacts in the South Korea network regularly share information and coordinate

---

96   Lee, H.T., "Interview with Denney, S." (July 17, 2013).
97   "4th Asia Pacific Consultation on Refugee Rights Concludes," *Asia Pacific Refugee Rights Network*, 30 August 2012, http://www.aprrn.info/1/index.php/news/123-4th-asia-pacific-consultation-on-refugee-rights-concludes
98   Lee, H.T., "Interview with Denney, S." (July 17, 2013).

strategies with their counterparts in Japan, Hong Kong, and other regional countries.

The functions of the APRRN and the Refugee Aid Network provide some measure of the extent to which South Korean civil society has aided the creation of and actively engaged in transnational networking to address the issue of refugee flows in South Korea and the broader region. Whereas these networks remain focused on a specific topic and are comprised of a number of small non-governmental organizations and legal groups within South Korea, other civil society organizations deliberately employed networks to build a broad regional and global community across a range of connected problems and solutions. These include the Jeju (formerly Peace) Forum, founded in 2001; the East Asia Institute, created in 2002; and the Asan Institute for Policy Studies, a uniquely positioned and well-funded think tank in the ROK, founded in 2008.

Case Study 4: Jeju (Peace) Forum

The Jeju Peace Forum is a good example of a multi-sectoral network initiated by private actors (scholars, universities) in partnerships with local government attracting support from the central government. It is also a good example of a ROK-led ideational network that promulgated a regional vision and process of change aimed at supplanting the prevailing security policies that dominated the Cold War.

The intellectual entrepreneurs behind the forum exploited opportunities for creative diplomacy in Northeast Asia at the end of the Cold War. In 1991, Mikhail Gorbachev visited Jeju, eschewing a visit to Seoul, and established diplomatic relations between the ROK and former Soviet Union. In the same year, Korean political scientist Moon Chung-in floated the idea in *Jemin Ilbo*, a local Jeju newspaper, that the Island should become a "hub of peace" similar to Geneva in the modern era. This idea took root the following year when *Jemin Ilbo* and a group of Jeju-based scholars (including Professors Choong-seok Koh, Koh Sung-joon, Yang Yeong-cheol, Kim Bu-chan, and Yang Gil-hyun of Jeju National University) began to advocate that Jeju should become an "island of peace" — an idea adopted in 1993 by the Jeju Provincial Assembly. In the nineties, a number of high-level visitors came to Jeju — China's president Jiang Zemin in 1995, for example, followed by US President Bill Clinton a year later for a US-Korea summit with ROK president Kim Young-sam. However, little systematic process ensued in

Jeju itself to support this role other than providing a conducive meeting place.

The historic June 2000 summit in Pyongyang between the two Korean leaders, Kim Dae-Jung and Kim Jong-il, raised hopes that inter-Korean relations could move forward towards ever-greater rapprochement and integration, and through a process of constructive dialogue and actual integration lead to transformational but peaceful change in the DPRK. Many cooperation agreements on sports, culture, public health, economic cooperation, and separated families, for example, were set in motion at the summit, and a series of implementation meetings were held in both Koreas. A number of the most important ministerial talks were held on Jeju Island in September 2000, including the special envoys meeting, the defense ministers meeting, and the third ministerial talks.

Jeju was chosen in part for its beauty, but also for its long history as a crossroads and independent province willing to negotiate peaceful outcomes rather than fight wars. This reputation is deeply engrained in Jeju's population. Without any direction from the central government, Jeju farmers donated thousands of tonnes of tangerines and carrots to the DPRK from 1998-2002.[99]

The big question after the Kims' Summit was how to capture this momentum and translate it into enduring habits of dialogue and cooperation between the two Koreas. An additional challenge for the ROK government was how to engage and even embrace the DPRK while managing American opposition to any dealings with the DPRK. The election of George W. Bush in December 2000, who viewed the DPRK as a rogue state and Kim Jong-il as a "pygmy," heralded the United States' adoption of a policy of "strategic neglect" towards the DPRK. The American posture collided head-on with Kim Dae-Jung's strategy, as well as that of his successor elected in 2003, Roh Moo-hyun. Indeed, due to the Bush Administration's opposition to engagement of the DPRK, inter-Korean relations froze.

One of Jeju's exports to the mainland was the security intellectual Moon Chung-in. Born and raised in Jeju, Moon graduated from the elite Yonsei University and after studying for advanced degrees at the University of Maryland, spent a decade teaching international relations and political economy at American universities. Distressed by the inability of the United

---

99   Ko, S.J. and Kang, K.H., "Assessing Inter-Korean Relations: Achievements, Setbacks and Prospects — in Relation to the Contribution of Jeju," in *2nd Jeju Peace Forum* (Jeju: Jeju Peace Institute, 2002).

States to resolve the DPRK issue during the Clinton Administrations, he returned to South Korea and rapidly rose in the academic hierarchy to become Dean of the Yonsei Graduate School of International Studies. As an advisor to Kim Dae-Jung, he attended the 2000 summit — one of only two scholars to do so (the other was Lee Jong-seok, who became Unification Minister during the Roh Moo-hyun government).

He was uniquely placed to connect his policy advisory role with Jeju Province, supported by his Yonsei and international networks. In 2000, Moon proposed to then-Jeju Governor Woo Geun-min that the provincial government convene the Jeju Peace Forum. Woo asked Yonsei to organize the forum along with the Jeju Development Institute. Woo was eager to establish Jeju as an international actor in its own right, thereby attracting visitors and business to Jeju by virtue of its peaceful reputation as well as its sheer beauty.

The first Jeju Peace Forum held on June 15-17, 2001 was, according to Moon, "convened partly to commemorate the first anniversary of the North-South summit and partly to enhance the status of the Jeju Island as an island of peace."[100] Moon conceived the Forum as a multi-layered, transnational process to conceptualize and implement a unique peace process to end the Korean conflict, and with it the DPRK's nuclear breakout. The Jeju Peace Forum was to answer the strategic question posed by the June 2000 summit: how could the two Koreas, so antagonistic in political culture, core economic structure, and military posture, resolve the Korean conflict? And, in this process, what role should third parties play, and, if they played it, how would resolving the Korean conflict set in motion a broader peace-building process in the region?

Moon drew on his scholarly and policy networks in South Korea and internationally, especially via the Pacific Century Institute in Los Angeles (the vehicle of Korean-American Spencer Kim, a pro-engagement businessman). He brought in the former US Defense Secretary, William Perry, and the former US Ambassador to the ROK, Don Gregg. Domestically, Lim Dong-won, then special assistant to President Kim, supported the forum and participated.[101] President Kim Dae-Jung's attendance at the first forum drew national and international attention.

The initial Jeju Peace Forum adopted the first of three Jeju forum declarations. The "Jeju Peace Declaration" linked explicitly the ideas

---

100 Moon, C.I., "Interview with Hayes, P." (September 7, 2013).
101 Ibid.

generated at the meeting and the contribution of Jeju Island, stating that: "We will institutionalize the convocation of the Jeju Peace Forum in order to promote common peace and common prosperity in Northeast Asia by inheriting the spirit of national reconciliation as enshrined in the June 2000 South-North Summit Meeting."[102]

Although the first forum decided to repeat the event every two years, the combination of the September 11, 2001 attacks on New York and the deteriorating Korean situation led to a "semi forum" in 2001, instigated in part by Bill Perry.[103] This meeting laid the groundwork for the second Jeju Peace Forum in November 2003. Until then, the Jeju Provincial Government had been the host, and the entire forum was co-organized by the Jeju Development Institute and the Yonsei Graduate School of International Studies. With Roh's inauguration in 2003, Moon became a cabinet-level appointee responsible for the Blue House's Presidential Committee on Northeast Asia Cooperation Initiative in 2004, but he had already played a key role in arranging President Roh's attendance at the third Jeju Forum in November 2003. The range of supporting institutions expanded rapidly to include the foreign affairs ministry.

The Forum's goal at this time was to generate support for a peace initiative in Northeast Asia focused on Korea. As Moon articulated the strategy at the third Jeju Peace Forum, in addition to making Northeast Asia an open, participatory, and integrated region, the ROK aimed to realize a "Network Northeast Asia." That is, a community that is interconnected with multiple layers of networks that overcomes all types of barriers by "building dense networks of people, goods and services, capital, infrastructure, and ideas and information." In this respect, Moon's vision prefigured the complex networked strategy for the ROK state advanced during the Lee Myung-bak Administration.[104] And Jeju was to play a leading role in orchestrating this networking strategy.

The third Jeju Peace Forum was held in June 2005. Co-organizers included the Jeju Provincial Government, Yonsei University, Jeju National University, and the East Asia Foundation. Prime Minister Lee Hae-chan attended. Meanwhile, the forum grew in size and Moon persuaded President

---

102 Jeju Forum World Leaders, *Jeju Peace Declaration* (Jeju: Jeju Forum, 2001).

103 *History – 2002* (Jeju: Jeju Forum, 2002).

104 Moon, C.I., *East Asia Community Building and ROK's Northeast Asian Cooperation Initiative*, Building a Northeast Asian Community: Toward Peace and Prosperity (Jeju: 3rd Jeju Peace Forum, 2003).

Roh to formally declare on January 27, 2005 that Jeju is "an island of world peace." Anticipating the drastic increase in its scope and scale in later years, the forum adopted the "Jeju Declaration on Northeast Asian Community," which stated, "Northeast Asian community-building cannot be left to the initiative of governments alone. Mutual understanding and cooperation among citizens through a shared regional identity, transcending parochial nationalism, are the most important determinants of community-building in the region. In this regard, the cultivation and expansion of intra-regional human networks should actively be sought."[105]

To lend weight to this networking and convening strategy, Moon set out to establish a research institute that would provide the intellectual impetus for this project as well as serve as the secretariat for the Jeju Peace Forum. Initially this entity was to be called the North-South Peace Institute, in line with the mission of the Jeju Peace Forum and its focus on solving the Korean conflict in a regional context. Funding this project entailed establishing a funding mechanism. Moon organized the International Peace Foundation in the ROK, co-funded by the foreign affairs ministry and the Jeju Provincial Government, to endow the Jeju Peace Institute. The Foundation was initiated by the Presidential Committee on Northeast Asian Cooperation Initiative (then directed by Moon), the Ministry of Foreign Affairs and Trade, and the Jeju provincial government. In March 2006, the Jeju Peace Institute was established as a non-governmental organization, though it was fully supported by the Ministry and the Jeju provincial government.[106]

The fourth Jeju Peace Forum was held during on June 26-28, 2007, and President Roh Moo-hyun again attended. The forum's agenda drew a parallel between the Jeju and Helsinki Processes. The "Jeju Declaration" from this forum declared that in similarity to the role played by Finland, Switzerland, and Yugoslavia in instigating the Helsinki Process, the ROK was well positioned to exercise catalytic power in "establishing the foundations for an effective security and political community in Northeast Asia." Therefore, the forum stated, "we advocate a new Jeju Process modeled on and drawing on the valuable lessons of the Helsinki Process."[107]

---

105 Jeju Forum World Leaders, *Jeju Declaration on Northeast Asian Community* (Jeju: Jeju Forum, 2005).

106 The Jeju Peace Institute provides a repository of presentations to the Jeju Forum from inception to present plus its own research publications. *Jeju Peace Institute* (Jeju: Jeju Peace Institute), http://www.jpi.or.kr/eng

107 Jeju Forum World Leaders, *Jeju Declaration* (Jeju: Jeju Forum, 2007).

In 2008, Lee Myung-bak became ROK president, and the ROK's *nordpolitik* shifted to a hard-line stance that disavowed most of the cooperative agreements flowing from the 2000 summit. By then, the Jeju Peace Forum had become a major international conference. The foreign affairs ministry took little time to assert control of its core budget and organizational apparatus, installing a former ambassador as president of the Jeju Peace Institute, removing "peace" from the Forum's name as of 2009, and importing big name speakers on themes unrelated to the "peace process." From 2008 onwards, the foreign affairs ministry also began to recruit foreign government officials to attend the forum.

For his part, Governor Woo, who was re-elected in 2010 after an electoral defeat in 2006, pushed to widen the scope of issues considered to emphasize economic and business affairs, especially with China, and to promote Jeju as an investment site.

This approach expanded the role of Jeju Forum as part of the "complex diplomacy" convening role played by the ROK on global and regional affairs, but also diverted it from its original purpose — to initiate a peace process with the DPRK. Consequently, the bulk of the Jeju Peace Institute's work is to organize the now enormous Jeju Forum involving thousands of participants, which became an annual event in 2011 at the instigation of the Jeju governor. Its research program is minimal (albeit impressive for its tiny staff) and largely unrelated to its original purpose.

Unsurprisingly, while remaining supportive of Jeju Forum, Moon's core network moved sideways to work through a new mechanism established in 2005, the East Asia Foundation. Although the Foundation was responsible for planning the entire Jeju Forum event and co-sponsored it financially alongside the provincial and national government agencies, it undertook a new but parallel project, the launching in 2006 of a leading journal of international affairs, *Global Asia*, which aimed to provide an open and creative forum for the exchange of ideas on regional cooperation and integration. Since then, the Foundation has been able to maintain a high profile for Jeju Forum participants in relation to peace and security issues, and the Foundation serves as a co-sponsor of the Forum.

In this manner, Moon and his colleagues inside and outside government, academia, think tanks, mass media, and, to a limited extent, civil society organizations, created a sustainable space for a Northeast Asian peace process via networked brainstorming and ideational innovation. Ultimately, this web of public diplomacy was curtailed and co-opted by the central state's complex diplomacy strategy. Nonetheless, it is the most successful Korean example of a partnership between the private sector (university plus foundation) and the public sector (local government, then central government) to address critical peace and security issues.

Although the emphasis and agenda have varied and shifted over the seven forums to date, the founding network lives on in the Jeju Forum, although many of the original participants have retired or died. The original inspiration and aspiration still invigorate many of its participants — not least Moon and his coterie, who remain as active as ever. As a network of networks, the Jeju Forum enables many weak links to become active and comprehensive approaches to multiple, interrelated problems to be explored — as at the 2013 panel on the impact of climate change on coastal and ocean fisheries in the Yellow Sea — a nexus of security, sustainability, and economic factors demanding simultaneous solutions.

The Jeju Forum is a unique hybrid of scholarly, civil society, market, and local government initiatives. Due to its momentum and resulting unpredictable impacts in far reaching corners of these constellated networks, this Forum does not represent a strategy that Seoul can control from the center. Indeed, attempting to do so would be self-defeating and counter-productive now that the network has begun to form its own networks and ideas. Thus, Moon's original vision may have far more staying power than might have appeared after it was eclipsed in 2008 by conservative South Korean foreign policies. Indeed, the intellectual framework appears to have re-emerged in Park Geun-hye's own Northeast Asia Peace and Cooperation initiative announced in 2013. In this sense, this network achieved its goal of diffusing a vision of the need for change and a concept for how to achieve it, irrespective of the eventual fate of the network itself.

Case Study 5: East Asia Institute's 21st-Century Knowledge Net

Think tanks come in many shapes and sizes, depending upon function, political culture, leadership, and orientation.[108] Their impact on foreign policy in a given country, therefore, is highly context-specific. In the United States, there is a long history of think tanks playing an important role in the formulation of foreign and security policy, both as insiders and as an

---

108 This section draws on Hayes, P., "The Role of Think Tanks in Defining Security Issues and Agendas," in *Presentation to Defence and Strategic Studies Course* (Canberra: Australian Defence College, 2004).

integral part of the national security state, and as outsiders banging on the door of the state to get their ideas incorporated into policy. Traditional think tanks such as the RAND Corporation and the Brookings Institution in Washington DC address the age-old problem of how to organize and deliver knowledge in ways that support the pursuit and exercise of political power.

McGann and Weaver define think tanks functionally as a part of civil society that mediates between governments and "the public"; that identifies, articulates and evaluates emerging issues; that participates in policy debates; and that provides a forum for exchange between key stakeholders in policy formulation.[109] What do traditional think tanks do? Their activity boils down to undertaking research and analysis, advocating for policies based on what they uncover, evaluating government programs, delivering knowledge to policymakers, and interpreting policy issues to the mass media. We observe four types: academic, contract-research, advocacy, and party-affiliated think tanks. Each undertakes these activities to various degrees, depending on the fragmentation, porosity, and openness of different political cultures to their contribution.

In the aftermath of the 1987 overthrow of the South Korean military dictatorship and the creation of a formally democratic political system, and concurrently with the collapse of the rigid Cold War international system in 1991, the ROK had only weak intellectual traditions and institutions in the fields of foreign policy and security, especially outside of academia or government-affiliated organizations such as the Korea Institute for Defense Analysis (Ministry of National Defense), Korea Institute of National Unification (Ministry of Unification), or Institute of Foreign Affairs and National Security (now the Korea National Diplomatic Academy). Many of the ROK's research institutes were created to house and support retiring presidents (for example, the Ilhae Institute, a corrupt charitable foundation established to support General Chun Doo Whan, overthrown in the 1987 democratic uprising, which later became the prestigious Sejong Institute) or ministers (for instance, the Ilmin International Relations Institute, Korea University, founded by former Foreign Minister Han Sung Joo in April 1995). Still others were essentially switchboards in which senior ROK diplomats, officials, and security intellectuals — often professors at a leading ROK university — could exchange views with overseas counterparts, especially

109 McGann, J.G. and Weaver, R.K., *Think Tanks and Civil Societies: Catalysts for Ideas and Action* (New Brunswick: Transaction Publishers, 2000).

Americans. The Seoul Forum for International Affairs, established in 1986 to promote "international understanding of Korea in the global community," is a good example of this kind of think tank.[110]

On this uneven and shifting terrain emerged the vision of Professor Kim Byung-kook. Kim had studied at Harvard, served as a presidential advisor in various capacities in the Kim Young-sam Administration and, by 2001, had become a major intellectual force in Korean political science from his home base at Korea University as the editor of the *Journal of East Asian Studies* and co-editor of the *Korean Political Science Review*. Positioned as he was at the nexus of knowledge, influence, and political power, he saw the opportunity to create the East Asia Institute (hereafter EAI), a think-tank conceived along the lines of the Brookings Institution.

In the spring of 2002, Kim began working with former ROK Prime Minister Lee Hong Koo and with Seok-Hyun Hong, then Chairman of the *JoongAng Ilbo* newspaper, and convened a Founding Committee of fifteen sectoral representatives to support the EAI, which consisted of Kim and one staffer.[111] From the outset, Kim understood the networked nature of the post-Cold War era, the need for powerful ideas that responded to the multi-dimensional, interconnected nature of domestic and international problems, and the need to reform the extraordinarily centralized presidential office inherited from the pre-democratic era in South Korea. This led to the production of a major retrospective research study on the nature of Park Chung Hee's regime and a two-volume proposal for restructuring the presidential office and powers[112] — which influenced directly its reform in the Roh administration.[113]

The EAI was particularly influential in its conceptualization of how ROK diplomacy, its alliance with the United States, and its response to China and the DPRK should incorporate the challenges posed by post-Cold War complexity in a new, grand, national strategy.[114] In 2004, this work began at the EAI with serious research led by Ha Young Sun (who chaired the EAI board of trustees and led many of its research taskforces) and with educational outreach to policymakers, leading to the full-fledged

---

110 *Brief History — History of 20 Years* (Seoul: Seoul Forum), http://seoulforum.or.kr/text. php?mid=m01_03

111 East Asia Institute, *EAI East Asia Institute: 2002-2012* (Seoul: East Asia Institute, 2012).

112 Ibid., p. 7.

113 Ibid., p. 14.

114 East Asia Institute, *East Asia Institute 2008-2009 Annual Report* (Seoul: East Asia Institute, 2009).

articulation in 2006 of "complex diplomacy" as outlined earlier in this chapter, which was embraced in 2011 by then-Minister of Foreign Affairs Sung-hwan Kim as the new paradigm for ROK diplomacy. Kim Byung-kook moved from the EAI to senior positions in ROK foreign policy in the Blue House, where he eventually served as Senior Secretary on Foreign Affairs and National Security to President Lee Myung-bak in 2008, and then as President of the Korea Foundation from 2010-2012.[115]

The EAI also undertook to create a global and regional network of advisors, fellows, and interns by convening conferences, hosting international fellows, and supporting bilateral and multilateral research projects, especially the Network of the Northeast Asian Security Challenge Cluster that brought together counterpart think tanks from China (Tsinghua University, Jiao Tong University, and the Center for RimPac Strategic and International Studies, Shanghai), Taiwan (National Chengchi University), South Korea (Korea University and Seoul National University), and the United States (the Peterson Institute for International Economics).[116] The EAI also convened bilateral dialogues with scholars and officials from China, Australia, and the United States. It further convened a social network of hundreds of former interns in its Exchange Panel for Interdisciplinary Knowledge (EPIK) Spiders in the belief that the next generation of leaders must be nurtured and shaped by new and creative ideas that break with the past.[117] (The name Spiders draws on a metaphor used by EAI's intellectual leader, Ha Young Sun, comparing regional networking strategy to a wolf spider web). The EAI's board of ROK and international advisors took on a publishing role in a stream of briefs, reports, and books, as well as the *Journal of East Asian Studies* (transferred from Seoul National University to EAI in 2002), making the EAI a highly competitive force in the marketplace for ideas on ROK foreign policy. No other ROK independent research institute has established such an intellectually potent presence in the think tank world, let alone proved as influential in shaping public and foreign policy in the ROK.

This result has been achieved on a remarkably small budget, roughly $1-$2 million US dollars per year. The EAI relies on the convening power

---

115 Kim, B.K., *Kim Byung Kook – Education and Work Experience* (Seoul: Political Science & International Relations, Korea University).

116 East Asia Institute (2009).

117 *EPIK Spiders — Background* (Exchange Panel for Interdisciplinary Knowledge network), http://epik.eai.or.kr/staff.asp

of its senior leadership to induce professors and intellectuals to contribute to its many task forces on key issues and thereby benefit from off-budget salaries paid for by other research and educational institutions.[118] In short, the EAI has created a global "knowledge-net" that sets the benchmark for competing institutions — such as the Asan Institute, the subject of the next section of this chapter — but still falls far short of a bottom-up transnational thinknet of the type driven by civil society organizations responding to critical issues on the ground, across borders, a type treated in later sections of this chapter.

Case Study 6: The Asan Institute for Policy Studies

Another cosmopolitan community formed in response to South Korea's civil society is the Asan Institute. In many ways, the Asan Institute is the antithesis of the Jeju Peace Forum. Founded in 2008, Asan framed itself not as a network to activate a peace-building process, convened by ROK civil society actors from universities and local government, but as a freestanding, long-term, and independent "think tank" undertaking policy-relevant research to "foster domestic, regional, and international environments that are conducive to peace and stability on the Korean peninsula and Korean reunification."[119]

The Asan Institute grew quickly from a small think tank to the fifth most influential think tank in East Asia in 2012, according to John McGann's annual ranking.[120] Asan was structured on the American think tank model. Its mandate was to become a central meeting place for networks in the region and — some trenchant observers suggest — to be the vehicle that creates an intellectual framework for the eventual presidential campaign of long-serving conservative National Assembly member Chung Mong Joon,

---

118 East Asia Institute (2012).

119 *About the Asan Institute* (Seoul: The Asan Institute for Policy Studies), http://en.asaninst. org/about/about-the-asan-institute/

120 The Asan Institute ranks fifth amongst think tanks in a geographical region that includes: China, India, Japan, and the Republic of Korea See McGann, J.G., *2012 Global Go to Think Tanks Report and Policy Advice* (Pennsylvania: Think Tanks and Civil Societies Program, University of Pennsylvania, 2013). The government-founded Korean Development Institute (KDI) ranks number three. What separates the two institutions, however, is the scope of their mandates. KDI is primarily domestic-oriented. It was founded in 1971 with a mandate to provide policy advice to those in the public and private sectors in Korea for development purposes. Asan, on the other hand, is far less domestic policy-oriented.

who inherited immense wealth from his father, the founder of the Hyundai Corporation.

The Asan Institute can engage in broad-based international civic diplomacy and networking because of its staff and strong funding. In this respect, it is unique among South Korean freestanding institutes. With over a dozen topic-specific research centers and more than 80 full-time staff (including interns), the Institute has an unmatched research and convening capacity in ROK civil society. Notably, many senior staff are bi/tri-lingual and have degrees from the world's most prestigious universities outside of South Korea, whether they are Korean or foreign nationals. Based on language ability and educational background, the Asan Institute is a cosmopolitan entity.

Asan's rapid ascendency began in 2010 when Hahm Chaibong became its president. Hahm is to the Asan Institute what Moon Kook-hyun was to Yuhan-Kimberley, Lee Ho-taeg to the early formation of the Refugee Aid Network, and Moon Chung-in to the Jeju Peace Forum — a true "insider-outsider."[121] Using his connections in both South Korea and the United States and making good use of his academic pedigree, Hahm envisioned connecting scholars in Korea and abroad within a transnational network anchored in Seoul. Hahm is fluent in both Korean and English. He holds degrees from Carleton College and Johns Hopkins University. He also has professional experience as a researcher at the RAND Corporation and has taught at the University of Southern California. "I often see myself as a proto-typical rootless cosmopolitan," Hahm told the authors during an interview. "During my college and graduate years, I studied political theory and epistemology. I wanted to know why Eastern and Western cultures were so different — a difference that I felt was reflected in my own identity."[122]

Hahm sees himself and the Asan Institute as playing the role of conduit between East and West and as a vessel to transmit information about Korea to the outside world. "Translating from one language or one culture to

---

121 Our informal conversations with Asan Institute staff confirm the extent to which Hahm is the central figure within the institute. Although opinions differ, those working at the Asan Institute all agree that Hahm is the core of the institute. Some see this as a wholly positive thing, while others are more reserved in their praise, citing problems associated with over-centralization.

122 Chaibong, H., "Interview with Denney, S." (July 24, 2013).

another is the role of a cosmopolitan and the role I want the Institute to play."[123]

The Asan Institute engages with and connects domestic and international audiences via informal meetings, networking lunches, special lecture series, forums, and, above all, at "Asan Plenums," huge multi-day events hosted at 5-star hotels where world-leading establishment figures, government officials, journalists, and other public intellectuals gather to discuss global problems and how to solve them.[124] There have been three Plenums thus far. At the 2011 Asan Plenum, entitled "Our Nuclear Future," nuclear scientists, engineers, policy experts, and other specialists from around the world gathered in Seoul to discuss nonproliferation, disarmament, peaceful use of nuclear power, nuclear security, and deterrence.[125] The 2012 Asan Plenum centered on the theme of "Leadership" at a time when leadership transitions in China, South Korea, Japan, and the United States were taking place.[126] The latest plenum, hosted in May of 2013, addressed the issue of the "New World Disorder," focusing on topics ranging from East Asian economic regionalism to the civil conflict in Syria.[127]

Since English is the medium of communication, the plenums are biased towards native and fluent English-speaking specialists from American and European-based institutions; even so, the composition of each plenum — in its participants and discussion topics — reflects the Asan Institute's efforts to foster discussion on regional issues that have global implications.

Asan Plenums bring together high-ranking officials. These include former assistant secretaries of state and vice ministers and leaders from leading global institutions and think tanks such as the US Committee for Human Rights in North Korea and the Centre for Economics and Foreign Policy Studies (Istanbul). They are convened at a single event in Seoul — a city not yet known as a global hub — enabling disparate contacts to network with each other at side events. Eileen Block, who plays a central role as a networking coordinator for the plenums, says the Asan Institute's

---

123 Ibid.
124 The official description can be found at the Asan Institute's website *About the Asan Institute*
125 Asan Institute, "Proceedings for the Asan Plenum 2011," in *Asan Plenum 2011* (Seoul: Asan Institute, 2011) http://asaninst.org/proceedings-for-the-asan-plenum-2011
126 Asan Institute, "Asan Plenum 2012 – Proceedings" in *Asan Plenum 2012* (Seoul: Asan Institute, 2012) http://en.asaninst.org/proceedings-for-the-asan-plenum-2012
127 Rapporteurs who work the events provide session sketches. *Sessions Sketches — 2013* (Seoul: The Asan Institute for Policy Studies, 2013), http://en.asaninst.org/events_category/asan-plenum/sub_category/session-sketches/?s_year=2013

goal of using them to build on its international network and to position South Korea within this network has proved successful thus far. "In the past, inviting individuals to the plenums was a task that required much effort on our part and reliance on colleagues. Now, with the contacts we've made and maintained through the plenums, people in Korea and abroad request an invitation to participate in the plenum or an opportunity to host a smaller event."[128]

From a broader theoretical perspective, the new domestic and transnational networks created through the plenums are opening opportunities for the institute's staff to establish their own networks outside of the ROK. Karl Friedhoff, Asan's program officer for the Public Opinions Studies Center, is the main contact point in English for Asan's monthly reports on public opinion polling data. As such, Friedhoff has become a key contact on public opinion for foreign media outlets based in Seoul (Reuters, AP, *The Wall Street Journal*). Furthermore, he relies on what he calls "persistence through networks" to establish himself as a bridge between the Asan Institute and policymakers from the White House, the State Department, and other DC-based institutions.[129]

Despite its meteoric rise in convening events and activating networks, many are skeptical of what they see as its partisan, highly politicized domestic agenda. Asan's founder and funder, Moon Mong-jung, for example, has argued for both the redeployment of tactical nuclear weapons to South Korea by the United States and the indigenous development of nuclear weapons. The former argument came at the March 2013 Nuclear Forum in February hosted by the Asan Institute and the latter at the Carnegie International Nuclear Policy Conference in Washington DC the next month.[130] This stance has led some to question whether Asan is in fact a non-partisan, independent think tank dedicated to research and solving global problems.[131] However, Moon's role at Asan is actually minimal (apart from providing ongoing funding).[132] Nor is Asan a monolith. Shin Chang-hoon,

---

128 Interview with Eileen Block, program officer at the Asan Institute for Policy Studies, July 22, 2013.
129 Friedhoff, K., "Interview with Denney, S." (July 22, 2013).
130 Hibbs, M., "South Korea's Nuclear Defense," *Arms Control Wonk*, 7 April 2013, http://hibbs. armscontrolwonk.com/archive/1617/south-koreas-nuclear-defense. Demick, B., "More South Koreans Support Developing Nuclear Weapons," *Los Angeles Times*, 18 May 2013, http://articles.latimes.com/2013/may/18/world/la-fg-south-korea-nuclear-20130519
131 Demick, B., 2013.
132 In our conversation with Hahm about the issue of independence from political pressure, he stressed that Chung, as chairman of the Asan Foundation, is a patron, not a client. He

director of the Asan Nuclear Policy and Technology Center (ANPTC) and host of the 2013 Nuclear Forum, is an ardent anti-proliferation advocate.[133] What is more, Choi Kang, vice president of research, is on record as saying that such positions are "[argued] for by the minority" in South Korea, and that the reintroduction of tactical nuclear weapons "would be a disaster."[134] A diversity of views and opinions are expressed at Asan.

As these six case studies show, ROK civil society is still developing. Its capacities relative to those of the ROK state and of the *chaebols* are still weak. However, it has established a powerful ability to convene and sustain networks that enable social entrepreneurs to place themselves and their partners in key positions. From these locations, they are able to propagate ideas and strategies, and to connect with otherwise isolated stakeholders whose views must be heard or whose interests must recognized for a cooperative solution to be visualized and implemented. ROK civil society has been effective in drawing together Northeast Asian networks, partly because Japanese counterparts chose to focus on less politicized, more distant issues and networks than those raised by the engagement of Chinese and South Korean civil society organizations, but also because South Korean groups work well with partners or proto-non-governmental organizations in China for cultural reasons. In almost all cases, a driving individual able to mobilize resources was a crucial enabling condition, albeit one insufficient to create networks that could visualize and implement solutions, and then scale them up to be used across borders.

Implementing strategies and sustaining them requires more resources than most ROK civil society organizations have been able to muster. One solution that may lend stamina to their efforts, by increasing reliable resourcing as well as demanding greater accountability from elected officials without being overwhelmed by the central state, is prefigured by the Jeju Peace Forum, which linked a civil network strategy to realize regional and inter-Korean peace with the leadership and commitment of a local government. The next section provides case studies that reveal

---

further emphasized that "Dr. Chung's views are his own" and that "he does not impose them on the Asan Institute." Chaibong, H., "Interview with Denney, S." (July 24, 2013).

133 In our conversations with Asan staff about the implications of Chung's political views have on perceptions of the institute's independence, this was a common response.

134 These comments were made in the summer of 2012 at a Brookings Institution event in Washington DC. *The Sixth Seoul-Washington Forum: Moving the United States-Korea Relationship Forward in Changing Environments* (Washington, DC: Brookings Institution, 2012), http://www.brookings.edu/events/2012/06/08-seoul-washington-forum

the potential for such public-private partnerships to emerge in the region, including examples drawn from the ROK, Japan, and China.

Networked Inter-City Cooperation

In *Reinventing Japan, From Merchant Nation to Civic Nation*, Yasuo Takao argues persuasively that independently elected and de facto autonomous local governments enable many local officials to act independently of the central state, to coordinate horizontally with civil society organizations, and thus to structure and facilitate the association and networking of independent civil society organizations.[135] For this reason, it is important to examine the role of local governments and cities in civic diplomacy and their cross-border activities in many dimensions of culture, economy, and ecology.

Above, we presented the leading role of the Jeju Provincial governor in establishing the Jeju Peace Forum — now one of the ROK's most important annual foreign policy events. In chapters 2 and 4, we examined how cities in Asia compete with each other for primacy within and between national urban hierarchies, for gateway dominance, and for survival and prosperity in the inevitable cycles of business up- and down-turns and the politically driven factors that determine the allocation of national resources to infrastructure. We found that without central planning or guidance, new patterns of mega and even giga-city corridor formation can be observed. Some of these corridors are likely to cross borders or drive cooperation transnationally in the search for mutuality, either in solving common problems or sharing common solutions — even if they are located far away from each other. Thus, bilateral and trilateral city-based networks have emerged involving the ROK and Japan, Japan and China, and China and the ROK. In the case of the Dalian-Kitakyushu relationship, we noted that the city officials not only coordinated to induce their central governments to fund their collaborative projects, they also created vibrant partnerships with local business and grassroots groups from civil society.

In South Korea, the Busan-Fukuoka inter-city network was an early example of Korean-Japanese networked strategy to create an economic,

---

135 Takao, Y., *Reinventing Japan: From Merchant Nation to Civic Nation* (New York: Palgrave Macmillan, 2003).

cultural, and social cross-border space managed collaboratively. As Lim Jung-Duk explains, this bilateral network did not emerge overnight:

> Major cities and regions of the KJSEZ (Korea-Japan Strait Economic Zone) form multi-layered interurban networks. First, the East Asia City Conference, which started with the Yellow Sea Rim Six-City Conference in 1991 and expanded in 2000 to include 10 port cities (Dalian, Qingdao, Tianjin, Yantai, Incheon, Busan, Ulsan, Kitakyushu, Fukuoka, and Shimonoseki), grew into the level of a "city alliance" by establishing the Organization for East Asian Economic Development [which] aimed at forming the Yellow Sea Rim Economic Bloc. Second, the Local Government Meeting for the Korea-Japan Strait Zone, established in 1992 between four prefectures of Northern Kyushu (Fukuoka, Saga, Nagasaki, and Yamaguchi) and one metropolitan city and three provinces [on South] Korea's southern coast (Busan, South Gyeongsang Province, South Jeolla Province, and Jeju Island), boasts of a competitive proximity. Third, the Northeast Asia Regional Government Association, with the participation of six Northeast Asian countries (Korea, North Korea, China, Mongolia, Russia, and Japan) [and] forty cities and provinces, is a city club established on transverse logic rather than proximity.[136]

This bilateral city network did not form only to facilitate the work of increasing trade and investment, as suggested by the first meeting of the Economic Cooperation Council of the Busan-Fukuoka Region in 2008, which aimed to nurture tourism and other forms of join economic gains. As Lim notes, it also led to the creation of a consortium of twenty-four universities from the two cities to foster scholarly exchange; to the Civic Group Council, consisting of forty-two civic groups; and to the Nippon Korea Citizen Exchange Network Fukuoka, formed by twenty-nine civic groups in Kyushu who signed the Busan-Fukuoka (Kyushu) NGO Agreement in 2008. These civil society networks aim to support student exchange and home stays, sports competitions, and systematic cultural exchange.[137] The goal, according to Lim, is to "spread a sense of identity of cross-border cooperation among citizens," arguably a precursor to a cosmopolitan citizen identity in this region.[138]

Lim notes that such cross-border initiatives remain "light" until they obtain financial and institutional autonomy from a central government,

---

136 Lim, J.D., "New Regionalism across Korea-Japan Strait: Cross-Border Region between Busan and Fukuoka," in *18th Northeast Asia Economic Forum* (Busan: Northeast Asia Economic Forum, 2009).
137 Ibid., p. 32.
138 Ibid., p. 33.

especially in regions dominated by geopolitical concerns. "The issue of forming a CBR [cross border region]," he concludes, "is a re-territorializing process involving the creation of a cooperative space for cross-border forces (market and society) based on networks, and this requires a process of unprecedented political discussion among actors whose countries give priority to territorial uniformity."[139] Moreover, after examining a number of such inter-city cooperative relationships, Yasuo Takao concluded that civil society organizations must make common cause with local governments at the provincial or city level in order to achieve long-term sustainability for their efforts.

Conclusion: Civic Diplomacy and ROK Foreign Policy

By now, it should be evident to the reader that civil society organizations in the ROK and in Northeast Asia provide capacities that state and market-based agencies cannot, capacities that are critically important to the resolution of global problems and various types of insecurity that originate or are manifest in the region. In comparison with "complex" state-based diplomacy, civic networked diplomacy is often more agile, better able to cross borders and circumvent communication barriers, and more capable of envisioning and propagating shared solutions with more credibility and at greater speed. Civil society organizations are also able to undertake tasks to which states are inherently ill suited due to their constitution — such as the formation of a cosmopolitan cultural identity, especially among youth leaders and civil society organizations, like that envisioned by the ROK's Northeast Asian Cooperation Initiative in 2004.[140] Such a hybrid cosmopolitan identity is already emerging bottom-up as younger generations of South Koreans, Chinese, Japanese, and Russians learn each other's languages, share popular culture, and travel widely within the region. Nonetheless, until systematic, cross-generational learning takes place involving young leaders from at least China, Japan, and the ROK to create a common discourse with defining moments and shared narratives, such an identity will remain limited at best by virulent nationalisms and provincialisms. When it does emerge, as William Callahan argues, it won't be a singular "Northeast Asian" identity. Rather,

---

139 Ibid., p. 34.
140 Moon, C.I. (2003).

it will be a kaleidoscopic, dizzying array of hybrid, post-modern identities incorporating local ethos and nativism, corporate loyalties, fashion, fads, Confucianism, religious orientations. It will commingle and contend with gendered, ethnic, diasporic, and virtual identities — in a cultural flux that disorients, dislocates, and redefines what it means to be a "good citizen" and a member of the nation-state.[141]

Because people who create transnational, networked civil society organizations are motivated more by universal values and norms than states, their civic diplomacy inevitably includes wider considerations than complex diplomacy and traditional foreign policy. Indeed, their orientation and demands may even clash with the narrow, introspective, and exclusive values and norms embodied in diplomacy that aims above all to establish and maintain territorial borders that separate self, nation-state, and "outsiders" of all kinds.[142] Civic diplomacy, as may be observed in the many case studies presented in this book, puts greater emphasis on realizing human and ecological security than on accumulating wealth and military power — the traditional goals of state-based foreign policy that drive complex diplomacy. Thus, civic diplomacy is likely to push for more open borders, in part to secure the labor needed to sustain graying economies in the ROK and Japan, but also to enable émigrés from China and the DPRK to obtain work and to make remittances that, via diasporic networks, finance local development in their countries of origin.

Some of these policy shifts driven in part by civic diplomacy may require states to respond with new regulations and controls. Increased cross-border mobility, for example, may result in new border screening and public health measures to respond to the increasing risk of pandemics arising from the cross-border transmission of disease vectors. This same mobility may also push states to innovate, for example, by expanding visa-less travel.

In other issue areas, expanded civic diplomacy may be highly congruent with complex diplomacy by providing unique or more efficient capacity to implement programs that embody the values and norms adhered to by states and by civil society organizations. Over time, the values and norms of civil society and states may converge both within and between states,

---

141 Callahan, W.A., *Contingent States: Greater China and Transnational Relations* (Minessotta: Minessotta University Press, 2004).

142 Ibid., p. 26.

because civil society organizations often draw their normative inspiration from shared global and universal sources.

At the most basic level, civil society organizations aim to realize peace, security, and sustainability based on community, whereas states aim to embody wealth and power, especially military power, based on territory. Let us explore the overlap and convergence, as well as the contradiction and divergence, between these overarching goals and their respective civic and complex foreign policies.

Earlier in this chapter, we noted that complex diplomacy aims to create social capital that enables the ROK to orient its allies and partners toward managing and resolving the DPRK threat on ROK terms. This is the foremost priority of its foreign policy. Concurrently, complex diplomacy sets out to position the ROK as a trading power in financial and investment networks, on a global and regional basis, and to use its positional power to convene influential networks on global and regional issues to enhance its reputation and negotiating ability.

In contrast, civic diplomacy aims to envision peaceful, secure, and sustainable futures; to create shared images of desirable futures based on collaboration; and to generate the common knowledge and discourse needed to identify and propagate strategies and solutions to specific problems at local sites, in part to exemplify generalized solutions, but also to construct a peaceful, sustainable future bottom-up, locale by locale. The strategies that support these goals are not based on wealth and military power, but rather on mutual learning and cultural realignment across generations and cultural-territorial borders. In addition to the individual and local-level changes needed to embody the reorientation of localities to sustainable and peaceful futures, civic diplomacy seeks to invoke changes in and hold state and corporate policies accountable to higher standards that reflect these values — even at the cost of immediate or medium-term gains in national wealth and military power. In addition to deepening and widening the autonomy and capacity of civil society in each country, civic diplomacy relies on ad hoc and enduring networks led by civil society rather than on military power or corporate wealth. To implement these strategies, civil society organizations create and maintain, sometimes with incredible tenacity, transnational networks based on divisions of labor that mix and match the strengths and offset the weaknesses of civil society across countries.

Due to its fundamental goals, the domain of complex diplomacy is relatively narrow. Foreign policy focuses on what enables the nation-state to accrue national wealth and power, often to the exclusion or subordination of other issues even where governments have agencies and programs (for example, on trans-boundary environmental problems) to reduce the complexity of the real world of scores and even hundreds of global problems to a small number of issues that can be managed using well-tested, often rigid methods. The cost of this approach is that the tools are often blunt, and policies aim to solve only a few top priorities at a time defined by leaders with short tenures and narrow attention spans. Consequently, rapid policy shifts by incoming administrations may exacerbate or suppress other related problems, only to have them re-emerge or even worsen over time. The ROK's vacillating *nordpolitik* is an obvious example.

By comparison, the domain of civic diplomacy is very wide — as wide as the range of concerns that motivate individuals, communities, and local governments to cooperate across borders. Because of the very large number of agile non-state actors involved, civil society often identifies many distinct and viable strategies to manage and even resolve linked problems at the same time. Due to their diversity and different locations in relation to the spatial, temporal, and socio-cultural dimensions of linked problems, they are able to construct peace, security and sustainability from the bottom-up, one person, one community, one region, and one issue at a time, in a mosaic of incremental, linked, partial solutions in each of these issues areas. Of course, civil society and its civic diplomacy are not seamless or perfectly consistent in addressing common problems across borders. The priority concerns of civil society as well as the definitions of urgent problems vary from country to country due to different income levels and cultural orientations. However, due to shared convictions that values and norms are universal in nature, civic diplomats often (but not always) find enough in common with their counterparts across borders to overcome residual divisiveness from the historical memory of past grievances inflicted by one country or sectarian group on another. They are also able to develop common agendas for concerted and even joint action in spite of varying socioeconomic levels and differential risk-perceptions.

In the realm of geopolitical security, complex diplomacy shares a priority concern with civic diplomacy on the need to reduce the risk of war and escalation, especially involving weapons of mass destruction such as nuclear weapons. Only states can mobilize, control, and calibrate the level of risk-taking by large-scale military forces such as those maintained by the ROK. Equally, sometimes only civil society personnel and organizations can communicate with the DPRK during a real crisis and shuttle information backwards and forwards between the protagonists to reduce the risk of war, including inadvertent war. Similarly, only states can maintain large-scale, highly technical functional capacities to sustain critical infrastructure such as air traffic control, watershed management, and sewage disposal, among other things. Equally, only civil society networks can instantly mobilize huge numbers of people to respond to contingencies in a massive, self-organizing fashion, as in China after earthquakes and Japan after cascading earthquake-tsunami catastrophes.

Historically, the ROK state has attempted to project a monolithically unified ROK against DPRK diplomatic overtures or military threats. At times of high tension, the ROK state often attempts to shut down these private channels by arresting ROK citizens engaged in this type of popular diplomacy, in part due to a concern that civil society representatives might be misunderstood as speaking on behalf of the state, and in part to suppress dissenting voices at home. Ironically, the DPRK itself often shuts down *all* private channels with the external world in order to ensure that only one line is articulated to the ROK and the United States, thereby isolating itself even more than is usually the case. Thus, the slender threads of disavowable, private communication to and from Pyongyang become most valuable at times of highest tension. During these periods, complex diplomacy is bereft of networked strategies to communicate with the DPRK "structural hole."

Before and after such crises occur, civic diplomats can build these enduring networks based on trust and sustained communication. This strategy overlaps and is reinforced by complex diplomacy wherein the ROK state sets out to establish itself as a "convening power" for regional meetings where minds meet and influential individuals from many sectors and countries connect. At such events, it is more important for habitual antagonists to be present than for people who already have aligned views. Networks of networks like the Jeju Peace Forum or the rapidly emerging Asan Plenums may be examples of disparate social connectivity that establish new layers of resilience for crisis management and conflict resolution.

Ironically, the proclivity of states for keeping most of their complex diplomacy on security issues secret and away from public view (unless revealed by managed leaks or via an uncontrolled revelation such as

Wikileaks) is a major handicap for ROK foreign policy. Many civic diplomats, by virtue of networks and/or presence in the field of a specific locale or problem-site, are better-informed and more up-to-date than foreign policy officials. Thus, one of the implications of enhanced civic diplomacy is a higher level of transparency — and related accountability — and a lesser reliance on secrecy, especially when civic and complex diplomacy are conducted in partnership. As the precept of one civil society organization states in relation to working with North Korea, "When there are no secrets, there are no lies." Of course, the same standards must apply to civic diplomacy and to the operations of civil society organizations — one reason they are often advised to link up closely with local government and city-level partners who will require more stringent accountability than civil society organizations standing alone.

An example of this kind of hybrid civic-complex diplomacy was the March 7-9, 2012 New York Conference on Peace and Cooperation in Northeast Asia, held shortly after the "Leap Day" Agreement between the DPRK and the United States and prior to the two satellite launches by the DPRK. The Friedrich Ebert Foundation convened this "Track 2" meeting in cooperation with the Korean Peninsula Affairs Center at the Maxwell School of Syracuse University, with Hanshin University, with the Pacific Century Institute, and with the National Association of Korean Americans. The Foundation assembled a group of experts from Europe, the ROK, China, the United States, Mongolia, and Germany to consider practical steps that could advance a process of denuclearization and peace on the Korean Peninsula.[143] In reality, the prime mover of this event was Hanshin University. At this event, the North and South Korean negotiators spoke frankly in a private capacity over breakfast, dinner, and for long days of candid meetings. As Henry Kissinger explained, the talks leading to the 1971 Mao-Nixon meeting were held no fewer than 136 times. The major achievement of such meetings is to enable the primary antagonists to talk and to understand each other — as the meeting's organizer put it, growing the buds of trust so that they can later flower and providing a space for peaceful conversation for all parties.[144]

---

143 *New York Conference "Peace and Cooperation in Northeast Asia" on March 8-9, 2012* (Seoul: Friedrich-Ebert-Stiftung, Korea Office, 2012), http://www.fes-korea.org/pages/english/events/2012.php

144 Yi, K., "The Purpose and Performance of the 2012 New York Conference for Peace and Cooperation in Northeast Asia (Korean)," 21 March 2012, http://weekly.catchkin.net/617?category=1

Another role for complex diplomacy that creates potential synergy with civic diplomacy is to enable civil society organizations to connect their visions with policy practitioners from across the region — as occurs at the Seoul Digital Forum each year. In this regard, civil society networks such as the Global Partnership for the Prevention of Armed Conflict-Northeast Asia (GPPAC-NEA), established in 2005; the trilingual EnviroAsia, a web-based project to share information about the environment between groups in South Korea, China, and Japan;[145] and the global Mayors for Peace, which originated in Japan and includes over 1,366 cities in Japan, 10 cities in the ROK, 4 cities in Mongolia, and 5 cities in China who have signed a petition for the abolition of nuclear weapons[146] — all work at an ideational level, propagating complementary visions of peace, security, and sustainability, with local programs to ground this vision in local communities.

GPACC-NEA, for example, adopted its Northeast Asia Regional Action Agenda in the presence of more than fifty activists and specialists at the Northeast Asian Conference on the Role of Civil Society in the Prevention of Violent Conflict in Tokyo on February 1-4, 2005.[147] At the event, the South Korean participants presented the *Northeast Asia Activity Report*, the result of months of prior case studies. It identified, for example, the need to include gender issues and the perspectives of women, hitherto conspicuously absent in official inter-Korean processes, in future official reconciliation and reunification efforts; it noted past attempts to enable North and South Korean women to meet against enormous obstacles; it called for the establishment of mechanisms for uninhibited exchange between North and South Korean women; and it noted that UN Security Council Resolution 1325 requires states to address the impact of war on women and women's contributions to conflict resolution and sustained peace.[148]

Similarly, as we noted in chapters 3 and 4, climate change requires that every community in Northeast Asia mitigate their emissions and adapt to new climate-generated stresses. As sociologist Ulrich Beck argues, global problems such as climate change have precipitated the nascent formation

---

145 For background in English, see *East Asia Environmental Information Center Enviro Asia.*

146 *Asia — Member Cities* (Hiroshima: Mayors for Peace), http://www.mayorsforpeace.org/english/membercity/asia/index.html

147 GPPAC Seoul Committee, *Northeast Asia Activity Report* (Global Partnership for Prevention of Armed Conflict, 2005).

148 GPPAC Seoul Committee, *Women's Exchange for Peace Building on the Korean Peninsula,* Northeast Asia Activity Report (Global Partnership for Prevention of Armed Conflict, 2005).

of new "imagined communities."[149] He argues that the rise of global threats unconfined to the territorial borders of states has "transformed ontological awareness and... expanded senses of belonging," much like the effect of nationalism on feudal communities in 18th-century Europe. Territorially confined communities, he suggests, are giving way to "new transnational constellations of social actors... thereby potentially enabling collective action, cosmopolitical decision-making, and international norm generation."[150] However, he argues that this shared vision is based in part on an apocalyptic sense of time due to the threat posed by climate change to progressive social and cultural narratives, rather than on a progressive regional version of the jointly constructed, shared future that drove post-World War II integration in Europe and earlier integration in North America.

We conclude this examination of the implications of civic diplomacy for ROK foreign policy and its complex official diplomacy by arguing that the balance between central, civilian, and local actors in formulating and implementing ROK foreign policy is shifting away from massively dominant central government agencies and increasingly moving towards civilian and local jurisdictions affected directly by cross-border issues. This shift in balance implies that civil society has begun to transform the nature of the central state as well as its complex diplomacy. In this transition, the role of complex diplomacy is no longer the direction of civic diplomacy as part of a total, unified national strategy, as suggested by Sanghun Lee from Sejong Institute in 2011.[151] It is rather to enable autonomous civic diplomacy, recognizing that many of the traditional functions of state-based diplomacy are better undertaken by civil society and local governments of provinces and cities than by centralized states relying on military and economic power. In this sense, civil society and its civic diplomacy are helping the traditional

---

149 Beck, U., *Cosmopolitan Vision* (Oxford: Polity, 2006). Beck, U., *et al.*, "Cosmopolitan Communities of Climate Risk: Conceptual and Empirical Suggestions for a New Research Agenda," *Global Networks*, 13(1) (2012), doi: http://dx.doi.org/10.1111/glob.12001

150 Beck, U., *et al.* (2012), p. 2.

151 "Complex diplomacy aims to accomplish a country's policy objectives through the use of all available means, including military diplomacy, trade diplomacy, development collaboration diplomacy, public diplomacy and private diplomacy, concerning specific diplomatic policy issues. To that end, it should be possible to mobilize network power resources as well as the hard power and soft power (i.e. knowledge, ideology, culture, etc.) that both the government and the private sector own." Lee, S.H., "Measures to Be Taken by South Korea to Carry out Complex Diplomacy," *JPI PeaceNet* (2011).

nation-state shift from the complex diplomacy and a foreign policy aimed at increasing wealth and power associated with the mercantile state to what Yasuo Takao suggests is the "civic state" (referring to Japan, but with relevance to the ROK) based on a partnership between the state and civil society.[152] As the process takes place slowly and unevenly, but pervasively and inexorably, civil society networks will not only reshape individual and national identities, as argued above, but will also redefine and expand the scope of national interest to include extra-territorial concerns of all kinds, based not on the exclusionary notion of the Other, but on the inclusionary notion of empathy.

In turn, this bottom-up construction of interdependent communities in border regions and in multi-dimensional reciprocal dependence — what Tatsujiro Suzuki has called "mutual assured dependence" — will generate a demand for regional governance that transcends the monopoly on foreign policy decision-making by nation-states. One possible form for such governance is the creation of a Council on Security established under the rubric of a Northeast Asian Treaty on Amity and Cooperation.[153] Another is to initiate a European-style integrative process that leads eventually to a political union — although that is much harder to imagine in Northeast Asia due to the enormous asymmetries in scale, interest, and ideology at this time.[154] Such high-level political and security concert would be matched by low-level functional integration of governance, as is prefigured already by scores of senior official regional meetings on specific issues, and by trans-governmental integration between low-level functional and regulatory agencies in coordinating and harmonizing policies and standards in many domains including policing, infrastructure, and public health.

If this portrayal of the end-state is correct, the process by which it is brought about is unlikely to be neat, linear, and orderly. Rather, the rise of civic states in the region will entail constant renegotiation of the cross-border relationships that are embodied in self and nation-state. The relationship between self, civil society, the residual nation-state, and evolving institutions of regional governance will remain ambivalent and contentious in this vision.

---

152 Takao, Y. (2003).

153 Halperin, M., *Promoting Security in Northeast Asia: A New Approach*, NAPSNet Policy Forum (Berkeley: Nautilus Institute, 2012).

154 Goodby, J., *Regional Framework for a Comprehensive Security Settlement: Does It Work?*, NAPSNet Policy Forum (Berkeley: Nautilus Institute, 2012).

Nonetheless, the rise of civic diplomacy working in concert with complex diplomacy, and the shift to the civic state and nation, provides the extra social capacity whereby the ROK can best respond to the challenges posed by global and regional problems. In this vision, there is no singular, unified civic foreign policy, but as many civic foreign policies as are needed to respond to the exigencies confronting communities and the issues evoking cross-border responses by civil society. The intrinsic multiplicity — some have called it multiplexity[155] — of civic diplomacy makes it impossible for the state to direct it as part of a unified complex diplomatic strategy. Instead of attempting to direct it, the state will become an enabler of "peer-to-peer" communities that, for the most part, sustain themselves largely independently of the central state.[156]

In this supporting rather than lead role, the civic state can do much to nurture the rise of civic diplomacy, even as it continues to rely on complex diplomacy to implement ROK foreign policy. Perhaps most significantly, it can provide support to capacity-building efforts for civil society in China, Mongolia, the Russian Far East, and, when feasible, to the "proto" non-governmental organizations that are already evident in the DPRK, notably in the social service sector in public health, nutrition, and reforestation. The civic state can also reduce the bureaucratic and legal controls on non-governmental organizations, even in the ROK, to make it easier and less expensive to establish such associations and to remove the requirement to report to a government ministry. It can also revise the tax laws to favor the emergency of a vibrant philanthropic sector that will deepen the independent resource base for a truly autonomous civil society.

The ROK can nurture authentically South Korean civic diplomacy in many ways. To some extent, this reform has already occurred in the shaping and implementation of the ROK's development aid program, used by non-governmental organizations to implement government programs and projects wherever possible. The ROK can give strong political and diplomatic support to local governments to establish strong collaborations with cross-border regional counterparts, whether city, civil society, or corporate, and delegate to these local governments and agencies the mandate to create and manage strong forms of interdependency within

---

155 Lejano, R.P. (2006), p. 576.
156 Ronfeldt, D., "Blond's 'civic state' . . . vis à vis TIMN," *Visions from Two Theories Blog*, 5 June 2010, http://twotheories.blogspot.com.au/2010/06/blonds-civic-state-vis-vis-timn. html

cross-border regions. It can increase the transparency of foreign policy deliberations and decision-making and consult closely with leading civil society organizations for input into these foreign policy processes, including them on official delegations as observers or even full members.

On a need-to-know basis, the ROK can make important information available to civil society organizations on urgent, critically important foreign policy issues and declassify the bulk of its foreign policy files — or reduce enormously the needless level of classification in any case. It can help civil society organizations in the foreign policy area to deepen their expertise in areas of conflict and cooperation with other states and to develop networking strategies that connect with their natural partners in other countries. It can increase its reliance on civil society organizations to report quickly from the field and to discern early warning signals of rising instability and tension in relation to core concerns of ROK foreign policy, namely the DPRK.

Finally, the state can promote multilingualism in ROK civil society, the importance of which cannot be over-estimated in the implementation of skillful civic diplomacy and the emergence of a new generation of talented civic diplomats.

7. Anticipating Complex Northeast Asian Futures

Peter Hayes, Joan Diamond, and Kiho Yi

In the previous chapter, we observed how civil society worked across borders in East Asia to create a shared memory of the past in the form of jointly written textbooks of the history of the Japanese invasion and atrocities in Korea, China, and in Japan itself. In this way, civil society started the healing process by creating a unified history of the region rather than a composite of national histories based on memories of horrific events. Far from forgetting or suppressing these events through crude historical revisionism, this civil society approach began a profound cultural reconciliation among these societies by reconstituting the meaning of the memories of grievous harms that resonated across generations and borders.

Another way that civil society has tried to embrace the uncertainty posed by rising complexity is to envision possible shared futures and to develop robust, joint strategies that anticipate the inevitable surprises that lie in store. Such utopias, dystopias, and diverse futures (sometimes called heterotopias) represent a normative or values-based response to high-impact or uncertain events. Just as we must create historical memory across generations and borders if former enemies are to reconcile, so must we imagine futures together to create "complex time" that embodies the universal values in regional and global community.

Some have attempted to outline national "meta-narratives" for the future, as in Hyeonju Son's scenarios for the ROK. Son identified five established cultural images of the ROK's future: (a) becoming a developed country, (b) apocalyptic discourse, (c) national unification, (d) advanced information society, and (e) feminist visions.[1] Some of these shared imaginary futures are dystopic (for example, those related to climate and nuclear catastrophes as delineated in chapters 4 and 5). Others are more utopian (for example, those involving "rurbanization," *in-situ* urbanization of rural areas, and sustainable cities as described in chapters 2 and 4). Other futures envisioned by civil society, such as the Korean DMZ Peace Park,[2] have been elevated from relatively isolated scientific thinking to state policy in less than two decades.[3] In one instance, scholars working with civil society organizations developed seven detailed "mini-scenarios" for managing the DMZ in an ambiguous, prolonged, and "frozen" present.[4] In another, one author presented a long-term macro-scenario for regional ecological security stretching from Russia and China to Japan via Korea based on the Korean notion of ridgeline-watershed management known as *Baekdudaegan*.[5]

Although such descriptions of collective orientations are insightful, they do not address how complex time emerges within, let alone across, borders in the modern era. By complex time, we mean the experience of time by civil society that arises from the decentralized interaction of different societies. Civil society organizations connect across borders to communicate, coordinate, and collaborate with each other for three reasons. The first is their commitment to universal human values. Citizens may become aware of the plight of people afflicted by a natural catastrophe or by human rights transgressions in neighboring states. Their *cross-border empathy* drives communication across borders between civil society organizations that share these values. Eventually, this leads to an awareness of the need to develop common images of shared futures based on reciprocity.

---

1   Son, H., "Images of the Future in South Korea," *Futures*, 52(0) (2013), doi: http://dx.doi.org/10.1016/j.futures.2013.06.001

2   Lee, S.H. (2010).

3   Hayes, P. and Cavazos, R., "An Ecological Framework for Promoting Inter-Korean Cooperation and Nuclear Free Future: A DMZ Peace Park," *NAPSNet Special Report* (2013).

4   See Ali, S., "Designing Ecological Peace in the Koreas," *National Geographic Newswatch*, 23 December 2011, http://voices.nationalgeographic.com/2011/12/23/designing-ecological-peace-in-the-koreas

5   Hayes, P. (2010). On Baekdudaegan, see Choi, Y., "Baekdudaegan, the Central Axis of the Korean Peninsular: The Path toward Management Strategies Regarding to Its Concepts," in *Ecological Issues in a Changing World Status, Response and Strategy*, ed. by Hong, S.-g. and Hong, S.-K., *et al.* (Berlin: Springer, 2004).

The second reason is that coordination is required to *create new value* by virtue of generally aligning goals and synchronizing specific actions — for example, between cities attempting to move their respective governments to adopt convergent policies to create common labor, industrial, logistical, or public health standards. Thirdly, collaboration is necessary to achieve a *transnational mobilization* to protect a regional or global commons — for example, by coastal communities and fishermen to prevent or respond to oil pollution — and to establish joint frameworks to manage shared problems based on enduring collaborations, such as the provision of training for environmental management across one border city to another.

Each of these types of cross-border communication, cooperation, and collaboration do not fit easily within the temporal framework of nation-states or national cultures. Communicating across borders, coordinating activities, and collaborating to bring about a joint result are lived experiences at the individual level that inform personal identity and change how individuals associate. Once touched, they can never again become isolated from the external world.

At the same time as civil society engages in specific, networked activities across borders, the external world is merging with internal, local worlds as lived by individuals and communities. Today, a vast, continuous web of instantaneous communication such as Voice-over-Internet Protocol (VoIP) connects individuals and communities who previously lived in disparate, asynchronous time (seasonal, cultural, work-related, or national). Such "concurrent" (simultaneously on-line) communications involve millions of individuals in China, South Korea, and Japan (the predominant VoIP users in the region who, when considered as an aggregate, are a majority of the global users of VoIP).[6] A significant fraction of these VoIP conversations — perhaps a million voices at a time — cross borders and form a constant, warm shower of "soft" social communication that bathes both sides of "hard" state-based territorial borders. Like a virtual "acid rain," this

---

6   See Point Topic, *VoIP Statistics – Market Analysis, Q1 2013* (London: Point Topic, 2013). Russell, J., "Think Skype Is Big? Go See How Many People Are Using Tencent's QQ Right Now," *Nextweb blog*, 27 June 2012, http://thenextweb.com/asia/2012/06/27/think-skype-is-big-go-see-how-many-people-are-using-tencents-qq-right-now. Caukin, J., "40 Million People: How Far We've Come," *Skype Big Blog*, 10 April 2012, http://blogs.skype.com/2012/04/10/40-million-people-how-far-weve/ Wireless Federation, "Regulators Enable Mobile Operators to Charge More Fees for VoIP (South Korea)," ICT Statistics Newslog, 17 July 2012, http://www.itu.int/ITU-D/ict/newslog/Regulators+Enable+Mobile+Operators+To+Charge+More+Fees+For+VOIP+South+Korea.aspx

communication corrodes border infrastructure even as it flows unhindered by the fences, gates, barbed wire, and minefields in some cases.

This flow of continuous communication transcends the state-based demarcation of time and space at national borders that separates people, preserves national identities, and reinforces diplomatic and military power. VoIP (and other forms of streaming culture, such as real time radio and video broadcasts over the Internet) supplant it with a civil society-based integration of space and time, a form of continuous virtual mobility that reaches into even the hardest state in the region, North Korea. It interrupts "heterochronicity"[7] or the dominant linear national historical narrative and its cyclical updating of the present state of affairs with reference to past Golden Ages or core events in the construction of the state such as wars, revolutions, or liberation from colonial occupation. It offers a hopeful future orientation to the lives of millions of people. Each VoIP call across borders is a tiny building block for creating a new regional identity and community, one person at a time, millions of people per second. It cannot obviate the need for face-to-face meetings and physical cross-border mobility, but it can substitute while such mobility is constrained by state border controls.

The unstoppable, cumulative effect of the civic diplomacy and networked civil society strategies outlined in previous chapters is to create a new form of shared time, congruent with the unified space of common problem-solving. We distinguish this shared time by its orientation towards joint problem-solving across borders — at the individual, familial, community, and city levels. In this regard, it subverts and recasts the past (backwards-looking time in Western cultures, as epitomized by the way time is referred to in the English language as linear and "behind" the present, whereas in the Chinese language, forwards-looking time refers to history lying on top of the present moment). These temporal frames are defined by and within each nation states. These latter time-frames that define national and individual identity are constituted by references to core historical events that punctuate time for different generations or cultures; by asynchronous time rooted in varying patterns of time in institutional domains; and by non-contemporaneity, or the coexistence of different societal time-frames due to co-evolving stages of social evolution — all of which tend to differentiate and separate people.[8] The new, shared temporality based on

---

7   Callahan, W.A. (2004), p. 28. Callahan refers to heterochronicity in relation to the cultural construction of "Greater China," but the point is generally applicable.

8   Bernhard Giesen distinguishes between three types of "temporal inconsistency"

joint problem-solving is a hybrid of these interrupted temporalities. In the context of cross-cultural "scenario" thinking, it incorporates backward-leaning time in the form of historical knowledge and wisdom with forward-leaning time driven by joint problem-solving, thereby expanding the cultural diversity incorporated into our understanding of the long "present" that includes at least six generations — three born roughly a century ago and three who will live for another century.

Northeast Asia 2050: Is There a Role for Civil Society in Meeting the Climate Change Challenge?

The explicit creation of imaginary futures is one way in which cross-cultural groups meeting across borders have explored the true uncertainty posed by complex global problems in Northeast Asia and envisioned shared futures and joint responses to the challenges posed by these imaginary futures. In 2009 and 2010, the authors convened and participated in just such an exercise involving participants from the ROK, China, Japan, and the United States.

The 2009 Seoul workshop posed the focal question: "Northeast Asia 2050: Is there a role for civil society in meeting the climate change challenge?" Rather than focusing on the mitigation of greenhouse gas emissions that contribute to the problem of global climate change, the workshop reframed the question to ask how best to adapt to climate change. They asked: "Who can possibly help us prevent the most devastating impacts of climate disruption and how can this be done given the great uncertainty associated with possible impacts?"[9]

We recognized that many drivers that would determine the effectiveness of civil society in bringing about adaptation to climate change in 2050 were

---

within a society, but the same types may be examined across cultures. Giesen writes: "'Noncontemporaneity' refers to the local and temporal coexistence of phenomena that are related to different historical periods or different stages of social evolution... 'asynchronicity' centres [on] the differences of pace and rhythms between different social systems or institutional domains... 'divided memories' are generated by different experiential backgrounds with respect to the perception of core events." Giesen, B., "Noncontemporaneity, Asynchronicity and Divided Memories," *Time & Society*, 13(1) (2004), doi: http://dx.doi.org/10.1177/0961463X04040741

9 Nautilus Institute, *et al.*, "Northeast Asia 2050: Is There a Role for Civil Society in Meeting the Climate Change Challenge," in *Civil Society Scenarios Workshop* (Seoul: Nautilus Institute, 2009). The description of the 2009 scenarios in this chapter are drawn from this report.

unpredictable in either occurrence or size of impact, but also that they were potentially very powerful. The degree to which climate impacts were incremental or highly disruptive, and whether the response to these impacts was based on regional cooperation or on uncoordinated national actions, framed the four scenarios developed in the workshop. A team representing multiple cultures, countries, ages, professions, and perspectives developed each scenario into a narrative format of a future time.

In the first scenario, "Asian Carbon Union," which combined regional cooperation and major climate disruption, catastrophic climate events force the countries of the region to cooperate to adapt to the new realities. The result is greater regional integration and a setting aside of historical differences. The two Koreas reunify. Regional cooperation occurs to overcome "mad pig disease" in China. Shanghai and Tokyo build massive seawalls that stave off a super-cyclone in 2020. By the end of the period, Asia establishes a common currency, super-cheap solar cells are in general use, and all countries participate in a carbon emissions control scheme that forms the basis of a global agreement in 2050.

The second scenario, "Divided World, United Regions," combines uncoordinated national actions and incremental climate change. The world is divided and climate change accelerates, but the region unites as climate shocks from super-typhoons that hit Osaka and Tokyo force it to work together on regional and/or bilateral levels to address environmental problems such as yellow sand and acid rain, with solutions including the transfer of clean coal technology from Japan to China. This allows countries to adapt so that, by 2050, they are on the path to low-carbon, sustainable societies.

In the third scenario, named "Out of the Ashes, a Lily is Born," a series of relatively small climate shocks force the countries of East Asia to come together to address climate change. Chinese air pollution greatly affects Korea and Japan. Civil society and private enterprise take the lead in promoting adaptive strategies and developing green technologies. A terrorist nuclear attack in the Middle East traced back to Japanese plutonium forces Japan to abandon reprocessing and begin accelerating renewable energy and battery technology. Economic recession leads to the collapse of China's auto industry and forces political transition, prompting the first green party in China. Based on the new battery, a green Chinese car is produced — the Lily — and it forms the foundation of a massive Chinese export industry. In turn, a regional "green summit" is held, and regional networks for sustainable transport, food production, and energy are constructed. By 2050, networked local communities focused on sustainable lifestyles are the basis of a regional community.

In the fourth scenario, based on major climate shocks and uncoordinated national action, the region enters the "Spring-Autumn Period," the name suggesting a continuous cycle of growth and decay. States are overwhelmed by the onslaught of massive climate change impacts and cities are rebuilt around fuel type as the key adaptation. World trade collapses and a series of super-typhoons hit Northeast Asia, devastating coastal cities such as Tokyo, Shanghai, and Busan. At first, people try to rebuild in the old places, but continuous typhoons and flooding force them to reconsider. By 2020, Tokyo starts rebuilding to withstand hurricanes, but Shanghai is abandoned, while in Busan, people move into hillier areas and away from the shore. With the destruction of sea ports, global trade is now practically nonexistent. This in turn undermines the tax base and thus the power of central governments. Cities must therefore survive by providing their own food and energy.

Three types of cities emerge — coastal-sea access, coal-based, and biofueled. Each type develops autonomous energy structures based on locally available resources. Cities with access to the sea, such as Tokyo, extract uranium from seawater to fuel nuclear power plants. Because of the focus on high technology, they develop highly technocratic and authoritarian systems. They also develop nuclear weapons as a means of defense. With widespread electrification, these cities rely on a combination of surveillance and electronic entertainment to keep the people pacified. Most people outside of the nuclear priesthood work in the service sector and entertainment industries. Those cities located near coal deposits, like Wuhan in China, rely on coal, but with large-scale carbon capture and storage to prevent emissions. This carbon capture and storage requires massive infrastructure with endless mazes of mines, factories, pipes, and tunnels to mine the coal, process it, burn it, and store the emissions. This requires large stores of unskilled labor, leading to frequent labor strikes and crackdowns on unions. The cities rely for defense on a kind of "doomsday device," whereby any attack on the city would release the carbon into the atmosphere, causing equal disaster for the attacker.

Cities with available arable land, such as Busan, develop bio-fuels to survive. Because environmental conditions have made the large-scale agriculture of the past unsustainable, new methods to grow plants for fuel with a minimum of land or water need to be developed. This, together with the actual transformation of plants into fuel, requires a highly skilled, scientifically literate population. As a result, the bio-cities have a highly educated population and more egalitarian system than in the other cities. But they too rely on the deterrence of weapons of mass destruction – in their case powerful biological weapons. The reduction of arable land forces people to turn to alternative food sources, largely developed in the biofuel cities. New forms of high-protein mushrooms are introduced that provide high amounts of nutrition with a minimum of input. Scientists also develop "in vitro meat" — cloned tissue cultures that provide animal protein without requiring actual livestock. These are popularly known as "stem-cell burgers." Outside of the cities is a sort of "wild west" of pirates, brigands, and rebels who disrupt trade between cities or serve as "cat's paws" for particular cities in their battles against others.

In these imaginary futures, participants not only envisioned radically divergent futures from those that might emerge from mere extrapolation from the present. They also identified how civil society might have intervened to move the worlds of 2050 to more secure and sustainable outcomes. They were able to identify robust strategies to this end that were relevant to all of the four future worlds. These strategies illustrate the inter-related nature of a spectrum of climate-driven problems and their respective solutions. We found that no fewer than five generic robust strategies warrant the development of civil society action plans today to embrace uncertainty about the future. These were:

1. Regulate and Reward: regulation and financing such as the Green Fund played a crucial adaptation role in managing climate change in more than one scenario.

2. Localization: strengthening local civil society and local governments, shifts in factories, farming, education, and green development can be implemented much more quickly than by waiting for central government to affect change at the small community level.

3. Legal Frameworks: governing responses to climate change at multiple levels led to the need to create new legal frameworks based on civil society such as a "Civil Court for Climate Change."

4. Sustainable Food: developing sustainable food supplies was identified to be critically important in Japan, China, and South Korea.

5. Adaptive Unification: integrating the DPRK in a climate-challenged region as an equal partner in the network of adaptive response was

critical, albeit more difficult than it sounds because the DPRK has almost no civil society today.

Identifying such visionary steps is vacuous unless accountabilities are specified and capacities to enforce compliance with new regimes and institutions are mobilized. That is exactly the task with respect to responding to the climate problem undertaken by many civil society organizations in the region, as we outlined in chapters 2, 3, and 4. To develop a common agenda for action that sets milestones for realizing such strategies requires that each participant incorporate his or her accountability in these joint strategies into his or her own temporality. This shared time must be constantly updated and renegotiated to overcome division, fragmentation, and conflict inherited from the past that otherwise precludes or obstructs communication, coordination, and collaboration across borders required to solve global problems. This shared time may be termed complex time, meaning the adjustment of pre-existing patterns of time inhabited by civil society actors to the demands for new patterns of activity generated by complex global problem-solving and synchronized in new ways across borders.

Will East Asia Mega-cities be Secure and Sustainable by 2050?

In the second workshop held in 2010,[10] also in Seoul, the focal question was: "Will East Asia Mega-cities be Secure and Sustainable by 2050?"

Like the 2009 workshop, the participants were from China, Australia, the ROK, and Japan, plus the United States, and were diverse in generation, gender, and disciplines. They enumerated drivers that would affect the answer to the focal question, including nanotechnology and energy-related developments; pandemics; the effects of climate change, including drought, sea level rise and changes in agriculture; shifts in public policy at the inter-governmental, city, state and local levels; the increasing ease of communication across languages; global economic crisis and recovery; migration and population diversity; regional vs. national identity; terrorism; global stress causing psychological meltdowns in the population; nuclear

---

10   Nautilus Institute, "Will East Asia Mega-Cities Be Secure and Sustainable by 2050?," in *Global Scenarios 2010* (Seoul: Nautilus Institute, 2010). The description of the 2010 scenarios in this chapter are drawn from this report.

war in Korea; low birth rates; and Korean unification, among others. This vast terrain of uncertainty boiled down to two spectra that framed four scenarios: (1) the degree to which the economies of the region become "green" (connoting sustainable and clean practices) and strong as opposed to "brown" (referring to fossil fuels and pollution) and struggling and (2) the extent to which the region becomes geopolitically secure and stable versus insecure and disorderly.

The first 2010 scenario, "The Dark Age of the Mega-city," combines regional instability with weak and struggling economies. By 2050, states in Northeast Asia have invested mostly in conventional fossil fuels and nuclear energy, and US forces are retreating from the region due to financial crisis. Energy supplies, including offshore gas, are increasingly subject to military considerations. In 2030, a nuclear meltdown near Shanghai that sends fallout over Korea and Japan triggers regional recession. Environmental degradation and the impacts of climate change lead to food shortages and disease, which heighten tensions within major cities in Northeast Asia, particularly between ethnic groups. Major cities are divided into ethnic enclaves with hostile relationships among neighbors. By 2050, in this dystopic future, despair results in a societal psychological meltdown characterized by high suicide rates, hopelessness, low productivity, and the deterioration of the family unit in Japan and Korea. By 2050, the megacities of Northeast Asia are economically and culturally depressed. They are dark, polluted places full of despair and ethnic conflict.

In the second scenario, "Droughts Yield a Green Tomorrow, or From Gulag to Garden," the world in 2050 is characterized by regional instability and a strong green economy. In this narrative, whole watersheds in China collapse ecologically and force refugees to move into North Korea and Russia. The resulting food shortages in the DPRK lead to a coup by the modernizing military who decide to rejoin regional intergovernmental dialogue. In 2025, the United States, China, and South Korea support the transformation of Pyongyang into a world-class Green City. Civil society, corporations, and the former DPRK military capabilities rapidly undertake various economic projects and soon the infrastructure for jobs and development is strong. In 2028, a light railway system is constructed in Pyongyang as the city evolves into the "New Dubai" with the development of "Pyongsong" fuels, a renewable energy source. The new wealth and living conditions trigger a "Pyongsong" population boom — the wider Pyongyang-Kaesong population hits 10 million and, by 2050, instability in the region returns because the infrastructure cannot support the burgeoning population in the DPRK.

In the third scenario, "Green Gold Giga-City," the world in 2050 is characterized by regional stability and successful green economic development. The transition from Kim Jong-il to political reforms under his son Kim Jong-un moves faster than expected. Russia rapidly completes a train and gas pipeline to the ROK via the DPRK. In 2018, the ROK and DPRK presidents share the Nobel Peace Prize for creating a regional nuclear weapons-free zone, and the influence of the United States diminishes by the day. In 2028, Pyongyang hosts the Olympic Games. In 2030, China adopts a multi-party system. Technological change — a bio-chip that makes it possible to talk and instantaneously understand conversations in other languages, plus bio-fuelled or nuclear-electric cars – is widely adopted.

With one common market, many small cell-cities are networked into a billion-person or giga-city connected functionally, but not subject only to hierarchical rule by states. By 2050, cooperation to solve the problems of the giga-city is strong. By 2050, the giga-city of Pusan-Seoul-Pyongyang-Sinijui runs across the border and all the way down the northeast coast of China from Dandong to Shanghai, and Shanghai is connected with a tunnel running across the Bohai Gulf. Food production relies on industry, nutrients from sewage recycling, and, on the oceanic side, aquaculture integrated with massive tidal power structures. The region becomes fortified against storm surge, storms, and extreme wind. It has mastered the art of adaptation to bring hope and happiness to the denizens of the world's first giga-city.

In the fourth scenario, "Jaws," the world in 2050 is characterized by a struggling green economy and by regional stability and cooperation. Between 2010 and 2030 nuclear energy grows at a rapid rate. By 2030, it supplies 65 percent of energy in the region in the name of green growth. Unfortunately, the decrease in climate disrupting emissions is too late to protect the region from 47cm of sea level rise. In 2028, the Olympics are held in North Korea, and while reunification does not occur in this scenario, the international validation and recognition of the DPRK fosters economic cooperation between the two Koreas and results in increasing stability for the entire region.

In 2040, a massive earthquake triggers a tsunami that is exacerbated by the increased weight of the sea wreaking havoc upon disaster as the region's nuclear plants located on coastal shores are destroyed. These seemingly innocuous nuclear plants on the Northeast Asia seaboard are the "Jaws," the invisible sharks beneath the surface, which once awakened by the earthquake destroy that most basic infrastructure system: energy. In addition to the meltdown of the nuclear power plants, the mega-cities themselves suffer extreme damage. Levees break and communities go underwater. Flooding, homelessness, disease, and suffering abound.

The region is saved from despair by the foundation of good-will built up over the preceding three decades, which triggers international aid, although it is soon clear that what is rebuilt will not look like what was destroyed. Individual communities feel their governments failed them by relying so heavily on nuclear power and begin to shift focus towards more local governance and decentralized political systems. More threatening, however, is the shift away from nuclear and back to fossil fuel and climate-changing energy technologies.

The Jaws scenario reveals the premonitory power of imaginative thinking by cross-cultural, diverse groups of people. Only five months after developing the Jaws scenario, the 3/11 earthquake and tsunami devastated northeastern Japan, with global ramifications. The catastrophe came three decades earlier than envisioned in the Jaws scenario, but the lesson learned — how civil society must act to save itself when governments fail — is still playing out. Moreover, the 2010 scenario was not the only cross-cultural recognition that such an event could occur, and that the possibility called for a multi-national response.

Indeed, in 2007, Japanese, South Korean, and American military officials met to discuss scenarios which presented decision-makers with a "chain of regional crises for which they must analyze various possible measures to enhance tripartite collaboration in dealing with disaster, particularly centered on the military's role and capabilities in support of overall national objectives."[11] In one of these scenarios, the US military posited a major earthquake near Hokkaido, which sends a tsunami shoreward that causes carnage along the coastline and in port cities and damages two nuclear reactors. "Communications and assistance to the affected areas are being

---

11   See "140 Chain of Disasters," in *Open Scenarios Repository* (Alexandria: United States Institute for Defense Analyses), http://openscenarios.ida.org/docs/Open-Scenario-Repository-06-25-2010-2.pdf The scenarios exercise involved IDA, Korean Institute of Defense Analysis (Seoul), National Institute of Defense Analysis (Tokyo) and the Office of the Secretary of Defense, U.S. Department of Defense. The description of the scenario is drawn from this spreadsheet.

hampered by the poor conditions of infrastructure resulting from the long cold spell. The picture at the moment is bleak and information sparse."

In reality, after 3/11, tripartite military cooperation to respond to the tsunami and the Fukushima catastrophe was nearly non-existent. The US military played a major role in supporting the Japanese Self Defense Force. But Japanese civil society was left to fend for itself while the Japanese central government response was weak, confused, and generally resistant to accepting external assistance, even when offered by the ROK. Civil society, however, responded strongly. South Koreans donated $32 million to the relief effort in the first few weeks,[12] and 3/11 still resonates in the region, especially by fuelling skeptical voices about the future of nuclear power in the ROK and China.

Conclusion

In this book, we argue that the future of global and regional security and sustainability is becoming more complex over time. As many will attest, the future itself is experienced as fractured, discontinuous, divergent across and within borders, and even regressive (as in the DPRK, where time stands still or goes backwards). In short, the future is increasingly uncertain in ways that cannot be predicted.

This uncertainty is inherent in the displacement and discontinuity caused by the globalization of every aspect of human existence — economic, political, cultural, technological, and even ecological — the basis of life. Also, the memories of key defining moments of the past — great catastrophes, wars, and protracted emergencies — are redefined or shed with each generation that passes. New crises form the basis of the identity and orientation of rising leaders towards the future. Some challenges such as climate change may lead to such radical outcomes that core elite beliefs — for example, that economic and technological modernization are inherently progressive — are rendered obsolete and even absurd, with consequences for the political legitimacy of the entire state. Although common causes drive problems such as climate change, the uneven distribution of positive

---

12   Borowiec, S., "Tsunami Diplomacy: South Korea and Japan," *The Global Post*, 3 April 2011, http://www.globalpost.com/dispatch/news/regions/asia-pacific/south-korea/110331/south-korea-japan-tsunami-aid

and negative climate impacts may subvert the notion that shared futures are desirable within and between nations and societies.[13]

Other global and regional problems that cross borders and make societies interdependent on a scale and pace never before seen in human history — the threat of global pandemics, for example — lurk in the wings, waiting for a tipping point to be exceeded that calls them to lurch onto center-stage. When they do, we can expect some states to close borders in a desperate attempt to stave off viral transmission — as if we could control the movement of birds or people in a timely manner from the viewpoint of mutating viruses.

Currently, historical disputes pitting China and the ROK against Japan divide and separate rather than integrate and unify the region. Indeed, in many respects, Northeast Asia is more of an anti-region than a regional community. Such antagonistic dynamics are more powerful for many people than those associated with universal values, common culture, and hybrid identities grounded in shared experience, especially when demagogic leaders stir the pot with nationalist narratives designed to scapegoat the other and the outsider — the true politics of ire. Such division, confrontation, and fragmentation make it more difficult to agree on the importance of common problems and the implementation of shared solutions.

The word complexity, or 複雑 in Chinese, suggests something that is complicated, intricate, and has many parts. 複雑 in Japanese, the phrase has connotations of "enfolding," as if hidden in layers of clothing, with resulting opacity as to what lies below the outermost layer. 복잡성 in Korean, it has a similar meaning, but carries no inherent connotation of goodness or badness — the significance of complexity is context-dependent. In Chinese, Japanese, and Korean, the noun does not carry the baggage that it has in English, wherein the original word has more of a sense of intertwined braids that are so snarled as to be not only complicated, but also incomprehensible or inexplicable — and therefore possibly to be feared (this English meaning in English originated in the 17th century from the Latin *complexus* and entered the lexicon via French). Only in English does the word carry the modern, scientific meaning of "complexity," referring to an open, self-organizing system constituted by many, diverse elements and characterized by non-linear change and discontinuous change (see

---

13   Beck, U., *et al.* (2012).

chapter 2). As the modern meaning of complexity in English carries many connotations of change, it is linked inherently to concepts of time, which flows differently in China, Korea, and Japan, depending in part on how "westernized" the society has become. Thus, how a given civil society or individual perceives complex global problems is laden with temporality, which will also inform their response, thereby contributing to a shared "complex time" when the response is cross-cultural and cross-border.

Just as cultural orientations towards "complexity" differ in subtle ways across cultures, borders, and languages, so nation-states employ different overarching strategies to absorb the impacts of unpredictable, catastrophic events such as tsunamis, financial crises, or wars. Thus, the Chinese state relies on the sheer mass of its economy and the breadth of its geography to absorb body blows and supplements local and provincial capacities with centrally directed resources, especially military ones.

In Japan, after its remaking by the American Occupation and its aftermath, the central state planned many aspects of life top-down in infinite detail, including for contingencies, although some areas were simply neglected or left to the corporate sector. The latter dynamic accelerated with deregulation and liberalization in the 1980s. Thus, when ambushed by real world catastrophes like the 3/11 earthquake and tsunami, the central state was immobilized and corporate management collapsed, whereas local civil society and local governments improvised recovery strategies from the bottom-up, relying on decentralized social capacity to respond to catastrophe. In contrast, the South Korean state relies heavily on its ability to redirect corporate entities to adjust quickly and mobilize capacity to respond to challenges and exploit opportunities with agility.

However, each of these state-centered strategies has fallen short of an effective response in the face of complex major events — the ROK in the face of the North Korean nuclear breakout in 2006 onwards, China in response to the 2008 Sichuan earthquake, and Japan in the aftermath of the 3/11 earthquake and tsunami. In each case, civil society organizations stepped forward to carry much of the load of emergency response. We suggest that in the case of many urgent regional security and sustainability issues, such as migration, energy and urban insecurity, nuclear weapons, and climate change adaptation, it is civil society organizations that cross borders to create transnational networks that anticipate future crises. By doing so, these civil society organizations create a new layer of social complexity commensurate with that of the emerging problem-terrain.

The conduct of civic diplomacy as outlined in this book requires inspirational vision as well as skillful networking and specialized capacities from civil society. In reality, all people inhabit civil society in some manner, including those located in formal institutions of the state and in the corporate-market sector. To be effective, civil society strategies of engagement and collaboration must involve ordinary citizens, not just officials, corporate leaders, or senior scholars such as mostly appear at the Asan Institute or the Jeju Forum. It must include the lowest-ranking member of status hierarchies as well as the super-elites, not least because the former do so much work that is invisible for much of the time, but because as farmers, fishermen, cleaners, miners, recyclers, they do many jobs on which everyone else depends.

If civil society is to be truly effective in solving linked global problems, then everyone must mobilize in one way or another. Everyone has a significant role to play. All voices must be heard. No one can be forgotten or left behind for the simple reason that no one can predict which butterfly amongst millions may cause a hurricane. No one knows who will invent desperately needed solutions to urgent global problems.

Bibliography

"4th Asia Pacific Consultation on Refugee Rights Concludes," *Asia Pacific Refugee Rights Network*, 30 August 2012, http://www.aprrn.info/1/index.php/news/123-4th-asia-pacific-consultation-on-refugee-rights-concludes

"6년만에 기업인으로 돌아온 문국현 '한솔섬유 히든챔피언 만들겠다," *Hankyoreh*, 4 July 2013, http://www.hani.co.kr/arti/economy/economy_general/594451.html

"140 Chain of Disasters," in Open Scenarios Repository (Alexandria: United States Institute for Defense Analyses), http://openscenarios.ida.org/docs/Open-Scenario-Repository-06-25-2010-2.pdf

The 13th Tripartite Environment Ministers Meeting (TEMM13) (Tripartite Environment Ministers Meeting), http://www.temm.org/sub05/view.jsp?id=20

Abuja, *et al.*, "A Man and a Morass," *The Economist*, 26 May 2011, http://www.economist.com/node/18741606

Aerts, J., *et al.*, *Connecting Delta Cities, Coastal Cities, Flood Risk Management and Adaptation to Climate Change* (Amsterdam: VU University Press, 2009).

Akaha, T., "Human Security in East Asia: Embracing Global Norms through Regional Cooperation in Human Trafficking, Labour Migration, and HIV/AIDS," *Journal of Human Security*, 5(2) (2009), doi: http://dx.doi.org/10.3316/JHS0502011

Ali, S., "Designing Ecological Peace in the Koreas," *National Geographic Newswatch*, 23 December 2011, http://voices.nationalgeographic.com/2011/12/23/designing-ecological-peace-in-the-koreas

Allison, G., "Confronting the Specter of Nuclear Terrorism," *ANNALS of the American Academy of Political and Social Science*, 607(Special Issue) (2006), doi: http://dx.doi.org/10.1177/0002716206290912

Allouche, J., "Does the Nexus Mask a Bigger Debate? Rethinking the Food-Energy-Water Nexus and a Low Water Economy," *Knowledge, Technology and Society*, 21 March 2014, http://www.water-energy-food.org/en/news/view__1607/does-the-nexus-mask-a-bigger-debate.html?-rethinking-the-food-energy-water-nexus-and-a-low-water-economy

Alvarez, R., *et al.*, "Reducing the Hazards from Stored Spent Power-Reactor Fuel in the United States," *Science and Global Security*, 11 (2003), http://dx.doi.org/10.1080/08929880309006

Anderson, D., *et al.*, *A Conceptual Design Tool for Exploiting Interlinkages between the Focal Areas of the GEF*, GEF working paper (Washington, DC: Global Environment Facility, 2004).

Anderson, D., *et al.*, *World Energy Assessment* (New York: United Nations Development Programme, 2004).

Anton, P.S., *et al.*, *The Global Technology Revolution*, Monograph Reports (Santa Monica: RAND Corporation, 2001).

Arai, M., "New Energy Systems in Railroads," in *Confederation of Asia-Pacific Chambers of Commerce and Industry* (East Japan Railway Company, 2009).

Arbatov, A., and Dvorkin, V., *The Great Strategic Triangle*, The Carnegie Papers (Moscow: Carnegie Moscow Center, Carnegie Endowment for International Peace, 2013).

Aronson, D., *Overview of Systems Thinking* (1998), http://www.thinking.net/Systems_Thinking/OverviewSTarticle.pdf

Asan Institute, "Asan Plenum 2012 – Proceedings," in *Asan Plenum 2012* (Seoul: Asan Institute, 2012), http://en.asaninst.org/proceedings-for-the-asan-plenum-2012

Asan Institute, "Proceedings for the Asan Plenum 2011," in *Asan Plenum 2011* (Seoul: Asan Institute, 2011), http://asaninst.org/proceedings-for-the-asan-plenum-2011

ASEAN Plus Three Cooperation (Jakarta: Association of Southeast Asian Nations, 2012), http://www.asean.org/asean/external-relations/asean-3/item/asean-plus-three-cooperation

Asia — Member Cities (Hiroshima: Mayors for Peace), http://www.mayorsforpeace.org/english/membercity/asia/index.html

Asia Pacific Energy Research Centre, *Electric Power Grid Interconnections in the APEC Region* (Tokyo: Japan Institute of Energy Economics, 2004).

Asia Pacific Refugee Rights Network (Bangkok: Asia Pacific Refugee Rights Network), http://www.aprrn.info/1

Asia Peace and History Education Network, "Look at the History of That Obligation for Future Generations!," *Asia Peace and History Education Network Blog*, 11 May 2001, http://yespeace.tistory.com/2

Asuka, J., *A Brief Memo on Environmental Security Regimes in the Asian Region*, PARES project (Berkeley: Nautilus Institute, 1997).

Babicz, L., "South Korea, Japan, and China: In Search of a Shared Historical Awareness," in *6th Biennial Conference of the Korean Studies Association of Australasia* (Sydney: University of Sydney, 2009).

Banks, D., *et al.*, *Environmental Crime, a Threat to Our Future* (London: Environmental Investigation Agency, 2008).

Bar-Yam, Y., *Complexity of Military Conflict: Multiscale Complex Systems Analysis of Littoral Warfare* (Cambridge: New England Complex Systems Institute, 2003).

Baranger, M., *Chaos, Complexity, and Entropy. A Physics Talk for Non-Physicists* (Cambridge: New England Complex Systems Institute, 2001).

Basic Universal Problems (Brussels: Union of International Associations), http://www.uia.be/node/328165

Bates, M., "Growth Prospects and the Potential for Progress in the DPRK's Agricultural Sector: Infrastructure and Incentives," *Sino-NK*, 23 June 2013, http://sinonk.com/2013/06/23/growth-prospects-and-the-potential-for-progress-in-the-dprks-agricultural-sector-infrastructure-and-incentives

Beck, U., *Cosmopolitan Vision* (Oxford: Polity, 2006).

Beck, U., *et al.*, "Cosmopolitan Communities of Climate Risk: Conceptual and Empirical Suggestions for a New Research Agenda," *Global Networks*, 13(1) (2013), doi: http://dx.doi.org/10.1111/glob.12001

Bennett, B.W., "North Korea's WMD Capability and the Regional Military Balance: A US Perspective," *Korean Journal of Security Affairs*, 14(2) (2009).

Bennett, B.W., *Uncertainties in the North Korean Nuclear Threat*, Document Briefing (Santa Monica: RAND Corporation, 2010).

Berry, B.J.L., *et al.*, "Adaptive Agents, Intelligence, and Emergent Human Organization: Capturing Complexity through Agent-Based Modeling," *Proceedings of the National Academy of the Sciences*, 99(Suppl 3) (2002), doi: http://dx.doi.org/10.1073/pnas.092078899

Beyea, J., *et al.*, "Damages from a Major Release of 137 Cs into the Atmosphere of the United States," *Science and Global Security*, 12 (2004), doi: http://dx.doi.org/10.1080/08929880490464775

Billé, F., *et al.*, *Frontier Encounters: Knowledge and Practice at the Russian, Chinese and Mongolian Border* (Cambridge: Open Book Publishers, 2012), doi: 10.11647/OBP.0026

Blackburn, J.O., and Cunningham, S., *Solar and Nuclear Costs — the Historic Crossover* (Durham: NC WARN: Waste Awareness & Reduction Network, 2010).

Blair, D.C., and Hanley, J.T., "From Wheels to Webs: Reconstructing Asia-Pacific Security Arrangements," *The Washington Quarterly*, 24(1) (2001), doi: http://dx.doi.org/10.1162/016366001561393

Bo, L., and Lianjun, T., "Vulnerability and Sustainable Development Mode of Coal Cities in Northeast China," *Chinese Geographical Science*, 18(2) (2008), doi: http://dx.doi.org/10.1007/s11769-008-0119-0

Bo, W., "Urban Security in China," in *Interconnections of Global Problems in East Asia, Green Economy, Urban Security And Energy Security* (Seoul: Nautilus Institute, 2010).

Bodeen, C., "SKorean President in Beijing for Summit with Xi," *Associated Press*, 27 June 2013, http://bigstory.ap.org/article/skorean-president-beijing-summit-xi

Borowiec, S., "Tsunami Diplomacy: South Korea and Japan," *The Global Post*, 3 April 2011, http://www.globalpost.com/dispatch/news/regions/asia-pacific/south-korea/110331/south-korea-japan-tsunami-aid

Bracken, P., *The Structure of the Second Nuclear Age*, E-Notes (Philadelphia: Foreign Policy Research Institute, 2003).

Bracken, P.J., *The Command and Control of Nuclear Forces* (New Haven: Yale University Press, 1983).

Braddock, J.V., *et al.*, *Targeting the Soviet Army Along the Sino-Soviet Border* (The BDM Corporation, released under US Freedom of Information Act request to Nautilus Institute, 1978).

Brief History — History of 20 Years (Seoul: Seoul Forum), http://seoulforum.or.kr/text.php?mid=m01_03

British Petroleum, *BP Statistical Review of World Energy* (British Petroleum, 2013).

British Petroleum, *BP Statistical Review of World Energy June 2011* (British Petroleum, 2011).

Brookings Institution, *The Sixth Seoul-Washington Forum: Moving the United States-Korea Relationship Forward in Changing Environments* (Washington, DC: Brookings Institution, 2012), http://www.brookings.edu/events/2012/06/08-seoul-washington-forum

Brown, K., "China: What We Think We Know Is Wrong," *Open Democracy*, 15 May 2013, http://www.opendemocracy.net/kerry-brown/china-what-we-think-we-know-is-wrong

Bunn, M., *et al.*, *Controlling Nuclear Warheads and Materials: A Report Card and Action Plan*, Project on Managing the Atom (2003).

Bureau of the Environment, *Guidelines for Heat Island Control Measures* (Tokyo: Tokyo Metropolitan Government, 2005).

Buys, A., *Proliferation Risk Assessment of Former Nuclear Explosives/Weapons Program Personnel: The South African Case Study*, NAPSNet Special Report (2011).

Byun, D.K., "S. Korea, Japan Inch Closer to Shared Perception of History," *Yonhap News Agency*, 23 March 2010, http://english.yonhapnews.co.kr/national/2010/03/23/24/0301000000AEN20100323004800315F.HTML

C40 Large Cities Climate Leadership Group, "The World Ports Climate Declaration and Endorsement Ceremony: Declaration," in *C40 World Ports Climate Conference* (Rotterdam: C40 World Ports, 2008).

Callahan, W.A., *Contingent States: Greater China and Transnational Relations* (Minessotta: Minessotta University Press, 2004).

Calmes, J., and Myers, S.L., "U.S. And China Move Closer on North Korea, but Not on Cyberespionage," *New York Times*, 8 June 2013, http://www.nytimes.com/2013/06/09/world/asia/obama-and-xi-try-building-a-new-model-for-china-us-ties.html?pagewanted=1&_r=0&ref=world

Cao, G.Y., *et al.*, "Urban Growth in China: Past, Prospect, and Its Impacts," *Population and Environment*, 33(2-3) (2012), doi: http://dx.doi.org/10.1007/s11111-011-0140-6

Caukin, J., "40 Million People: How Far We've Come," *Skype Big Blog*, 10 April 2012, http://blogs.skype.com/2012/04/10/40-million-people-how-far-weve/

CBS/Associated Press, "Shots Fired as North Koreans Cross DMZ," *CBS News*, 11 February 2009, http://www.cbsnews.com/stories/2006/10/07/world/main2072358.shtml

Central Intelligence Agency, *The World Factbook* (Washington, DC: Central Intelligence Agency, 2011), https://http://www.cia.gov/library/publications/the-world-factbook/index.html

Chaibong, H., "Interview with Denney, S." (July 24, 2013).

Chaihark, H., "Human Rights in Korea," in *Human Rights in Asia: A Comparative Legal Study of Twelve Asian Jurisdictions, France and the USA*, ed. by Peerenboom, R., *et al.* (Abingdon: Taylor & Francis, 2006), pp. 265-97.

Chavez-Dreyfuss, G., "FOREX-Dollar Falls as Oil Prices Rise on Iran News," *Reuters*, 9 July 2008, http://www.reuters.com/article/2008/07/09/markets-forex-idUSN0943813620080709

Chen, X., and Liu, C., "The Reluctant Powerful Participant: China on, in, and out of the Pan-Yellow Sea Rim," in *2010 Presidential Committee on Regional Development International Conference* (Jeju, 2010).

Chen, Y., *Energy Science and Technology in China: A Roadmap to 2050.* ed. by Sciences, C.A.o. (Berlin: Springer, 2010).

China Daily staff writer, "British Media Says North Korean 3G Mobile Phone Users to Reach One Million," *China Daily*, 21 November 2011, http://news.163.com/11/1121/11/7JCM79DL00014JB5.html

China Institute of Spatial Planning & Regional Economy, *et al.*, *Proposal for Promotion of the Realization of the BESETO Corridor Vision – toward Sustained Development in the Northeast Asia Region* (Tokyo: National Institute for Research Advancement, 2007).

China Internet Statistics Whitepaper (Singapore: China Internet Watch, 2013), http://www.chinainternetwatch.com/whitepaper/china-internet-statistics

Chinese Nuclear Arms Control and Disarmament: Principal Players and Policy-Making Processes (Monterey: Center for Nonproliferation Studies, James Martin Center for Nonproliferation Studies, 2009), http://cns.miis.edu/opapers/op15/chart_11x17_china.pdf

Cho, M., "Is the Green Economy Secure in Korea? Dissecting Korea's Green Growth Strategy," in *Interconnections of Global Problems in East Asia, Green Economy, Urban Security And Energy Security* (Seoul: Nautilus Institute, 2010).

Cho, M., "Trends and Prospects of Urbanization in Korea: Reflections on Korean Cities" (Korean Language), *Economy and Society*, 30(29) (2003).

Choe, S.C., "The Evolving Urban System in North-East Asia," in *Emerging World Cities in Pacific Asia*, ed. by Yeung, Y. and Lo, F. (Tokyo: United Nations University Press, 1996).

Choe, S.C., "Incheon City-Region in Korea: Gateway to Northeast Asia – Aspiring to Be an Innovative and Learning Region," in *2nd International Conference on the Process of Innovation and Learning in Dynamic City-Region* (Bangalore: United Nations Industrial Development Organization, 2005).

Choe, S.C., *Status and Role of Seoul for the 21st Century* (Seoul: Seoul Development Institute, 1994).

Choi, J.J., "The Democratic State Engulfing Civil Society: The Ironies of Korean Democracy," *Korean Studies*, 34 (2010), https://muse.jhu.edu/journals/korean_studies/v034/34.choi.html

Choi, Y., "Baekdudaegan, the Central Axis of the Korean Peninsular: The Path toward Management Strategies Regarding to Its Concepts," in *Ecological Issues in a Changing World Status, Response and Strategy*, ed. by Hong, S.-g. and Hong, S.-K. (Berlin: Springer, 2004).

Chuanjiang, J., and Ruixue, Z., "Shandong's 'Solar Valley' Basks in Success," *China Daily*, 11 August 2010, http://www.chinadaily.com.cn/cndy/2010-08/11/content_11134110.htm

Chun, H.M., *et al.*, "South Korea as an Emerging Donor: Challenges and Changes on Its Entering OECD/DAC," *Journal of International Development*, 22(6) (2010), doi: http://dx.doi.org/10.1002/jid.1723

Chung, S.-Y., "Climate Change and Security in East Asia: Mapping Civil Society Organizations' Contributions," in *A Growing Force: Civil Society's Role in Asian Regional Security*, ed. by Sukma, R. and Gannon, J. (Tokyo: Japan Center for International Exchange, 2013).

City Safety Agency of Seoul, *Report of Disasters in Seoul 2010* (Seoul: City Safety Agency of Seoul, 2011).

Clawson, P., "Energy Security in a Time of Plenty," *Strategic Forum*, 130 (1997), file:///Users/arabellaimhoff/Downloads/ADA394273%20(2).pdf

Climate Change and Environmental Risk Atlas 2013 (Bath: Verisk Maplecroft, 2013), http://maplecroft.com/about/news/ccvi_2013.html

Cockle, J., "The Army's Role," *NBC Report* (1998), http://www.hsdl.org/?view&doc=11715&coll=limited

Cole, E.A., and Barsalou, J., *Unite or Divide?: The Challenges of Teaching History in Societies Emerging from Violent Conflict*, Special Report (Washington, DC: United States Institute of Peace, 2006).

Concluded Working and Study Groups (Kuala Lumpur: Council for Security Cooperation in the Asia Pacific), http://www.cscap.org/index.php?page=concluded-working-and-study-grups

Council of Local Authorities for International Relations, *Local Authorities International Cooperation Network* (Council of Local Authorities for International Relations, 2003),

Countries (Washington, DC: Energy Information Administration, US Department of Energy), http://www.eia.gov/countries/

Coward, M., Network-Centric Violence, "Critical Infrastructure and the Urbanization of Security," *Security Dialogue*, 40(4-5) (2009), doi: http://dx.doi.org/10.1177/0967010609342879

CTBR staff writer, "Australia's Rudd Government Invites Industry Bids to Transform Its Energy Grid through Smart Grid, Smart City Initiative," *Clean Technology Business Review*, 29 October 2009, http://www.cleantechnology-business-review. com/news/australias_rudd_government_invites_industry_bids_to_transform_ its_energy_grid_through_smart_grid_smart_city_initiative_091029

Cumming, G.S., and Norberg, J., *Complexity Theory for a Sustainable Future, Complexity in Ecological Systems* (New York: Columbia University Press, 2008).

Data Sets, Global Rural-Urban Mapping Project (New York: SocioEconomic and Applications Data Center, Colombia University), http://sedac.ciesin.columbia. edu/data/collection/grump-v1/sets/browse

Davis, M., *Planet of Slums* (London: Vigo, 2006).

De Wit, A., *Japan's Nuclear Village Wages War on Renewable Energy and the Feed-in Tariff*, NAPSNet Policy Forum (Nautilus Institute, 2011).

Demick, B., "More South Koreans Support Developing Nuclear Weapons," *Los Angeles Times*, 18 May 2013, http://articles.latimes.com/2013/may/18/world/la-fg-south-korea-nuclear-20130519

Deng, Q., "Natural Disasters, Migration and Urban Insecurity in China," in *Interconnection Among Global Problems in Northeast Asia Workshop* (Paju: Nautilus Institute, 2009).

Denney, S., "The Public Sphere in South Korea: Kim Young-Hwan on the National Security Act," *Sino-NK*, 26 September 2012, http://sinonk.com/2012/09/26/the-public-sphere-in-south-korea-kim-young-hwan-on-the-national-security-act

di Nicola, A., "Trafficking in Human Beings and Smuggling of Migrants," in *The Handbook of Transnational Crime and Justice*, ed. by Reichel, P.L. (New York: Sage Publications, 2005).

Diamond, J.M., *Collapse : How Societies Choose to Fail or Succeed* (New York: Viking, 2005).

The DMZ Forum (New York: The DMZ Forum, 2010), http://www.dmzforum.org

Douglass, M., "Toward Participatory Governance of Transborder Intercity Regions in Asia," in *Interventions in the Political Geography of Asia's Transborder Urban Networks: Working Paper Series 193*, ed. by Miller, M.A. and Bunnell, T. (Singapore: Asia Research Institute, National University of Singapore, 2012).

Drexler, M., *Influencing Complex Systems – a Systemic Overview*, Young Global Leaders: Guide to Influencing Complex Systems (Geneva: World Economic Forum, 2012).

Ducruet, C., and Notteboom, T., "The Worldwide Maritime Network of Container Shipping: Spatial Structure and Regional Dynamics," *Global Networks*, 12(3) (2012), doi: http://dx.doi.org/10.1111/j.1471-0374.2011.00355.x

East Asia Environmental Information Center (Tokyo: Asia 3R Citizen's Network), http://www.asia3r.net/en/link/eden-j.html

East Asia Institute, *EAI East Asia Institute: 2002-2012* (Seoul: East Asia Institute, 2012).

East Asia Institute, *East Asia Institute 2008-2009 Annual Report* (Seoul: East Asia Institute, 2009).

Ebenhack, B.W., and Martinez, D.M., "Understanding of the Role of Energy Consumption in Human Development through the Use of Saturation Phenomena," *Energy Policy*, 36 (2008), doi: http://dx.doi.org/10.1016/j.enpol.2007.12.016

Ebinger, J., and Vergara, W., *Climate Impacts on Energy Systems: Key Issues for Energy Sector Adaptation* (Washington, DC: The World Bank, 2011).

The Economist, "Could Asia Really Go to War over These?," *The Economist*, 22 September 2012, http://www.economist.com/node/21563316

Encyclopedia of World Problems and Human Potential (Wikipedia), http://en.wikipedia.org/wiki/Encyclopedia_of_World_Problems_and_Human_Potential

Endicott, J.E., "Limited Nuclear-Weapon-Free Zones: The Time Has Come," *Korean Journal of Defense Analysis*, 20(1) (2008), doi: http://dx.doi.org/10.1080/10163270802006305

Energy Data and Modeling Center, *Handbook of Energy & Economic Statistics in Japan '08*, Japan Energy Conservation Center (Tokyo: Institute of Energy Economics, 2009).

Enviro Asia (East Asia Environmental Information Centre), http://www.enviroasia.info/

Environmental Ship Index ESI (World Ports Climate Initiative), http://esi.wpci.nl/Public/Home

EPIK Spiders — Bakground (Exchange Panel for Interdisciplinary Knowledge network), http://epik.eai.or.kr/staff.asp

Fan, C.C., "Foreign Trade and Regional Development in China," *Geographical Analysis*, 24(3) (1992), doi: http://dx.doi.org/10.1111/j.1538-4632.1992.tb00264.x

Ferris, E., and Solís, M., "Earthquake, Tsunami, Meltdown – the Triple Disaster's Impact on Japan, Impact on the World," 11 March 2013, http://www.brookings.edu/blogs/up-front/posts/2013/03/11-japan-earthquake-ferris-solis

Fischer-Kowalski, M., *et al.*, *Decoupling Natural Resource Use and Environmental Impacts from Economic Growth* (Nairobi: United Nations Environment Programme, 2011).

Fisk, D.J., and Kerhervé, J., "Complexity as a Cause of Unsustainability," *Ecological Complexity*, 3(4) (2006), doi: http://dx.doi.org/10.1016/j.ecocom.2007.02.007

Friedhoff, K., "Interview with Denney, S." (July 22, 2013).

Fujino, J., "Backcasting and a Dozen Actions for 70% CO2 Emissions Reductions by 2050 in Japan," in *Low Carbon Society Symposium* (Tokyo, Japan, 2009).

Fujino, J., "Japan and Asian Low-Carbon Society Scenarios and Actions," in *East Asia Low Carbon Green Growth Roadmap Informal Brainstorming Meeting* (Bangkok, 2010).

Fujita, E.S., "Middle Power Diplomatic Strategy of Brazil and Policy Recommendations for South Korea's Middle Power," in *The Third Roundtable Discussion for Middle Power Diplomacy* (Seoul: East Asia Institute, 2013).

Futrell, W.C., "Environmental Networks and Flows in Northeast Asia: NGOs and Institutes Working on Sandstorms and Migratory Birds," in *ISA's 49th Annual Convention, Bridging Multiple Divides* (San Francisco: International Studies Association, 2008).

Futrell, W.C., "Shallow Roots: Transnational Environmental Civil Society in Northeast Asia," in *American Sociological Association's 103rd Annual Convention* (Boston: American Sociological Association, 2008).

Gabel, M., and Bruner, H., *Global Inc: An Atlas of the Multinational Corporation* (New York: New York Press, 2003).

Gaffney, O., "Tracking China's Urban Emissions," *Global Change Magazine*, 1 December 2009, http://www.igbp.net/news/opinion/opinion/trackingchinasurb anemissions.5.1b8ae20512db692f2a680003075.html

Gangzhe, L., *Research Trends: Research on a Grand Design for Northeast Asia* (Tokyo: National Institute for Research Advancement, 2006).

Gao, G., "1,000 New-Energy Cars to Have Trial Run in 10 Cities," *Gasgoo.com*, 24 October 2008, http://autonews.gasgoo.com/china-news/1-000-new-energy-cars-to-have-trial-run-in-10-citi-081024.shtml

Gaye, A., *Access to Energy and Human Devel* (New York: United Nations Development Programme, 2008).

GDP (Current US$) (Washington, DC: The World Bank), http://data.worldbank.org/indicator/NY.GDP.MKTP.CD?order=wbapi_data_value_2011+wbapi_data_value+wbapi_data_value-last&sort=desc

Geanakoplos, J., "Common Knowledge," *The Journal of Economic Perspectives*, 6(4) (1992), http://www.jstor.org/stable/2138269

Giesen, B., "Noncontemporaneity, Asynchronicity and Divided Memories," *Time & Society*, 13(1) (2004), doi: http://dx.doi.org/10.1177/0961463X04040741

Gitay, H., et al., "Interlinkages: Governance for Sustainability, Section D: Human Dimensions of Environmental Change," in *Global Environmental Outlook GEO 4* (Kenya: United Nations Environment Programme, 2007).

Global Asia (Seoul: East Asia Foundation), http://www.globalasia.org/

Goldin, I., and Mariathasan, M., *The Butterfly Defect: How Globalization Creates Systemic Risks, and What to Do About It, Princeton University* (Princeton: Princeton University Press, 2014).

Goodby, J., *Regional Framework for a Comprehensive Security Settlement: Does It Work?*, NAPSNet Policy Forum (Nautilus Institute, 2012).

Gormley, D.M., *Missile Contagion: Cruise Missile Proliferation and the Threat to International Security* (Santa Barbara: Praeger Security International, 2008).

GPPAC Seoul Committee, *Northeast Asia Activity Report* (Global Partnership for Prevention of Armed Conflict, 2005).

GPPAC Seoul Committee, *Women's Exchange for Peace Building on the Korean Peninsula*, Northeast Asia Activity Report (Global Partnership for Prevention of Armed Conflict, 2005).

Gray, D., "Keeping Its Head above Water," *Associated Press*, 27 October 2007, http://v1.theglobeandmail.com/servlet/Page/document/hubsv3/Travel/travelPages?activities=floods

Green Economy and Sustainable Development (New York: United Nations Conference on Sustainable Development, Rio +20).

Gries, P., "Disillusionment and Dismay: How Chinese Netizens Think and Feel About the Two Koreas," *Journal of East Asian Studies*, 12(1) (2012), http://journals.rienner.com/doi/abs/10.5555/1598-2408-12.1.31

Gupta, E., "Oil Vulnerability Index of Oil-Importing Countries," *Energy Policy*, 36(3) (2008), doi: http://dx.doi.org/10.1016/j.enpol.2007.11.011

Ha, Y.S., *Path to an Advanced North Korea by 2032: Building a Complex Networked State*, EAI Asia Security Initiative Working Paper (East Asia Institute, 2011).

Haas, E.B., "Turbulent Fields and the Theory of Regional Integration," *International Organization*, 30(02) (1976), doi: http://dx.doi.org/10.1017/S0020818300018245

Halford, G.S., *et al.*, "How Many Variables Can Humans Process?," *Psychological Science*, 16(1) (2005), doi: http://dx.doi.org/10.1111/j.0956-7976.2005.00782.x

Halperin, M., *The Nuclear Dimension of the U.S.-Japan Alliance*, NASPNet Special Report (n.d., circa 2000).

Halperin, M., *Promoting Security in Northeast Asia: A New Approach*, NAPSNet Policy Forum (Nautilus Institute, 2012).

Han, Y.J., *The Necessity and Role of a Cooperative System among the Northeast Asian Mega-Cities; the Future of Northeast Asian Mega-Cities* (Seoul: Seoul Development Institute, 1994).

Hankyoreh, "S. Korea Becomes First Former Aid Recipient to Join OECD Development Assistance Committee," *The Hankyoreh*, 26 November 2009, http://english.hani.co.kr/arti/english_edition/e_editorial/389918.html

Harlan, C., "Japanese Prime Minister Naoto Kan Calls for Phase-out of Nuclear Power," *Washington Post*, 13 July 2011, http://www.washingtonpost.com/world/japans-prime-minister-calls-for-phase-out-of-nuclear-power/2011/07/13/gIQAXxUJCI_story.html

Harrison, H., "Popular Responses to the Atomic Bomb in China 1945-1955," *Past & Present*, 218(Supplement 8) (2013), doi: http://dx.doi.org/10.1093/pastj/gts036

Harrison, N.E., *Complexity in World Politics: Concepts and Methods of a New Paradigm* (New York: State University of New York Press, 2006).

Harrison, N.E., "Thinking About the World We Make," in *Complexity in World Politics: Concepts and Methods of a New Paradigm*, ed. by Harrison, N.E. (Albany: State University of New York Press, 2006).

Hassig, K.O., *Northeast Asian Strategic Security Environment Study* (Alexandria: Institute for Defense Analyses, 2001).

Hayes, P., "Fukushima's Implications for Korea's Nuclear Dilemmas," *East Asia Forum*, 14 May 2011, http://www.eastasiaforum.org/2011/05/14/fukushima-s-implications-for-korea-s-nuclear-dilemmas

Hayes, P., *Pacific Powderkeg: American Nuclear Dilemmas in Korea* (Lanham: Lexington Books, 1991).

Hayes, P., *The Potential for Environmental Action: Report to the UNEP* (Geneva: NGO Environment Liaison Board, 1976).

Hayes, P., "The Role of Think Tanks in Defining Security Issues and Agendas," in *Presentation to Defence and Strategic Studies Course* (Canberra: Australian Defence College, 2004).

Hayes, P., *The Stalker State: North Korean Proliferation and the End of American Nuclear Hegemony*, NAPSNet Policy Forum (Nautilus Institute, 2006).

Hayes, P., "The Status Quo Isn't Working: A Nuke-Free Zone Is Needed Now," *Global Asia* (2010).

Hayes, P., "Sustainable Security in the Korean Peninsula: Envisioning a Northeast Asian Biodiversity Corridor," *The Korean Journal of International Studies*, 8(10) (2010), http://japanfocus.org/-Peter-Hayes/3423

Hayes, P., "Wonpok," in *Pacific Powderkeg, American Nuclear Dilemmas in Korea* (Lanham: Lexington Press, 1991).

Hayes, P., and Bruce, S., "Translating North Korea's Nuclear Threats into Constrained Operational Reality," in *North Korean Nuclear Operationality: Regional Security and Nonproliferation*, ed. by Moore, G. (Baltimore: John Hopkins university Press, 2013), pp. 15-31.

Hayes, P., and Cavazos, R., "An Ecological Framework for Promoting Inter-Korean Cooperation and Nuclear Free Future: A DMZ Peace Park," *NAPSNet Special Report* (2013). http://nautilus.org/napsnet/napsnet-special-reports/an-ecological-framework-for-promoting-inter-korean-cooperation-and-nuclear-free-future-a-dmz-peace-park

Hayes, P., and Cavazos, R., *Internet Events, Social Media and National Security in China*, NAPSNet Special Reports (Nautilus Institute, 2013).

Hayes, P., and Hamel-Green, M., "Paths to Peace on the Peninsula: The Case for a Japan-Korea Nuclear Weapon Free Zone," *Security Challenges*, 7(2) (2011), http://www.securitychallenges.org.au/ArticlePDFs/vol7no2HayesandHamelGreen.pdf

Hayes, P., *et al.*, "The Impact of the Northeast Asian Peace and Security Network in US-DPRK Conflict Resolution," in *Internet and International Systems: Information Technology and American Foreign Policy Decision-making Workshop* (San Francisco: Nautilus Institute, 1999).

Hayes, P., and Tannenwald, N., "Nixing Nukes in Vietnam," *Bulletin of the Atomic Scientists*, 59(3) (2003), http://thebulletin.org/2003/may/nixing-nukes-vietnam

Hayes, P., and von Hippel, D., *Foundations of Energy Security for the DPRK: 1990-2009 Energy Balances, Engagement Options, and Future Paths for Energy and Economic Redevelopment*, NAPSNet Special Report (Nautilus Institute, 2012).

Hayes, P., and von Hippel, D., "Growth in Energy Needs in Northeast Asia: Projections, Consequences, and Opportunities," in *2008 Northeast Asia Energy Outlook Seminar, Korea Economic Institute Policy Forum* (Washington, DC: Korean Economic Institute, 2008).

Hayes, P., *et al.*, *After the Deluge: Short and Medium-Term Impacts of the Reactor Damage Caused by the Japan Earthquake and Tsunami* (Nautilus Institute, 2011).

Hayes, P., and Zarsky, L., "Environmental Issues and Regimes in Northeast Asia," *International Environmental Affairs*, 6(4) (1994), http://nautilus.org/staff-publications/environmental-issues-and-regimes-in-northeast-asia

Helbing, D., "Globally Networked Risks and How to Respond," *Nature*, 497 (2013), doi: http://dx.doi.org/10.1038/nature12047

Held, D., *Global Transformations: Politics, Economics and Culture* (Redwood City: Stanford University Press, 1999).

Henderson, J.V., and Wang, H.G., "Urbanization and City Growth: The Role of Institutions," *Regional Science and Urban Economics*, 37(3) (2007), doi: http://dx.doi.org/10.1016/j.regsciurbeco.2006.11.008

Herman, S., "Japan Urged to Invite Foreign Expertise When Re-Building Tsunami Communities," *City Mayors Development*, 4 March 2012, http://www.citymayors.com/development/japan-post-tsunami.html

Hibbs, M., "South Korea's Nuclear Defense," *Arms Control Wonk*, 7 April 2013, http://hibbs.armscontrolwonk.com/archive/1617/south-koreas-nuclear-defense

Iida, T., "Changing Climate Change & Energy Policy and Politics in Japan," in *Interconnections of Global Problems in East Asia, Green Economy, Urban Security And Energy Security* (Seoul: Nautilus Institute, 2010).

Hiromichi, U., "Toward a Northeast Asia Nuclear Weapon-Free Zone," *Japan Focus* (2005), http://www.japanfocus.org/-Umebayashi-Hiromichi/1784

History – 2002 (Jeju: Jeju Forum, 2002).

Hodson, M., and Marvin, S., "Urban Ecological Security: A New Urban Paradigm?," *International Journal of Urban and Regional Research*, 33(1) (2009), doi: http://dx.doi.org/10.1111/j.1468-2427.2009.00832.x

Holling, C.S., "Resilience and Stability of Ecological Systems," *Annual Review of Ecology and Systematics*, 4(1) (1973), doi: http://dx.doi.org/10.1146/annurev.es.04.110173.000245

Holt, M., and Andrews, A., *Nuclear Power Plant Security and Vulnerabilities*, Report for Congress (Congressional Research Service, 2008).

Horner, D., *Pyroprocessing Is Reprocessing: U.S. Official*, Arms Control Today (Arms Control Association, 2011).

Huang, Y., "Urban Development in Contemporary China," in *China's Geography: Globalization and the Dynamics of Political Economic and Social Change*, ed. by Gregory Veeck, Clifton Pannell, Christopher J. Smith, and Youqin Huang (Boulder: Roman & Littlefield Publishers 2006).

Hwang, B.Y., "Korea: A Model for Southeast Asia?," *The Diplomat*, 17 April 2012, http://thediplomat.com/2012/04/korea-a-model-for-southeast-asia

Hwang, J.S., and Choe, Y.H., *Smart Cities Seoul: A Case Study*, ITU-T Technology Watch Report (International Telecommunications Union, 2013).

IAEA Staff Reporter, "Asia Leads Way in Nuclear Power Development," *International Atomic Energy Agency*, 30 October 2007, http://www.iaea.org/newscenter/news/2007/asialeads.html

Inajima, T., and Okada, Y., "Japan to Have Surplus Power in Summer without Additional Nuclear," *Bloomberg*, 9 April 2013, http://www.bloomberg.com/news/2013-04-09/japan-to-have-surplus-power-in-summer-without-additional-nuclear.html

International Energy Agency, *World Energy Outlook 2008* (Paris: International Energy Agency, 2008).

The Internet and International Systems: Information Technology and American Foreign Policy Decision-Making Workshop (Berkeley: Nautilus Institute, 1999), http://oldsite.nautilus.org/gps/info-policy/workshop/papers/

Jacobs, W., *et al.*, "Integrating World Cities into Production Networks: The Case of Port Cities," *Global Networks*, 10(1) (2010), doi: http://dx.doi.org/10.1111/j.1471-0374.2010.00276.x

Japan for Sustainability, "Walking on New Power-Generating Floor Creates Electricity," 22 March 2007, http://www.japanfs.org/en/pages/026618.html

Japanese-Chinese-Korean Committee for Common History Teaching Materials of the Three Countries, *A History That Opens the Future — Unauthorised English Language Translation* (Washington, DC: Memory and Reconciliation in the Asia-Pacific, George Washington University), http://www.gwu.edu/~memory/issues/textbooks/jointeastasia.html

Jeju Forum World Leaders, *Jeju Declaration* (Jeju: Jeju Forum, 2007).

Jeju Forum World Leaders, *Jeju Declaration on Northeast Asian Community* (Jeju: Jeju Forum, 2005).

Jeju Forum World Leaders, *Jeju Peace Declaration* (Jeju: Jeju Forum, 2001).

Jeju Peace Institute (Jeju: Jeju Peace Institute), http://www.jpi.or.kr/eng/

Jeon, S.W., et al., "Policies on Conservation of the DMZ District Ecosystem," Environmental Policy Bulletin, 5(1) (2007), http://eng.me.go.kr/eng/file/readDownloadFile.do;jsessionid=Y28x82xD8E3OEgw0la yrej5Cu41aWczpadsgTd3gbNg1iVD1qvvsXJxQpVaF9IU0.meweb2vhost_servlet_engine 3?fileId=92441&fileSeq=1

Jeong, N.-k., "Former Japanese Prime Minister Criticizes Abe's Remarks," *The Hankyoreh*, 21 May 2013, http://www.hani.co.kr/arti/english_edition/e_ international/588357.html

Jho, W., and Lee, H., "The Structure and Political Dynamics of Regulating 'Yellow Sand' in Northeast Asia," *Asian Perspective*, 33(2) (2009), http://210.101.116.28/W_ files/ksi2/02106467_pv.pdf

Jiawei, Z., "Korean Mobile Phone Users to Reach One Million Four Years after Mobile Phone Ban Lifted (in Chinese)," *Reuters*, 21 November 2011, http:// cn.reuters.com/article/CNAnalysesNews/idCNCHINA-5247520111121? pageNumber=2&virtualBrandChannel=0

Jun, J., "Dealing with a Sore Lip: Parsing China's 'Recalculation' of North Korea Policy," 29 March 2013, http://38north.org/2013/03/jjun032913

Jung, H.Y., *Seoul-toward a Regional Hub City in the Northeast Asia* (Seoul: Seoul Development Institute, 2005).

Kafchinski, J., "Global Counterfeit Trade" (George Mason University, 2009).

Kang, J., *An Initial Exploration of the Potential for Deep Borehole Disposal of Nuclear Wastes in South Korea*, NAPSNet Special Report (Nautilus Institute, 2010).

Kaplan, D.E., and Dubro, A., *Yakuza: Japan's Criminal Underworld* (Oakland: University of California Press, 2003).

Kassenova, T., *A 'Black Hole' in the Global Nonproliferation Regime: The Case of Taiwan*, NAPSNet Policy Forum (Nautilus Institute, 2011).

Kato, C., *TED Case Studies: Taiwan Nuclear Waste Exports (NKORNUKE)* (Washington, DC: American University, 1977), http://www1.american.edu/ ted/nkornuke.htm

Kazimi, M., *et al.*, "Postscript," in *The Future of the Nuclear Fuel Cycle* (Massachusetts: Massachusetts Institute of Technology, 2011).

Keane, J., *Global Civil Society?*, *Contemporary Political Theory* (Cambridge: Cambridge University Press, 2003).

Kebede, R., "Oil Hits Record above $147," *Reuters*, 11 July 2008, http://www.reuters. com/article/2008/07/11/us-markets-oil-idUST14048520080711

Keep Northeast Asia Green (Seoul: Northeast Asia Forest Forum) http://www.neaff. org

Keum, H., "Globalization and Inter-City Cooperation in Northeast Asia," *East Asia*, 18(2) (2000), doi: http://dx.doi.org/10.1007/s12140-000-0029-y

Key Outcomes of Soms: Som-14 (8-9 April 2009; Moscow, Russian Federation) (Incheon: North-East Asian Subregional Programme for Environmental Cooperation), http://www.neaspec.org/key-outcomes-soms

Key World Energy Statistics (Paris: International Energy Agency, 2009), http://large. stanford.edu/courses/2009/ph204/landau1/docs/key_stats_2009.pdf

Khatib, H., *et al.*, "Energy Security," in *World Energy Assessment*, ed. by United Nations Development Programme (New York: United Nations Development Programme, 2000).

Kim, B.K., *Kim Byung Kook — Education and Work Experience* (Seoul: Political Science & International Relations, Korea University).

Kim, C., "A Step Forward to Refugee Protection? South Korea's New Refugee Act," *Oxford Monitor of Forced Migration,* 2(1) (2012), http://oxmofm.com/wp-content/uploads/2012/06/A-Step-Forward-to-Refugee-Protection.pdf

Kim, D., and McGoldrick, F., *Decision Time: US-South Korea Peaceful Nuclear Cooperation,* Academic Paper Series (Korea Economic Institute, 2013).

Kim, G.E., and Seliger, B., *Tackling Climate Change, Increasing Energy Security, Engaging North Korea and Moving Forward Northeast Asian Integration – "Green Growth" in Korea and the Gobitec Project,* Gobitec Outline Paper (2010).

Kim, J.E., *et al.,* "Disaster Management of Local Government: Comparison between the UK and South Korea," in *Korea Association of Public Administration 2012 Summer Conference* (Korea Association of Public Administration, 2012).

Kim, K.G., *Urban Development Model for the Low-Carbon Green City: The Case of Gangneung* (London: University College London), http://www.weitz-center.org/uploads/1/7/0/8/1708801/urban_development_model_kwi_gon_kim.pdf

Kim, S., "International History Textbook Work from a Global Perspective: The Joint Franco-German History Textbook and Its Implications for Northeast Asia," *Journal of Northeast Asian History,* 6(2) (2009), http://contents.nahf.or.kr/chinese/item/downloadItemFile.process?fileName=jn_010_0030.pdf&levelId=jn_010e_0030

Kim, S., "Roles of Middle Power in East Asia: A Korean Perspective," in *International Conference on the Role of Middle Power in the 21st Century International Relations* (Seoul: Korean Association of International Studies, 2013).

Kingston, J., *Ousting Kan Naoto: The Politics of Nuclear Crisis and Renewable Energy in Japan,* NAPSNet Policy Forum (Nautilus Institute, 2011).

Kipp, J., *Asian Drivers of Russia's Nuclear Force Posture* (Arlington: Nonproliferation Policy Education Center, 2010).

Kissinger, H., *Diplomacy* (New York: Simon & Schuster, 1994).

Kitakyushu Office for International Environmental Cooperation, *Eco, Thereby Enhancing Global Partnership* (Kitakyushu: City of Kitakyushu, 2007).

Ko, S.J., and Kang, K.H., "Assessing Inter-Korean Relations: Achievements, Setbacks and Prospects — in Relation to the Contribution of Jeju," in *2nd Jeju Peace Forum* (Jeju: Jeju Peace Institute, 2002).

Korea DMZ, "Fish Hunting of the North Korean Soldiers," *Korea DMZ* (n.d., circa 2001), http://www.korea-dmz.com/en/s/sa/ssa_01_en.asp

Korea Energy Economics Institute, *Korea Energy Statistics Information System* (Seoul: Korea Energy Economics Institute, 2011), http://www.kesis.net/flexapp/KesisFlexApp.jsp?menuId=Q0109&reportId=&chk=Y-app=5dd0&7a56-selectedIndex=2

Korea Energy Management Corporation, *Handbook of Energy and Climate Change* (Yongin City: Korea Energy Management Corporation, 2010).

Korea Environment Institute, *Research on Policies for Mitigating Heat Island Phenomenon to Adapt to Climate Change in Urban Area* (Seoul: Korea Environment Institute, 2009).

Korea Nuclear Energy Promotion Agency, *Survey Results of People's Nuclear Awareness in 2010* (Seoul: Korea Nuclear Energy Promotion Agency, 2010).

"Korea-Japan Joint Research Project for New Era," *KBS World Radio*, 27 January 2009, http://world.kbs.co.kr/english/archive/program/news_zoom.htm?no=4709&current_page=44

Korean Ministry of Economy and Knowledge, *Reports of Energy Census* (Seoul: Korean Ministry of Economy and Knowledge, 2008).

Krauthammer, C., "The Unipolar Moment," *Foreign Affairs*, 70(1) (1990), http://www.foreignaffairs.com/articles/46271/charles-krauthammer/the-unipolar-moment

Kroenig, M., and Pavel, B., "How to Deter Terrorism," *The Washington Quarterly*, 35(2) (2012), doi: http://dx.doi.org/10.1080/0163660X.2012.665339

Kurokawa, K., *et al.*, *The Official Report of the Fukushima Nuclear Accident Independent Investigation Commission: Executive Summary* (Tokyo: The National Diet of Japan, 2012).

Kwon, W.T., "Changes in Land Use Resulting from Abnormal Climate and Natural Disaster," *Kugto*, 353 (2007).

Lall, S., and Wang, H.G., "China Urbanization Review: Balancing Urban Transformation and Spatial Inclusion. An Eye on East Asia and Pacific" (The World Bank, 2011).

Lang, G., and Miao, B., "Food Security for China's Cities," *International Planning Studies*, 13(1) (2013), doi: http://dx.doi.org/10.1080/13563475.2013.750940

LEAP: Long-Range Energy Alternatives Planning System (United States: Stockholm Environment Institute), http://www.energycommunity.org/–sthash.g5LLFKXm.dpbs

Lee, H.T., "Interview with Denney, S.," (July 17, 2013).

Lee, S., "Climate Change and Green Cities in South Korea," in *Interconnections of Global Problems in East Asia, Green Economy, Urban Security And Energy Security* (Seoul: Nautilus Institute, 2010).

Lee, S., "Latent Layers beneath the Relationship between Urban Insecurity and Climate Change: Case of South Korea," in *Interconnection Among Global Problems in Northeast Asia* (Paju: Nautilus Institute, 2009).

Lee, S.H., "Measures to Be Taken by South Korea to Carry out Complex Diplomacy," *JPI PeaceNet* (2011), http://www.jpi.or.kr/eng/regular/policy_view.sky?code=EnOther&id=3917

Lee, S.H., "A New Paradigm for Trust-Building on the Korean Peninsula: Turning Korea's DMZ into a UNESCO World Heritage Site," *The Asia-Pacific Journal*, 35(2) (2010), http://www.japanfocus.org/-Seung_ho-Lee/3404

Lee, S.H., *et al.*, "Ubiquitous and Smart System Approaches to Infrastructure Planning: Learnings from Korea, Japan and Hong Kong," in *Sustainable Urban and Regional Infrastructure Development: Technologies, Applications and Management*, ed. by Yigitcanlar, T. (Hershey: IGI Global, Information Science Reference, 2010).

Lee, S.J., *South Korea as New Middle Power Seeking Complex Diplomacy*, EAI Asia Security Initiative Working Paper (East Asia Institute, 2012).

Lee, S.J., *et al.*, *The Vision of the Korean Peninsula and Territorial Networking Strategies* (Korea Research Institute for Human Settlements, 2009).

Lee, S.J., and Kim, W.B., "Recent Trends of Cross-Border Cooperation and Spatial Strategies of the Northeast Asian Countries," in *Presidential Committee on Regional Development, 2010 International Conference* (Seoul, 2010).

Lejano, R.P., "Theorizing Peace Parks: Two Models of Collective Action," *Journal of Peace Research*, 43(5) (2006), doi: http://dx.doi.org/10.1177/0022343306066565

Levin, N.D., and Han, Y., *Sunshine in Korea: The South Korean Debate over Policies toward North Korea* (Santa Monica: Rand Corporation, 2002).

Levin, S., "Ecosystems and the Biosphere as Complex Adaptive Systems," *Ecosystems*, 1(5) (1998), doi: http://dx.doi.org/10.1007/s100219900037

Li, J., "From Strong to Smart: The Chinese Smart Grid and Its Relation with the Globe," *Asian Energy Platform News*, 2009, http://www.aepfm.org/ufiles/pdf/ Smart Grid - AEPN Sept.pdf

Liang, X., *The Six-Party Talks at a Glance* (Washington, DC: Arms Control Association, 2012), http://www.armscontrol.org/factsheets/6partytalks

Lijun, M., "Study on Problem of Trans-Border Drugs Crimes on Sino-DPRK Border," *Journal of Chinese People's Armed Police Force Academy* (2009), http:// www.wanfangdata.com.cn

Lim, D.-w., *Peacemaker: Twenty Years of Inter-Korean Relations and the North Korean Nuclear Issue* (Stanford: Shorenstein Asia-Pacific Research Center, 2012).

Lim, J.D., "New Regionalism across Korea-Japan Strait: Cross-Border Region between Busan and Fukuoka," in *18th Northeast Asia Economic Forum* (Busan: Northeast Asia Economic Forum, 2009).

Lin, G.C.S., "The Growth and Structural Change of Chinese Cities: A Contextual and Geographic Analysis," *Cities*, 19(5) (2002), doi: http://dx.doi.org/10.1016/ S0264-2751(02)00039-2

List of Track II Activities 1994-2012 (Jakarta: ASEAN Regional Forum) http:// aseanregionalforum.asean.org/library/arf-activities/list-of-arf-track-i-activities-by-inter-sessional-year.html

Liu, Y., and Chen, D., "Why China Will Democratize," *The Washington Quarterly*, 35(1) (2011), doi: http://dx.doi.org/10.1080/0163660X.2012.641918

Lopez, G., A., *et al.*, "The Global Tide," *The Bulletin of the Atomic Scientists*, 51(4) (1995).

Lovins, A., "Hypercars, Hydrogen, and Distributed Utilities: Disruptive Technologies and Gas-Industry Strategy," in *Operations & Marketing Conferences, American Gas Association* (Denver: Rocky Mountain Institute, 2000).

Mann, S.R., "Chaos Theory and Strategic Thought," *Parameters* (1992), http://strategicstudiesinstitute.army.mil/pubs/parameters/Articles/1992/1992%20mann.pdf

Mansourov, A., *Bytes and Bullets: Information Technology Revolution and National Security on the Korean Peninsula* (Honolulu: Asia Pacific Center for Security Studies, 2005), http://nautilus.org/wp-content/uploads/2011/12/DPRK_Digital_Transformation.pdf

Mansourov, A., *North Korea on the Cusp of Digital Transformation*, NAPSNet Special Report (Berkeley: Nautilus Institute, 2011).

Margolis, J., "Sinking Bangkok," *PRI's The World*, 2007.

Martinot, E., *et al.*, *Global Status Report on Local Renewable Energy Policies* (REN21, *et al.*, 2009).

Masayoshi, S., *Creating a Solar Belt in East Japan: The Energy Future*, NAPSNet Policy Forum (Nautilus Institute, 2011).

Matsuhashia, R., *et al.*, "Sustainable Development under Ambitious Medium Term Target of Reducing Greenhouse Gases," *Procedia Environmental Sciences*, 2 (2010), doi: http://dx.doi.org/10.1016/j.proenv.2010.10.135

Matthew, R.A., *Environmental Security: Demystifying the Concept, Clarifying the Stakes*, Environmental Change and Security Program Report (Environmental Change and Security Program, 1995).

Matthias, R., and Coelho, D., "Understanding and Managing the Complexity of Urban Systems under Climate Change," *Climate Policy*, 7(4) (2007), doi: http://dx.doi.org/10.1080/14693062.2007.9685659

McDonald, M., "'Crisis Status' in South Korea after North Shells Island," *New York Times*, 23 November 2010, http://www.nytimes.com/2010/11/24/world/asia/24korea.html?pagewanted=all&_r=0

McEvoy, D., and Mullett, J., *Enhancing the Resilience of Seaports to a Changing Climate: Research Synthesis and Implications for Policy and Practice* (Gold Coast: National Climate Change Adaptation Research Facility and RMIT University, 2013).

McGann, J.G., *2012 Global Go to Think Tanks Report and Policy Advice* (Pennsylvania: Think Tanks and Civil Societies Program, University of Pennsylvania, 2013).

McGann, J.G., and Weaver, R.K., *Think Tanks and Civil Societies: Catalysts for Ideas and Action* (New Brunswick: Transaction Publishers, 2000).

McPhee, J., *The Curve of Binding Energy* (New York: Ballantine, 1974).

Meeting on Nature Conservation in Transboundary Areas in North East Asia Expert Group (Incheon: North-East Asian Subregional Programme for Environmental Cooperation), http://www.neaspec.org/article/neaspec-meeting-nature-conservation-transboundary-areas-north-east-asia

Melissen, J., "Concluding Reflections on Soft Power and Public Diplomacy in East Asia," in *Public Diplomacy and Soft Power in East Asia*, ed. by J., M. and Lee, S.J. (New York: Palgrave MacMillan, 2011).

Meng, L., "Study on Problem of Trans-Border Drugs Crimes on Sino-DPRK Border," *The Journal of Chinese People's Armed Police Force Academy*, 1 (2009).

The Metropolitan Area Underground Discharge Channel (Tokyo: Japan Ministry of Land, Infrastructure, Transport and Tourism), http://www.ktr.mlit.go.jp/edogawa/gaikaku/

The Millennium Development Goals (New York: United Nations Development Programme), http://www.undp.org/content/undp/en/home/mdgoverview/mdg_goals.html

Minakir, P.A., "Russia and the Russian Far East in Economies of the APR and NEA," in *Economic Cooperation between the Russian Far East and Asia-Pacific Countries* (RIOTIP, 2007).

Minato, T., "Urban Security," in *Interconnections of Global Problems in East Asia, Green Economy, Urban Security And Energy Security* (Seoul: Nautilus Institute, 2010).

Minato, T., and Sutheerawatthana, P., "Exploring Possible Cooperation for Climate Change Adaptation: How Civil Society Could Work with Government Strategies," in *Interconnections of Global Problems in East Asia: Climate Change Adaptation and its Complexity from the Perspective of Civil Society* (Paju: Nautilus Institute, 2009).

Ministry of Economics, Trade, and Industry, *Energy Balance of Japan for Fiscal Year 2009* (Tokyo: Japan Ministry of Economics, Trade, and Industry, 2011).

Ministry of Economy, Trade and Industry, *Innovative Energy Technology Plan* (Tokyo: Japan Ministry of Economy, Trade and Industry, 2007).

Ministry of Foreign Affairs and Trade, *Introduction to New Asia Initiative* (Seoul: Korean Ministry of Foreign Affairs and Trade, 2009).

Ministry of Knowledge and Economy, and Korea Energy Economics Institute, *Yearbook of Energy Statistics* (Japan Ministry of Knowledge and Economy and Korea Energy Economics Institute, 2011).

Ministry of Land, Infrastructure, Transport and Tourism, *Climate Change Adaptation Strategies to Cope with Water-Related Disasters Due to Global Warming (Policy Report)* (Tokyo: Japan Ministry of Land, Infrastructure, Transport, and Tourism, 2008).

Ministry of Land, Transportation and Maritime Affairs, *Report on Status of Roads* (Seoul: Korean Ministry of Land, Transportation and Maritime Affairs, 2009).

Ministry of the Environment, *FY 2007 Greenhouse Gas Emissions in Japan (Provisional Data)* (Tokyo: Japan Ministry of Environment, 2008).

Ministry of the Environment, 地球温暖化の日本への影響 (Tokyo: Japan Ministry of the Environment, 2001).

Ministry of Water Resources, *Bulletin of Flood and Drought Disasters in China* (Beijing: China Ministry of Water Resources, 2010).

Mo, J., *Middle Powers and G20 Governance* (Basingstoke: Palgrave Macmillan, 2013).

Modi, N., "Introduction to Rurban and Rurbanisation," in *Panel Discussion on Rurbanisation* (Ahmedabad, 2011).

Moench, M., and Gyawali, D., *Desakota: Reinterpreting the Urban-Rural Continuum* (Ecosystem Services for Poverty Alleviation, 2008).

Monitor 360, *Master Narratives Country Report: China* (Open Source Center, 2012).

Moon, C.I., *The Sunshine Policy : In Defense of Engagement as a Path to Peace in Korea* (Seoul: Yonsei University Press, 2012).

Moon, C.I., *East Asia Community Building and ROK's Northeast Asian Cooperation Initiative*, Building a Northeast Asian Community: Toward Peace and Prosperity (Jeju: 3rd Jeju Peace Forum, 2003).

Moon, C.I., "Interview with Hayes, P." (7 September 2013).

Moon, K.H., and Park, D.K., "The Role and Activities of NGOs in Reforestation in the Northeast Asian Region," *Forest Ecology and Management*, 201(1) (2004), doi: http://dx.doi.org/10.1016/j.foreco.2004.06.013

Morgan, P.M., "Deterrence and System Management: The Case of North Korea," *Conflict Management and Peace Science*, 23(2) (2006), doi: http://dx.doi.org/10.1080/07388940600665768

Morgan, P.M., *Deterrence Now* (Cambridge: Cambridge University Press, 2003).

Mori, N., "A Grand Design for Northeast Asia," in *15th Northeast Asia Economic Forum* (Khabarovsk, 2006).

Morris-Suzuki, T., *The Past within Us: Media, Memory, History* (Brooklyn: Verso, 2005).

Morrison, T., "Interview with Denney, S." (July 2013).

Mostashari, A., *et al.*, "Cognitive Cities and Intelligent Urban Governance," *Network Industries Quarterly*, 13(3) (2009), http://newsletter.epfl.ch/mir/index.php?module=Newspaper&func=viewarticle&np_id=267&np_eid=43&catid=0

Mufson, S., "Executive Resigns in Storm over Sleeping Guards," *Washington Post*, 10 January 2008, http://www.washingtonpost.com/wp-dyn/content/article/2008/01/09/AR2008010903368_pf.html

Nair, D., "Regionalism in the Asia Pacific/East Asia: A Frustrated Regionalism?," *Contemporary Southeast Asia*, 31(1) (2008), https://muse.jhu.edu/journals/contemporary_southeast_asia_a_journal_of_international_and_strategic_affairs/v031/31.1.nair.html

Nakamichi, T., and Ito, T., "Tokyo Estimates Disaster Costs of Almost $200 Billion," *Wall Street Journal*, 24 March 2011, http://online.wsj.com/news/articles/SB10001424052748704050204576217852022676740

Nakata, M., *et al.*, *Carbon Dioxide Emissions Reduction Potential in Japan's Power Sector—Estimating Carbon Emissions Avoided by a Fuel-Switch Scenario* (World Wildlife Fund Japan, 2003).

Nakicenovic, N., and Swart, R., *Emissions Scenarios* (Intergovernmental Panel on Climate Change, 2000).

National Development and Reform Commission, *China's National Climate Change Programme* (Beijing: China's National Development and Reform Commission, 2007).

National Energy Technology Laboratory, *A Compendium of Smart Grid Technologies* (Pittsburgh: United States Department of Energy, Office of Electricity Delivery and Energy Reliability, 2009).

National Energy Technology Laboratory, *A Vision for the Modern Grid* (Pittsburgh: United States Department of Energy, Office of Electricity Delivery and Energy Reliability, 2007).

National Institute for Population and Social Security Research, *Social Security in Japan* (National Institute for Population and Social Security Research, 2011).

National Intelligence Council, *Disruptive Civil Technologies: Six Technologies with Potential Impacts on US Interests out to 2025* (National Intelligence Council, 2008).

Nautilus Institute, "Will East Asia Mega-Cities Be Secure and Sustainable by 2050?," in *Global Scenarios 2010* (Seoul: Nautilus Institute, 2010).

Nautilus Institute, *et al.*, "Northeast Asia 2050: Is There a Role for Civil Society in Meeting the Climate Change Challenge," in *Civil Society Scenarios Workshop* (Seoul: Nautilus Institute, 2009).

Neff, T.L., *Improving Energy Security in Pacific Asia: Diversification and Risk Reduction for Fossil and Nuclear Fuels*, Pacific Asia Regional Energy Security (PARES) Project (Nautilus Institute, 1997).

New York Conference "Peace and Cooperation in Northeast Asia" on March 8-9, 2012 (Seoul: Friedrich-Ebert-Stiftung, Korea Office, 2012), http://www.fes-korea.org/pages/english/events/2012.php

The Nexus Network (Brighton: The Nexus Network), http://thenexusnetwork.org

Nicholls, R.J., *et al.*, *Ranking Port Cities with High Exposure and Vulnerability to Climate Extremes*, OECD Environment Directorate Working Paper (Organization for Economic Co-operation and Development, 2008).

Nissan Motor Company, "Urban Mobility: Breaking the Chain of Urban Traffic Congestion," *Nissan Technology Magazine*, 19 July 2010, http://www.nissan-global.com/EN/TECHNOLOGY/MAGAZINE/report1.html

Northeast Asian Conference on Environmental Cooperation (Tokyo: Environmental Cooperation Office, Japan Ministry of Environment, 2005).

The Northeast Asia Cooperation Dialogue (La Jolla: University of California Institute on Global Conflict and Cooperation), https://igcc.ucsd.edu/research-and-programs/programs/regional-issues/northeast-asia/northeast-asia-cooperation-dialogue.html

Nozaki, Y., and Selden, M., "Japanese Textbook Controversies, Nationalism, and Historical Memory: Intra- and Inter-National Conflicts," *The Asia-Pacific Journal*, 24-5-09 (2009), http://japanfocus.org/-mark-selden/3173

Nuclear Power in South Korea (London: World Nuclear Association, 2013), http://www.world-nuclear.org/info/Country-Profiles/Countries-O-S/South-Korea/-.UgPXcW33M5s

Nuclear Security Summit leaders, "Seoul Communiqué at 2012 Nuclear Security Summit," *Council on Foreign Relations*, 27 March 2012, http://www.cfr.org/proliferation/seoul-communiqu-2012-nuclear-security-summit/p27735

Nye, J., *Soft Power: The Means to Success in World Politics* (New York, United States: PublicAffairs, 2004).

O'Donnell, M.A., "Laying Siege to the Villages: Lessons from Shenzhen," *openSecurity*, 28 March 2013, https://http://www.opendemocracy.net/opensecurity/mary-ann-o%E2%80%99donnell/laying-siege-to-villages-lessons-from-shenzhen

Ochmanek, D., and Schwartz, L., *The Challenge of Nuclear-Armed Regional Adversaries* (Santa Monica: RAND Corporation, 2008).

On-Fat Wong, J., "Security Requirements in Northeast Asia" (University of Wisconsin, 1982).

Onishi, N., and Belson, K., "Culture of Complicity Tied to Stricken Nuclear Plant," *New York Times*, 26 April 2011, http://www.nytimes.com/2011/04/27/world/asia/27collusion.html?_r=1&hp=&pagewanted=print

Pachauri, R., and Reisinger, A., *Climate Change 2007: Synthesis Report. Contribution of Working Groups I, II and III to the Fourth Assessment Report of the Intergovernmental Panel on Climate* (Geneva: Intergovernmental Panel on Climate Change, 2007).

Paik, H., "Northeast Asian Energy Corridor Initiative for Regional Collaboration," *Journal of East Asian Economic Integration* 16(4) (2012), http://www.jeai.org/download.jsp?filePath=/j_data/JE0001/2012/v16n4/&fileName=JE0001_2012_v16n4_395.pdf

Park, D.K., "Interview with Denney, S.," (22 July 2013).

Park, J.H., *et al.*, "Potential Effects of Climate Change and Variability on Watershed Biogeochemical Processes and Water Quality in Northeast Asia," *Environment International*, 36(2) (2010), doi: http://dx.doi.org/10.1016/j.envint.2009.10.008

Park, S.H., "Post-Cold War Trans-Border Networks in Northeast Asia: The Busan-Fukuoka Network," in *Interventions in the Political Geography of Asia's Transborder Urban Networks: Working Paper Series 193*, ed. by Miller, M.A. and Bunnell, T. (Singapore: Asia Research Institute, National University of Singapore, 2012).

Participants of the 1st Asian Solidarity Conference, "The Joint Resolution of the First Asian Solidarity Conference on Military Sexual Slavery by Japan" (1992).

Perkovich, G., *et al.*, *Universal Compliance, a Strategy for Nuclear Security* (Washington, DC: Carnegie Endowment for International Peace, 2007).

Petroleum and Other Liquids: Europe Brent Spot Price Fob (Washington, DC: Energy Information Administration, United States Department of Energy, 2013), http://www.eia.gov/dnav/pet/hist/LeafHandler.ashx?n=PET&s=RBRTE&f=D

Pingel, F., "Old and New Models of Textbook Revision and Their Impact on the East Asian History Debate," *Journal of Northeast Asian History*, 7(2) (2010), http://www.historyfoundation.or.kr/?bmode=view&stype=2&sidx=239&page=8&mode=&s_word=&bidx=106&search=

Pingel, F., *UNESCO Guidebook on Textbook Research and Textbook Revision* (UNESCO, 2010), http://unesdoc.unesco.org/images/0011/001171/117188E.pdf

Point Topic, *VoIP Statistics – Market Analysis, Q1 2013* (London: Point Topic, 2013).

Politics (Seoul: Trilateral Cooperation Secretariat), http://www.tcs-asia.org/dnb/board/list.php?board_name=3_1_1_politics

Power Grid Interconnection in Northeast Asia (Seoul: Nautilus Institute), http://nautilus.org/projects/by-name/asian-energy-security/workshop-on-power-grid-interconnection-in-northeast-asia/

Prasad, N., *et al.*, *Climate Resilient Cities: A Primer on Reducing Vulnerabilities to Disasters* (Washington, DC: The World Bank, 2009).

Presidential Committee on Green Growth, *Greenhouse Gas Reduction Target* (Green Growth Korea, 2011).

Prime Minister of Japan and his Cabinet, *Japan Revitalization Strategy-Japan Is Back* (Government of Japan, 2013).

Ramberg, B., *Nuclear Power Plants as Weapons for the Enemy: An Unrecognized Military Peril* (Berkeley: University of California Press, 1984).

Ranger, S., and Kim, Y.G., *The Balance of Power in a "Complex" Northeast Asia* (East Asia Institute, 2012).

Rauhala, E., "How Japan Became a Leader in Disaster Preparation," *Time*, 11 March 2011, http://content.time.com/time/world/article/0,8599,2058390,00.html

Razavi, H., *Economic, Security and Environmental Aspects of Energy Supply: A Conceptual Framework for Strategic Analysis of Fossil Fuels* (Nautilus Institute, 1997).

Redick, J., "A Differentiated Entry into Force Procedure" (1997).

Renwick, N., *Northeast Asian Critical Security: Exploring Democratic Freedoms and Social Justice* (Basingstoke: Palgrave Macmillan, 2004).

Research Organization for Information Science & Technology (Tokyo: Research Organization for Information Science & Technology), http://www.rist.or.jp/ehome.html

Resonance, *China Social Media Usage* (Shanghai: Resonance).

Reuters Staff Writer, "U.N. Fears Nine North Korean Defectors Sent Home by China," *Reuters*, 31 May 2013, http://www.reuters.com/article/2013/05/31/us-mhh-korea-north-rights-idUSBRE94U0GM20130531

Rischard, J.F., *High Noon: Twenty Global Problems, Twenty Years to Solve Them* (New York: Basic Books, 2002).

Risse-Kappen, T., *Bringing Transnational Relations Back In: Non-State Actors, Domestic Structures and International Institutions* (Cambridge: Cambridge University Press, 1995).

Roberts, B., *Deterrence and WMD Terrorism: Calibrating its Potential Contributions to Risk Reduction* (Alexandria: Institute of Defense Analysis, 2007).

Robichaud, C., "The Consequence of a Dirty Bomb Attack," *The Hill*, 12 April 2011, http://thehill.com/blogs/congress-blog/homeland-security/155493-the-consequence-of-a-dirty-bomb-attack

Ronfeldt, D., "Blond's 'civic state' . . . vis à vis TIMN," *Visions from Two Theories Blog*, 5 June 2010, http://twotheories.blogspot.com.au/2010/06/blonds-civic-state-vis-vis-timn.html

Rosenau, J.N., "Many Damn Things Simultaneously: Complexity Theory and World Affairs," in *Complexity, Global Politics, and National Security*, ed. by Alberts, D.S. and Czerwinski, T.J. (Honolulu: University Press of the Pacific, 2002).

Rosenau, J.N., *Turbulence in World Politics: A Theory of Change and Continuity* (Princeton: Princeton University Press, 1990).

Rotterdam Climate Initiative, *Port of Rotterdam CO2 Hub: Crucial Stepping Stone Towards Sustainable Economic Growth* (Rotterdam Climate Initiative, 2012).

RTCC staff writer, "Mayor of Seoul Aims to 'Cancel out' a Nuclear Power Plant with Climate Action," *Responding to Climate Change*, 25 October 2012, http://www.rtcc.org/mayor-of-seoul-aims-to-cancel-out-a-nuclear-power-plant-with-climate-action

Russell, J., "Think Skype Is Big? Go See How Many People Are Using Tencent's QQ Right Now," *Nextweb blog*, 27 June 2012, http://thenextweb.com/asia/2012/06/27/think-skype-is-big-go-see-how-many-people-are-using-tencents-qq-right-now

Ryall, J., "Japan Struggles to Cope with Heatwave, with 26 Dead of Heatstroke," *The Telegraph*, 18 July 2011, http://www.telegraph.co.uk/news/worldnews/asia/japan/8645326/Japan-struggles-to-cope-with-heatwave-with-26-dead-of-heatstroke.html

Rynikiewicz, C., "European Port Cities as Gateways to a Green Economy?," *Network Industries Quarterly*, 13(4) (2011), http://newsletter.epfl.ch/mir/index.php?module=Newspaper&func=viewarticle&np_id=285&np_eid=44&catid=0

Samuels, R., "The MIT Japan Program Science, Technology and Management Report," in *Securing Asian Energy Investments: Geopolitics and Implications for Business Strategy* (Massachusetts Institute of Technology, 1997).

Schattle, H., and McCann, J., "The Pursuit of State Status and the Shift toward International Norms: South Korea's Evolution as a Host Country for Refugees," *Journal of Refugee Studies* (2013), doi: http://dx.doi.org/10.1093/jrs/fet003

Schmitt, J.F., "Command and (out of) Control: The Military Implications of Complexity Theory," in *Complexity, Global Politics, and National Security*, ed. by Alberts, D.S. and Czerwinski, T.J. (Honolulu: University Press of the Pacific, 2002).

Schneider, A., *et al.*, "A New Map of Global Urban Extent from MODIS Satellite Data," *Environmenal Research Letters*, 4 (2009), doi: http://dx.doi.org/10.1088/1748-9326/4/4/044003

Schneider, C., "The Japanese History Textbook Controversy in East Asian Perspective," *The ANNALS of the American Academy of Political and Social Science*, 617(1) (2008), doi: http://dx.doi.org/10.1177/0002716208314359

Schneider, M., *et al.*, *Nuclear Power in a Post-Fukushima World: 25 Years after Chernobyl Accident* (Washington, DC: Worldwatch Institute, 2011).

Schreurs, M.A., and Hyun, I., *The Environmental Dimension of Asian Security : Conflict and Cooperation over Energy, Resources, and Pollution* (Washington, DC: United States Institute of Peace Press, 2007).

Security of Spent Nuclear Fuel (Berkeley: Nautilus Institute), http://nautilus.org/projects/by-name/security-of-spent-nuclear-fuel/

Sekiguchi, T., and Nishiyama, G., "Japan's Kan Seeks Exit from Nuclear Power," *The Wall Street Journal*, 14 July 2011, http://online.wsj.com/article/SB10001424052702304911104576443542422110936.html

"Senate Committee Calls on Edward Mazria to Testify on Building Energy Efficiency," in *United States Senate Committee on Energy and Natural Resources* (Washington, DC: United States Senate Committee on Energy and Natural Resources, 2007).

Seoul Development Institute, and Seoul 21st Century Research Center, *Building the BESETO Cooperation System* (Seoul Development Institute and Seoul 21st Century Research Center, 1995).

Sessions Sketches — 2013 (Seoul: The Asan Institute for Policy Studies, 2013), http://en.asaninst.org/events_category/asan-plenum/sub_category/session-sketches/?s_year=2013

Shambaugh, D.L., "China Engages Asia: Reshaping the Regional Order," *International Security*, 29(3) (2004), https://muse.jhu.edu/journals/international_security/v029/29.3shambaugh.html

Shaplak, D., *et al.*, *A Question of Balance Political Context and Military Aspects of the China-Taiwan Dispute* (Santa Monica: RAND Corporation, 2009).

Shelley, L.I., "Trafficking in Nuclear Materials: Criminals and Terrorists," *Global Crime*, 7(3-4) (2006), doi: http://dx.doi.org/10.1080/17440570601073335

Shen, D., "North Korea's Strategic Significance to China," *WSI China Security*, 2(3) (2006), http://www.isn.ethz.ch/Digital-Library/Publications/Detail/?ots591=0c54e3b3-1e9c-be1e-2c24-a6a8c7060233&lng=en&id=31934

Shin, H.B., "Development and Dissent in China's 'Urban Age,'" *openSecurity*, 25 February 2013, http://www.opendemocracy.net/opensecurity/hyun-bang-shin/development-and-dissent-in-chinas-urban-age

Shin, S., "East Asian Environmental Co-Operation: Central Pessimism, Local Optimism," *Pacific Affairs*, 80(1) (2007), doi: http://dx.doi.org/10.5509/20078019

Simmons, P.J., and de Jonge Oudraat, C., *Managing Global Issues: Lessons Learned* (Washington, DC: Carnegie Endowment for International Peace, 2001).

Singlaub, J.K., and McConnell, M., *Hazardous Duty: An American Soldier in the Twentieth Century* (Mandaluyong City: Summit Books, 1991).

Slack, G., "Electric Vehicles for Energy Storage to Stabilize Utility Grid," 11 April 2012, http://citris-uc.org/electric-vehicles-for-energy-storage-to-stabilize-utility-grid

Snyder, S., "China-Korea Relations: Establishing a 'Strategic Cooperative Partnership,'" *Comparative Connections* (2008), http://csis.org/files/media/csis/pubs/0802qchina_korea.pdf

Snyder, S., "Envisioning a Northeast Security Framework: The Korean Peninsula," in *Towards a Northeast Asian Security Community: Implications for Korea's Growth and Economic Development*, ed. by Seliger, B. and Pascha, W. (New York: Springer, 2011), pp. 27-38.

Soh, C., "Enhancing Human Security in North Korea through Development of a Human Rights Regime in Asia," *Korea Review of International Studies*, 10(1) (2006).

Sohn, Y., "Middle Powers' Like South Korea Can't Do without Soft Power and Network Power," *Global Asia*, 7(3) (2012), http://globalasia.org/issue/charm-offensive/

Sohn, Y., "Searching for a New Identity: Public Diplomacy Challenges of South Korea as a Middle Power," in *Opening New Horizons for Public Diplomacy and Culture in the 21st Century, 2012 Korean Association of International Studies-Korea Foundation International Conference* (Seoul: Korea Foundation, 2012).

Sokolski, Henry, "Nuclear Abolition and the Next Arms Race," in *In the Eyes of the Experts: Analysis and Comments on America's Strategic Posture, Selected Contributions by the Experts of the Congressional Commission on the Strategic Posture of the United States*, ed. by Taylor Bolz (United States Institute of Peace Press, Washington, DC), pp. 207-08, http://www.usip.org/files/In%20the%20Eyes%20of%20the%20Experts%20full.pdf

Soligo, R., "Facilitating Development of the Natural Gas Market in Japan: Pipelines Gas and Law," in *New Enerty Technologies in the Natural Gas Sectors: A Policy Framework for Japan* (Institute for Public Policy, Rice University, 2001).

Son, H., "Images of the Future in South Korea," *Futures*, 52(0) (2013), doi: http://dx.doi.org/10.1016/j.futures.2013.06.001

Spiegel, "Germany to Reconsider Nuclear Policy: Merkel Sets Three-Month 'Moratorium' on Extension of Lifespans," *Spiegel*, 14 March 2011, http://www.spiegel.de/international/world/germany-to-reconsider-nuclear-policy-merkel-sets-three-month-moratorium-on-extension-of-lifespans-a-750916.html

Statistics Korea, *Survey on Agricultural Land* (Daejeon: Statistics Korea, 2009).

Stenek, V., *et al.*, *Climate Risk and Business: Ports* (Washington, DC: International Finance Corporation, 2011).

Streets, D., *Energy and Acid Rain Projections for Northeast Asia*, NAPSNet Policy Forum (Nautilus Institute, 1997).

Study Groups (Kuala Lumpur: Council for Security Cooperation in the Asia Pacific), http://www.cscap.org/index.php?page=study-groups

Suh, S.-w., and Moon, C.I., "Burdens of the Past: Overcoming History, the Politics of Identity and Nationalism in Asia," *Global Asia*, 2(1) (2007), http://globalasia.org/issue/barbs-of-nationalism/

Sukma, R., and Gannon, J., *A Growing Force: Civil Society's Role in Asian Regional Security*, ed. by Sukma, R. and Gannon, J. (Tokyo: Japan Center for International Exchange, 2013).

Bibliography 435

Suzuki, T., *et al.*, *A Framework for Energy Security Analysis and Application to a Case Study of Japan*, Synthesis Report for the Pacific Asia Regional Energy Security (PARES) Project, Phase 1 (Nautilus Institute, 1998).

Swaine, M.D., *et al.*, *China's Military and the U.S.-Japan Alliance in 2030: A Strategic Net Assessment* (Washington, DC: Carnegie Endowment for International Peace, 2013).

Swilling, M., *Decoupling Natural Resource Use and Environmental Impacts from Economic Growth* (United Nations Environment Programme, 2011).

Tainter, J.A., "Problem Solving: Complexity, History, Sustainability," *Population and Environment*, 22(1) (2000), doi: http://dx.doi.org/10.1023/A:1006632214612

Taiwan Bureau of Energy, *Energy Balance Sheet of Taiwan, 2010* (Taiwan Ministry of Economic Affairs, 2011).

Takao, Y., *Reinventing Japan: From Merchant Nation to Civic Nation* (New York: Palgrave Macmillan, 2003).

Takao, Y., "Transnational Coalitions in Northeast Asia: Search for a New Pathway of Japanese Local Government," *Ritsumeikan Annual Review of International Studies*, 2 (2003).

Takase, K., "Energy Security in Japan," in *Interconnections of Global Problems in East Asia, Green Economy, Urban Security And Energy Security* (Seoul: Nautilus Institute, 2010).

Takase, K., and Suzuki, T., "The Japanese Energy Sector: Current Situation, and Future Paths," *Energy Policy*, 39(11) (2011), doi: http://dx.doi.org/10.1016/j.enpol.2010.01.036

Tan, J., *et al.*, "The Urban Heat Island and Its Impact on Heat Waves and Human Health in Shanghai," *International Journal of Biometeorology*, 54(1) (2010), doi: http://dx.doi.org/10.1007/s00484-009-0256-x

Tan, Z., *et al.*, "Agent-Based Modeling of Netizen Groups in Chinese Internet Events," *Society for Modeling & Simulation International Magazine*, 3(2) (2011), http://www.scs.org/magazines/2012-04/index_file/Files/Tan.pdf

Tanker NAKHODKA Oil Spill in the Sea of Japan (Fukui: Environmental Research Centre, Fukui Prefectural Institute of Public Health and Environmental Science), http://www.erc.pref.fukui.jp/news/Eoil.html

Tanter, R., and Hayes, P., "Beyond the Nuclear Umbrella: Re-Thinking the Theory and Practice of Nuclear Extended Deterrence in East Asia and the Pacific," *Pacific Focus*, 26(1) (2011), doi: http://dx.doi.org/10.1111/j.1976-5118.2011.01053.x

TED Case Studies: Japan Oil Spill (Washington, DC: American University), http://www1.american.edu/ted/japanoil.htm

TED Case Studies: Taiwan Nuclear Waste Exports (NKORNUKE) (Washington, DC: American University), http://www1.american.edu/ted/nkornuke.htm

Thompson, G., *Robust Storage of Spent Nuclear Fuel: A Neglected Issue of Homeland Security* (Institute for Resource and Security Studies and Citizens Awareness Network, 2003).

Tikhonov, V., *Russia's Nuclear and Missile Complex: The Human Factor in Proliferation* (Washington, DC: Carnegie Endowment For International Peace, 2001).

Tokyo Electric Power Company, *Roadmap Towards Restoration from the Accident at Fukushima Daiichi Nuclear Power Station* (Tokyo: Tokyo Electric Power Company, 2011).

Tokyo Times staff writer, "Kan: Nuclear Energy to Take a Back Seat," *Tokyo Times*, 11 May 2011, http://www.tokyotimes.com/2011/Kan-Nuclear-energy-to-take-a-back-seat

Torres, I., "Abe's Government Will Reconsider Previous Nuclear Power Phase out Policy," *Japan Daily Press*, 28 December 2012, http://japandailypress.com/abes-government-will-reconsider-previous-nuclear-power-phase-out-policy-2820569

Trilateral Cooperation Secretariat Website (Seoul: Trilateral Cooperation Secretariat), http://www.tcs-asia.org/dnb/main/index.php

"Truth Can Never Be Distorted, the History Compiled by Three East Asian Countries, an Interview with Zhu Chengshan," *Xinhua News Agency*, 5 July 2007, http://www.js.xinhuanet.com/xin_wen_zhong_xin/2005-07/05/content_4569047.htm

Um, J.W., "Refugees Still Not Cared for with New Law on the Way," *The Hankyoreh*, 20 June 2013, http://www.hani.co.kr/arti/english_edition/e_international/592578.html

UN Economic and Social Commission for Asia and the Pacific, "Subregional Cooperation for Shipping and Port Development in North-East Asia," in *Development of Shipping and Ports in North-East Asia* (New York: 2005).

UNESCO, "Human Security in East Asia," in *International Conference on Human Security in East Asia* (Seoul: Korean National Commission for UNESCO, 2003).

Under Secretary for Public Diplomacy and Public Affairs (Washington, DC: United States Department of State), http://www.state.gov/r

Union of International Associations, *Encyclopedia of World Problems and Human Potential*. 3 vols (Munich: K.G. Saur, 1994).

Union of International Associations, *Yearbook of International Organizations 2012-2013: Geographical Index: A Country Directory of Secretariats and Memberships* (Boston: Brill, 2012).

United Nations High Commissioner for Refugees, "New UNHCR Report Says Global Forced Displacement at 18-Year High," 19 June 2013, http://www.unhcr.org/51c071816.html

United Nations, Department of Economic and Social Affairs, Population Division, *World Population Prospects: The 2012 Revision, DVD Edition* (United Nations, Department of Economic and Social Affairs, Population Division, 2013).

United Nations, Department of Economic and Social Affairs, Population Division, *World Urbanization Prospects, the 2009 Revision* (United Nations, Department of Economic and Social Affairs, Population Division, 2010).

United Nations Development Programme, *About GEI: What Is the "Green Economy?"* (n.d.), http://www.unep.org/greeneconomy/AboutGEI/WhatisGEI/tabid/29784/Default.aspx

United Nations Development Programme, *Human Development Report: New Dimensions of Human Security* (New York: United Nations Development Programme, 1994).

United Nations Development Programme, *Towards a Green Economy: Pathways to Sustainable Development and Poverty Eradication* (United Nations Development Programme, 2011).

United Nations Economic and Social Commission for Asia and the Pacific, *Saving the Flagship Species of North-East Asia: Nature Conservation Strategy of NEASPEC* (New York: United Nations).

United Nations High Commissioner for Refugees, *Asylum Levels and Trends in Industrialized Countries – 2012* (Geneva: United Nations High Commissioner for Refugees, 2013).

United Nations High Commissioner for Refugees, *UNHCR's Comments on the Republic of Korea 2009 Draft Bill on Refugee Status Determination and Treatment of Refugees and Others* (Geneva: United Nations High Commissioner for Refugees, 2009).

United States Department of Defense, *Quadrennial Defense Review* (Washington, DC: United States Department of Defense, 2010).

United States Department of Energy, *Country Analysis Briefs — Japan* (United States Department of Energy, 2011).

United States Department of State, "Minutes of Washington Special Actions Group Meeting, Washington, August 19, 1976, 8:12-9:15 A.M," in *Foreign Relations of the United States, 1969-1976, Volume E–12, Documents on East and Southeast Asia, 1973-1976, Document 285* (Washington, DC: United States Office of the Historian, 1976).

Vanderschraaf, P., and Sillari, G., *Common Knowledge* (Stanford: Stanford Encyclopedia of Philosophy, 2002), http://plato.stanford.edu/entries/common-knowledge

Vassilieva, A., and Akaha, T., *Crossing National Borders Human Migration Issues in Northeast Asia* (Tokyo: United Nations University Press, 2005), http://search.ebscohost.com/login.aspx?direct=true&scope=site&db=nlebk&db=nlabk&AN=148044

Vervaeck, A., and Daniell, J., "Japan – 366 Days after the Quake… 19000 Lives Lost, 1.2 Million Buildings Damaged, \$574 Billion," *Earthquake-Report*, 12 March 2012, http://earthquake-report.com/2012/03/10/japan-366-days-after-the-quake-19000-lives-lost-1-2-million-buildings-damaged-574-billion

von Hippel, D., *et al.*, "Northeast Asia Regional Energy Infrastructure Proposals," *Energy Policy*, 39(11) (2011), doi: http://dx.doi.org/10.1016/j.enpol.2009.08.011

von Hippel, D., and Hayes, P., *Deep Borehole Disposal of Nuclear Spent Fuel and High Level Waste as a Focus of Regional East Asia Nuclear Fuel Cycle Cooperation*, NAPSNet Special Report (Nautilus Institute, 2010).

von Hippel, D., and Hayes, P., "DPRK Energy Sector Development Priorities: Options and Preferences," *Energy Policy*, 39(11) (2011), doi: http://dx.doi.org/10.1016/j.enpol.2009.11.068

von Hippel, D., and Hayes, P., *Foundations of Energy Security for the DPRK: 1990-2009 Energy Balances, Engagement Options, and Future Paths for Energy and Economic Redevelopment* (Nautilus Institute Special Report: Sustainability, N.I.f.S.a., 2012).

von Hippel, D., and Hayes, P., "Future Northeast Asian Regional Energy Sector Cooperation Proposals and the DPRK Energy Sector: Opportunities and Constraints," *ERINA Report*, 82 (2008).

von Hippel, D., *et al.*, "Overview of the Northeast Asia Energy Situation," *Energy Policy*, 39(11) (2011), doi: http://dx.doi.org/10.1016/j.enpol.2009.07.004

von Hippel, D., *et al.*, "Energy Security and Sustainability in Northeast Asia," *Energy Policy*, 39(11) (2011), doi: http://dx.doi.org/10.1016/j.enpol.2009.07.001

von Hippel, D., *et al.*, "Evaluating the Energy Security Impacts of Energy Policies," in *The Routledge Handbook of Energy Security*, ed. by Sovacool, B.K. (Abingdon: Taylor & Francis, 2010).

von Hippel, D., and Takase, K., *The Path from Fukushima: Short and Medium-Term Impacts of the Reactor Damage Caused by the Japan Earthquake and Tsunami on Japan's Electricity Systems*, NAPSNet Special Report (Nautilus Institute, 2011).

von Hippel, D., *et al.*, "Energy Security (East Asia)," in *Berkshire Encyclopedia of Sustainability: China, India, and East and Southeast Asia: Assessing Sustainability* (Great Barrington: Berkshire Publishing Group, 2012).

Walker, B., and Meyeres, J., "Thresholds in Ecological and Social-Ecological Systems: A Developing Database," *Ecology and Society*, 9(3) (2004), http://www.ecologyandsociety.org/vol9/iss2/art3/

Wang, M., and Li, G., "The Shenyang-Dalian Mega-Urban Region in Transition," *International Development Planning Review*, 30(1) (2008), doi: http://liverpool.metapress.com/content/l03530t8627u023t/?genre=article&id=doi%3a10.3828%2fidpr.30.1.1

Wang, Q.E., "Remember the Past; Reconciling for the Future: A Critical Analysis of the China-Japan Joint History Research Project (2006-2010)," *The Chinese Historical Review*, 17(2) (2010), doi: http://dx.doi.org/10.1179/tcr.2010.17.2.219

Wang, W.-C., *et al.*, "Urban Heat Islands in China," *Geophysical Research Letters*, 17(13) (1990), http://dx.doi.org/10.1029/GL017i013p02377

Wang, Y., "China's Approach to Green Development and Transformation of Economic Development Pattern," in *Interconnections of Global Problems in East Asia, Green Economy, Urban Security And Energy Security* (Seoul: Nautilus Institute, 2010).

Wang, Z., "Old Wounds, New Narratives: Joint History Textbook Writing and Peacebuilding in East Asia," *History and Memory*, 21(1) (2009), http://www.jstor.org/stable/10.2979/HIS.2009.21.1.101

Ward, R., and Mabrey, D., "Organized Crime in Asia," in *The Handbook of Transnational Crime and Justice*, ed. by Reichel, P. (Sage Publications, 2005).

The Way to New Energy (St. Paul-lez-Durance: ITER Organization), http://www.iter.org/

Wesley, M., *The Regional Organizations of the Asia Pacific: Exploring Institutional Change* (Basingstoke: Palgrave Macmillan, 2003).

What Is Green Home? (Dublin: An Taisce and the Ireland Environmental Protection Agency, 2011), http://www.greenhome.ie/

What Is PD? (Los Angeles: Center on Public Diplomacy, University of Southern California), http://uscpublicdiplomacy.org/page/what-pd

Whiteneck, D., "Deterring Terrorists: Thoughts on a Framework," *The Washington Quarterly*, 28(3) (2005), doi: http://dx.doi.org/10.1162/0163660054026452

Wilkening, K.E., *et al.*, "Trans-Pacific Air Pollution," *Science*, 290(5489) (2000), doi: http://dx.doi.org/10.1126/science.290.5489.65

Willrich, M., and Taylor, T., *Nuclear Theft: Risks and Safeguards: A Report to the Energy Policy Project of the Ford Foundation* (Pensacola: Ballinger, 1974).

Wilson, P., "Does 'Strategic Stability' Have a Future in Northeast Asia?," in *Strategic Stability in a Turbulent World: SAIC Report of 5th Nuclear Stability Roundtable to Defense Threat Reduction Agency, Advanced Systems Concepts Office* (McLean: Science Applications International Corporation Strategies Group, 2003).

Wireless Federation, "Regulators Enable Mobile Operators to Charge More Fees for VOIP (South Korea)," ICT Statistics Newslog, 17 July 2012, http://www.itu.int/ITU-D/ict/newslog/Regulators+Enable+Mobile+Operators+ To+Charge+More+Fees+For+VOIP+South+Korea.aspx

World Economic Forum, *Global Risks 2014*, Insight Report (Geneva: World Economic Forum, 2014).

World Economic Forum, "Young Global Leaders: Guide to Influencing Complex Systems," in *The Forum of Young Global Leaders* (Nuevo Vallarta: World Economic Forum, 2012).

World Economic Forum, *et al.*, *Global Risks 2009, a Global Risk Network Report* (Geneva: World Economic Forum, 2009).

World Economic Forum, *et al.*, *Global Risks 2007, a Global Risk Network Report* (Geneva: World Economic Forum, 2007).

World Economic Forum, *et al.*, *Global Risks 2008, a Global Risk Network Report* (Geneva: World Economic Forum, 2008).

World Economic Forum, *et al.*, *Global Risks 2006* (Geneva: World Economic Forum, 2006).

World Economic Forum, *et al.*, *Global Risks 2013* (Geneva: World Economic Forum, 2013).

World Economic Forum, *et al.*, *Global Risks 2012* (Geneva: World Economic Forum, 2012).

World Economic Forum in collaboration, and Merrill Lynch, *Global Risks to the Business Environment, 2005* (Geneva: World Economic Forum, 2005).

World Nuclear Association, "Nuclear Power in the United Arab Emirates," February 2010, http://www.world-nuclear.org/info/Country-Profiles/Countries-T-Z/United-Arab-Emirates

World Nuclear News, "Japan to Reconsider Energy Policy," *World Nuclear News*, 11 May 2011, http://www.world-nuclear-news.org/NP-Japan_to_reconsider_energy_policy-1105114.html

Xie, L., *China's Environmental Activism in the Age of Globalization* (London: City University London, Department of International Politics, 2009).

Xie, Y., *et al.*, *Simulating Emergent Urban Form: Desakota in China* (London: Centre for Advanced Spatial Analysis, University College London, 2005).

Xu, J., *et al.*, "Participatory Agroforestry Development for Restoring Degraded Sloping Land in DPR Korea," *Agroforestry Systems* (2012), doi: http://dx.doi.org/10.1007/s10457-012-9501-0

Xu, X., "Internet Facilitated Civic Engagement in China's Context: A Case Study of the Internet Event of Wenzhou High-Speed Train Accident" (Columbia University, 2011).

Yale Center for Environmental Law & Policy, and Center for International Earth Science Information Network, C.U., *Environmental Performance Index 2010, South Korea* (New Haven: Yale University, 2010).

Yamaji, K., *Long-Term Techno-Management for Mitigating Global Warming*, PARES project (Nautilus Institute, 1997).

Yamamoto, T., ed., *Emerging Civil Society in the Asia Pacific Community: Nongovernmental Underpinnings of the Emerging Asia Pacific Community* (Tokyo: Japan Center for International Exchange, 2006).

Yang, M., *Talks of History in Civil Society for the Reconciliation of East Asia, Transcending Boundaries of Historical Perspectives in East Asia* (Seoul: Asia Peace and History Education Network, 2008).

Yasu, M., and Shiraki, M., "Hitachi, Ge Submit Proposal to Dismantle Crippled Fukushima Nuclear Plant," *Bloomberg*, 13 April 2011, http://www.bloomberg.com/news/2011-04-13/hitachi-ge-file-proposal-to-scrap-fukushima-dai-ichi-plant.html

Ye Qi, *et al.*, "Translating a Global Issue into Local Priority: China's Local Government Response to Climate Change," *The Journal of Environment & Development*, 17(4) (2008), doi: http://dx.doi.org/10.1177/1070496508326123

Yeh, A.G.O., and Xu, J., "China's Post-Reform Urbanization: Trends and Policies," in *IIED-UNFPA Research on Population and Urbanization Issues* (London, 2009).

"Yellow Dust Be Gone-Thanks to Youth Groups," *Nature's Crusaders*, 7 November 2009, http://naturescrusaders.wordpress.com/2009/11/07/yellow-dust-be-gone-thanks-to-youth-groups

Yeo, A., *Bilateralism, Multilateralism, and Institutional Change in Northeast Asia's Regional Security Architecture*, EAI Fellows Program Working Paper Series (East Asia Institute, 2011).

Yi, K., "The Purpose and Performance of the 2012 New York Conference for Peace and Cooperation in Northeast Asia (Korean)," 21 March 2012, http://weekly.catchkin.net/617?category=1

Yi, K., *et al.*, *Development Model for the Increased Cooperation for Northeast Asian Social Culture Exchange: A Network Based on Peace, History and Knowledge (in Korean)* (Seoul: National Research Council for Economics, Humanities and Social Sciences, 2006).

Yonhap News Agency staff writer, "Chinese 'Power Microbloggers' to Visit S. Korea This Week," *Yonhap News Agency*, 1 July 2013, http://www.globalpost.com/dispatch/news/yonhap-news-agency/130701/chinese-power-microbloggers-visit-s-korea-week

Yonhap News Agency staff writer, "The Consortium of Korea Electric Power Corporation Won a Nuclear Power Contract of 40 Billion Dollars," *Yonhap News*, 27 December 2009.

Yonhap News Agency staff writer, "S. Korea to Conduct Worldwide Survey on National Image," *Yonhap News Agency*, 28 July 2013, http://english.yonhapnews.co.kr/news/2013/07/28/0200000000AEN20130728000900315.html

Yoo, S.J., "Issues in Climate Change and Energy Security in Northeast Asia," in *Interconnections of Global Problems in East Asia: Climate Change Adaptation and its Complexity in Perspective of Civil Society Initiative* (Paju: Nautilus Institute, 2008).

Yoon, E., "The Growth of Environmental Cooperation in Northeast Asia: The Potential Roles of Civil Society," *The Good Society*, 12(1) (2003), doi: http://dx.doi.org/10.1353/gso.2003.0032

Yoon, E., *et al.*, "The State and Nongovernmental Organizations in Northeast Asia's Environmental Security," in *The Environmental Dimension of Asian Security: Conflict and Cooperation over Energy, Resources, and Pollution*, ed. by Schreurs, M.A. and Hyon, I.-T. (Washington, DC: United States Institute of Peace Press, 2007).

Yun, S.J., "Energy Security of Cities in Korea," in *Interconnections of Global Problems in East Asia, Green Economy, Urban Security And Energy Security* (Seoul: Nautilus Institute, 2010).

Yun, S.J., *et al.*, "The Current Status of Green Growth in Korea: Energy and Urban Security," *The Asia-Pacific Journal*, 9(44) (2011), http://www.japanfocus.org/-sun_jin-yun/3628

Zhang, L., *et al.*, "Analyzing and Forecasting Climate Change in Harbin City, Northeast China," *Chinese Geographical Science*, 21(1) (2011), doi: http://dx.doi.org/10.1007/s11769-011-0441-9

Zhou, N., *et al.*, *Energy Use in China: Sectoral Trends and Future Outlook* (Berkeley: Lawrence Berkeley National Laboratory, 2008).

Zhou, W., *et al.*, "Energy Consumption Patterns in the Process of China's Urbanization," *Population and Environment*, 33(2-3) (2012), doi: http://dx.doi.org/10.1007/s11111-011-0133-5

Zhou, Y., *An Initial Exploration of the Potential for Deep Borehole Disposal of Nuclear Wastes in China*, NAPSNet Special Report (Nautilus Institute, 2012).

Zittel, W., and Schindler, J., *Crude Oil, the Supply Outlook* (Energy Watch Group, 2007).

Index

This book need not end here...

At Open Book Publishers, we are changing the nature of the traditional academic book. The title you have just read will not be left on a library shelf, but will be accessed online by hundreds of readers each month across the globe. We make all our books free to read online so that students, researchers and members of the public who can't afford a printed edition can still have access to the same ideas as you.

Our digital publishing model also allows us to produce online supplementary material, including extra chapters, reviews, links and other digital resources. Find *Complexity, Security and Civil Society in East Asia* on our website to access its online extras. Please check this page regularly for ongoing updates, and join the conversation by leaving your own comments:

http://www.openbookpublishers.com/isbn/9781783741120

If you enjoyed this book, and feel that research like this should be available to all readers, regardless of their income, please think about donating to us. Our company is run entirely by academics, and our publishing decisions are based on intellectual merit and public value rather than on commercial viability. We do not operate for profit and all donations, as with all other revenue we generate, will be used to finance new Open Access publications.

For further information about what we do, how to donate to OBP, additional digital material related to our titles or to order our books, please visit our website: http://www.openbookpublishers.com

OpenBook Publishers

Knowledge is for sharing